BUSINESS AND SOCIETY
Corporate Strategy, Public Policy, Ethics

McGRAW-HILL SERIES IN MANAGEMENT

Fred Luthans and Keith Davis, Consulting Editors

ARNOLD and FELDMAN: Organizational Behavior
BARTOL and MARTIN: Management
CASCIO: Managing Human Resources: Productivity, Quality of Work Life, Profits
CERTO and PETER: Selected Cases in Strategic Management
CERTO and PETER: Strategic Management: A Focus on Process
CERTO and PETER: Strategic Management: Concepts and Applications
DAUGHTREY and RICKS: Contemporary Supervision: Managing People and Technology
DAVIS and NEWSTROM: Human Behavior at Work: Organizational Behavior
DOBLER, BURT, and LEE: Purchasing and Materials Management: Text and Cases
DUNN and RACHEL: Wage and Salary Administration: Total Compensation Systems
FELDMAN and ARNOLD: Managing Individual and Group Behavior in Organizations
FREDERICK, POST, DAVIS: Business and Society: Corporate Strategy, Public Policy, Ethics
HAMPTON: Management
HAMPTON: Inside Management: Readings from *Business Week*
HODGETTS: Effective Supervision: A Practical Approach
HODGETTS and LUTHANS: International Management
JAUCH and GLUECK: Business Policy and Strategic Management
JAUCH and GLUECK: Strategic Management and Business Policy
JAUCH and TOWNSEND: Cases in Strategic Management and Business Policy
KARLINS: The Human Use of Human Resources
KAST and ROSENZWEIG: Experiential Exercises and Cases in Management
KATZ and KOCHAN: An Introduction to Collective Bargaining and Industrial Relations
KNUDSON, WOODWORTH, and BELL: Management: An Experiential Approach
KOONTZ and WEIHRICH: Essentials of Management
KOONTZ and WEIHRICH: Management
KOPELMAN: Managing Productivity in Organizations: A Practical, People-Oriented Perspective
LEVIN, RUBIN, STINSON, and GARDNER: Quantitative Approaches to Management
LUTHANS: Organizational Behavior
LUTHANS and THOMPSON: Contemporary Readings in Organizational Behavior
MILES: Theories of Management: Implications for Organizational Behavior and Development
MILES and SNOW: Organizational Strategy, Structure, and Process
MILLS: Labor-Management Relations
MITCHELL and LARSON: People in Organizations: An Introduction to Organizational Behavior
MOLANDER: Responsive Capitalism: Case Studies in Corporate Social Conduct
MONKS: Operations Management: Theory and Problems
NEWSTROM and DAVIS: Organizational Behavior: Readings and Exercises

PEARCE and ROBINSON: Corporate Strategies: Readings from *Business Week*
PORTER and MCKIBBIN: Management Education and Development: Drift or Thrust into the 21st Century?
PRASOW and PETERS: Arbitration and Collective Bargaining: Conflict Resolution in Labor Relations
QUICK and QUICK: Organizational Stress and Preventive Management
RUE and HOLLAND: Strategic Management: Concepts and Experiences
RUGMAN, LECRAW, and BOOTH: International Business: Firm and Environment
SAYLES: Leadership: Managing in Real Organizations
SCHLESINGER, ECCLES, and GABARRO: Managing Behavior in Organizations: Text, Cases and Readings
SCHROEDER: Operations Management: Decision Making in the Operations Function
SHARPLIN: Strategic Management
STEERS and PORTER: Motivation and Work Behavior
STEINER: Industry, Society, and Change: A Casebook
STEINER and STEINER: Business, Government, and Society: A Managerial Perspective, Text and Cases
STEINHOFF and BURGESS: Small Business Management Fundamentals
SUTERMEISTER: People and Productivity
WALKER: Human Resource Planning
WEIHRICH: Management Excellence: Productivity through MBO
WERTHER and DAVIS: Human Resources and Personnel Management
WOFFORD, GERLOFF, and CUMMINS: Organizational Communications: The Keystone to Managerial Effectiveness
YOFFIE: International Trade and Competition

Also Available from McGraw-Hill

SCHAUM'S OUTLINE SERIES IN ACCOUNTING, BUSINESS, & ECONOMICS

Most outlines include basic theory, definitions, and hundreds of solved problems and supplementary problems with answers.

Titles on the Current List Include:

Accounting I, 3d edition
Accounting II, 3d edition
Advanced Accounting
Advanced Business Law
Advertising
Bookkeeping & Accounting
Introduction to Business
Business Law
Business Mathematics
Introduction to Business Organization & Management
Business Statistics, 2d edition
College Business Law
Contemporary Mathematics of Finance
Cost Accounting I, 2d edition
Cost Accounting II, 2d edition
Development Economics
Financial Accounting
Intermediate Accounting I, 2d edition
International Economics, 3d edition
Macroeconomic Theory, 2d edition
Managerial Accounting
Managerial Economics
Managerial Finance
Marketing
Mathematics for Economists, 2d edition
Mathematics of Finance
Microeconomic Theory, 3d edition
Money and Banking
Operations Management
Personal Finance
Personal Finance & Consumer Economics
Principles of Economics
Statistics and Econometrics
Tax Accounting

Available at your College Bookstore. A complete listing of Schaum titles may be obtained by writing to: Schaum Division
McGraw-Hill, Inc.
Princeton Road, S-1
Hightstown, NJ 08520

BUSINESS AND SOCIETY

Corporate Strategy, Public Policy, Ethics

SEVENTH EDITION

William C. Frederick
University of Pittsburgh

James E. Post
Boston University

Keith Davis
Arizona State University

McGraw-Hill, Inc.
New York St. Louis San Francisco Auckland Bogotá
Caracas Lisbon London Madrid Mexico Milan
Montreal New Delhi Paris San Juan Singapore
Sydney Tokyo Toronto

BUSINESS AND SOCIETY:
Corporate Strategy, Public Policy, Ethics

Copyright © 1992, 1988, 1984, 1980, 1975 by McGraw-Hill, Inc. All rights reserved. Previously published under the titles of: *Business, Society, and Environment: Social Power and Social Response*, copyright © 1971 by McGraw-Hill, Inc., all rights reserved; *Business and Its Environment*, copyright © 1966 by McGraw-Hill, Inc., all rights reserved. Printed in the United States of America. Except as permitted under the United States Copyright Act of 1976, no part of this publication may be reproduced or distributed in any form or by any means, or stored in a data base or retrieval system, without the prior written permission of the publisher.

2 3 4 5 6 7 8 9 0 HAL HAL 9 0 9 8 7 6 5 4 3 2

ISBN 0-07-015613-1

This book was set in Zapf by Arcata Graphics/Kingsport.
The editors were Alan Sachs and Dan Alpert;
the designer was Joan Greenfield;
the production supervisor was Annette Mayeski.
Project supervision was done by The Total Book.
Arcata Graphics/Halliday was printer and binder.

Library of Congress Cataloging-in-Publication Data

Frederick, William Crittenden, (date).
Business and society: corporate strategy, public policy, ethics.
—7th ed. William C. Frederick, James E. Post, Keith Davis.
p. cm.—(McGraw-Hill series in management)
Includes index.
ISBN 0-07-015613-1
1. Social responsibility of business. I. Post, James E.
II. Davis, Keith, (date). III. Title. IV. Series.
HD60.F72 1992
658.4'08—dc20 91-26776

ABOUT THE AUTHORS

William C. Frederick is Professor of Business Administration in the Graduate School of Business at the University of Pittsburgh. Corporate social performance, business ethics, and managerial values are his primary areas of interest and research. His coauthored and coedited books include *Social Auditing; Research in Corporate Social Performance and Policy: Empirical Studies of Business Ethics and Values; Business Ethics: Research Issues and Empirical Studies;* and four editions of *Business and Society*. He has been chairperson of the Social Issues in Management division of The Academy of Management, President of The Society for Business Ethics, and the Charles Dirksen Professor of Business Ethics at the University of Santa Clara. He is on the editorial boards of the *Academy of Management Review* and *Business Ethics Quarterly*. He holds a doctorate in economics from the University of Texas.

James E. Post is Professor of Management and Public Policy at Boston University. He has degrees in law and management and teaches courses in business and public policy, public affairs management, and management of environmental issues. He has lectured throughout the United States and internationally. Publications include such books as *Private Management and Public Policy* (with Lee Preston), *Corporate Behavior and Social Change,* and *Research in Corporate Social Performance and Policy,* an international research volume for which he has served as series editor. He has been a consultant and advisor to the National Wildlife Federation's Corporate Conservation Council, the World Health Organization, Rockefeller Foundation, and The Population Council, and been an expert witness before various committees of the U.S. Senate and House of Representatives. He is past chairperson of the Social Issues in Management division of the Academy of Management and has served as an editorial board member or reviewer for such journals as the *Academy of Management Review, California Management Review,* and *Sloan Management Review.* In 1989, his book, *Private Management and Public Policy,* was cited by the Academy of Management for "its lasting contribution to the study of business in society."

Keith Davis is Professor Emeritus of Management at Arizona State University. He has a Ph.D. from Ohio State University and formerly taught at Indiana University and the University of Texas. He is a former president of The Academy of Management and is a Fellow in both The Academy of Management and the International Academy of Management. He is coauthor of numerous books and articles, including *Human Behavior at Work* and *Human Resources and Personnel Man-*

agement; was named a Beta Gamma Sigma Distinguished Scholar; and has lectured at many universities in the United States and abroad. The first edition of *Business and Society,* coauthored with Robert L. Blomstrom, won a national book award in 1966; and several of his books have been translated into other languages. He has been an active consultant and a contributor to the business and society field for over thirty years. Prior to becoming a professor he worked in industry and served in the military as a personnel officer.

CONTENTS

PART THREE THE CORPORATION AND PUBLIC POLICY

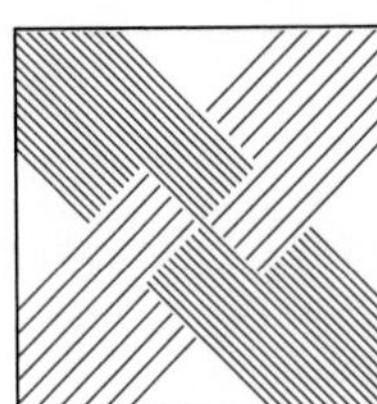

PART FIVE SOCIAL ISSUES IN MANAGEMENT

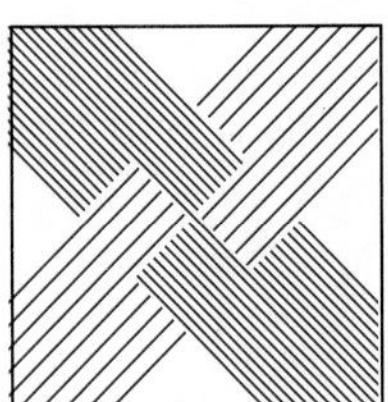

CASE STUDIES IN CORPORATE SOCIAL POLICY

PREFACE

At no moment in the entire twentieth century has it been more obvious that business operates within a complex web of social relationships. These broad societal networks now extend throughout the world. It is literally true that nowhere in the world can business go forward—nor can any business decision be made—without encountering human, social, political, governmental, legal, and ethical linkages. This awesome realization, while known earlier, has received greatly increased attention within the last half of the twentieth century. A sophisticated knowledge of the social environment now shapes managers' careers. It helps to guide corporate strategy. It defines many of business's central problems and frequently provides helpful solutions to them.

The last decade of the twentieth century is witnessing an immense transformation of business systems everywhere—from tightly regulated markets to freer markets, from centralized authoritarian controls to more horizontal systems, from a monopoly of decision making by a few to more widespread participation by widening circles of employees, from labor-intensive companies to greater reliance on computerized work processes, from isolated domestic markets to worldwide ones, from a narrow technical concept of business to one in which people and their communities demand a voice.

This enormously complex, continuously evolving, and tightly interlinked business-and-society system is the subject of this book. We invite those who read it to explore with us the multiform problems and issues that are typical of the business and society interface. That intersection, where business and society come together, constantly generates a whole host of tough human and social problems. It also complicates the life of business managers and professionals, thrusting on them the need to develop new perspectives and new approaches to traditional business problems. Our main audience—college and university students who plan or already are pursuing careers in business or whose lives will be strongly affected by business activities—will find here the kinds of insights they need to plan their professional futures and to understand some of the central puzzles and dilemmas of modern business, as well as the hopeful initiatives being taken by leading business firms to resolve those issues.

This book, now in its seventh edition, has a long and widely respected record. The first edition of *Business and Society,* written by Keith Davis and Robert L. Blomstrom, won a national book award in 1966. The book's successive editions have been an authoritative repository of the major research findings of scholars who have studied business and society relations, as well as the thoughts and actions of business practitioners who have struggled both successfully and unsuccessfully with these kinds of problems.

Over the years, the issues discussed have changed as the social environment of business has been transformed. This seventh edition is no exception, as readers will discover. Some issues have become less compelling and new ones have taken their place on the business agenda, while others endure through the years. The major changes and improvements we have introduced can be briefly summarized.

- **The discussion of business ethics has been greatly expanded throughout the text, and an entirely new chapter on ethics has been added.** A careful distinction is now made between different types of ethics issues that occur in the workplace. New research findings and analytic concepts are used to clarify ethics dilemmas in business and to suggest what can be done about them.
- **A theme of global enterprise—worldwide business, international trends, and multinational corporate operations—runs throughout the book.** This theme reflects the dramatic global changes that continue to create both opportunities and problems for today's business firms. Part Two is devoted entirely to some of these core issues, and other individual chapters provide appropriate analysis and discussion.
- **The various issues surrounding the entry of women into the workplace receive attention in a new chapter on this topic.** Questions of equal opportunity, professional advancement, needed changes in business practices, and the impact of these on family life are discussed. No other text in this field contains such a comprehensive treatment of these matters.
- **Ecological problems, issues, and progress are discussed in greater detail, with much new material introduced.** One of the authors, James Post, has been a major figure in a nationwide effort sponsored by the National Wildlife Federation's Corporate Conservation Council to develop teaching materials about the environment for use in the nation's business schools. Throughout the book, timely examples connect ecological concerns to fundamental business-and-society concepts and themes.
- **A greater diversity of case studies—including several new ones written by guest authors—appear in this edition.** These cases, in a special section at the end of the text, exhibit more comprehensiveness and are chosen to match several of the book's major themes. Seven of these case studies are new, while three of the "classic" cases have been updated with recent developments.
- **Special new features appear in each chapter.** These include Key Questions and Chapter Objectives, Key Terms and Concepts, Summary Points linked to the Key Questions and Chapter Objectives, and a somewhat longer Discussion Case keyed to the chapter's major themes. As in previous editions, several illustrative figures help explain major points, and these are supplemented by new boxed exhibits intended to drive home especially important perspectives.
- **As adopters would expect, all existing chapters have been thoroughly revised and updated based on new research findings and current developments.**

- **The color format and improved artwork not only enhance the book's attractiveness but also focus greater attention on major discussion points.** No other book in the business and society field has adopted this appealing feature.

ACKNOWLEDGMENTS

This seventh edition has benefited greatly from collaborative authorship, which we are pleased to acknowledge. Colin Boyd, Deborah Crimmins, Robbin Derry, Anne Lawrence, Jeanne Logsdon, Forest Reinhardt, Barbara Ley Toffler, and James Weber wrote the case studies bearing their respective names. Each is an acknowledged expert concerning those topics. James Weber and Sandra Waddock are major authors of Chapters 13 and 15, respectively.

For research assistance or for reading portions of the manuscript and offering suggestions for improvement, we thank Denis Collins, Robbin Derry, Susan Key, Nancy Kurland, Mary Mallott, Lyman Reed, Peter Simpson, Diane Swanson, and William Wubbenhorst. We are especially grateful for the numerous helpful comments made by the following reviewers appointed by McGraw-Hill editors: Raymond E. Alie, Western Michigan University; Arnold J. Bornfriend, Worcester State College; Eleanore A. Chong, Chaminade University of Hawaii; Oya Culpan, Pennsylvania State University; Richard T. Dailey, University of Montana; D. Kirk Davidson, The George Washington University; Leonard E. Goodall, University of Nevada; Robert H. Hogner, Florida International University; Patricia C. Kelley, Western Washington University; John Kohls, Gonzaga University; David L. Mathison, Loyola Marymount University; Judith K. Thompson, The University of New Mexico; and Paul L. Wilkens, The Florida State University. Cathie Chatowski and Margaret Jonnet of the University of Pittsburgh, and Kay Beck and Matthew Martin of Boston University, provided essential and reliable administrative and secretarial support.

Since textbooks describe the central ideas that make up any field of study, we also acknowledge, with much professional admiration, the work of our colleagues in colleges and universities here and abroad. Particularly noteworthy are those members of the Social Issues in Management division of The Academy of Management and the members of The Society for Business Ethics. They are largely responsible for producing the research data and theoretical insights that undergird the study of business and society relations. We salute them for their many imaginative and creative efforts to forge a coherent field of study. We hope that we have captured the essence of their work and contributions.

For continuing the high-quality publishing tradition that has characterized this book since its inception, we thank Alan Sachs, Management Editor, Kaitlin Quistgard, Editorial Assistant, and Annette Bodzin, Project Supervisor, all of McGraw-Hill.

William C. Frederick
James E. Post
Keith Davis

INTRODUCTION AND OVERVIEW

In this introduction, we wish to explain the overall design of the book, which is divided into five major parts plus a group of case studies. Each chapter displays several common features designed to enhance learning, and these will be explained, along with additional design elements of the book.

PART ONE: THE CORPORATION IN SOCIETY

Part One's basic theme: The corporation conducts business within a surrounding environment of political, governmental, and social institutions which exert a powerful influence on the company and its managers. The general public expects corporate managers to be economically efficient, socially responsible, and ethically sensitive as they make decisions and set corporate policies. Corporations that are socially and ethically responsive to their stakeholders gain widespread public approval.

PART TWO: THE CORPORATION IN A GLOBAL SOCIETY

Part Two's basic theme: Today's business firms—whether large or small, whether serving local markets or far-flung global markets, whether highly profitable or just struggling to stay alive—are enormously influenced by worldwide events and trends. For that reason, each company needs to think of its present and future in global terms, knowing that international political, social, and economic developments can mean the difference between survival and failure. This global outlook is especially critical for multinational corporations, which operate in diverse economic, social, cultural, and national systems.

PART THREE: THE CORPORATION AND PUBLIC POLICY

Part Three's basic theme: The public policies of any nation provide a broad framework of laws, regulations, and public expectations that serve as guides for corporate actions. The legal and political environment of business—domestic and international—is constantly shifting, requiring close attention to each nation's public policies and political attitudes toward business. The competitive strength and success of businesses in any one nation often depend on an up-to-date and advanced knowledge of geopolitical trends at home and abroad.

PART FOUR: RESPONDING TO CORPORATE STAKEHOLDERS

Part Four's basic theme: Any company normally interacts with a wide variety of stakeholders. Especially important are four stakeholder groups: stockholders, employees, consumers, and the community. Corporate managers must be responsive to their needs, interests, and powers if the corporation is to achieve its profit goals. These stakeholders expect to be treated fairly, ethically, and responsibly when corporate actions affect their well-being.

PART FIVE: SOCIAL ISSUES IN MANAGEMENT

Part Five's basic theme: Some social issues in management are more critical than others, reflecting widespread public concern plus a belief that business can be highly influential in finding solutions to these problems. By the early 1990s, four of these issues had assumed a special importance in the public mind: the treatment of women in the workplace, the media's enormous influence on business and society, accelerating technological and scientific trends, and public awareness of environmental and ecological problems.

CASE STUDIES IN CORPORATE SOCIAL POLICY

The ten case studies in this section represent a wide variety of business-and-society issues that call for responsible corporate social policies. Included are product recalls, doing business across national and cultural boundaries, industrial accidents and disasters, environmental hazards, public-private partnerships, community activism, ethical dilemmas, and others. The cases represent both positive and negative actions taken by business firms, and they demonstrate responsible social performance as well as less desirable outcomes. Business operations in several nations are depicted, with emphasis on the unique features that arise in such circumstances. These case studies can be used in any order desired by instructors and students. Each case has links to two or more chapters in the text and can be assigned according to the emphasis desired by an instructor and the interests of students.

LEARNING FEATURES OF EACH CHAPTER

Preview Paragraph: The first page of each chapter contains a short paragraph giving a condensed introduction to that chapter's content.

Key Questions and Chapter Objectives: Five or six key questions outline the major issues to be explored in the chapter.

Opening Examples: Each chapter begins with two or three examples that illustrate the issues, problems, or major themes to be discussed.

Illustrative Examples: Throughout each chapter, color-highlighted examples from the actual world of business illustrate the relevance of the chapter's concepts to business operations.

Figures: Graphic figures and tables are integrated into the textual material, to illustrate relationships and to condense detailed information.

Exhibits: From one to three boxed and color-highlighted quotations are included in most chapters to reinforce major points by demonstrating their relevance to actual business operations.

Summary Points: The chapter's major content is summarized in several condensed points at the end of each chapter. Each of these summary points matches the Key Questions and Chapter Objectives that appear at the chapter's beginning.

Key Terms and Concepts: The terms and concepts most important for understanding the chapter's content are listed. For easy identification and review, each of these terms and concepts is printed in boldface type in the chapter.

Discussion Case: Each chapter ends with a short Discussion Case that illustrates the chapter's major themes and demonstrates their application in the business world. Discussion Questions accompany each Discussion Case.

OTHER LEARNING FEATURES

Glossary: A list of technical terms used in the text, together with their definitions, appears after the Case Studies at the end of the book. This glossary can be used by students to review key meanings as they read through the text and before examinations.

Bibliography: A select bibliography is included for each of the five major parts of the book. These books can be consulted for additional information, diverse points of view, preparing term papers, and studying for examinations.

Indexes: A name index and a subject index are included to aid in finding a specific topic or person in the text or case studies.

CENTRAL IDEAS AND THEMES

Throughout all chapters and case studies in the book, we emphasize the following ideas many times:

- Corporate social responsibility
- Corporate social responsiveness
- Corporate ethical challenges
- Corporate stakeholders and responding to them
- Global diversity and economic competition
- Government-business interface
- Critical social issues confronting business
- Improving corporate social policies and performance

These are the sinews that bind the book's arguments together. They are the major components of the business-and-society relationship. Grasping these central concepts and putting them to work in business will greatly improve the quality of life for all who are affected by business operations in today's world society.

BUSINESS AND SOCIETY
Corporate Strategy, Public Policy, Ethics

PART ONE

The Corporation in Society

1

The Corporation and Its Stakeholders

Business has complex relationships with many segments of society. The existence and power of these segments require careful management attention and action. A company's success can be affected—negatively or positively—by its stakeholders. Failure to respond to stakeholder concerns can lead to conflicts and serious public issues.

Key Questions and Chapter Objectives

This chapter focuses on these key questions and objectives:

- Why are business, government, and society an interactive system?
- What kind of involvement does business have with other elements of society?
- Who are a corporation's primary and secondary stakeholders?
- Why are stakeholders important to a corporation, and how can they affect its success?
- What kinds of interests and powers do stakeholders have, and how do coalitions of stakeholders pursue their objectives?
- What is the performance-expectations gap, and how do corporate managers respond to it?

On February 12, 1990, Perrier Group of America, the U.S. subsidiary of the French company, Source Perrier S. A., withdrew over 70 million of the familiar green bottles of Perrier water from stores and restaurants throughout North America. County water testers in North Carolina, who used Perrier bottled water as a gauge for purity, were testing local water quality when they discovered that the Perrier water had excessive levels of benzene, a liquid solvent that has been shown to cause cancer in laboratory animals. The U.S. Food and Drug Administration was notified, and it conducted testing which showed high benzene levels in 13 other bottles of Perrier water. Although the FDA stressed that the level of benzene in these bottles posed no immediate health risk to the public, Perrier executives took swift action to remove the mineral water from stores, restaurants, and other outlets. Initially, the company claimed that an employee at Perrier's French bottling plant had used a fluid containing benzene to clean machinery on the assembly line that filled the bottles sent to North America. A few days later, however, random testing of bottles being sent to other markets indicated that they too were affected. As a precautionary measure, Source Perrier issued a worldwide recall of its product, an action estimated to cost $70 million.

In addition to the recall, Perrier executives announced that the contamination was not caused by cleaning the machines. A failure to replace the charcoal filters (used in the bottling process to screen out benzene) led to the excess level of benzene in the product. A certain minute amount of benzene is evident in the natural gases which carbonate the natural spring water. Although the amount of benzene was not immediately dangerous to the consumer, the company recalled all of its product because Perrier's image stresses the purity of the product. Gustave Levin, Perrier's chairman, was quick to stress that the source spring for Perrier water was *not* contaminated; the contamination was caused by human error. After the filters at the bottling plant were replaced, normal production (of approximately 6 million bottles a day) resumed. The plant returned to working 6 days a week, 24 hours a day, to replenish the recalled stock.

Since the company's brand market image has been based on purity, some speculated that the recall did not harm Perrier; it only enhanced the product integrity. However, the complete removal of the product from the market led some market analysts to believe that it could harm Perrier's dominance in the bottled water market. Although officials at Source Perrier speculated that it could take up to three months before the famous green bottles would reappear on U.S. shelves, in France it was available within a few days. And French consumers appeared unaffected by the contamination recall.

During its absence from store shelves, Perrier's competitors scrambled for a larger percentage of market share. While other brands of bottled water launched advertisements playing on this incident, Perrier began the difficult struggle of keeping its product in consumers' minds while it was unavailable. By spending over $25 million on a U.S. advertising campaign alone, Perrier tried to keep consumers thinking about its bottled water product.

Public opinion surveys conducted after the recall seemed to support the company: 82 percent of Perrier drinkers were aware that Perrier had a problem (80 percent knew that it was benzene contamination); over 95 percent felt the company had acted responsibly; 84 percent said that they intended to purchase Perrier again as soon as it was returned to the market; and 47 percent of non-Perrier drinkers indicated they would begin drinking Perrier. Perrier hoped that its customers would return and that its desire to "do the right thing" would be vindicated in time.[1]

Every corporation has complex involvements with other people, groups, and organizations in society. Some of these are intended and desired; others are unintentional and not desired. The people and organizations with which cor-

[1] "Perrier: The Promise," *New York Times*, Mar. 7, 1990, p. A9; "Getting Perrier Out of Hot Water," *Business Week*, July 30, 1990, p. 7.

porations are involved have an interest or stake in the decisions, actions, and practices of the firm. They are **stakeholders,** and they are a critical factor in determining the success or failure of a modern business enterprise.

BUSINESS—GOVERNMENT—SOCIETY: AN INTERDEPENDENT SYSTEM

As the Perrier episode demonstrates, business, government, and other elements of society are highly interdependent. Few business actions are without an impact on others in society, just as few actions by government are without direct or indirect impact on business. And, of course, business and government decisions continuously affect all segments of the general public. To manage these interdependencies, corporate managers need both a conceptual understanding of the relationships and practical skills for responding.

A Systems Perspective

Management thinking has been influenced by general systems theory. According to this theory, all living organisms (systems) interact with, and are affected by, other forces in their host environments. The key to survival is the ability to adapt—to be responsive to the changing conditions in the environment. For an organism such as the modern business corporation, systems thinking provides a powerful tool to help managers appreciate the relationships between their companies and the rest of the world.

Figure 1–1 illustrates the "systems" connections between very broad, abstract ways of thinking about business-government-society relationships and very specific, practical ways of doing so. The broadest view of that relationship is a societal perspective that emphasizes the "systems" connections between a society's economic activity, its political life, and its culture. Michael Novak, a prominent socio-economist, writes that every society is a mixture of economic, political, and cultural influences, each generated by its own "system" of people, institutions, and ideas.[2] In other words, reality for all of us is a mixture of economic, political, and cultural influences.

> In the case of Perrier, for example, Europeans have long consumed bottled water from pure springs. In North America, bottled water is a more recent phenomenon, and Perrier was at the forefront of economic and cultural change. Indeed, to some, the little green Perrier bottle became one of the symbols of the Yuppie generation. When Perrier recalled its product, some commentators called it the official end of the Yuppie era of the 1980s.

A somewhat narrower perspective is illustrated in the middle panel of Figure 1–1. "Business" is composed of many segments, industries, and sectors; "gov-

[2] Michael Novak, *The Spirit of Democratic Capitalism,* New York: Simon & Schuster, 1982.

FIGURE 1–1
A range of levels at which to conceptualize business, government, society relations.

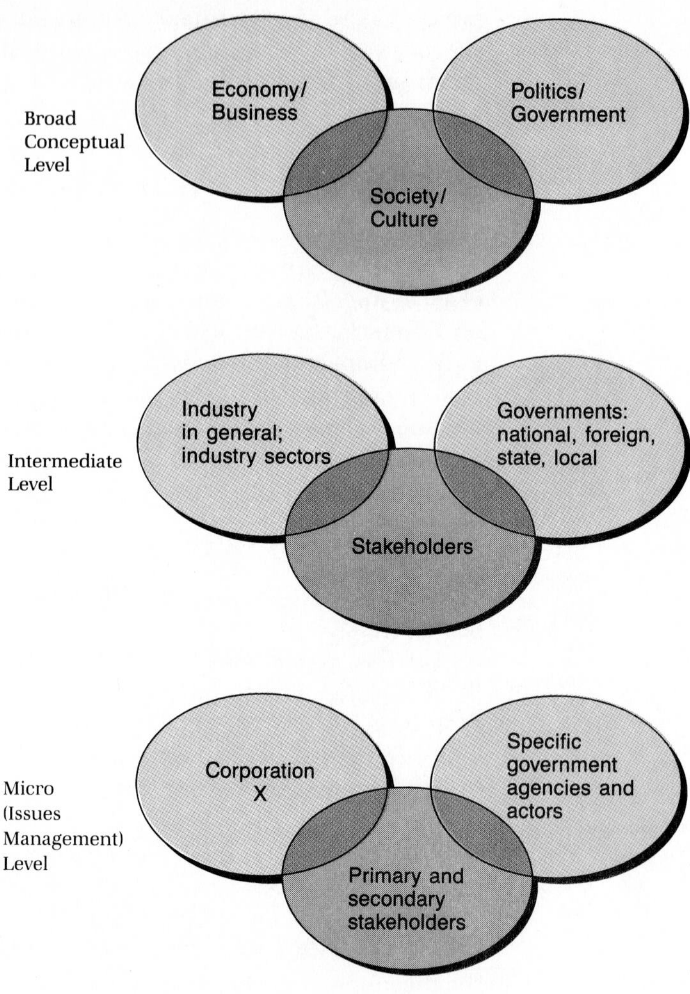

ernment" involves political life at the national, state, local, and international levels; and "society" is composed of many segments, groups, and stakeholders. In the Perrier case, an entire industry of bottled water companies was affected by the situation, and governments in the United States, France, and many local jurisdictions participated in dealing with the problem. But it is at the most specific level (lower panel in Figure 1–1) that we can understand best the actions that Perrier's managers took to respond to the issue.

The company (Group Perrier in the United States and Source Perrier S. A. in France) responded to a problem brought to its attention by government agencies in the United States (state and federal) and of importance to its stakeholders (customers, including retail stores and restaurants, employees, distributors, and the general public who consumed Perrier water). Perrier's managers had to have the practical skills to know how to recall the product, deal with the media, communicate with customers and consumers, and understand the broader issues of business responsibility and business-government-society relations that were involved. Whether or not they understood it explicitly, Perrier's managers were behaving with an appreciation of the complex social system in which they and their company exist.

Once, it was widely believed that business interacted with others in society only through the marketplace. But that view has long since been replaced by an understanding that business and society have many nonmarket interactions as well. Many social influences on business come from the political and cultural forces in society; business also has an influence on the political life and culture of any society. The impact of computer technology, for example, has certainly not been confined to those with whom IBM or Apple Computer have done business directly. Indeed, the computer has become a pervasive social influence, affecting our very culture. These cultural effects are due in large measure to the success of IBM, Apple Computer, and other firms in developing the technology, marketing it widely to many types of customers, and finding many ways to encourage the public to solve problems, do new kinds of work with computers, and even play games.

One result of this close, inseparable relationship between business and society is that all business decisions have a social impact, much as a pebble thrown into a pond creates ever-widening ripples. Another result is that the vitality and survival of business depend on society's actions and attitudes. Business can be smothered under a heavy blanket of social demands. For example, a labor union may demand wages that exceed a company's ability to pay. Local taxes may be set at a punitive level, thereby driving businesses to other regions. Environmental regulations may prove to be too costly, leading to plant closures and job losses. So, while business decisions can have both positive and negative impacts on society, the actions of a society often can determine whether a business firm will prosper or die.

That is why business and society, taken together, are in **interactive system.** Each needs the other. Each can influence the other. They are intertwined so completely that an action taken by one will inevitably affect the other. The boundary line between the two is blurred and indistinct. Business is a part of society, and society penetrates far and often into business. They are both separate and connected. And in a world where global communication is rapidly expanding, the connections are closer than ever before.

THE STAKEHOLDER CONCEPT

When business interacts so often and so closely with society, a shared interest and interdependence develops between a company and other social groups. When this occurs, corporate stakeholders are created. Stakeholders are all the groups affected by a corporation's decisions, policies, and operations. The number of stakeholders, and the variety of interests, that a company's management must consider can make decisions quite complex.

For example, executives at Lederle Laboratories faced a difficult business problem several years ago. Lederle was the exclusive distributor of DPT vaccine manufactured by Wyeth Laboratories, a division of American Home Products. Wyeth was one of the few manufacturers of the vaccine, which is given to millions of children to prevent diphtheria, whooping cough, and tetanus. However, fifty to seventy children die annually from the millions of vaccinations that are given. This created a crisis for the vaccine manufacturers, who faced skyrocketing liability insurance costs. The cost of the vaccine distributed by Lederle, for example, rose from $0.68 per dose to $2.80 per dose within three years, largely because of the cost of liability insurance and legal fees.

Many stakeholders were affected by this crisis. Children, parents, doctors, and hospitals all faced serious health problems if the production of vaccine were to be stopped; thousands of children would be at risk if Lederle stopped distribution. In the 1930s, before vaccine was widely distributed, more than 9,000 children died of whooping cough alone each year. Lederle faced a serious economic problem, however. According to company officials, the dollars demanded in DPT lawsuits against the company were more than 100 times Lederle's annual vaccine sales. Insurance costs were predicted to continue rising, and it was feared that insurance might become completely unavailable. That would probably force Lederle out of the business.

Government officials also were very concerned. Most states require that children be vaccinated with DPT before entering school. Without vaccine, that would be impossible. Various proposals had been offered: government agencies might directly produce the vaccine, or legislation might place a limit on the damages that could be given to a family whose child died as a result of the vaccine. Yet, it was argued, should not the families of children who died receive damages for their suffering and that of their child?[3]

Although the government—a stakeholder—can create conditions that would influence a company to stay or withdraw from a given market, the company itself—in this case, Lederle—is the one to make the final decision. However, a company cannot act without regard to stakeholder interests. In addition to profit and business considerations, Lederle must consider the possibilities of a lawsuit by an injured consumer, plus the fact that production of the vaccine is necessary. Weighing conflicting considerations such as these is a part of any manager's job.

Stakeholders and stakeholder relationships have changed over the years. Previously, managers had only to focus their attention on the product-market framework; they could concentrate on bringing products and services to market as efficiently and effectively as possible. The number of stakeholders was limited.

[3] Adapted from Peter W. Bernstein, "A Vaccine Crisis Lands in Congress," *Fortune* (April 29, 1985), p. 238.

Thomas J. Watson, Sr., chairman of IBM in the 1950s, is said to have descr management's role as one of balancing a "three-legged stool" consisting of em ployees, customers, and shareholders. To emphasize their equality, he insisted on systematically changing the order in which he mentioned these three groups in his talks and speeches. In those days, it could be assumed that these were the important stakeholders. In contrast, the 1990 book about IBM by Thomas J. Watson, Jr., emphasized the great number and variety of publics with which the company works.

The interests of all corporate stakeholders need to be given consideration by the company. If their concerns are disregarded, they may damage or halt the company's operations. The key point about corporate stakeholders is that they may, and frequently do, share decision-making power with a company's managers. Their justification for doing so is that they are affected by the company's operations. The interest created between a company and its stakeholders can be a powerful aid to business, or it can be turned against a company. When stakeholders demand a voice in decision making and policy making, corporation managers need to respond with great skill if their primary business mission—producing goods and services—is to be achieved.

On the positive side, corporate stakeholders also can be enlisted to aid and support a company that is in trouble.

> For example, when the Norton Company, an abrasives manufacturer located in Worcester, Massachusetts, received an unsolicited and unwelcome buyout offer from BTR, a British conglomerate, Norton's management asked for the help of employees, community officials, the governor and state legislative leaders, and prominent business leaders. The state legislature passed an anti-takeover law in record time to help prevent the Norton takeover. Fears of lost jobs, closed plants, and a loss of local charitable support contributed to the prompt response. Norton's network of stakeholders was concerned and eager to help the company resist the unwanted purchase by BTR. The state's congressional representatives and senators even called on President Bush to invoke a federal law preventing takeovers by foreign companies when the U.S. company is involved in critical defense-related businesses. In the end, BTR was thwarted in its attempt to acquire Norton.[4]

There are many examples of companies disregarding their stakeholders' wishes, either out of the belief that the stakeholder was wrong or out of arrogance and the sense that "one unhappy customer, employee, or regulator doesn't matter!" Such attitudes are foolish and often have proved costly to the company whose employees share the view. Builders of nuclear power plants have learned that they have virtually no ability to build a plant over community objections. The only way to build a power plant or an incinerator facility to destroy solid waste is to work with the community, to respond to concerns, and to invest in

[4] "Lawmakers Join Foes of Norton Takeover," *Boston Globe,* Apr. 20, 1990, pp. 65–66; "No End in Sight in Norton Battle," *New York Times,* Apr. 19, 1990, p. D-2.

a business

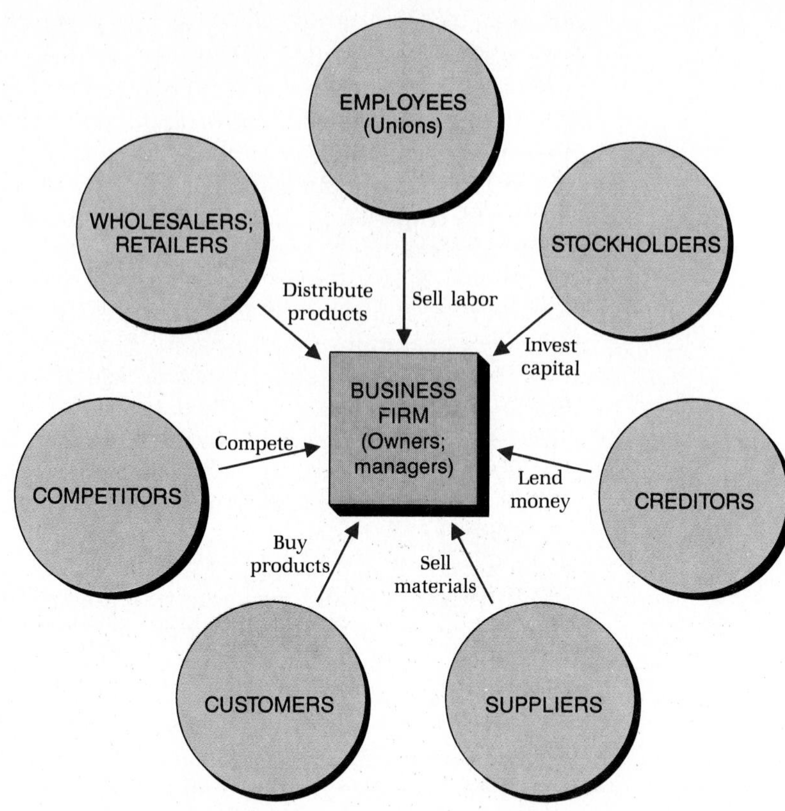

creating and maintaining a relationship of trust. John deButts, who served as chairman of AT&T during the late 1970s, commented about the "three-legged stool": "The only image which recurs with uncomfortable persistence is not a piece of furniture at all. It's a porcupine—with quills reversed."[5]

Today, comprehensive approaches are needed for the successful management of business—approaches that take into consideration the needs of a larger and more diverse group of stakeholders. Business cannot be done in a vacuum and business planning must take into account this web of considerations.

Primary and Secondary Stakeholders

In spite of the close relationship of business and society, not all business ties to society are the same. Some are closer than others and more directly related to a company's main economic functions in society.

Figure 1–2 shows business interacting with other groups necessary to carry

[5] John deButts, "A Strategy of Accountability," in William Dill, ed., *Running the American Corporation*, Englewood Cliffs, NJ: Prentice-Hall, 1978, p. 141.

out its primary purpose of effectively providing society with goods and services. Stockholders and creditors provide capital funds; employees contribute their work skills; suppliers sell raw materials, energy, and other needed supplies; and wholesalers, dealers, and retailers help move the product from the plant to sales outlets and on to consumers. All business firms need customers willing to buy what is produced, and most companies compete with other companies that are selling identical or similar products and services. These are the fundamental interactions that a company has with society. They tell us why that company is in business and what its economic mission is.

A business's primary involvement with society includes all the direct relationships necessary for it to perform its major mission of producing goods and services for society. These primary interactions are usually conducted through the free market, which is a buying and selling process. In other words, business buys employees' time and skills, buys supplies, borrows capital, and, of course, sells products to its customers in competition with other firms. The free market system, discussed in Chapter 7, is one of the main ways in which business interacts with society.

Thus a firm's primary involvements reflect its strategy, the policy decisions of its managers, and the stakeholders who are critical to its existence and activities. These market-driven customers, suppliers, employees, and investors are its **primary stakeholders.**

However, as Figure 1–3 reveals, a business's relationships go beyond those primary involvements to others in society. Another level of interaction occurs when other groups express an interest or concern in the organization's activities. A business's secondary involvements are the result of the impacts caused by the company's primary mission or function. And **secondary stakeholders** are those groups in society who are affected, directly or indirectly, by the company's secondary impacts and involvements.

Calling these involvements and stakeholders "secondary" does not mean that they are less important than business's primary relationships with society. It means that they occur as a *consequence* of the normal activities of conducting business. Primary and secondary areas of involvement are not always sharply distinguished; often, one area shades into the other. For example, although two companies may have very different primary activities (e.g., one produces automobiles, the other hair spray), the secondary involvements (e.g., safety and environmental issues) may be similar.

These secondary interactions normally do not occur through the free market. As Figure 1–4 illustrates, an extensive network of social groups may interact with business. All it takes to bring them into the picture is for the people they represent to be affected one way or another by a business firm's operations. The problems with which these groups are concerned are not easily approached or resolved by market action alone.

Consumers, for example, may not trust the market to establish fair prices. Plant closures may create semipermanent pockets of unemployment when workers either cannot or will not leave their home communities for jobs or higher wages elsewhere. Or coal miners may feel safer if government officials, rather than

FIGURE 1–3
Relations between a business firm and its secondary stakeholders.

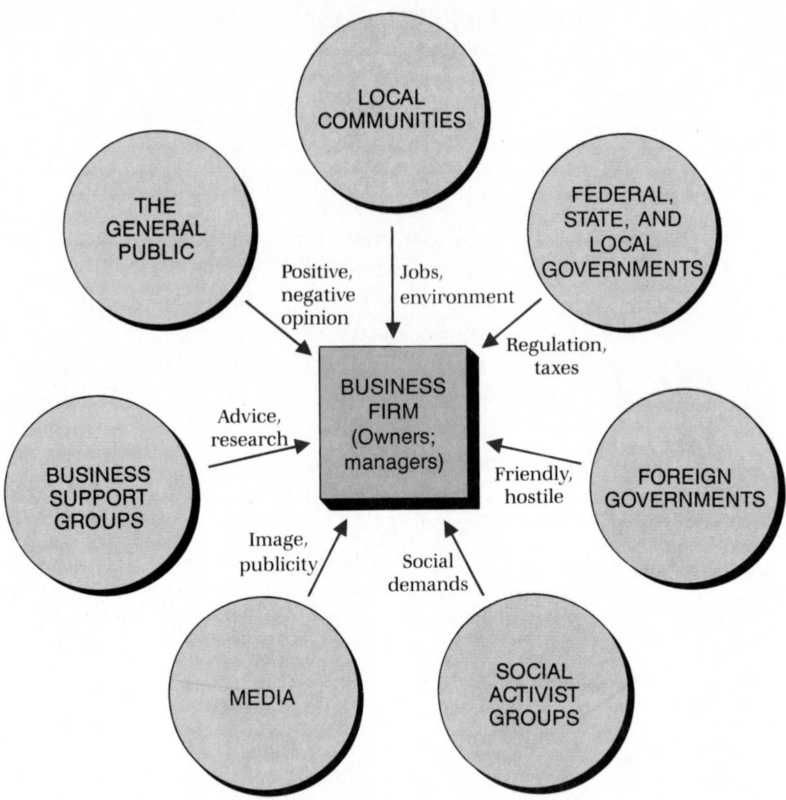

the owners, inspect mines for safety hazards. In these and similar cases, people form self-help groups or turn to the government for aid, often believing that their goals are better achieved by nonmarket means.

Combining business's primary and secondary interactions gives an **interactive model of business and society,** as shown in Figure 1–4. Primary interactions conducted through the free market are shown on the left. The secondary interactions, which are carried out through nonmarket institutions, are depicted on the right. The main lessons that emerge from this interactive model are the following ones:

- In making decisions, business shares power with all primary and secondary groups. Shared decision making has become more and more typical of all businesses, large and small, domestic and foreign.
- The managers of business firms need to become skilled in the social and political factors involved in their secondary relations, as well as in the economic and financial aspects of their primary relations. Neither skill alone will suffice.
- A business firm's acceptance by society—its legitimacy as an approved institution—depends upon its performance in both the primary *and* sec-

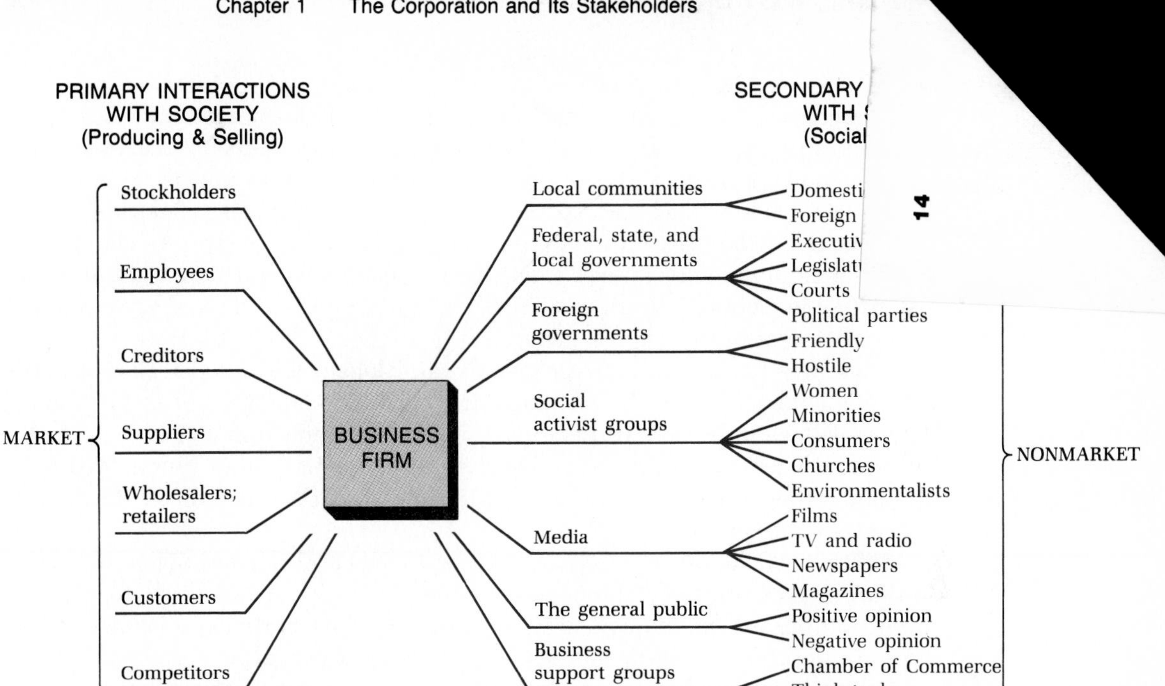

FIGURE 1–4
An interactive model of business and society relations.

ondary spheres. An automaker may be a successful manufacturer of reasonably priced cars that make a profit for the company but will encounter public disapproval if those cars are unsafe, polluting gas guzzlers.

The interactive model of business and society defines clearly the fundamental role of the business corporation in society. It recognizes that corporate decision makers need to take actions that protect and improve the welfare of society as a whole along with their own interests. The net effect is to enhance the quality of life in the broadest possible way, however the quality of life is defined by society. An effective relationship between business's actions and society's wants is thus achieved. Business acts in a manner that will accomplish social benefits along with the traditional economic gains that it seeks. It becomes concerned with its social as well as economic outputs and with the total effect of its economic and institutional actions on the society.

Stakeholder Interests and Powers

Stakeholder groups exist in many forms, some being well organized, others much less so. This variety makes it more difficult for a company's managers to understand and respond to stakeholder concerns. Each stakeholder has a unique involvement with the organization, and managers must understand the differing interests and respond accordingly. For example, stockholders have an ownership interest in the organization. The economic health and success of the corporation affect these people financially; their personal wealth is at stake. Customers, suppliers, and retailers have a different interest. Owners are most interested in realizing a return on their investment, while customers and suppliers are most interested in gaining fair value in the exchange of goods and money. Neither has a great interest in the other's stake.

Governments, public interest groups, and local communities have another sort of relationship with the company. In general, their stake is broader than the financial stake of owners or persons who buy products and sell services to the company. They may wish to protect the environment, assure human rights, or advance other broad social interests. Managers need to track these stakeholder interests with great care.

Different stakeholders also have different types and degrees of power. **Stakeholder power,** in this instance, means the ability to use resources to make an event happen or to secure a desired outcome. One authority describes three types of stakeholder power: voting power, economic power, and political power.[6]

Voting power (not referring to political, electoral voting) means that the stakeholder has a legitimate right to cast a vote. For example, each stockholder has a voting power proportionate to the percentage of the company's stock that he or she owns. Stockholders typically have an opportunity to vote on such major decisions as mergers, acquisitions, and other extraordinary issues. Through the exercise of informed, intelligent voting, they may influence company policy so that their investment is protected and will produce a healthy return.

Customers, suppliers, and retailers have a direct economic influence on a company. Their power is economic. Suppliers can withhold supplies or refuse to fill orders if a firm does not meet its contractual responsibilities. Customers can choose to boycott products or an entire company for any number of reasons; they may consider the goods to be too expensive, poorly made, unsafe, or inappropriate for consumption. Other customers may refuse to buy a company's products if the company enacts an improper policy.

Government exercises political power by creating legislation, making regulations, or bringing lawsuits against corporations. In an open political system, other stakeholders may exercise political power, too, using their resources to pressure government to adopt new laws or regulations or to take legal action against a company.

> In a landmark case, a group of citizens in Woburn, Massachusetts, sued W. R. Grace Company and Beatrice Foods for allegedly dumping toxic chemicals that leaked into underground wells used for drinking water. The deaths and illnesses of family members led the survivors to mobilize political power against Grace and Beatrice. Investigations were conducted by private groups and public agencies, and the toxic waste issue became politically important.

[6] R. Edward Freeman, *Strategic Management: A Stakeholder Approach,* Marshfield, MA: Pitman, 1984.

Of course, a single stakeholder is capable of exercising more th of power. The Woburn families sued the two corporations (political they had other powers, too. They could have led a boycott (econo against the companies, or purchased shares of stock in the companies and attempted to oust the directors and management through a proxy fight (voting power). Thus stakeholders who are intent on forcing a corporation to change its behavior have a variety of options for doing so. A company's managers must therefore understand the type of power each stakeholder group has or can readily acquire. Exhibit 1-A illustrates the nature of the interest and power of the key stakeholders identified in Figure 1–4.

EXHIBIT 1–A

PRIMARY AND SECONDARY STAKEHOLDERS: NATURE OF INTEREST AND POWER

Stakeholder	Nature of Interest—Stakeholder Wishes To:	Nature of Power—Stakeholder Influences Company By:
PRIMARY STAKEHOLDERS		
EMPLOYEES	■ Maintain stable employment in firm ■ Receive fair pay for work ■ Work in safe, comfortable environment	■ Union bargaining power ■ Work actions or strikes ■ Publicity
OWNERS/ STOCKHOLDERS	■ Receive a satisfactory return on investments (dividends) ■ Realize appreciation in stock value over time	■ Exercising voting rights based on share ownership ■ Exercising rights to inspect company books and records
CUSTOMERS	■ Receive fair exchange: value and quality for dollar spent ■ Receive safe, reliable products	■ Purchasing goods from competitors ■ Boycotting companies whose products are unsatisfactory or whose policies are unacceptable
SUPPLIERS	■ Receive regular orders for goods ■ Be paid promptly for supplies delivered	■ Refusing to meet orders if conditions of contract are breached ■ Supplying to competitors
COMPETITORS	■ Be profitable ■ Gain a larger share of the market ■ See the entire industry grow	■ Technological innovation, forcing competitors to "keep up" ■ Charging lower prices

Stakeholder	Nature of Interest—Stakeholder Wishes To:	Nature of Power—Stakeholder Influences Company By:
RETAILERS/ WHOLESALERS	■ Receive quality goods in a timely fashion at reasonable cost ■ Offer reliable products that consumers trust and value	■ Buying from other suppliers if terms of contract are unsatisfactory ■ Boycotting companies whose goods or policies are unsatisfactory
CREDITORS	■ Receive repayment of loans ■ Collect debts and interest	■ Calling in loans if payments are not made ■ Utilizing legal authorities to repossess or take over property if loan payments are severely delinquent
SECONDARY STAKEHOLDERS		
LOCAL COMMUNITIES	■ Employ local residents in the company ■ Ensure that the local environment is protected ■ Ensure that the local area is developed	■ Refusing to extend additional credit ■ Issuing or restricting operating licenses and permits ■ Lobbying government for regulation of the company's policies or methods of land use and waste disposal
SOCIAL ACTIVISTS	■ Monitor company actions and policies to ensure that they conform to legal and ethical standards, and that they protect the public's safety	■ Gaining broad public support through publicizing the issue ■ Lobbying government for regulation of the company
MEDIA	■ Keep the public informed on all issues relevant to their health, well-being, and economic status ■ Monitor company actions	■ Publicizing events that affect the public, especially those which have negative effects

Stakeholder	Nature of Interest—Stakeholder Wishes To:	Nature of Power—Stakeholder Influences Company By:
BUSINESS SUPPORT GROUPS (e.g., trade associations)	■ Provide research and information which will help the company or industry perform in a changing environment	■ Using its staff and resources to assist company in business endeavors and development efforts ■ Providing legal or "group" political support beyond that which an individual company can provide for itself
FOREIGN GOVERNMENT	■ Promote economic development ■ Encourage social improvements	■ Granting permits to do business ■ Adopting regulations
FEDERAL, STATE AND LOCAL GOVERNMENTS	■ Raise revenues through taxes ■ Promote economic development	■ Issuing regulations, licenses, and permits ■ Allowing or disallowing industrial activity
THE GENERAL PUBLIC	■ Protect social values ■ Minimize risks ■ Achieve prosperity for society	■ Supporting activists ■ Pressing government to act ■ Condemning or praising individual companies

Stakeholder Coalitions

Stakeholder coalitions are not static. The stakeholders that are highly involved with a company today may be less involved tomorrow. Issues that are most salient at one time may be replaced by other issues at another time; stakeholders who are most dependent on an organization at one time may be less dependent at another. To make matters even more complex, the process of shifting coalitions may not occur uniformly in all parts of a large corporation. Stakeholders involved with one part of a large corporation often will have little or no involvement with another part of the company.

Groups are always changing their relationships to one another in society. **Stakeholder coalitions** are the temporary unions of stakeholder groups that come together and share a common point of view on a particular issue or problem. There are very broad coalitions whose member organizations span the nation and the world. "Movements" such as the environmental movement or the consumer movement involve hundreds of state, national, and local affiliated organizations and may operate with little or no coordinated policymaking. Other movements, such as the Coalition for the Homeless, involve many groups and affiliates with a core policy-making board or group.

Coalitions of stakeholders have become internationalized as well. Sophisticated communications technology, coupled with political freedom and a shared sense of the need to be concerned about the behavior of multinational business, have created networks of sophisticated international activists. Coalitions have formed to monitor and protest multinational business behavior on such diverse issues as the marketing of infant formula products in developing nations and the sale, distribution, and use of commercial pesticides around the world.

> Consider the case of the Scott Paper Company, a U.S. multinational corporation headquartered in Philadelphia. In the late 1980s, Scott negotiated an agreement with the government of Indonesia to build a new paper and pulp processing plant in Sumatra, one of Indonesia's principal islands. Indonesian environmentalists were outraged at the proposal, however, and fought to prevent it. Sumatra holds some of Indonesia's rainforest, and it was feared that the presence of the plant would inevitably lead to rainforest destruction. In addition, paper and pulp plants are notorious for their air and water pollution discharges. The Indonesian environmentalists contacted friends in the U.S. environmental movement, including the Natural Resources Defense Council (NRDC). NRDC planned a national boycott of Scott Paper products, including such highly visible consumer products as Scotties tissues. Scott Paper's executives recognized their company's vulnerability to a consumer boycott and reluctantly withdrew from the Indonesian project. The Indonesian government was disappointed as well, having anticipated tax revenues and the creation of jobs. To keep the project alive, the government turned to a Japanese company to build and operate the paper and pulp plant.[7]

The combination of improved skills, national and international networks of experienced activists, and media interest in a wide range of local, national, and international issues makes coalition development and issue activism an increasingly powerful factor in business.

STAKEHOLDER EXPECTATIONS AND CORPORATE PERFORMANCE

Social issues often arise because a company's performance fails to meet the expectations of a stakeholder or stakeholder group. For example, when a company dumps normal garbage into a landfill or dump, that action is unimportant to everyone except the company's maintenance crew and the dump staff. If, however,

[7] This account is based on an interview by one of the authors with the head of the Indonesian Environmental Federation in 1990.

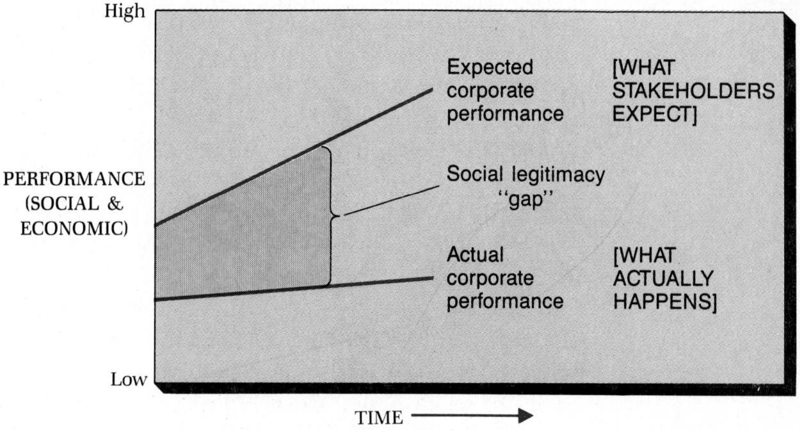

FIGURE 1–5
The performance-expectations gap is a measure of corporate social legitimacy.

the company includes toxic waste in its garbage, local residents, environmental groups, and government agencies—as well as the dump operator's staff—will have concerns because of new threats to their health and well-being. The company's performance in dumping regular solid waste met public expectations in the first instance; but disposing of toxic waste in this manner failed to meet expectations in the second instance.

Often, the first sign of a problem is a complaint, objection, or protest from a stakeholder group whose expectations are not being met. For example, a group of residents may object to the odor or smoke from a local plant, or others may protest the use of monkeys or mice for scientific research at a local university. Or an employee may claim that he or she became ill after working in a plant and breathing fumes from hazardous chemicals.

The Performance-Expectations Gap

What has happened in each of these instances is that a gap has developed between the expectations of the stakeholder (person or group) and the actual performance of the corporation. (See Figure 1–5.) Stakeholder expectations are a mixture of the opinions, attitudes, and beliefs of people about what constitutes responsible business behavior. The residents do not believe the air emissions constitute responsible behavior; people who care about animals do not believe it is morally responsible to inflict pain on animals in the name of scientific research; employees who choke on fumes do not believe it is ethically responsible to endanger their health in this way.

At this point, an unhappy or concerned group may try to build support by recruiting other citizens to their cause. They may print pamphlets, newsletters, and brochures or attract media attention. They are striving for visibility. The residents may picket the plant that is spewing foul smoke into the air. Animal rights groups may contact their local government representatives and demand that the university or commercial laboratory be prohibited from conducting painful experiments on animals. The employees may contact a local health department or government agency that is concerned with worker safety. Such actions may be the beginning of a course of action that escalates and gets progressively more hostile.

Managers have a responsibility to identify such emerging issues as early as possible. Failure to understand the concerns of stakeholders and to respond appropriately will permit the performance-expectations gap to grow larger. Real problems may exist and need correction. Ethical norms may be at stake. Stakeholders also may devise ways to draw more people, groups, and organizations into the fray. If they succeed, the issue may become exceedingly complex for the company and its managers. Individuals or groups of stakeholders who are concerned about an issue may direct their actions toward the company itself in hopes of producing a favorable response, or they may appeal to an appropriate level of government in hopes that governmental action will prompt the desired response from business. In practice, stakeholders may employ both types of action in a coordinated plan.

RESPONDING TO STAKEHOLDERS

The commitment by a company's managers to "manage the gap" between its own performance and stakeholders' expectations may be motivated by various factors. As illustrated in Figure 1–6, business is inclined to respond voluntarily to an issue when the requested action is consistent with management values and beliefs. On the other hand, involuntary responses can be prompted by a need to comply with the law, where failure to do so can lead to civil and criminal penalties. Stakeholder pressure is a middle ground approach, consisting of actions that

FIGURE 1–6
Different motivations produce different business responses.

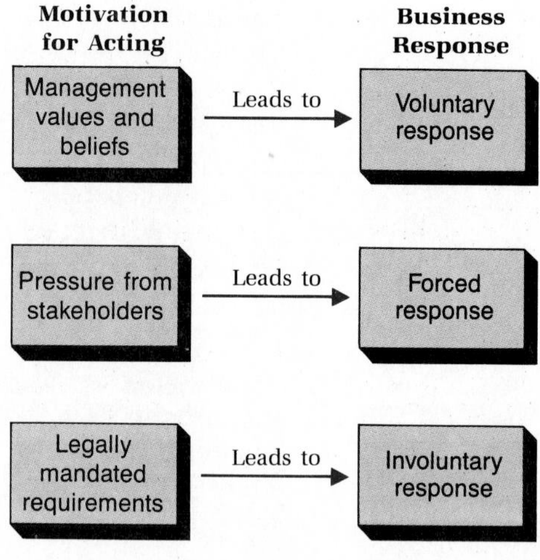

prompt quasi-voluntary responses (e.g., Perrier's recall of the benzene-contaminated water).

Whatever the motivation, managers may decide to focus on individual issues in an ad hoc, one-at-a-time way. Or the corporation may be redesigned to respond in a more systematic, strategic way. In the latter case, the company's management may try to anticipate problems before they arise, rather than react to them after they have occurred. Each of these approaches is discussed below.

Ad Hoc Responses

Some companies seem to approach problems on a "solve them as you see them" basis. That is, as a problem arises, and stakeholders press for action, management attention will turn to the issue. The greater the stakeholder pressure, the quicker the management response. This has been called the **pressure-response model** of corporate response to social issues.[8] As discussed above, Scott Paper Company moved quickly to reduce tensions once a consumer boycott was threatened. There are times, of course, when a company will respond as soon as it becomes aware of the problem. In large organizations, there are some types of issues that management simply cannot know about until a stakeholder points them out. Perrier's quick response to the existence of benzene illustrates this situation.

Ad hoc responses usually involve a company's secondary relationships and do not generate fundamental and continuing changes in the company's primary activity.[9] A plan to purchase products from minority vendors, or monitor the well-being of elderly customers, for example, may be very extensive but is still not part of the core primary activity of the company. One such voluntary program is described in Exhibit 1-B.

Strategic Responses

Strategic responses to stakeholder concerns usually do involve the company's primary activities and involvements. Strategic adjustments imply that the organization is altering its chosen course of action in a core area of activity because of stakeholder concerns about the company's conduct. The decision to add certain safety features to a new facility it is building is an ad hoc response; the decision to build the plant and conduct the operations has not changed. However, a decision to cancel the project itself is a strategic adjustment, reflecting a recognition that a *fundamental* premise of the decision was flawed.

> For example, when Consumers Power, a Michigan public utility, began to build a nuclear plant in Midland, Michigan, major opposition from stakeholders erupted. The battle dragged on for years, and finally the company

[8] James E. Post, *Corporate Behavior and Social Change*, Reston, VA: Reston Publishing Co., 1978.

[9] Lee Preston and James E. Post, *Private Management and Public Policy*, Englewood Cliffs, NJ: Prentice-Hall, 1975.

EXHIBIT 1-B

"In addition to providing low-cost, dependable service to our customers, and a good overall return to our shareholders, we are committed to being a caring and supportive corporate citizen. As an example, Empire was the first investor-owned company in Missouri to institute the Gatekeeper's Program. . . . In this program, trained employees recognize danger signs of the frail, elderly, homebound senior citizens in our service territory and report findings of these danger signs to appropriate agencies for investigation. Since its inception, we believe we have prevented at least two deaths, four exploitations of the elderly, and have extended the quality of life with integrity to many other senior citizens.

"I would like to go through some of the values we feel are important and govern our actions in business. First, recognition and satisfaction of our customer needs remain our number one priority. We take customer satisfaction personally. We are committed to providing superior value in our services on a continuing basis. When we take care of the customer first, everything else falls into place. Secondly, we are dedicated to creating value for our customers and financial communities by performing in a manner that will enhance returns on investment. And thirdly, we respect the individuality of each employee and foster an environment in which our employees' creativity and productivity can be encouraged, recognized, and rewarded."

R. L. Lamb, president of The Empire District Electric Company, an investor-owned electric company based in Joplin, Missouri. The Empire District Electric Company, *Quarterly Report to Stockholders and Report to Annual Meeting,* March 31, 1989 (letter dated May 10, 1989).

was forced to withdraw plans for the nuclear facility. In its place, a more conventional form of power plant technology was used and a new company (formed after CP filed for bankruptcy) took over the project. Consumers Power was forced to make a major strategic adjustment in order to accommodate stakeholders' concerns.

Companies may be slow to make strategic adjustments because such decisions usually involve basic and important aspects of the company's business. Yet the necessity of adapting to stakeholder concerns is one of the characteristics of successful businesses.

Partnerships

James O'Toole, author of *Vanguard Management,*[10] has written that some of America's best-managed companies (the ones he calls "Vanguard") believe that shareholders are best served when corporations attempt to satisfy the legitimate claims of all parties that have a stake in their companies. The task of management, as O'Toole sees it, is to resolve conflicts among competing claims of stakeholder groups. One way to do so is to incorporate the views of all into the decision

[10] James O'Toole, *Vanguard Management: Redesigning the Corporate Future,* New York: Berkley Books, 1987, pp. 42–43.

process. An alternative is to make the stakeholder a direct part of the process. In doing so, the stakeholder group is drawn into a partnership with the company.

> In the late 1970s, General Motors got into trouble by ignoring the needs of suppliers, dealers, employees, customers, and the society of which the company was a part. It lost market share of the U.S. automobile business, and all of the stakeholders suffered. GM approached the United Autoworkers' Union (UAW) and sought a number of "give backs" from unionized employees to help reduce costs and restore the company to health. Recognizing that everyone, including their members, had a big stake in GM's long-term position, the UAW made concessions that helped reduce GM's costs. GM's management then made the mistake of providing large raises for themselves! The union and its members were outraged, as was the public and GM's shareholders.
>
> In contrast to General Motors, Levi Strauss, maker of famous jeans and other clothing, faced comparable problems of costs and competition in the early 1980s. At one point, Robert Haas, the company's chief executive officer, had to go to the union and ask for wage concessions, including postponement of a previously negotiated raise. The union agreed, and no conflict ensued. Levi Strauss's management also took a wage freeze. Unlike GM's leaders, Levi's managers understood that it was important to the company that both union employees and managers demonstrate their common stake in helping the company through a difficult economic period. There was a "symmetry," in O'Toole's terms, between the interests of employees and managers. They were in partnership with one another.

Managing the Performance-Expectations Gap

Companies respond to their stakeholders in many ways. Some are very positive and productive; others are sometimes negative and produce serious conflicts. On some issues, corporations are known to have changed their approaches to managing the performance–expectations gap over time.

Research has shown that an organization's response to stakeholder concerns will vary depending on the situation. As illustrated in Figure 1–7, a company's response will reflect management's "stake" in preserving the current situation or status quo. If animal rights groups are asking for the shutdown of the company's only research facility, management may believe that keeping the facility open is its highest priority. If so, it may try to find ways to collaborate with the animal rights stakeholders or, alternatively, it may resist their efforts. Managers form mental pictures of their critics, just as critics form mental images of the company. If the management believes that animal rights activists are totally wrong about the issue ("there is a need for this research, and the animals do not feel pain"), it is likely to resist the requested changes.

There are times when the company and the stakeholders will cooperate because they believe they share a common stake. When the Norton Company was the target of an unfriendly takeover attempt by the British firm, BTR, the local

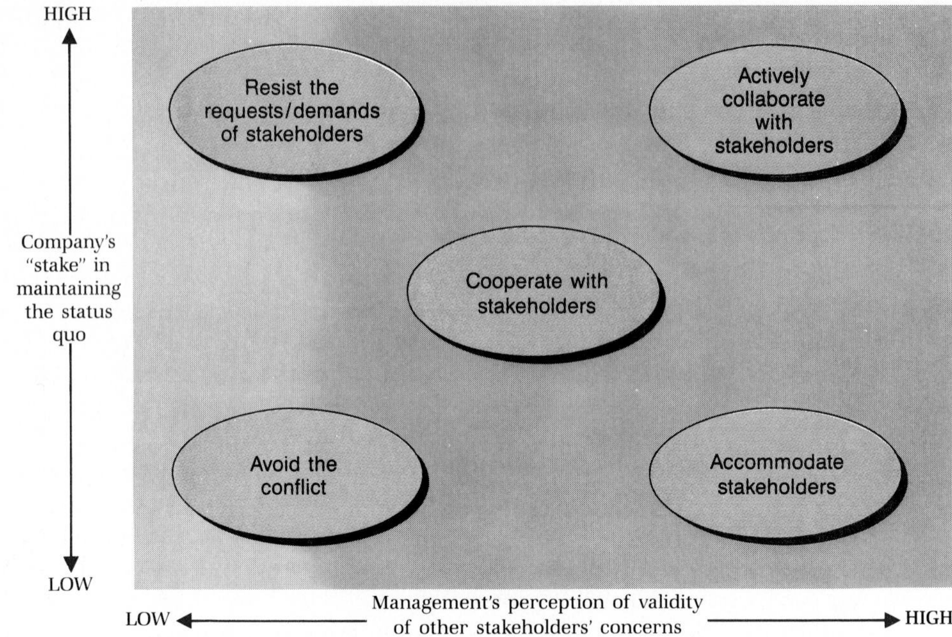

FIGURE 1–7 Responses to stakeholders depend on "stake" in status quo and how critics' concerns are perceived.

community, state legislators, and many others came to its assistance. Together, the company and many of its stakeholders collaborated on finding a way to prevent the unwanted acquisition. Eventually, the collaboration produced a result that the company and the stakeholders found acceptable.

There are times when a company's managers will conclude that it is best to meet stakeholder expectations by changing behavior in a way that delivers the results the stakeholders are seeking. Again, the company's management may see itself in agreement or disagreement with others, but because the company has little at stake, it seems prudent to accommodate the stakeholders by doing what is asked or trying to avoid the entire issue.

CONCLUSION

The relationship between business, government, and society is highly interdependent and complex. General systems theory states that all organisms or systems are affected by their host environments; thus an organization must be appropriately responsive to changes and conditions in its environment in order to survive and succeed.

The web of interactions between business, government, and society naturally generates a corresponding system of stakeholders—groups affected by and influential in corporate decisions and actions. Stakeholder analysis helps managers define specifically who the company's stakeholders are, what their interests and sources of power are, and how these change over time.

SUMMARY POINTS OF THIS CHAPTER

- Business, government, and society are an interactive system because each affects and influences the other and because neither can exist without the others. Economic, political, and cultural life are thoroughly entwined in one another in every nation. Together, they are the key distinguishing features of a society.
- Every business firm has complex involvements and interactions with others in society. Some are intended, some unintended; some are positive, others negative. Those related to the basic mission of the company are primary involvements; those which flow from those activities but are more indirect are secondary involvements.
- The people, groups, and organizations that interact with the corporation and have an interest in its performance are its stakeholders. Companies have both primary and secondary stakeholders.
- Stakeholders have a variety of powers, including economic, social, and political influence. Stakeholders have legitimate expectations of how a business firm should behave. If those expectations are not met, actions may pressure the company to change its behavior.
- When a gap exists between the expectations of stakeholders and a company's actual performance, action must be taken to adjust the corporation's behavior or change the expectations of the stakeholders. The response is likely to be affected by the company's ability to change its behavior and management's view of the validity of the stakeholders' concerns.

KEY TERMS AND CONCEPTS USED IN THIS CHAPTER

- Stakeholders
- Primary and secondary stakeholders
- Interactive model of business and society
- Stakeholder power
- Stakeholder coalitions
- Performance-expectations gap
- Pressure-response model

DISCUSSION CASE

FOOD MART STORES

Joe Smith, midwestern area manager of Food Mart Stores, was faced with a problem. Two stores in a suburban area of a medium-sized city in Missouri were scheduled to be closed. Just as this announcement was made, and with only one week left until closing, the townspeople sent hundreds of letters of protest to the president of the company, asking that the decision be reconsidered. The president turned the problem over to Smith.

When Smith visited the town, he found that one of the stores located in the Stone Hill area seemed to be highly desired, while local citizens were indifferent to the other. At the former store, he was met by picketers and media representatives, all of whom seemed to have an unfavorable opinion of the company for closing the store. Smith found the residents of the Stone Hill area to be highly organized and community oriented; they had formed a strong, united front, complete with petitions, form letters, and protest banners, in less than 24 hours.

After investigating, Smith discovered the major reasons for the protest. The senior citizens, numbering one in ten in the community, were the most ardent opponents. Because they could not carry heavy loads long distances, these people shopped frequently. If the store closed, they would be forced to take a bus in and out of the central city several times a week, and few of them could afford to do so. Another group opposed to the closing were local families in low-income brackets. Family incomes averaged $9,000 in the neighborhood, compared with the city average of $11,000. Jane Katz, the protest organizer, also mentioned that when the Food Mart Store had first come to the area, it had forced all other local stores out of business; they would not be there now to serve the residents if the only store left were to close.

The problem was not a simple one. Food Mart had been overhauling its operations for some time. Most of its small stores had been replaced with stores that not only were two or three times bigger, but which carried a much more diverse line of products than the basic food lines carried at the Stone Hill store. Renovations of older, smaller stores were rarely done because they were costly yet produced no increases in sales. The company, through this expansion program, had increased its efficiency, which allowed it to offer lower prices. Therefore, all the patrons (stakeholders) of the new stores were receiving benefits from the program.

On the other hand, customers of the Stone Hill store would suffer if it closed, or even if a new, larger location were opened which was not within walking distance. Jane Katz felt that Food Mart, as a large corporation, could easily absorb the costs of running one store that produced somewhat lower revenues than the rest. She asserted that, for humanitarian reasons, the store should stay open.

Smith had to take several factors into consideration. The profits of the company would probably increase if the two stores were closed and relocated to a larger site. This was important to the company, since it currently earned less than 2 percent on sales (before taxes and after operating costs). It also would be important to Smith, whose performance was evaluated on the profitability of this area. In addition, the patrons of the other new stores were benefiting from lower prices produced by the expansion program.

On the other hand, Smith could not ignore the protesters and the needs of the people in the community. The Food Mart Store had forced out all of its local competition. The local citizens of Stone Hill would have no convenient alternative. Since Food Mart had been the cause of the public's dependence on it, did not the corporation owe something to this public? Perhaps if the store had to be closed for economic reasons, the closing could be held off until a new store had moved to the area to service the customers. On returning to his office, Smith had to determine what to recommend to Food Mart's president.

Discussion Questions

1. Who are the stakeholders in this case? Which are primary, and which are secondary? What is the nature of each stakeholder's influence, and how much influence does each seem to have? Use illustrations from throughout the chapter to shape your answers.
2. If Smith decides to close the store immediately, how will the business-government-society relationship come into play? How might the issue unfold?
3. How should Smith handle the situation? Defend your recommendations and compare them with the viewpoints of others in the class.

2

Corporate Social Responsibility

Corporate social responsibility expresses the idea that business firms should help solve social problems as they pursue traditional economic goals. The general public expects business to be socially responsible, and many companies have responded by making social goals a part of their overall business operations. Guidelines for acting in socially responsible ways are not always clear, thus producing controversy about what constitutes such behavior, how extensive it should be, and what it costs to be socially responsible.

Key Questions and Chapter Objectives

This chapter focuses on these key questions and objectives:

- What is the basic meaning of corporate social responsibility?
- Where and when did the idea of social responsibility originate?
- What must a company do to be considered socially responsible?
- Are laws required to make corporations act in socially responsible ways, or can we count on voluntary corporate actions?
- How does social responsibility affect profits?

"I felt that a lot of people were being consigned, in many cases to what were human warehouses, prematurely, because families didn't quite know what to do with aging parents. I also felt that a lot of older people had time and energy to give and love. And here we had a day-care center for children who were somewhat deprived of contact with older people. It just kind of evolved."[1] So said Arnold Hiatt, chairman of Stride Rite Corporation, the maker of children's shoes and sports shoes, about an intergenerational care center located on the fourth floor of his corporation's headquarters. The center, which costs $500,000 a year to operate, provides care for children and older persons who interact with each other. Reflecting on this unusual corporate initiative, Hiatt said, "We invest in plants, we invest in equipment and we invest in research and development. But

[1] *Boston Globe*, July 11, 1989, pp. 25ff.

I think we're beginning to discover that a much more important investment are the people that make a difference in this country."

"There was an epic debate, almost theological in tone," declared Anthony J. F. O'Reilly, chairman of H. J. Heinz Company.[2] He was speaking of the company's board of directors, who in April 1990 had just announced that its subsidiary, Star-Kist Seafood Company, would no longer buy tuna caught by nets that also kill dolphins. Lobbied by environmentalists, boycotted by many consumers, and facing threatened new federal regulations to protect dolphins, Heinz and the other two leading tuna producers adopted this new environmental policy. The three companies normally sell around 70 percent of all tuna in the United States. Each can of the "dolphin-safe" tuna was expected to cost from 2 to 10 cents more. Star-Kist's president said, "We had been uncomfortable with the whole dolphin issue for a long time. Killing dolphins is undesirable for everyone." One financial analyst added, "The negative publicity of doing nothing would probably have harmed Heinz. Heinz would have looked like it was not being run by socially conscious people."

"I'm following the moral convictions of myself, our people, my company and my country. I generally believe in what our government does, but personally I'm embarrassed for our government right now." This comment came from Nick H. Prater, president of Mobay Corporation, a producer of thionyl chloride.[3] Mobay had just refused to fill a U.S. government order for the chemical, which is an ingredient of nerve gas. Prater cited a five-year-old company policy against use of its products in chemical weapons. He also criticized the U.S. government for continuing to manufacture these weapons while it was urging other nations to stop making them. The Defense Production Act of 1950 allows the government to force companies to supply materials necessary for national defense. Knowing this, Prater said, "If the Department of Commerce directs us to sell the product, we will do so; but, we will do so under protest."

These examples reveal some of the complexities of trying to act in socially responsible ways. In each case, some people believed the company was being socially responsible, while others thought the opposite. The top executives of these companies felt much pressure from those most affected, whether families with children and aging parents, environmentalists, or national defense officials. Stockholders, consumers, employees, and government regulators also had a stake in these decisions. All three episodes make it obvious that social responsibility involves questions of ethics, legality, economic costs, and management judgment.

In this chapter we discuss the advantages and drawbacks of being socially responsible. Most of all, though, we argue that social responsibility is an inescapable demand made by society. Whether businesses are large or small, make goods or services, operate at home or abroad, willingly try to be socially responsible or fight against it all the way—there is no doubt about what the public expects.

[2] "Lobbying, Research Convinced Heinz 'Dolphin-Safe' Tuna Made Business Sense," *New York Times News Service*, reprinted in *Pittsburgh Post-Gazette*, Apr. 17, 1990, pp. 1, 7.

[3] *Pittsburgh Press*, Mar. 29, 1990, pp. B7–B8; "Defense: A Chemical Reaction," *Newsweek*, Apr. 23, 1990, p. 25; Mobay Corporation news release, Mar. 28, 1990.

Many business leaders also subscribe to the idea of social responsibility. A 1990 *Business Week*–Louis Harris poll revealed that U.S. top-level corporate executives (69 percent of those polled) and MBA students (89 percent) believe that corporations should become more involved in solving social problems. Similar beliefs were recorded in a study of 107 European corporations, with prosocial attitudes being especially strong in Scotland and West Germany.[4] Corporate social responsibility may be complex, controversial, costly, and even risky, but it is an idea and a social demand that is here to stay.

THE MEANING OF CORPORATE SOCIAL RESPONSIBILITY

Corporate social responsibility means that a corporation should be held accountable for any of its actions that affect people, their communities, and their environment. It implies that negative business impacts on people and society should be acknowledged and corrected if at all possible. It may require a company to forgo some profits if its social impacts are seriously harmful to some of the corporation's stakeholders or if its funds can be used to promote a positive social good.

However, being socially responsible does not mean that a company must abandon its primary economic mission. Nor does it mean that socially responsible firms cannot be as profitable as others less responsible (some are and some are not). Social responsibility requires companies to balance the benefits to be gained against the costs of achieving those benefits. Many people believe that both business and society gain when business firms actively strive to be socially responsible. Others are doubtful, saying that business's competitive strength is weakened by taking on social tasks.

The social responsibilities of business grow directly out of two features of the modern corporation: (a) the essential functions it performs for society and (b) the immense influence it has on people's lives. We count on corporations for job creation, much of our community well-being, the standard of living we enjoy, the tax base for essential municipal, state, and national services, and our needs for banking and financial services, insurance, transportation, communication, utilities, entertainment, and a growing proportion of health care. These positive achievements suggest that the corporate form of business is capable of performing a great amount of good for society, such as encouraging economic growth, expanding international trade, and creating new technology.

The power and influence of the modern corporation are unmatched, as described by a leading expert:

> The large corporation generally—and the megacorporation in particular—has become a social institution which embraces the thousands of human beings whose lives are

[4] "A Kinder, Gentler Generation of Executives?" *Business Week*, Apr. 23, 1990, p. 86; and David L. Mathison and David Boje, "Have European CEOs' Social and Strategic Priorities Changed with the New Europe? A Preliminary Report," unpublished manuscript, College of Business Administration, Loyola Marymount University, n. d.

> affected by it and which provides an important focus for the employees' social relationships. In the more complex society, with greater mobility, the loosening of community ties, and urban anonymity, the neighborhood social unit has lost its cohesion and the corporation has assumed some of its role. . . . With the expansion of group health insurance programs, pension plans, and personal counselling services, the corporation is further strengthening the areas of its participation in the nonbusiness portion of its employees' lives.[5]

This "megacorporation" wields great political and governmental influence, according to an experienced U.S. business executive:

> Large corporations . . . have . . . moved a long way toward rivaling or surpassing the power of government on issues that are of special importance to them. . . .
>
> [In a sense] the large corporation becomes a part of government. This is the real character of the large companies that constitute a major part of the economic base of this country, a nation that still contains the greatest concentration of economic power in the world.[6]

Many people are concerned about potential corporate influence. In 1989, two-thirds of a national sample believed that "Business has gained too much power over too many aspects of American life."[7] The focused power found in the modern business corporation means simply that every action it takes can affect the quality of human life—for individuals, for communities, and for the entire globe. With such corporate technology as computers, communications satellites, and television networks drawing the world into a tighter and tighter "global village," the entire Planet Earth has become the corporation's most important stakeholder. All societies are now affected by corporate operations. As a result, social responsibility has become a worldwide expectation.

Social Responsibility in Other Nations

Social responsibility, however, takes different forms in different societies. Richard Wokutch, an experienced observer of Japanese industry, reveals the contrasting social environment found there:[8]

- In spite of heavy environmental pollution, and even some environmental disasters, "victims of environmental tragedies who have lobbied for compensation and recognition of environmental hazards have been treated as social outcasts by their fellow citizens."
- Racial discrimination, while illegal, is "a generally accepted social practice" that does not cause much public outcry or business action.

[5] Phillip I. Blumberg, *The Megacorporation in American Society*, Englewood Cliffs, NJ: Prentice-Hall, 1975, pp. 2–3.

[6] Alfred C. Neal, *Business Power and Public Policy*, New York: Praeger, 1981, pp. 136, 150.

[7] "The Public Is Willing to Take Business On," *Business Week*, May 29, 1989, p. 29.

[8] Richard E. Wokutch, "Corporate Social Responsibility Japanese Style," *The Academy of Management Executive*, May 1990, pp. 56–74.

- "It is not at all clear that significant changes in [sex discrimination] are in the offing. Japanese women seem resigned to a type of permanent second-class citizenship." The women's movement there is "ineffectual."
- Japanese stockholders and consumers are not as well protected against corporate abuses as in the United States. "It has been a traditional practice for [Japanese] corporations to employ thugs to physically intimidate dissident shareholders to keep dissent at annual meetings to a minimum."
- On the positive side, the Japanese corporate record of job safety is superior to that of the United States.

These striking differences occur because the culture of Japan is not the same as U.S. culture. According to Wokutch, the business climate in Japan is more placid, leaving Japanese firms relatively free of widespread protest by stakeholders. But when operating in other nations where social responsibility is actively promoted by organized stakeholders, some Japanese companies have been criticized for disregarding stakeholders' needs.

Corporate social responsibility also assumes a different form in several European nations because governments there provide many social services often demanded from private corporations in the United States. In addition, European

FIGURE 2–1
Opinions of corporate executives concerning selected social issues, 1990.

OPINIONS OF CORPORATE EXECUTIVES CONCERNING SELECTED SOCIAL ISSUES, 1990
(N = 107)

	Percent Answering Yes				
	USA	France	UK	Scotland	West Germany
Should corporations routinely test new employees for AIDS and drug use, or not?	59	27	8	32	19
Should corporations provide a separate career track for women executives to work part-time so they can continue to pursue a professional career without having to sacrifice the rewards of motherhood, or not?	46	39	52	69	60
Do women and minorities have the same opportunities to advance in [the respondent's country's] business as white males, or not?	44	24	31	7	50

SOURCE: Adapted from David L. Mathison and David Boje, *Have European CEOs' Social and Strategic Priorities Changed with the New Europe? A Methodological Study of France, U.K., and Germany: A Preliminary Report*, unpublished manuscript, Los Angeles, CA: College of Business Administration, Loyola Marymount University, n.d. Used with permission of the authors.

trade unions have promoted social goals without waiting for corporations to act. Figure 2–1 compares the contrasting attitudes of European and United States corporate executives toward two social responsibility issues: testing new employees for AIDS and drug use, and job opportunities for women and minorities.

In many of the world's developing nations where poverty is widespread or civil strife is frequent, economic goals and military activities tend to be given a higher priority than the pursuit of social goals. Environmental protection, for example, may be considered less critical than having a polluting steel plant that creates jobs. In these cases, social responsibility initiatives by business tend to be slow in coming.

HOW CORPORATE SOCIAL RESPONSIBILITY BEGAN

In the United States, the idea of corporate social responsibility appeared in the early part of the twentieth century. Corporations at that time came under attack for being too big, too powerful, and guilty of antisocial and anticompetitive practices. Critics tried to curb corporate power through antitrust laws, banking regulations, and consumer-protection laws.

Faced with this kind of social protest, a few farsighted business executives advised corporations to use their power and influence voluntarily for broad social purposes, rather than for profits alone. This approach appealed to those who opposed more government restrictions on business, because it allowed business to retain its power and influence while meeting some of society's demands. As one commentator noted, "For the corporate prince, then, it is better to be loved than feared. . . . American corporate officials moved from a denial of power to a denial of selfishness."[9]

Some of the wealthier business leaders—steelmaker Andrew Carnegie is a good example—became great philanthropists who gave much of their wealth to educational and charitable institutions. Others like automaker Henry Ford developed paternalistic programs to support the recreational and health needs of their employees. The point to emphasize is that these business leaders believed that business had a responsibility to society that went beyond or worked in parallel with their efforts to make profits.[10]

As a result of these early ideas about business's expanded role in society, two broad principles emerged. These principles have shaped business thinking about social responsibility during the twentieth century. They are the historical foundation stones for the modern idea of corporate social responsibility.

[9] Neil J. Mitchell, *The Generous Corporation: A Political Analysis of Economic Power,* New Haven: Yale University Press, 1989, p. 143.

[10] Morrell Heald, *The Social Responsibilities of Business: Company and Community, 1900–1960,* Cleveland: Case–Western Reserve Press, 1970. For a history of how some of these business philanthropists acquired their wealth, see Matthew Josephson, *The Robber Barons: The Great American Capitalists,* New York: Harcourt Brace, 1934.

The Charity Principle

The idea that the wealthier members of society should be charitable toward those less fortunate is a very ancient notion. Royalty through the ages have been expected to provide for the poor. The same is true of those with vast holdings of property, from feudal times to the present. Biblical passages invoke this most ancient principle, as do the sacred writings of other world religions. When Andrew Carnegie and other wealthy business leaders endowed public libraries, supported settlement houses for the poor, gave money to educational institutions, and contributed funds to many other community organizations, they were continuing this long tradition of being "my brother's keeper."

This kind of private aid to the needy members of society was especially important in the early decades of this century. At that time, there was no Social Security system, no Medicare for the elderly, no unemployment pay for the jobless, no United Fund to support a broad range of community needs, few Veterans Administration hospitals for war veterans, and no federal disaster relief system for the victims of storms and floods. There were few organizations capable of helping immigrants adjust to life in a new country, counseling troubled families, sheltering women and children victims of physical abuse, aiding alcoholics, treating the mentally ill or the physically handicapped, or taking care of the destitute. When wealthy industrialists reached out to help others in these ways, they were accepting some measure of responsibility for improving the conditions of life in their communities. In doing so, their actions helped counteract the critics who claimed that business leaders were uncaring and interested only in profits.

Before long, these community needs outpaced the riches of even the wealthiest persons and families. When that happened, beginning in the 1920s, much of the charitable load was taken on by business firms themselves rather than by the owners alone. The symbol of this shift from *individual* philanthropy to *corporate* philanthropy was the Community Chest movement in the 1920s, the forerunner of today's United Fund drives that are widespread throughout the United States. Business leaders gave vigorous support to this form of corporate charity, urging all business firms and their employees to unite their efforts to extend aid to the poor and the needy. In other words, what once had been a responsibility of wealthy individuals and families now became more of a shared responsibility of business firms, their employees, and their top-level managers.

Business leaders "established pension plans, employee stock ownership and life insurance schemes, unemployment funds, limitations on working hours, and high wages. They built houses, churches, schools, and libraries, provided medical and legal services, and gave to charity."[11]

For many of today's business firms, corporate social responsibility means this kind of participation in community affairs—making paternalistic, charitable contributions. However, charitable giving is not the only form that corporate social responsibility takes. The founders of the doctrine also had another principle in mind.

[11] Mitchell, op. cit., p. 3.

The Stewardship Principle

Many of today's corporate executives see themselves as stewards o act in the general public's interest. Although their companies are priva and they try to make profits for the stockholders, the company is man directed by professional managers who believe they have an obligation that everyone—not just those in need—benefits from the company's ac According to this view, corporate managers have been placed in a position public trust. They control vast resources whose use can affect people in fun damental ways. Because they exercise this kind of crucial influence, they incur a responsibility to use those resources in ways that are good not just for the stockholders alone but for society generally. In this way, they have become stewards, or trustees, for society. As such, they are expected to act with a special degree of social responsibility in making business decisions.[12]

This kind of thinking eventually produced the modern theory of stakeholder management, which was described in the opening chapter of this book. According to this theory, corporate managers need to interact skillfully with all groups who have a "stake" in what the corporation does. If they do not do so, their firms will not be fully effective economically or fully accepted by the public as a socially responsible corporation. As one former business executive declared, "Every citizen is a stakeholder in business whether he or she holds a share of stock or not, is employed in business or not, or buys the products and services of business or not. Just to live in American society today makes everyone a stakeholder in business."[13]

MODERN FORMS OF CORPORATE SOCIAL RESPONSIBILITY

These two principles—the charity principle and the stewardship principle—established the original meaning of corporate social responsibility. Figure 2–2 shows how these two principles have coalesced to form the modern idea of corporate social responsibility. **Corporate philanthropy** is the modern expression of the charity principle. The stewardship principle is given meaning today when corporate managers recognize that business and society are intertwined and interdependent, as explained in Chapter 1. This mutuality of interests places a responsibility on business to exercise care and social concern in formulating policies and conducting business operations. Exhibit 2–A shows how this idea is expressed by a leading insurance industry executive.

[12] Two early statements of this stewardship-trustee view are Frank W. Abrams, "Management's Responsibilities in a Complex World," *Harvard Business Review*, May 1951, and Richard Eells, *The Meaning of Modern Business*, New York: Columbia University Press, 1960.

[13] James E. Liebig, *Business Ethics: Profiles in Civic Virtue*, Golden, CO: Fulcrum, 1990, p. 217. For stakeholder theory, see R. Edward Freeman, *Strategic Management: A Stakeholder Approach*, Boston: Pitman, 1984.

	Charity Principle	Stewardship Principle
	Business should give voluntary aid to society's needy persons and groups.	Business, acting as a public trustee, should consider the interests of all who are affected by business decisions and policies.
[illegible] Expression	■ Corporate philanthropy ■ Voluntary actions to promote the social good	■ Acknowledging business and society interdependence ■ Balancing the interests and needs of many diverse groups in society
Examples	■ Corporate philanthropic foundations ■ Private initiatives to solve social problems ■ Social partnerships with needy groups	■ Stakeholder approach to corporate strategic planning ■ Optimum long-run profits, rather than maximum short-run profits ■ Enlightened self-interest attitude

EXHIBIT 2–A

"The [*1989 Social Report of the Life and Health Insurance Business*] shows unequivocally that this business is continuing to provide the corporate resources and leadership to address social problems and contribute to the quality of life in the nation. Through cash and in-kind contributions, socially responsive investments, and participation in hundreds of community projects, insurance companies are proving the extent of their concerns about better education and more affordable housing, shelter for the homeless, and vital services for people with AIDS. The range and scope of these activities reflect both the diversity within our industry and the willingness of companies to adjust their efforts to meet new and emerging needs.

[Our industry's] 17-year record of corporate public involvement . . . demonstrates a tradition of caring—about the people we serve, the communities in which we do business, and our own employees."

E. James Morton, chairman, Committee for Corporate Public Involvement, Social Report of the Life and Health Insurance Business, American Council of Life Insurance, and Health Insurance Association of America, in *1989 Social Report of the Life and Health Insurance Business,* cover page. Used with permission of the publisher.

Socially Responsible Activities

The best way to see what social responsibility involves is revealed in Figure. 2–3 and 2–4. These two sets of social priorities—one from the early 1970s and one in 1989—were developed by prominent business leaders and recommended to other companies. The Committee for Economic Development is a group of about 200 top-level business executives who advocated one of the first industry-wide programs of social responsibility. The insurance association's categories show the directions taken by social responsibility in the life and health insurance industry. Several of the categories in these two figures are identical or similar, while the differences tend to reflect the evolving horizon of social problems facing the United States. For example, AIDS education and treatment programs, along

FIGURE 2–3

Recommended social responsibility actions—Committee for Economic Development.

SOURCE: *Social Responsibilities of Business Corporations*, New York: Committee for Economic Development, 1971.

BUSINESS ACTIVITIES TO IMPROVE SOCIETY (Committee for Economic Development, 1971)

- **Economic growth and efficiency**
  Improving productivity
  Cooperating with government
- **Education**
  Giving aid to schools and colleges
  Assisting in managing schools and colleges
- **Employment and training**
  Training disadvantaged workers
  Retraining displaced workers
- **Civil rights and equal opportunity**
  Ensuring equal job opportunities
  Building inner-city plants
- **Urban renewal and development**
  Building low-income housing
  Improving transportation systems
- **Pollution abatement**
  Installing pollution controls
  Developing recycling programs
- **Conservation and recreation**
  Protecting plant and animal ecology
  Restoring depleted lands to use
- **Culture and the arts**
  Giving aid to arts institutions
- **Medical care**
  Helping community health planning
  Designing low-cost medical care programs
- **Government**
  Improving management in government
  Modernizing and reorganizing government

37

insurance industry.

SOURCE: *1989 Social Report of the Life and Health Insurance Business*, Washington, D.C.: American Council of Life Insurance and Health Insurance Association of America, 1989, pp. 4, 6.

TYPES OF COMMUNITY PROJECTS MOST FREQUENTLY SUPPORTED BY 175 LIFE AND HEALTH INSURANCE CORPORATIONS IN 1988

Community Project	Percent of Companies
Education	91
Arts and cultural programs	88
Local health programs	81
Youth activities	74
Neighborhood improvement programs	72
Minority affairs	60
AIDS education and treatment	59
Drug or alcohol abuse programs	57
Programs for the handicapped	55
Programs for hungry and homeless people	51
Health and Wellness Activities for Employees	
Exercise-fitness	85
Smoking cessation	79
Weight control	72
Periodic health examination	71
Nutrition	69
Stress management	64
Cardio-pulmonary resuscitation	64
Hypertension screening	60
Heart attack risk reduction	53

with support for homeless and hungry people, had become more important by the late 1980s. The lower half of Figure 2–4 gives a detailed breakdown of the employee health and wellness programs adopted by the companies.

Figure 2–5 shows how corporate social responsibility looks from outside the corporation. The Council on Economic Priorities (CEP) is a corporate watchdog organization that reports periodically on the social behavior of large corporations. In 1987 the Council began to "accentuate the positive" by citing companies that had demonstrated an outstanding record of socially responsible behavior. 1990's winners were Cummins Engine for its generous charitable contributions, Pitney Bowes for being responsive to employee needs, US West for encouraging equal opportunity and workplace diversity, AT&T for environmental programs, and Xerox for community action programs. That same year, three companies were given "dishonorable mentions"—Exxon for various environmental failures, Perdue Farms for dangerous conditions in its meatpacking plants, and USX for employee discrimination, unsafe working conditions, and pollution. Companies are ineligible for CEP's annual "corporate conscience award" if their charitable contributions are less than 1 percent of pretax earnings, if they operate in South Africa, if they have no women or minorities on the board of directors, if they have seriously violated environmental standards, if they make nuclear, chemical, or biological

FIGURE 2–5 Social responsibility actions cited by the Council on Economic Priorities.

SOURCE: *The Third (and Fourth) Annual America's Corporate Conscience Awards and Twentieth Anniversary Celebration.* New York: Council on Economic Priorities, 1989, 1990.

JUDGING THE CORPORATE CONSCIENCE— COUNCIL ON ECONOMIC PRIORITIES

Social Responsibility Category	Representative Annual Winner
Charitable contributions	Cummins Engine (1990) Dayton Hudson (1989)
Employer responsiveness (to employees)	Pitney Bowes (1990) Federal Express (1989)
Equal opportunity	US West (1990) Avon Products (1987)
Environment	AT&T (1990) 3M Corporation (1988)
Community action	Xerox (1990) IBM (1987)
South Africa operations	Polaroid (1987)
Opportunities for the disabled	General Mills (1988)

weapons, or if they are among the top ten weapons contractors for the Department of Defense.

The Business Enterprise Trust, founded in 1989 by prominent leaders in business, academia, labor, and the media, recognizes business leaders and other individuals who have significantly advanced the cause of social responsibility through "acts of courage, integrity, and social vision." The Trust's annual awards go to corporate executives and employees who have been responsible for socially useful products, creative crisis management, innovative human resource policies, responsible management of plant closings and hazardous waste disposal, or creating corporate cultures that support and encourage social responsibility. Several hundred individuals were nominated for the initial awards. The 1991 winners were cited for environmental improvements, meeting social needs, aiding the poor, and a sustained record of social responsibility leadership. The Trust's goals are summarized in Exhibit 2–B.

THE LIMITS OF CORPORATE SOCIAL RESPONSIBILITY

Social responsibility is widely expected of business, but it has limits. The main limits are cost, efficiency, relevance, and scope. As a result of these constraints, the amounts and kinds of social actions pursued by business are sometimes less than the public wants to see.

EXHIBIT 2–B

"The Business Enterprise Awards seek to identify and celebrate exemplary acts of business responsibility. The goal of the Awards is to spark a new awareness of farsighted, socially responsible business behavior—and to inspire others in business, especially the next generation, to emulate examples of this behavior. Stories about Award winners can promote new standards of business excellence and dispel the suspicion among some that responsibility and success are incompatible. . . .

"Given its importance, business has a special obligation of leadership. It must consider how it affects the common good and must develop responsible business practices that address the needs of its various constituencies. Yet, in the changing economic climate of the 1990s, finding innovative, effective and morally thoughtful strategies can be difficult. Overcoming short-term pressures that undermine long-term business needs can require ingenuity and vision. Standing firm on principles in the face of intense competition can require great courage. . . .

"Every day, individual managers and employees in companies of all sizes, confronted with difficult choices, are responding with creativity and integrity. They are pursuing enlightened new business strategies and initiatives—quietly, persistently and successfully."

The Business Enterprise Awards for Courage, Integrity, and Social Vision in Business, Stanford, CA: Business Enterprise Trust, 1990, pp. 8–9. Used with permission of the Business Enterprise Trust.

Costs

Every social action is accompanied by costs of one kind or another. A company's contributions to a worthy charity, or establishing a child care center for its employees, or adopting a dolphin-safe tuna-buying policy imposes costs on someone. A United Fund contribution could have been paid instead to company stockholders as a dividend. Money spent on a child care center could have been used instead to boost employees' wages. Dolphin-safe tuna is more costly to consumers. Building oil tankers with double hulls to prevent harmful oil spills boosts the price of gasoline. As worthy as some of these social actions may be, they do impose costs either on the business firm or on some groups in society.

Efficiency

The costs of social responsibility, like all business expenses, can potentially reduce a company's efficiency and affect its ability to compete in the marketplace. For example, if a company is pressured by a local community to keep an outmoded, inefficient plant in operation because closing it would mean a big job loss for local people, while its competitors close their old plants and move operations to foreign nations where wage rates are lower, which company is more likely to survive in the long run? The socially responsible managers who care for local employees, even though making what seems to be an admirable decision, may not be able to compete with their lower-cost, more efficient competitors.

Relevance

"Is this social problem any of our affair?" is a question worth asking by corporate officials. "Is it seriously affecting our business?" "Do we have the needed in-house talent?" "Can solving it help us, as well as others?" A "yes" answer to these questions might cause a company to take socially responsible action. If, for example, drug usage is causing serious safety problems in a plant, a company might be justified in spending money on a drug-education and treatment center that can help its employees and others in the community. Or when Eddie Bauer, the sporting goods company, supports the March of Dimes' programs for the physically handicapped, it gives tangible help while exhibiting its own concern.

However, a "no" answer or an "I'm not sure" answer to the questions should cause company executives to think twice. Social expenditures by corporations can be justified, and are considered to be a lawful use of stockholders' funds, if they promote the interests of the company while simultaneously helping society. This legal principle was established in a famous 1951 lawsuit when a judge ruled that corporations were justified in contributing company funds to a university because these corporate gifts benefited the company in the long run. Judgments about the relevance of any social activity are usually made by a firm's top-level executives who, in the words of the court, must take "a long-range view of the matter" and exercise "enlightened leadership and direction."[14]

Scope and Complexity

Some of society's problems are simply too massive, too complex, and too deep-seated to be solved by even the most socially conscientious company or even by all companies acting together.

Examples are environmental problems such as acid rain, ozone depletion in the upper atmosphere, and destruction of rainforests. What is required is joint action by corporations and governments in several nations, as happened when companies producing the chemicals that destroy the planet's high-level ozone layer agreed to phase out production gradually.

Some of today's health problems—AIDS, on-the-job drug abuse, and tobacco use—frequently reflect complex social conditions. While socially responsive businesses can adopt workplace policies and programs regarding these and other health problems, solutions are most likely to be found through joint actions of government, business, community groups, and the individuals involved.

Other social problems are even more persistent. These may include the deep-seated issues of race relations, sex discrimination, and ethnic and religious animosities. No single business firm can be expected to root out these long-standing features of society. The most it can do is to adopt socially responsible attitudes and policies about these issues, being certain that company practices do not make things worse.

[14] For a discussion of the precedent-setting A. P. Smith Manufacturing Company case, see Clarence C. Walton, *Corporate Social Responsibilities*, Belmont, CA: Wadsworth, 1967, pp. 48–52.

One respected authority on corporate social performance has identified another fundamental limitation on business's social responsibility. Social actions are limited, he maintains, because most people in society put their jobs and desire for material goods ahead of most social concerns. In other words, corporations who limit their social performance do so mainly in response to these unspoken but very real pressures from the public.[15]

These four limits often produce disagreements among those who want corporations to be socially responsible and those who think business is doing enough. The latter group usually declare, "Business cannot do more because of these limits." Their opponents in the debate usually respond by saying, "Business should be socially active in spite of these constraints, because business is obligated to help society solve its problems." Exhibit 2–C gives a flavor of these different viewpoints.

VOLUNTARY RESPONSIBILITY VERSUS LEGAL REQUIREMENTS

Do we need laws and government regulations to ensure socially responsible conduct by business? Or will business, knowing that society expects a high standard of social behavior, decide voluntarily to be socially responsible?

Oddly enough, the answer to both of these questions is "Yes." Business does need social guidance from laws and public policies.[16] Without them, companies would be uncertain about which social goals they should pursue and in which order of priority. For example, since the early 1970s, the public has signaled clearly that it wants the environment cleaned up, and lawmakers have responded by adopting strong pollution control laws and updating them every few years. These new legal rules set standards for business to follow. They tell business that environmental protection is an important social goal with a high priority.

Laws and regulations also help create a "level playing field" for businesses that compete against one another. By requiring all firms to meet the same social standards—for example, for the safe disposal of hazardous wastes—one firm cannot gain a competitive advantage over its rivals by dumping its wastes carelessly without the risk of lawsuits, fines, possible jail terms for some of its managers and employees, and unfavorable publicity for the lawbreaking firm.

Businesses that comply with laws and public policies are meeting a *minimum* level of social responsibility expected by the public. According to one leading scholar of corporate social performance, even legal compliance is barely enough to satisfy the public:

> The traditional economic and legal criteria are necessary but not sufficient conditions of corporate legitimacy. The corporation that flouts them will not survive; even the

[15] Neil Chamberlain, *The Limits of Corporate Responsibility,* New York: Basic Books, 1973.

[16] Chapter 9 in this book discusses public policy in greater detail. For further information, see Rogene A. Buchholz, *Essentials of Public Policy for Management,* Englewood Cliffs, NJ: Prentice-Hall, 1985, chaps. 1 and 2.

EXHIBIT 2–C

CORPORATE SOCIAL RESPONSIBILITY = SHAREHOLDER WEALTH

"In a market-based economy that recognizes the rights of private property, the only social responsibility of business is to create shareholder value and to do so legally and with integrity. Yet we do have important unresolved social challenges—from drug abuse to education and the environment—that require collective action. Corporate management however has neither the political legitimacy nor the expertise to decide what is in the social interest. It is our form of government that provides the vehicle for collective choice via elected legislators and the judicial system.

"Whether corporate social responsibility is advocated by political activists or the chief executive officer, the costs of these expenditures, which don't increase the value of the company or its stock, will be passed on to consumers by way of higher prices, or to employees as lower wages, or to shareholders as lower returns."

Alfred Rappaport, "Let's Let Business Be Business," *New York Times*, Feb. 4, 1990, p. F13.

CORPORATE SOCIAL RESPONSIBILITY = ALL STAKEHOLDERS

"Increasingly, responsible corporate behavior is being defined as taking into account the values, concerns, and needs of a wide variety of stakeholders, those parties—including those external to the organization—who have a legitimate stake, or interest, in the organization, its conduct and performance. Traditionally in business, these stakeholders have been identified solely as the company's shareholders, and the objective function of business was tidily summed up as maximizing the shareholders' wealth. . . .

"There are too many other competing interests in today's pluralistic society to ignore. Stakeholders other than shareholders have important claims on a business which also must be met if the company is to survive and flourish. Meeting these claims probably means less profit in the short term and may mean some reduction in potential shareholder wealth in the long term. Nonetheless, such outside groups and their demands cannot be ignored."

Edwin A. Murray, "Ethics and Corporate Strategy," in Robert B. Dickie and Leroy S. Rouner (eds.), *Corporations and the Common Good*, Notre Dame, IN: Notre Dame University Press, © 1986, pp. 108–109. Reprinted by permission of the publisher.

mere satisfaction of these criteria does not ensure the corporation's continued existence. . . .

Although relatively few corporations have been accused of violating the laws of their nations, they have been increasingly criticized for failing to meet societal expectations and failing to adapt their behavior to changing social norms. Thus, social responsibility implies bringing corporate behavior up to a level where it is in congruence with currently prevailing social norms, values, and performance expectations. . . . [Social responsibility] is simply a step ahead—before the new societal expectations are codified into legal requirements.[17]

[17] S. Prakash Sethi, "A Conceptual Framework for Environmental Analysis of Social Issues and Evaluation of Business Response Patterns," in S. Prakash Sethi and Cecilia M. Falbe (eds.), *Business and Society: Dimensions of Conflict and Cooperation*, Lexington, MA: Lexington Books, 1987, pp. 42, 43.

Not only are laws and regulations the least that the public expects from business performance, but by being stated in broad general terms they require interpretation to know just how they should be applied. So a company's version of how to comply with, for example, an equal opportunity hiring law may be quite different from how the hiring rules are seen by government regulators. If these differences result in a lawsuit, then the courts may interpret the law in yet another way. This means that business must use its own best judgment in interpreting and honestly trying to comply with the law. One such approach is called "enlightened self-interest."

Enlightened Self-Interest

Being socially responsible by meeting the public's continually changing expectations requires wise leadership at the top of the corporation. Companies with an ability to recognize profound social changes and anticipate how they will affect operations have been shown to be "survivors." They get along better with government regulators, are more open to the needs of the company's stakeholders, and often cooperate with lawmakers as new laws are developed to cope with social problems. Corporate leaders who possess this kind of social vision believe that business should help create social change rather than try to block it. With such an attitude, they know that their own companies will have a better chance of surviving in the turbulent social currents of today's world.[18]

Companies with this outlook are guided by **enlightened self-interest,** which means that they are socially aware without giving up their own economic self-interest. The Committee for Economic Development described it this way:

> By acting on its own [socially responsible] initiative, management preserves the flexibility needed to conduct the company's affairs in a constructive, efficient, and adaptive manner. And it avoids or minimizes the risk that governmental or social sanctions, produced out of a crisis atmosphere, may be more restrictive than necessary. . . .
>
> Enlightened self-interest thus has both "carrot and stick" aspects. There is the positive appeal to the corporation's greater opportunities to grow and profit in a healthy, prosperous, and well-functioning society. And there is the negative threat of increasingly onerous compulsion and harassment if it does not do its part in helping such a society.
>
> [This approach] has gradually been developing in business and public policy over the past several decades to the point where it supports widespread corporate practices of a social nature. . . .[19]

Voluntary Action versus Legal Compulsion

Should a company get credit for being socially responsible if its actions are required by law or government regulations? Some people say "No." They argue

[18] Robert H. Miles, *Managing the Corporate Social Environment: A Grounded Theory,* Englewood Cliffs, NJ: Prentice-Hall, 1987.

[19] Committee for Economic Development, *Social Responsibilities of Business Corporations,* New York: Committee for Economic Development, 1971, pp. 27, 29.

that the only truly socially responsible corporations are those who are motivated by a strong desire to do social good and who are willing voluntarily to "put their money—or their actions—where their mouth is." According to this view, a company that must be legally coerced to act in responsible ways falls short of the true meaning of social responsibility.

> For example, manufacturers of infant formula have been criticized for marketing this product in Third World nations where poverty and unsanitary conditions prevent its proper use. The resulting malnourishment, as many mothers give up breastfeeding their babies, contributes to high infant mortality rates in some countries. Only after many years of public protests and boycotts, and the threat of new laws to control marketing practices, were the manufacturers persuaded to modify their selling tactics.
>
> By contrast, in the famous Tylenol product-tampering case of the early 1980s, Johnson & Johnson immediately withdrew this endangered product from the shelves and voluntarily took other very costly steps to ensure the safety of consumers using this popular pain reliever. Company executives acted well in advance of legal pressures and collaborated closely with regulatory officials to safeguard the public.

Socially responsible actions frequently occur as a result of mixed motives—partly from a genuine desire to promote worthy social goals, partly from wanting to project a caring image of the company, and partly from the knowledge that government may step in if business fails to act on its own.

PROFITS AND SOCIAL RESPONSIBILITY

Do socially responsible companies sacrifice profits by working conscientiously to promote the social good? Do they make higher profits, better-than-average profits, or lower profits than corporations that ignore or flout the public's desires for a high and responsible standard of social performance?

Unfortunately, there is no precise answer to these questions, in spite of several attempts to discover the relationship between a company's financial performance and its social performance. Some studies seem to demonstrate that a good social performer also has a good record of profit making, but other research contradicts this finding.[20]

Faced with this kind of uncertainty, corporate executives who favor a positive and proactive approach to social responsibility have developed the following broad principles about how social activities can be reconciled with business's need for profits.

[20] A useful summary and discussion of these studies can be found in Kenneth E. Aupperle, Archie B. Carroll, and John D. Hatfield, "An Empirical Examination of the Relationship between Corporate Social Responsibility and Profitability," *Academy of Management Journal*, June 1985, pp. 449–459.

Long-run Profits versus Short-run Profits

Any social program—for example, an in-company child care center, a drug education program for employees, or lending company executives as advisers to community agencies—will usually impose immediate monetary costs on the participating company. These short-run costs certainly have a potential for reducing the company's profits unless the social activity is designed to make money, which is not usually the purpose of these programs. Therefore, a company may sacrifice **short-run profits** by undertaking social initiatives.

But what is lost in the short run may be gained back over a longer period. For example, if a drug education program prevents and reduces on-the-job drug abuse, the firm's productivity may be increased by lower employee turnover, fewer absences from work, a healthier workforce, fewer accidents and injuries, and lower health insurance costs. In that case, the company may actually experience an increase in its **long-run profits,** although it had to make an expensive outlay to get the program started.

Optimum Profits versus Maximum Profits

Maximum profits are the "official" goal of all business activities. Sometimes, however, business judgments are deliberately made that result in less than a maximum return. In these cases, companies seem willing to settle for **optimum profits** rather than maximum profits. An optimum profit is a return that is considered to be satisfactory by the managers or owners of a business. It may be lower than what is actually possible, and it is higher than the minimum return necessary to keep the company in business. An optimum profit may be the best a company can earn when operating in unfavorable economic conditions or under tough government regulations.

Social responsibility decisions may lead to optimum profits by diverting funds that otherwise could be used to drive profits close to the maximum level. For example, the drug education funds might have been used to purchase a more productive computer system. Or a favorable financial opportunity might be avoided in order to escape public protest, as happened to many U.S. firms who withdrew their generally profitable operations from South Africa during the 1980s.

Stockholder Interests versus Company Interests

Top-level managers, along with a corporation's board of directors, are generally expected to produce as much value as possible for the company's stockholders. This can be done by paying high dividends regularly and by running the company in ways that cause the stock's value to rise. Not only are high profits a positive signal to Wall Street investors that the company is being well run—thereby increasing the stock's value—but those profits make possible the payment of high dividends to stockholders. Low profits have the opposite effects and put great pressure on managers to improve the company's financial performance.

However, stockholders are not the only stakeholder group that management must keep in mind. All stakeholders must be considered. None can be ignored. The top manager's job is to interact with the totality of the company's stakeholders, including those groups who advocate high levels of social responsibility by business. Management's central goal is to promote the interests of the entire company, not just any single stakeholder group, and to pursue multiple company goals, not just profit goals.

This broader and far more complex task tends to put more emphasis on the long-run profit picture rather than an exclusive focus on immediate returns. It also leads to taking optimum profits rather than maximum profits. When this happens, dividends paid to stockholders may be less than they desire, and the value of their shares may not rise as rapidly as they would like.

These are the kinds of risks faced by corporate managers who have a fiduciary responsibility to produce high value for the company's stockholder-owners but who also must try to promote the overall interests of the entire company. Some of the corporate takeovers that occurred during the 1980s were brought on by a low-value, low-dividend record of the target company. Corporate raiders charged management with not producing high economic value for stockholder-owners. Takeovers often ousted one management team and put another in its place.

This dilemma continues to be a puzzle in the 1990s. Putting all of the emphasis on short-run maximum profits for stockholders can lead to policies that overlook the interests and needs of other stakeholders. Social responsibility programs that increase short-run costs also may be downgraded, although it is well known that socially responsible companies are strongly approved by the general public. To handle this problem, an enlightened self-interest point of view may be a useful and practical approach. That means incurring reasonable short-run costs to undertake socially responsible activities that benefit both the company and the general public. The results might satisfy stockholders' pressures for short-run profits while generating long-run positive public attitudes toward business.

SUMMARY POINTS OF THIS CHAPTER

- Corporate social responsibility means that a corporation should be held accountable for any of its actions that affect people, their communities, and their environment.
- The idea of corporate social responsibility in the United States first appeared in the early twentieth century and was adopted by business leaders as a new philosophy of corporate enterprise.
- The central themes of social responsibility have been charity—which means giving aid to the needy—and stewardship—which means acting as a public trustee and considering all corporate stakeholders when making business decisions.
- Business is limited in its efforts to be socially responsible by actions that impair business efficiency, are too costly, are unrelated to company goals and abilities, and are highly complex.

- Social responsibility is a result of both voluntary initiatives taken by business and laws that promote desirable social goals.
- Social responsibility does not necessarily lower profits but may encourage firms to focus on long-run profits rather than short-run profits, optimum profits rather than maximum profits, and promoting the interests of the entire company and all stakeholders rather than just the stockholders' interest.

KEY TERMS AND CONCEPTS USED IN THIS CHAPTER

- Corporate social responsibility
- Charity principle
- Stewardship principle
- Corporate philanthropy
- Enlightened self-interest
- Short-run profits
- Long-run profits
- Maximum profits
- Optimum profits

DISCUSSION CASE

CUMMINS ENGINE COMPANY

One admirer called it "capitalism at its best." Another said its chief executive officer "believed in superb products, concern for employees, involvement in the community—all those qualities that made American corporations the envy of the world."[21]

But as the 1990s began, this paragon of social responsibility appeared to be in trouble. It had lost over $100 million in 1986, almost as much in 1988, and had only a tiny net profit in 1987. It had fended off one British corporate raider at a cost of $72 million but faced another potential hostile takeover by a Hong Kong investor who held around 15 percent of the company's stock.

In spite of shaky profits, the company refused to cut long-term research spending to improve its products or to reduce charitable contributions which were among the highest in industrial America. Neither would company officials listen to those who urged a move from its Midwestern home to nonunion lower-cost areas in the South. When Hurricane Hugo devastated large sections of South Carolina in 1989, the company sent free engines and generators to some of the victims. Near its new factory in Brazil, it helped build a school, a clinic, and a gymnasium in a poor neighborhood.

[21] All quotations are from Robert Johnson, "Survivor's Story: With Its Spirit Shaken but Unbent, Cummins Shows Decade's Scars," *Wall Street Journal,* Dec. 13, 1989, pp. A1, A6; and Letters to the Editor, *Wall Street Journal,* Jan. 15, 1990, p. A11. See also Rogene A. Buchholz, William D. Evans, and Robert A. Wagley, *Management Response to Public Issues: Concepts and Cases in Strategy Formulation,* Englewood Cliffs, NJ: Prentice-Hall, 1985, pp. 239–249; and "Mr. Rust Belt," *Business Week,* Oct. 17, 1988, pp. 72–83.

Viewing this situation, one financial analyst declared, "Cummins is one big social slush fund. An incredibly naive attitude exists at the company. . . ."

The subject of all this commentary, both positive and negative, was Cummins Engine Company, a leading maker of heavy-duty diesel engines for trucks. From its founding in 1919, Cummins was known for a benevolent attitude, mainly a result of the religious convictions and social philosophy of Clessie Cummins, the founder. It also was famous for high-quality, reliable, and efficient engines, which earned profits for the company for 43 straight years until 1980. During the 1980s, Cummins began to feel the combined pressures of foreign competition, a recession, and takeover threats from raiders impatient with a spotty profit picture.

Cummins' long record of social responsibility is well known. Its headquarters town of Columbus, Indiana, is sprinkled with public buildings designed by some of the world's leading architects whose fees were paid by Cummins. The management staff was racially integrated as early as the 1960s, and Cummins became an early leader in reducing pollution caused by its engines. Employees are protected against unwarranted use of personal data in company files, and Cummins' chairman helped develop privacy guidelines for other employers. Many local causes draw upon the company's charitable funds, along with the voluntary help of company executives and employees. Townspeople remained fiercely loyal to the company, even after over 4,000 were laid off during the 1980s. Cummins employees receive good wages and benefits and take much pride in producing high-quality engines.

Faced with the tough competitive environment of 1990, Henry B. Schacht, Cummins' chairman, said, "Some say the company's main goal should be to maximize shareholder value . . . I say no. [The company's goal is] being fair and honest and doing what is right even when it is not to our immediate benefit." Hearing this, a Wall Street skeptic declared that Cummins has been "in a long-term mode for 10 years. . . . Schacht sounds great, but at some point there's got to be a payout for all this spending."

An outside observer responded by saying, "Wall Street stubbornly ignores the success of Japanese industrial enterprises—success achieved in long-term planning for market penetration, in lieu of a consuming emphasis on short-term results. If the financial community would lay off the hounding of public-company managements [like Cummins], allowing them to run their businesses instead of wasting valuable time reacting to the ill-conceived criticisms of these Wall Street gurus, domestic enterprises would be all the better for it."

A former chairman of the company summed up his own view: "Cummins has a fantastic future because it isn't just factories, machines and cash. It's outstanding people who take intense pride in their work and their community."

Demonstrating that his social skills are matched by an equal financial ability, Cummins' CEO in mid-1990 sold a 27 percent stake of the company to Ford Motor, Tenneco, and Kubota, a Japanese firm. The deal gave Cummins needed new business for its diesel engines and $250 million to reduce debt and invest in modernization.[22]

[22] "Turning Cummins into the Engine That Could," *Business Week*, July 30, 1990, p. 20.

Discussion Questions

1. Is Cummins' commitment to social responsibility fair to the company's stockholders? If you were Cummins' CEO, would you cut back on social expenditures so you could pay higher dividends to the company's owners? Would that keep the corporate raiders at bay?
2. Which principle of social responsibility—the charity principle or the stewardship principle—is the basis of Cummins' approach to social responsibility? Give some examples from the case.
3. Of the four major limits to social responsibility discussed in this chapter, which ones seem to apply to Cummins?
4. Is Cummins an example of what this chapter calls "enlightened self-interest?" Explain your answer.

3

Ethical Dilemmas in Business

People who work in business—managers and employees alike—frequently encounter and must deal with on-the-job ethical problems. Learning how to recognize the different kinds of ethical dilemmas and knowing why they occur is an important business skill. The costs to business and to society of unethical and illegal behavior are very large. A business firm is more likely to gain public approval and social legitimacy if it adheres to basic ethical principles and society's laws.

Key Questions and Chapter Objectives

This chapter focuses on these key questions and objectives:

- What is ethics? What is business ethics? Are they the same?
- Why should business be ethical?
- What major types of ethical dilemmas are found in business?
- Why do ethics problems occur in business?
- Are ethical behavior and legal behavior the same?

Roger Worsham had just graduated as an accounting major with an MBA degree and had landed a job with a small regional accounting firm in northern Michigan. Working there would give him the experience he needed to qualify as a certified public accountant (CPA). He, his wife, and their two small children settled in to enjoy small-town life. Roger's employer was experiencing tough competition from Big Eight companies who were able to offer more varied services, including management consulting, computerized data processing services, and financial advice. Losing a big client could mean the difference between staying open or closing down one of the local offices.[1]

During one of his first audit assignments of a local savings and loan (S&L) company, Roger uncovered evidence of fraud. The S&L was restricted by law to mortgages based on residential property, but it had loaned money to a manu-

[1] More details about this episode are in LaRue Tone Hosmer, *The Ethics of Management*, Homewood, IL: Irwin, 1987, pp. 143–147. See also "Big Eight Firms Woo Little Guy in an Effort to Grow," *Wall Street Journal*, Jan. 17, 1989, p. B2.

facturing company. To conceal this illegal loan from Roger, someone had removed the file before he began the audit. Roger suspected that the guilty party might have been the S&L president, who, in addition to being the largest owner of the manufacturing firm, was also a very influential lawyer in town.

Roger took the evidence of wrongdoing to his boss, expecting to hear that the accounting firm would include it in the audit report, as required by standard accounting practices. Instead, he was told to put the evidence and all of his notes through a shredder. His boss said, "I will take care of this privately. We simply cannot afford to lose this client." When Roger hesitated, he was told, "You put those papers through the shredder or I'll guarantee that you'll never get a CPA in Michigan, or work in an accounting office in this state for the rest of your life."

Question: If you were Roger, what would you do? If you were Roger's boss, would you have acted differently? What is the ethical thing to do?

Roger Worsham was not alone in grappling with an ethical dilemma at work, as revealed in the words of one manager in a large high-tech company:[2]

> There are a number of times when you know as manager that a particular individual has been identified to be laid off, . . . and everyday, and it may go on for several weeks, you have to come to work and acknowledge the person, deal with them, work with them, knowing that at a given point in time they are going to be out of a job literally. And yet, you can't prepare them, because your job as a manager is to try to get the pieces done, work with the company, and maintain the morale. It's a moral difficulty because I always feel that if I know that a particular individual is going to have something like that happen, that I should tell him. . . . However, I also understand . . . that in the business we do need his services for three more months.

Question: If you were this manager, what would you do? How would you feel if you were the employee? What is the ethical thing to do?

Ethical puzzles like these occur frequently in business. They are troubling to the people involved. Sometimes, a person's most basic ideas of fairness, honesty, and integrity are at stake. This chapter explores the meaning of ethics, identifies the different types of ethical problems that occur in business, and tells why these dilemmas arise. A discussion of corporate crime illustrates the relationship of law and ethics. The next chapter then tells how ethical performance in business can be improved by providing some tools for grappling with on-the-job ethical dilemmas.

THE MEANING OF ETHICS

Ethics is a conception of right and wrong conduct. Ethics tells us when our behavior is moral and when it is immoral. Ethics deals with fundamental human relationships—how we think and behave toward others and how we want them

[2] Quoted in Robbin Derry, "Moral Reasoning in Work-Related Conflicts," in William C. Frederick (ed.), *Research in Corporate Social Performance and Policy*, vol. 9, Greenwich, CT: JAI Press, 1987, p. 39.

to think and act toward us. Ethics principles are guides to moral behavior. example, in many societies lying, stealing, deceiving, and harming others a considered to be unethical and immoral. Honesty, keeping promises, helping others, and respecting the rights of others are considered to be ethically and morally desirable behavior. Such basic rules of behavior are essential for the preservation and continuation of organized life everywhere.

These notions of right and wrong come from many sources. Religious beliefs are a major source of ethical guidance for many. The family institution—whether two parents, a single parent, or a large family with brothers and sisters, grandparents, aunts, cousins, and other kin—imparts a sense of right and wrong to children as they grow up. Schools and schoolteachers, neighbors and neighborhoods, friends, admired role models, ethnic groups—and of course, the ever-present television—influence what we believe to be right and wrong in life. The totality of these learning experiences creates in each person a concept of ethics, morality, and socially acceptable behavior. This core of ethical beliefs then acts as a moral compass that helps to guide a person when ethical puzzles arise.

Ethical ideas are present in all societies, all organizations, and all individual persons, although they may vary greatly from one to another. Your ethics may not be exactly the same as your neighbor's, or one particular religion's notion of morality may not be identical to another's, or what is considered ethical in one society may be forbidden in another society. These differences raise the important and controversial issue of **ethical relativism,** which is the question of whether ethical principles should be defined by personal opinion, a society's traditions, various periods of time in history, or the special circumstances of the moment. If so, the meaning given to ethics would be relative to time, place, circumstance, and the person involved. In that case, there would be no universal ethical standards on which people around the globe could agree. For companies conducting business in several societies at one time, this question can be vitally important, and we discuss those issues in more detail later in this chapter.

For the moment, however, we can say that, in spite of the diverse systems of ethics that exist within our own society and throughout the world, all people everywhere do depend on ethical systems to tell them whether their actions are right or wrong, moral or immoral, approved or disapproved. Ethics, in this sense, is a universal human trait, found everywhere.

What Is Business Ethics?

Business ethics is the application of general ethical ideas to business behavior. Business ethics is not a special set of ethical ideas different from ethics in general and applicable only to business. If dishonesty is considered to be unethical and immoral, then anyone in business who is dishonest with employees, customers, stockholders, or competitors is acting unethically and immorally. If protecting others from harm is considered to be ethical, then a company that recalls a dangerously defective product is acting in an ethical way. To be considered ethical, business must draw its ideas about what is proper behavior from the same sources as everyone else. Business should not try to make up its own definitions of what is right and wrong. Employees and managers may believe at times that they are permitted or even encouraged to apply special or weaker ethical rules to business situations. But society does not condone or permit such an exception. People who work in business are bound by the same ethical principles that apply to others.

Figure 3–1 shows what executives from 300 U.S. and non-U.S. corporations consider to be ethical issues in business. Nearly half (45 percent) of the issues involve employee relations—in other words, the way people interact with each

FIGURE 3–1
Ethics issues identified by corporate executives.

SOURCE: Ronald E. Berenbeim, *Corporate Ethics*, Conference Board Research Report 900, New York: Conference Board, 1987, p. 3. Copyright The Conference Board, Inc. All rights reserved. Used with permission of The Conference Board.

IS THIS AN ETHICAL ISSUE FOR BUSINESS?

The Views of 300 Corporate Executives in the United States, Canada, Europe, Japan, and Australia, 1987

Issue	Percent Saying "Yes"
Widespread Agreement [High majority]	
Employee conflicts of interest	91%
Inappropriate gifts to corporate personnel	91
Sexual harassment	85
Unauthorized payments	84
Affirmative action	84
Employee privacy	84
Environmental issues	82
Moderate Level of Agreement [High to moderate majority]	
Employee health screening	79
Conflicts between company's ethics and foreign business practices	77
Security of company records	76
Workplace safety	76
Advertising content	74
Product safety standards	74
Corporate contributions	68
Shareholder interests	68
Corporate due process	65
Whistle blowing	63
Employment at will	62
Disinvestment [e.g., from South Africa]	59
Government contract issues [e.g., overcharging]	59
Financial and cash management procedures	55
Plant/facility closures and downsizing	55
Political action committees	55
No Consensus [Less than a majority]	
Social issues raised by religious organizations	47
Comparable worth [of men's and women's jobs/salaries]	43
Product pricing	42
Executive salaries	37

other and are treated on the job. About one-fifth of the issues deal with customer relations. Community ethical concerns account for another one-fifth of the list.

These same executives, when asked to name the ethical issues they believed would be very important in the next five years, identified six as particularly important: environmental issues (86 percent said it would be a serious or critical issue), product safety (78 percent scored it serious or critical), employee health screening (77 percent), security of company records (73 percent), shareholder interests (70 percent), and workplace safety (70 percent). These are the coming ethical challenges in business, as they see them.[3] All of these issues are given special attention in later chapters of this book.

Why Should Business Be Ethical?

Why should business be ethical? What prevents a business firm from piling up as many profits as it can, in any way it can, regardless of ethical considerations? For example, what is wrong with Roger Worsham's boss telling him to destroy evidence of a client's fraudulent conduct? Why not just shred the papers, thereby keeping a good customer happy (and saving Roger's job, too)?

We mentioned one reason when discussing social responsibility in Chapter 2. The general public expects business to exhibit high levels of ethical performance and social responsibility. Companies that flout this public attitude can expect to be spotlighted, criticized, curbed, and punished. Measuring up to public expectations of high ethical behavior is one way for business to gain widespread public approval. It means that business and society, working together in partnership, have found ways to enjoy the economic benefits of business while adhering to ethical principles of conduct.

A second reason why businesses and their employees should act ethically is to prevent harm to the general public and the corporation's many stakeholders. One of the strongest ethical principles is stated very simply: "Do no harm." A company that is careless in disposing of toxic chemical wastes that cause disease and death is breaking this ethical injunction. Many ethical rules operate to protect society against various types of harm, and business is expected to observe these commonsense ethical principles.

A third reason for promoting ethical behavior is to protect business firms from abuse by unethical employees and unethical competitors. A study commissioned by the International Retail Merchant Association reported that the average retail firm lost $21 million in 1989 from employee theft. Other estimates put the total amount of employee theft from all retail stores at $4 billion to $25 billion yearly. Unethical competitors also cause harm to businesses. "One New York apparel vendor says he lost a $4 million account with one of the nation's largest retailers because he, unlike one competitor, didn't bribe the buyer with $20,000 cars and pricey stereo systems."[4]

[3] Ronald E. Berenbeim, *Corporate Ethics*, New York: The Conference Board, 1987, pp. 3–4.

[4] "Bribery of Retail Buyers Is Called Pervasive," *Wall Street Journal*, Apr. 1, 1985, p. 6; and "Theft Shrinks Profits of Retailers," *Pittsburgh Post-Gazette*, Dec. 12, 1990, pp. 17, 19.

FIGURE 3–2
Reasons why business should be ethical.

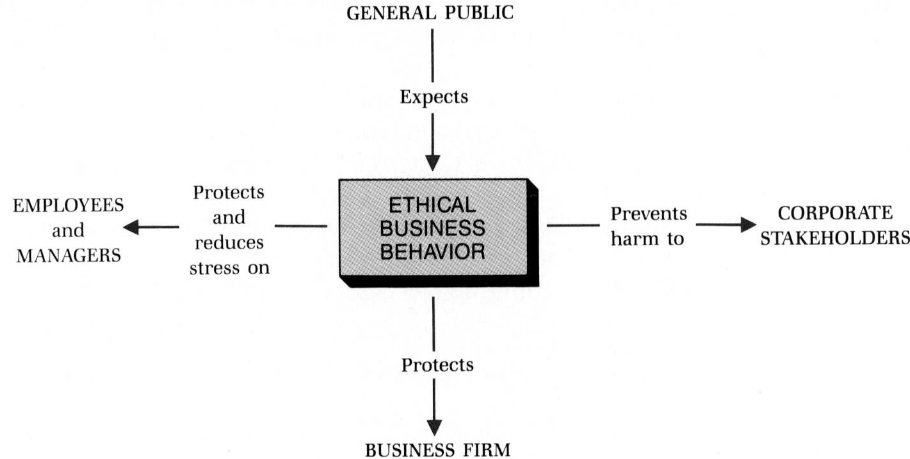

High ethical performance also protects people who work in business. Employees resent invasions of privacy (such as unjustified polygraph tests) or being ordered to do something against their personal convictions (such as falsifying an accounting report) or being forced to work in hazardous conditions (such as entering unventilated coal mines or being exposed to dangerous agricultural pesticides in the fields). Businesses that treat their employees with dignity and integrity reap many rewards in the form of high morale and improved productivity. It is a win-win-win situation for the firm, its employees, and society.

A fifth reason for promoting ethics in business is a personal one. Most people want to act in ways that are consistent with their own sense of right and wrong. Being pressured to contradict their personal values creates much emotional stress. Knowing that one works in a supportive ethical climate contributes to one's sense of psychological security. People feel good about working for an ethical company because they know they are protected along with the general public.[5]

Figure 3–2 diagrams these major reasons why business firms should promote a high level of ethical behavior.

TYPES OF BUSINESS ETHICS ISSUES

Not all ethics issues in business are the same. Some occur as people interact with each other on the job. These are everyday face-to-face ethical dilemmas related to people's jobs. Ethics dilemmas at this level often have a very human, personal dimension. Other ethics issues deal with large-scale problems such as oil spills, hazardous waste disposal, and a company's attitudes about honesty in advertising or sponsoring television programs that feature violence. These com-

[5] For a discussion of this kind of personal on-the-job stress, see James A. Waters and Frederick Bird, "The Moral Dimension of Organizational Culture," *Journal of Business Ethics*, vol. 6, 1987, p. 18.

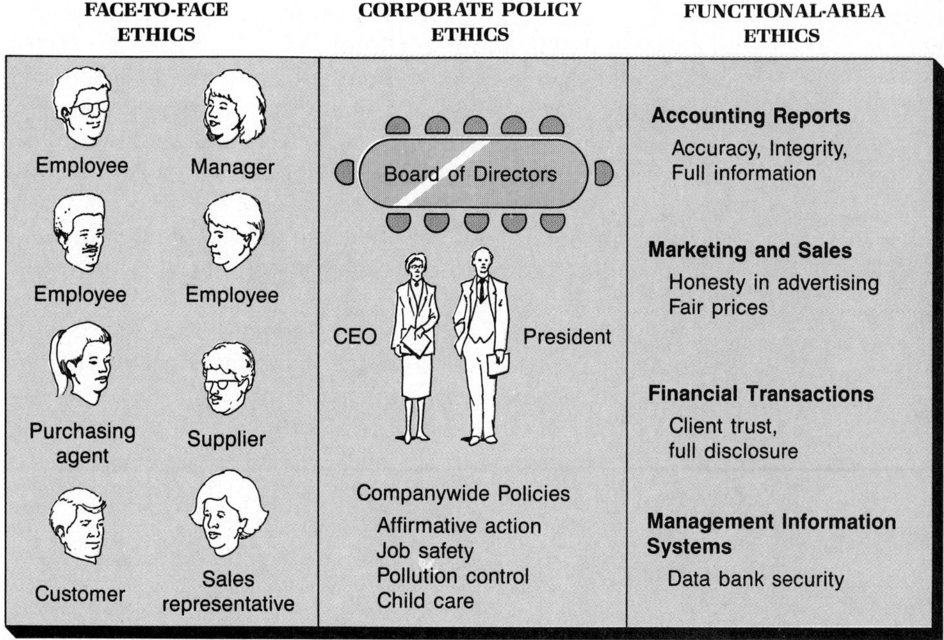

FIGURE 3–3 Diverse types of ethics issues in business.

panywide problems are focused at a higher level of organizational authority and require top-management policy decisions. Still other kinds of ethical puzzles appear in the different operational areas of business, such as accounting, marketing, finance, and others. These three types of ethics issues—**face-to-face ethics, corporate policy ethics,** and **functional-area ethics**—are depicted in Figure 3–3 and discussed next.

Face-to-Face Ethics

Problems having an ethical dimension appear frequently in most business firms. That is because there is a human element in most business transactions. For example, it is normal for a supervisor who works with a group of employees on a day-to-day basis to get to know something about their personal lives, whether they have children or elderly parents, what their professional goals are, and the various kinds of personal and family crises they encounter. The same kind of personal relationship may develop between a purchasing agent and the sales representative who sells supplies to a company; they frequently know one another on a first-name basis, have lunch together, and talk often on the telephone. As one purchasing manager said, "Good things can happen at lunch."[6] A company's best customers may be well known to people in the production department; it

[6] "Vendors' Gifts Pose Problems for Purchasers," *Wall Street Journal,* June 26, 1989, p. B4.

helps to ensure that the company's products fit the customer's needs. And every business firm has an informal network or "grapevine" that links employees together into small groups whose members interact closely with one another.

Because business is composed of these human interactions, it should not be surprising that face-to-face ethics issues occur from time to time. Studies have shown that managers and employees commonly encounter these "everyday moral issues" as they go about their work. Figure 3–4 shows that relations with employees, customers, and suppliers are most likely to generate this kind of ethical dilemma, and Exhibit 3-A lets managers tell in their own words how they view some of these situations.

As mentioned earlier, managers and employees face conflicts when their own personal standards differ from job demands. Particularly difficult are the giving of gifts and kickbacks to gain business, unfair discrimination in dealing with others, unfair pricing, and firings and layoffs that harm people. The unethical practices that one group of business executives most wanted to eliminate included unfair pricing, gift giving, cheating customers, and unfairness to employees.[7]

Corporate Policy Ethics

Companies are sometimes faced with ethical dilemmas that affect their operations across all departments and divisions of the firm. Top managers and the board of directors then are faced with establishing companywide policies to cope with the issues, such as the following.

- Should our company adopt a drug abuse policy, including required screening of employees for drug use and a remedial program for abusers? Will this policy violate our employees' privacy rights?
- When some of our employees who are members of National Guard units are called up for active duty in such places as Panama or the Middle East, should we have a policy that continues their pay and guarantees them their job back when they return? If so, will this practice lower our efficiency by having to rely on temporary replacements? What would be ethical?
- Even though our company is not a government contractor and does not receive any federal government funds, should we voluntarily develop an affirmative action program to hire and promote Hispanics, Native Americans, African Americans, and women of all races? Are we ethically obligated to promote social goals that are not required by law?

The ethical burden of deciding corporate policy normally rests on a company's leaders. The top managers and directors are responsible for making policies and seeing that they are carried out. The ethical content of their policies can have enormous influence throughout the company. It can set an ethical tone and send a forceful message to all employees as well as to external stakeholders.

[7] Scott J. Vitell and Troy A. Festervand, "Business Ethics: Conflicts, Practices and Beliefs of Industrial Executives," *Journal of Business Ethics*, vol. 6, 1987, pp. 115–16.

FIGURE 3–4
Face-to-face ethical issues and the groups most often involved.

SOURCE: Adapted from J. A. Waters et al., "Everyday Moral Issues Experienced by Managers," *Journal of Business Ethics,* vol. 5, 1986, p. 375; S. J. Vitell and T. A. Festervand, "Business Ethics: Conflicts, Practices and Beliefs of Industrial Executives," *Journal of Business Ethics,* vol. 6, 1987, p. 114; and R. Sandroff, "How Ethical Is American Business?" *Working Woman,* September 1990, p. 116.

TYPICAL MORAL ISSUES EXPERIENCED BY MA

Group	Percent of Issues	Typical I
With employees	36	Fair treat Help bey work Performance feedback and standing
With customers	21	Truthfulness in pricing, quality, and service Questionable selling practices
With suppliers	19	Maintaining professional relations Fair and impartial treatment

CONFLICTS BETWEEN COMPANY INTERESTS AND PERSONAL ETHICS REPORTED BY INDUSTRIAL EXECUTIVES

Group	Percent of Executives Reporting Conflict	
	Sometimes	Often
With customers	45.6	4.4
With suppliers	45.2	4.3
With employees	40.0	0

UNETHICAL ACTS PERSONALLY OBSERVED BY READERS OF *WORKING WOMAN*

Fairness Violations	
Favoritism or nepotism	70
Taking credit for others' work	67
Doing business with sexist clients	52
Discrimination	47
Sexual harassment	41
Stealing	
Expense-account abuses	52
Bribery	5
Dishonesty	
Lying to employees	52
Violating confidentiality	64
Lying to make a sale	31
Sexual trading	
Flirting to make a sale	43
Sexual intimacy with boss	29
Sex with co-worker on company time	19
Sex with client to make a sale	10

3-A

MANAGERS TALK ABOUT ETHICS

Regarding Employees

"We have a lot of people in my company who don't know where they stand. Half-truths or incomplete pictures are drawn in performance appraisals. The truth is bent and the employee is not dealt with in a forthright and honest fashion with respect to his performance and his prospects."

"We go out of our way to help an employee hit with a personal problem (e.g., drinking, financial crisis); we have intervened with creditors, negotiated better payback terms, all on a confidential basis."

Regarding Customers

"We have been forced to compromise quality in order to remain competitive. We secretly cheapen a product and keep selling it as if it met the standards of the original product and rationalize it as 'good enough for the application.' "

"We don't buy business but we do offer use of our ski chalet, fishing camp and Florida condo to our customers. It's a question of secretiveness and level of recipient. In our case we only offer it to top executives."

Regarding Suppliers

"I took over as works manager and discovered a great deal of 'patronage,' e.g., suppliers subsidizing parties, providing contracting services to the management club, tire suppliers providing tires to several foremen, etc.; I told the group that they had till the end of the month for 'confession' and that the practices were to stop immediately."

"Shades of truth are required in negotiating with suppliers. One may offer me a product at $3.50/unit and I tell him I have a promotion and need it at $3.00. After he says okay, I tell him to hold on and then go out to look for a promotion."

(Selected quotations from James A. Waters, Frederick Bird, and Peter D. Chant, "Everyday Moral Issues Experienced by Managers," *Journal of Business Ethics,* vol. 5, 1986, pp. 376–378. Reprinted by permission of Kluwer Academic Publishers.)

Functional–Area Ethics

Because business operations are highly specialized, ethics issues can appear in any of the major functional areas of a business firm. Each function tends to have its own particular brand of ethical dilemmas, as discussed next.

FIGURE 3–5
Ethical issues in the accounting profession.

SOURCE: Don W. Finn, Lawrence B. Chonko, and Shelby D. Hunt, "Ethical Problems in Public Accounting: The View from the Top," *Journal of Business Ethics*, vol. 7, 1988, p. 609. Reprinted by permission of Kluwer Academic Publishers.

ETHICAL ISSUES IN THE ACCOUNTING PROFESSION (Responses of 332 Practitioner Members of American Institute of Certified Public Accountants)

Rank	Issue	Frequency Mentioned
1	Client proposals of tax alteration and tax fraud	47%
2	Conflict of interest and independence	16%
3	Client proposals of alteration of financial statements	12%
4	Fee problems (billing, collection, contingent fee problems, or competitor bids)	10%
5	Other issues	15%
		100%

Accounting ethics

The accounting function is a critically important component of every business firm. Accounting reports tell owners and managers whether the firm is doing well or poorly. Company managers, external investors, government regulators, tax collectors, and labor unions rely on accounting data to make key decisions. Honesty, integrity, and accuracy are absolute requirements of the accounting function. Roger Worsham's dilemma, discussed at the beginning of this chapter, highlights the importance of honest accounting.

Professional accounting organizations—such as the American Institute of Certified Public Accountants and the Financial Accounting Standards Board—have developed generally accepted accounting principles whose purpose is to establish uniform standards for reporting accounting and auditing data. When they are followed, these standards go far toward ensuring a high level of honest and ethical accounting behavior. Failure to observe them, however, can produce the kinds of ethical issues shown in Figure 3–5. Such problems also occur in other nations; and member nations of the European Economic Community have discussed the desirability of adopting uniform accounting rules that would apply to all members.[8] The U.S. Foreign Corrupt Practices Act requires U.S. companies with foreign operations to adopt accounting procedures that ensure a full disclosure of the company's relations with sales agents and government officials; the purpose is to prevent bribery and other legally questionable payments.

[8] Andrew Likierman, "Ethical Dilemmas for Accountants: A United Kingdom Perspective," *Journal of Business Ethics*, vol. 8, 1989, pp. 617–629. For several excellent examples of ethical dilemmas in accounting, see Steven M. Mintz, *Cases in Accounting Ethics and Professionalism*, New York: McGraw-Hill, 1990; and "Battle of the Books: Audit Firms Are Hit by More Investor Suits for Not Finding Fraud," *Wall Street Journal*, Jan. 24, 1989, pp. A1, A12.

Marketing ethics

Relations with customers tend to generate many ethical problems. Pricing, promotions, advertising, product information, relations between advertising agencies and their clients, marketing research—all of these are potential problem areas. To improve the marketing profession, the American Marketing Association in 1987 adopted a code of ethics for its members. The AMA code advocates professional conduct guided by ethics, adherence to applicable laws, and honesty and fairness in all marketing activities. The code also recognizes the ethical responsibility of marketing professionals to the consuming public and specifically opposes such unethical practices as misleading product information, false and misleading advertising claims, high-pressure sales tactics, bribery and kickbacks, and unfair and predatory pricing. These code provisions have the potential for helping marketing professionals translate general ethical principles into specific working rules.[9]

Financial ethics

Finance produced some of the most spectacular ethics scandals of the 1980s. Wall Street financiers such as Ivan Boesky, Michael Milken, and Dennis Levine were found guilty of insider trading, illegal stock transactions, and various other financial shenanigans. E. F. Hutton, a leading stock brokerage firm, pleaded guilty to 2,000 counts of mail fraud for defrauding banks by illegally earning interest on phantom overnight deposits. Hundreds of savings and loan associations failed after their managers misused their depositors' funds, rewarded themselves and family members with lavish salaries and "perks," misled bank examiners, published false accounting reports, and left U.S. taxpayers to pay the cost of the largest corporate bailout in the nation's history.

Several other kinds of financial transactions are potential ethical minefields: investment banks that finance hostile corporate takeovers that threaten employees' jobs and local communities; trust departments charged with safely investing funds entrusted to them; money market managers who must vote on shareholder resolutions dealing with controversial ethical issues; whether a bank should side with a corporation's management team that has been a good customer even though management's policies cause damage to the company's stockholders; and a stockbroker's relationship with clients who seek sound investment advice.[10]

Other functional areas

Ethics issues also arise in purchasing departments where strong pressures are felt to obtain the lowest possible prices from suppliers and where suppliers feel a similar need to land lucrative contracts. Bribes, kickbacks, and discriminatory pricing are temptations to both parties.

[9] *Marketing News,* Sept. 11, 1987, pp. 1, 10; reprinted in John E. Richardson (ed.), *Business Ethics 89/90,* Guilford, CT: Dushkin, 1989, pp. 179–180. For additional information on marketing ethics, see O. C. Ferrell and K. Mark Weaver, "Ethical Beliefs of Marketing Managers," *Journal of Marketing,* July 1978, pp. 69–73.

[10] For several good examples of these and other areas, see John L. Casey, *Ethics in the Financial Marketplace,* New York: Scudder, Stevens & Clark, 1988.

Production and maintenance functions, which may seem to be remote from ethics considerations, can be at the center of some ethics storms. Dangerously defective products can injure or kill innocent persons, and toxic production processes may threaten the health of workers and the general public. A failure to follow recommended maintenance procedures caused the crash of an American Airlines DC-10, killing over 200 people in Chicago. Union Carbide's pesticide plant in Bhopal, India, was allegedly not properly maintained, and this failure was believed to be a contributing cause of the tragic leak that killed over 2,000 people.

One of the newest areas of ethical concern is management information systems and the data banks made possible by computer applications, where issues of privacy, confidentiality, and misuse of data arise.

These examples make one point crystal clear: all areas of business, all people in business, and all levels of authority in business encounter ethics dilemmas from time to time. Ethics issues are a common thread running through the business world.

WHY ETHICAL PROBLEMS OCCUR IN BUSINESS

Obviously, ethics problems in business appear in many different forms. While not common or universal, they occur frequently. Finding out just what is responsible for causing them is one step that can be taken toward minimizing their impact on business operations and on the people affected. Some of the main reasons are summarized in Figure 3–6 and are discussed next.

Personal Gain and Selfish Interest

Personal gain, or even greed, causes some ethical problems. Business sometimes employs people whose personal values are less than desirable. They will put their own welfare ahead of all others, regardless of the harm done to other employees, the company, or society. In the process of hiring employees there is an effort to weed out ethically undesirable applicants, but ethical qualities are difficult to anticipate and measure. The embezzler, the expense account padder, the bribe taker, and other unethical persons can slip through. Lacking a perfect screening system, business is not likely to eliminate this kind of unethical behavior entirely. Moreover, business has to proceed carefully when screening applicants, taking care not to trample on individuals' rights in the search for potentially unethical employees.

A manager or an employee who puts his or her own self-interest above all other considerations is called an **ethical egoist.** Self-promotion, a focus on self-interest to the point of selfishness, and greed are traits commonly observed in an ethical egoist. The ethical egoist tends to ignore ethical principles accepted by others, or to believe that "ethical rules are made for others." Altruism—which

FIGURE 3–6
Why ethical problems occur in business.

WHY ETHICAL PROBLEMS OCCUR IN BUSINESS

Reason	Nature of Ethical Problem	Typical Approach	Attitude
Personal Gain and Selfish Interest	Selfish interest vs. others' interests	Egotistical mentality	"I want it!"
Competitive Pressure on Profits	Firm's interest vs. others' interests	Bottom-line mentality	"We have to beat the others at all costs!"
Business goals vs. Personal values	Boss's interests vs. subordinates' values	Authoritarian mentality	"Do as I say, or else!"
Cross-cultural Contradictions	Company's interests vs. diverse cultural traditions and values	Ethnocentric mentality	"Foreigners have a funny notion of what's right and wrong!"

is acting for the benefit of others when your own self-interest is sacrificed—is seen to be sentimental or even irrational. "Looking out for Number One" is the ethical egoist's motto.[11]

Competitive Pressures on Profits

When companies are squeezed by tough competition, they sometimes engage in unethical activities in order to protect their profits. This may be especially true in companies whose financial performance is already substandard. Research has shown that poor financial performers and companies with lower profits, as compared with those with higher profits, are more prone to commit illegal acts.[12] However, a precarious financial position is only one reason for illegal and unethical business behavior, because profitable companies also can act contrary to ethical principles. In fact, it may be simply a single-minded drive for profits, regardless of the company's financial condition, that creates a climate for unethical activity.

Price-fixing is a practice that often occurs when companies compete vigorously

[11] For a compact discussion of ethical egoism, see Tom L. Beauchamp and Norman E. Bowie, *Ethical Theory and Business,* 3d ed., Englewood Cliffs, NJ: Prentice-Hall, 1988, pp. 18–21.

[12] For a discussion, see Peter C. Yeager, "Analyzing Corporate Offenses: Progress and Prospects," in William C. Frederick (ed.), *Business Ethics: Research Issues and Empirical Studies,* Greenwich, CT: JAI Press, 1990, pp. 168–171; and Philip L. Cochran and Douglas Nigh, "Illegal Corporate Behavior and the Question of Moral Agency: An Empirical Examination," in William C. Frederick (ed.), *Research in Corporate Social Performance and Policy,* vol. 9, Greenwich, CT: JAI Press, 1987, pp. 73–91.

in a limited market. Besides being illegal, price-fixing is unethical behavior toward customers, who pay higher prices than they would if free competition set the prices. Companies fix prices to avoid fair competition and to protect their profits, as happened in the following case.

> The nation's two largest waste haulers, Waste Management and Browning-Ferris, pled guilty in 1987 to price-fixing and allocating customers between themselves in the Toledo, Ohio, area; each company paid a fine of $1 million. A similar charge in 1984 led to their conviction for price-fixing in Atlanta. In 1988, yet another lawsuit was brought against them—this time by some of their biggest customers—charging a conspiracy to fix prices nationwide for container-refuse service. The two corporations denied these latest charges, as they had the earlier ones.[13]

Price-fixing among competing companies is not the only kind of unethical behavior that can occur.

> According to a committee of outside directors of Miniscribe, a producer of computer disk drives, competitive pressures caused the company to falsify sales figures, inflate inventories, ship drives that had not been ordered, accumulate defective drives that had been returned and then sell them again as new products, package bricks and ship them to distributors as disk drives, secretly break into auditors' files to change inventory figures on the auditors' reports, and file misleading and inaccurate financial reports. Miniscribe's top managers allegedly resorted to these tactics from 1985 to 1988 when the computer industry was suffering a general decline and after Miniscribe had lost IBM, one of its biggest customers.[14]

Other kinds of unethical behavior also occur under competitive pressures. Suppliers can be forced to lower their prices to companies, thereby receiving less than a fair price. When company officials have a strict "bottom-line mentality" shaped almost exclusively by market competition, they may overlook the ethical claims of their many stakeholders. Doing so has the unfortunate and needless effect of pitting business against society.

Business Goals versus Personal Values

Ethical conflicts in business sometimes occur when a company pursues goals or uses methods that are unacceptable to some of its employees. "Whistle-blowing" may be one outcome, if an employee "goes public" with a complaint after failing to convince the company to correct an alleged abuse. Another re-

[13] "Waste Management, Browning-Ferris Face Charges of Nationwide Price Fixing," *Wall Street Journal,* Feb. 17, 1988, p. 15.

[14] "Cooking the Books: How Pressure to Raise Sales Led MiniScribe to Falsify Numbers," *Wall Street Journal,* Sept. 11, 1989, pp. A1, A8; and "MiniScribe's Investigators Determine That 'Massive Fraud' Was Perpetrated," *Wall Street Journal,* Sept. 12, 1989, p. B4.

course for employees caught in these situations is a lawsuit, as happened in the following cases.

> A pilot for Eastern Airlines charged in court that he had been given undesirable flight assignments and was suspended from work for insisting, without success, that certain safety improvements should be made on cockpit equipment that later was implicated in a fatal airplane crash.
>
> A senior design engineer for Ford Motor Company brought suit after the company had demoted him and later brought about his termination because he objected to hazardous design features of the Ford Pinto's windshield and gas tank. The placement of the gas tank was allegedly responsible for fiery rear-end crashes that killed and injured many Pinto drivers and rear-seat passengers. He said, "Our main purpose as Ford employees was to increase corporate profits. . . . In short we were forced to indulge in poor engineering practices, and had to assume responsibility for components we knew were marginal in design—or worse."[15]

The protesting employees in these companies were not troublemakers. They tried to work through internal company procedures to get the problems corrected. The ethical dilemma arose because the company's goals and methods required the employees to follow orders that they believed would harm themselves, other employees, customers, the company, and the general public. As far as they were concerned, they were being asked or ordered to do something unethical. Their own internal ethical compass was at odds with the goals and methods of their company.

Cross-Cultural Contradictions

Some of the knottiest ethical problems occur as corporations do business in other societies where ethical standards differ from those at home. Today, the policymakers and strategic planners in all multinational corporations, regardless of the nation where they are headquartered, face this kind of ethical dilemma. Consider the following situations:

> U.S. sleepwear manufacturers discovered that the chemicals used to flameproof childrens' pajamas might cause cancer if absorbed through the child's skin. When these pajamas were banned from sale in the United States, some manufacturers sold the pajama material to distributors in other nations where there were no legal restrictions against its use.

Question: Although the foreign sales were legal, were they ethical? Is "dumping unsafe products" unethical if it is not forbidden by the receiving nation?

[15] These episodes are described in greater detail in Alan F. Westin, *Whistle-Blowing! Loyalty and Dissent in the Corporation*, New York: McGraw-Hill, 1981. The quotation is from pp. 120–121.

When Honda began building automobile plants in Ohio, it located them in two mostly white rural areas and then favored job applicants who lived within a 30-mile radius of the plant. This policy excluded blacks who lived in Columbus, the nearest big city. Earlier, Honda also had agreed to pay nearly half a million dollars to settle an age-discrimination suit brought by older job applicants who had been refused work there.

Question: Were Honda's job-hiring policies, which would have caused few problems in Japan, unethical in Ohio?

These episodes raise the issue of ethical relativism, which was defined earlier in this chapter. Should ethical principles—the ones that help chart right and wrong conduct—take their meaning strictly from the way each society defines ethics? Are Japanese attitudes toward job opportunities for minorities, older workers, and women as ethically valid as U.S. attitudes? Were the children's pajama makers on solid—or shaky—ethical ground when they sold the cancer-risky pajama cloth in countries where government officials did not warn parents about this possible health risk? Who should assume the ethical responsibility? What or whose ethical standards should be the guide?

As business becomes increasingly global, and as more and more corporations penetrate overseas markets where cultures and ethical traditions vary, these questions will occur more frequently. Employees and managers need ethical guidance from clearly stated company policy if they are to avoid the psychological stresses mentioned earlier. One U.S. corporate executive emphasized this point by saying that he and his company "recognize that the world consists of a wide array of races, religions, languages, cultures, political systems and economic resources. We accept these differences as legitimate and desirable; we recognize that each country must determine its own way. . . . However, we must not use local custom as an excuse for violating applicable laws or corporate policies. We regard observing local law to be the minimum acceptable level of conduct; PPG's own standards frequently oblige us to go beyond that legal minimum and to conduct our affairs according to a higher standard."[16]

Some who study international business ethics say that such higher standards of ethics already exist. They point to the numerous treaties and codes of conduct for regulating the activities of multinational corporations regarding environmental protection, equitable treatment of employees, laws against bribery and other questionable payments in international trade, and protection of basic human rights in the workplace. Thomas Donaldson, a leading ethics scholar, has outlined a set of fundamental human rights—including the right to security, to freedom of movement, to subsistence income, and other rights—that should be respected by all multinational corporations.[17]

[16] Vincent A. Sarni, chairman, PPG Industries, Inc., *Worldwide Code of Ethics,* Pittsburgh, PA, n.d.

[17] Thomas Donaldson, *The Ethics of International Business,* New York: Oxford University Press, 1989. For a discussion of international codes of ethics, see William C. Frederick, "The Moral Authority of Transnational Corporate Codes," *Journal of Business Ethics,* vol. 10, 1991, pp. 165–177.

ETHICS, LAW, AND ILLEGAL CORPORATE BEHAVIOR

Before discussing specific ways to improve business's ethical performance (in the next chapter), we want to consider the relationship of law and ethics. Some people have argued that the best way to assure ethical business conduct is to insist that business firms obey society's laws. However, this approach is not as simple as it seems.

Law and ethics are not quite the same. Laws are similar to ethics because both define proper and improper behavior. In general, laws are a society's attempt to formalize—that is, to reduce to written rules—the general public's ideas about what constitutes right and wrong conduct in various spheres of life. However, it is rarely possible for written laws to capture all of the subtle shadings that people give to ethics. Ethical concepts—like the people who believe in them—are more complex than written rules of law. Ethics deals with human dilemmas that frequently go beyond the formal language of law and the meanings given to legal rules. The following situations demonstrate that there is not always a perfect match between the law and important ethical principles.

In 1986, some of the nation's largest convenience chains decided to quit selling *Playboy* and *Penthouse* because some of their customers objected to the magazines' sexually explicit photographs and articles. Although selling these magazines was not illegal, protesters argued that it was immoral because the material degraded women and encouraged sexual promiscuity among readers. For these groups, pornography laws were inadequate for coping with what they saw as an ethical crisis.

About the same time, many groups in the United States objected to U.S. corporations doing business in South Africa. They claimed that South Africa's racial laws deprived the majority black population of fundamental human rights and therefore were in direct conflict with basic ethics principles. On the other hand, those opposed to business withdrawal from South Africa pointed out that their companies were not breaking the law by conducting business there. Their attitude was, "As long as it is legal, it is not unethical."

These episodes suggest that legality cannot always define when something is believed to be ethical or unethical. Although laws attempt to codify a society's notions of right and wrong, they are not always able to do so completely. Obeying the law is usually one way of acting ethically, and the public generally expects business to be law-abiding. But at times, the public expects business to recognize that ethical principles are broader than the law. Because of the imperfect match between law and ethics, business managers who try to improve their company's ethical performance need to do more than comply with the law. Society will generally insist that they heed ethical principles *and* the law.[18]

[18] For a discussion, see Richard McCarty, "Business, Ethics and Law," *Journal of Business Ethics*, vol. 7, 1988, pp. 881–889.

EXHIBIT 3-B

LAWBREAKING IN BUSINESS

"Nearly two-thirds of the Fortune 500 corporations were charged with violations of corporate law over a two-year period (1975–1976); one-half of these were charged with a serious or a moderately serious violation. At least one sanction was imposed on 321 of the corporations. Using imposed court sanctions, one study found that 11 percent of the Fortune 500 were involved in a major law violation between 1970 and 1979. A more recent study found that 115 corporations of the Fortune 500 had been convicted between 1970 and 1980 of at least one major crime or had paid civil penalties for serious illegal behavior. Allowing for size, the largest of the Fortune 500 corporations have been found to be the chief violators. Moreover, they have received a widely disproportionate share of the sanctions for serious and moderate violations.

"These corporate violations . . . include pricefixing, false advertising claims, the marketing of unsafe products, environmental pollution, political bribery, foreign payoffs, disregard of safety regulations in manufacturing cars and other products, the evasion of taxes, and the falsification of corporate records to hide illicit practices. . . .

"On the other hand, a sizable proportion of these large corporations maintain high ethical standards and exhibit significant social responsibility in their dealings with the public, consumers, and workers. A two-year study (1975–1976) found that 40 percent of the Fortune 500 corporations had not been charged with any violations of law by any of the 25 federal agencies during that period of time."

Marshall B. Clinard, *Corporate Ethics and Crime: The Role of Middle Management*, Beverly Hills, CA: Sage, 1983, pp. 15–16. References to the various studies cited have been omitted. Used with permission of the publisher.

Corporate Lawbreaking and Its Costs

Although estimates vary, lawbreaking in business is not unusual, as revealed in Exhibit 3-B. This kind of illegal business behavior causes serious financial losses.

> A Department of Justice estimate put the total annual loss to taxpayers from reported and unreported violations of federal regulations by corporations at $10 to $20 billion. The Chamber of Commerce of the United States (1974), a conservative probusiness organization, has estimated that various white-collar crimes cost the public some $40 billion a year. One of the most thorough attempts to calculate the financial loss to the country from corporate crimes was that of [a U.S. Senate subcommittee which] put the cost of corporate crime at between $174 and $231 billion a year. Compared to even the lesser of these estimates, the $3 to $4 billion annual loss to street crime [robbery, burglary, assault, etc.] represents only a small proportion of the economic cost of crime.[19]

Beyond these dollar costs of illegal behavior are the physical and social costs. Over 100,000 deaths each year are attributed to occupational diseases, and most

[19] Ronald C. Kramer, "Corporate Criminality: The Development of an Idea," in Ellen Hochstedler (ed.), *Corporations as Criminals*, Beverly Hills, CA: Sage, 1984, p. 19.

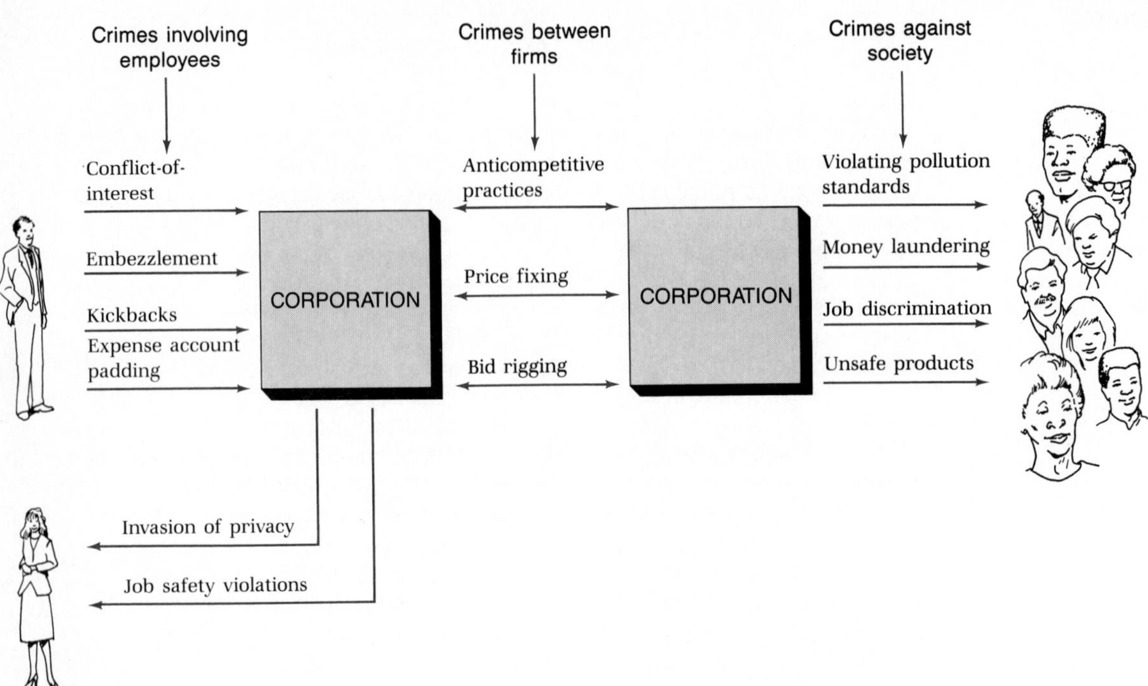

FIGURE 3–7
Major types of corporate crime.

of these are a result of violations of health and safety laws. Over 14,000 workers are killed annually in industrial accidents; 2 million others receive disabling injuries on the job. The blame for these deaths and injuries can be shared by careless employees and by employers who fail to adhere to occupational health and safety laws.

Consumers also suffer the costs of illegal business behavior. The U.S. Consumer Product Safety Commission has estimated that some 20 million serious injuries occur each year because of unsafe food and drugs and defective consumer products. The general public also is injured when companies violate environmental protection laws.[20]

Types of Illegal Business Behavior

Not all lawbreaking in business is alike. Some violations are committed by employees against their own company. In other cases, employees violate laws that benefit the company. Sometimes, company lawbreaking harms the general public; at other times, a company's own employees may bear the brunt of illegal activities. These different types of illegal actions are diagramed in Figure 3–7 and are discussed next.[21]

[20] Kramer, op. cit., pp. 19–21.
[21] For a discussion of the different types of illegal business behavior, see Marshall B. Clinard, *Corporate Ethics and Crime: The Role of Middle Management,* Beverly Hills, CA: Sage, 1983, pp. 12–19.

Crimes involving employees

As noted earlier, employees can harm their own company when they take bribes from suppliers, embezzle company funds, falsify expense accounts, or have conflicts of interest such as hiring unqualified family members or channeling company business to outside firms in which they have a financial interest. These actions are usually called **occupational crimes** because the opportunities for lawbreaking and for personal gain arise from a person's occupation or job.

In these cases, employees have violated their legal and ethical duty of loyalty and fidelity to their employer. They have enriched themselves unjustly at the employer's expense. Companies try to combat occupational crime by carefully screening prospective employees, installing surveillance systems, establishing tight accounting controls, and issuing detailed guidelines in the form of codes of conduct.

However, employees themselves can be harmed if their employing firm does not comply with employee-protection laws. Examples are failure to provide equal job opportunities or not enforcing job safety regulations or allowing unauthorized use of personal medical information in an employee's file.

Corporate crimes

Another kind of illegal behavior occurs when employees deliberately and consciously break laws in ways that benefit their own business firm. These violations are usually called **corporate crimes** because the corporation is the primary beneficiary. However, the individual employee also may benefit by demonstrating a willingness to put the firm's goals ahead of legal compliance.

Crimes against other companies

Some illegal actions are taken by one company against another for the purpose of financial or competitive gain. If a group of electrical contractors agrees secretly to fix the prices of its services and to divide the available business among its members, their industrial customers will have to pay unfairly high prices. Such actions are forbidden by law.

Insider trading is another violation of law and of stock exchange rules. It occurs when someone in a position of trust gets secret, proprietary information about a potential change in the price of a company's stock and then uses this "inside" information to buy or sell the stock. As a result, others who did not have access to the same inside information could not take advantage of the opportunity to buy or sell the stock. They therefore lose money or lose an opportunity to profit from such an investment. Insider trading can be either an occupational crime—when an individual employee personally gets the benefits of the illegal transaction—or it can be a corporate crime—when the illegal profits go to a stock brokerage firm or investment banking firm.

Crimes against the government

Several defense contractors during the 1980s were found guilty of fraud against the Department of Defense. An example is Sunstrand, an aerospace manufacturer that pleaded guilty to billing the government for cost overruns on fixed-price contracts and charging taxpayers for expenses incurred by company executives for baby-sitting, saunas, golf, movies, dog kennels, servants, and snowplowing at their homes. Sunstrand also admitted buying wine, liquor, meals, and sporting event tickets for Defense Department employees and their wives "to improve its ability to market its products to the Defense Department." The company paid penalties of $199 million and was temporarily suspended from bidding on future military contracts.[22]

Crimes against community stakeholders and the public interest

When corporations carelessly dump dangerous wastes where they may harm people or the environment, their actions harm the general public.[23] The same is true when a company produces consumer goods, such as children's toys, that are defective and dangerous for an entire group of people in society. Society has acted through its legal system to forbid such harmful behavior, so business has an obligation and an ethical duty to comply with such laws. If it does not do so, the general public interest and the rights of many community stakeholders are violated.

Acting both legally and ethically pays many dividends to corporations. They enjoy the goodwill of the general public and of the many stakeholders whose lives are affected by business operations. Their managers and employees have the satisfaction of working for a company whose practices reflect their own personal ethical commitments as well as society's general conceptions of what is considered to be right and moral. While it is true that ethical conduct may impose short-run costs on a business firm, it is also true that the long-run gain in public approval and in the personal satisfaction of those who work for the company goes far to offset those costs. In the following chapter, we discuss specific steps that businesses can take to improve their ethical performance.

SUMMARY POINTS OF THIS CHAPTER

- Ethics is a conception of right and wrong behavior, defining for us when our actions are moral and when they are immoral.
- Business ethics is the application of general ethical ideas to business behavior.
- Ethical business behavior is expected by the public, prevents harm to society, protects business against unscrupulous employees and competitors, pro-

[22] "Sunstrand to Plead Guilty to Fraud on Defense Work, Pay U.S. $115 Million," *Wall Street Journal,* Oct. 13, 1988, p. A3; "Defense Agency Bars Sunstrand from New Jobs," *Wall Street Journal,* Oct. 20, 1988, p. B2; and "Sundstrand Former Officials Cleared of Fraud," *Wall Street Journal,* Oct. 11, 1990, p. A4.

[23] For several examples of severe injuries, see "Toxic Turpitude: Environmental Crime Can Land Executives in Prison These Days," *Wall Street Journal,* Sept. 10, 1990, pp. A1, A6.

tects business employees from harmful actions by their employer, and allows people in business to act consistently with their personal ethical beliefs.

- Business ethics issues usually appear in three different forms: face-to-face personal interactions on the job; corporate policy ethics involving companywide ethical concerns; and functional–area ethics in accounting, personnel, marketing, and other core business functions.
- Ethical problems occur in business for many reasons, including selfishness by a few, competitive pressures on profits, a clash of personal values and business goals, and cross-cultural contradictions in global business operations.
- Although law and ethics are closely related, they are not the same; ethical principles tend to be broader than legal principles.
- Illegal behavior by business and its employees imposes great costs on business and the general public.

KEY TERMS AND CONCEPTS USED IN THIS CHAPTER

- Ethics
- Ethical relativism
- Business ethics
- Face-to-face ethics
- Corporate policy ethics
- Functional-area ethics
- Ethical egoist
- Law
- Occupational crimes
- Corporate crimes

DISCUSSION CASE

IT'S A SHORT LIFE, SO GO AHEAD AND LIGHT UP!

"You can't turn around to a guy who is going to die at age 40 and tell him that he might not live two years extra at age 70," said a British tobacco company executive. He was defending cigarette sales to smokers in poor Third World nations where average life expectancy is much lower than in advanced nations.[24]

The world's tobacco companies in the last quarter century have turned to overseas sales to bolster profits made at home. These foreign markets are especially important for their long-term survival. Numerous scientific studies link smoking to many life-threatening diseases such as cancer, stroke, and heart disease. Governments in North America, Western Europe, and other advanced regions began restricting tobacco sales in the 1960s and 1970s. Health warnings are required

[24] Except when otherwise noted, quotations and examples used in this case are from Steve Mufson, "Smoking Section: Cigarette Companies Develop Third World as a Growth Market," *Wall Street Journal*, July 5, 1986, pp. 1, 19. Reprinted by permission of the *Wall Street Journal*, © 1986 Dow Jones & Company, Inc. All rights reserved worldwide.

on cigarette packages and in tobacco advertisements; television ads for tobacco products are banned in the United States and several other nations; sports figures may not be depicted in cigarette ads in Israel; nonsmoking seating arrangements are required in many restaurants, public buildings, and entertainment centers; by 1990 many globe-straddling airlines banned all smoking except on the longest flights; and city ordinances often attempt to make cigarette vending machine sales to minors especially difficult.

Third world markets are an especially attractive prospect for the tobacco companies. A large and youth-weighted population there is growing rapidly, government smoking regulations are absent or less onerous, and in some nations an expanding middle class is eager to identify itself with the symbols of wealth and success that are seen as typical of life in advanced countries. The third world "is where the growth is," according to one expert on the tobacco industry; estimates put third world sales at about one-third of the world total. In most of these nations, no health warnings are required and radio and television advertising is not restricted.

Because average incomes are low, individual cigarettes are sold. Even so, tobacco use burdens family budgets. In Bangladesh, according to a British medical journal, people spend about 20 percent of their incomes on tobacco, thereby threatening the family's dietary needs.

Cigarette ads are appealing. B.A.T. Industries' Ambassador cigarette billboard in Zaire is labeled "La classe" and shows a business-suited man stepping from a chauffeured Mercedes. Another promotion for Graduate cigarettes in Nigeria features a university student in cap and gown. The Gold Leaf brand depicts a lawyer in the traditional British white wig, claiming Gold Leaf to be "a very important cigarette for very important people."

Defending these ads, one tobacco company representative said, "Every cigarette manufacturer is in the image business. [In these countries] a lot of people can't understand what is written on the ads anyway, so you'll zero in on the more understandable one and usually on a visual image."

As these ads take hold in the third world, smokers there get a bigger dose of tar and nicotine than smokers in the advanced nations. "These people are used to smoking their own locally made product, which might have several times as much tar and nicotine," said a spokesperson for B.A.T., the London-based manufacturer. "It's a black lie that we sell higher tar and nicotine in the third world," countered a Philip Morris vice president; but a study of Benson & Hedges Special Filter cigarettes showed tar and nicotine content ranged from 31 to 83 percent higher in some developing nations.

Speaking of the lax regulatory attitude toward tobacco use in poorer nations, one tobacco industry representative said, "If there is no ban on TV advertising, then you aren't going to be an idiot and impose restrictions on yourself. If you get an order and you know they've got money, no one is going to turn down the business."

Third world governments are usually strapped for funds to meet the crushing burdens of their large populations, so they are glad to get the revenues from tobacco sales. China, which welcomed R. J. Reynolds in a joint venture to make cigarettes, takes in $5 billion each year from its state-owned tobacco industry. The Soviet Union struck a deal in 1990 with Philip Morris and RJR Nabisco to import 34 billion cigarettes to help overcome a shortage caused by that nation's transition toward a market-directed economy. A tobacco company representative said, "We think our American-blend cigarettes will be very popular there—this is a wonderful opportunity for us."[25]

Discussion Questions

1. Do you believe that tobacco companies have an ethical problem when selling their products in third world nations? Defend your answer.
2. Of the four reasons given in this chapter for ethical problems occurring in business, which one or more may be operating in this situation? Which do you consider to be the most important?
3. Does this case illustrate face-to-face ethical problems, corporate policy ethical problems, or functional-area ethical problems? Give examples from the case to illustrate your answer.

[25] "Smokeless Soviets Say 'Da' to Philip Morris and RJR," *Wall Street Journal*, Sept. 14, 1990, pp. B1, B7.

4

Improving Ethical Performance in Business

Tangible steps can be taken by business to improve ethical performance. The most important components leading to ethical reform are the values and personal character of a company's employees, especially its managers. Corporate culture and ethical climate also play leading roles. A positive approach involves a careful analysis of on-the-job ethical issues, as well as designing and adopting practical ways to handle these issues when they arise.

Key Questions and Chapter Objectives

This chapter focuses on these key questions and objectives:

- What are managers' major goals and values? How do they affect a company's ethical performance?
- What role does personal character play in business ethics?
- How do a company's culture and work climate influence the ethical views of managers and employees?
- When analyzing ethics issues, how much weight should be given to harms and benefits, to human rights, and to social justice?
- What are the strengths and weaknesses of ethics codes, ethics training programs, ethics "hot lines," and similar reform efforts?

"Here's an up-from-the-ranks guy who's now head of the division and suddenly running into profit problems. He's seen what had happened to his former boss, and he's scared." The government prosecutor was referring to the vice president of AEL Industries, a Philadelphia defense contractor. Earlier in his career when the vice president was a junior manager, he was demoted and his boss had been fired when their division had lost money on a contract.[1]

Now, AEL's Emtech division had landed two jobs, one to develop radar equipment for the U.S. army and a similar contract with South Korea. The U.S. army contract was profitable, but the Korean one was not. Knowing that top manage-

[1] "Pressure for Profits: Tough Goals Put a Strain on Honesty," *Los Angeles Times,* June 27, 1986, p. 24.

ment frowned on poor financial performance, Emtech's vice president allegedly directed clerks to change entries on the time cards of 26,000 employees during a three-year period. These falsely inflated costs—amounting to $1.6 million—were then charged to the government. When auditors uncovered the scheme, the vice president was sent to jail for six months and AEL paid a fine of $2.66 million.

Around the company, the vice president was known as a "kind and conscientious" person. He was admired for working his way up the hard way—going to night school and then moving through the ranks. A Pentagon defense official had been impressed with his "honest good deeds" after he had saved the government money by recommending a cost-saving material. His own attorney, referring to the time when the young manager and his boss had been penalized for the money-losing contract, said, "It does not require a psychiatrist's insight to sense the impact of that decision on the defendant."

This episode raises some disturbing questions: Can top-down pressure for profitable performance corrupt middle-level managers and employees, causing them to take dishonest actions in order to save their jobs? Can it happen even when those who feel the pressures have a good personal character?

More importantly, what steps can companies take to guard against such ethical abuses? Following the court action, AEL agreed to appoint an ethics director and to tighten up its accounting systems. During the 1980s, several other leading defense contractors who were charged with similar ethical lapses began ethics training programs and wrote ethics codes.

In this chapter, we examine ways to improve business's ethical performance. The keys to success are a blend of managers' values, personal character, a company's culture and ethical climate, the tools available for analyzing moral dilemmas, and practical changes in company procedures that permit high ethical performance along with profitable operations.

THE CORE ELEMENTS OF ETHICAL REFORM

Whether a company improves its ethical performance depends on three core components: the goals and values of its managers; the personal character of its managers and other employees; and the traditions, attitudes, and business practices built into the company's culture. Good ethical practices not only are possible but they become normal with the right combination of these three components.

Managers' Goals and Values

Managers are one of the keys to whether a company will act ethically or unethically. As major decision makers, they have more opportunities than others to create an ethical tone for their company. The values held by these managers, especially the top-level managers, will serve as models for others who work there.

FIGURE 4–1
A comparison of managers' goals for their companies.

SOURCE: 1982 goals are from Barry Z. Posner and Warren H. Schmidt, "Values and the American Manager: An Update," *California Management Review*, Spring 1984, p. 205. 1967 goals are from George W. England, "Personal Value Systems of American Managers," *Academy of Management Journal*, March 1967, p. 62.

A COMPARISON OF MANAGERS' GOALS FOR THEIR COMPANIES, 1967, 1982

Rank	1967 Goals	1982 Goals
1	Organizational efficiency	Organizational effectiveness
2	High productivity	High productivity
3	Profit maximization	Organizational leadership
4	Organizational growth	High morale
5	Industrial leadership	Organizational reputation
6	Organizational stability	Organizational efficiency
7	Employee welfare	Profit maximization
8	Social welfare	Organizational growth
9		Organizational stability
10		Organizational value to community
11		Service to the public

Figure 4–1 shows that managers' on-the-job goals are pretty much what one would expect. Most important is organizational effectiveness—"Are we getting the job done?" They also seek high levels of productivity, along with the kind of leadership that will make the company stand out. The managers in this study clearly want to promote company-centered goals. They worry less directly about their company's value to the community or its service to the public. That appears to be an indifferent attitude toward society, but managers probably tend to believe that service to the public will be one result of a well-managed, efficient company.

Do managers' goals change over time? Figure 4–1 shows the goal rankings from another study conducted during the mid-1960s. The goals are ranked in a different order, but the same general pattern is present. The most popular goals are those that promote the welfare of the company. Employee welfare and social welfare are ranked at the bottom.

The same tendency to think of the company first was revealed when these managers were asked to identify the groups that were most important to their work. In the mid-1960s study, the top four groups were my company, customers, managers, and my boss.[2] By the early 1980s, the groups considered most important were customers, myself, subordinates, and employees.[3]

Having a practical, work-oriented, company-centered attitude is a characteristic trait of most managers, although the emphasis can vary from nation to nation,

[2] George W. England, "Personal Value Systems of American Managers," *Academy of Management Journal*, March 1967, pp. 53–68.

[3] Barry Z. Posner and Warren H. Schmidt, "Values and the American Manager: An Update," *California Management Review*, Spring 1984, p. 206.

FIGURE 4–2
Major decision-making orientations of managers from five nations.

SOURCE: George W. England, *The Manager and His Values*, Cambridge, MA: Ballinger, 1975, p. 20. Used with permission.

	U.S.A.	Japan	Korea	Australia	India	Internati… Sample
Will it work? (pragmatic approach)	57.3%	67.4%	53.1%	40.2%	34.0%	52.9%
Is it right? (ethical approach)	30.3	9.9	9.0	40.2	44.1	24.4
Is it pleasant? (affective approach)	1.2	7.0	8.5	5.4	2.2	5.1
Mixed (Combination of the three approaches)	11.2	15.8	29.4	14.2	19.6	17.6
Number of managers	997	374	211	351	623	750*

* 150 managers from each of the five nations.

as shown in Figure 4–2. Almost six of every ten U.S. managers approach a decision by asking "Will what I am about to do produce practical results?" Only three of the ten begin by asking "Is it right or ethical?" In both Australia and India, this pragmatic tendency is less pronounced, while Japanese managers are far more practical-minded than others.[4]

However, this inward-looking, company-centered tendency is not the entire story of managers' goals and values. In their everyday work, managers have a high regard for integrity in their coworkers, as diagramed in Figure 4–3. They bring several moral standards to bear as they make decisions, and these are listed in Figure 4–4.[5]

How managers' values can promote ethics reform

Managers are authority figures and role models in their companies. By setting a personal example of high ethical behavior, they can influence others around them. Repeated studies over the years have arrived at the same conclusion: *The behavior and ethical attitudes of an employee's boss are seen as the most important factors determining whether the employee will behave unethically on the job.*[6]

Managers can be a powerful force for improving a company's ethical performance. To do so, they need to be keenly aware of—and on guard against—their tendencies to put the company's interests before all other considerations. Being sensitive to the ethical perspectives of others, particularly the company's many diverse stakeholders, is a step in the right direction.

[4] For additional information about variations in ethical viewpoints in different societies, see Helmut Becker and David J. Fritzsche, "Business Ethics: A Cross-Cultural Comparison of Managers' Attitudes," *Journal of Business Ethics*, vol. 6, 1987, pp. 289–295.

[5] For details and additional discussion, see Frederick Bird and James A. Waters, "The Nature of Managerial Moral Standards," *Journal of Business Ethics*, vol. 6, 1987, p. 11.

[6] For a summary of these studies, see Posner and Schmidt, op. cit., p. 212.

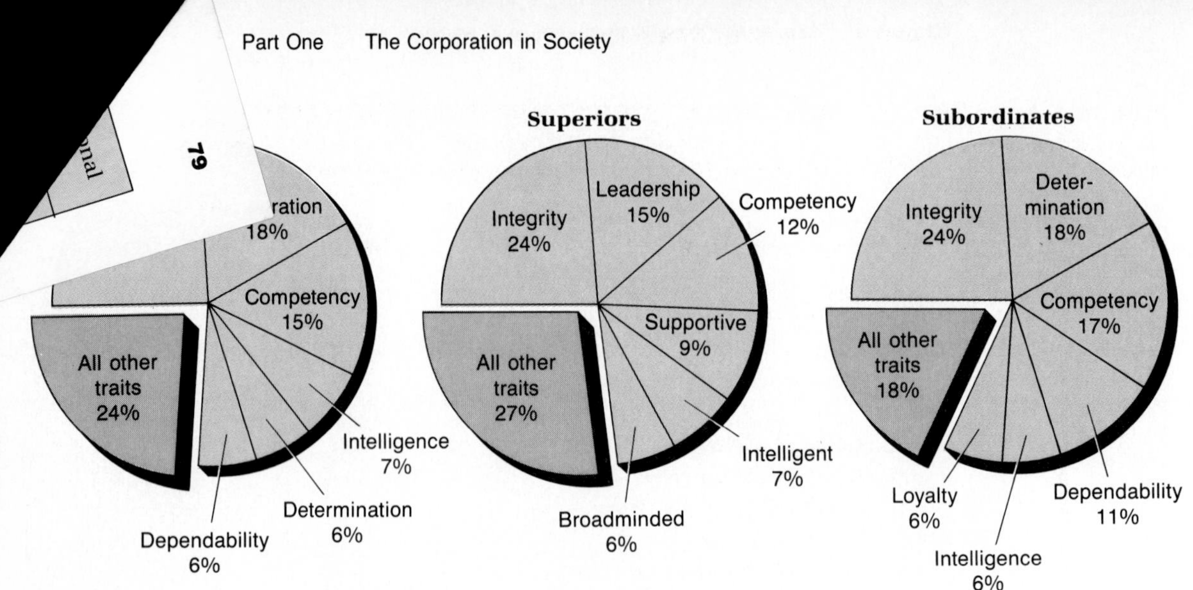

FIGURE 4–3

Qualities most admired in peers, superiors, and subordinates.

SOURCE: Barry Z. Posner and Walter Schmidt, "Values and the American Manager: An Update," Copyright 1984 by the Regents of the University of California. Reprinted from the *California Management Review*, vol. 26, no. 3, p. 209. By permission of the Regents.

Another step toward better ethics is simply acknowledging that an ethical outlook has become central to the job of managing today's complex, global corporation, as noted by a leading ethics scholar.

> Few kinds of decision making are exempt from moral or social factors. The issue is whether the manager has chosen to deal with the factors. Moral issues in management are not isolated and distinct from traditional business decision making but right smack in the middle of it. . . . [*M*]*oral* competence is an integral part of *managerial* competence. . . . [T]he moral manager sees every evolving decision as one in which an ethical perspective must be integrated. This view to the future is an essential executive skill.[7]

Personal Character and Moral Development

Clarence Walton, a seasoned observer of managerial behavior, says that personal character is one of the keys to higher ethical standards in business. "People of integrity produce organizations with integrity. When they do, they become moral managers—those special people who make organizations and societies better."[8]

Others agree, including one long-time business executive who did an in-depth study of twenty-four business managers who were notable for high-quality ethical standards in their companies. He emphasizes the close connection between personal character and a person's belief system or values.

> Virtuous leaders are persons of honesty, integrity and trust. As popularly defined in business literature today, they are concerned about excellence. Facing the rough-and-

[7] Archie B. Carroll, "In Search of the Moral Manager," *Business Horizons*, March–April 1987, p. 14.

[8] Clarence C. Walton, *The Moral Manager*, Cambridge, MA: Ballinger, 1988, p. 33 and Part III, The "Ethic" of Character.

FIGURE 4–4
Moral standards used by managers.

SOURCE: Adapted from Frederick Bird and James A. Waters, "The Nature of Managerial Moral Standards," *Journal of Business Ethics*, vol. 6, 1987, pp. 1–13.

MORAL STANDARDS USED BY MAN

Standard	
Fair treatment of employees, customers, suppliers, coworkers, and other managers	[illegible]
Fair competition regarding pricing, dealing with suppliers and customers, and avoiding favoritism	29.5
Honesty in communications regarding job evaluations, advertising, labelling, expense accounts, and public relations	25.9
Organizational responsibility that promotes efficiency, reduces waste, and advances the organization	21.2
Special consideration regarding personal problems of employees, handicapped employees, long-term customer and supplier relationships, and similar unique situations	15.0
Respect for law, including obeying both the spirit and letter of the law	9.3
Social responsibility regarding community impacts, environmental pollution, hazardous consumer goods, and corporate philanthropy	5.7

tumble of competition, and its ancillary temptations, they must exhibit moral courage. But virtue requires more than techniques and personal integrity. Virtue requires the acceptance of equity in human relationships and a commitment to act accordingly. It involves that core element, the belief system of a person.[9]

The most important formative influences discovered by this particular study were a person's religious upbringing, critical events or crises that brought forth what the person really believed in, and seeing the actions and absorbing the beliefs of inspirational role models such as family members, church leaders, teachers, friends, and others. Personal character was forged over a long period of years and depended largely on the contacts and experiences of each of the managers.[10] Business schools also play a part in forming students' personal character, sometimes reinforcing business attitudes and values.[11]

[9] James E. Liebig, *Business Ethics: Profiles in Civic Virtue,* Golden, CO: Fulcrum, 1990, p. 5.
[10] Ibid., pp. 196–197.
[11] John A. Ruhe and Robert Drevs, "Character Development in Management Education," Midwest Business Administration Associates meeting, Chicago, IL, Mar. 19, 1989; and John A. Ruhe, "Value Importance for Success: A Longitudinal Study," *Society for Advancement of Management Journal,* 1990.

Managers' moral development

Personal character and personal values—taken together—exert a powerful influence on the way ethical work issues are treated. Since people have different personal histories and have developed their character and values in different ways, they are going to think differently about ethical problems. This is as true of corporate managers as it is of other people. In other words, the managers in a company are liable to be at various **stages of moral development.** Some will reason at a high level, others at a lower level.

A summary of the way people grow and develop morally is diagramed in Figure 4–5. From infancy to mature adulthood, most people move steadily upward from Stage 1. Over time, they become more developed and advanced in moral reasoning. At first, they are almost entirely ego-centered—the original "Me Generation"—not considering anyone's wishes but their own. Slowly and sometimes painfully, the infant learns that what is considered to be right and wrong is pretty much decided by parents. As adolescence comes along and the child enters a wider world, it learns the give-and-take of group life among small circles of friends,

FIGURE 4–5
Stages of moral development and ethical reasoning.

SOURCE: Adapted from Lawrence Kohlberg, *The Philosophy of Moral Development*, New York: Harper & Row, 1981.

STAGES OF MORAL DEVELOPMENT AND ETHICAL REASONING

DIRECTION OF MORAL DEVELOPMENT ↑

Age Group	Development Stage and Major Ethics Referent	Basis of Ethics Reasoning
Mature Adulthood	**Stage 6** UNIVERSAL PRINCIPLES Justice, fairness, universal human rights	Principle-centered reasoning
Mature Adulthood	**Stage 5** MORAL BELIEFS ABOVE AND BEYOND SPECIFIC SOCIAL CUSTOM Human rights, social contract, broad constitutional principles	Principle-centered reasoning
Adulthood	**Stage 4** SOCIETY AT LARGE Customs, traditions, laws	Society-and-law centered reasoning
Youth, Adolescence, Early Adulthood	**Stage 3** SOCIAL GROUPS Friends, school, coworkers	Group-centered reasoning
Childhood	**Stage 2** SELF AND PARENTAL CONTROL Parental punishment and reward	Parent-centered reasoning
Infancy	**Stage 1** SELF AND EGO Self-seeking needs and demands	Ego-centered reasoning

school mates, and similar close-knit groups; and this process continues into youth and early adulthood. At this point, pleasing others and being admired by them are important clues to proper behavior. Most people are now "other-directed" rather than "me-directed." Upon reaching full adulthood—the late teens to early twenties in the United States—most people accept the society's customs, traditions, and laws as the proper way to define what is right and wrong. Stages 5 and 6 in Figure 4–5 lead to a special kind of moral reasoning, because people begin to get above and beyond the specific rules, customs, and laws of their own societies. They base their ethical reasoning on broad principles and relationships, such as human rights and constitutional guarantees of human dignity, equal treatment, and freedom of expression. In the highest stage of moral development, the meaning of right and wrong is defined by universal principles of justice, fairness, and common rights of all humanity.[12]

Research has demonstrated that most people, including managers, get only as far as Stages 3 and 4. Their ethical horizons are defined by their family, close friends, neighborhood groups, and society's laws and customs. For managers, who typically reason at Stages 3 and 4, the company's rules and customary ways of doing things become their main ethical compass. While at work, the company is their ethical reference group. For them, the right way to do business depends upon what the boss and one's coworkers accept as right and wrong (this is Stage 3 reasoning), as long as everyone also shows a respect for society's laws (this is Stage 4 reasoning).[13]

Another way to think about the development of moral character has been developed by Carol Gilligan. She suggests that men's and women's personal characters are distinct because boys and girls are raised differently. Boys and young men learn that fairness and justice result from obeying rules and principles. For them, being ethical means adhering to rules laid down by parents, teachers, friends, and society's customs and laws. Girls and young women follow a somewhat different path in their moral development. Their ethical orientation is toward responsibility to others, caring for others' well-being, being involved in and wanting to preserve close relationships, and valuing direct actions over dependence on rules when facing an ethical dilemma. Corporate managers with this more caring attitude about others would have an important impact on the way companies cope with on-the-job ethical issues.[14]

The development of a manager's moral character—regardless of whether it arises from a rule-based ethics or a caring-based ethics—can be crucial to a company. Some ethics issues—an example is the defense-contractor vice president mentioned at the beginning of this chapter—require managers to move beyond selfish interest (Stages 1 and 2), beyond company interest (Stage 3 reasoning), and even beyond sole reliance on society's customs and laws (Stage 4

[12] For details and research findings, see Lawrence Kohlberg, *The Philosophy of Moral Development*, San Francisco, CA: Harper & Row, 1981.

[13] James Weber, "Managers' Moral Reasoning: Assessing Their Responses to Three Moral Dilemmas," *Human Relations*, vol. 43, 1990, pp. 687–702. See also Robert Jackall, *Moral Mazes: The World of Corporate Managers*, New York: Oxford University Press, 1988.

[14] Carol Gilligan, *In a Different Voice*, Cambridge, MA: Harvard University Press, 1982.

reasoning). Needed is a manager whose personal character is built on a caring attitude toward others, recognizing others' rights and their essential humanity (a combination of Stage 5 and 6 reasoning and care-based reasoning). The moral reasoning of upper-level managers, whose decisions affect companywide policies, can have a powerful and far-reaching impact both inside and outside the company.

Corporate Culture and Ethical Climate

Personal values and moral character play key roles in improving a company's ethical performance. However, they do not stand alone, because personal values and character can be affected by a company's culture.

Corporate culture is a blend of ideas, customs, traditional practices, company values, and shared meanings that help define normal behavior for everyone who works in a company. Culture is "the way we do things around here." Two experts testify to its overwhelming influence:

> Every business—in fact every organization—has a culture. . . . [and it] has a powerful influence throughout an organization; it affects practically everything—from who gets promoted and what decisions are made, to how employees dress and what sports they play. . . . When [new employees] choose a company, they often choose a way of life. The culture shapes their responses in a strong, but subtle way. Culture can make them fast or slow workers, tough or friendly managers, team players or individuals. By the time they've worked for several years, they may be so well conditioned by the culture they may not even recognize it.[15]

Hewlett-Packard, the California-based electronics manufacturer, is well known for a culture that stresses values and ethics. Called "The HP Way" by employees, the most important values of the culture are confidence in and respect for people, open communication, sharing of benefits and responsibilities, concern for the individual employee, and honesty and integrity. "Particular values, defining ethical and human concerns, have driven all the Company's relationships with its employees, its customers, its suppliers, and the communities in which it has operated. These values have been integrated into and are central to the company's strategy, its objectives and its self-image."[16] The impact of this ethics-oriented culture is evident to managers and employees alike. A Hewlett-Packard manager commented that "It is not easy to get fired around HP, but you are gone before you know it if it is an ethics issue." Another manager said, "Somehow, the manipulative person, the person who is less open and candid, who shaves the truth or the corners of policies, doesn't last. They either get passed over for promotion or they just don't find this a comfortable environment."

[15] Terrence E. Deal and Allan A. Kennedy, *Corporate Cultures: The Rites and Rituals of Corporate Life,* Reading, MA: Addison-Wesley, 1982, pp. 4, 16.

[16] Kirk O. Hanson and Manuel Velasquez, "Hewlett-Packard Company: Managing Ethics and Values," *Corporate Ethics: A Prime Business Asset,* New York: The Business Roundtable, February 1988, p. 75.

FIGURE 4–6
The components of ethical climates.

SOURCE: Adapted from Bart Victor and John B. Cullen, "The Organizational Bases of Ethical Work Climates," *Administrative Science Quarterly*, vol. 33, 1988, p. 104.

THE COMPONENTS OF ETHICAL CLIMATES

	Focus of Ethical Concern		
Ethical Criteria	**Individual Person**	**Company**	**Society**
Egoism (Self-centered approach)	Self-interest	Company Interest	Economic Efficiency
Benevolence (Concern-for-others approach)	Friendship	Team Interest	Social Responsibility
Principle (Integrity approach)	Personal Morality	Company Rules and Procedures	Laws and Professional Codes

Ethical climates

In most companies, a "moral atmosphere" can be detected. People can feel the way the ethical winds are blowing. They pick up subtle hints and clues that tell them what behavior is approved and what is forbidden. This unspoken understanding among employees is called an **ethical climate.** It is the part of corporate culture that sets the ethical tone in a company.[17]

One way to view ethical climates is diagramed in Figure 4–6. Three different types of ethical yardsticks are egoism (self-centeredness), benevolence (concern for others), and principle (respect for one's own integrity, for group norms, and for society's laws). These ethical yardsticks can be applied to dilemmas concerning individuals, or one's company, or society at large. For example, if a manager approaches ethics issues with benevolence in mind, he or she would stress friendly relations with an employee, emphasize the importance of team play and cooperation for the company's benefit, and recommend socially responsible courses of action. However, if the manager used egoism to think about ethical problems, he or she would be more likely to think first of self-interest, promoting the company's profit, and striving for efficient operations at all costs. A company's ethical climate depends on which combination it has of these nine possibilities.

Research has demonstrated that different companies have different ethical climates. The pioneering study diagramed in Figure 4–6 discovered five types of corporate ethical climate.[18]

[17] Karen N. Gaertner, "The Effect of Ethical Climate on Manager's Decisions," in Richard M. Coughlin, *Socio-Economic Perspectives 1990*, Armonk, NY: M. E. Sharpe, 1990; and Mary E. Guy, *Ethical Decision Making in Everyday Work Situations*, New York: Quorum Books, 1990, chap. 5.

[18] Bart Victor and John B. Cullen, "The Organizational Bases of Ethical Work Climates," *Administrative Science Quarterly*, vol. 33, 1988, pp. 101–125.

- *A caring climate.* A benevolence yardstick was predominant here. Employees said such things as, "The most important concern is the good of all the people in the company as a whole."
- *A law-and-code climate.* A principles yardstick produced a positive attitude toward society's laws and professional codes. A typical employee statement here was, "People are expected to comply with the law and professional standards over and above other considerations."
- *A rules climate.* Company rules and regulations were the principles emphasized here. In this climate, employees agreed that "Successful people in this company go by the book."
- *An instrumental climate.* An egoism yardstick was typical in this climate, and it was focused on the self-interest of the company and of employees. Employees agreed that "People are expected to do anything to further the company's interests, regardless of the consequences." They also said, "In this company, people are mostly out for themselves."
- *An independence climate.* People in this climate preferred a yardstick that put the emphasis on personal beliefs. A typical attitude was "In this company, people are guided by their own personal ethics."

The researchers concluded that "Employees were more satisfied with the ethics of their company when they observed greater levels of caring . . . and lower levels of instrumentalism. . . ."[19]

Ethical impact of corporate culture and ethical climates

By signaling what is considered to be right and wrong, corporate cultures and ethical climates can put much pressure on people to channel their actions in certain directions desired by the company. Among over 1,000 U.S. corporate managers, four out of ten supervisory managers said they had to compromise their personal principles to conform to company expectations, and about seven out of ten managers at all levels believed that such pressures were strong.[20]

This kind of pressure can work both for and against good ethical practices. In a caring ethical climate, the interests of the company's employees and external stakeholders most likely would be given high priority. But in an instrumental ethical climate, employees and managers might be encouraged to disregard any interests other than their own.

ANALYZING ETHICAL PROBLEMS IN BUSINESS

Business managers and employees need a set of guidelines that will guide their thinking when on-the-job ethics issues occur. The guidelines should help them (a) identify and analyze the nature of an ethical problem, and (b) decide which

[19] Ibid., p. 117.

[20] Posner and Schmidt, op. cit., p. 211.

FIGURE 4–7
Three methods of ethical reasoning.

Method	Critical Determining Factor	An Action Is Ethical When . . .	Limitations
Utilitarian	Comparing benefits and costs	Net benefits exceed net costs	Difficult to measure some human and social costs Majority may disregard rights of minority
Rights	Respecting rights	Basic human rights are respected	Difficult to balance conflicting rights
Justice	Distributing fair shares	Benefits and costs are fairly distributed	Difficult to measure benefits and costs Lack of agreement on fair shares

course of action is likely to produce an ethical result. The following three methods of ethical reasoning can be used for these analytical purposes, as summarized in Figure 4–7.

Utility: Comparing Benefits and Costs

One approach to ethics emphasizes the utility—the overall amount of good—that can be produced by an action or a decision. Should a company close one of its older plants and move production to its modern facility in another part of the country (or world)? The answer would depend on how much good is produced by the move, compared to the harm that could result. If the company is better off after the move than before, then it would claim that the move was ethical because more good than harm resulted. On the other hand, the workers left jobless by the plant closing would probably say that the company was unethical to move away because the harm done to them and their community was great.

This ethical approach is called **utilitarian reasoning.** It is often referred to as cost-benefit analysis because it compares the costs and benefits of a decision, a policy, or an action. These costs and benefits can be economic (expressed in dollar amounts) or social (the effect on society at large) or human (usually a psychological or emotional impact). After adding up all the costs and all the benefits and comparing them with one another, the net cost or the net benefit should be apparent. If the benefits outweigh the costs, then the action is ethical because it produces "the greatest good for the greatest number" of people in society. If the net costs are larger than the net benefits, then it is probably unethical because more harm than good is produced.

The main drawback to utilitarian reasoning is the difficulty of accurately measuring both costs and benefits. Some things can be measured in monetary terms—goods produced, sales, payrolls, and profits. But other items are trickier—employee morale, psychological satisfactions, and the worth of a human life. Human and social costs are particularly difficult to measure with precision. But unless they can be measured, the cost-benefit calculations will be incomplete, and it will be difficult to know whether the overall result is good or bad, ethical or unethical.

Another limitation of utilitarian reasoning is that the rights of those in the minority may be overridden by the majority. Closing an outmoded plant may produce "the greatest good for the greatest number," but this good outcome will not change the fact that some workers left behind may be unable to find decent jobs. The problem is especially difficult for older workers or those not well educated or members of minority groups. A utilitarian solution may leave them in the lurch. They will not agree that this method of reasoning produces an ethical outcome.

In spite of these drawbacks, cost-benefit analysis is widely used in business. Because this method works well, when used to measure economic and financial outcomes, business managers sometimes are tempted to rely on it to decide important ethical questions without being fully aware of its limitations or the availability of still other methods that may improve the ethical quality of their decisions. One of these other methods is to consider the impact of business decisions on human rights.

Rights: Determining and Protecting Entitlements

Human rights are another basis for making ethical judgments. A right means that a person or group is entitled to something or is entitled to be treated in a certain way. The most basic human rights are those claims or entitlements that enable a person to survive, to make free choices, and to realize one's potential as a human being. Denying those rights or failing to protect them for other persons and groups is normally considered to be unethical. Respecting others, even those with whom we disagree or whom we dislike, is the essence of human rights, provided that others do the same for us. This approach to ethical reasoning holds that individuals are to be treated as valuable ends in themselves just because they are human beings. Using others for your own purposes is unethical if, at the same time, you deny them their goals and purposes. For example, a union that denies a group of women employees an opportunity to bid for all jobs for which they are qualified is depriving them of some of their rights. Or a company that carelessly disposes of hazardous wastes may be guilty of ignoring the rights of others and simply using the environment for its own selfish purposes.

The main limitation of using rights as a basis of ethical reasoning is the difficulty of balancing conflicting rights. For example, an employee's right to privacy may be at odds with an employer's right to protect the firm's cash by testing the employee's honesty. Some of the most difficult balancing acts have occurred when minorities and women have competed with white males for the right to hold jobs in business and government. Rights also clash when United States multinational corporations move production to a foreign nation, causing job losses at home but creating new jobs abroad. In such cases, whose job rights should be respected?[21]

In spite of this kind of problem, the protection and promotion of human rights is an important ethical benchmark for judging the behavior of individuals and organizations. Surely most people would agree that it is unethical to deny a person's fundamental right to life, freedom, privacy, growth, and human dignity. By defining the human condition and pointing the way to a realization of human potentialities, such rights become a kind of common denominator of ethical reasoning, setting forth the essential conditions for ethical actions and decisions.

Justice: Is It Fair?

A third method of ethical reasoning concerns **justice.** "Is it fair or just?" is a common question in human affairs. Employees want to know if pay scales are fair. Consumers are interested in fair prices when they shop. When new tax laws are proposed, there is much debate about their fairness—where will the burden fall, and who will escape paying their fair share?

Justice (or fairness) exists when benefits and burdens are distributed equitably and according to some accepted rule. For society as a whole, social justice means that a society's income and wealth are distributed among the people in fair proportions. A fair distribution does not necessarily mean an equal distribution. The shares received by people depend on the society's approved rules for getting and keeping income and wealth. These rules will vary from society to society. Most societies try to consider people's needs, abilities, efforts, and the contributions they make to society's welfare. Since these factors are seldom equal, fair shares will vary from person to person and from group to group.

Determining what is just and unjust is often a very explosive issue because the stakes are so high. Since distributive rules usually grant privileges to some groups based on tradition and custom, sharp inequalities between groups can generate social tensions and demands for a fairer system. An "equal opportunity" rule—that is, a rule that gives everyone the same starting advantages in life (to health, to education, and to career choices)—can lead to a fairer distribution of society's benefits and burdens.

Justice reasoning is not the same as utilitarian reasoning. A person using utilitarian reasoning adds up costs and benefits to see if one is greater than the other; if benefits exceed costs, then the action would probably be considered ethical. A person using justice reasoning considers who pays the costs and who gets the benefits; if the shares seem fair (according to society's rules), then the action is probably just. Is it ethical to move a factory from Boston to Houston? The utilitarian would say "yes" if the net benefits to all parties are greater than the costs incurred by everyone. A person using justice reasoning would say "yes"

[21] For a discussion, see Patricia H. Werhane, *Persons, Rights, and Corporations*, Englewood Cliffs, NJ: Prentice-Hall, 1985.

if the benefits and costs caused by the move were fairly borne by all parties affected by the move. The utilitarian reasoner is interested in the net sum. The justice reasoner is interested in fair shares.

Applying Ethical Reasoning to Business Activities

Anyone in the business world can use these three methods of ethical reasoning to gain a better understanding of ethical issues that arise at work. More often than not, all three can be applied at the same time. Using only one of the three methods is risky and may lead to an incomplete understanding of all the ethical complexities that may be present. It also may produce a lopsided ethical result that will be unacceptable to others.

Figure 4–8 diagrams the kind of analytical procedure that is useful to employ when one is confronted with an ethical problem or issue. Two general rules can be used in making such an analysis.

The unanimity rule

If you want to know whether a decision, a policy, or an activity is ethical or unethical, you first ask the three questions listed in Figure 4–8. If the answers to all three questions are "yes," then the decision or policy or activity is probably ethical. If answers to all three are "no," then you probably are looking at an unethical decision, policy, or activity. The reason why you cannot be absolutely certain is that different people and groups (1) may honestly and genuinely use different sources of information, (2) may measure costs and benefits differently, (3) may not share the same meaning of justice, or (4) may rank various rights in different ways. Nevertheless, anytime an analyst obtains unanimous answers to these three questions—all "yeses" or all "noes"—it is an indication that a strong case can be made for either an ethical or an unethical conclusion.

The priority rule

What happens when the unanimity rule does not apply? What if there are two "yeses" and one "no," or another combination of the various possibilities? In that case, a choice is necessary. A corporate manager or employee then has to assign priorities to the three methods of ethical reasoning. What is most important to the manager, to the employee, or to the organization—utility? rights? or justice? What ranking should they be given? A judgment must be made, and priorities must be determined.

These judgments and priorities will be strongly influenced by a company's culture and ethical climate. A company with an instrumental ethical climate—or one with a rules ethical climate—would probably assign high value to a utilitarian approach that calculates the costs and benefits to the company. A caring ethical climate will bring forth a greater respect for the rights of employees and the just treatment of all stakeholders. Obeying the law would be a top priority in a law-and-code ethical climate.

The type of ethical reasoning chosen also depends heavily on managers' values,

FIGURE 4–8
An analytical approach to ethical problems.

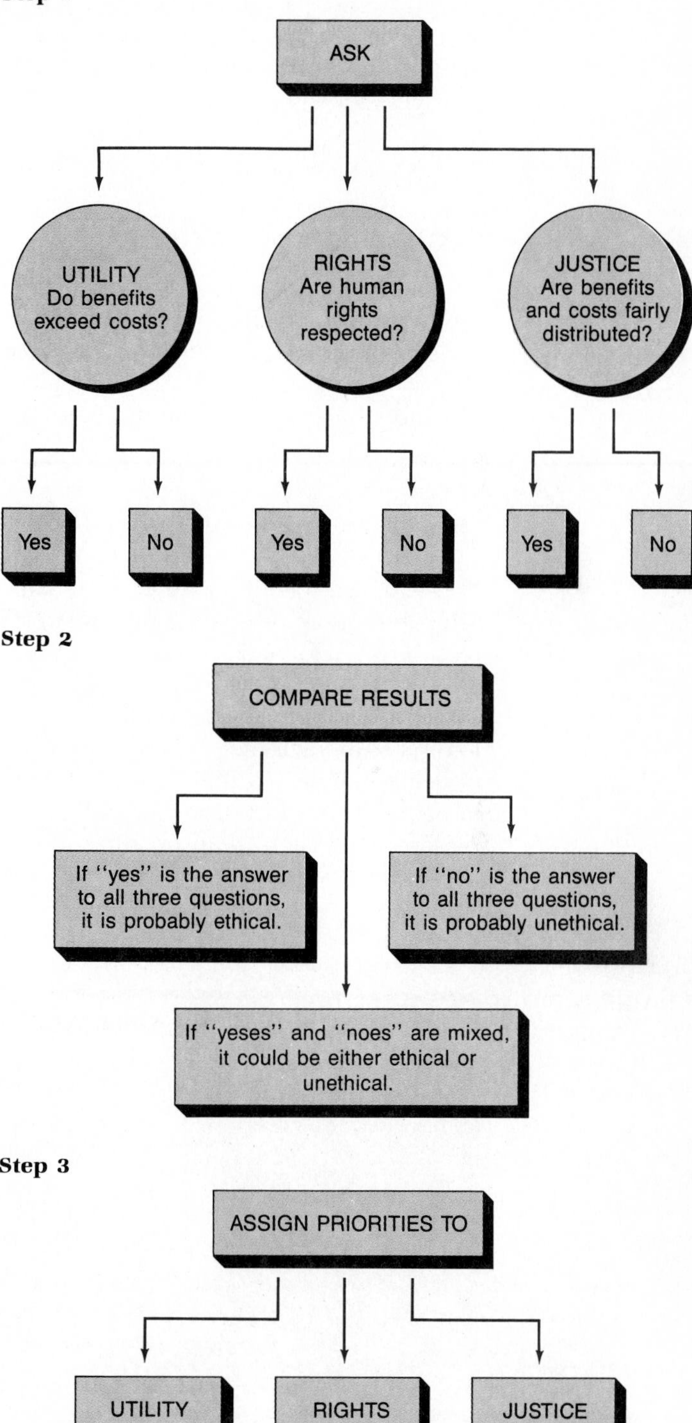

especially those held by top management, and on the personal character of all decision makers in the company. Some will be sensitive to people's needs and rights, while others will put themselves or their company ahead of all other considerations.

MAKING ETHICS WORK IN CORPORATIONS

Any business firm that wishes to do so can improve the quality of its ethical performance. Doing so requires two fundamental steps. The first step is to legitimize moral discourse or "ethics talk." The second step requires a company to build ethical safeguards into its everyday routines.

"It's OK to Talk about Ethics Here"

The language of ethics—that is, talking about utility, rights, justice, honesty, integrity, and fairness—is a foreign language in most business firms. Some of the reasons are depicted in Figure 4–9. Study after study has made the same point. Managers "did not feel much support from others for making moral choices. . . . as moral actors they were on their own. . . . Because managers do not feel able to discuss moral issues with peers and superiors, they often experience the stress of being morally on their own. . . . In a very real sense, morality needs to be brought 'out of the organizational closet' and collectively recognized as an important dimension of an organization's culture and as an important aspect of

FIGURE 4–9
Why managers are reluctant to talk about ethics.

SOURCE: Frederick Bird and James A. Waters, "The Moral Muteness of Managers." Copyright 1989 by the Regents of the University of California. Reprinted from the *California Management Review*, vol. 32, no. 1, 1989. By permission of the Regents.

WHY MANAGERS ARE RELUCTANT TO TALK ABOUT ETHICS

Moral talk is viewed as creating these negative effects . . .	. . . because of these assumed attributes of moral talk.
■ Threat to Harmony	■ Moral talk is intrusive and confrontational and invites cycles of mutual recrimination.
■ Threat to Efficiency	■ Moral talk assumes distracting moralistic forms (praising, blaming, ideological) and is simplistic, inflexible, soft and inexact.
■ Threat to Image of Power and Effectiveness	■ Moral talk is too esoteric and idealistic and lacks rigor and force.

everyday managerial life."[22] Until people in business feel comfortable "talking ethics," progress may be slow in making ethics work in corporations.

Overcoming the ethics language barrier is almost entirely in the hands of a company's senior-level managers. By injecting ethics into their policy statements, by insisting that ethics problems be brought out into the open, and by setting a personal example through their own behavior, top management signals others in the company that "it's OK to talk about ethics here." This approach can extend to special ethics training programs and workshops, where the real ethics dilemmas that come up every day can be aired. Lower-level managers and supervisors can be encouraged—and rewarded for doing so—to be more open with their subordinates when ethics problems emerge. When this kind of ethics dialogue occurs, the manager and employee need not feel alone and isolated in grappling with a tough ethics problem. "Talking it out" is the beginning of corporate ethics reform.

Building Ethical Safeguards into the Company

Managers and employees need guidance on how to handle day-to-day ethical situations; their own personal ethical compass may be working well, but they need to receive directional signals from the company. Several organizational steps can be taken to provide this kind of ethical awareness and direction.

Top management commitment and involvement

When senior-level managers signal employees that they believe ethics should receive high priority in all business decisions, a giant step is taken toward improving ethical performance throughout the company. By personal example, through policy statements, and by willingness to back up words with actions, top management can get its message across. Johnson & Johnson's famous Credo—a 24-point statement of the company's basic beliefs—is used in just this way. Managers are expected to be familiar with the Credo and to use it in decision making. Failure to follow it can lead to reprimand or dismissal.[23]

Codes of ethics

Surveys show that about three out of four U.S. corporations have **ethics codes.** Their purpose is to provide guidance to managers and employees when they encounter an ethical dilemma. A typical code discusses conflicts of interest that can harm the company (for example, guidelines for accepting or refusing gifts

[22] James A. Waters and Frederick Bird, "The Moral Dimension of Organizational Culture," *Journal of Business Ethics,* vol. 6, 1987, p. 18. For similar findings, see Barbara Toffler, *Tough Choices: Managers Talk Ethics,* New York: Wiley, 1986; and Kathy E. Kram, Peter C. Yeager, and Gary E. Reed, "Decisions and Dilemmas: The Ethical Dimension in the Corporate Context," James E. Post (ed.), *Research in Corporate Social Performance and Policy,* vol. 11, Greenwich, CT: JAI Press, 1989.

[23] Laura L. Nash, "Johnson & Johnson's Credo," *Corporate Ethics: A Prime Business Asset,* New York: The Business Roundtable, February 1988, pp. 77–104.

from suppliers, hiring relatives, or having an interest in a competitor's firm). Rules for complying with various laws, such as antitrust, environmental, and consumer protection laws, also are popular code provisions. The most effective codes are those drawn up with the cooperation and widespread participation of employees. An internal enforcement mechanism, including penalties for violating the code, puts teeth into the code. A shortcoming of many codes is that they tend to provide more protection for the company than for employees and the general public. They do so by emphasizing narrow legal compliance—rather than taking a positive and broad view of ethical responsibility toward all company stakeholders—and by focusing on conflicts of interest that will harm the company.[24]

Ethics codes are more popular in U.S. corporations than among foreign-based companies. The Conference Board revealed in a 1987 study of 200 companies worldwide that only 30 percent of non-U.S. corporations reported having an ethics code. About one-half of large Canadian companies were found to have a code, while a survey of British corporations turned up just 42 percent with codes. These results are generally compatible with a survey of 189 British, French, and West German business firms, where only 41 percent relied on codes of ethics, compared with 75 percent of U.S. companies. Most of the European codes were introduced in the mid-1980s, about a decade later than U.S. experience. A big difference also appears in topics covered in the European and U.S. codes. Employee conduct was included in all of the European business codes but in only 55 percent of U.S. company codes, and local community and environmental affairs were more frequently mentioned in European (65 percent) than in U.S. codes (42 percent). However, U.S. companies seemed to be more attentive to customers, suppliers, and contractors than the Europeans. The authors of this comparative study concluded that corporate ethics codes vary considerably from country to country, reflecting differences in political, governmental, and social approaches to business ethics issues.[25]

Ethics committees

Some companies—about one in three *Fortune* 1000 companies, according to a 1989 survey by the Ethics Resource Center—have created an **ethics committee** to give guidance on ethics matters. It can be a high-level committee of the board of directors, usually chaired by an outside board member (to create an arm's-length relationship with top management). In other cases, the committee's members are drawn from the top ranks of management. For example, "Boeing's Ethics

[24] Center for Business Ethics, "Are Corporations Institutionalizing Ethics?" *Journal of Business Ethics*, vol. 5, 1986, pp. 85–91; Bernard J. White and B. Ruth Montgomery, "Corporate Codes of Conduct," *California Management Review*, Winter 1980, pp. 80–87; and M. Cash Mathews, *Strategic Intervention in Organizations: Resolving Ethical Dilemmas*, Newbury Park, CA: Sage, 1988, chaps. 4 and 5.

[25] Ronald E. Berenbeim, *Corporate Ethics*, New York: Conference Board, 1987, chap. 3; Leonard J. Brooks, "Corporate Codes of Ethics" [in Canadian companies], *Journal of Business Ethics*, vol. 8, 1989, pp. 117–129; Bodo B. Schlegelmilch and Jane E. Houston, "Corporate Codes of Ethics in Large UK Companies, *European Journal of Marketing*, vol. 23, no. 6, 1989, pp. 7–24; and Catherine C. Langlois and Bodo B. Schlegelmilch, "Do Corporate Codes of Ethics Reflect National Character? Evidence from Europe and the United States," *Journal of International Business Studies*, vol. 21, no. 4, 4th quarter 1990, pp. 519–539.

and Business Conduct Committee is chaired by . . . a senior vice president. It also includes staff vice presidents for finance and human resources, as well as the heads of the company's three operating divisions—commercial, computers, and military."[26]

These committees field ethics questions from employees, help a company establish policy in new or uncertain areas, advise the board of directors on ethics issues, and sometimes oversee ethics training programs.

Ethics advisers, advocates, and directors

Pacific Bell, once part of American Telephone and Telegraph, sailed into rough ethical waters when on its own. It was charged with abusive, high-pressure sales tactics, it was sued for allowing dial-a-porn companies to use its telephone lines, and consumers charged that their privacy was violated when Pacific Bell announced plans to sell lists of its customers to telemarketers and direct mail firms. As part of its response, the company established an "ombudsman" office. Its function is to give a private and confidential hearing to ethics complaints of employees who might be reluctant to report their concerns to their immediate supervisor. The staff then investigates and acts as a go-between. "We're trying to create an environment where employees feel safe raising [ethics] issues, trying to create a support system within the company," according to the company's director of external affairs.[27]

Ethics hot lines

In some companies, when employees are troubled about some ethical issue but may be reluctant to raise it with their immediate supervisor, they can place a call on the company's "ethics hotline." The ethics director or perhaps a member of the ethics committee receives the confidential call and then quietly investigates the situation. Elaborate steps are taken to protect the identity of the caller, so as to encourage more employees to report ethically questionable activities. In other words, ethics hotlines encourage internal whistle-blowing, which is better for a company than to have disgruntled employees take their ethical complaints to the media.[28]

Ethics training programs

Nearly all companies who take ethics seriously provide ethics training for their managers and employees. After all, firms frequently train their employees in accounting methods, marketing techniques, safety procedures, and technical systems, so why not also give them training in ethics? These programs acquaint company personnel with official company policy on ethical issues, and they show how those policies can be translated into the specifics of everyday decision making. Sometimes, simulated case studies based on actual events in the company

[26] "The Ethics Committee: 'A Vehicle to Keep the Process Moving,' " *Ethikos*, September–October 1990, p. 6.

[27] "Pacific Bell: Dial E for Ethics," *Ethikos*, May–June 1990, p. 5.

[28] For an example, see "Bell Helicopter Seeks a Safe Landing for Ethical Employees," *Ethikos*, July–August 1990, pp. 6–8.

are used to illustrate how to apply ethical principles to on-the-job problems.[29] When these training sessions are truly open, they offer an opportunity to overcome "the moral muteness of managers" by establishing an ongoing dialogue about a broad range of ethical dilemmas that may arise from time to time.

Ethics audits

Dow Corning's face-to-face **ethics audit** is well known. Its purpose is "to get people to a level of understanding where they can make their own decisions." Members of the company's Business Conduct Committee meet with employees to discuss ethics problems, such as kickbacks to sales representatives or how to deal with regulatory agencies in a foreign location. These face-to-face meetings may require interpretation of various provisions in Dow Corning's code of conduct, thus converting the code's broad principles into practical work procedures. One result is to decentralize ethical responsibility by placing more of it on the employee. Another is to define ethics in practical terms that can be better understood at the point where an ethics dilemma occurs.[30] Exhibit 4–A describes the thor-

EXHIBIT 4–A

HEWLETT-PACKARD'S ETHICS AUDIT

"During the annual audit, the auditor is required to note any deviations from HP's [ethics] standards that become evident during the audit and bring them to the attention of the audit supervisor. In addition, the managers of each operating entity must make a report to the auditor on the corrective actions they have taken to deal with any deviations from the standards that emerged in the prior year's audit. Managers must also report on the written procedures they have established for informing new employees of the standards and for providing ongoing review of the standards with other employees. If a manager is deficient in either of these areas, an appropriate comment is placed on the manager's letter of evaluation.

"In addition, the auditing team must interview the top managers of each entity (in Marketing entities this includes the General Manager, the Business Manager, the Sales Manager, and the Support Manager; in manufacturing entities this includes the General Manager, the Marketing Manager, the Manufacturing Manager, the R&D Manager, and the Controller). During the interview each manager is asked [both general and detailed] questions. . . .

"Upon completion of the audit, the auditor is required to sign the following statement: 'As a result of the audit tests and procedures performed during the audit of the entity, I did not detect any violations of HP Standards of Business conduct policies, except for those referenced above.' "

Kirk O. Hanson and Manuel Velasquez, "Hewlett-Packard Company: Managing Ethics and Values," *Corporate Ethics: A Prime Business Asset*, New York: The Business Roundtable, February 1988, pp. 72–73.

[29] For several examples of these training programs, see The Business Roundtable, op. cit.

[30] "The Ethics Committee," op. cit., p. 7; and Patrick E. Murphy, "Implementing Business Ethics," *Journal of Business Ethics*, vol. 7, 1988, pp. 909–910.

oughgoing ethics audit of Hewlett-Packard, showing how managers in that company are held accountable for emphasizing ethics during each year.

SUMMARY POINTS OF THIS CHAPTER

- Improving a company's ethical performance depends on the values and goals of its managers, the personal character of employees and managers, and the company's culture and ethical climate.
- Managers' on-the-job values tend to be company-oriented, assigning high priority to company goals.
- The quality of personal character and moral development varies within any company; moral courage and principled reasoning can greatly assist in coping with ethical dilemmas.
- A company's culture and ethical climate tend to shape the attitudes and actions of all who work there, sometimes resulting in high levels of ethical behavior and at other times contributing to less desirable ethical performance.
- People in business can analyze ethics dilemmas by using three major types of ethical reasoning: utilitarian reasoning, rights reasoning, and justice reasoning.
- Companies can improve their ethical performance when top management leads the way and when organizational safeguards are adopted, such as ethics codes, ethics committees, ethics training programs, and ethics audits.

KEY TERMS AND CONCEPTS USED IN THIS CHAPTER

- Stages of moral development
- Corporate culture
- Ethical climate
- Utilitarian reasoning
- Human rights
- Justice
- Ethics codes
- Ethics committees
- Ethics audits

DISCUSSION CASE

ORGANIZING FOR ETHICS REFORM

In the mid-1980s, General Dynamics, headquartered in St. Louis, was one of several U.S. defense contractors charged with fraudulent accounting practices and overbilling the government. Until it had made certain management changes, the U.S. Secretary of the Navy suspended all of General Dynamics' contracts with the Navy. One of the changes demanded was the establishment and enforcement of "a rigorous code of ethics for all General Dynamics officers and employees with mandatory sanctions for violation."[31]

Within three months, General Dynamics initiated a comprehensive ethics program, which the company described as follows:[32]

> The organization of the Ethics Program begins with the Board Committee on Corporate Responsibility. The Committee has broad oversight responsibility for company programs and policies in relation to employees, customers, suppliers, shareholders, and community. The Committee consists entirely of outside directors. . . .
>
> In addition to the Board Committee, a Corporate Ethics Steering Group, made up of the heads of major functional departments within the corporation, has responsibility for providing policy guidance and general administrative direction for the Ethics Program corporatewide. Similar groups at some of the divisions provide divisionwide direction for the program. Company attorneys, at both the Corporate Office and at each division, support the Ethics Program with legal counsel concerning the laws, regulations, and government rules that lie behind the specific guidelines for conduct found in the Standards booklet. Corporate and division counsel also play important roles in investigations concerning violations of the Standards.
>
> At the Corporate Office, and at each division, subsidiary, and major location, there are Ethics Program Directors responsible, on a day-by-day basis, for assisting management in the implementation and maintenance of the Ethics Program. The Ethics Program Directors provide advice to employees with questions about the application of the Standards, and they are responsible for screening allegations concerning possible violations of the Standards. Many of the directors maintain hotlines.
>
> Altogether, at the close of 1986, there were 39 individuals serving as Ethics Program Directors around the corporation. There is a full-time Corporate Ethics Program Director at the Corporate Office who reports to the Chairman and Chief Executive Officer. There are full-time directors at each of the defense division headquarters. These persons report directly to their General Manager or President. The directors at the commercial subsidiaries serve on an added-task basis but are available full-time if necessary. As Ethics Program Directors, they report directly to their President. At any of the satellite locations of the divisions, there are individuals serving on a part-time basis as Ethics Program Directors. In their capacity as Ethics Program Directors, they report directly to the Manager of their facility.
>
> General Dynamics is a corporation where leadership is most visibly and effectively exercised through line management. Line management has been particularly important in the implementation of the Ethics Program and integration of the Standards. Line management defines expectations and sets the example. Ethical conduct depends on alertness and information. It is not a product of a specialized skill and requires no expert knowledge of philosophy, theology, psychology, law or other academic disciplines. It depends heavily on commitment. 'You gotta wanna,' as the phrase goes, and in the area of employee attitude, management—up and down the line—has a special

[31] Andrew Singer, "General Dynamics Corporation: An Ethics Turnaround?" *Ethikos,* March–April 1990, pp. 1–5, 11.

[32] Reported in Berenbeim, op. cit., p. 29.

responsibility for setting an example. Functional departments also play an important supporting role, especially Human Resources, Legal, Security, and Internal Audit. In the midst of all this, the role of the Ethics Program Director is to assist management in its leadership role and to assist employees generally in their understanding and application of the Standards to daily business conduct.

Discussion Questions

1. Using the major ideas of this chapter, evaluate the strengths and weaknesses of General Dynamics' ethics program. In doing so, identify the specific organizational reforms introduced into the company's routines.
2. What factors that contribute to a company's ethical performance (and which are discussed in this chapter) are not included in this description of General Dynamics' ethics program? How important do you consider their omission to be? Could it make the difference between a high level of ethical conduct and something less desirable?
3. Discuss possible reasons why General Dynamics did not begin their ethics program prior to the Navy's suspension of its contracts. In your discussion, refer to Chapter 3 as well as the material in this chapter.

5

Socially Responsive Management

A corporation's core activities have the greatest impact on society. Current business activities, and future business plans, define the company's primary involvements with its stakeholders. The socially responsive corporation considers and carefully plans for the effects of its decisions and policies. This chapter discusses how businesses integrate social responsiveness into the management decision process and infuse social responsibility into the organization and its activities.

Key Questions and Chapter Objectives

This chapter focuses on these key questions and objectives:

- What are four basic strategies of corporate response to the social environment?
- How are strategic decisions formulated with an awareness of environmental issues?
- What is the model of management responsiveness to environmental issues and social demands?
- What has to happen within a company for social responsiveness to become effective?
- What is the purpose of the corporate public affairs function?

As the world's population continues to expand, it places new pressures on global natural resources such as energy, water, and food. These resources can be enhanced by technologies to improve energy efficiency, new methods to distribute water from places where it is plentiful to places where it is scarce, and chemical and biological advancements to improve agricultural productivity. Central to agricultural improvement is the genetic engineering industry, which is leading the technological way into the twenty-first century.

Genetic engineering is a powerful application of scientific knowledge to create organisms that have attributes of the sort necessary to achieve desired results. For example, one of the famous early genetic field experiments occurred in the mid-1980s when Steven E. Lindow, a scientist at the University of California, sought to spray a 200-foot row of potato vines with "ice-minus," a synthetic bacterium created to prevent frost from damaging the plants. It was hoped that "ice-minus" might eventually protect food crops from destruction due to frost and cold temperatures. Environmental activist Jeremy Rifkin went to court and attempted to halt the testing of the "ice-minus" bacterium in the open environment. Rifkin contended that scientists did not know how to control the side effects of a release of such an organism into the open environment, thereby placing all living creatures at risk. Some cartoonists even suggested that we would see genetic monsters destroying the earth.

This was just the first of several court actions initiated by Rifkin which halted or slowed the development of genetically altered organisms. Delays present a serious problem for firms in the genetic engineering industry. Although they continue to conduct research, usually at great expense, the firms have no guarantee that they will have a return on their investment. To make matters more complex, a company receives no guarantee that it will have an exclusive patent on any product it develops. In one case, Hoffman-La Roche, a Swiss pharmaceutical multinational company, was awarded a United States patent for alpha interferon (a potential cancer fighter) in early 1985; Biogen, a Swiss biotechnology firm, had been awarded a European patent for the same product six months earlier. In such an unstable, unpredictable environment, strategic planning becomes both increasingly difficult and increasingly important.

The dilemma hinges on an ongoing argument: biotechnology firms and scientists insist that the products they are developing will be so valuable to humanity that they should not be stopped by critics. Critics agree that the potential rewards from genetic testing and development may be great, but they fear that too much unregulated progress may be dangerous. If testing is allowed to proceed unwatched, the environment may be permanently and adversely altered.[1]

This example highlights several key truths about managing in the 1990s. First, economic needs alone will not justify actions that risk injury to the public. The industry will have to find a way to test its products safely. Second, although the message of the industry's critics may sound harsh and strident to business leaders, it cannot be ignored. The critics are stakeholders with legitimate interests and powers to influence the firm and cannot be ignored. Third, all of these social expectations require that corporations have a consciously developed social strategy that meshes with traditional economic concerns. This kind of corporate social strategy requires business leaders to "reinvent" their corporations. They must find a place for social needs and goals without abandoning business's traditional emphasis on meeting economic needs and goals.

STRATEGIES OF RESPONSE

As managers attempt to plan and implement business strategies, they frequently encounter pressures and problems from the external environment. Usually, ex-

[1] Michael Bowker, "The Hawkers of Heredity," *Sierra Club Bulletin*, January–February, 1985, p. 28.

ternal problems and pressures can be associated with other organizations, groups, or stakeholders. In societies where power is diffused and where individuals can freely make decisions in their own self-interest, managers are likely to find their actions challenged by others outside the organization. Some managers believe such outside interferences are illegitimate, and they respond with an attitude that R. Edward Freeman calls "blame the stakeholder."[2] Government, environmentalists, and consumer activists are among the most popular villains.

> Winston J. Brill, vice president of research and development for Agracetus, a Wisconsin biotechnology firm, illustrates such a position. In response to claims of impending disaster, he says, "It's very easy to gain the media's attention by crying 'the sky is falling.' But the fact is, I couldn't make an organism that could cause a significant problem even if I wanted to. And to create one by accident is virtually impossible."[3]

There are, however, other approaches for coping with a changing environment. Some firms steadfastly adhere to their plans, no matter how strong the opposition or pressure from other actors in society. Some firms change only when forced to do so by strong outside pressures. Others actively attempt to move society in directions that will be to the company's advantage. A fourth approach is to try to find ways to harmonize a company's own goals with the changing needs, goals, and expectations of the public. These approaches are referred to, respectively, as an **inactive strategy,** a **reactive strategy,** a **proactive strategy,** and an **interactive strategy** of response to the environment. They are shown in Figure 5–1.

An Inactive Strategy

Many managers are apt to respond initially by resisting, altering their policies only as pressure and criticism mount. Occasionally, however, a company will absolutely refuse to change its behavior in response to the concerns of others. For example, Quarex Industries, a publicly traded company that the President's Commission on Organized Crime reported had ties to organized crime, repeatedly failed health inspections by authorities in New York, paid small fines, and continued to "short weight" customers, sell unfit food, and operate some of the most unsanitary supermarkets in New York State.[4] For such companies, nothing less than a government edict, court order, or imprisonment of managers will force a modification of behavior. A well-publicized example occurred in 1990 when Eastern Airlines was charged with criminal violations of airline safety rules. The indictment charged that during the late 1980s Eastern's management failed to

[2] R. Edward Freeman, *Strategic Management: A Stakeholder Approach,* Marshfield, MA: Pitman, 1984, p. 23.
[3] Bowker, op. cit., p. 28.
[4] Walt Bogdavich, "A Food Firm Prospers Despite Often Failing Sanitary Inspections," *Wall Street Journal,* July 25, 1986, pp. 1, 12.

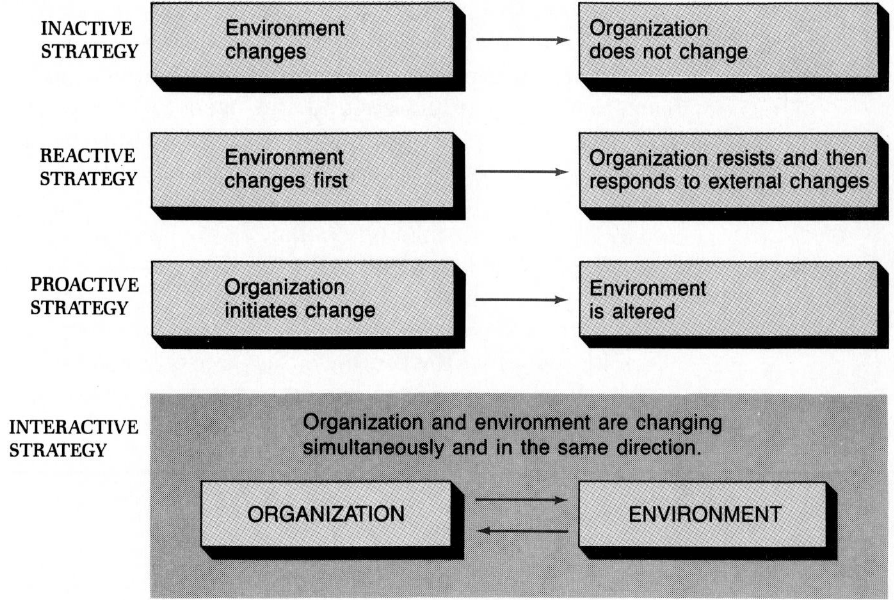

FIGURE 5–1 Four basic strategies of social response.

implement mandated safety procedures and falsified safety records. This occurred in defiance of federal safety regulations and rules.

A Reactive Strategy

Utilizing a reactive strategy, a firm tries to cope with an unanticipated change in its environment after the significant change has occurred. Often, company practices will be modified only as strong pressures are applied.

Consider the actions of the makers of aerosol spray products. Scientists discovered in the mid-1970s that chemical propellants, once released into the air, posed a threat to the protective ozone layer in the earth's atmosphere. Without this protection, the earth would be exposed to harmful solar radiation that can cause skin cancer and mutations in plants and animals. The manufacturers initially attempted to defend their products, but after mounting pressure, they acceded to a 1978 government regulation banning the use of damaging aerosols.

In the mid-1980s, the controversy again heated up, as a large "hole" in the ozone layer was discovered over Antarctica. Pressure was exerted to have chlorofluorocarbons (CFCs), widely used as refrigerants, and industrial solvents using CFCs banned. Environmental groups pushed for an international agreement of nations to ban the damaging substances. A large number of companies that manufactured or used CFCs in their products began to switch to non-CFC alternatives. Although costly, there was a sense that it was necessary to react to new evidence and mounting political pressure.

A Proactive Strategy

Companies utilizing proactive strategies are a step ahead of those that merely react, because they understand the need to "get ahead" of changes that are occurring in their environments. Such companies may try to manipulate the environment in ways that will be to their own advantage.

> Although an ongoing conflict exists between environmentalists and biotechnology firms, many in the industry take a very proactive approach and actively promote regulation for a number of reasons. First, it would create some stability where none now exists because many companies literally have no idea whether the products they are spending millions of dollars to develop will ever be sold. Second, if regulations are developed and published, and if a biotechnology firm follows them, the company may be protected from future prosecution should some environmental harm occur.

An Interactive Strategy

When a company is able to anticipate environmental change and blend its own goals with those of the public, it has adopted an interactive strategy. An interactive strategy promotes harmonious relations between a firm and the public by reducing the gap between public expectations and business performance. This is often accomplished through a serious management commitment to dialogue with its stakeholders.

> As concerns for protection of the natural environment have grown, for example, many people have criticized the fast-food industry for promoting a "throw-away" culture that ignores the ecological consequences of such practices. McDonald's Corporation, the largest fast-food company in the world, faced a major strategic challenge. The company's business strategy has rested on speed, service, quality, and consistency. Recycling laws, new packaging, and other ecological issues could seriously affect the way the company does business. To enhance the search for creative solutions, McDonald's reached an agreement with the Environmental Defense Fund (EDF), a leading environmental organization, to cooperate in finding practical options for dealing with the environmental dimensions of McDonald's business. The heart of the agreement is the company's commitment to a continuing dialogue.[5]

Research has demonstrated that, under various conditions, the inactive, reactive, and proactive response strategies may produce temporary, short-run successes for companies. However, evaluations of longer-term successes strongly suggest that an interactive approach brings greater, more lasting benefits for both

[5] "McDonald's Waste Study Planned," *New York Times,* Aug. 2, 1990, p. D18; Peter Nulty, "Recycling Becomes a Big Business," *Fortune,* Aug. 13, 1990, pp. 81–86; "Big Mac Joins with Big Critic to Cut Trash," *Wall Street Journal,* Aug. 3, 1990, p. B-1.

EXHIBIT 5-A

CORPORATE CONSERVATION COUNCIL

As the pressure of a growing concern for environmental issues has increased on business, some companies have sought new ways to break out of the old adversarial relationship with environmental groups. One such effort was begun in 1982 when the Corporate Conservation Council was formed.

The council is a division of the National Wildlife Federation (NWF), an environmental organization with nearly 6 million members. Jay Hair, president of NWF, believed that a dialogue with members of industry could occur and would further the cause of conservation and the wise use of natural resources. With a group of corporate leaders from companies such as Du Pont, Dow Chemical, ARCO, Weyerhauser, and USX (formerly U.S. Steel), the Corporate Conservation Council set out to expand the dialogue between industry and the environmental community. Beginning with quarterly meetings at which candid "off the record" discussions were held on key environmental issues such as waste reduction and global warming, the council has expanded into developing policy statements on such problems as hazardous waste and wetlands protection.

In 1988, the council used its Outreach Program to begin a program to create environmental education for business and management students. By 1991, environmental courses were being taught and case studies were being used in universities and colleges in the United States, Europe, and Asia. The commitment to dialogue and the search for "win-win" solutions continues among the current CCC members, including many leading U.S. companies. According to the council's executive director, Barbara Haas, the objective is to use the council as a forum for dialogue.

business and society.[6] Exhibit 5-A describes an organization of companies that is pursuing an interactive strategy with leading environmentalists.

A strategy of response to the social and physical environment depends on how well a manager understands that the environment is changing and that a strategic approach is needed to respond to it. Only then can any of these specific responses be employed. As one author says: "Major strategic shifts in the business environment require conceptual shifts in the minds of managers."[7] Thus managers need to reexamine their assumptions and think about the present and future environment in a way that is accurate, practical, and up-to-date.

FORMULATING SOCIALLY RESPONSIVE STRATEGIES

Social considerations permeate both the formulation and implementation of an organization's strategy. The strategy of a business involves basic decisions about its mission, purpose, and reason for being. These are value-laden decisions, affected by the values and ethics of management, the interests of various stake-

[6] James E. Post, *Corporate Behavior and Social Change,* Reston, VA: Reston, 1978; Robert Miles, *Managing the Corporate Social Environment: A Grounded Theory,* Englewood Cliffs, NJ: Prentice-Hall, 1987.

[7] Freeman, op. cit., p. 24.

FIGURE 5–2
Strategy and social responsiveness.

SOURCE: Adapted from R. Edward Freeman, *Strategic Management: A Stakeholder Approach,* Marshfield, MA: Pitman, 1984, p. 92.

CORPORATE STRATEGY

STAKEHOLDER ANALYSIS	VALUES ANALYSIS	SOCIETAL ISSUES
• Who are our stakeholders?	• What are the dominant organizational values?	• What are the major issues (economic, political, social, technological) facing our society over the next ten years?
• What effects do we have on each in political, economic, and social terms?	• What are the values of the key executives and board members?	• How do these issues affect our company and our stakeholders?
• How do these stakeholders perceive these effects?	• What are the values of the key stakeholders?	

holders, and the web of social issues and problems that are a vital dimension of the environment. In other words, a business strategy that will effectively guide an enterprise over time cannot possibly be formulated without taking company, stakeholder, and societal values and interests into account. These relationships are shown in Figure 5–2.

The Relevant Environment

In order to begin formulating a socially responsive strategy, a framework of environmental information is needed. Managers must understand what is occurring in many sectors of the external world. According to two authorities, the environment that is relevant for businesses and their managers consists of four distinct segments: social, economic, political, and technological.[8] The environment consists of an almost unlimited amount of information, including facts, trends, issues, and ideas. Each of these segments represents a focused area of information, a portion of which is important and relevant to the business.

The social segment focuses on information about (1) demographics, (2) life-styles, and (3) social values of a society. Managers have a need to understand changes in population patterns, characteristics of the population, emergence of new life-styles, and social values that seem to be in or out of favor with the majority of the population.

[8] Liam Fahey and V. K. Narayanan, *Macroenvironmental Analysis for Strategic Management,* St. Paul, MN: West, 1986, pp. 28–29.

FIGURE 5–3
The macroenvironment of business.

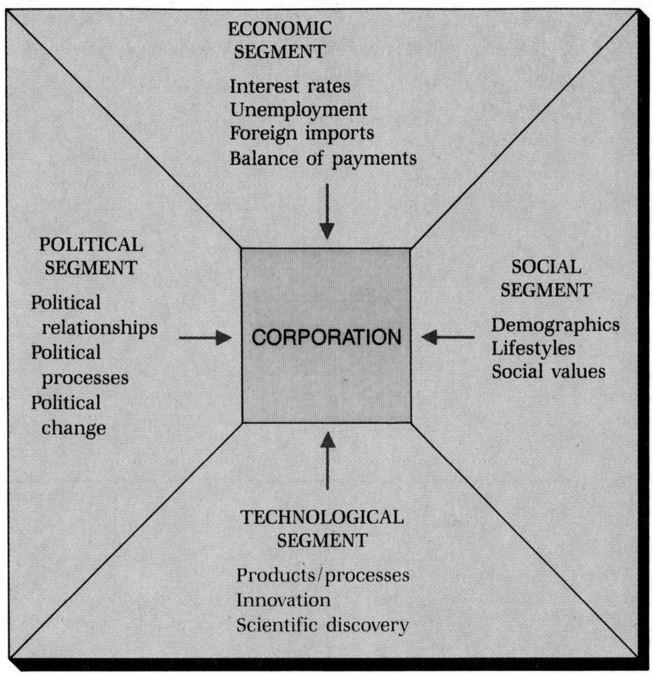

The economic segment focuses on the general set of economic factors and conditions confronting industries in a society. For example, information about interest rates, unemployment, foreign imports, and many other such factors is relevant to virtually all businesses. The economic segment obviously has a large impact on all business organizations.

The political segment deals with specific political relationships in society, changes in them, and the processes by which society makes political decisions. Changes in the tax code, for example, redistribute income and tax burdens. This involves political relationships between various segments of society. The creation and dissolution of regulatory institutions that set standards for business behavior are examples of changes in the political process.

The technological segment is concerned with the technological progress and potential hazards that are taking place in a society. New products, processes, or materials, including any negative social impacts; the general level of scientific activity; and advances in fundamental science (e.g., biology) are the key concerns in this area.

The macroenvironment, as presented in Figure 5–3, is a system of interrelated segments, each one connected to and influencing the others. The developments in genetic science, for example, occur in the technological segment. Their impact is evident in the economic segment, where new businesses are formed. They also affect the political segment, where regulation is discussed, and the social segment, where the ethical dimensions of genetic engineering are debated. By understanding each of these segments, their interrelationships, and those facts which are of direct and indirect importance to the corporation, a manager will improve his or her understanding of the relevant environment in which strategies must be formulated.

Scanning and Environmental Analysis

There are many different ways for managers to learn about the external environment. **Environmental scanning** is a term that generally describes a managerial process of analyzing the external social, economic, technological, and political environment. Scanning can be done informally or formally, and by individual managers or by teams. It is largely an information collection, analysis, and processing activity, and it is a valuable first step in building a socially responsive strategy for an organization.

Generally, scanning can be done by focusing on one or more of the following: trends that are occurring in government, society, or segments thereof; issues that are emerging in one's industry, sector of the economy, or nations in which the company conducts business; and stakeholders who are important to the organization currently or who appear to be potentially important in the future.

Trend analysis attempts to understand and extrapolate the implications and consequences of current trends into the future. Companies whose products or services have particularly long life spans have a special need for an understanding of long-term trends. The life insurance industry, for example, regularly enters into individual contracts that have a life span of 20, 30, or even 50 years. Policyholders may pay premiums on a life insurance policy for decades before the company is required to make payment on the policy. Trends such as increasing lifespan and more active life-styles also can alter the calculation of how many years an insurer may have to pay out on a pension plan or annuity. The failure to understand such trends and their implications can result in poor financial planning that injures the company and the insurance beneficiary or pension recipient.

Issues analysis involves a careful assessment of specific concerns that are having, or may have, an impact on the company. In many companies, public affairs managers do detailed tracking and monitoring of taxation proposals in state legislatures and the Congress. Because tax proposals frequently involve highly technical and specific aspects of a company's business (e.g., depreciation rates for different types of equipment), it is often crucial for a company's top management to know the specific dollar effects of proposed bills or regulations. In manufacturing and natural resource industries, for example, it is not unusual for companies to have one or more specialists whose entire job is to track the development of such proposals and assess each one's impact on the company. This analysis becomes the basis for the company's lobbying or other political activities.

Because most corporations face many issues at one time, they need to set priorities for public issues in terms of their imminent development and/or their

FIGURE 5–4
Identifying high priority issues for action.

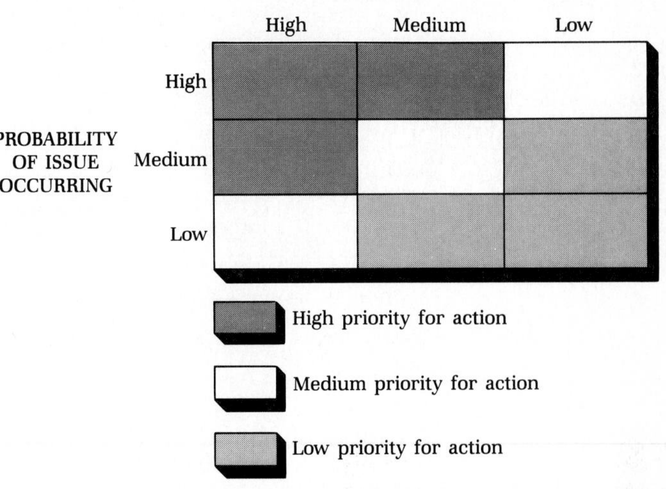

impact on the firm. In Figure 5–4, a matrix presentation of emerging public issues is illustrated. The General Electric Company pioneered this type of environmental analysis in the 1970s and regularly updated its "high priority" issues list. This helps provide a guide to top management and the company's lobbyists as to where they should focus attention in the political arena. Issues analysis can be utilized with trend analysis to provide a more accurate picture of current issues and their probable future development.

Stakeholder analysis places the scanner's focus on the people, groups, and organizations that populate the external environment. By trying to understand the issues that are of concern to the company's primary and secondary stakeholders, managers are better able to predict what types of demands are going to be made in the months ahead. There are many ways to collect such information, ranging from professional reporting services that track leaders of activist groups to direct contacts and discussions with stakeholder representatives. Informal discussions with union leaders or local environmentalists can go a long way toward providing managers with an understanding of what is critical to these groups and why.

In practice, companies and managers try to integrate all three types of information into a complete view of the external environment. Some firms have large staffs that try to systematically tie all of the pieces together into a coherent report, often in conjunction with the company's strategic planning effort. Others prefer a less formal, and less costly, approach. Not surprisingly, companies which have had bad experiences or have been surprised in the past tend to pay attention to the external issues and problems to avoid repeating past experiences.

Some experts prefer to see scanning as part of a broader process of environmental analysis that includes other specific steps. For example, experts on corporate strategic planning believe that the process of environmental analysis occurs

FIGURE 5–5
Four phases of environmental analysis.

SOURCE: Adapted from Liam Fahey and V. K. Narayanan, *Macroenvironmental Analysis for Strategic Management*, St. Paul, MN: West, 1986.

Phase 1.	IDENTIFYING Identify warning signals of environmental change
Phase 2.	MONITORING Track specific issues and trends in the environment
Phase 3.	FORECASTING Anticipate the future direction of environmental change
Phase 4.	ASSESSMENT Interpret the influence and importance of changes for the company

in four stages: identifying warning signals of potential environmental change or environmental changes already taking place, monitoring specific environmental trends and patterns, forecasting the future direction of environmental changes, and assessing current and future environmental changes.[9] Figure 5–5 illustrates the relationships between the four phases of the environmental analysis process.

Identification

Identification involves a general surveillance of all segments of the relevant environment to detect changes already under way and to identify hints of coming changes. It is both present-oriented and prospective, looking toward the "unknown future."

Environmental scanners study newspapers, magazines, research reports, government publications, futurist publications, and obscure periodicals. They always look for basic trends and changes in the social, political, economic, and technological environments of business. Artistic trends expressed in contemporary painting, drama, literature, or "pop" music may contain hints of underlying changes in public moods or values. What may appear to be trivial style or fashion movements—for example, shorter hairstyles for men or space-age toys for children—may signify to an environmental scanner that cultural shifts are occurring. Environmental scanning also involves contacting professional, scientific, governmental, and special interest groups.

Monitoring

After potential changes and trends have been identified, sequences of events and streams of activities must be tracked and monitored. The monitoring activity allows the firm's management to keep track of important developments and respond to them more quickly and effectively. It also allows managers to separate true signals from false signals. Signals picked up during the original scanning may hint at a trend or development; they need to be verified before organizational decisions are made.

> For example, in the 1980s, the early signs of a new alliance of conservatives, old-style liberals, and Americans with interests ranging from Eastern mysticism

[9] Ibid., pp. 36–45.

and the occult to holistic medicine appeared. These strands in a "thread of alternative thought" began working their way increasingly into the nation's cultural, religious, social, economic, and political life. Some people believed that these alternative ideas and "human potential" or "self-help" programs might be used to help executives compete in the world marketplace. One scholar described the trend as "the most powerful force in the country today. I think it's as much a political movement as a religious movement, and it's spreading into business management theory and a lot of other areas. But if you look at it carefully, you see it represents a complete rejection of Judeo-Christian and bedrock American values."[10]

Years may pass before a purported trend can be verified and understood, so the monitoring phase will be lengthy and complex. In general, effective monitoring by all companies should produce a specific description of environmental trends and patterns that are occurring, identification of specific trends that need further monitoring, and identification of areas that need further scanning.

Forecasting

Since strategic planning and decision making require an orientation toward the future, managers try to project, or forecast, what will happen in the future as well as describe current events.

Forecasting can be conducted on two fronts. Some trends are more predictable than others; thus some forecasting is done in the realm of "the expected." For example, much demographic information can be projected, with a small margin of error, for five or ten years into the future. School enrollments, the number of entry-level jobs, and school dropout or graduation rates can be forecast with a reasonable degree of accuracy because of experience and the ability to double-check past forecasts.

This situation is not true for all developments, however. Many future situations and circumstances are sudden and unexpected. They cannot be projected based on available data and figures. The sudden action of Iraq to invade Kuwait in 1990, for example, was entirely unexpected by many people. Yet the event produced major economic and political consequences. Public skepticism of nuclear power also was not predicted by those who built the first nuclear power plants. Warning signals did exist in both situations, however, which could have been used to construct pictures of a "possible future."

Despite the problems and ambiguities involved in forecasting, most companies recognize its importance and value. Today, many corporations have discovered that new techniques enable managers to integrate forecasts into their strategic planning processes.[11]

[10] Robert Lindsey, "Spiritual Concepts Drawing a Different Breed of Adherent," *New York Times*, Sept. 29, 1986, pp. A1, B12; Frank Rose, "A New Age for Business," *Fortune*, Oct. 8, 1990, pp. 156–164.
[11] Fahey and Narayanan, op. cit., chap. 13.

EXHIBIT 5-B

SOURCE: Adapted from Edward Cornish, "A Short List of Global Concerns," *The Futurist*, January–February 1990, pp. 29–36.

A SHORT LIST OF GLOBAL CONCERNS

The start of a decade, or a new century, prompts futurists and others to assess how things stand now and how they might look in ten years. Not long ago, the Union of International Associations in Brussels produced a list of 10,000 world problems. These were the broad headings used to "cluster" the experts' opinions of critical world problems:

Category	Basic Theme
International tensions	Peace is an elusive goal
The fragile economy	A global economy at risk
Growing pollution	Bad and getting worse
The drug crisis	A social phenomenon
Disappearing resources	Ecological disasters
The struggle against poverty	Problems of social underclass
Rampant lawlessness	Danger lurks everywhere
Population problems	Size, composition, and mobility
Medical dilemmas	Hard choices riddle the system
The changing family	Survival needs of the family unit
Media maladies	Information overload in the modern world

Assessment

Identification, monitoring, and forecasting produce information which is then assessed and interpreted to determine how the trends and developments might affect the company. The assessment phase therefore involves a great amount of interpretation and judgment on the part of the manager. Assessment requires identifying how, why, in what time frame, and to what degree certain predicted trends will affect the strategic plan of the company. As Exhibit 5-B highlights, various global "futures" can be understood.

IMPLEMENTING SOCIAL RESPONSIVENESS

Companies do not become socially responsive overnight. The process takes time. New attitudes have to be developed, new routines learned, and new policies and action programs designed. Many obstacles must be overcome in implementing socially responsive strategies. Some are structural, such as the reporting relationships between groups of managers; others are cultural, such as a historical pattern of only men or women in a particular job category.

FIGURE 5–6
A three-stage model of corporate social responsiveness.

Source: Adapted from Robert W. Ackerman, *The Social Challenge to Business,* Cambridge, MA: Harvard University Press, 1975; and Robert W. Ackerman and Raymond A. Bauer, *Corporate Social Responsiveness: The Modern Dilemma,* Reston, VA: Reston, 1976.

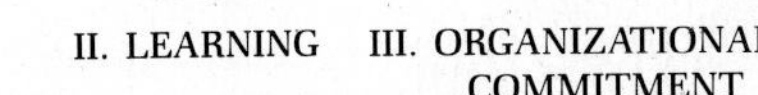

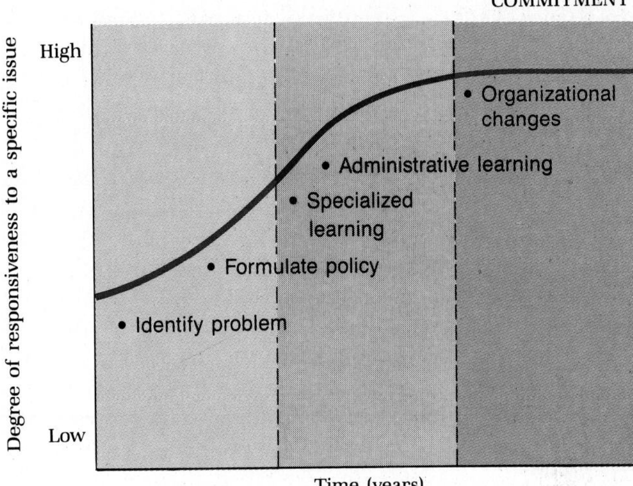

A Model of Corporate Social Responsiveness

An early model of how large corporations effectively implement socially responsive policies is illustrated in Figure 5–6.[12] There are three stages to the responsiveness process depicted in this model. Each is dicussed below.

The policy stage

The first stage of social responsiveness involves being aware of which part of the surrounding environment needs to be responded to and acted upon by the company. The process may occur after stakeholder expectations change, or it may result from a systematic environmental analysis. Whether or not stakeholder pressure exists, a company's management may think, based on the company's own environmental analysis, that a response is needed to emerging issues, concerns, or social trends.

For example, a group of Boston businesses announced a $6 million program designed to guarantee financial aid to all graduates of the city's public high schools who get into college and to provide jobs for those who complete their education. This action reflected a continuing policy commitment by the chief executives of these companies. The businesses, mostly banks and insurance companies, were responding to statistics indicating that roughly 50 percent of the students in an entering high school class dropped out over the four-

[12] Robert W. Ackerman, *The Social Challenge to Business,* Cambridge, MA: Harvard University Press, 1975; and Robert W. Ackerman and Raymond A. Bauer, *Corporate Social Responsiveness: The Modern Dilemma,* Reston, VA: Reston, 1976.

year attendance period.[13] Since the Boston school population was declining, the number of graduating students had been decreasing drastically. This trend meant a drastic shortage of applicants for entry-level jobs at many of the local insurance companies and banks. The businesses formulated a plan to support local schools and education. In addition to the funds provided, 350 Boston-area companies pledged to help provide jobs to high school graduates, and many offered to help pay for guidance counselors in the schools. This commitment served two purposes: the students and schools were helped, and the companies ensured themselves a future pool of applicants for entry-level jobs.

Social responses need to be guided by policies that are carefully and deliberately developed by top management and the board of directors. Those policies provide a framework for shaping other aspects of the organization's response. New production policies, for example, may result in better quality control for consumer products, may remove job hazards, and may reduce water pollution all at the same time.

The learning stage

Once a social problem—for example, excessive numbers of high school dropouts—has been identified, and once a general policy—for example, an educational opportunity policy—has been adopted, the company must learn how to tackle the problem and make the new policy work. Two kinds of learning are needed: specialized learning and administrative learning.

Specialized learning occurs when a "sociotechnical" expert—for example, an inner-city educator who is thoroughly familiar with the culture, life-styles, motivations, and special problems of high school youth—is employed to advise company officers and managers. The kind of specialized knowledge that the sociotechnical expert brings to the company is particularly helpful in the early stages of social responsiveness when the company is dealing with an unfamiliar social problem, whether it be high school dropouts, prejudice against minorities in hiring practices, excessive pollution, or toxic chemical hazards.

Administrative learning occurs when a company's supervisors and managers—those who administer the organization's daily affairs—become familiar with new routines that are necessary to cope with a social problem. A technical expert can assist the company in taking its first steps to solve a problem but cannot do the whole job alone. Social responsiveness requires the full cooperation and knowledge of line managers as well as staff experts. Personal involvement is essential.

Managers of businesses involved in supporting the education systems in their cities have had to learn many new skills. For example, Dianne Sullivan, the president of Miraflores Designs in New York, pledged to help 60 East Harlem students. Then, the day before school started in September, she learned

[13] Fox Butterfield, "Funds and Jobs Pledged to Boston Graduates," *New York Times*, Sept. 10, 1986, p. D25.

that they did not know which junior high school they were supposed to attend. Sullivan immediately telephoned the local school superintendent and worked to solve the problem. Had she not done so, many of the students might have missed the program's beginning.[14]

The organizational commitment stage

One final step is needed to achieve full social responsiveness: an organization must "institutionalize" its new social policy.[15] The new policies and routines learned in the first two stages should become so well accepted throughout the entire company that they are considered to be a normal part of doing business. In other words, they should be a part of the company and its standard operating procedures. For example, when managers respond to the needs of the local education system or to the students without having to rely upon special directives from top management, the socially responsive policy can be considered to be institutionalized.

The normal organizational pressures to resist change mean that both effort and time are needed to improve a corporation's responsiveness. In the past, it took large corporations an average of six to eight years to progress from the first stage to the third stage on any given social issue or problem such as equal employment opportunity or pollution control. Yet some firms are more flexible than others, and some social problems are easier to handle than others, so the time involved may vary considerably. It is clear, however, that a combination of internal factors, especially management willpower, and external factors, especially continued stakeholder action on the problem, is necessary for effective change to occur.[16]

MAKING A SOCIAL STRATEGY WORK

Countless obstacles impede effective implementation of management policy in the modern corporation. As illustrated in Figure 5–7, top management often changes the factors that most affect resistance to change: organizational structures, evaluation and reward systems, administrative systems, and corporate culture. Companies that have demonstrated significant success in being socially responsive to their stakeholders and the environment have recognized that new structures, as well as new attitudes and new incentives, are needed.

Organizational Structure

A corporation cannot achieve any strategy if it is organized improperly. An organization's structure is the "architecture" that helps determine how it will look to others and how it will perform for its stakeholders.

[14] Jane Perlez, "Public Schools and the Private Sector," *New York Times*, Sept. 14, 1986, p. 14.
[15] Robert Ackerman, "How Companies Respond to Social Demands," *Harvard Business Review*, July–August 1973, pp. 88–98.
[16] Miles, *op. cit.*

FIGURE 5–7
"Levers" through which a corporation's business and social strategy is managed.

Board of directors

As shown in Figure 5–8, corporate response often begins with the board of directors. The board is responsible for the basic policy and strategy of the firm. Many corporate social actions are major ones that require broad approval. The board needs to improve its interaction with the environment in order to gain more social understanding. The directors need to learn what is happening in the social world in the same way that they historically have sought to know what is happening in the economic world.

One way to increase social inputs to the board is to increase the number of "outside" members, as compared with insiders who also are top managers of the company. Outside directors generally have a broader perspective and sometimes may possess specialized social knowledge. Another suggestion is to appoint stakeholder representatives as board members: minorities, women, consumers, labor-union representatives, and others who might contribute distinctive social viewpoints to corporate policies.

Many large corporations have a public responsibility or public policy committee of the board of directors. The job of such a committee is to monitor the social environment, identify social and political issues most likely to affect the firm, and make recommendations to the full board for appropriate actions.[17]

The chief executive officer

The chief executive officer (CEO) is the link between the board's policies and the top management group that must put policies into action. CEOs often spend substantial amounts of time on external affairs that affect their companies. A

[17] John Kohls, "Corporate Board Structures, Social Reporting, and Social Performance," in L. Preston (ed.), *Research in Corporate Social Performance and Policy*, vol. 7, Greenwich, CT: JAI Press, 1985, pp. 165–189.

FIGURE 5–8
Actions required by different management groups for corporate social responsiveness.

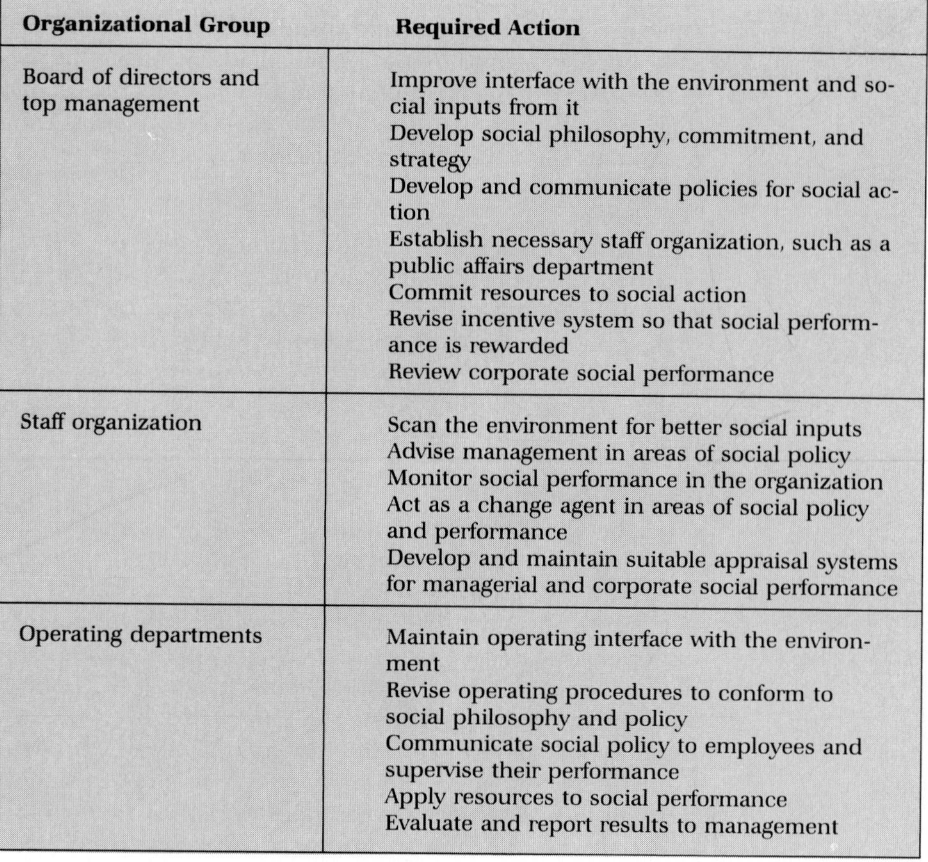

Organizational Group	Required Action
Board of directors and top management	Improve interface with the environment and social inputs from it Develop social philosophy, commitment, and strategy Develop and communicate policies for social action Establish necessary staff organization, such as a public affairs department Commit resources to social action Revise incentive system so that social performance is rewarded Review corporate social performance
Staff organization	Scan the environment for better social inputs Advise management in areas of social policy Monitor social performance in the organization Act as a change agent in areas of social policy and performance Develop and maintain suitable appraisal systems for managerial and corporate social performance
Operating departments	Maintain operating interface with the environment Revise operating procedures to conform to social philosophy and policy Communicate social policy to employees and supervise their performance Apply resources to social performance Evaluate and report results to management

study undertaken by the Conference Board revealed that the majority of top executives surveyed spend one-quarter of their time managing external affairs and that a sizable percentage of them devote up to 50 percent of their workweek to such duties.[18] An active and socially alert CEO can keep both the board and top management well informed, thereby increasing the firm's chances of responding meaningfully to external pressures.

Top management

While the board of directors and the CEO can work together to establish general social policies for a company, the top management group should translate these broad guidelines into operational plans and programs. For example, the board of directors of a large food manufacturer wanted to demonstrate the company's concern for members of the city's poorer neighborhoods. Top officers of the company, after consulting with production and marketing departments, decided

[18] Seymour Lusterman, *The Organization and Staffing of Corporate Public Affairs*, New York: The Conference Board, 1987.

to donate excess inventories of canned goods to selected community agencies. The costs of the program were absorbed by the public affairs department. In this way, a policy favored by the public affairs managers became a practical reality through top management planning. The participation of many business firms in such major activities as Live-Aid, Hands across America, and the Statue of Liberty restoration effort was implemented in similar ways.[19]

The staff role

Companies large enough to have staff units will depend on them for a number of support functions related to social policy. The staff is the firm's specialized organ for reaching out into the world and learning directions of social change so the firm may respond appropriately. Staff experts may advise top management on social developments, monitor the company's social performance from inside, and help evaluate how well the firm is meeting its social program objectives. The role of public affairs staffs, discussed below, is crucial to this effort.

Operating units

Change eventually affects operating departments, and usually its impact is greatest there. Since traditional ways of work must be revised to conform with new programs, change always brings some operating costs, regardless of the benefits that eventually may occur. In the case of social involvement, there often are high beginning costs, while the benefits are long-range, often indirect, and sometimes not very evident to an individual department. As a result, from a department's point of view a cost-benefit analysis may be negative; therefore, management faces an additional task of providing resources that can help departments to develop a long-term perspective. Nevertheless, it is in the plant, the office, the mine, and the field location—where a company actually conducts its business—that top-level social policies and goals either succeed or fail.

Rewards and Evaluation

Success or failure in social programming generally depends on the same kinds of factors that operate in normal business situations. Is there enough money allocated for the program? Is a qualified person in charge? Is there proper follow-up and review? And, most importantly, are managers and employees motivated to be socially responsive? As Peter Jones, former senior vice president and corporate counsel of Levi Strauss, a company that has often appeared among lists of the most socially responsive companies in America, stated the problem succinctly: "The key to getting the desired type of behavior in the modern corporation is providing enough contervailing pressures—either incentives or sanctions—to overcome the incentives to behave in the undesired way."[20]

[19] Sandra Waddock and James E. Post, "Catalytic Alliances for Social Problem-Solving," *Academy of Management Best Papers Proceedings*, 1990.

[20] Peter R. Jones, "Sanctions, Incentives and Corporate Behavior," in R. B. Dickie and L. Rouner (eds.), *Corporations and the Common Good*, South Bend, IN: University of Notre Dame Press, 1986, pp. 118–137.

When Du Pont's chief executive, E. S. Woolard, committed the company to become a leader in corporate environmentalism, the compensation of all managers was tied to the speed and effectiveness of their environmental program. This approach is a vital way of convincing operating managers that the policy is not mere "window dressing"; if they wish to receive their "normal" bonuses, they must make environmental improvement part of their normal performance.[21]

Administrative Systems

The flow of information, communications, and data is part of the administrative circulatory system in any organization. In order to evaluate its social strategy and social performance, a firm needs some form of specialized **social performance reporting** process. The study of a firm's social performance is conducted much like other management studies. What has been called a **social audit** provides management with information about the firm's social impact; it may be presented as a report for managers only or for the public as well.[22]

Public disclosure of the data collected in a social evaluation is an important issue. At one time, only financial performance data were presented in annual reports. By 1990, however, the pressure for greater disclosure of social performance information had led 90 percent of the top 500 corporations to include information about their social activities in the company's annual report to shareholders. A few companies, such as General Motors, Bank of America, and Atlantic Richfield, published special yearly reports detailing the company's efforts to be a socially responsible member of the community. In the insurance industry, the Clearing House for Corporate Social Involvement has collected and published reports about member companies' performance in such socially important areas as equal employment opportunity, inner-city investments, and charitable contributions.

Perhaps the most visible example of systematic social reporting by United States companies involved reports filed by more than 100 companies that agreed to abide by the Sullivan Principles in South Africa.[23] The principles specified standards of conduct toward black workers in hiring, wage rates, and working conditions. Companies that signed an agreement to abide by the principles publicly reported on their performance annually.

Social performance reporting in general is done on a mostly voluntary basis in the United States, but it is required in nations such as Germany, France, and Spain.[24] Social performance reporting is more highly advanced in Europe because

[21] E. S. Woolard, Address to National Wildlife Federation/Corporate Conservation Council, Jan. 30, 1990.

[22] A discussion of the original social audit concept is found in Raymond A. Bauer and Dan H. Fenn, Jr., *The Corporate Social Audit,* New York: Russell Sage, 1972; David H. Blake, William C. Frederick, and Mildred S. Myers, *Social Auditing: Evaluating the Impact of Corporate Programs,* New York: Praeger, 1976; and John J. Corson and George A. Steiner, *Measuring Business's Social Performance: The Corporate Social Audit,* New York: Committee for Economic Development, 1974.

[23] See Investor Responsibility Research Center, *South Africa Review Service,* Washington, DC: IRRC, Annual Reports, 1986–1991.

[24] Meinolf Dierkes and Ariane Berthoin Antal, "Whither Corporate Social Reporting: Is It Time to Legislate?" *California Management Review,* Spring 1986, pp. 106–121.

of the commitment of both government and companies (e.g., the Swiss company Migros) to its implementation, and because of pressure from activist trade unions and national political parties.

Corporate Culture

The culture or climate in an organization affects employees and the stakeholders with whom they deal. In companies with a strong commitment to social strategy, top management uses a variety of tools to encourage a climate of respect for social values and stakeholder interests. These may include a demonstrated personal commitment by top-level managers to desirable social goals, symbolic company actions (such as developing and enforcing a code of conduct) to dramatize a strong social commitment, and training programs that teach employees and managers how to respond positively to stakeholders' demands. Additionally, creation and maintenance of a socially responsive culture can be achieved by using many of the tools mentioned above.

As illustrated previously in Figure 5–7, a corporation's culture is directly, and critically, linked to the social strategy top management is trying to achieve. Moreover, it is indirectly but clearly connected to the organization's administrative systems, rewards and evaluation activities, and structure. All of these areas of organizational life contribute to the development of a corporation that "stands for something" in the eyes of the employees, customers, community members, and other stakeholders. The corporate culture is the practical means that managers have for translating their social and ethical "vision" into actions that reach all of the corporation's stakeholders.

THE PUBLIC AFFAIRS FUNCTION

In many companies, specialized staff departments have been created to manage stakeholder relationships. The emergence of the corporate **public affairs function** has been a major innovation in U.S. management, replacing and often combining the specialized departments such as government relations, community affairs, media relations, and public relations.

According to one group of experts:

> [T]he essential role of public affairs units appears to be that of a *window out* of the corporation through which management can perceive, monitor, and understand external change, and simultaneously, a *window in* through which society can influence corporate policy and practice. This boundary-spanning role primarily involves the flow of information to and from the organization. In many firms it also involves the flow of financial resources in the form of political contributions to elected and would-be officials, and charitable contributions to various stakeholder groups in society.[25]

[25] Boston University Public Affairs Research Group, *Public Affairs Offices and Their Functions: A Summary of Survey Results* (Boston, MA: Boston University School of Management, 1981), p. 1.

FIGURE 5–9
Public affairs activities and functions of 400 corporations.

Does your company consider the activity or function to part of public affairs?

Activity	Percentage of Respondents: Yes	No
Community relations	84.9%	15.1%
Government relations	84.2	15.8
Corporate contributions	71.5	28.5
Media relations	70.0	30.0
Stockholder relations	48.5	51.5
Advertising	40.4	59.6
Consumer affairs	38.5	61.5
Graphics	33.5	66.5
Institutional investor relations	33.5	66.5
Customer relations	23.8	76.2
Other	26.3	73.7

Yes No

("Other" includes grass-roots lobbying and political action committees.)

Between 1970 and 1980 more than half (58 percent) of 400 corporations in the Boston University study had established a public affairs unit; an update of that study showed that the trend toward establishing public affairs continued during the 1980s.[26] Today, medium-sized and small businesses are joining larger companies in using the public affairs function as a means of coordinating political, social, and economic initiatives. Figure 5–9 summarizes a broad range of activities that are normally associated with public affairs management. Community relations and government relations (at both federal and state levels) account for much of the activity, but many companies also recognize the need to include corporate contributions and media relations.

Most companies have a high-ranking executive to head the public affairs

[26] James E. Post, "The Corporation and Public Policy in the 1990s," *Journal of Organizational Change Management*, forthcoming, 1991.

PUBLIC AFFAIRS (WORLDWIDE)

- Chairman, Political action committee
- V. Chairman, Crisis management team
- Ex. Secy., Board public policy committee
- Ex officio, Corporate contributions committee

INTERNATIONAL PUBLIC AFFAIRS

CORPORATE PHILANTHROPY

- Contributions committee
- Corporate foundation
- Trade group memberships

CORPORATE/MARKETING COMMUNICATIONS

- Corporate ID program
- Corporate P.R.
- Product P.R.
- Product advertising services
- Customer inquiry system
- Sales promotion items

EMPLOYEE/FINANCIAL COMMUNICATIONS

- Financial P.R.
- Shareholder/investor communications
- Employee publications
- Executive speechwriting

FEDERAL GOVERNMENT RELATIONS

- Federal marketing support
- Legislative support
- Political relations
- Executive support
- Trade group relations

STATE/COMMUNITY RELATIONS

- Legislative support
- Political relations
- Executive support
- Community involvement
- United Way

FIGURE 5–10
Public affairs organization for a large corporation.

function, so the public affairs unit usually has a direct input or voice in the company's major strategy and policy decisions. According to a former senior vice president and director of public affairs at First Interstate Bank in California, this arrangement is an important key to infusing social responsiveness into the organization.

> This policy role involves asking many difficult questions. The task of public affairs should be to ask: What are the public policy ramifications of a new product or service? What will this do to the community? Who will be offended or hurt, and who is helped? What are the social forces out there that will try to stop this action, and why? Are there outsiders we should be consulting with, such as "think tanks," foundations, or people in academia? How do we bring the "outside" key players "in" and make them feel part of the process? What will the press say? How will the political community react? And, if we can't do it this way, how about rethinking and redesigning it so we can get to the same result? In other words, the question should always be: Are we anticipating as many facets of the issues as we can, and how much can we learn *before* we make a decision?[27]

[27] Lloyd B. Dennis, "Redefining the Role of Public Affairs," *New Management*, June 1986, pp. 50–53.

Many companies have developed a public affairs function that meshes with the company's decision-making system in three key ways. First, public affairs often is responsible for collecting, analyzing, and preparing **political and social intelligence** for top management. Issues are identified, trends forecast, and the environment analyzed. Second, public affairs is responsible for communicating important information to a variety of other management groups within the company. Special reports may be prepared for the board of directors, the chief executive officer, strategic planners, and operating managers in different product divisions.[28] Third, public affairs is responsible for developing and executing action programs that target key external stakeholders. Thus a public affairs department may have a media contacts program, community affairs operations, and federal government lobbying activities. The public affairs organization chart depicted in Figure 5–10 shows how these programs and functions are arranged at a large manufacturing company.

CONCLUSION

The true measure of a company's social responsiveness is how well its core activities—its primary involvements—reflect a concern for stakeholders. Companies display basic strategies for responding to these issues. This chapter has focused on the relationship between a company's business and social strategies, their interconnections, and the actions needed to infuse social responsibility into the organization and its activities.

SUMMARY POINTS OF THIS CHAPTER

- This chapter has described the relationship between the strategic business decisions made by managers and the social responsiveness concerns of corporate stakeholders. The challenge for modern management is to effectively make near-term and longer-term decisions that integrate stakeholder interests with the actions and values of management and emerging social trends.
- Environmental analysis is crucial to integrating social responsiveness and long-term strategic decisions. Through scanning, monitoring, forecasting, and assessment, managers can anticipate the future business environment.
- The implementation of socially responsive strategies and policies also is a major challenge to business. By understanding the stages in the responsiveness process and the devices that have been utilized to make social responsiveness operational in organizations, the integration of business and social concerns can be achieved.

[28] Thomas G. Marx, "Strategic Planning for Public Affairs," *Long Range Planning*, vol. 23, no. 1, February 1990, pp. 9–16.

- Managers have a number of "levers" to effect change in organizations. Policy, structure, rewards, and evaluation processes can all be managed to improve corporate social responsiveness. The objective is to build a corporate culture that encourages and rewards socially responsible, ethical behavior.
- The public affairs function is the mechanism many companies use to organize and manage their political and other external relationships.

KEY TERMS AND CONCEPTS USED IN THIS CHAPTER

- Strategies of response: inactive, reactive, proactive, interactive
- Environmental analysis and scanning
- Corporate social responsiveness model
- "Levers" of organizational change
- Social performance reporting
- Social audit
- Public affairs function
- Political and social intelligence

DISCUSSION CASE

APPLIED ENERGY SYSTEMS

During the 1980s, scientists assembled more conclusive proof that the buildup of carbon dioxide (CO_2) in the earth's atmosphere was having a serious effect on global temperatures. The discovery of global warming has led to great concern about the effects: melting of the earth's polar ice caps, thereby increasing the level of oceans, flooding many coastal-plain areas, and destroying the agricultural and industrial bases of many nations around the world. Hundreds of millions of people could be directly affected, many being forced to relocate their homes and families. While there is considerable disagreement about the precise timetable on which global warming is occurring, there is a broad consensus that discharges of carbon dioxide should be halted or reduced wherever possible.

One of the carbon dioxide culprits is industrial activity. The burning of fossil fuels, such as coal and the oil which is refined into gasoline, emits large quantities of carbon dioxide into the atmosphere. Virtually all industries contribute to the CO_2 emissions problems, but the heaviest users of fossil fuels are naturally the target for action. Power producers, including public and private utilities in the industrialized world, are near the top of the fossil fuel users and CO_2 emitters. Not surprisingly, they are under considerable pressure from environmentalists to reduce their emissions.

In 1988, Applied Energy Systems (AES), an independent producer in Virginia, announced an innovative response to its own carbon dioxide emissions. AES owns and operates power plants in various states, including Connecticut, where it had been planning to build a 180-megawatt coal-fired plant. AES planners realized that such a plant, while needed by the citizens of Connecticut, would emit 15.5 million tons of carbon dioxide. No technology exists to eliminate such emissions entirely, and so the challenge was to "balance" the emissions in some manner.

Live trees, especially young trees that are growing rapidly, absorb carbon dioxide. Thus, one way to balance the negative effect of 15.5 million tons of CO_2, reasoned AES managers, is to add enough trees to the ecosystem to absorb an equivalent amount of carbon dioxide emissions. After considerable research and active collaboration with environmental groups, Applied Energy Systems executives announced a plan to invest $2 million to plant trees in tropical Guatemala to offset the effects of the new Connecticut plant emissions. This pilot project was the first practical application of the concept of offsetting emissions in the industrial world with tropical tree planting. The technique is known as "carbon sequestration forestry." Third world tropical areas are particularly attractive for reforestation projects because forests have been lost rapidly and because trees grow quickly and can be planted at a fraction of the cost of replacing temperate region forests. It would be nearly impossible to find enough land for such planting in Connecticut, and the land price would surely be prohibitive. In Guatemala, the land is available, people will be employed to plant the trees, and the global environmental effect will "balance" the emissions in Connecticut.

Discussion Questions

1. What social pressures do you think Applied Energy Systems' managers faced prior to deciding on this action?
2. Does it concern you that the "balance" is not occurring in an area that is geographically close to the AES plant? Discuss this concern from a global point of view.
3. What stakeholders are involved in this situation? What are their interests?
4. Identify the various stages of social response mentioned in this chapter which were taken by AES.

PART TWO

The Corporation in a Global Society

6

Corporate Social Strategy: Global Challenges

Corporations of the 1990s must have a well-developed social strategy to accompany their economic strategy. Combining financial and social goals is expected by the public, and it improves profitable performance. Business faces a dizzying blend of global competition, new and powerful forms of technology, worldwide political changes, and the turbulence that accompanies regional conflicts. A well-thought-out social strategy can help companies around the globe to cope with these challenges.

Key Questions and Chapter Objectives

This chapter focuses on these key questions and objectives:

- How is corporate social strategy affected by international trends?
- What economic, political, technological, and social changes have been largely responsible for the major global challenges facing business in the 1990s?
- Why is it necessary to reinvent corporate strategy?
- What are the central questions that every corporate social strategy must address?

By late 1986, the directors of Barclays Bank, one of Britain's most prominent commercial banks, knew what they had to do. After almost two decades of public protest, after disruptive sit-ins at many of their branch offices, after seeing deposits withdrawn by churches, local governments, trade unions, and universities, and after taking a hard look at Barclays' future profit opportunities, the directors decided to pull out of South Africa. They sold their interest in Barclays National Bank Ltd. of South Africa to a group of South African companies and investors. It was the largest corporate pullout on record and ended 60 years of Barclays' banking services to that nation. A Barclays official in London said, "We were concerned about the longer term economic prospects of that part of Africa. We were concerned that there didn't seem to be an ending to apartheid. We were concerned that our business was being affected both here and to a lesser extent in the United States by certain groups, particularly in the student area. But perhaps more importantly than any of those factors was that in fact we have seen for some time our areas of potential and future investment as being Europe, Western Europe, North America, and Australia-Asia."[1]

A few years earlier, Japanese television audiences watched as a Japanese woman's husband walked into the bathroom as she was bathing. While she told him about the new beauty soap she was using, he stroked her shoulder and hinted that he was interested in more than her soap. Many Japanese viewers were offended, feeling that the man was displaying bad manners to intrude on his wife's bath. Procter & Gamble's efforts to sell its Camay soap to Japanese consumers were set back by this advertisement. P&G had similar troubles marketing its U.S. brand of bulky disposable diapers to Japanese buyers, who preferred cloth diapers or Japanese brands that were better fitting for Japanese babies. When they advertised P&G laundry detergent as working in all temperatures of water, they discovered that many Japanese wash clothes in cold water and did not care about P&G's claim. Problems like these caused the company to lose $200 million in its first years of entering Japanese markets. In Europe, the company's liquid laundry detergent could not be used in European-made washing machines which were designed to take only powdered laundry detergent. In trying to design portable liquid dispensers to be included in P&G's detergent package, the company discovered that each brand of washing machine required a different design. Procter & Gamble's marketing staff eventually overcame these blunders encountered in entering foreign markets so well that the company expected over half of its total revenues to come from foreign sales in the 1990s. The lesson was clear: Successful marketing requires a thorough knowledge of differing cultural attitudes and practices.[2]

Japanese companies expanding rapidly into foreign markets have had their own troubles adjusting to business life in other nations. NEC Corporation, the electronics and communications giant, found out that its home-grown executives needed special training in how to conduct business overseas. Especially troublesome areas were labor negotiations, which tend to be more direct in the United States than in Japan, how to handle lawsuits, and working with a multinational workforce. The United States stress on individualism contrasts with a Japanese penchant for group decision making. A weakness in understanding U.S. antitrust laws brought lawsuits against NEC by some distributors. Honda Corporation, another Japanese-based company, was charged with discrimination against blacks, women, and older workers, and agreed to a $6 million back-pay settlement to these groups. On the other hand, Sumitomo Rubber Industries convinced British employees in its newly purchased Dunlop tire plant in Birmingham,

[1] Quoted in Karen Paul and Sharyn Duffy, "Corporate Responses to the Call for South African Withdrawal," in Lee E. Preston (ed.), *Research in Corporate Performance and Policy,* vol. 10, Greenwich, CT: JAI Press, 1988, p. 234.

[2] "After Early Stumbles, P&G Is Making Inroads Overseas," *Wall Street Journal,* Feb. 6, 1989, p. B1.

England, to adopt many Japanese management and work practices, resulting in higher productivity and turning losses into profits.[3]

Both NEC and Honda—like Barclays Bank and Procter & Gamble—were learning that the road to multinational business success includes more than financial skill alone. A workable corporate strategy, they found out, requires a sophisticated knowledge of the social customs, the political systems, and the deeply felt human values of the societies in which they conduct business.

This chapter explains why corporate social strategy must be based upon a knowledge of worldwide trends. The best-managed corporations are the ones that devote much time and energy to designing and implementing such social strategies. They also turn out to be the companies most admired and approved by the general public.

BUSINESS'S TURBULENT OPERATING ENVIRONMENT

Today's business firms do not operate in a social or political vacuum. They find themselves in a virtual whirlwind of social and political problems and controversies. Business managers are buffeted by complicated and threatening forces, many of them global in scope. These trends now intrude into the very core of business operations, thus requiring careful attention and planning. Even small business firms that serve local markets are affected by disruptions in supply, price fluctuations, regional warfare, and uncertainty stemming from international political and economic events. Figure 6–1 lists the major environmental forces at work during the 1980s and early 1990s. These are discussed next.

Global Economic Changes

Beginning in the 1970s and continuing unabated into the early 1990s, dramatic changes transformed the world's economic scene. Some of the most far-reaching economic developments were Japanese industrial expansion, Third World economic development, western European economic integration, eastern European economic transformations, and world population growth. Global changes of this magnitude create more than just sharper economic competition. As economies changed, so have established governments, politics, and social systems. Operating a business in this shifting climate greatly complicates the job of management. Reaching business goals often requires a keen understanding of social, political, and cultural trends, and having an effective social strategy can mean the difference between business success or failure. Japan's impressive economic expansion demonstrates the importance of linking business goals with social awareness.

[3] "Japanese Executives Going Overseas Take Anti-Shock Courses," *Wall Street Journal,* Jan. 12, 1987, pp. A1, A18; "Blacks, Women at Honda Unit Win Back Pay," *Wall Street Journal,* Mar. 24, 1988, p. A2; and "Britain's 'Intransigent' Rubber Workers Bow to Japanese Management Practices," *Wall Street Journal,* Mar. 29, 1988, p. 20.

FIGURE 6–1
Business's major environmental challenges.

BUSINESS'S MAJOR ENVIRONMENTAL CHALLENGES

- **GLOBAL ECONOMIC CHANGES**
  Japanese industrial expansion
  Third world economic competition
  Western European economic integration
  World population growth
- **GLOBAL POLITICAL CHANGES**
  Deregulation and privatization
  Glasnost and *perestroika* (USSR)
  Eastern European political reforms
- **SCIENTIFIC AND TECHNOLOGICAL INNOVATIONS**
- **ECOLOGICAL IMPACTS**
- **COMPETITIVE PRESSURES VS. COMMUNITY NEEDS**
- **HUMAN PROBLEMS AND DIVERSITY IN THE WORKFORCE**
- **ETHICAL EXPECTATIONS**

The Japanese economic sun rises

By 1990, no business leader anywhere in the world could afford to ignore Japan's determined drive to become a global economic power. Best known for its prowess in electronics and automobile production, Figure 6–2 shows that Japan also has the world's eight largest banks, four of the top ten insurance companies, and four of the ten largest securities firms. In 1989, exactly half of the world's 100 largest public corporations were Japanese. By contrast, only 35 were United States corporations. Europe was represented by 15 giant companies.[4]

Such a shift in overall industrial and financial power brought profound economic repercussions around the globe, as the following examples show.

> Japan's efforts to stockpile oil during the Iranian revolution in the late 1970s drove world oil prices up sharply, although oil stocks were adequate to meet world demands. Japan's industrial expansion included constructing plants abroad near rich markets, as happened in Britain, which saw 100 Japanese plants open there during the 1970s and 1980s. In the United States, Toyota, Nissan, Honda, Mazda, Fuji, and Isuzu opened auto and truck plants, while Mitsubishi joined with Chrysler in a joint venture to produce cars. Other Japanese economic surges were felt in consumer electronics, industrial process equipment, steel, banking, securities trading, and the foreign exchange market where Japan took third place behind Britain and the United States. And as the European Economic Community prepared to open its economic borders wider, the Japanese doubled their investments there in the late 1980s. As one Japanese banking official said, "The [Japanese] companies are becoming part of the economic fabric of Europe."[5]

[4] "The World's 100 Largest Public Companies," *Wall Street Journal,* Sept. 22, 1989, p. R14.

[5] "The Japanese Invade Europe," *Newsweek,* Oct. 2, 1989, pp. 28–29; and "Japanese Influence Grows in Global Currency Market," *Wall Street Journal,* Sept. 14, 1989, pp. C1, C12.

FIGURE 6–2
The world's largest banks, insurers, and securities firms.

SOURCE: "The World's 100 Largest Banks," "The World's 50 Largest Insurers," and "The World's 25 Largest Securities Firms," *Wall Street Journal*, Sept. 22, 1989, pp. R-16, R-18.

THE WORLD'S TEN LARGEST BANKS, INSURERS, AND SECURITIES FIRMS, 1988

Ten Largest Banks (ranked by assets)			
1	**Dai-Ichi Kangyo Bank** (Japan)	6	**Industrial Bank of Japan** (Japan)
2	**Sumitomo Bank** (Japan)	7	**Norinchukin Bank** (Japan)
3	**Fuji Bank** (Japan)	8	**Tokai Bank** (Japan)
4	**Mitsubishi Bank** (Japan)	9	Citicorp (U.S.)
5	**Sanwa Bank** (Japan)	10	Banque Nationale de Paris (France)
Ten Largest Insurers (ranked by assets)			
1	Prudential (U.S.)	6	Aetna (U.S.)
2	**Nippon Life** (Japan)	7	Equitable Life (U.S.)
3	**Dai-Ichi Mutual** (Japan)	8	Cigna (U.S.)
4	Metropolitan Life (U.S.)	9	Prudential Corp. (U.K.)
5	**Sumitomo Life** (Japan)	10	**Meiji Mutual** (Japan)
Ten Largest Securities Firms (ranked by capital)			
1	**Nomura Securities** (Japan)	6	**Nikko Securities** (Japan)
2	Salomon (U.S.)	7	**Yamaichi Securities** (Japan)
3	Merrill Lynch (U.S.)	8	Dean Witter (U.S.)
4	**Daiwa Securities** (Japan)	9	Goldman Sachs (U.S.)
5	Shearson Lehman Hutton (U.S.)	10	Morgan Stanley (U.S.)

With this new and highly effective competitor on the economic scene, business firms were put on notice. Market competition would sharpen. Corporate economic strategies would have to be adjusted to deal with this new element. Corporate social strategies also would have to change, because Japanese business managers would be forced to adjust their companies' behavior to the diverse social customs and values of nations in which they planned to do business. And Japan's competitors would have to fathom the secrets and traits of a Japanese business culture unfamiliar to many. Fashioning an effective social strategy could be the key to profitable operations for Japanese firms and their competitors, because business in all societies is conducted within a surrounding social and cultural network that exerts a powerful influence on business practices.

The third world stirs

While the Japanese economic thrust continued apace, some of the world's less developed nations also began to make their economic influence felt. Nations that earlier had occupied only the outer margins of the world economy emerged as strong competitors during the 1970s and 1980s.

> Korea, Hong Kong, Taiwan, Singapore, Brazil, Spain, and Mexico first became major players in markets for clothing, footwear, toys, and electronics assemblies. Soon they moved into such basic industries as steel; by 1978, Korea's steel exports to the United States were increasing at a faster rate than Japan's. As they shifted production to capital-intensive industries, even poorer countries with lower wage rates began to produce simple consumer items such as clothing and footwear. These included Malaysia, Thailand, the Philippines, Sri Lanka, the Dominican Republic, Nicaragua, and Mauritius.
>
> Before long, the strongest third world economic leaders produced automobiles, consumer electronics, ships, aircraft, generators, petrochemical plants, and other products that before had been the province of the highly developed countries in North America and western Europe.[6]

These new players in the world economy greatly intensified competition. They also disrupted economic and social relations in other nations. By giving jobs to their own deserving people, they sometimes took jobs away from workers in the developed countries. By opening new plants in the third world, they forced closure of older operations in Europe and North America, creating economic and social distress there. By proving their prowess and skill in producing electronics products, they stripped the advanced nations of important markets. It was a dramatic development, signaling economic hope for the poorer nations but sending a competitive chill into the ranks of corporations in the highly industrialized nations. Managers in both camps would be forced to deal with both social and economic consequences of this startling shift in the world's markets. The competitive strategies of third world nations forced a reshaping of both economic and social strategies in the advanced industrial nations.

Western European integration

The 1980s saw twelve members of the European Economic Community (EEC), popularly known as the Common Market, agree to integrate their economies more closely with one another by the end of 1992. The move would create a large market of great global significance, with trade barriers greatly scaled back.[7] Figure 6–3 shows the EEC nations and their 322 million integrated consumers. Exhibit 6-A reveals the great saving one company was able to make by serving one large market rather than several smaller ones.

Not all cultural barriers would fall immediately. After all, the people in these twelve nations speak thirteen different languages, cherish their own national customs and values, and are proud of their nations' long and distinctive histories. These cultural and national differences would continue to be a fact of life for most business managers. Although the economic environment might become simpler by establishing a common monetary unit and establishing uniform eco-

[6] Robert B. Reich, *The Next American Frontier,* New York: Penguin Books, 1983, pp. 121–127.

[7] Philip Revzin, "Getting Together: Despite Difficulties, Moves to Strengthen Common Market Gain," *Wall Street Journal,* Feb. 23, 1988, p. 1; and Shawn Tully, "Europe Gets Ready for 1992," *Fortune,* Feb. 1, 1988, p. 84.

FIGURE 6–3
Common Market nations and their populations.

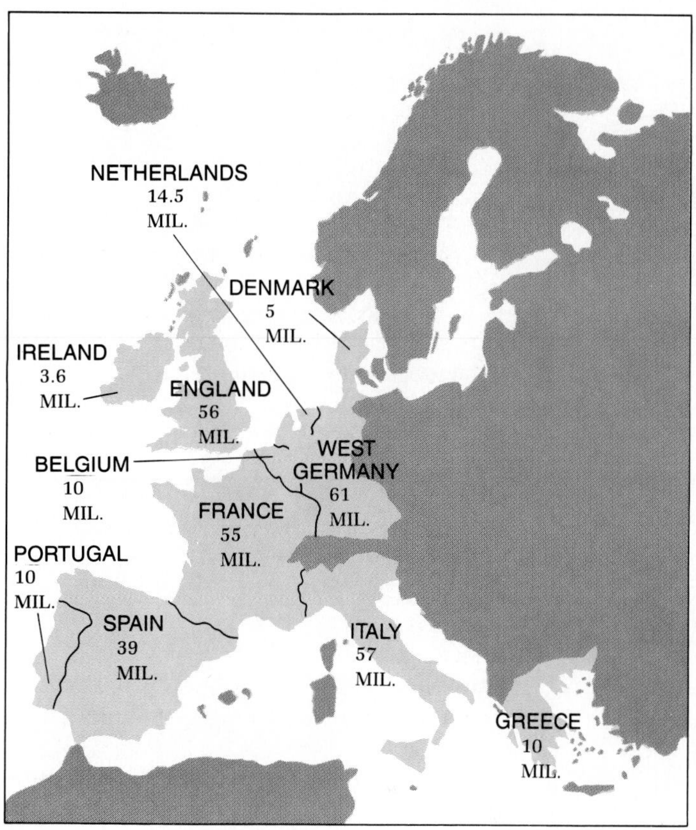

nomic standards and regulations, the social and political environment would remain diverse.

In addition to dealing with the national laws of each member country, companies would be subject to the EEC governing machinery. This included the EEC Commission, which issues regulations, the Council of Ministers, which decides EEC policies, and the European Parliament, which is largely advisory but can veto the commission's budget. Their combined 18,000 employees are sometimes called "Eurocrats." Here is a whole new set of political institutions whose policies and decisions can affect all companies doing business in the European community. Their presence—and potential power—complicate the manager's job by adding yet another layer of political complexity and regulation to the business environment.[8]

Firms planning to do business in this integrated Common Market would obviously need a sophisticated understanding of European customs, social in-

[8] Philip Revzin, "United We Stand . . . ," *Wall Street Journal,* Sept. 22, 1989, pp. R5–R6, a special section entitled "World Business: The Uncommon Market."

EXHIBIT 6-A

SOURCE: Shawn Tully, "Europe Gets Ready for 1992," *Fortune*, Feb. 1, 1988, p. 83. © 1988 Time Inc. All rights reserved.

TEARING DOWN POLITICAL OBSTACLES TO BUSINESS EFFICIENCY

"Philips [a Dutch electronics corporation] is a prime example of how [EEC] reforms in customs procedures and product standards will help the bottom line. . . .

"As local standards vanish, Philips plans to shrink its vast range of washing machines, hair dryers, fluorescent light bulbs, and above all TV sets, a crucial, $3-billion-a-year business. Europe now has two standards for television reception, Secame in France and PAL for the rest of Europe. To make matters worse, Germany, Italy, and Denmark impose different norms for radio interference, ostensibly to ensure that the TV's audio signal doesn't block shortwave radio reception in passing police cars.

"To meet those standards, Philips' plant in Brugge turns out seven types of TV sets equipped with different tuners, semiconductors, and even plugs. A staff of 70 engineers does nothing but adjust new models to local requirements. Assembly lines are revamped weekly to produce TVs for different countries. All told, the extra cost of meeting national standards comes to $20 million a year, including $8 million for the assortment of components and $2 million for the array of plugs.

"Philips is now preparing to streamline production, thanks in part to a recent EEC directive harmonizing regulations for radio interference. By 1990 it will reduce the types of TVs produced at Brugge to two or three. In a few [more] years it should be turning out just one model."

stitutions, and political systems. That is only another way of saying that they would need a well-thought-out social strategy.

Eastern European economic transformations

The remarkable economic, political, and ideological upheavals that occurred in eastern Europe beginning in the late 1980s are discussed more fully in a later section of this chapter as well as in Chapter 7. However, the lesson for corporate social strategy is generally similar to the one that applies to western European integration: fundamental social and political change pressures business to adjust the way it conducts operations. A firm's economic and financial strategy is vitally affected by political events and changing public attitudes. Successful economic strategy calls for an equally effective social strategy.

World population growth

In midsummer 1990, more than 5 billion people lived on earth. Even more were on the way, perhaps reaching around 6 billion by the year 2000. As Figure 6–4 shows, the largest population masses are in Asia, especially China, which alone has over 1.25 billion citizens. Africa, where mass starvation has struck a number of times in the 1970s and 1980s, has the highest annual population growth rate in the world, far ahead of other continents and regions. The declining birth rates in several Western nations could not offset the overall world population surge because of the large numbers of young people of childbearing age in many other countries.[9]

[9] For more information on population growth and its consequences, see Lester R. Brown et al., *State of the World, 1984*, New York: Norton, 1984; and Stanley P. Johnson, *World Population and the United Nations: Challenge and Response*, Cambridge: Cambridge University Press, 1987.

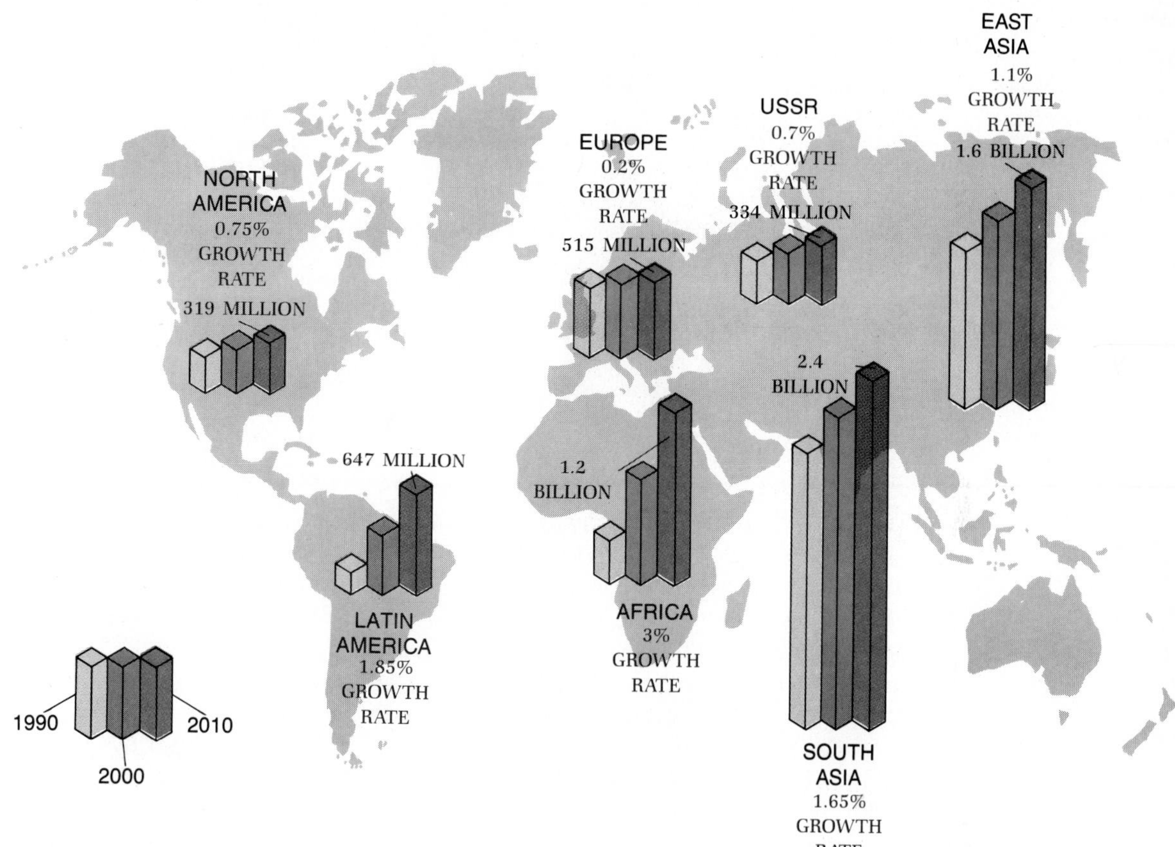

FIGURE 6–4
Population and annual growth rates, 1990, 2000 and 2010.

What do these population figures mean for business? It might seem that more people should mean more potential sales and therefore good times for business. In some parts of the world, such positive opportunities do exist. But overshadowing the good news are two crushing issues of immense significance for businesses and governments around the globe.

The first problem is poverty. According to reports by the World Bank and the United Nations Population Fund, one out of every five persons in the world—over 1 billion in all—live in poverty; and their numbers actually increased from the mid-1970s to the mid-1980s. These people, most of them in the third world, live very near the margin of subsistence. They have only a fraction of the goods and services enjoyed by those in the industrialized nations. Relief agencies report that about 10 million of the world's people (30,000 each day) were expected to die of hunger and hunger-related diseases in 1989; most of them were children. Thirty-four third world nations whose populations are among the fastest-growing face certain declines in per capita incomes; and nearly half the world's people face stagnation of income. So, rather than being customers with money in their pockets, many of the world's poor people are cut off from the economic benefits

FIGURE 6–5
Ecological problems that can occur when population expands.

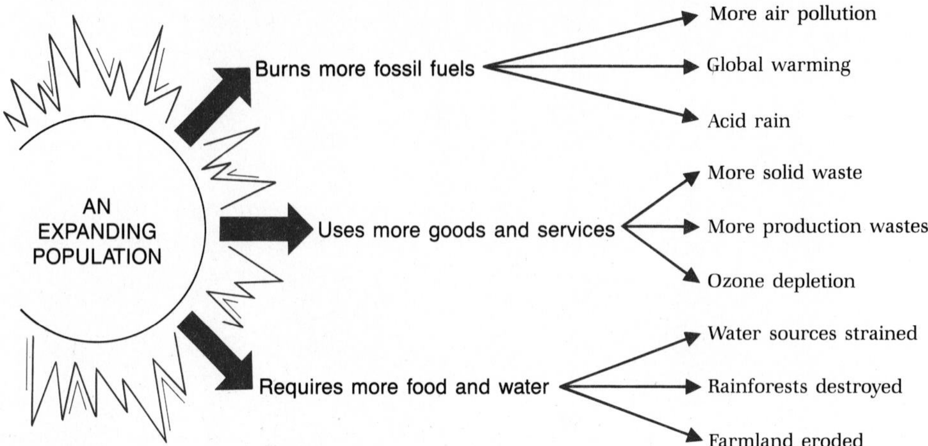

enjoyed by industrial nations. Their huge numbers often hinder their nation's prospects for further economic development and an improved standard of living.

Another equally serious problem that comes with high population increase is pollution and ecological crisis. Figure 6–5 depicts some kinds of ecological problems that occur when population expands.[10]

Corporations charting their future understand that widespread poverty, global pollution, and ecological imbalance are far from the ideal conditions in which they can expect to prosper. Great political unrest can be generated by downtrodden populations. National political leaders may resort to authoritarian or dictatorial ways to keep order. Poor people do not make good or reliable consumers. Governments may generate only meager tax revenues to provide for their people or to create stable business conditions. Corruption and bribery may become a way of life. Local economies can become distorted, national currencies unreliable, and qualified workers scarce. Business may become a target of environmental activists protesting the ecological harm being done by industrial operations.

This unstable climate resulting from population growth is likely to remain a fact of business life for a long time. It is a frightening blend of many diverse and highly emotional forces: nationalistic pride, family traditions, economic necessity, social customs, religious beliefs, and individual choice. The combined and largely unpredictable influence of these complex social and political elements is capable of upsetting the most carefully laid strategic plans of any corporation. The best corporations will develop an awareness of such possibilities and uncertainties, factoring their potential impact into the company's overall social strategy.

Global Political Changes

Beginning sometime in the 1960s and 1970s, new winds of change began to blow through many of the world's economic, political, and social institutions. No one

[10] For additional information about the ecological impacts of high-growth populations, see Paul R. Ehrlich and Anne H. Erlich, *The Population Explosion*, New York: Simon & Schuster, 1990.

knew exactly what had set these new currents of reform in motion. They were not felt with the same strength in all nations. Nor were all kinds of institutions in any one nation challenged. But wherever these currents blew, they seemed to have one trait in common: Focal points of centralized power and authority came under attack.

Demands were made to disperse power more widely within any given society or nation. "Power to the people" became a popular rallying cry that captured the essence of this new social force. Leaders in all areas of society discovered that their grip on institutional power was not as secure as it had been in earlier times. The public seemed to be less trusting of its leaders. They wanted "a piece of the action." They believed that too much power had been concentrated at the top of society's major institutions. They demanded reform.

The best known of these political changes are deregulation and privatization in the western world, *glasnost* (openness) and *perestroika* (reform, reconstruction, renewal) in the Soviet Union, China's move toward freer markets and a more decentralized economic system until slowed by the turmoil accompanying the student-led democracy movement in 1989, and the sweeping political upheavals in eastern Europe beginning in the late 1980s. In all of these cases (including China up to 1989), centralized governmental power was being dispersed and moved out from the center toward the periphery.

What does this globe-straddling reform movement mean for business? It creates new business opportunities but it also poses new business risks. When free markets open up where none existed before, corporations can take advantage of profit opportunities. European, Japanese, and American business firms flocked to China in the early days of its reform movement. But just as quickly, they became more cautious when government authorities showed signs of reinstalling centralized power over all business decisions. When the Soviet Union and eastern European nations relaxed government controls and welcomed economic ties with Western nations, many corporations crossed over into that formerly forbidden territory, seeking profitable opportunities. The business risks were considerable, though, because these former socialist nations frequently lacked free and open market systems, stable currencies, and competitive traditions.

As eastern Europe struggled to transform its economic and political institutions, governments there faced formidable problems, such as inflation, unemployment, and declines in national income. Speaking of this difficult period, a Hungarian political scientist said, "The cold war is over, but this will be a very dangerous peace. . . . Conflicts are growing between nationalities, between rich people and poor, between the government and street protesters, between industrialists and laborers. . . ."[11]

The main point is that the global movement toward more freedom and democracy and away from centralized authoritarian governments carries both pluses and minuses for corporations. Once again, they have found themselves facing large measures of uncertainty. These volatile political and ideological forces had become a central part of the world business climate by the late 1980s. Ignoring them could be fatal. Integrating them into strategic approaches was essential.

[11] "East Europe Offers Investors Big Profits and Big Perils," *Wall Street Journal*, Jan. 11, 1991, p. A6.

Revolutions in Science and Technology

Another kind of global change is the accelerating revolution in science and technology. Few forces in the modern world produce more powerful impacts and more far-reaching changes in human affairs than science and technology. For example, few people understood, just after the Second World War, how enormous would be the impact of a single new invention called the transistor, which laid the groundwork for the modern computer and the electronics age in which we now live.

Corporate strategists understand that a technological world is a world of rapid and sometimes unexpected change. New devices and inventions tumble out of research laboratories at a furious pace. Companies that get on top of these innovations gain a crucial competitive edge over their rivals.

> At Westinghouse Electric, for example, executives live inside an electronics cocoon composed of personal desktop computers, teleconferencing networks, electronic mail, voice-message systems, telephone answering machines, portable cellular phones, facsimile machines, and laptop computers. These electronic systems help the company to boost the productivity of its white-collar workforce by reducing costs and speeding up information flows. E-mail, for example, costs 90 percent less than overseas telephone calls and letters. One Westinghouse vice president said, "People are amazed at how quickly we can move information around. It gives us a competitive edge."[12]

But all was not rosy in this new technological Eden. When Japan and third world steel producers installed new computerized steel-making equipment, they took business and jobs away from U.S. and European companies which continued to rely on older technology. The robots now making new autos have displaced thousands of auto workers around the world, bringing social and economic distress to many communities. Other technological doubts were expressed by video terminal workers who have complained of eyestrain, on-the-job stress, and other serious health problems. Biotechnology firms have been stymied by public fears of what might happen if genetically engineered forms of life are released into the environment. Employees and customers resent and fear invasion of their privacy made possible by massive computerized data banks containing personal information.

These "down-side" effects of science and technology serve as a warning to corporate strategic planners. New technology creates many new corporate stakeholders who want to know how their lives will be affected. What scientific innovation gives with one hand, public opposition and fear may take away with the other hand. To counteract such fears, when IBM learned that consumers were worried about the safety of video display terminals, the company introduced new models that emit less electromagnetic radiation.[13]

[12] *Business Week,* Oct. 10, 1988, p. 110.

[13] "IBM to Reduce Radiation from Future VDT Models," *Wall Street Journal,* Nov. 22, 1989, p. B-1.

The lesson that emerges from scientific and technological change is similar to the one learned from economic change: New worlds are on the way. Older customs, traditions, and many human values will be challenged and perhaps even obliterated. People may decide that the technological benefits are not worth the human costs involved. Any corporation not ready to factor this simple lesson into its strategic plans will certainly face a shaky and dim future.

Ecological Impacts

One of the most important social challenges to business is to find a happy medium between industrial production and nature's limits. Industrial production, mining, and farming are bound to produce waste and pollution, along with needed goods and services. Pollution and waste are a price society pays for abandoning a quieter, more serene rural life. All industrial societies—whether the United States, Japan, the Soviet Union, or others—create a portion of the world's pollution and waste simply because these are the unavoidable by-products of a high level of economic activity. The industrializing nations of the third world, mentioned earlier, also are part of the problem.

Consumers too are responsible for much litter and pollution because they demand, buy, and use pollution-generating products (automobiles, refrigerators, air conditioners), solid-waste products (all kinds of packaging and wrapping, cans, bottles, fast-food containers), and hazardous waste products (household and lawn chemicals, batteries, antifreeze).

Ecological impacts extend far beyond national boundaries. High-level ozone depletion threatens health on a worldwide basis. The industrial accident at Chernobyl's nuclear power station spread dangerous radiation across several European nations and sent a radiation cloud around the globe. Oil spills have fouled the oceans and beaches of several nations. Clearing of tropical rainforests has the potential to affect weather climates throughout the world.

Corporate managers in the 1990s therefore face the social challenge of reducing harmful ecological impacts. Pollution and waste cannot be stopped entirely, but their volume can be reduced through improved product designs, better controls, and recycling reusable materials. Environmental accidents such as oil spills can be prevented by careful planning, and cleanup efforts can be pursued vigorously. The basic goal is to achieve a livable balance between human needs and nature's limits.

Balancing Competitive Pressures and Community Needs

A goal of most business firms is high productivity, which refers to the efficient use of resources. Financial, technological, and human resources are channeled to their best uses in a highly productive company. A high-productivity company makes a strong competitor, usually because its cost-revenue structure is more favorable than those of its rivals. Foreign competition puts a premium on productivity and cost-effective operations. Less efficient firms feeling these competitive pressures are forced to take steps to improve their productivity.

Most of the time, when a corporation improves its productivity, the benefits are felt throughout society. For example, when IBM or Apple Computer brings out a new, lower-cost, more productive computer model, many individuals and companies welcome it as a more efficient and cheaper way to get work done. Because IBM and Apple became more productive, others in society also can be more productive.

Sometimes, however, steps taken by a company to improve its own productivity can work against the interests and productivity of another group or an entire community. While *economic* costs may be lowered for the company, *social* costs may be simultaneously increased for the community. This situation is illustrated by the following episode.

> In early 1988, Chrysler Corporation announced plans to close its auto assembly plant in Kenosha, Wisconsin, just one year after spending $200 million intended to make it more productive. Chrysler's chairman, Lee Iacocca, blamed stiff foreign competition for the shutdown. Plant employees, Kenosha citizens, and government officials at city, county, and state levels protested vigorously, saying that the community, region, and state would be seriously damaged by the closure. They also said that Chrysler had promised to keep the plant open for five years after buying it from American Motors.
>
> Several months later, Chrysler agreed to a $250 million plan that eased the closing's impact on employees and on the community of Kenosha. A $20 million trust fund would help meet housing, educational, and welfare needs of families affected by the shutdown, the plant would be kept open a few extra months beyond the planned closing date, $60 million would repay workers who invested some of their own money in the plant, and numerous other unemployment, health, and pension benefits were paid by the company.[14]

This episode demonstrates that the productivity needs of both business and the community have to be considered together, because business decisions that are made to improve *company* productivity can actually lower *a community's* overall productivity. This problem can be especially severe in international business when multinational corporations move production or assembly facilities from high-wage areas to low-wage regions, as many U.S. corporations have done in locating operations near the U.S.-Mexican border or putting them in faraway locales in eastern and southeastern Asia.

Productivity is something in which everyone has a stake. Therefore, it becomes the job of corporate managers not only to improve their own company's productivity but to work for the well-being of other community stakeholders whose lives may be touched by these corporate decisions. Doing so is a good example of a corporate strategy that has blended economic and social factors.

[14] "Chrysler to Donate Wisconsin Profits to Fund for Workers from Closed Plant," *Wall Street Journal*, Feb. 17, 1988, p. 4; "Chrysler to Pay $250 Million to Settle Dispute over Wisconsin Plant Closing," *Wall Street Journal*, Sept. 26, 1988, p. 4.

Human Problems and Diversity in the Workforce

No part of the business environment is more important than the people who work there. Productivity depends very largely on the skills and talents of human workers. Knowing how to organize, motivate, and direct the energies of employees is perhaps the central task of corporate management. Because work is done by people (as well as machines), an enormous number of complex human issues occur in the workplace.

These include the desire of employees to be recognized as the unique individuals they are and to be treated with personal dignity on the job. Safeguarding employees' privacy has become more important, especially since computer data banks contain personal medical records, job performance evaluations, and other sensitive materials. Safety and health at work are given higher priority because on-the-job injuries are more likely with the use of complex machinery and exotic chemicals in production. Employees, unions, activist groups, and government officials have demanded an end to workplace discrimination against ethnic minorities, women, handicapped persons, and older employees. Retirement security and pension benefits are important to an aging workforce, especially since competitive pressures and corporate takeovers sometimes result in threats to employee pension plans.

Acknowledging the importance of these kinds of human workplace needs, the 12-nation European Economic Community adopted a Social Charter in 1989. The Charter obliges EEC members to promote a wide range of "fundamental social rights" of people who work in business, as summarized in Exhibit 6-B. In effect, the Charter defines common levels of social security for employees throughout the EEC and attempts to set minimum standards for wages, health benefits, and safety practices. Some of its provisions, especially those encouraging worker participation in management decisions, were strongly opposed by some industrialists.[15]

Adding to this complex picture is the growing globalization and cultural diversity of the corporate workforce. Worker migration across national boundaries has been common in Europe for many years, and enterprises there have learned to cope with the changes it introduces into the workplace. U.S. executives foresee similar diversity in their companies' worldwide operations. One study revealed that 75 percent of chief executive officers of large U.S. corporations expected to hire more people worldwide by the year 2000 and that most of these new jobs would be filled by workers from abroad. Their own jobs as CEO also were expected to become more globalized: "The next century's corporate chief," said one executive, "must have a multienvironment, multicountry, multifunctional, maybe even multicompany, multi-industry experience."[16]

[15] George M. Kraw, "The Community Charter of the Fundamental Social Rights of Workers," *Hastings International and Comparative Law Review,* Spring 1990, pp. 467–477; and Michael Farr, "1992: The Workers' Stake," *International Management* (Europe edition), November 1989, pp. 50–54.

[16] "Going Global: The Chief Executives in Year 2000 Will Be Experienced Abroad," *Wall Street Journal,* Feb. 27, 1989, pp. A1, 27.

EXHIBIT 6-B

SOURCE: Summarized from George M. Kraw, "The Community Charter of the Fundamental Social Rights of Workers," *Hastings International and Comparative Law Review*, Spring 1990, pp. 467–477.

THE EUROPEAN COMMUNITY'S SOCIAL CHARTER

The Social Charter, officially known as The Community Charter of the Fundamental Social Rights of Workers, was adopted in October 1989 by the Commission of the European Community. The Charter establishes standards that must be maintained by businesses operating within the member states of the European Community. Its main provisions are the following:

Freedom of movement for nationals and nonnationals
Workers may move freely within the community to take any job offered to them, regardless of their home nation.

Job choice and pay
Workers should be paid wages sufficient to support a decent standard of living for themselves and their family.

Working and living conditions
Weekly rest periods, annual vacations, and layoff procedures are required.

Social protection
Each member state should provide adequate social security benefits.

Collective bargaining
Workers have the right to engage in collective bargaining with employers.

Vocational training
Worker training is required on a permanent and continuing basis.

Equal treatment of men and women
Pay, job opportunities, and other job benefits are to be equal for men and women. Family support programs for employees are to be developed.

Worker participation in management decisions
Where technological change, corporate restructuring, large layoffs, and similar developments threaten jobs, employees must be consulted and allowed to participate in resolving company policy.

Safety and health
Safe and healthful working conditions are required.

Protection of children, retired workers, and disabled persons
Safeguards for these groups of employees are specified.

With such workplace diversity, the human problems and concerns of employees need to be at the forefront of corporate thinking.

Ethical Expectations

Chapters 3 and 4 demonstrated that ethical expectations are a vital part of the business environment. The public expects business to make decisions ethically. They want corporate managers to apply ethical principles—in other words, guidelines about what is right and wrong, fair and unfair, and morally correct—when they make business decisions.

In the global arena, ethical standards—and even what is meant by ethics—can vary from one society to another, and these kinds of problems and how to deal with them are discussed in Chapters 3 and 4. In spite of differences in ethical meanings, the cultural variation does not automatically rule out common ethical agreement being reached among people of different societies. A good example of that possibility is the European Economic Community's Social Charter, which promotes common job rights and humane workplace treatment in highly diverse nations.

The question for global corporate strategists is not, should business be ethical? Nor is it, should business be economically efficient? Society wants business to be both—at the same time. The challenge to business is to find a balance between these two social demands—high economic performance and high ethical standards.

REINVENTING CORPORATE STRATEGY

This enormously unsettled global environment of the 1990s presents business leaders with bewildering, mind-boggling complexity. Their companies confront a complicated array of forces—economic, technological, political, social, and nationalistic—that somehow must be understood. Business cannot succeed unless its leaders learn how to maneuver their firms through this tumultuous environment. Figure 6–6 graphically summarizes the main forces at work.

One thing is clear: Satisfying economic needs alone will not be enough. Every economic system, each business firm, is deeply embedded in society. True, people everywhere look to business to produce needed goods and services. But they also expect business to show respect for social needs and goals, wherever business is conducted.

Reinventing corporate strategy along these lines is more a matter of mind and attitude than anything else. It takes a business executive who is willing to look at more than the "bottom line." Social sensitivity is possessed by a manager who realizes that employees are people first and producers second. Employees may take pride in their work, but at the same time they are family members, citizens of their communities, religious communicants, political adherents, people with aspirations, problems, hopes, and desires who are often emotional, sometimes rational, and frequently confused.

Research has shown that companies with the best social reputations and the best social performance records have top managers who take a very broad view of their company's place in society. In fact, these managers believe that their corporations should take the lead in helping society to solve its problems. Corporations with this attitude generally take a long-run view of the company, rather than focusing exclusively on short-term gains. Social goals, as well as economic goals, are given high priority in planning the company's future.[17] One result is

[17]For example, Robert H. Miles has demonstrated this to be true in the insurance industry; see his *Managing the Corporate Social Environment: A Grounded Theory*, Englewood Cliffs, NJ: Prentice-Hall, 1987.

FIGURE 6–6
Major forces causing turbulence in the business environment.

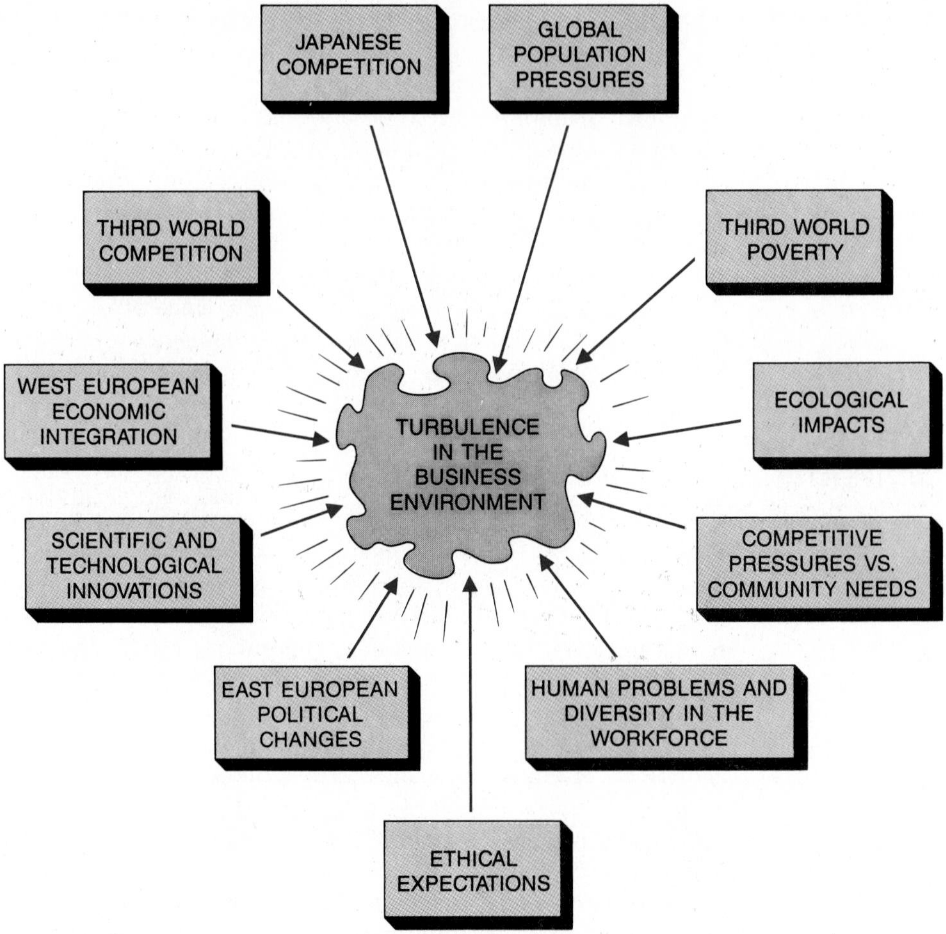

that the corporation takes on many more social functions, such as child care, parental leaves, retirement planning, and health care, than a company that focuses on economic goals alone. In the words of one observer, "The workplace is becoming the center of social services for a large portion of America's population."[18]

When asked to reflect on what they had learned during the turbulent decade of the 1980s, twenty-four leading corporate CEOs identified ten major lessons. Figure 6–7 shows that *all ten lessons involved ways in which corporations interact with the social, political, governmental, and global environment.* This kind of social awareness is encouraging to see. It means that corporate leaders are developing the social vision necessary for today's business climate. These prominent CEOs are role models for many other corporate managers, so it is likely that the lessons they learned will be absorbed by others as well.

[18] Reich, op. cit., pp. 246–251. See also "Company School: As Pool of Skilled Help Tightens, Firms Move to Broaden Their Role," *Wall Street Journal,* May 8, 1989, pp. A1, A4.

FIGURE 6–7
Ten lessons of the 1980s: The views of twenty-four chief executive officers.

SOURCE: Adapted by permission of *Forbes*, Jan. 8, 1990, pp. 100–114. © Forbes Inc., 1990.

TEN LESSONS OF THE 1980s
The Views of 24 Chief Executive Officers

The Lesson	Social-Political Implications
"Go Global or Die"	■ Organizational and job changes for managers and employees. ■ Joint ventures with foreign companies. ■ Operating in different social systems.
"When the Money Markets Talk, Politicians Listen"	■ Business decisions help determine government policies.
"Time to De-Leverage"	■ The debt load resulting from the corporate merger movement threatens both profits and jobs.
"Deregulation Helps but It Also Hurts"	■ Deregulation may have gone too far in the airline industry and the savings and loan industry. Is re-regulation a desirable government policy?
"A Poorly Educated Labor Force May Cost the U.S. Dearly"	■ Poor education is a major social problem that penalizes the efficiency of U.S. business.
"Entrepreneurs Could Face a Tougher Decade"	■ Corporate takeovers and restructurings destroyed many jobs, weakened company loyalty, and changed labor relations. Political reactions can be expected.
"Energy Prices Are Likely to Stay Low: The Market Works!"	■ Energy decontrol, new oil discoveries, and the weakness of OPEC oil producers lessens the likelihood of another oil and energy crisis.
"Economic Growth Is a Must, but It Must Be Reconciled with the Environment"	■ Corporations have responded to new environmental laws and to public concern about pollution.
"Technology Is Crucial, Especially Process Technology"	■ Corporate survival and employees' jobs depend on technological innovation. Cuts in government funding and corporate restructuring have hurt R&D
"Computers Should Solve Problems, Not Make Them"	■ Computers enhance productivity but change the way work is done. Human adjustment is difficult.

THE CENTRAL QUESTIONS OF CORPORATE SOCIAL STRATEGY

Corporate social strategy, if it is to be effective, has to be focused on the biggest and most central questions in the public's mind. People now expect business, while making a profit, to be active in three core areas: the social arena, the political arena, and the ethical arena.

Corporate Strategy in the Social Arena

The central social questions that all corporations must try to answer are three in number:

- Are we being socially responsible in all that we do? Putting it another way, are we using the power and influence that society has granted to us in ways that are socially acceptable? The general public wants business to be accountable for its actions and social impacts. People expect business to take responsibility for their actions.
- Are we being socially responsive to our stakeholders whose lives we affect by our day-to-day and year-to-year activities? People who have a stake in what we do will demand that we consider their interests as well as our own. They want us to respond to their needs. Managing our stakeholder relations with care and concern is what it takes to be a socially responsive company.
- Is our social vision broad enough to see global as well as domestic problems, tomorrow's issues as well as today's, human concerns as well as economic ones? Our social perspective, as a business firm, must reach as far as the boundaries of our operating environment, which is constantly restless and shifting.

The real test of a company's strategy in the social arena is whether it is able to answer these three questions affirmatively. A "no" to any one of them spells trouble ahead.

Corporate Strategy in the Political Arena

What a corporation must do to be an effective political actor is fully discussed in later chapters. For now, though, we can say that four kinds of actions form the core of corporate political strategies.

- Companies need to participate actively in political life, while respecting legal limitations and safeguards against too much corporate political influence. Holding back from politics might mean that a company's interests are ignored or given lower priority than they deserve.
- When public policies that affect business are being debated, it is proper for

corporations to try to influence public policy. As corporate citizens, companies also are in position to provide political leadership.

- Government and business continually interact with each other. Governments are one type of corporate stakeholder. Managing this government-business interface well is as important as managing any other stakeholder relationship.
- Business political influence is one part of a pluralistic society where power is widely shared by many kinds of institutions. For business's own sake as well as society's, business influence should be used in ways that preserve and safeguard this pluralistic balance of power.

A corporate strategy in the political arena that is based on these principles gives business the political "clout" it needs without risking public disapproval.

Corporate Strategy in the Ethical Arena

The ethical content of corporate strategy aligns a company with ethical values and moral principles. More than any other component of strategy, it helps to harmonize a company's goals with society's goals, in those situations where conflict may develop. This kind of ethics-centered strategy requires a firm to do the following:

- Pursue business goals within the bounds set by society's values and moral principles. Business decisions and policies that show disrespect for these cherished beliefs are generally condemned by most members of the general public.
- Respect human value diversity that is found among people and groups at home and abroad, in the workplace and the community. People's notions of right and wrong vary considerably among societies, religions, historical periods, and ethnic groups. The wise corporation knows this and acts with care and understanding.
- Accept responsibility for nurturing ethical attitudes in business operations and for any negative impacts caused by the company. Business pressures that lead employees into unethical practices are a common problem. Ways exist for lessening these episodes.

Adopting this kind of corporate strategy in the ethical arena is no longer an option for business. Acting ethically is a central requirement.

Companies employing this three-pronged strategic approach—social, political, and ethical—increase their chances of being favorably accepted by their stakeholders and the general public. This happens because the corporation and its managers, while continuing to seek profits, lift their sights beyond the bottom line and broaden their view of what it takes to run a business firm in today's unusually complicated environment.

SUMMARY POINTS OF THIS CHAPTER

- Business leaders and managers—in large firms and small ones—must have strategies based on international developments because complex forces throughout the world help determine business opportunities and create business risks.
- The major social challenges facing business in the 1990s and beyond have been created by economic changes in Japan, Europe, and third world nations, rapid population growth, political changes in many nations, scientific and technological revolutions, ecological impacts, and a desire to harmonize community needs, human factors in production, and ethical values with business's profit goals.
- Corporate strategy needs to be reinvented if business is to carry out needed economic functions with full public approval.
- The general public approves business actions when they are socially responsible, politically influential without upsetting society's pluralistic balance of power, and ethically responsive to moral values and principles.

KEY TERMS AND CONCEPTS USED IN THIS CHAPTER

- Turbulent global business environment
- Major environmental challenges
- Reinventing corporate strategy
- Central questions of corporate social strategy

DISCUSSION CASE

NAVIGATING THROUGH TURBULENT GLOBAL SKIES

In the late summer months of 1989, two of the world's largest airlines faced uncertain and separate futures. United Air Lines (UAL) had an immediate crisis on its hands because it was threatened with a hostile takeover by an outside investor. British Airways (BA) was concerned about the much greater competition it would face beginning in late 1992. That was the year Europe's Common Market planned to relax restrictive government regulation of airlines and encourage more competition.

Events of the next few weeks would draw these two companies together in unexpected ways, as each company struggled to survive in a tough business world. They would encounter new challenges typical of today's global marketplace. Their survival strategies would depend almost entirely on a sophisticated knowledge of the social and political environment at home and abroad.

It all began when Marvin Davis, a Los Angeles investor who owned 3.5 percent of UAL, made a bid for controlling interest in the airline. He offered to pay $275 per share for the 22.5 million shares of UAL stock—a hefty price tag of $6.19 billion. Davis's bid stimulated Robert Bass, a Texas investor with the image of corporate raider, to consider making a counteroffer. With the takeover wolves circling, the UAL board of directors found themselves under much pressure to respond. UAL stock rose, signaling Wall Street's belief that the stock had been undervalued. If he gained control, Davis was believed ready to shake up United's management and put pressure on the airline's unions as a way to cut costs.

Faced with this threat, UAL's top managers, 35 in all, then joined forces with the airline's unionized pilots and British Airways, proposing that this group buy out all UAL stock. Their offer was $300 per share, a total of $6.75 billion. In mid-September, the UAL board accepted this higher offer. Pilot-employees would then own 75 percent of the airline, BA 15 percent, and top managers 10 percent. Most of the equity capital—$750 million—would be put up by the British airline, which would get some common stock and a large amount of nonvoting preferred stock. The pilots would get three seats on the new board of directors, managers three seats, and BA one seat, with eight directors to be chosen from outside. UAL would then become the largest employee-owned firm in the United States.

BA's willingness to rescue UAL from a hostile raider—and UAL's eagerness to be saved—reflect the kinds of corporate strategies demanded by today's business climate. Both airlines were strengthening themselves for the heated-up competition expected during the 1990s. A 1988 marketing agreement had already enabled BA and UAL to interchange their passengers flying between the United States and Europe. This arrangement allowed United to penetrate parts of Europe, Africa, and the Middle East. The British airline could send some of its passengers to cities in the United States and Mexico where UAL operates.

Earlier strategic moves by BA included buying into UAL's computer reservation system and purchasing British Caledonian Airways, Britain's second largest air carrier. While negotiating the UAL deal, it was simultaneously proposing to buy 20 percent of Sabena World Airlines. By becoming bigger through these mergers, BA's financial base would expand and it would gain access to world markets previously closed to it. Anticipating approval of their merger, an October 1989 UAL-BA advertisement in *The Wall Street Journal* trumpeted, "We've got a better handle on the world. It's a partnership of global proportions. We're making the world far easier to handle."

These rosy hopes were soon dashed. Neither company anticipated the backlash that would come from some of their most important stakeholders. One such stakeholder was the U.S. government.

U.S. law forbids foreign ownership of more than 25 percent of any U.S. airline. Although BA would own only 15 percent of UAL stock, it had agreed to provide 78 percent of the equity capital needed for the buyout. In a similar case, the U.S. Transportation Secretary had forced the Dutch airline, KLM, to reduce its equity capital stake in Northwest Airlines (NWA) from 69 to 25 percent. The secretary believed that the size of the KLM investment would enable it to exercise control over NWA's policies. If he applied that same reasoning to the BA-UAL case, it might unravel the entire package.

Another major stumbling block was UAL's largest union, the machinists. They were not part of the employee buyout plan. Feeling left out, they registered early opposition to the proposal. Some observers believed that union leaders were simply jockeying for bargaining advantages under the new management arrangement. Nevertheless, the 23,000 UAL machinists could be the critical factor determining success or failure of this proposed employee stock ownership plan (ESOP).

The buyout plan required very large bank loans. Perhaps no one had a bigger financial stake in the merger than the lending banks. They turned it down, saying the proposed financial plan was unsound. The price to be paid was too high, and the crushing debt load to be assumed by both companies was potentially ruinous, especially if worldwide passenger traffic were to slump.

Because they overlooked the interest, power, and influence of these three stakeholders—government, unions, and banks—British Airways and United Air Lines failed to achieve their strategic objectives. They had to pick their way through a minefield of government agencies, union leaders, hostile raiders, political figures in the United States and Britain, and skeptical financial backers. The flying public was another big stakeholder since they worried about air safety, possible hijackings, and equipment reliability. They feared that taking on a huge debt load to finance the merger might cause the two airlines to compromise on safety and security by scrimping on costs.

A successful corporate strategy that would strengthen both companies' competitive chances would have to be built on both economic and social factors. Global strategists would have to master the complexities of deregulation in Europe, the motives of corporate raiders, the U.S. fear of foreign ownership of its companies, the tensions of labor-management relations, and the public's concern about safety. Only then would it be possible to achieve each company's twin strategic objectives of a profitable future and general public approval.[19]

Discussion Questions

1. Identify three major kinds of economic, social, and political challenges that British Airways and United Air Lines faced in trying to combine their two companies. Which of these challenges played the biggest role in the failed merger attempt?
2. Make a list of all of the corporate stakeholders involved in the BA-UAL merger negotiations. If you had been in the BA-UAL group that wanted to buy out

[19] For details of these events, consult issues of *The Wall Street Journal* and *Business Week*, for the period August 1989 through October 1990. After the BA-UAL buyout effort collapsed, other investor groups continued to try to buy United Air Lines but British Airways dropped out. A new coalition of UAL unions—pilots, machinists, and flight attendants—made a bid for ownership control in 1990, but this initiative failed to obtain financial backing. See James E. Ellis, "Ego, Greed, and Hokum: Why the UAL Deal Crashed," *Business Week*, Oct. 22, 1990, p. 33.

UAL, which stakeholder groups would you consider to be the most critical to the buyout's success? Tell why you think so.

3. In this case, the corporate strategies of British Airways and United Air Lines misfired, since they were unable to join forces. In your opinion, what steps might have been taken by the BA–UAL buyout group to design and carry out a more successful strategy?

7

Contrasting Socioeconomic Systems: Their Impact on Business

People around the globe tend to organize their lives according to one of three major types of socioeconomic system. These are free enterprise, central state control, and mixed state-and-private enterprise. These systems create both opportunities and risks for business. Corporate managers therefore must understand what these socioeconomic systems are, what they permit and forbid, and how they change over time.

Key Questions and Chapter Objectives

This chapter focuses on these key questions and chapter objectives:

- What are the major features of free enterprise, central state control, and mixed state and private enterprise?
- What major changes occurred in the world's socioeconomic systems during the 1980s and early 1990s?
- Is it possible for systems of central state control to transform themselves into free enterprise societies?
- What is privatization and why has it appealed to so many nations?
- What are the major lessons business needs to learn when socioeconomic systems undergo major change?

In early 1990, the managers of Digital Equipment Corporation (DEC), the U.S. computer maker, must have been shaking their heads in disbelief and wonderment. DEC had just signed a joint venture agreement to sell and service its computers in Hungary. Hungary was one of the first of the eastern European nations formerly in the Soviet bloc of socialist economies to open itself up for business with private corporations. The head-shaking did not arise just from the surprising shift of events that brought dramatic economic exchanges between Eastern bloc and Western bloc nations, which had previously viewed each other with great suspicion.

The surprising element was that DEC's new business partners in Hungary had been the very two firms that had illegally copied the U.S. firm's computer designs, then manufactured clones, and sold them in Hungary for a profit. U.S. military security laws had forbidden DEC to sell their computers behind the iron curtain. Now the joint venture's sales personnel would be faced with competition from illegally copied DEC computers! Digital's partners were Szamalk and KSzKI, Hungarian computer-systems designers and researchers, who promised to discontinue the cloning. The joint venture gave DEC a 51 percent stake and the Hungarian firms 24.5 percent each.[1]

The ultimate success of this joint venture would depend largely on political, not economic, factors. The sale of high-technology items to nations considered to be security threats to the United States had been forbidden by several Presidential administrations and by Congressional legislation. Unless and until that policy was liberalized, Digital sales would be severely limited.[2] Even so, DEC managers were optimistic that future sales would be permitted, especially to help modernize Hungary's banking and telecommunications systems, which had suffered neglect during the period of domination by the Soviet Union. Clearly, the business outlook for profits—the supply and demand for computers—was almost totally a matter of international political developments that extended far beyond the financial horizons of the U.S. and Hungarian business firms involved.

DEC's experience in Hungary is not at all unusual. It reveals the unique kinds of problems that many corporations face when they begin to do business in nations that have strikingly different kinds of socioeconomic systems. In Hungary's case, it was a socialist system that had been dominated by the Communist Party since the Second World War. Hungary's Communist leaders were hostile toward all aspects of capitalism, especially large multinational corporations. Private property was generally forbidden. Free markets were unknown. The profit motive was absent. Joint ventures with foreign companies—of the kind DEC had just successfully completed—were not approved. Even in the early 1990s, Hungary's economy was not entirely free of government-imposed restrictions. DEC's managers would have to remain alert to swift political, economic, and social currents that could spell the difference between profits and losses. They realized that the "rules of the game" in Hungary's socioeconomic system were not going to be the same as those in the United States.

This chapter presents the main outlines of the world's three major types of socioeconomic systems. It discusses their pros and cons from a business point of view. It shows the pitfalls they represent, as well as the opportunities they offer, to politically aware business leaders. Since many multinational corporations do business in nations around the globe, these diverse socioeconomic systems become the main staging ground for their business operations. Knowing what these different systems require and what they expect from business becomes a

[1] "Computer Firm Moves to Create Base in Hungary," *Wall Street Journal,* Feb. 12, 1990, p. A9A.

[2] By midsummer 1990, the controls were significantly loosened. See "East Awaits Flow of Western Technology," *Wall Street Journal,* May 30, 1990, p. A9; and "High-Tech Exports: Is the Dam Breaking?" *Business Week,* June 4, 1990, p. 128.

vital part of business planning. As revealed in Chapters 1 and 6, a company's social strategy must consider all of the political, ideological, social, and cultural factors that become intertwined with its financial and economic goals. Because socioeconomic systems organize each nation's economic, political, and social life, they can be the key to a successful corporate social strategy.

BASIC TYPES OF SOCIOECONOMIC SYSTEMS

The world's peoples, faced with solving their economic and social problems, generally organize themselves according to one of three basic systems: **free enterprise, central state control,** or **mixed state-and-private enterprise.** In each system there is some combination of private efforts and government controls. In all systems attention is given to social problems as well as economic ones; thus, they are called **socioeconomic systems.** As shown in Figure 7–1, varying amounts of freedom and coercion are present in each system. Some systems are politically democratic and socially open, while others are dominated by a single

FIGURE 7–1
Major types of socioeconomic systems.

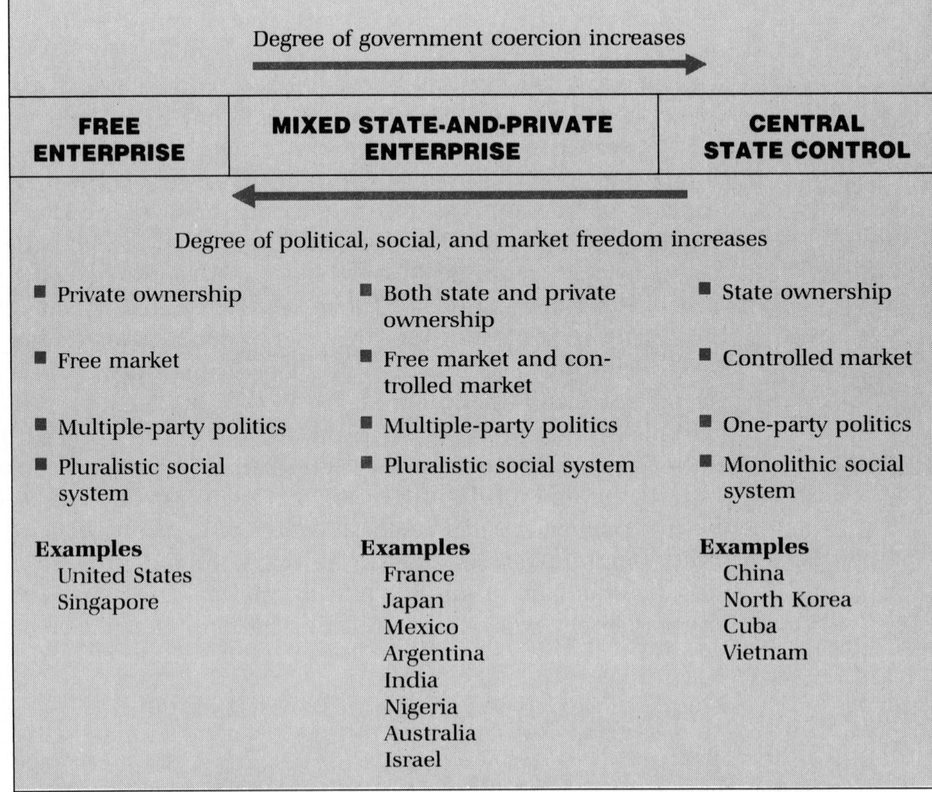

political party that controls the government and centralizes economic and social decisions.

The kind of socioeconomic system any nation has depends greatly on that nation's history. For example, the strong ties between government and business in Japan result from a long tradition of close cooperation between public authorities and private merchants. China owes its present centralized socioeconomic system to a historical tradition in Chinese culture showing respect for a male-dominated family, an honorable standing for elderly persons, a rigid bureaucratic system of government, and a custom of relying on a central authority figure in most areas of life. A long history of Confucian religious thought tended to encourage such practices. These ancient cultural attitudes were reinforced and given modern forms when the Chinese Communist Party led a successful revolution in 1949 to gain control of the Chinese government.[3]

But history is not the whole story. Socioeconomic systems can change, sometimes with dramatic speed. The best example is what happened in eastern Europe in the late 1980s, as Communist-dominated nations transformed themselves into political democracies. South Africa provides another example, when decades of racial separatism began to give way in 1990 to more equitable ways of life. These shifts show that socioeconomic systems are not "set in concrete." They can and do change.

Wise business leaders know that the grounds on which they do business are constantly shifting. They can reduce the uncertainties and risks by having a thorough knowledge of the more stable features of the world's socioeconomic systems. That is the topic we discuss next.

FREE ENTERPRISE

A free enterprise economy is based on the principle of voluntary association and exchange. People with goods and services to sell take them voluntarily to market, seeking to obtain a profit from the sale. Other people with wants to satisfy go to market voluntarily, hoping to find the things they want to buy. No one forces anybody to buy or to sell. Producers are drawn voluntarily to the market by their desire to make a profit. Consumers likewise go willingly to the marketplace in order to satisfy their many wants. The producer and consumer then make an economic exchange in which normally both of them receive an economic benefit. The producer earns a profit, and the consumer has a new good or service personally valued more highly than its cost.

A modern supermarket is a good example of how free enterprise works. The owners of the supermarket stock the shelves with hundreds of food items, knowing from past experience that their customers will pay enough money

[3] Oiva Laaksonen, *Management in China during and after Mao in Enterprises, Government, and Party*, Berlin: Walter de Gruyter, 1988, pp. 330 ff.

for the supermarket to earn a profit. No one has to force the supermarket to try to sell groceries or to meet government-imposed sales quotas. The owners voluntarily sell in order to make a profit.

The customers are willing to shop in the supermarket because in the past they have found the items they need. They may shop around among several supermarkets for the best buys in order to stretch the family grocery budget as far as possible. They also may try to avoid the supermarket entirely by raising their own food, but most people now prefer the convenience of supermarket shopping and the wide variety of choices there.

As Figure 7–2 demonstrates, in such a market economy, production is for profit and consumption is for the satisfaction of wants. People try to promote their own interests in the marketplace. To make the system work fairly, competition must be present. In other words a producer—the supermarket operator—has to sell at prices at about the same level as competing supermarkets or run the risk of losing customers and profits to lower-priced stores. All prices are the result, not of actions by monopolists or government officials, but of completely impersonal forces of supply (by producers) and demand (by consumers). When these conditions occur, producers voluntarily produce what consumers want, for that is the way to make a fair profit. At the same time, consumers achieve an optimum satisfaction of their wants at the lowest cost. In free competitive markets, the consumer is "king" or "queen" because producers must obey the wishes and demands of consumers if they want to make a profit.

In this kind of market system, the members of society satisfy most of their economic wants through these voluntary market transactions. Business firms (like the supermarket) that sell goods and services to consumers for a profit are at the same time fulfilling a social or public need. Consider society's need for cars,

FIGURE 7–2
Basic components of a free market system.

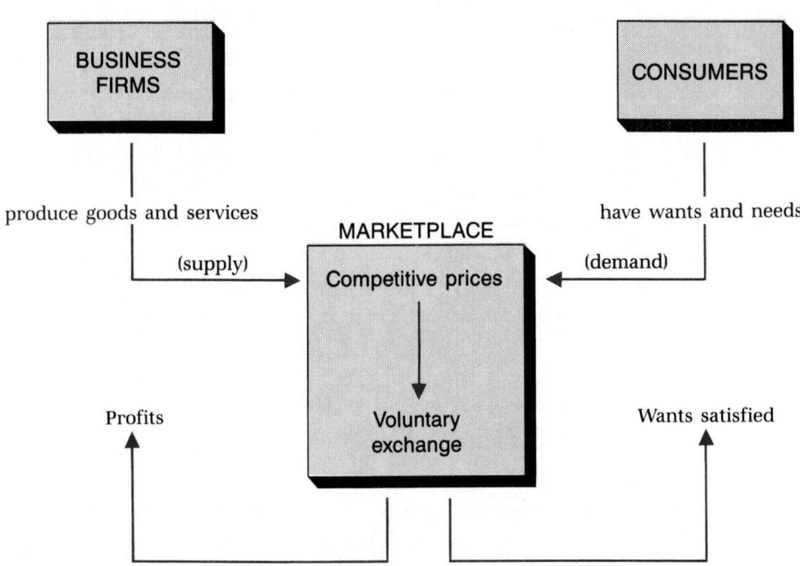

housing, energy, and entertainment—all produced mostly by private enterprise. Usually there is a very large overlap between society's needs and business's efforts to provide those needs through profit-making activities.

Of course, some serious problems can occur in this kind of socioeconomic system. If people cannot earn an adequate income, for whatever reason, they will not be able to satisfy their wants very well. Large numbers of such persons can create a serious poverty problem for society. Other difficulties arise if some business firms find ways to charge noncompetitive prices, or if labor unions manage to drive wages to unfair levels, or if government regulations impose unnecessary costs on society.

Very few economic systems conform strictly to the ideal conception of a free enterprise system. The United States comes the closest of any of the major industrial powers, partly because its historical traditions have favored free markets and partly because the American public prefers the economic and social freedom as well as the less-centralized government typical of free enterprise. The economies of Singapore and Hong Kong also exhibit many features of a free enterprise system.

Free Enterprise Ideology

All socioeconomic systems have an ideology—a guiding philosophy—that explains and justifies the way economic activities are organized. This philosophy shapes the attitudes and general outlook of corporate managers and government officials. It channels their thinking about how economic problems should be approached and solved.

In free enterprise societies, special attention is given to the major economic role that should be played by private business. Government is assigned the tasks that cannot be undertaken by the private sectors of society. Government also is expected to maintain order, protect national security, and enforce the business "rules of the game," such as free competition and private property.

The advocates of a free enterprise system build their case on several basic principles. These principles have become deeply embedded in the business mind, guiding the thinking of many business people today. The following ideas make up the core of this **free enterprise ideology.**

- *Individualism.* The individual person is considered to be more important than society or its institutions. Society's institutions exist to protect and promote the interests of individual persons. The opposite is true in a collectivist state, where individuals are subordinated to the power of government, the military, or organized religion.
- *Freedom.* All individuals must be free to promote and protect their own personal interests. This means they must have freedom to own property, to choose a job and career, to move freely within the society and to other societies, and to make all of life's basic decisions without being coerced by others. In business affairs, it means companies should be left free to pursue profits, and markets should be free of government intervention.

- *Private property.* The bedrock institution on which free enterprise is founded is private property. Unlike socialist states where the government owns the productive system, property is held by private individuals or companies. The ownership and use of property allows one to control one's own destiny, rather than to have important decisions made by someone else.
- *Profit.* Profit is a gain made by owners who use their property for productive purposes. Although profits are sometimes made by using property unproductively—or, as in the case of some government-supported farmlands, from not using the property at all—a free enterprise economy tends to draw all property into productive uses because that is the way to make profits. Profits are a reward for making a productive contribution to society. They act as a powerful incentive to needed production.
- *Equal opportunity.* Equality of opportunity has long been an ideal of free enterprise thinking. This notion does not guarantee that everyone is, or should be, equal in life. It says only that each person should have an opportunity to begin life's race on about the same footing as all others. No special advantages—in education, access to jobs, or treatment at work—should be allowed to tip the scales in favor of one person over another.
- *Competition.* Competition is an indispensable part of free enterprise thinking. Once equality of opportunity is achieved for everyone, the way is open for competition to encourage the most skilled, the most ambitious, and the most efficient to rise to the top. Competition is society's way of encouraging high levels of economic performance from all of its citizens. Adam Smith's "invisible hand" of competition regulates and curbs economic power, rather than the "visible hand" of government regulators. It keeps business on the alert to do its best, or else a competititor will win customers away with a better product or service.
- *The work ethic.* Most Americans believe that work is desirable, good for one's health and self-esteem, necessary if society is to achieve high levels of productivity, and even a fundamental right that should not be denied. This "work ethic" has fluctuated from period to period but remains an important part of free enterprise ideology. In the older Calvinist version of the work ethic, work was considered to be a way of using God-given talents to improve oneself. Eventually, this quasi-religious notion of work helped justify the pursuit of worldly wealth by merchants, financiers, and others in business.
- *Limited government.* The founders of free enterprise thinking advocated a government of very limited economic functions. "That government is best which governs least" was the ideal. Beyond protecting private property, enforcing contracts, and providing for general security, the government was expected to do little. A "hands off" policy toward business—often called *laissez faire*—is a preferred ideal of free enterprise theory, although obviously many changes have occurred since this ideal theory was first advanced.

This free enterprise ideology originated over 200 years ago in Great Britain. Adam Smith, the Scottish philosopher, first outlined the main components of

FIGURE 7–3
Central elements of today's United States business ideology.

- Free enterprise ideals: Profits, freedom, individualism
- More free market, less government intervention
- Socially responsive corporations
- Government-business cooperation in social problem-solving
- Policies to promote free trade and U.S. competitive strength

this capitalist philosophy in 1776 when he wrote *The Wealth of Nations.* It has guided business thinking in free market systems ever since. Its basic principles have been ignored or rendered impractical in many cases, and some people have argued that it has lost much of its relevance for today's business needs. However, its core ideas continue to have a strong appeal in free enterprise societies, as well as in other types of socioeconomic systems, especially eastern European nations as they broke away from domination by the Soviet Union in the late 1980s.

Business ideology in the United States retains much of the flavor of Adam Smith's views, but with a recognition that changing times have required an updating of free enterprise philosophy. The main features of today's business ideology, as found in the United States, are summarized in Figure 7–3. The traditional United States business belief system, which was based on pure free enterprise principles, gave way partly to the idea of socially responsive corporations run by socially aware business leaders. A larger and more active government that works in close partnership with private business has been accepted as necessary for handling some of society's bigger problems, including policies that promote greater trade and U.S. competitive strength. Corporate stakeholder groups organized by minorities, environmentalists, consumers, women, and others may place curbs and regulations on the private enterprise system, but business believes that these should be kept to a minimum because of the costs they impose on business and the public. Above all, the business community prefers a free enterprise system based on profits and one where government intervention in business is not allowed to lower efficiency and productivity. The older ideals of freedom, equal opportunity, and the right to make one's own decisions remain at the core of today's business ideology.[4]

CENTRAL STATE CONTROL

Corporations who do business under a system of central state control encounter an entirely different set of rules.[5] Most economic and political power is concen-

[4] For a more detailed account, see Gerald F. Cavanagh, *American Business Values*, 2d ed., Englewood Cliffs, NJ: Prentice-Hall, 1984.

[5] For a description of these systems in their heyday, see Barry M. Richman, *Soviet Management*, Englewood Cliffs, NJ: Prentice-Hall, 1965, chaps. 1, 5; and Barry M. Richman, *Industrial Society in Communist China*, New York: Random House, 1969, chap. 1. For more recent developments, see Rosalie L. Tung, *Chinese Industrial Society after Mao*, Lexington, MA: Lexington, 1982; and Laaksonen, op. cit.

trated in the hands of government officials and political authorities. The central government owns most property that can be used to produce goods and services. Private ownership may be forbidden or greatly restricted, and most private markets are illegal. Citizens are required to get government permission to move from one job to another. Wages and prices are strictly controlled by government planners. Foreign corporations, if permitted to operate at all, may find it difficult or impossible to take their profits out of the country.

The political system also is different. Usually only one political party is authorized to nominate candidates for public office. Not all citizens are permitted to join this one party, so the party's members may form a privileged elite of powerful people. With no political opposition, elections are only a formality, used by the nation's leaders to reinforce their control over politics, government, and most other spheres of society. Obviously, these leaders can and do set the terms under which foreign corporations are allowed to do business there. This means that the company's managers need to be skilled in political negotiations with government bureaucrats. Since these systems frequently are slow-moving and bureaucratic, corporations also need to exercise much patience as they wait for decisions to be made by government agencies.

By the early 1990s, this system of central state control and one-party rule could be found, for example, in China, North Korea, Vietnam, and Cuba.

Usually a government plan sets economic and social goals for one year, five years, or longer. Government officials then allocate budget money to achieve these goals. Factories, hospitals, schools, and farms strive to achieve production quotas set by government directive. In such a system, the government performs all the functions of a free enterprise system—deciding what will be produced; allocating resources and money to plants, offices, and farms; deciding how goods and services will be distributed to the people; and determining wages, costs, and prices.

In this type of socioeconomic system, the government has to make deliberate choices about which economic and social goals to pursue. Priorities have to be assigned.

> For many years in the Soviet Union, top officials in government and in the Communist party chose to emphasize military strength and basic industrial development in their five-year plans. Consumer goods and services were deliberately downgraded in the overall priority system. Steel, rubber, and chemicals were used to produce tanks, missiles, airplanes, and other weapons rather than to satisfy consumer desires for refrigerators, cars, and television sets. This centralized planning system dominated the Soviet Union's economy until the early 1990s, when reforms were introduced.

Government goals in this kind of system can include deliberate attempts to solve social problems. For example, where a particular industry such as coal mining is known to be especially hazardous to workers, the government plan can include special allocations of money for installing safety equipment, alarm systems, and ventilation fans in the mines. Or if a certain class of workers—for example, those who manufacture steam locomotives—becomes obsolete, due in this case to the introduction of diesel locomotives, the government can channel special money to retrain these workers.

Under central state control, a political ideology usually guides government planners and party leaders in setting production targets and social priorities. The official ideology may promote the broad interests of the masses of workers, or it may warn against the perils of external threats from unfriendly neighbors, or it may praise the virtues of the traditional ways unique to its own people. Production goals of China's economy for many years reflected Chairman Mao's ideological principles that the Chinese people should concentrate on making themselves secure from foreign attacks. The work force was exhorted to exceed production quotas in order to carry forward the Chinese people's revolution. All social goals and economic goals were determined by Chairman Mao's political ideology.

Under such circumstances, government planners and party leaders may decide that economic production is more important than safe factories, clean air and water, and an esthetically pleasing environment. Central state control, exercised through the officially approved political party, gives them the power to make such decisions. Coercion is the dominant feature of this type of socioeconomic system, as diagramed in Figure 7–1. Although large numbers of the population may accept the dominant political ideology, they can do little to change it if they do not like it. The government and party have a monopoly on economic and social decision making.

Figure 7–4 contrasts the "top-down" system typical of central state control

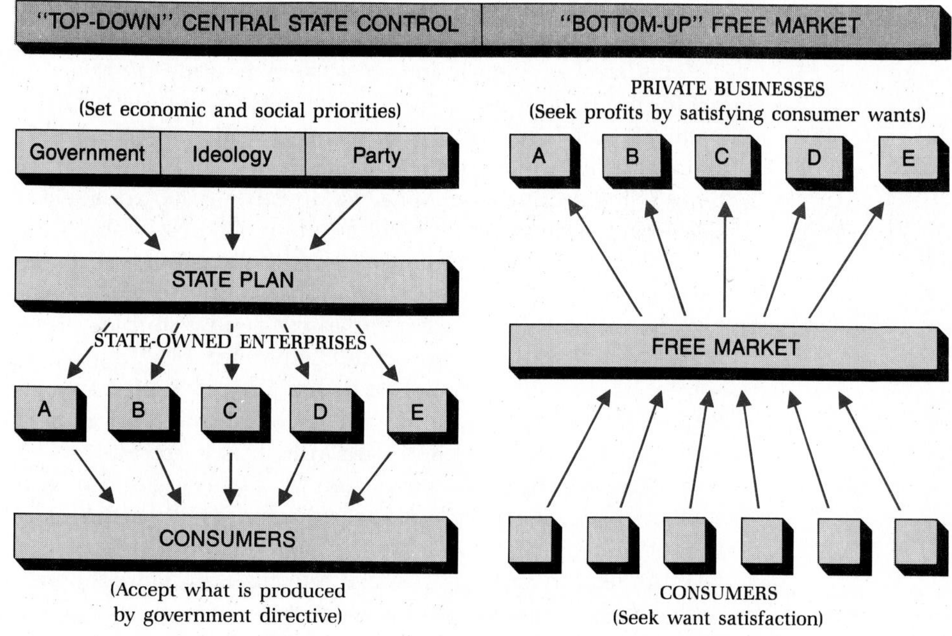

FIGURE 7–4 "Top-down" versus "bottom-up" decision making under central state control and in a free market.

with the "bottom-up" decision making in a free enterprise system. In a system of central state control, government and party planners at the top decide what and how much consumers will get, and the state-owned enterprises are ordered to produce these goods and services according to an overall plan. Consumers have no choice but to take what is decided by others at the top. By contrast, in a free enterprise system, consumers are the ones who give the orders, and private business firms produce goods and services to satisfy consumer wants. A free market is the principal difference between the two systems, allowing consumers by their purchases to direct production into channels they prefer and permitting businesses that cater to consumers to survive and make a profit.

MIXED STATE-AND-PRIVATE ENTERPRISE

Standing between the two opposite poles of free enterprise and central state control is another type of socioeconomic system that combines some elements of both of those systems. Not all, but some portion, of the industrial and financial sectors is owned and operated by the state. These may include the central bank through which the country's overall monetary policies are determined; the railroads, bus lines, and airline company; public utilities such as telephone, telegraph, electricity, water, and gas companies; and basic industries such as steel manufacturing, coal mining, nuclear power, and health care.

In spite of state ownership of these key parts of the business system, most businesses are owned and operated by private individuals and corporations. They coexist with the state enterprises and transact business according to free market principles; they make profits for their stockholders and take the normal risks of failure faced by free enterprisers everywhere.

This kind of socioeconomic system is quite popular in many parts of the world, as indicated in Figure 7–1. These countries enjoy a greater degree of political, social, and market freedom than the citizens who live under a central state control system. Political elections are open and free, and the social system tends to be pluralistic and diverse. However, when compared with free enterprise systems, the amount of market freedom is considerably less.

As with all socioeconomic systems, the benefits and costs need to be balanced against each other in judging the system's worthwhileness. Some of these nations—West Germany and Japan are good examples—have achieved spectacular economic growth and productivity rates, but their record of social problem solving has not always matched their economic performance. Tokyo, for example, has one of the worst air pollution records in the world, and the Rhine River in Germany is heavily polluted with industrial by-products.

Social problems may be tackled by a combination of government initiatives, socially responsive corporations, and a politically active trade union movement. Unions are especially watchful of the welfare of their members, and often they take the lead in proposing social reforms that will enhance the quality of work life. In both France and West Germany, for example, social audits of private and state enterprises were first proposed by trade unions.

In 1989 and the early 1990s, several nations of eastern Europe broke away from primary reliance on central state control and single-party politics. Included were Poland, Hungary, Bulgaria, Czechoslovakia, and Romania, as well as East Germany, which joined with West Germany to form a single German nation. While moving in the general direction of free enterprise, some of these nations have preferred to retain parts of their former socialist regimes, such as government-sponsored health care, housing, retirement pension plans, and "safety nets" for the jobless. Others have been reluctant, or have found it politically impossible, to abandon all government-imposed price controls, as well as subsidies paid to businesses and farmers. Some nations have held onto their government-owned central banks, railroads, airlines, and other public utilities. As a result, these countries may be described as having mixed state-and-private enterprise systems. They have gone only part way toward becoming full-fledged private enterprise systems.[6]

MILITARIZED NONDEMOCRATIC SOCIOECONOMIC SYSTEMS

In addition to the three classic types of socioeconomic systems already described, other subtypes also exist. Corporations frequently must decide whether to begin, or to continue, doing business in these nations.

The most frequently encountered subsystem is dominated by military factions or even a military dictatorship. A small, wealthy class is sometimes allied with the military government, with its members serving in high-level government posts. Human rights and democratic freedoms may be severely curtailed by the government. The press and media are normally government-controlled and used for propaganda purposes. Labor unions, religious organizations, and some professional groups (for example, artists, teachers, writers) are watched carefully by government authorities to keep them from becoming the focus of political opposition.

Outwardly, the socioeconomic system may appear to be a mixed system of state-and-private enterprise. Private markets may be tolerated, and many large privately owned business firms may be present. The government may welcome foreign investment and foreign corporations. There may even be a semblance of political opposition, although opposition parties normally cannot expect to win at the polls because elections are not free and fair.

Military-political regimes of this kind have appeared with unfortunate frequency during the last half of the twentieth century. They have been found in advanced industrial nations, as well as in the third world, and on most of the world's continents.

[6] For some examples, see "Prudent Pioneers: Even Entrepreneurs in East Bloc Shy Away from Total Capitalism," *Wall Street Journal*, Mar. 30, 1990, pp. A1, A12.

Their importance to business is plain, because corporate leaders must decide whether, or to what extent, they should do business where these plutocratic systems exist. Where wage rates are held down by government decree, questions of basic fairness arise. Where political rights are denied, a free and open society cannot exist. Where human rights are suppressed, business leaders may question the wisdom of doing business in such a climate of fear and deprivation. In addition, a dictatorial government may be an arbitrary government, leaving business open to abuses by corrupt officials. Taxes on business may be set at punitive levels, or regulations may be suddenly tightened. When these things happen, corporate leaders have to review their long-run strategic goals and decide whether the benefits of doing business in such systems are worth the economic, human, and social costs.

SYSTEMS IN TRANSITION

Socioeconomic systems change over time. During the 1980s, for example, some of the world's most important nations began to shift their position on the scale shown in Figure 7–1. Some moved away from central state control to greater reliance on market forces. Others—France was one example—shifted in the opposite direction by nationalizing key industries.

When changes like these occur, business must adjust to the new conditions. Unexpected but profitable opportunities might open up. Of course, the opposite also can happen if markets are closed down or costs are driven up by new government restrictions. Whether good or bad for business, one fact stands out above all others: A company's social strategy will always be affected. This happens because the company's relations with some of its most important stakeholders—e.g., government officials, the labor force, and local communities—are usually changed in significant ways.

China and Hungary are good examples of the ways in which socioeconomic systems change, and how those changes can affect corporate social strategy. These systems are discussed next.

China's Socioeconomic Pendulum Swings Back and Forth

China's current system of central state control dates from 1949, when Mao Zedong founded the Communist People's Republic of China. A one-party system gave exclusive political power to the Communists. Private ownership of businesses and farms was abolished; by the mid-1960s all industrial output was produced by state-owned and collectively owned firms. Exhibit 7–A explains how power is shared by officials in government and in the Communist party of China (CPC).

Faced with the gargantuan task of feeding a large and rapidly expanding population, Chinese planners have wanted to stimulate economic development of their country. One early attempt in the late 1950s, called The Great Leap

EXHIBIT 7–A
China's state and one-party control system.

SOURCE: Oiva Laaksonen, *Management in China during and after Mao in Enterprises, Government, and Party*, Berlin: Walter de Gruyter & Co., 1988, p. 29. Used with permission of the publisher. All rights reserved.

"In China two parallel, hierarchical administrative structures, that of the state and of the CPC [Communist Party of China] run through the whole society from the highest societal top to the bottom of the microlevel organizations [shown below]. The two administrative lines are bound tightly together with many personal and organizational ties."[1]

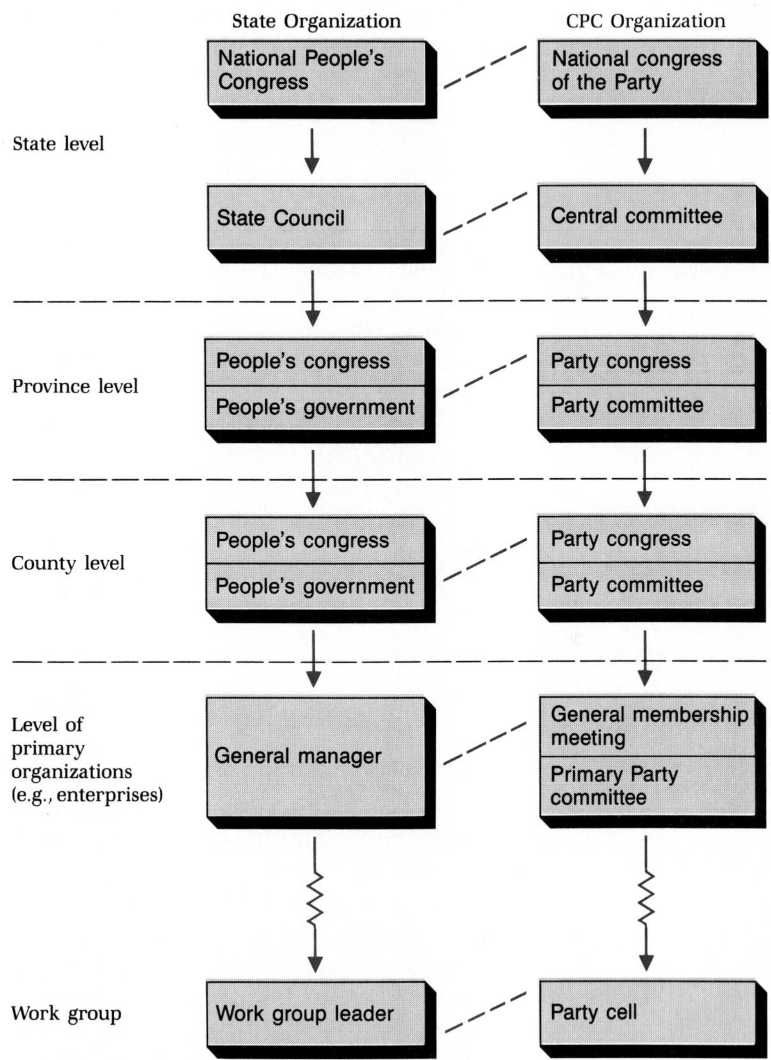

1. Oiva Laaksonen, *Management in China during and after Mao in Enterprises, Government, and Party*, Berlin: Walter de Gruyter, 1988, p. 29.

Forward, was a dismal failure. Mao's Great Proletarian Cultural Revolution, launched in 1966, was an even greater disaster for the nation. China adopted a "go it alone" policy with a vengeance. Ideological purity and loyalty to the Communist regime were elevated to the status of a quasi-religion. Doctors, engineers, university professors, and many other professional and technical persons were sent to the country to help with farming chores. Plant managers were subject to the whims of unskilled and inexperienced Communist party officials and members of the youth-oriented radical Red Guards. Scientific education was severely restricted, and Chinese experts were denied opportunities to make contact with scholars in other nations. Anyone thought to have a favorable opinion of capitalism was in danger of being jailed, often being called a "capitalist roader" or a "running dog of capitalism." Deng Xiaoping, who succeeded Mao as China's leader, was himself labeled a "capitalist roader" during this period and was accused of having a "lust for foreign technology and equipment, blatantly opposing the principles of independence and self-reliance."[7] In spite of official Communist party enthusiasm for Mao's two big economic programs, they did not succeed in their goals of converting China into a modern industrial nation.

Mao died in 1976 and was succeeded by Deng Xiaoping in 1978. Deng's attitude toward economic development and capitalism was strikingly different from Mao's antagonistic anticapitalist views. Deng and his supporters took a pragmatic view of relations with free enterprise systems. What China needed was technology, foreign capital, an infusion of up-to-date scientific and technical knowledge, and a renewal of contacts with other industrial nations. The United States, European nations, and even former archenemy Japan were invited to explore possible trade, scientific, and educational exchanges. Management know-how was sought from American business schools. Chinese students were sent to universities and technical schools in the West.

Deng also loosened a number of centralized controls. Plant managers were allowed to set their own production targets rather than take orders from government planners, and some plants were permitted to keep and invest some of their profits rather than give them back to the central government. Small entrepreneurs—for example, the owner of a noodle stand in Canton or of a small restaurant in Chongqing—no longer had to risk jail for owning property and making small profits. In the all-important countryside, farmers could raise crops and sell them in private markets, a forbidden practice that could lead to jail during the Mao regime. Deng also broke up China's single state-owned airline into five competing companies in an effort to improve efficiency and service.

Another innovation was the establishment of Special Economic Zones along China's coast. These carefully restricted regions are reserved for foreign corporations that wish to do business in China. They allow China to "have its (centrally planned) cake and eat it (that is, free enterprise advantages), too." Figure 7–5 shows how both China and foreign multinational corporations benefit from these zones.

[7] Quoted in Kwan-yiu Wong and David K. Y. Chu, *Modernization in China,* Oxford: Oxford University Press, 1985, p. 27.

FIGURE 7–5
Benefits of China's Special Economic Zones.

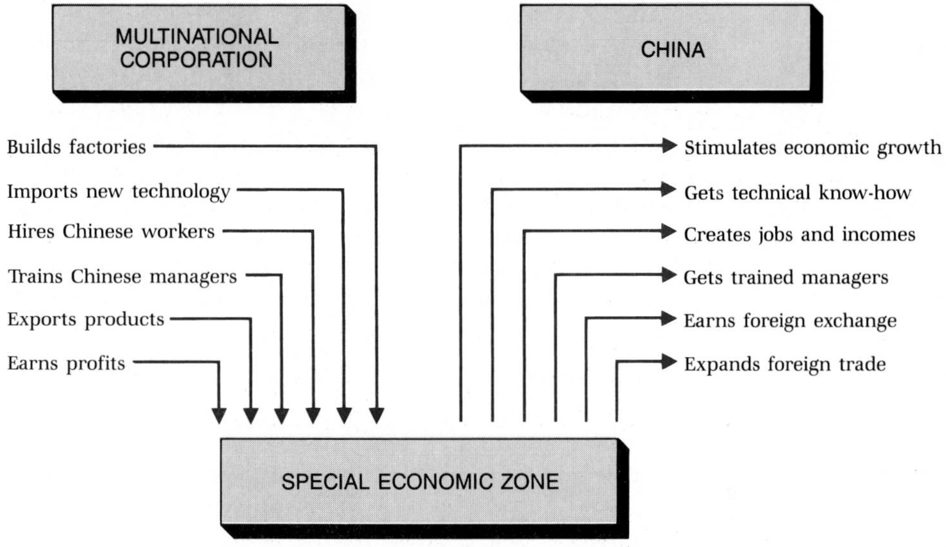

Then in 1989, just as China appeared to be adopting some free enterprise practices, the pendulum swung back toward central state control. The student-led democracy movement threatened the supremacy of one-party control by the Communists and it was crushed by military force. Some of Deng's economic reforms contributed to inflation, created income disparities, and encouraged political corruption. Relaxed controls over regional industries and farms made it harder for central planners to meet their goals. "Recentralization"—which meant drawing power back to the central government-and-party mechanism—became the new policy. Price controls, which had been relaxed, were tightened. Selling some state enterprises to Chinese citizens and workers was halted. Some semi-private rural factories were closed. State-owned industries were given preferential treatment and subsidies. Profit-sharing plans between provincial governments and factories were no longer encouraged. Over 2 million private enterprises were closed. As one Chinese economist said, "A single theme prevails—centralization, politically and economically. [This] officially marks the beginning of the undoing of China's decade-long economic reform."[8]

This turnabout was nearly disastrous for many foreign companies with operations in China.

> For example, Givaudan Far East, Ltd., a Swiss company, found it harder to sell chemicals to shampoo and soap factories in China because government restrictions had slowed the factories' supplies of working capital. Things got worse after the government's crackdown on student protesters, and several

[8] "Beijing Is Reasserting Centralized Control," *Wall Street Journal,* Nov. 28, 1989, p. A10; "China's Economic Reform Program Stalls," *Wall Street Journal,* Sept. 26, 1989, p. A20; and "Nervous Holdouts for a Hardline," *Newsweek,* Jan. 15, 1990, p. 35.

months passed without any new orders being placed with Givaudan. The company expected its business to drop by as much as 40 percent.

PepsiCo had the same kind of experience, although its bottling plant was in one of the privileged Special Economic Zones. Its explosive growth was halted when China's central planners stopped issuing permits for Chinese distributors to buy Pepsi. The planners preferred to direct Chinese entrepreneurial efforts toward other purposes.

Most foreign corporations that had been doing business in consumer products and light-industry sectors found their business and profits drying up as China turned back toward a system of central state control.[9]

Hungary's Move from East to West

Hungary's experiences in the last half of the twentieth century carry important lessons for business. Starting in the 1950s with a post–World War II system of central state control that was imposed by the Soviet Union, Hungary moved by the early 1990s sharply away from central planning toward the free enterprise end of Figure 7–1's continuum. Unlike China, Hungary's reforms occurred slowly over a period of three decades, and progress was steadier. Of course, Hungary's leaders did not face the crushing population pressures of China, and its history gave the European nation industrial and commercial advantages not enjoyed so widely in the vast expanses of China. As one of the Soviet Union's economic satellites, Hungary also gained certain benefits that enabled it to experiment with its own economic system. Those experiments were startling, partly because they occurred right under the nose of the Soviet Union's system of central state control.

Hungary: a blend of two systems

By the early 1990s, Hungary was neither a central state control system nor a free enterprise system but a blend of the two. It had become a type of mixed state-and-private enterprise system while retaining features of its former socialist core. Although it continued to adopt more and more free enterprise practices and institutions, government officials retained much influence over national economic policies and the practices of business firms.

Figure 7–6 summarizes the major components of Hungary's socioeconomic system. The *state sector* includes all enterprises owned by the government, such as the National Bank of Hungary, major manufacturers, construction firms, service companies, and public utilities. These enterprises are the largest in Hungary, often enjoy an official monopoly in their market, and usually receive favorable government treatment including subsidies and even bailouts if in serious financial trouble. Until 1985, their managers were appointed by government authorities, but they are now elected by their employees. *Agricultural and nonagricultural cooperatives* are a form of collective ownership favored by socialist ideology. They

[9] "China Trade Slumps after June Killings," *Wall Street Journal*, Oct. 23, 1989, p. A5E; and "Beijing's Economic Ills Pose a New Threat of Social Upheaval," *Wall Street Journal*, Aug. 3, 1989, pp. A1, A11.

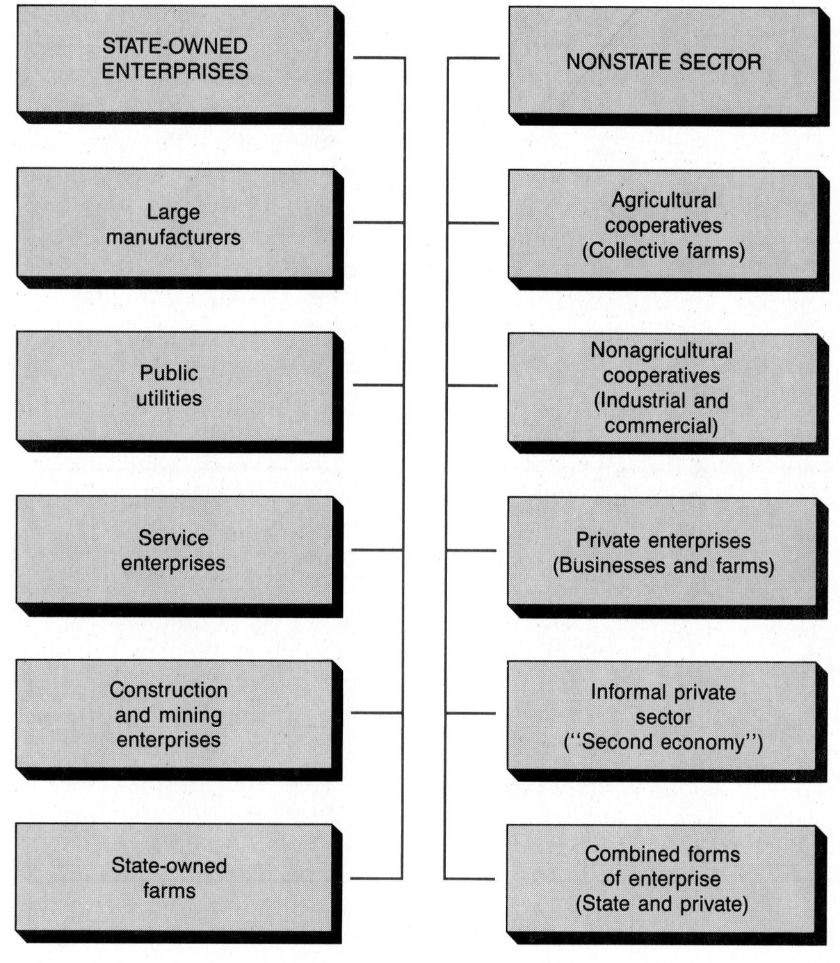

FIGURE 7–6 State and nonstate sectors of Hungary's socioeconomic system.

are a "halfway house" between state ownership and private ownership by individuals. These enterprises rely somewhat on market pricing, have a stronger profit motivation, and cannot count on being saved by government subsidies and bailouts.

The *private sector* includes small entrepreneurial business initiatives by private citizens, who operate on a profit-and-loss basis. Typical firms include restaurants, shopkeepers, craft workers, and small-scale construction contractors. They receive little or no government support and may keep their profits but also must accept whatever losses they incur. Private farms also belong in this category.

The *informal private sector,* sometimes called "the second economy," is all kinds of economic activity and income not included in the "official" sectors. Examples are "moonlighting" work to earn extra income, private housing construction, car repair and maintenance, child care, and other ways of providing for a household's own consumption. The *combined (state and private) forms* refer to joint ventures between the Hungarian government and foreign private business firms, leasing state property for private gain, and "business work partnerships" that act somewhat like a consulting group within a Hungarian business firm.

The boundaries between some of these sectors are hazy, thus revealing the government's willingness to tolerate and experiment with new ways of organizing economic life. According to a leading Hungarian economist, "The appearance of a vital nonstate sector represents something brand new and important in the history of socialist countries."[10]

The dominant trait of Hungary's socioeconomic system at the beginning of the 1990s was a blend of bureaucratic government control and free market transactions. The state sector was by far the largest component, generating two-thirds of national income. It operates under direct bureaucratic control of government officials but also is influenced by market pressures. Exhibit 7–B gives a bird's-eye view of these state-owned firms.

The nonstate sector is market-oriented but still must contend with strong bureaucratic restrictions, such as some price controls, credit controls, restrictions on foreign trade, restricted access to foreign exchange, and a complex and often arbitrary tax system. These bureaucratic controls work on Figure 7–4's "top-down" principle. Market activities, even though restricted, tend to work on a "bottom-up" principle. To free themselves from bureaucratic constraints, or to gain advantages, the managers of most Hungarian business firms constantly engage in active bargaining and negotiating with government officials. This "regulator bargaining," as it is called, "goes on about all issues all the time. This is a bargaining society, and the main direction is vertical, namely bargaining between the levels of the hierarchy, or between bureaucracy and firm, not horizontal, between seller and buyer."[11]

One other feature of central state control prevailed in Hungary through the 1980s—a one-party political system. Until the Communist party's monopoly was officially broken in late 1989, party officials exerted much influence on Hungary's economic and social policies. Party committees had a hand in appointing enterprise managers, deciding wage policies, approving a firm's export plans, and weighing the merits of plant construction. A multiparty system and free elections in 1990 moved the nation further away from this kind of political interference in business management.[12]

[10] Janos Kornai, "The Hungarian Reform Process: Visions, Hopes, and Reality," *Journal of Economic Literature,* December 1986, p. 1710.

[11] Kornai, op. cit., p. 1700.

[12] Laura D'Andrea Tyson and Steve Popper, "The New Hungarian Economic Reforms and Their Effects on Enterprise Behavior," *Advances in the Economic Analysis of Participatory and Labor Managed Firms,* vol. 3, Greenwich, CT: JAI Press, 1988, pp. 329–333.

EXHIBIT 7–B

HOW HUNGARY'S STATE-OWNED FIRMS WORK

"Hungarian state-owned firms do not operate within the framework of market socialism. The reformed system is a specific combination . . . of bureaucratic and market coordination. . . . The market is not dead. It does some coordinating work, but its influence is weak. The firm's manager watches the customer and the supplier with one eye and his superiors in the bureaucracy with the other eye. Practice teaches him that it is more important to keep the second eye wide open: managerial career, the firm's life and death, subsidies and credit, prices and wages, all financial 'regulators' affecting the firm's prosperity, depend more on the higher authorities than on market performance."

SOURCE: Janos Kornai, "The Hungarian Reform Process: Visions, Hopes, and Reality," *Journal of Economic Literature*, December 1986, pp. 1699–1700.

As shown in Figure 7–7, Hungary reformed its socioeconomic system by a series of important steps taken over a long period of years. Some of the significant results also are listed in the figure.

As Hungary's dramatic reforms took shape, new business opportunities opened up.

> US West installed eastern Europe's first cellular-phone network in cooperation with the Hungarian Post Office. American Express made its credit cards available to Hungarian citizens. *Playboy* magazine sold its first Hungarian edition. General Electric bought a majority stake in Tungsram, Hungary's light bulb manufacturer, for $150 million, and the French computer maker Cie. des Machines Bull invested $5 million in a joint computer-assembly and sales venture with Hungary's main electronic enterprise, Videoton. A consortium of Swiss and Hungarian holding companies purchased the nation's largest fertilizer company. Other joint ventures with foreign corporations were undertaken in computer software, pharmaceuticals, and chemicals. A big U.S. consulting firm, Arthur D. Little, used its expertise to introduce Western-style accounting to Hungarian enterprises.[13]

Some experts believe that Hungary's slow but steady shift from a central state control system toward a market-oriented one might be a beneficial model that can be followed by other socialist economic systems. Unlike those in China, Hungary's reforms have been peaceful. Prior to the political upheavals of late 1989, compromises, bargaining, and negotiating between advocates of change and defenders of the older system were reached without serious economic disruption. When faced with massive political protests, government and party leaders ac-

[13] "Cowboy Capitalism Goes East," *U.S. News and World Report*, Jan. 22, 1990, p. 34; "Computer Firm Moves to Create Base in Hungary," *Wall Street Journal*, Feb. 12, 1990, p. A9A; and "Ventures in Hungary Test Theory That West Can Uplift East Bloc," *Wall Street Journal*, Apr. 5, 1990, pp. A1, A18.

FIGURE 7–7
Major stages of reform in Hungary, 1950 to 1990.

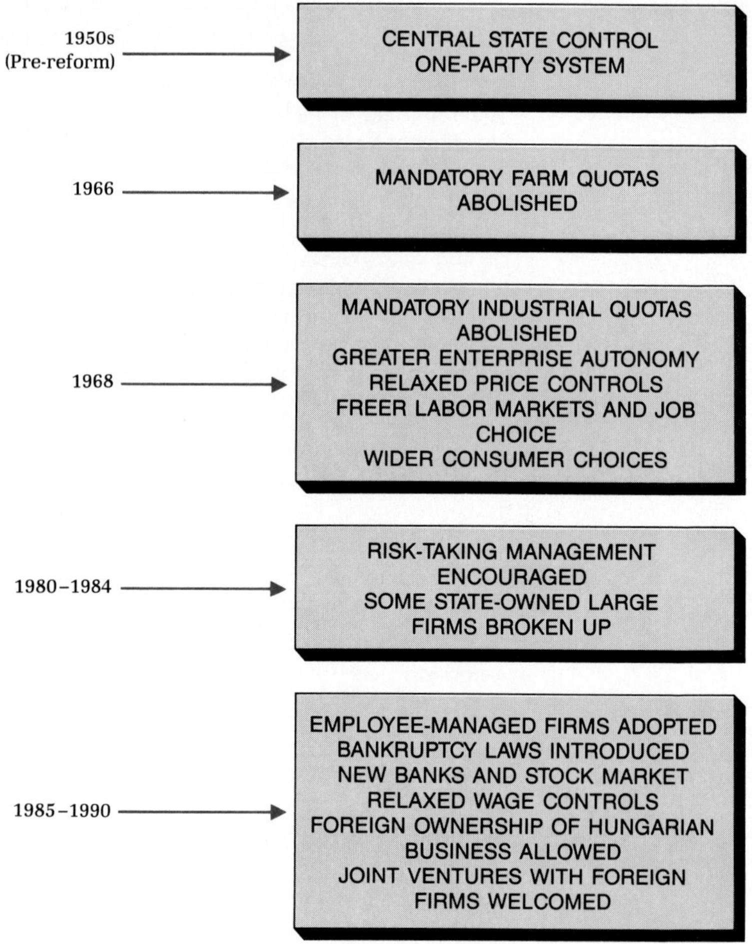

cepted the need for change. Hungary's "Third Way" might prove to be a model worth copying.[14]

Changes in Other Nations

The 1980s and early 1990s will probably be remembered as a time when the map of the world's socioeconomic systems was drastically altered. A gigantic shift was underway. A startling number of nations decided to introduce or reinvigorate the free market and private profit making. Reliance on centralized economic planning by government officials was out of favor in a surprising number of countries.

[14] For a discussion of this point, see Jacob Naor and Peter Akos Bod, "Innovative State-Guided Economic Institution Building in Hungary—Some Developmental Lessons for Countries with Insufficiently Competitive Markets," *Journal of Global Marketing*, vol. 2, no. 1, 1988, pp. 7–32.

FIGURE 7–8
Selected privatized companies on four continents.

SOURCE: Richard Hemming and Ali M. Mansoor, *Privatization and Public Enterprises*, Washington, DC: International Monetary Fund, January 1988, pp. 7–9; and "Mexico's Been Bitten by the Privatization Bug," *Wall Street Journal*, Sept. 15, 1989, p. A13.

PRIVATIZED COMPANIES

Britain
British Airways
Jaguar Cars
British Gas
British Telecom
British Steel
Rolls-Royce
Cable & Wireless

France
St. Gobain (glass)
Paribas
Compagnie Generale d'Electricite
Societe Generale

West Germany
VEBA (energy, chemicals)
VIAG (aluminum, chemicals)
IVG (transportation, property)
Volkswagen (cars)

Japan
Nippon Telegraph & Telephone
Japan Air Lines

Chile
Banco de Santiago
CHILMETRO (urban transport)
CHILQUINTA (electricity)
SOQUIMICH (nitrates)
CAP (iron ore)

Mexico
Aeromexico
Mexicana de Aviacion
National Hotel Group

Malaysia
Malaysian Airline System
Malaysian International Shipping
Port Kelong container terminal

"**Privatization**" was in the air. This movement took two forms: the sale of government-owned enterprises to private investors, and turning over some government services and functions (such as prisons and refuse collection) to private enterprise. Privatization thus meant that nations were allowing more economic decisions to be made by the free market, rather than by government officials and regulators. The reasoning went like this: If private business can make a profit by providing services formerly delivered by government, and if it can do so more efficiently and at a fair price, so much the better.

Privatization's popularity is indicated in Figure 7–8, which lists some of the better-known companies that were moved from government ownership to private ownership. This impulse toward free enterprise was not limited to any one type of socioeconomic system. Britain took the lead in selling off most of its nationalized industries. Saskatchewan, a Canadian province with a strong socialist tradition, announced plans to privatize a mammoth potash-mining company, a natural gas distribution firm, and the provincial insurance business. Canada's federal government had already sold a majority of Air Canada as well as its holdings in two aircraft makers and a telecommunications company. Turkey, whose state-owned companies in the 1980s accounted for about half of that nation's industrial production, decided to sell many of these enterprises to private citizens. Argentina in 1989 initiated the sale of 30 state-run companies, including Aerolineas Argentinas and parts of Yacimientos Petroliferos Argentinos. By 1989, Mexico had divested itself of over half of the 1,155 public entities it owned in 1982, according to that nation's undersecretary of finance. Portugal, Indonesia, Thailand, Venezuela, Chile, and others joined the privatization parade. Even Vietnam, which remained firmly committed to a centrally planned system, permitted private consumer-goods shops to open, approved an increase in trade with foreign corporations, and gave private entrepreneurs the right to hire a workforce and pay unlimited bonuses to them. Not everyone went along with privatization. Cuba's President Fidel Castro declared, "We will never renounce the glorious title of Socialists and Communists. We . . . [are] dedicated to advancing the Party and the Revolution."[15]

The Lessons for Business

What do these fast-paced changes mean for business? What are the main lessons to be learned? How can socioeconomic systems, and changes in them, affect a company's social strategy?

In one sense, business resembles a complex game. The world arena in which the game of business is played is far from uniform. The playing field is divided into diverse spheres, each with a different set of rules. To win the game, companies must learn each set of rules and be ready to adjust their play as they cross from one part of the field into another. Failure to do so can bring a big penalty; in severe cases, the game itself (that is, the opportunity to make a profit) may be forfeited. As this chapter demonstrates, profit-seeking business is not even allowed to play in some parts of the world where the rules forbid free enterprise.

This picture of business as a global game adds up to some specific lessons for corporations, their top managers, and those in charge of the company's strategic planning.

The first lesson is clear. A socioeconomic system's "rules of the game" can have a life-or-death impact on business by helping to decide the following central questions.

- Whether a company will be allowed to conduct business at all.
- What products and services will be approved for production.
- How the company is organized for business there, that is, whether it operates as a separate entity or is linked in joint ventures with the government or other enterprises.
- The source of its supplies, materials, and resources, including employees, capital funds, and technology.
- Its cost structure, especially wages and taxes.
- How prices for its products and services are determined, whether by government decree or by market forces.
- The level of profits permitted and the company's ability to take its profits out and recycle them.

[15] Ron Chepesiuk, "Castro against the Tide," *The New Leader*, Jan. 8, 1990, p. 10. For more information, see E. S. Savas, *Privatization*, Chatham, NJ: Chatham House, 1987; and Cento Veljanovski, *Selling the State: Privatisation in Britain*, London: Weidenfeld and Nicolson, 1987.

A second lesson follows from the first. Since these central functions of business can be shaped by the type of socioeconomic system involved, corporate managers and strategic planners cannot hope to conduct business successfully unless they learn each system's "rules of the game." This puts a great premium on social and political knowledge and skills. A culture's values must be understood and respected. Government contacts must be cultivated. Political negotiating skills must be learned and applied. Learning the "pace" and "feel" of a society's institutions is important. Anticipating when and how political reforms are likely to occur may prove to be crucial to the timing of a business strategic plan. In other words, a company's financial goals can be achieved only if its managers have a sophisticated knowledge of the social, cultural, political, and governmental features of the socioeconomic systems in which the company does business.

A third lesson for business is to remember that each society and each socioeconomic system is different from all others. This unique character means that each nation needs to find its own way, based on its history, its culture, its political traditions, the needs of its people, and its unique place in the world community. The most that business can be expected to do is to help each society achieve the goals that it has set for itself. It can do this by carrying out its economic mission effectively while at the same time showing respect for each nation's laws, values, and traditions.

SUMMARY POINTS OF THIS CHAPTER

- Free enterprise, central state control, and mixed state-and-private enterprise differ from one another mainly in the amount of freedom permitted for making economic choices, as well as how much government coercion and regulation is present.
- Free enterprise ideology favors individualism, private property, free markets, competitive prices, profits, and limited government.
- Central state control ideology usually favors central planning by government officials, state-owned property, strong allegiance to the government and nation, and one-party political control.
- The major changes that occurred in the world's socioeconomic systems during the 1980s and early 1990s were a shift away from central state control in the direction of free enterprise practices. Privatization was the principal form taken by these changes.
- The experiences of China and Hungary reveal that systems of central state control can be reformed to be more like free enterprise systems, but the transition is difficult, occurs unevenly, and normally takes many years.
- Socioeconomic systems and changes in them can affect the core functions of a business firm, making the difference between profit and loss.
- Corporate managers can be most effective in achieving their financial goals if they have a sophisticated understanding of the socioeconomic systems in which they do business.

KEY TERMS AND CONCEPTS USED IN THIS CHAPTER

- Socioeconomic system
- Free enterprise
- Central state control
- Mixed state-and-private enterprise
- Free enterprise ideology
- One-party political system
- Privatization

DISCUSSION CASE

CHEROKEES IN CHINA

"Are you sure Chrysler wants us to just walk out of this place? To leave, to risk wiping out our whole investment?"

"Yep. We're out."

Following this exchange between two top-ranking U.S. executives in the Beijing Jeep factory, they and their families bought tickets, rode to the Beijing airport along a road lined with armored personnel carriers, and flew out of a nation that seemed to be on the verge of civil war.[16] It was early June 1989 just after the people's Liberation Army, acting on orders of Chinese government leaders, had massacred hundreds of prodemocracy demonstrators in Tiananmen Square, the symbolic center of Beijing, the nation's capital city.

To these Beijing-based managers, it seemed to be an inglorious and disappointing end to a ten-year effort to bring U.S. capital, technology, and managerial skills to the world's most populous nation. In doing so, they and their company had hoped to get an early foothold in what many believed to be the potentially richest market in the world.

Back in 1979, the first team of U.S. automotive experts arrived in China at the invitation of high-level government officials. They worked for American Motors Corporation (AMC), which was famous the world over for its four-wheel-drive vehicle, the jeep. Their task was to explore the possibilities of helping the Chinese to modernize the factory that made a poor copy of the AMC jeep, as well as to produce a new model that could be sold in China and overseas. The People's Liberation Army was especially interested in getting a jeep designed for military purposes. The agreement that was signed also included the idea that automotive parts and components would eventually be manufactured in China for export to other nations, thus providing China with much-needed foreign exchange to finance its drive for modernization.

Believing the deal was almost clinched, the AMC officials were baffled by the slow progress in getting a formal contract drawn up. Two years went by without tangible progress, followed by another long period of frustrating negotiations.

[16] This quotation and several other details cited here are from Jim Mann, *Beijing Jeep: The Short, Unhappy Romance of American Business in China,* New York: copyright © 1989 by Jim Mann. Reprinted by permission of Simon & Schuster, Inc.

One problem was Chinese unfamiliarity with the way free market economies work. Some Chinese negotiators showed no interest in production costs, sales prices, or profits, because their centrally planned socialist system made such decisions far from the factories where production occurred. Another problem was the government bureaucracy, whose decisions were very cumbersome, requiring many layers of approval.

Finally, in the spring of 1983, the joint venture was officially launched. AMC and its partner, the Beijing Automotive Works (BAW) which was a large state-owned enterprise, formed Beijing Jeep Company. The American company would contribute cash and technology; the Chinese side would put in more than two-thirds of the total assets needed. The board of directors was to be controlled by the Chinese, with an AMC executive to be the first chief executive officer and a Chinese to be chairman of the board.[17] Coming just a few years after Deng Xiaopeng's economic reforms that were opening China to foreign investment, AMC indeed had gained its sought-after foothold. Beijing Jeep was the first major manufacturing joint venture under Deng's regime. It was important enough to warrant a signing ceremony in the Great Hall of the People, attended by high-level officials.

When factory operations began in early 1984, AMC managers found an entirely new world of manufacturing. Workers came to work late, took very long tea breaks, took naps on company time, left work long before the work day ended, often punched time cards for friends who did not bother to come in, and could be absent for a week by getting a note from a doctor. Under communist ideology, wages were kept nearly equal for most workers, leaving little incentive for greater effort. Since wages were not tied to efficiency, few people thought much about keeping costs down or being careful not to waste materials. If the assembly line was halted by a power shortage, workers took naps or went home, not waiting to see if the line would start moving shortly.

The biggest hassles, though, centered around the product to be made and the number of jeeps to be produced. The Chinese wanted, and had been led to believe that they would get, a newly designed jeep that would replace their older model and that could be sold at home and abroad. AMC wanted to send Detroit-made parts for the Cherokee model to Beijing for assembly; they argued that a new jeep would cost too much to produce and would be out of the price range of most Chinese and export customers. AMC also wanted to make 40,000 vehicles by 1990, but the Chinese were talking far fewer numbers. In what proved to be a fateful move, the Chinese officials of Beijing Jeep finally agreed to the AMC plan for importing Cherokee parts from Detroit; acting in the spirit of Deng's new drive to decentralize economic decisions, they gave their approval without the blessings of central government authorities.

The stumbling block was China's supply of foreign exchange. It was needed to buy new technology (such as the Cherokee jeep) so that the nation could continue to modernize. But the ups and downs of government policy and the

[17] Jim Mann reports that the new Chinese chairman told AMC's chairman and CEO, "I've never been a chairman before. Can you tell me what a chairman does?" Mann, op. cit., p. 91.

continuing power struggles within the upper reaches of the central government hindered Deng's program to get foreign companies to invest there. A big chunk of this precious foreign exchange was needed to buy the American-made Cherokee parts. Beijing Jeep did not have the needed amount. The central government in Beijing would not provide the funds. Production slowed and came close to stopping altogether.

In desperation, Beijing Jeep's American CEO broke Chinese custom and leaked stories to the press in other countries about the company's troubles. Chinese officials were both infuriated and embarrassed. The nation's deputy premier passed the word that the necessary foreign exchange should be made available. Because Beijing Jeep was a showcase model of the kind of joint venture China wanted to encourage, the CEO's strategy worked. But he had to settle for a production figure of only 12,500.

Following this crisis, production hummed along, jeeps rolled off the line, demand for them increased rapidly, AMC was making money at last—and then the roof fell in. In March 1987, Renault, the French car maker that owned a controlling interest in AMC, agreed to sell its AMC stake to Chrysler. The news hit like a thunderbolt in Beijing, where government officials were largely in the dark about the merger mania that had gripped U.S. corporations during the 1980s. For a while, the Chinese seemed ready to block the deal by arguing that the 1983 contract prevented any sale of AMC shares in Beijing Jeep without the approval of its joint venture partner. In the end, though, they were convinced that Chrysler was a bigger, richer company with more advanced technology than AMC, so the buyout might be better for China in the long run.

Not wanting to put all of its technology eggs into the basket of the advanced Western nations, China in the late 1980s began reaching out to the Soviet Union, eastern Europe, and such developing nations as Taiwan and South Korea. It was a way to find technology without paying the high price in foreign exchange needed when dealing with the advanced nations. In the upper circles of government policy, fierce behind-the-scenes struggles for power were going on, some wishing to open to greater foreign trade and others preferring to go slower in welcoming foreigners into China.

In the spring of 1987, students from Beijing's universities began protest demonstrations in Tiananmen Square, making various demands on China's leaders, including more democracy. By May, hundreds of thousands of students, factory workers, and other citizens were crowding into the square, some remaining all night. Workers at Beijing Jeep found it difficult to get to work on time because of the crowded streets; some joined the demonstrations.

Faced with growing tumult in the streets, the government declared martial law. By early June, army troops and tanks were ordered into the square to clear the demonstrators. Hundreds were killed by machine guns, rifles, and tanks.

Chrysler advised its Beijing employees and their families to leave immediately, and they did. Many other foreign companies did likewise. Business attitudes toward China changed abruptly. High-level government officials who had favored an open-door policy toward foreign business firms were deposed. In the ensuing months, China seemed to turn away from the market reforms that Deng had introduced earlier. Many observers believed that it would take many years for business prospects to brighten in China.[18]

In Detroit, Chrysler headquarters was the scene of student demonstrators from nearby universities, demanding that the company pull out of Beijing Jeep entirely. The company refused. It sent its managers back to Beijing about a month after the massacre in Tiananmen Square. A company representative said, "We feel what we're doing is consistent with the policies of the United States."[19]

Discussion Questions

1. Was AMC right to enter into the joint venture to make jeeps in China? Was it a good strategy?
2. Of the various social, cultural, and political factors that affected Beijing Jeep, which ones proved to be critical to the success of the joint venture? Could these environmental factors have been foreseen by AMC's planners and top-level executives? Should they have been made a part of the company's strategy?
3. Do you believe Beijing Jeep's CEO, who was a foreigner, should have gone so far as to publicly embarrass high-level Chinese officials in order to achieve the company's business goal? Did his actions show a respect for China's traditions? Was the business result worth the risk?
4. What do you think about Chrysler's decision to return to China after the Tiananmen Square massacre? Was it good business? Was it ethical? Did it show a respect for human rights?

[18] "Long March: How the Twisting Path of China's Reform Led to Guns of Tiananmen," *Wall Street Journal*, June 16, 1989, pp. A1, A4; Denis Fred Simon, "After Tiananmen: What Is the Future for Foreign Business in China?" *California Management Review*, Winter 1990, pp. 106–123.
[19] Mann, op. cit., p. 303.

8

The Multinational Corporation

The multinational corporation is a basic means of conducting business activities in much of the world. As business becomes more internationalized, the multinational corporation has become a primary agent of economic and social change. Corporations and their managers must develop and implement policies that build a positive relationship with each society in which they do business.

Key Questions and Chapter Objectives

This chapter focuses on these key questions and objectives:

- Why is the multinational corporation the most prominent actor in international commerce?
- What private and public roles does the corporation play in modern society?
- How do principles of national sovereignty and business legitimacy shape the business-society relationship in different nations?
- Why do some business leaders favor the idea of the "stateless corporation"?
- What impact can multinational business have on a host nation, and what impact can a host nation have on a multinational company?
- Why are cultural conflicts between a multinational company's home nation and the host country a most difficult type of problem for the company's managers?

Chrysler Corporation announced a joint venture with Renault in 1989 to build small recreational vehicles called "Junior Jeeps" (JJs).[1] The announcement brought joy to the people of Valladolid, Spain, where—it was announced—the manufacturing operation would be established. The prospect of jobs, increased local income, and other economic benefits was good news for the town that is about 100 miles north of Madrid. One year later, joy turned to disappointment

[1] "Chrysler-Renault Project Is Ended," *New York Times,* June 13, 1990, p. D-1.

when Chrysler and Renault announced a joint decision to terminate the JJ venture. The companies had been unable to successfully organize the business they hoped to create. For the citizens of Valladolid there would be no jobs and no improvement in their town's economic future.

Question: What responsibility do Chrysler and Renault have to the citizens of Valladolid?

The strength of the Japanese yen as an international currency has given Japanese investors an economic opportunity to purchase assets in other nations at relatively low prices. One place in which that opportunity has created a boom is Hawaii.[2] Japanese tourists have long favored the Hawaiian islands as a vacation destination. With their increased purchasing power, they have chosen to invest directly in real estate, purchasing many of Hawaii's expensive homes, hotels, and commercial properties. By the early 1990s, Japanese investors acquired commercial and residential property worth billions of dollars. Many Hawaiians were openly concerned about the effects of this ownership on Hawaii's future.

Question: What should Japanese investors do to respond to the concerns of Hawaiian citizens?

Following nearly eighteen months of negotiations, the General Motors Corporation entered an agreement with the Soviet Union to sell automobile parts to the Volga Automobile Works.[3] The agreement requires GM to supply fuel injectors, wiring, electronic controls, and catalytic converters to the Soviet Union's largest auto manufacturer for an estimated $1 billion. The agreement is scheduled for a five-year period, during which the Soviets plan to export their Lada automobiles to western Europe. The Soviets agreed to pay GM in dollars rather than rubles, the official Soviet currency. The Soviets had previously adhered to the ruble exchange rule to preserve their scarce foreign currency reserves. Because rubles cannot be easily converted to other currencies, they could only be used in the USSR. The GM agreement thereby signaled an important break with the past.

Question: Was it responsible for GM to press the Soviets to compromise on the ruble exchange rule?

These examples illustrate the complexity of international business relationships and responsibilities. Most businesses can no longer consider just one country as their entire sphere of operations. Increasingly, corporations operate and conduct business with parties in many other nations. Managers, in turn, must recognize that the policies they create and implement have an impact on all of the countries in which the company does business. In each of the incidents above, key economic, political, and social issues exist involving stakeholders, business responsibility, and corporate power. These are issues at home and abroad.

[2] Martin Tolchin, "Foreign Investors Hold $2 Trillion in U.S. in '89," *New York Times,* June 13, 1990, p. D-2.

[3] "GM and Moscow in $1 Billion Pact," *New York Times,* June 8, 1990, p. A-1.

THE MODERN CORPORATION

Today, much of the world's commerce is done through corporations. Corporations, in turn, are growing larger, with the assets of some even exceeding those of nations, as illustrated in Figure 8–1. As they become more global in their operations, many corporations recognize the importance and necessity of harmonizing global business goals with social responsibility in each nation. This view was expressed by a recent chairman of General Motors, the world's largest corporation, in Exhibit 8–A.

FIGURE 8–1
Comparison of multinational's sales and GNPs of several nations.

SOURCE: Company sales from *Fortune*, Apr. 23, 1990, and June 4, 1990; country data derived from *National Geographic*, "States in Turmoil: The Middle East," February 1991, special insert.

Company Annual Sales 1989–90 (billions)		Country Annual GNP 1989–90 (billions)	
General Motors	$126.9	Iran (pop. 55.6 mil.)	$100.1
Ford Motor	96.9	Saudi Arabia (pop. 15 mil.)	92.6
IBM	63.4	Israel (pop. 4.6 mil.)	39.7
Sears	50.2	Egypt (pop. 54.7 mil.)	35.5
AT&T	35.2	Kuwait (pop. 2.1 mil.)	28.7

EXHIBIT 8–A

THE NEED FOR A GLOBAL VIEW

"(A) major theme highlighted in this year's report concerns the importance of adopting a unitary perspective—to see the globe as a whole, an integrated human community with a common destiny. General Motors has operated around the world for most of its lifetime. Throughout, the Corporation has followed a policy of conforming with the laws and customs of the countries in which it operates.

"We will continue that policy, but we must also take account of vast changes in technology, communications, and economic interdependence. In short, General Motors is increasingly a global organization, and it must compete with a world view. This may not be a new thought, but it must become the dominant perspective for policy and action if we are to serve our customers and remain competitive.

"The need for a global view reaches beyond structural changes in the international automotive industry. Few of the major public issues now before us can be resolved within a strictly national context—not the environment, not economic stability, not drugs or AIDS, nor even the quality of life itself. All of these issues will yield only to the combined efforts of an interdependent world to realize the marvelous potential of the 21st Century."

SOURCE: Roger B. Smith, chairman, *General Motors Corporation Public Interest Report*, May 15, 1990, p. 2.

Throughout much of the world, the business corporation is the powerful engine through which economic transactions occur. In many countries, the number of corporations is quite small. But corporations account for an overwhelming amount of the wealth created in the global economy. While there may be a greater number of proprietorships and partnerships, the economic wealth created by them is only a small fraction of that created by corporations.

The legal concept of the corporation is very simple: in law, it is an "artificial legal person," with the same rights and powers given to other persons except as modified by the laws of the nation. In the United States and most industrialized nations, a corporation can own property in its name, buy and sell goods and services, employ others, pay taxes, incur legal obligations, and do everything else that is needed to run a business. Among the things a corporation cannot do are vote in elections and participate as a "citizen" in political activities except as allowed by special laws.

Responsibility is fundamental to legal existence; the United States and foreign nations have laws to establish the minimum responsibilities of corporations. If a corporation fails to meet its legal responsibilities, it can be disciplined by financial penalties and, in extreme cases, lose its right to exist.

Public and Private Roles

Every society tries to strike a balance between business's role as a generator of wealth and its role as an employer of large numbers of people, a seller of goods to customers, and a resource in the communities where it operates. This public role must be acknowledged by corporate managers and creatively linked to private, wealth-generating activities.

Two ideas guide much of the modern understanding about a corporation's private and public roles. First, it is generally accepted that a business is responsible for the consequences that flow directly from its chosen business activities. Thus, a company is accountable for the chemicals it discharges into local rivers, the quality of its products, and the safety of its operations.

A second idea that shapes corporate accountability, but which remains an unsettled issue, is the extent of legal responsibility arising from very remote effects of a corporation's activities. At some point, for example, the chemicals discharged by a local plant cannot be distinguished from chemicals discharged by dozens of other facilities. Products that have been modified by buyers for years after purchase and which cause injury may be too distant from the seller to hold it responsible, and an injury that results from an employee's own reckless action may not be the employer's fault. Some laws and court opinions hold corporations responsible for negative impacts even under these circumstances. Where that happens, business's private and public roles coalesce and its accountability is very extensive.

The Multinational Corporation

In practice, business managers try to reconcile and integrate private, profit-seeking activities with public responsibilities. Nowhere is the reconciliation of private and public purposes more important, or more at issue, than with the **multinational corporation** (MNC). The MNC functions in more than one or two countries, establishes ownership of affiliate or subsidiary firms in each nation, and controls those firms through the design of a common strategy. In practice, this means that a group of managers in one country can make decisions that affect thousands, perhaps millions, of people in dozens of countries around the world. Understandably, people in those countries are anxious to know that their interests are being helped, not harmed, by those decisions. That is why governments often play an especially active role in negotiating terms of entry for MNCs and establishing rules of conduct to guide their behavior in the foreign nation.

THE INTERNATIONAL IMPERATIVE

Nearly all large businesses in the United States, Europe, and Japan are involved in international business. Many own subsidiary businesses in foreign nations and have other forms of direct investment in other countries. Most have various types of business relations with foreign companies, and nearly all employ foreign citizens. In some instances, the number of foreign employees may actually exceed those from the company's home nation.

Many factors lead companies to become involved in international business. Companies seek to acquire natural resources not available elsewhere or at lower cost; to expand revenues and profits by selling products and services to foreign customers; to acquire technology that improves business activities; to take advantage of special tax laws that are financially beneficial; or to develop relationships with people and governments whose presence can be valuable to the company. For some companies, all of these reasons apply.

Only a few decades ago, the opportunities for global business were limited. International communications systems were much slower; travel and shipping took longer and were more expensive. Today, people can get to virtually any place on the globe in a day or less, and international communication is almost instantaneous. It is possible to manage and control operations in many countries simultaneously, and it can be done effectively and profitably. Resources are sometimes more plentiful and less costly in other countries; labor may be cheaper; taxes may be lower. In some cases, it is beneficial because the weather is better.

In the 1990s, new factors are encouraging the internationalization of business. Old barriers are disappearing. Western Europe's democratic nations agreed to move ahead with an important program of more than 200 steps to promote economic integration by 1992. Social and political reforms in the communist nations of eastern Europe opened those nations and millions of customers to market transactions and international business. Forty-five years after Germany was divided into East and West at the end of World War II, reunification became a political and economic reality. A great wave of change also occurred in the Pacific Rim during the 1980s. The rise of Japan as a leading economic power was coupled with the increasing economic importance of Asian nations such as

Taiwan, South Korea, Malaysia, Indonesia, and Thailand. China, the world's most heavily populated nation, held great economic promise because of its size and need to modernize.

Doing Business in International Settings

Expansion beyond national boundaries is much more than a step across a geographical line. It is also a step into different social, educational, political, and cultural settings. Even businesses operating in only one country cannot operate successfully without taking into consideration a wide variety of stakeholder needs and interests. This view has not always prevailed. At one time companies that operated internationally reflected an **ethnocentric perspective.** This perspective views the home nation as the major source of the company's capital, markets, and managerial talent. The home country's laws are the foundation of security and justice, and the company is an emissary or representative of the home country's culture. Such a company is ethnocentric in the sense that its standards are based on the home country's customs, markets, and laws. It assumes that practices that are successful in the home nation will be equally successful in other countries and that managers should be supplied by the home nation, while the host nation supplies nonmanagerial workers.

Today's international businesses have found they must consider the world, not just one nation, as their "home." Companies which have a **geocentric view** adapt their practices to different national cultures and environments while continuing to maintain worldwide identity and policies. They develop managers at all levels from a worldwide pool of talent and seek to use the best people for all jobs regardless of their country of origin. Placing host-country nationals on a company's board of directors is one example of a geocentric approach. European companies have outpaced other multinational businesses in globalizing their boards. Forbo, Asea Brown Boveri, and Nestle, for example, have had directors from America, Britain, Sweden, Germany, Switzerland, Holland, and Luxembourg.[4]

Ideas, technology, people, and economic resources can all be moved around the world through the multinational business firm. As managers participate in this flow, they usually become more geocentric in their outlook and perspective. It is not farfetched for today's students to imagine themselves being Americans working for a European corporation negotiating an agreement with a Japanese company to distribute products to a developing nation in Africa. That is a reality that many managers are experiencing today.[5]

Small and medium-sized companies also are involved in international business dealings. This may take many forms, including export or import activity, support for international trade (e.g., freight forwarders, customs brokers), or professional

[4] "Coping with Foreigners," *The Economist*, Mar. 26, 1988, p. 61.

[5] Robert B. Reich, "Who Is Us?" *Harvard Business Review*, January–February, 1990, pp. 53–64; Michael C. Jensen, "The Eclipse of the Public Corporation," *Harvard Business Review*, September–October 1989, pp. 61–74; Amanda Bennett, "The Chief Executives in Year 2000 Will Be Experienced Abroad," *Wall Street Journal*, Feb. 27, 1989, pp. 1, 7.

FIGURE 8–2
Examples of international business activity.

SOURCE: Adapted from Robert Grosse and Duane Kujawa, *International Business: Theory and Managerial Applications,* Homewood, IL: Richard D. Irwin, Inc., 1988, p. 6.

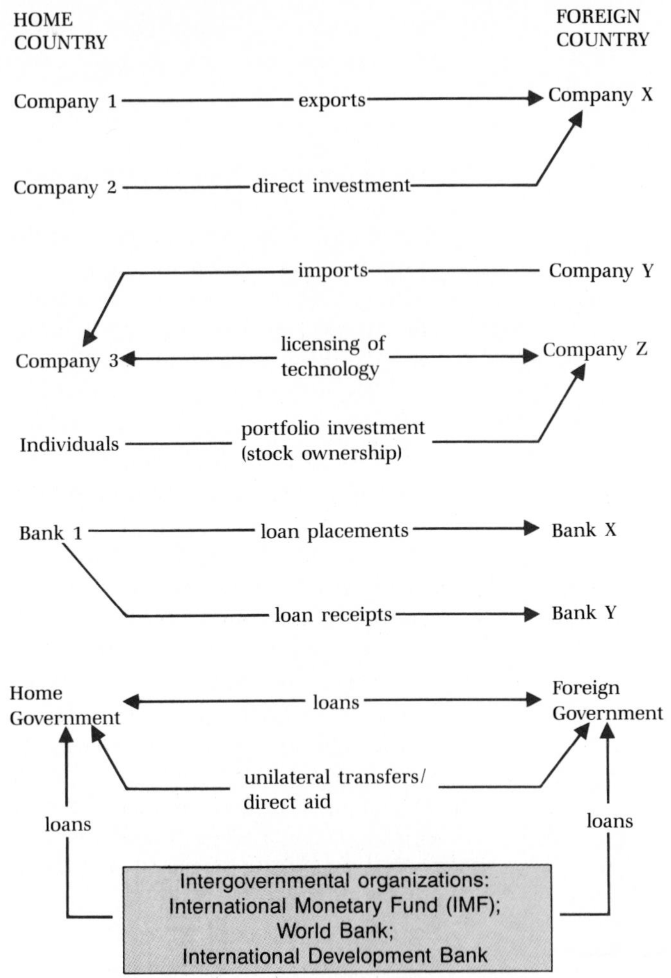

services such as accounting, banking, or legal counsel. Many small and medium-sized businesses also are involved in overseas plant investment and licensing arrangements with foreign firms.[6]

International business activity is carried on in many different ways and forms. Figure 8–2 illustrates a few of the more common examples of such transactions. It is important to recognize that both companies and governments are actors in these arrangements. In many nations, the government itself is a direct participant in the business activity being conducted. State-owned enterprises are a form of government-owned business in which the activities of the organization are guided by government policies and directives. In countries such as Brazil, state-owned

[6] Robert Grosse and Duane Kujawa, *International Business: Theory and Managerial Applications,* Homewood, IL: Richard D. Irwin, Inc., 1988, p. 6.

enterprises in industries such as steel and aircraft manufacturing have been an important part of the nation's modern economic history.

National Sovereignty and Business Legitimacy

Two principles shape the relationship between multinational businesses and foreign governments. The first is the **principle of national sovereignty.** This principle holds that a nation is a sovereign state whose laws, customs, and regulations must be respected. It means that the government of any nation has the power to create laws, rules, and regulations regarding the conduct of business within its borders. The second is the **principle of business legitimacy.** This principle holds that a company's behavior is legitimate if it complies with the laws of a nation and is in conformance with the expectations of the affected stakeholders. In theory, the principles of national sovereignty and business legitimacy are not in conflict. In practice, however, there are times when conflicts occur.

> For example, the government of India has had a long and difficult struggle with foreign corporations such as Coca-Cola to establish terms that the country and the company could live with. In 1977, Coca-Cola was forced to leave India for refusing to disclose the secret of its concentrate formula. It was not until 1989 that Coca-Cola successfully negotiated reentry into India by setting up a bottling plant in an export processing zone (free trade zone). The plant would ship about 75 percent of its production outside India, the rest to the domestic market. This arrangement will help India's foreign trade balance.[7]

Multinational companies and foreign governments each worry about the other in two areas: ownership and control. A foreign government may believe that the multinational firm must agree to some degree of local ownership in the business to be conducted in that nation. The company may argue that local ownership is inappropriate because no local investment is being made or for other reasons. Often, there is the fear that ownership will lead to influence and control of the operations of the local business. Host governments often have concerns about controlling the activities of multinational companies. A web of laws, regulations, and restrictions may be created to place limitations on the MNC's behavior in areas such as employment practices, safety standards, and movement of funds in and out of the nation.

MULTINATIONAL CORPORATE POWER

The multinational enterprise is the single most important actor in international business. National governments and other non-multinational firms that partici-

[7] Sanjoy Hazarika, "Effort by Coke Challenged in India," *New York Times*, Feb. 6, 1989, p. D-10.

FIGURE 8–3
The multinational corporation spans home and host countries.

SOURCE: Adapted from Robert Grosse and Duane Kujawa, *International Business Theory and Managerial Applications*, Homewood, IL: Richard D. Irwin, Inc., 1988, p. 23.

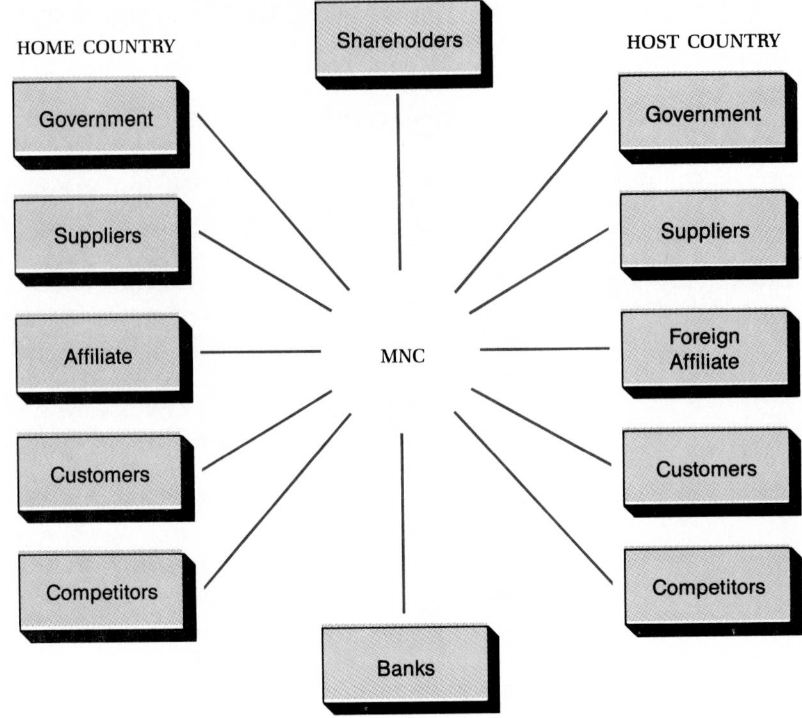

pate in international business also are significant. But the MNC dominates by virtue of the size and scope of its international transactions, the frequency of those transactions, and other measures of international business, including the visibility of its activities in the public eye.[8]

As illustrated in Figure 8–3, the MNC has stakeholders in home and host countries and organizes a web of international transactions involving money, goods, and information. Through transactions with internal and external stakeholders, multinational firms export and import products; they move funds internally through loans, payments for technology, overhead, and so on; they borrow from and lend funds to unrelated parties; they exchange ownership of assets across national borders; and they pass huge volumes of information internationally among affiliate companies and others. These are the sources of power.

The essence of multinational enterprises is that they are made up of affiliated firms in different countries that share several distinguishing characteristics:[9]

[8] Grosse and Kujawa, op. cit., p. 24.

[9] This definition is provided by R. Vernon and L. Wells, *Manager in the International Economy*, 4th ed., Englewood Cliffs, NJ: Prentice-Hall, 1981, p. 4. An up-to-date discussion is found in Christopher Bartlett and Sumantra Ghoshal, *Managing across Borders: The Transnational Solution*, Cambridge, MA: Harvard Business School Press, 1989.

- They are linked by ties of common ownership.
- They draw on a common pool of resources, such as money and credit, information systems, trade names, and patents.
- They respond to some common strategy.

Multinational businesses may be privately or governmentally owned and may vary in size. Their use of resources and their common strategy across boundaries make them powerful and different from one-nation businesses.

Foreign Direct Investment

Foreign direct investment (FDI) involves the ownership of a company in a foreign country, with the investor usually transferring some of its financial, managerial, technological, or other resources to the foreign country. The ability to utilize more than one country as the firm's market or production site creates the competitive advantage peculiar to multinational firms. Companies such as Du Pont, Gillette, Dow Chemical, and Toyota have dozens of direct investments in foreign nations as they have created global businesses in industrial and consumer products.[10] Natural resource companies in the petroleum, natural gas, forest products, and minerals industries have long had foreign direct investments. As illustrated in Figure 8–4, manufacturing has been a fast-growing sector for FDI since the 1950s. But new areas are emerging: Disney spent billions of dollars of foreign direct investment in building recreational theme parks in Japan and France in the 1980s and 1990s. In each instance, the company involved sought to create a competitive advantage for itself through the acquisition and control of a foreign business.

Foreign direct investment has social consequences that may concern a host country's government and other stakeholders. Foreign control of assets may raise local concerns. As described at the beginning of this chapter, one of the fears of residents in Hawaii is that Japanese ownership and control of assets will have a negative effect on them. Concerns about foreign ownership in the United States are similar in many ways to concerns expressed by other nations when American investors bought businesses overseas in the past.

The Stateless Corporation

As companies continuously reshape themselves to compete in the global business environment, a new phenomenon is emerging: Companies that appear capable of acting apart from any single nation, including their home country. **Stateless corporations** are truly citizens of the world; their facilities, ownership, and customers are everywhere. Therefore, they seem to owe loyalty to no single nation and are able to organize and reorganize in dozens of countries around the globe.[11]

[10] Grosse and Kujawa, op. cit., pp. 89–90.

[11] "The Stateless Corporation," *Business Week*, May 14, 1990, pp. 98–106.

FIGURE 8–4
Patterns of direct investment.

SOURCE: Various issues of *Survey of Current Business*. See also N. J. Glickman and D. P. Woodward, *The New Competitors: How Foreign Investors Are Changing the U.S. Economy*, New York: Basic Books, 1989.

U.S.-BASED FIRMS' DIRECT INVESTMENT IN FOREIGN COUNTRIES AND FOREIGN-BASED FIRMS' DIRECT INVESTMENT IN THE UNITED STATES (based on Year-end Book Values in Billions of U.S. dollars)

	1950	1960	1970	1980	1985	1989
U.S.-based firms in foreign countries						
Total	11.8	31.8	75.5	213.5	251.7	358.6 (+9.7% from 1988)
Manufacturing	3.8	11.0	31.0	89.0	87.1	n/a
Petroleum	3.4	10.8	19.8	47.0	55.0	n/a
Other	4.6	10.0	24.7	77.5	109.6	n/a
Foreign-based firms in the United States						
Total	n/a	6.9	13.3	65.5	182.9	214.6 (+22% from 1988)
Manufacturing	n/a	2.6	6.1	24.1	60.8	n/a
Petroleum	n/a	1.2	3.0	12.3	28.1	n/a
Other	n/a	3.1	4.2	29.1	94.0	n/a

There are important economic and political advantages to companies for being, or appearing to be, "stateless."

> For example, when countries impose trade bans on products from another country, a company may be able to continue its business if it operates through a subsidiary that is incorporated in a nation that is not being banned. Taiwan and South Korea have banned Japanese cars as part of their trade policy. But because Honda Motor Co. has U.S. operations in Marysville, Ohio, it has been able to circumvent the restrictions by shipping Honda Accord sedans from the United States to Taiwan and South Korea. For the purpose of such trade, Honda is a U.S. corporation.

Statelessness may allow a company's management to avoid various political problems, regulatory hurdles, and powerful labor unions. But statelessness does not eliminate corporate responsibilities. As the chief executive officer of SmithKline Beecham, a pharmaceutical company, notes in Exhibit 8–B, a company's management must always recognize its obligations to its stakeholders wherever it does business.

EXHIBIT 8–B

STATELESS IS JUST A STATE OF MIND

"The rapid flow of technology and the means of production around the globe and the clear trend for many companies to gear their strategies and management attitudes to the global market all point to the emergence of new global enterprises. Indeed, our company, SmithKline Beecham, is a prototype of the company you describe.

"But I object to the term stateless in describing companies such as ours. The dictionary describes stateless as meaning "without political community." The new global companies—I prefer the term transnational companies—are not "untethered from their home countries." The essence of the concept, and increasingly the practice, is to be "tethered" in more than one country. If tethered means fully accountable to national laws and security regulations, then SmithKline Beecham, with nearly equal share ownership in Britain and the U.S., is certainly tethered in both countries.

"With respect to "multiple identities," most of the companies you mention—Electrolux, Colgate-Palmolive, Honda, IBM, etc.—work very hard to establish one strong global identity. In fact, most of them work hard to establish a single identity worldwide for major products or brands, from mainframe computers to toothpastes.

"As our corporations become globalized, we assume more responsibility, not less. In the process, we help to define the world market and become a major force for global interdependence, wealth creation, and higher and increasingly common standards for the quality of life."

SOURCE: Harry Wendt, Chairman, SmithKline Beecham, Philadelphia, "Letters to the Editor," *Business Week*, July 9, 1990, p. 8.

THE CHALLENGES OF DOING BUSINESS ABROAD

Business and society are challenged by multinational business in three distinct areas: political, economic, and sociocultural. In each of these areas, the multinational corporation, the host nation, and the company's home country have a stake in harmonizing one another's goals and objectives.

Political Challenges

International business is affected by political and governmental factors on two levels. First, in the broadest sense, business operates in an environment shaped by the relations between governments, which may range from friendly to hostile. Second, even in an atmosphere of normal relations between governments, companies must recognize their host governments to be powerful political forces.

Intergovernmental relations

The relations between governments have a great impact on international business. If two countries are at war, for example, there will be no trade between them.

But even in the absence of major hostilities, the shape of international transactions may be influenced by political relations of the home and host country governments.

Consider trade relations between the United States and two leading world powers: China and the Soviet Union. After years of isolation, diplomatic relations were reestablished between the United States and China in the 1970s. China's planned economy did permit some market transactions, and two-way (bilateral) trade between the United States and China topped $6 billion by the mid-1980s. The improvement in economic relations seemed to benefit both nations. When the student-led uprising in 1989 was crushed by Chinese leaders, however, trade relations cooled as U.S. anger created political pressure to impose sanctions. Gradually, this pressure subsided, but by the early 1990s only a cautious resumption had occurred.

Trade between the United States and the Soviet Union also changed greatly between the 1970s and 1980s. A political accord in the early 1970s led to growth in U.S. exports, especially grain. In response to the Soviet invasion of Afghanistan, however, a grain embargo was imposed by President Carter. Exports dropped, and by 1984, for example, exports of machinery and transportation equipment were only one-sixth of their 1976 levels. When the political relationship between President Reagan and Soviet leader Mikhail Gorbachev warmed in the 1980s, trade opportunities once again expanded. Companies such as General Motors (mentioned at the beginning of this chapter) were encouraged to do business with the Soviets, and in the early 1990s, the United States even permitted export of high technology to Eastern Bloc nations.[12]

The shifts in U.S. relations with China and the Soviet Union illustrate the manner in which economic relations are affected, for better or worse, by political change. Export-oriented industries such as agriculture and high-technology equipment are especially vulnerable to the consequences of intergovernmental relations. As global markets for all types of products have developed, business has become a partner with government in achieving political and economic goals. When the United States reestablished economic relations with Nicaragua in 1990, for example, not only did the United States remove economic sanctions previously in force, but it also pledged $500 million to assist in restoring a stagnant economy. Much of that was in the form of credits to buy products and services from U.S. companies.[13]

Host government influence

When a multinational firm enters another nation, it is usually subject to a variety of ownership regulations, controls, licenses, and foreign exchange rules imposed

[12] Jia Shi, "Future Prospects for Broadening U.S.–China Economic and Trade Cooperation," *Columbia Journal of World Business*, Twentieth Anniversary Issue 1966–1986, Fall 1986, p. 57; Marshal I. Goldman, "U.S.–Soviet Trade: What Went Wrong and What about the Future?" *Columbia Journal of World Business*, Twentieth Anniversary Issue 1966–1986, Fall 1986, pp. 45–48; Alan Riding, "U.S. to Relax Standards on High Tech Exports," *New York Times*, June 8, 1990, p. D6.

[13] Bill Keeler, "Joint Ventures, Russian Style," *New York Times*, Jan. 6, 1987, pp. D1, D6.

by the government. This web of bureaucratic restrictions can be complicated a[illegible] burdensome for business and counterproductive for the nation.

For example, King Hassan II of Morocco announced on September 14, 1989, that foreign investors, if not hearing within two months of their investment proposal, could consider their project automatically approved for that country. Foreign investments in Morocco are subject to a pre-Investment Code to ensure that Moroccan values and objectives are met. The Investment Code, cited by the king as a slow and uncommunicative but important process, actually deterred foreign investment in Morocco. This process was counterproductive to the national goal of economic development. In effect, the king attempted to reduce this bureaucratic process which was impeding the economic growth of Morocco.[14]

The host government may use a variety of sanctions and incentives ("sticks and carrots") to shape and regulate foreign investment, attempting simultaneously to lure investors and prevent excessive manipulation by these investors.[15] A host country can derive many benefits from foreign investors, such as technology transfer and training, increased employment, and increased local productivity. On the other hand, because of the potential power of the multinational, many host governments fear that their sovereignty may be in jeopardy. For example, U.S. law forbids foreign corporations from owning more than 25 percent of any U.S. airline. That was a factor when British Air sought to acquire United Airlines in 1989, as illustrated in Chapter 6's discussion case.

In the most serious cases, a host country might exert power of a possessive nature on multinationals. In some nations, the government may insist on being partial owner of a foreign business, especially a basic industry. In situations of sudden social upheaval or changes in government control, a country may nationalize, or expropriate, the assets of a company or plant. That is, the government will take ownership and control of the property and may or may not pay for what it takes. This can be very costly to the multinational. There are several extreme examples, such as Cuba's nationalization of $1.5 billion of assets in 1960 and Iraq's seizure of all Kuwaiti assets in 1990. Still, the overall level of expropriation has remained below 5 percent of total foreign-owned assets.[16]

When nationalization does occur, an equal or greater loser sometimes is the expropriating nation itself. It can only nationalize property. It cannot nationalize managerial skills, technical know-how, international markets, and the many benefits that multinational business offers a nation.[17]

[14] "Royal Decision in Favour of Foreign Investors," *Wall Street Journal,* Sept. 14, 1989, p. A-2.

[15] William A. Stoever, "The Stages of Developing Country Policy toward Foreign Investment," *Columbia Journal of World Business,* Fall 1985, p. 3.

[16] Dennis Encarnation and Sushil Vachani, "Foreign Ownership: When Hosts Change the Rules," *Harvard Business Review,* September–October 1985, pp. 152–160.

[17] John Paul Newport, Jr., "Risky Business," *Fortune,* Aug. 5, 1985, p. 71; see also J. Daniels et al., "U.S. Joint Ventures in China: Motivation and Management of Political Risk," *California Management Review,* Summer 1985, pp. 46–58.

Economic Challenges

Economic issues such as high interest rates, capital shortages, and restrictions on repatriation of profits affect business. Moreover, nations make public policy choices that make them more attractive to companies in the world economy.[18] Four factors—MNC power, inflation, trade, and debt—are central long-term problems of the international environment. They greatly affect economic and social policy in every nation.

MNC power

Multinational companies have the power to employ, or not employ, hundreds of local people. They can support or compete with local businesses, buying their products or blocking them out of the market. They can strengthen or weaken the nation's economy. They can enhance the socioeconomic infrastructure by supporting schools, hospitals, and housing, or they can restrict uses of all of their resources to their own operations.

At times, companies have a negative impact on their host nations. In some cases, a multinational has built a plant, drawn farmers from the countryside, and thus disrupted the social structure of the people. Then when the plant is closed because of political unrest in the country, a change in the company's strategy, or for some other reason, the people are let go, and they have no means to support themselves.

Inflation

From the 1960s to the 1980s, inflation was the single most critical issue facing the world's economies. A high level of inflation creates so much instability and social unrest that it restricts business's capacity to operate successfully and a society's ability to function. In some countries, the value of local money has been cut to one-hundredth or even one-thousandth of its value.[19] What formerly cost one unit of currency now costs 1,000 or more: in other words, an ice cream cone that originally cost 20 cents would now cost 20,000 cents, or $200!

Since inflation weakens confidence in money, it often causes capital to flee from the inflated country to one with a more stable currency. The development of global currency markets keeps national currencies closely related to investor assessments of each economy. Investor knowledge thus may increase capital shortages and further limit business and national development. Hyperinflation, black markets, food shortages, and eventually, sociopolitical unrest can follow in a spiral of social and economic illness.[20]

Trade

Another economic challenge for nations and business is the balance of trade. The country that imports much more than it exports may be in a weaker financial

[18] Michael Porter, *The Competitive Advantage of Nations,* New York: Basic Books, 1990.

[19] "Hyperinflation, Taming the Beast," *The Economist,* Nov. 15, 1986, p. 55; see also Alan Riding, "Brazilian Debt Crisis Flames Again," *New York Times,* Feb. 16, 1987, pp. 43, 48; Thomas Kamm, "Daily Inflation Struggle Obsesses Brazil," *Wall Street Journal,* Jan. 29, 1990, p. A10.

[20] James Austin, *Doing Business in Developing Countries,* New York: Free Press, 1990.

FIGURE 8–5
Top U.S. trade partners in 1988 (billions of U.S. dollars).

SOURCE: *Survey of Current Business,* various issues, 1988–1989.

	Total Trade	Exports to	Imports from	U.S. Net
Canada	$151.8	70.9	80.9	(−10.0)
Japan	127.5	37.7	89.8	(−52.1)
Mexico	43.9	20.6	23.3	(−2.7)
West Germany	40.8	14.3	26.5	(−12.2)
Taiwan	36.9	12.1	24.8	(−12.7)
Britain	36.4	18.4	18.0	(+0.4)

position than a country that exports much more than it imports. Figure 8–5 illustrates U.S. balances with its leading trade partners. Economic development tends to be unevenly distributed around the world. Many third world countries still struggle with enormous debts caused by trade deficits. For example, nations such as Mexico, which depended heavily on oil revenues, suffered greatly when oil prices dropped from $30 per barrel to less than $15 per barrel in the late 1980s. A nation's ability to address such social needs as health care, education, and social services is directly affected by trade balances.

Debt

A fourth problem affecting international business operations is international debt. During the 1980s, third world debt exceeded $1 trillion, and many of the countries with severe inflation problems (Argentina, Brazil, Mexico, and Israel) were also some of the heaviest borrowers. To meet their debt payments, major cutbacks were required in other areas of public spending. To alleviate some of these economic problems, lenders from Japan, Europe, and the United States created arrangements that permitted a debtor nation to pay the interest due on the loan but postpone the principal payment to a later date. By the late 1980s, United States foreign indebtedness—the difference between all known foreign holdings of equity and debt in the United States and similar U.S. investments abroad—exceeded $200 billion. Japan, with very large surpluses, replaced the United States as the "world banker" by lending billions to debtor nations, including the United States.

Social and Cultural Factors

The social and cultural differences among nations present formidable challenges for the multinational firm, its managers, and their families. Differences in language, physical surroundings, and values of the population can create important business and human conflicts. Business has discovered that social and cultural differences may pose difficult problems in its relations with the host country and in establishing a productive and capable workforce in its foreign affiliates.

EXHIBIT 8–C

KIKKOMAN'S SEARCH FOR HARMONY

Multinational companies make an effort to respect a host country's culture and social systems. For example, Kikkoman Corporation, headquartered in Tokyo, Japan, has developed a credo or statement of principles for all of its operations in foreign countries, including the United States. "In order to create a friendlier world," says Yuzaburo Mogi, the company's managing director, "I believe we need many types of cultural exchanges. Kikkoman believes that soy sauce marketing is the promotion of the international exchange of food culture." Kikkoman has developed a policy for maintaining "harmony" with society and the local community. According to Mogi, "It is needless to say that a foreign concern should try to prosper *together* with society and the local community in order to promote the success of the entire operation."

Kikkoman tries to carry out the following commitments in its Wisconsin plant: They are committed to employing as many local people as possible; they try to participate in local activities and events, and contribute to society through their business activities; they try to avoid the "Japanese village" stereotype by advising their Japanese employees to spread themselves among the community rather than living in ethnic groups; they try to do business with many local companies, rather than with Japanese companies; and they delegate most authority to local management and try to avoid a "remote-control situation with letters or telephone calls from Japan."

SOURCE: Yuzaburo Mogi, "The Conduct of International Business: One Company's Credo—Kikkoman Soy Sauce and the U.S. Market," *Columbia Journal of World Business,* Twentieth Anniversary Issue, 1966–1986, Fall 1986, p. 94.

Host country environment

The widespread variation in culture among people and nations makes each operating situation unique. There are important variations in social understandings of such concepts as human rights, equal employment opportunities for women, and corporate giving. The amount of difference between two social systems is called **cultural distance,** and in many situations it may be substantial. Extensive cultural distance can make it difficult for employees and their families to adapt to foreign job assignments. One leading researcher noted that in several studies on expatriate assignments (assignments outside one's home country) the incidences of expatriate failure of United States multinationals are sometimes as high as 30 to 40 percent.[21] Some companies, such as Kikkoman (see Exhibit 8–C), go to great lengths to encourage harmonious relations.

When a business establishes a major operation abroad, it may find that support facilities such as schools, hospitals, roads, and public utilities either are not available or are in such short supply that efficient operation of business is prevented. Essentially, the economic and social infrastructure is inadequate for the

[21] Rosalie L. Tung, "Corporate Executives and Their Families in China: The Need for Cross-Cultural Understanding in Business," *Columbia Journal of World Business,* Spring 1986, pp. 21–25. Thomas O'Boyle, "Little Benefit for Careers Seen in Foreign Stints," *Wall Street Journal,* Dec. 12, 1989, p. B1.

new operation. The whole system must be upgraded, and this results in substantial social overhead costs as well as additional start-up time.

An example is Marcona Mining Company, which opened a new iron ore mine in Peru on the western edge of the Andes Mountains. In this desolate area (the nearest major city was eight hours by road), it was necessary for the company to build a completely new city for its workers and support personnel. The company built streets, houses, schools, stores, and utilities. It was necessary to build a hospital, employ physicians and nurses, and bring water to this desert region.

Cultural conflicts

Adherence to a host country's cultural norms may be complicated by the multinational's home country values. The public in the home nation will be watching the company's actions abroad; if it finds some policy or method of operation unacceptable, it will pressure the company to change.

The classic example in recent decades concerned the situation in South Africa. The South African government had enforced for decades a system of apartheid, under which black people were segregated in the workplace and in everyday life from the white population. Finding this system abhorrent, church and human rights groups, as well as government officials and private citizens, exerted pressure on businesses with South African operations to challenge apartheid or cease doing business in South Africa. In 1986, the United States Congress enacted economic sanctions against South Africa that further pressured many major companies to close their South African operations.

In the case of South Africa, a nearly worldwide consensus was reached that condemned the system of apartheid. Many situations are less clear. The Arab-Israel conflict, for example, demonstrates how U.S. multinational firms are confronted with opposing host and home nation values and laws.

In 1987, NCR Corporation, a U.S. computer manufacturer, was fined $381,000 for allegedly cooperating with an Arab boycott against Israel. According to the U.S. Commerce Department, nine NCR subsidiaries disclosed information to several Arab League nations on their ties to Israeli companies. This information could have been used by the Arab League to discriminate against companies that have business relations with Israel. U.S. law prohibits the disclosure of such information on the grounds that firms doing business with Israel may be disadvantaged. While NCR paid the largest civil fine ever imposed for this violation at that time, it was not the first company to be charged with this infraction. Companies including Citibank, a unit of the New York–based Citicorp, and Safeway Stores, a food retailer, have been investigated and fined for their alleged boycott participation.[22]

[22] "Agency Fines NCR $381,000 over Law on Arab Boycott," *Wall Street Journal,* Aug. 26, 1987, p. B-18.

Conflicts between the home and host nations in the multinational business environment arise for many reasons. In extreme cases, these conflicts may lead to government trade embargoes, harassment of business, bombing of business properties, kidnapping of managers, and protests by partisan groups. Value conflicts can be the most difficult to manage due to the emotional intensity that surrounds them.

One of the thorniest problems for U.S. multinational firms, for example, has involved payments to customs inspectors, government officials, and other agents in international trade. The issue arises primarily because of differences in customs, ethics, and laws among the nations of the world. **Questionable payments** by business are those that raise significant ethical questions of right and wrong in the host or home nation. Some people condemn all questionable payments as bribes, but real situations are not simple. Managers of the foreign subsidiary may find themselves forced to choose between the host country's laws or customs and the policies of corporate headquarters.

The Foreign Corrupt Practices Act regulates questionable payments of all United States firms *operating in other nations.* It was passed in 1977 in response to disclosure of a number of questionable foreign payments by United States corporations. The law has the following major provisions:

- It is a criminal offense for a firm to make payments to a foreign government official, political party, party official, or candidate for political office to secure or retain business in another nation.
- Sales commissions to independent agents are illegal if the business has knowledge that any part of the commission is being passed to foreign officials.
- Government employees "whose duties are essentially ministerial or clerical" are excluded, so expediting payments to persons such as customs agents and bureaucrats are permitted.
- Payments made in situations of genuine extortion are permitted.
- In addition to the antibribery provisions that apply to all businesses, all publicly held corporations that are subject to the Securities Exchange Act of 1934 are required to establish internal accounting controls to assure that all payments abroad are authorized and properly recorded.

It can be seen that the basic purposes of the law are (1) to establish a worldwide code of conduct for any kind of payment by United States businesses to foreign government officials, political parties, and political candidates, and (2) to require appropriate accounting controls for full disclosure of the firm's transactions. The United States law applies even if a payment is legal in the nation where it is made. The idea is to assure that United States businesses meet United States standards wherever they operate.

CONCLUSION

The fundamental challenge to multinational corporations is similar to that faced by domestic companies: to manage their affairs in ways that meet society's social and economic goals. In meeting this challenge, businesses need a strategy that is responsive to society's expectations, or they risk losing their power and influence to other forces and institutions. Building such a strategy requires managers to recognize and respond to new realities of international business.

SUMMARY POINTS OF THIS CHAPTER

- Modern companies need to think and act globally in conducting their business activities. The ability of the multinational corporation to operate globally has made it the most powerful actor in international commerce.
- The corporation has both private and public roles. Its private role is to generate wealth through economic success. Its public role includes meeting the legitimate expectations of its stakeholders in each country where it does business.
- Nations of the world want to develop their economies and make more productive use of their human and natural resources. The multinational corporation is a means through which this development can occur. National sovereignty guarantees each society the right to determine how it will pursue its own objectives. Business legitimacy requires a company to act in conformance with national laws, customs, and expectations.
- Some business leaders believe that a corporation that is not identified with the home country in which it was created and headquartered is better able to avoid political and economic conflicts among governments. The "stateless corporation" is becoming a new reality in international business activity.
- Multinational business can affect a nation's economic prosperity, its position in international trade, and its overall financial health. It can also influence a nation's culture, social norms, and values. The host nation environment creates the economic, social, political, and cultural context in which a company's activities must be conducted. These conditions directly affect business activity.
- A host nation's culture and social customs affect the manner in which a company and its managers will behave. Social norms in a host nation may conflict with those in a company's home country, thereby creating conflict. The making of questionable payments to officials in some host nations exemplifies this type of cultural conflict.

KEY TERMS AND CONCEPTS USED IN THIS CHAPTER

- Multinational corporation (MNC)
- Foreign direct investment
- Geocentric and ethnocentric perspectives
- National sovereignty principle
- Business legitimacy principle
- Stateless corporation
- Cultural distance
- Questionable payments

DISCUSSION CASE

MITSUBISHI AND ROCKEFELLER CENTER

On October 30, 1989, the Mitsubishi Estate Company purchased a controlling interest in Rockefeller Center, one of America's most famous landmarks. A world-renowned business address, Rockefeller Center has been home to such companies as NBC, Time-Warner, General Electric, McGraw-Hill, and Price Waterhouse. To many, this purchase appeared to be another case of Japanese investors gobbling up American jewels. Only one month earlier, SONY Corporation, the Japanese electronics giant, had purchased Columbia Productions, a major movie company.

Mitsubishi paid $846 million for a 51 percent interest in the Rockefeller Group, which also owns Radio City Music Hall and a number of other mid-Manhattan office buildings. According to Richard Voell, president and chief executive officer of the Rockefeller Group, the transaction was a way of enhancing the financial strength of the Rockefeller Group and guaranteeing the group's ability to continue its management of existing properties and diversify into some new areas of interest.

Both sides reaffirmed the commitment of the new partnership to maintaining Rockefeller Center as a modern and prestigious commercial complex that would add to the character of New York City. David Rockefeller, grandson of John D. Rockefeller, Jr., who in 1934 initiated the Rockefeller Center development, said that the arrangement with Mitsubishi "preserves the abiding commitment to Rockefeller Center and New York City" that was evident in his grandfather's action decades before.

Mitsubishi is one of Japan's largest real estate companies and one of the wealthiest investment institutions in the world. Aging properties at home, combined with a need to remain competitive in the global real estate business, led Mitsubishi to look for various opportunities to acquire property outside Japan. Beyond the prestige of owning Rockefeller Center, Mitsubishi's partnership with the Rockefeller Group could lead to other developments in the United States. At a news conference, Jotaro Tagaki, president of Mitsubishi, stressed that "We are participating in the (entire) future of the Rockefeller Group."

Initially, Mitsubishi had planned to acquire 80 percent of the Rockefeller Group. In an attempt to mute public reaction, however, it bought only 51 percent. Many Americans were wary of seeing well-known United States assets purchased by wealthy Japanese interests. (In one 1989 survey by the U.S. Commerce Department, Japan had the largest direct foreign investment in the United States. Japanese investments were being courted by U.S. states, cities, and towns attracted by the potential economic benefits from increased employment, development, and taxation.) Japanese officials and business executives were surprised by the negative publicity surrounding Sony's $3.4 billion deal for Columbia Pictures; several commentators indicated American reaction was equivalent to racism toward the Japanese. Earlier in 1989, an official at one of Mitsubishi's Japanese rival real estate firms was asked not to bid on the Sears Tower in Chicago because of growing American sensitivity to Japanese holdings. The cover of an issue of *Fortune* that appeared shortly after the Mitsubishi deal was announced was entitled, "Fear and Loathing of Japan."[23]

As a result, the Japanese government has informally cautioned its business leaders against purchasing conspicuous properties in the United States. A further step by Japanese business leaders is the creation of a Committee on Public Affairs at Keidanren, the largest Japanese business association. The committee urged Japanese companies investing in the United States to take steps to become a "good corporate citizen." These should include corporate contributions to philanthropic groups and working with local governments to ease public concerns.[24]

Discussion Questions

1. What economic, political, and cultural issues do Mitsubishi's actions raise?
2. What actions would you suggest that Mitsubishi's leaders take to reassure Rockefeller Center tenants and employees? What actions should the Rockefeller Group take to respond to criticism of their decision to sell to Japanese interests?
3. Several months after the Mitsubishi acquisition, a Swiss pharmaceutical firm, Roche Holding, Ltd., acquired Genentech Inc., the leading U.S. biotechnology firm. What similarities and differences do you see in the two situations? Is either one a long-term threat to U.S. interests? Why?

[23] Lee Smith, "Fear and Loathing of Japan," *Fortune,* Feb. 26, 1990, pp. 50–60.

[24] Robert J. Cole, "Control of Rockefeller Center Is Sold to Japanese Company," *New York Times,* Oct. 31, 1989, pp. A-1, D-6; James Sterngold, "Mitsubishi's U.S. Deal Surprises Many in Japan," *New York Times,* Nov. 11, 1989, p. D-1; Steven R. Weisman, "Japanese Are Concerned about Rockefeller Deal," *New York Times,* Nov. 11, 1989.

PART THREE

The Corporation and Public Policy

9

Public Policy and the Political Environment

Business decision making and political decision making are closely connected. Business decisions affect politics; political decisions affect business. Government actions shape the business environment in important ways and are the expression of a nation's public policies. Managers must understand how public issues emerge, the dynamics of the public policy process, and ethical and strategic aspects of corporate political activity.

Key Questions and Chapter Objectives

This chapter focuses on these key questions and objectives:

- How do stakeholder concerns evolve into public issues?
- What is public policy?
- What are the key elements and stages of the public policy process?
- Why is it important for business to be involved in public policy decision making?
- What form does corporate political activity take?

When Henry Ford organized the Ford Motor Company in 1903, his relationships with government were relatively simple. There was only one important antitrust law on the books, and his business was too small to be bothered by it. The federal government did not tax the income of his company or its employees or their capital gains. Although rival car makers in this country were gearing up to compete with Ford, foreign competitors were no threat. No unions were permitted in the Ford plant, and government regulations concerning wages, hours, working conditions, and safety and health were unheard of. The government exacted no payments from the company for employee retirement and pension plans for the simple reason that none existed. Nor was the fledgling automaker plagued with problems of a polluted environment, an energy shortage, or consumer complaints about auto safety, all of which in later years would bring the wrath of the government down on the Ford company. His main legal worry in those early years was a patent infringement suit brought against him by competitors, but he eventually won the suit in the courts.

By the 1970s, Henry Ford II, the founder's grandson and then chief executive officer of the company, faced a different world. He could scarcely make a move without government taking an active hand or peering over his shoulder. That single antitrust law known to his grandfather had grown into a tangle of antitrust laws and court rulings regulating competition, pricing practices, mergers, and acquisitions. Labor laws legalized unions and controlled wages, hours, working conditions, safety and health, and employee discrimination. Federal, state, local, and foreign governments levied taxes on company income, its plant and equipment, capital gains, auto and truck sales, and salaries.

The members of the Ford family who are part of the company's management in the 1990s are witnessing dramatic changes as well. In many industries, government and business are cooperating, even jointly planning how to compete in a global economy. In the space of 75 years, the leaders of Ford Motor Company have seen their relationship with government become much more complex and change in character from one of adversaries to potential partners.

This chapter focuses on government as an important reality with which all businesses must reckon. In no country in the world does business have an absolute right to exist and pursue profits; those rights are always conditioned on business compliance with appropriate laws and public policy. Government imposes major costs on business through regulation and holds the power to grant or refuse permission for many types of business conduct and activity. Even the largest multinational companies, operating in dozens of nations, must obey the laws and public policies of those nations if they are to retain the right to do business.

The topics in this chapter are closely related to some of the major ideas developed in earlier chapters, including the interactive model of business and society (Chapter 1), corporate stakeholders (Chapters 1 and 6), and the relationship of corporate business strategy to social strategy (Chapters 5 and 6). One of the main features of the interactive model is the involvement of business with government. Stakeholders have persuaded governments to regulate business activities in order to promote or protect interests. Public policy also is used to encourage business to meet major social challenges such as drug use, education, and job creation. Global business competition has sharpened the understanding of U.S. business and political leaders about alternative ways that governments and business can relate to one another. As a result, business and government are interacting more often in the public policy process. The relationship between corporations and government, like that of business and all of society, is dynamic and continues to change.[1]

EVOLUTION OF PUBLIC ISSUES

A society's members have the right and the power to ask that business and government respond to problems, needs, and expectations. Of course, neither

[1] Louis Galambos and Joseph Pratt, *The Rise of the Corporate Commonwealth: United States Business and Public Policy in the 20th Century*, New York: Basic Books, 1988; George C. Lodge, *Comparative Business Government Relations*, Englewood Cliffs, NJ: Prentice-Hall, 1990.

business nor government can agree to each request or demand, but the existence of such issues is critical to understanding how business, government, and the public influence one another. When stakeholders have concerns and want a company or government agency to respond to those concerns, pressures can be exerted to encourage a response.

From Social Concerns to Public Action

It is widely believed in the United States and other nations that government is created to serve the needs and interests of citizens. This principle, deeply rooted in history, means that individuals, groups, and organizations have the right to petition government—federal, state, or local—to respond to perceived problems and needs. As public pressure builds, elected officials and government appointees pay more attention to the citizens' concerns and demands. Frequently, social concerns focus on relatively specific problems or **public issues.** A group of neighbors may worry that an intersection is particularly dangerous for children to cross because no traffic signal or stop signs are present. A small town's residents may be concerned that a proposed power plant will affect the character of the community and destroy its peace and quiet. People who live and work in a large city may worry that crime has made it unsafe to live and work in certain areas. People may clamor for government to take action and respond to these concerns.

The Public Issues Life Cycle

Social concerns generally evolve through a series of phases which, because of their natural evolution, can be thought of as a **public issues life cycle.** By recognizing the pattern through which issues evolve, and spotting the early warning signs, a corporation's management can anticipate problems and act to resolve them before they reach crisis proportions. As shown in Figure 9–1, the public issue life cycle includes four phases: changing stakeholder expectations; political action; legislative and regulatory action; and legal implementation.

Changing stakeholder expectations

Public issues begin to develop when a stakeholder group's expectations of how business or government should behave are not met by actual performance. This failure to meet expectations can take many forms, ranging from small groups of residents objecting to a local manufacturer's fouling of the air to the concern of animal lovers for the welfare of monkeys being used in scientific research in a laboratory. As the history of the tobacco industry illustrates, once an expectations-performance gap develops, as explained in Chapter 1, the seeds of another public issue have been sown.[2]

> The tobacco industry has had to battle against an increasingly pervasive antismoking climate. In the 1920s, 1930s, and 1940s, smoking was considered

[2] Richard McGowan, "Public Policy Measures and Cigarette Sales," in J. E. Post (ed.), *Research in Corporate Social Performance and Policy,* vol. 11, Greenwich, CT: JAI Press, 1989, pp. 151–179.

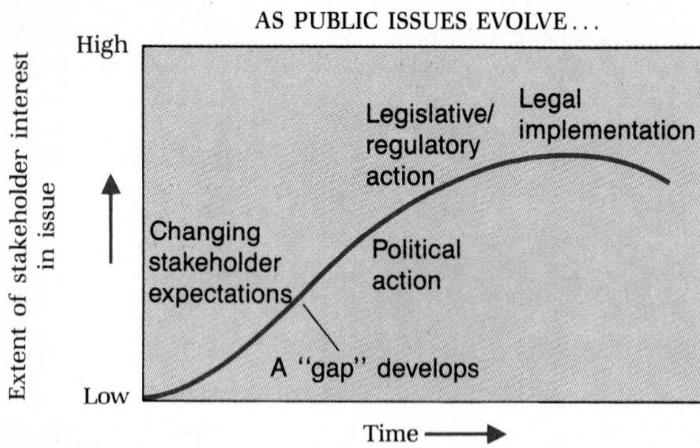

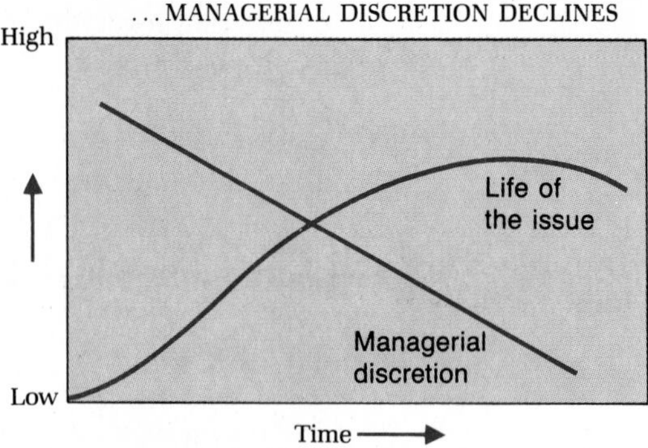

FIGURE 9–1
Phases of the public issues life cycle.

SOURCE: Adapted from James E. Post, *Corporate Behavior and Social Change,* Reston, VA: Reston, 1978.

to be glamorous and sophisticated. Advertisements during the 1940s featured movie stars dressed in military garb, which gave the impression that smoking was not only glamorous but patriotic. The perception of smokers and smoking is very different today. The public has increasingly defined smoking as unacceptable. As Dr. David Harris, the Suffolk County (NY) Health Commissioner, said, "(The public) is demanding the right to live free from smoke, the right to life, liberty and the pursuit of happiness without smoke." Although tobacco industry representatives dispute the validity of studies linking health hazards to smoking, they agree "that in a society enamored with youth, beauty, and fitness, smokers are increasingly seen as misfits." An official of the industry trade group, the Tobacco Institute, said, "They've turned smokers into social pariahs."[3]

Political action

It may take months or even years for an unhappy or concerned group of stakeholders to build a base of support sufficient to challenge a corporation. If an issue persists, however, the group may organize formally and campaign for its point of view through pamphlets, newsletters, posters, and other forms of communication. They may attract the attention of the media, which will result in newspaper, television, or radio coverage. Such attention helps move the issue from generalized citizen concern to political importance.

The political drive against passive smoking began in the 1960s. The landmark "turning of the tide," however, came in 1973, when the Civil Aeronautics Board gave in to antismoking pressure and ruled that smokers had to be separated from nonsmokers on airline flights.

Political efforts included the formation of various antismoking groups, most notably the Group Against Smoking Pollution (GASP). GASP received calls from people complaining of illness caused by "passive smoke"—smoke from other people's cigarettes. In time, they assisted companies wishing to establish

[3] Lindsey Gruson, "Employers Get Tough on Smoking at Work," *New York Times,* Mar. 14, 1985, p. B-8.

smoking restrictions. Antismoking activists attribute corporate willingness to set up such policies to dozens of legal cases in which nonsmokers have successfully sued companies for failing to protect them from passive smoke. Environmental Protection Agency statistics show that passive smoke kills thousands of people each year, and courts have increasingly sided with nonsmokers in passive-smoking lawsuits.

Politicians are interested in citizen concerns and often are anxious to advocate action on their behalf. The government officials become new stakeholders with different types of power to use in closing the gap between public expectations and business performance. For the company, resolution of an issue will now require action that is satisfactory to government officials as well as to local citizens. The company's managers have lost some of their discretion to resolve the issue. The issue has become more complex for the company and its managers.

Legislative and regulatory action

The political phase of an issue's life can be quite long. As more people are drawn into a conflict, there may emerge some ideas—or even a consensus—about a new law or regulation that can help to solve the problem. When legislative proposals or draft regulations begin to emerge, the public issue moves to a new level of action and managerial importance.

Much legislative and legal action has been taken in favor of antismoking activists during the past decade.[4] Antismoking legislation has been enacted nationally and in many states and cities. The federal government has required that health warnings on cigarette labels and advertisements be much larger and that messages be rotated quarterly to provide more effective warnings. New laws now limit the areas in restaurants that can be used by smokers, and nonsmokers in the workplace have the right to declare their "immediate work area" a no-smoking zone. Several years ago, the city commissioner in Gainesville, Florida, approved smoking restrictions that require smokers to ask for and receive permission from every employee in their work area before smoking. The New Jersey legislature approved bills that prohibit smoking on buses and trains and in supermarkets and require restaurants to post their smoking policies on the door. In the 1990s, a number of cities have banned cigarette vending machines from public places.

When a company faces legislative and regulatory action, it is represented by lawyers, lobbyists, and professional political consultants. Top management sometimes may testify before government committees or regulatory agencies, but for the most part, corporate lawyers and lobbyists are deciding what proposals are best and worst for the company. The managers have lost most of their direct decision-making discretion.

[4] McGowan, op. cit.

Legal implementation

Once a new law is passed or a regulation developed, government agencies take action to see that corporations comply with the new rules. A corporation may still challenge the validity of the law by testing it in a lawsuit. Thus, implementation of new laws and regulations is often accompanied by litigation. Managers may be called to testify as the court proceedings continue. The company's lawyers are primarily responsible until the litigation is ended. At that point, the corporation is expected to implement the new rules and involve appropriate levels of management in meeting the new requirements.

> In the case of smoking restrictions, most businesses are more than willing to comply. Most companies have financial incentives for meeting or even exceeding smoking restrictions. The owner of a New Jersey plumbing and heating supply business gave his employees a $2 per week bonus for not smoking. "Nonsmokers are worth more than people who smoke," he said. "They're out sick less. And smoking takes time from the job. Smokers are always stopping for a pack and running out of matches." An in-house survey at Goodyear estimated that the almost 3,000 employees at the Akron headquarters cost the company about $2 million each year in smoking-related problems.[5]

Stakeholder interest in an issue tends to decline as a new law or regulation is implemented. If the law is violated or ignored, however, the issue will reemerge, as a gap once again develops between stakeholder expectations and the corporation's actual performance.

PUBLIC POLICY

Public policy is a plan of action undertaken by government to achieve some broad purpose affecting a substantial segment of the citizenry. As U.S. Senator Patrick Moynihan is reported to have said: Public policy is simply what a government chooses to do or not to do. In general, these ideas are consistent. Governments typically do not choose to act unless a substantial segment of the public is affected and some public purpose is to be achieved. In modern economies throughout the world, the role of government is broad and expanding. As world population increases, individual societies have more members whose needs have to be met and whose interests and concerns have to be reconciled into reasonable plans of action. These are the roles that government—whatever its specific form—has to play in the modern world. Public policy, while different from nation to nation, is the basic set of goals, plans, and actions that each nation and government will follow in achieving its purposes.

The governmental action of any nation can be understood in terms of several

[5] Gruson, op. cit., pp. B-1, B-8.

FIGURE 9–2
The key elements of public policy.

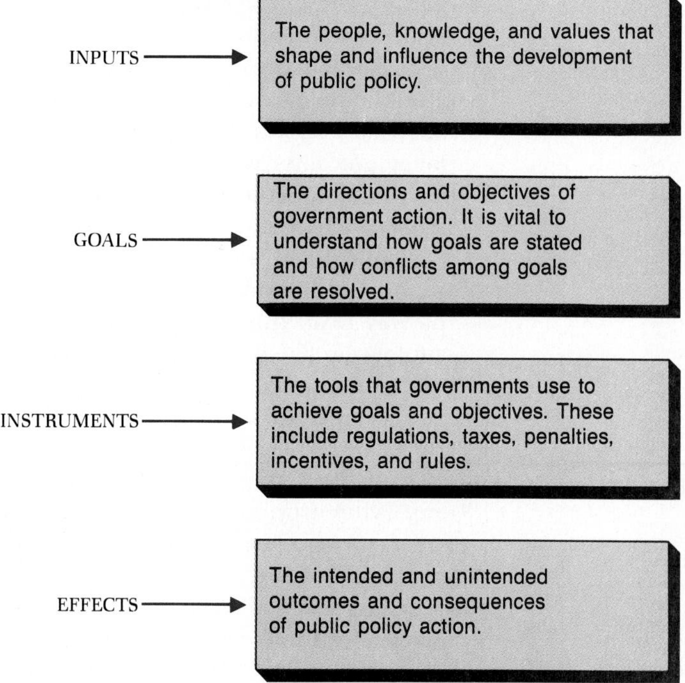

basic **elements of public policy.** As shown in Figure 9–2, these elements are the basic building blocks of government action and can guide managers in their understanding of how public policy is formed.

Many factors, or **inputs,** influence the development of a public policy. A government may determine its course of action on the basis of economic or foreign policy considerations, or domestic political pressure from constituents and interest groups. Public policy also may be influenced by technical studies of complex issues such as taxation or development of new technologies such as fiber optic electronics. All of these factors can help shape what the government chooses to do and how it chooses to do it.

Public policy **goals** can be lofty and high-minded or narrow and self-serving of the national interest. National values, such as freedom, democracy, and equal opportunity for citizens to share in economic prosperity—that is, public policy goals—can lead to the adoption of civil rights laws, liberal immigration laws, and assistance programs for those in need (e.g., the poor, aged, disabled, or refugees). Narrow, self-serving goals are more evident when, for example, nations negotiate trade agreements or decide how tax legislation will allocate the burden of taxes among various interests and income groups. In short, public policy goals may vary widely, but it is always important for citizens and managers to inquire "What public policy goals are being pursued in this action?"

Governments use different tools or **instruments** to achieve their policy goals. In budget negotiations, for example, much discussion is likely to focus on alternative ways to raise revenue—higher tax rates for individuals and businesses, reduced deductions, new sales taxes (e.g., luxury automobiles), or increased taxes on selected items (e.g., gasoline, tobacco, or alcohol). In general, the instruments of public policy are those combinations of incentives and penalties that government uses to stimulate citizens, including business, to act in ways that achieve policy goals. As we discuss in Chapter 10, government regulatory powers are broad and constitute one of the most formidable instruments for accomplishing public purposes.

Public policy actions always have **effects.** Some are intended and deliberate; some are unintended and not desired. Regulations may cause business to improve the way toxic substances are used in the workplace and reduce health risks to employees. Yet it is possible that some other goals may be obstructed as an unintended effect of compliance with a regulation. For example, when health risks to pregnant women were associated with exposure to lead in the workplace, some companies removed women from those jobs. That action was seen as a form of discrimination against women that conflicted with the goal of equal employment opportunity. The unintended effect (discrimination) of one policy action (protect employees) conflicted head-on with another public policy goal (equal opportunity).

In assessing the action of government, it is important for managers to find answers to the questions posed by these four elements. What inputs will affect the public policy? What goals are to be served? What choices will be made about the instruments to be used? And what effects, intended or unintended, are likely to occur? These elements are a cornerstone of understanding any nation's public policy actions.

Stages in the Public Policy Process

The process through which public policy is developed and implemented has several distinct stages, as shown in Figure 9–3. Businesses and their managers must understand the process as well as the elements in order to understand what to do and when to do it.

Stage 1. Agenda building

The public policy agenda consists of those major issues or problems to which officials give serious attention and upon which they feel compelled to act. Not all public issues or problems get enough attention or support to become agenda items. Each year, people ask government to respond to thousands of issues and problems. But response to each one is not possible. In other words, many issues do not have a chance of being converted from public concern into public policies, as the following examples illustrate:

> Auto safety did not become a major public issue worthy of much congressional attention until Ralph Nader, who was then an unknown lawyer,

FIGURE 9–3
Major stages of the public policy process.

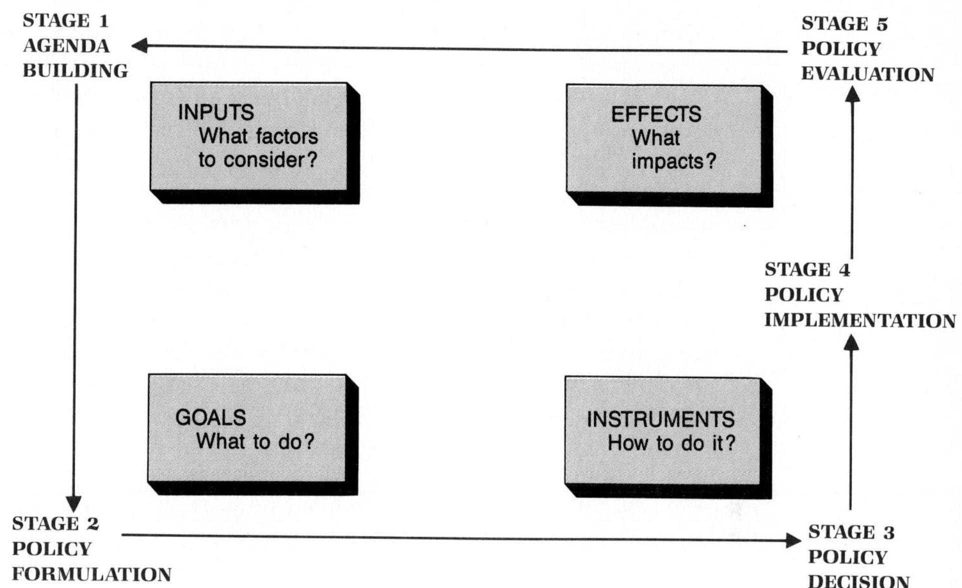

charged General Motors with manufacturing a car that was "unsafe at any speed."[6] Auto fatalities in the mid-1960s totaled nearly 50,000 annually, were the sixth leading cause of death in the United States, and had been climbing steadily for two decades. Although an obvious public safety problem had existed long before Nader made his charges, the highway death toll had not resulted in new public policies to reduce auto deaths by making cars safer. Not all vehicle accidents were the result of unsafe cars, but some were, and Nader's book convinced many people, both in and out of government, that government should do something to make motor vehicles safer. Now, 25 years later, extensive federal and state laws have created a huge body of safety rules, including seat belts and air bags, to increase automobile safety and reduce fatalities.

What does it take to put a problem on the public policy agenda for action by government?[7] A charismatic leader, such as Nader, may capture enough public attention to lead a reform movement. Or in the case of environmental pollution, a dramatic crisis or tragedy may galvanize public opinion. This occurred in Woburn, Massachusetts, in the mid-1980s, when several children contracted leukemia believed to be associated with local drinking water allegedly contaminated by W. R. Grace Company. Eventually, the parents of the children settled their grievances out of court with the company. The town of Woburn then decided to

[6] Ralph Nader, *Unsafe at Any Speed,* New York: Grossman, 1965.

[7] Robert B. Reich (ed.), *The Power of Public Ideas,* Cambridge, MA: Ballinger Publishing, 1988. For a classic discussion of agenda building, see Roger W. Cobb and Charles D. Elder, *Participation in American Politics: The Dynamics of Agenda Building,* Boston, MA: Allyn & Bacon, 1972.

sue the company because several of its wells had been contaminated and had to be closed down and water supplies had to be rerouted. In November 1986, a referendum question on the state ballot asked voters whether or not they favored a statewide mandatory toxic sites cleanup. The vote was overwhelmingly in favor of the proposal.[8]

The actions of an interest group also may put an issue on the public policy agenda, as the group swings into action to protect its members by advocating greater government participation. It is extremely important for business to be aware of what is happening during the agenda-building stage. At first, General Motors executives did not believe that Ralph Nader was very important. They did not realize that he would later arouse the attention and support of the car-buying public and influential politicians, thus increasing greatly the number of regulations imposed on auto manufacturers. Socially aware and politically alert corporations are constantly scanning the social and political environments for developments that might bring new issues onto the public policy agenda. Business itself often wants to promote its own interests by proposing new laws or advocating repeal of old ones, thereby adding items to the public policy agenda.

Stage 2. Policy formulation

Policy formulation occurs when interested groups take a position on some public issue and try to persuade others to adopt their viewpoint as public policy. If consensus among the participating groups can be reached, the proposed public policy moves toward the decision stage. If consensus cannot be reached, the issue may drop off the public policy agenda, or another similar effort may be made in the future to convert the agenda item into a public policy.[9]

Business's stake in policy formulation is high. Lawmakers and other government officials often seek the support of the business community for the policies they are trying to push through Congress, as President Bush did in actively promoting a cut in capital gains taxes in 1990. The administration spent considerable time and effort trying to enlist the support of business leaders and organizations representing business interests. Similarly, business looks to government leaders for public policies that will help businesses. Tax cuts during a recession can stimulate a sluggish economy and help business recover customers and expand activity. In both of these ways, business can and often does participate actively in helping to formulate public policy.

Stage 3. Policy decision

A policy decision occurs when some arm of government either authorizes, or fails to authorize, a course of action. For example, a city council may authorize a new bond issue to pay for building a convention center or a stadium for professional sports. Or the President may issue an executive order forbidding trade with another country. The courts—another branch of government—may

[8] Andrew J. Dabilis, "Focusing on Referendums: Ballot Questions May Spark More Voter Interest than the Races," *Boston Globe*, Nov. 3, 1986, pp. 1, 6.

[9] Philip B. Heyman, "How Government Expresses Public Ideas," in Reich, op. cit., pp. 85–107.

hand down a decision that becomes a precedent for paying claims to victims of airline disasters.

When these steps are taken, the government is putting into effect a new public policy or reaffirming an existing one. The policy decision occurs when a law is passed, when a regulation is adopted, when an executive order is issued, or when a court opinion is announced. Failing to act can also be a form of policy decision. If, after much debate, Congress or a city council turns down or defeats a proposed new law regulating plant closings, for example, it has made a policy decision.

Business normally has no direct role to play in policy decisions since, by definition, all such decisions are made by government officials. But the influence of business and other interest groups is felt before, during, and after the decision itself through political lobbying.

Stage 4. Policy implementation

Passing a law, issuing a judicial opinion, or adopting a new government regulation—in other words, making a public policy decision—does not automatically mean that the public policy will be carried out. Policy implementation occurs when action is taken to enforce a public policy decision. When a new tax law is passed by Congress, for example, the Internal Revenue Service sends out notices to taxpayers explaining the new law and then tries to collect what is owed to the government. When a president forbids trading with another nation for national security reasons, he may penalize any company that continues to do business there, thus sending a message to other companies that he is prepared to enforce the new policy.

At this stage, does business have a chance to influence public policy? Once a law is passed or a court decision handed down, business can still wield significant influence in the implementation of public policy.

A company may negotiate with a regulatory agency for extending compliance deadlines, as steel companies have done concerning pollution controls and auto makers concerning fuel economy standards. Legal steps can be taken by appealing an agency's actions to a higher court. Or an industry may play off one branch of government against another; for example, an aggressive presidential policy on raising gasoline taxes may be checked by appeal to a more cautious congressional attitude.

Business has greatly improved its understanding of, and participation in, the formulation and implementation of public policy. This understanding of how the political process works can be most beneficial to management. Rather than just reacting to laws and regulations, business can be an effective participant in implementing public policies.[10]

Stage 5. Policy evaluation

Policy evaluation occurs when the impact of a public policy becomes evident. Groups who initially were opposed to a policy may take an "I told you so" attitude

[10] Hedrick Smith, *The Power Game: How It Works*, New York: Random House, 1988; David Vogel, *Fluctuating Fortunes—The Political Power of Business*, New York: Basic Books, 1989.

and try to prove that it has been a bad one from beginning to end. Its supporters, on the other hand, may try to see mainly its good points and ignore the bad ones.

Basically, policy evaluators try to find out whether the benefits have been worth more than the costs incurred, and whether the same goals could have been achieved in another, more efficient, less expensive way. This kind of evaluation is tricky. Costs and benefits are difficult to measure. Government agencies and corporations are reluctant to release cost data that may make them look bad. Also, the cause-and-effect relationships are not always clear; for example, if the economy recovers from a recession after a tax cut is enacted by Congress, did the tax cut cause the recovery or would conditions have improved anyway? It is often difficult to know the answer.

Business uses several approaches to public policy evaluations. Some companies, particularly those with public affairs or government relations departments, make their own studies of how public policies affect the company. Trade associations such as the National Association of Manufacturers or the United States Chamber of Commerce also evaluate the impact of government programs on business costs, profits, investments, and foreign competition. Business also supports "think tanks" such as the American Enterprise Institute, which issues probusiness reports either critical or in praise of selected government programs and policies. Additionally, the prestigious Business Roundtable, composed of the top executives of 200 large corporations, occasionally meets directly with high-level government officials as a way of expressing the business community's view on the effectiveness of various public policies.

These five stages of the public policy process often overlap and interweave with one another, creating a very complex web of government policies, programs, laws, regulations, court orders, and political maneuvers. At any one time, something is happening in all five stages on a wide range of issues. For business or for any other interest group, this means that public policy is constantly being made and that the political process is a part of the social environment in which business operates. Knowing how to participate in that process is vital to the prosperity, survival, and vitality of business.

BUSINESS, PUBLIC POLICY, AND THE POLITICAL SYSTEM

Beyond participation in the resolution of specific public policy issues, business also can play a role in the life of the larger political system. Politics is the means through which society makes decisions about who shall have power to make important decisions (who governs), and for what purposes and in what ways will that power be used (toward what ends).[11] It is clear, for example, that business has a stake in the outcome of discussions of whether free enterprise, central state control, or mixed state-and-private enterprise shall prevail.

[11] James Q. Wilson, *American Government*, 2d ed., Lexington, MA: D. C. Heath, 1984, chap. 1.

There has been a long debate about how politics and public policy interrelate. Marxists believe that those who control the economic system also will control the political system. Pluralists, on the other hand, think that many different interests compete for influence in the political system. Other people believe that the bureaucracy of government itself dominates the political system and that all interests are secondary in importance to civil servants and the institutions of government. A fourth view holds that a social elite, including business leaders and others, will make key decisions without much regard to popular wishes.

It is a debate to which there is no clear answer. Individual issues often produce contradictory evidence that seems to favor one or another of these viewpoints. The United States at the beginning of the 1990s remains a mostly pluralistic political system. Interest groups abound, and they have an important influence on political life. Because there are so many different interests in modern America, coalitions have to be formed to advance certain ideas, specific legislation, or regulations. According to some experts, all areas of modern American political life—including legislation, regulation, and executive policy action—reflect coalition politics, which means that no special interest is ever powerful enough, by itself, to determine how an issue should be resolved.[12]

Political parties are a vital ingredient of a pluralistic society. They represent "grand coalitions" of individuals and various interest groups who wish to promote their own welfare through political action. Although political parties are not mentioned in the United States Constitution, they nevertheless are an important part of the system of representative government. Not only do they make the electoral process possible by providing a means for nominating and supporting candidates for public office, but they also serve as a rallying point for the expression of political philosophies, a way for individuals and groups to identify and work with others who hold similar ideas about how to run the government.[13]

BUSINESS AND POLITICAL PARTICIPATION

Business and politics are different, and these differences need to be well understood if business is to be an effective participant in the public policy process. Three of the most important differences are the following:

- The primary goal of business is to produce goods and services for profit. The primary goal of politics is to allocate power among various groups in society. The politician strives to acquire the power of a public office and to hold it as long as possible. Votes and the influence of powerful allies are the lifeblood of a politician. Without these, the politician is as powerless as the business without profits.

[12] Thomas J. Eagleton, *Issues in Business and Government*, Englewood Cliffs, NJ: Prentice-Hall, 1990, p. 5.

[13] Arthur M. Schlesinger, Jr., *The Cycles of American History*, Boston, MA: Houghton Mifflin, 1986.

- Ideally, business decisions are made by applying rational, objective, carefully calculated standards. Ideally, a new product will not be brought out nor will a capital investment be made unless business experts have considered all aspects and repercussions of such an action with great care and precision. Political decisions, on the other hand, often are made on economically irrational, emotional grounds, where hard-to-measure social and philosophical factors are involved. A city government may place great pressure on a business to keep a failing plant open to preserve local jobs for a while longer, although good business reasons would dictate that the plant be closed.
- The primary stakeholders for a business are relatively few in number and easy to identify: stockholders, employees, customers, and suppliers. The important stakeholders in politics are much more numerous and diverse, and they place an astonishing array of demands at the politician's doorstep. The politician has more constituents to satisfy than does the business executive of even the largest corporation. Satisfying stakeholders in politics is generally messier and less precise, and it involves more contradictions and inconsistencies than in business.

These differences between business and politics create real difficulties and frustrations when business people enter the world of politics. The gap that is born of different ways of thinking and acting on problems is not easily closed. To some, the answer is for business to stay out of politics and politicians out of business. But in the modern business environment, business and politics are increasingly brought together. Gradually, many business leaders have come to recognize that business survival is dependent on political activism.

The Case for and against Political Involvement by Business

Those people who argue that business should be an active political participant cite four main justifications:

- A representative political system gives business the right to express its views, just as other interest groups do. A workable pluralistic society depends on active participation of all groups.
- The importance of business-government relations, whether supportive or regulatory, requires active involvement in politics to safeguard business interests.
- Business political activity is needed to counteract political activity by other groups that affect business, such as labor unions, consumer groups, and environmentalists.
- Because of its position as one of society's central institutions, business's political views may at times promote the interests of other related groups, including workers, consumers, suppliers, and local communities.

Those who argue for less political participation by business say that political action by business can lead to trouble and should be avoided for the following reasons:

- Politics should be left to politicians because people in business are not qualified or knowledgeable in the field of politics or their viewpoints are too narrow (this may be true of other interest groups as well).
- Business leaders can sometimes be naive about the complexities of the political world. This leads to points of view that are foolish in the real world of political action.
- Because of the size of many corporations, business political involvement can unbalance pluralism and tend to substitute a dominant private interest for the public welfare.
- Much political activity by business, particularly if successful, makes business a target of public criticism, causing a loss of customers and inviting even more government controls. According to this view, a low-profile approach to government policy is more effective and less risky.

The clear trend has been for expanded business involvement in political debate and discussion. Managers seem to have concluded that in the modern business environment, it is simply unrealistic and unwise to stand on the sidelines while political leaders make decisions with far-ranging consequences for the economy and competitiveness of business enterprises.

Tools of Corporate Political Activity

There are many tools that business and other interests use to directly influence the development of public policy. Most involve efforts to transmit information, express a point of view, or communicate a "message" to a legislator, executive branch official, or regulator.[14] **Lobbying** involves direct contact with a government official to influence the thinking or actions of that person on an issue or public policy. It is usually done through face-to-face contact, sometimes in lengthy discussions or in meetings that may last only minutes. **Grassroots programs** are organized efforts to get constituents to influence government officials to vote or act in a favorable way. Many companies have asked their shareholders to participate in grassroots efforts to persuade their congressional representatives to reduce capital gains taxes and thereby make stock purchases and other investments more lucrative. These programs send a strong message to elected officials that the desired action is supported by a large number of voters.

Other direct forms of political action include letter writing campaigns, "fax attacks," telegrams, and telephone calls to register approval or disapproval of an official's position on an important issue. In addition, businesses often invite government officials to make visits to local plant facilities, give speeches to employees, attend awards ceremonies, or participate in activities that will improve the official's understanding of management and employee concerns. These ac-

[14] See Robert L. Heath and Richard Alan Nelson, *Issues Management: Corporate Public Policymaking in an Information Society*, Beverly Hills, CA: Sage, 1986.

tivities help to "humanize" the distant relationship that can otherwise develop between government officials and the public.

Political Influence

Business exercises political influence of two different types: (1) efforts that shape government policies, forthcoming legislation, and the actions of regulatory agencies; and (2) business influence on the outcome of elections. These are called **governmental politics** and **electoral politics.**[15]

Governmental politics

The techniques used by business to participate in governmental politics are similar to those of other interest groups. Many large corporations place a full-time representative and staff in Washington to keep abreast of developments in government that may affect the company (this is a type of environmental scanning) and to exert influence on members of Congress and other officials. Company lobbyists may be active in city halls and state capitols as well.

Smaller companies, as well as many large ones, join trade associations such as the National Association of Manufacturers or the U.S. Chamber of Commerce, where they count upon strength of numbers and a centralized staff to promote their interests with government officials. The Chamber of Commerce, for example, has a membership of 200,000 companies, operates with a large annual budget, publishes a widely circulated business magazine, and has a satellite television network to broadcast its political messages.

Ad hoc coalitions that bring diverse business groups together to lobby for or against a particular piece of legislation have proved to be effective. Defeat in 1990 of proposed federal laws establishing day-care programs and strengthening affirmative action programs was attributed, in part, to the work of ad hoc business coalitions.

Electoral politics

Direct contributions by corporations to political candidates running for federal offices are forbidden by federal law, and some states also place similar restrictions on corporate contributions in state elections. Since the mid-1970s, however, companies have been permitted to spend company funds to organize and administer a **political action committee** (PAC). PACs may solicit contributions from stockholders and employees and then channel the funds to those seeking political office. Even companies that have organized PACs, though, are not permitted to donate corporate money to the PAC or to any political candidate. All donations to a company-organized PAC must come from individuals. Similarly, unions and other organizations may solicit contributions from members and supporters for their PACs.

The Federal Election Commission has established rules to regulate PAC activities. For example, PACs are not allowed to give more than $5,000 to a single candidate for each election, although the winner of a primary election may be

[15] Edwin M. Epstein, *The Corporation in American Politics*, Englewood Cliffs, NJ: Prentice-Hall, 1969, chap. 5.

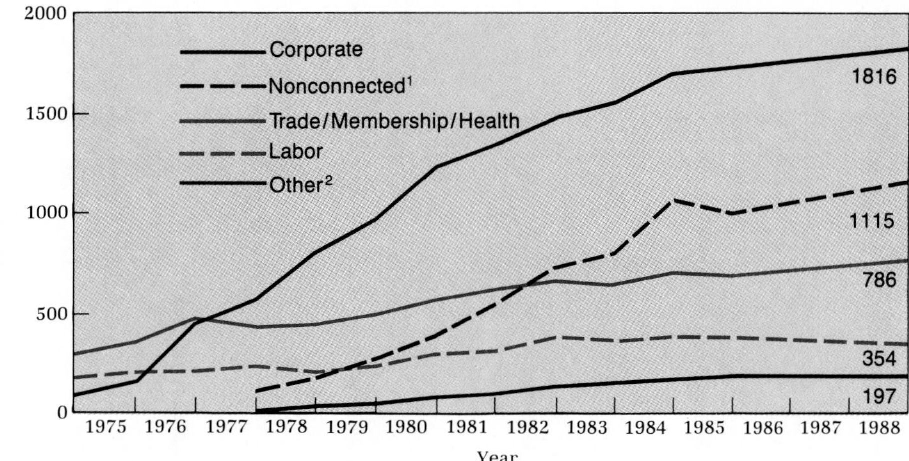

FIGURE 9–4
Political Action Committee growth from 1975 to 1988.

SOURCE: Federal Election Commission, reported in *Almanac of Federal PAC's, 1990*, pp. 595–599.

given another $5,000 for the general election. These limits were imposed on all PACs to reduce the role of concentrated wealth in determining the outcome of elections to public office. But new ways are constantly being found to get around the rules. In recent congressional campaigns, for example, PACs took advantage of loopholes that allowed them to spend as much as they wanted indirectly on candidates so long as they did not cooperate or consult with candidates or their campaigns. Thus PACs spent money on television commercials, telephone banks, and mass mailings in addition to funds they were permitted to contribute directly to the candidate.[16]

As Figure 9–4 shows, PACs have proved to be very popular with business as well as with other groups. Although corporate PACs were the most numerous, accounting for 43 percent of the total, they were not the biggest money raisers or spenders. As illustrated in Figure 9–5, nonconnected organizations—an example would be the National Association of Realtors—ranked highest in money raised and spent. Some labor unions are among the biggest contributors, although as a whole they represent only 8 percent of all PACs. For several years, labor union PACs outstripped business in raising money, but in the 1980s, they fell behind the combined efforts of corporate and trade association PACs. Interestingly, the number of PACs seems to have peaked in the late 1980s, although money raised has continued to reach new high levels into the 1990s.

RESPONSIBLE BUSINESS POLITICS

We agree with others who say that political action by business—whether to influence government policy or the outcome of elections—is a natural outgrowth

[16] Michael Oreskes, "The Trouble with Politics," *New York Times*, Mar. 18, 1990, p. 11; "PACs Turning to Indirect Way to Aid Hopefuls," *New York Times*, Nov. 2, 1986, pp. 1, 35.

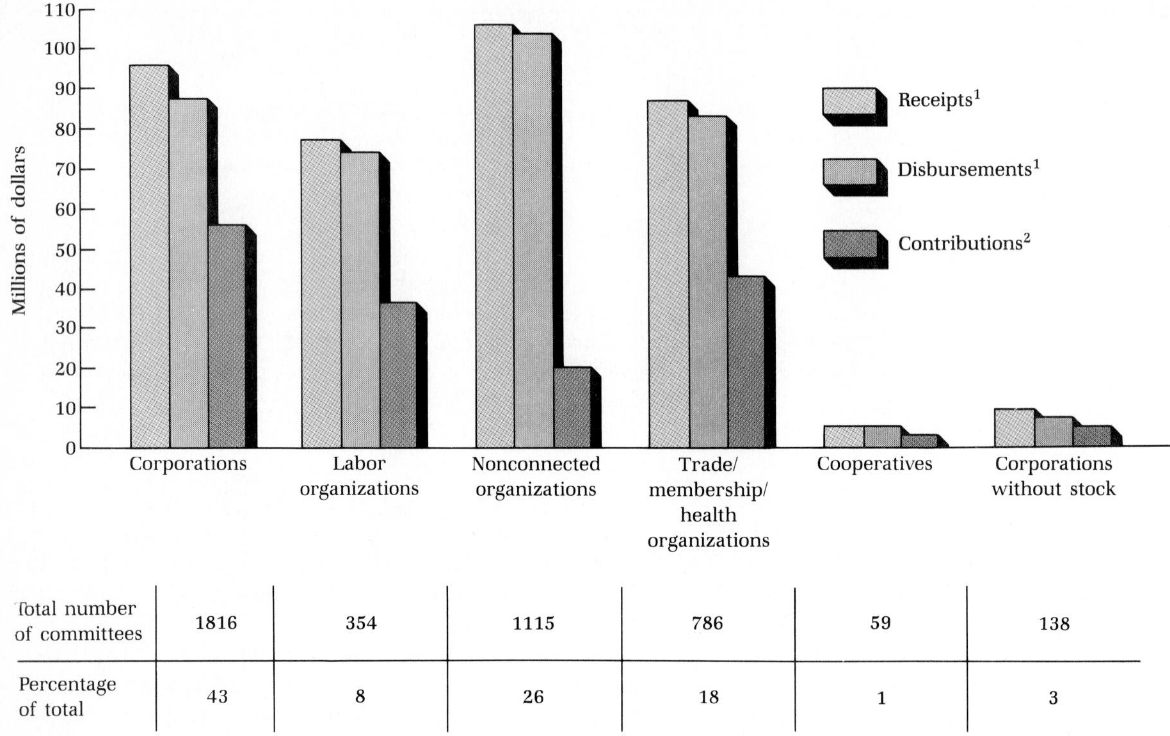

	Corporations	Labor organizations	Nonconnected organizations	Trade/ membership/ health organizations	Cooperatives	Corporations without stock
Total number of committees	1816	354	1115	786	59	138
Percentage of total	43	8	26	18	1	3

[1]Receipts and disbursements do not include funds transferred between affiliated committees.

[2]Includes contributions to committees of 1986 House and Senate candidates: and all federal candidates (for House, Senate and Presidency) campaigning in future elections or retiring debts of former campaigns.

FIGURE 9–5
Financial activity of PACs, 1987–1988.

SOURCE: Federal Election Commission, reported in *Almanac of Federal PAC's, 1990,* pp. 595–599.

of a pluralistic society. Business has a legitimate right to participate in the political process, just as consumers, labor unions, environmentalists, and others do.

The principal danger arising from corporate political activity is that corporations may wield too much power. If that power were to "tip the scales" unfairly in favor of business and against the many pluralistic interests in society, both business and society would be losers. A careful use of business influence is therefore an ideal goal to be worked for, as is true of union power, religious power, consumer power, or any concentrated power that may exist in an organizational society.

Money and Politics

The great expense of modern political campaigns has made campaign financing an increasingly serious problem. Candidates need money to run effective political campaigns, and business has become an important source of funds.

EXHIBIT 9–A

BUSINESS LOSES ON CAMPAIGN CONTRIBUTIONS

A 1990 United States Supreme Court decision (*Austin v. Michigan State Chamber of Commerce*) gave states the power to limit political campaign contributions by corporations. The decision upheld a Michigan law which prohibited corporations from spending their own funds (as opposed to PAC donations) on behalf of political candidates. The Michigan Chamber of Commerce had argued that its member companies had a right to political expression (free speech) which was not adequately protected by the alternative of setting up political action committees. But the Supreme Court ruled that the state of Michigan had a "compelling rationale" for imposing limits on "the corrosive and distorting effects of immense aggregations of wealth that are accumulated with the help of the corporate form." The chamber had planned to place an advertisement in a Grand Rapids newspaper in support of a Republican candidate for state office. Fearing that the ad would be illegal, the chamber filed a federal suit seeking to have the Michigan law declared unconstitutional as applied to the chamber.

SOURCE: Based on the following published articles: Linda Greenhouse, "Justice Restricts Corporate Gifts for Politicians," *New York Times*, Mar. 28, 1990, pp. A–1, A–7; "Michigan Retains Law Limiting Campaign Funding," *Investor's Daily*, Mar. 26, 1990, p. 27.

An old adage states that "money is the mother's milk of politics." The 1990s are reaffirming the truth of that century-old slogan in new and extraordinarily expensive ways. While the cost of campaigning for political office has risen to all-time high levels, with television advertising driving much of the escalation, legislatures and the courts—as described in Exhibit 9–A—wrestle with proper limitations.

Some observers worry that special-interest groups, including business, are able to wield too much influence on elections and on government. According to these critics, officeholders who seek reelection may be "bought off" by PAC contributions, especially since election campaigning has become so expensive in an electronic age. Others counter this argument by claiming that it is better to have political contributions out in the open, as required by the current law, than to go back to the old system of secret slush funds.[17]

Winning elections has become a full-time business involving professional associations and magazines, computers, continuous polling, and ubiquitous television coverage and advertising. In 1990, more than half a billion dollars was spent on House and Senate races, more than 10 times the amount spent in 1974. Business is an important factor in the electoral process. Businesses supply many of the services needed to run modern political campaigns, from airplanes to computers to polling data. Politicians and political parties solicit the support of business and business leaders for their campaigns. PAC spending, and managers acting in their capacity as individual citizens, further contribute to the involvement of business in politics. Sometimes, as in the exploits of savings and loan executive Charles Keating, there are improper motives behind the actions. Business depends

[17] James A. Barnes, "Paying the Piper," *National Journal*, Sept. 23, 1989, pp. 2323–2326.

FIGURE 9–6
What other countries do to control money in politics.

SOURCE: Michael Oreskes, "The Trouble with Politics: Running versus Governing," *New York Times*, Mar. 21, 1990, pp. A-1, A-22.

WHAT OTHER COUNTRIES DO

	Public Financing	Limits on Fund Raising or Spending	Television
U.K.	No	Yes	Free time based on party's strength in previous election
France	Reinburse candidates based on votes received	Yes	Free and equal time to candidates
Japan	No	Yes	Candidates given some free time for speeches; no negative advertising
Germany	Reinbursement to parties according to votes received	No	Free time to candidates on public stations

greatly on honest government, and business executives have an ethical responsibility not to corrupt or be corrupted by the political system.

Money spent on all political advertising during election years rose from $50 million in 1972 to more than $250 million in 1990 for congressional elections. The average cost of running for a congressional seat grew from $250,000 in 1982 to more than $600,000 in 1990; a U.S. Senate campaign increased from $2.1 million in 1982 to more than $4.5 million in 1990. PAC disbursements totaling about $360 million for 1987–1988 senatorial and congressional elections are shown in Figure 9–5.

Campaign reform proposals take many forms. Some advocate absolute dollar limitations on campaign spending and fund raising. Others believe a system of public financing (total or matching funds) would serve to level the campaign playing field. A number of political leaders have offered proposals to require television networks and stations to provide free time for candidates' advertising. As shown in Figure 9–6, other democratic nations utilize a combination of such ideas to reduce the impact of money on electoral politics. Business leaders must address these issues because business has an important stake in a healthy, honest political system.

SUMMARY POINTS OF THIS CHAPTER

- Stakeholder expectations, if unmet, trigger action to transform social concern into pressure on business and government. A gap between what is expected and actual performance stimulates the formation of a public issue.

- Public policies are government actions intended to accomplish a broad public purpose. By affecting business, they give business an important incentive to influence public policies.
- Public policy consists of inputs, stated goals, alternative instruments to achieve those goals, and effects, both intended and unintended. These elements interact throughout five distinct stages of the public policy process: agenda building, policy formulation, decision making, implementation, and evaluation.
- Business is involved in public policy decision making because government influences business activity, government can be helpful to business, and public policy guides business's social policies.
- Corporate political activity is focused on governmental policies and decision making and on electoral politics. Lobbying, grassroots programs, and political action committees are among the most popular types of corporate political activities.

KEY TERMS AND CONCEPTS USED IN THIS CHAPTER

- Public issues and the public issues life cycle
- Public policy
- Elements of public policy: inputs, goals, instruments, effects
- Stages of the public policy process
- Lobbying
- Grassroots programs
- Political action committees
- Governmental politics
- Electoral politics

DISCUSSION CASE

THE CLEAN AIR ACT OF 1990

As the 101st Congress limped toward conclusion in October 1990, important pieces of national business remained unresolved. The federal budget was caught in a political gridlock, with President Bush at loggerheads with the Democratic and Republican leaders in the Congress over spending limits, taxation provisions, and ways to reduce the huge federal budget deficit. The overriding presence of the budget debate cast a political pall on many other pieces of pending legislation, including an environmental law that had been thirteen years in the making!

When George Bush was elected president in 1988, he campaigned on a promise to become the "environmental president." Once elected, he took a number of quick steps to signal his commitment to that pledge. Foremost among his early acts was the appointment of William Reilly, formerly the head of the World Wildlife

Fund, to become the Environmental Protection Agency's administrator. Within months of his appointment, Reilly was on Capitol Hill introducing the administration's proposed clean air legislation. Environmentalists hailed the administration's desire to see a clean air bill passed before the end of 1989, but political insiders knew that was an unlikely timetable at best, an impossibility at worst.

The EPA had long been interested in strengthening the nation's laws regarding air quality. The original Clean Air Act was passed by the Congress in 1970, an achievement greatly shaped by Senator Edmund Muskie of Maine, who had chaired the Senate committee that drafted the bill. When President Richard Nixon signed the bill into law, it was felt that the United States government had the tools needed to reduce health risks attributable to dangerous airborne contaminants. The newly created EPA staff quickly discovered the limitations of the legislation and its own powers to deal effectively with air quality problems. EPA staff members began pressing for more powerful tools to clean up the nation's air.

It took time, but by 1976 the Congress was ready to act. Representative Paul Rogers of Florida and Senator Edmund Muskie were the champions of tougher standards, each chairing an important legislative committee. David Hawkins was the Deputy Administrator for Air Quality at EPA and worked with the congressional staffs to shape effective legislation. One particularly prominent opponent was Representative John Dingle of Michigan, who was deeply concerned about the effects of auto emissions controls on the automobile industry that was such a large part of Michigan's economy. A long, difficult struggle followed, but in 1977 Clean Air Act amendments were enacted by the Congress and signed into law by President Jimmy Carter.

During the 1980s, many of the nation's air quality problems grew worse. In California, smog became an increasingly serious health hazard to more than 12 million residents of the Los Angeles basin. Dozens of other U.S. cities faced serious air quality problems because of the emissions of pollutants from increasing numbers of automobiles. In New England, acid rain caused by chemicals spewed into the air from coal burned by utilities in the Midwest caused the "death" of lakes and streams, corrosion of buildings and other physical property, and serious harm to forests. The burning of hydrocarbons from fossil fuels (coal and oil) was the primary contributor to dirty air. The clean air proposals favored by health experts and environmentalists to address these problems encountered steadfast political resistance during the eight years of the Reagan presidency. But in 1988, public opinion polls showed George Bush that environmental issues—and air quality in particular—were high-priority public issues. The promise to act, to become the "environmental president," proved one of the most effective themes in his successful campaign for the presidency.

To succeed, Bush's clean air proposal needed strong support in both the House of Representatives and the Senate. The President successfully enlisted the assistance of John Dingle and Henry Waxman of California (who had succeeded Paul Rogers as chair of the key House committee) and had the Senate majority leader, George Mitchell of Maine (a protégé of former Senator Muskie), and Senator Robert Dole (Republican of Kansas) to lead a bipartisan effort to enact clean air legislation. After thirteen years of obstacles, it appeared that a new clean air law might be achievable.

Automobile manufacturers quickly objected to various provisions, including a proposed average 40 miles per gallon standard for fuel efficiency. Midwestern utilities objected to strict acid rain provisions, fearing that costs of control technology would increase user costs and damage local industries. The petroleum industry objected to "clean fuels" provisions that would create tax subsidies for ethanol and methanol, fuels made from nonpetroleum sources. Clean air advocates, including David Hawkins, now a top environmental lobbyist, pressed hard for all of those provisions, citing high levels of public support for the legislation.

After months of wrangling, a compromise bill emerged from the Congress for President Bush to sign. The 1990 Clean Air Act included a large number of near-term and long-term steps to improve the nation's air quality. But some special needs were recognized. Utilities in the middle west, for example, received an exemption from having to install equipment to reduce mercury, which has polluted the Great Lakes. Clean-burning gasoline requirements were "stretched out" to 1995. The benefits for ethanol remained in the bill, however.

The benefits for ethanol depended on the inclusion of a special tax provision in the budget legislation that was also moving through Congress. Archer Daniels Midland Co. (ADM), producer of 70 percent of the nation's ethanol, a gasoline substitute distilled from corn, had a strong interest in it. Senator Dole of Kansas, a corn producing state, saved a 60 cents per gallon tax credit for companies that turn ethanol into gasohol used in cars. Coincidentally, ADM's PAC and top managers contributed $10,000 to Senator Dole's reelection campaign.[18]

Discussion Questions

1. Using the major ideas discussed in this chapter, evaluate the process that produced the clean air legislation. In doing so, identify the various inputs, goals, instruments, and effects discussed by the participants. Can you trace the process through the five stages of the public policy process?
2. What type of corporate political activity—governmental politics or electoral politics—did companies such as Archer Daniels Midland, the large petroleum producers, or the automobile manufacturers engage in when dealing with the "clean fuels" provisions of the bill?
3. How might contributions from the political action committee of Exxon, the American Medical Association, and Archer Daniels Midland have been used before or after the legislation was passed? What factors should influence the decisions of PACs in making those contributions?

[18] "A Little Help for Some Friends," *Time*, Nov. 5, 1990, p. 31.

10

The Government-Business Interface: Regulation, Deregulation, and Collaboration

The regulatory system is a primary means through which government tries to harmonize business behavior and the public interest. Many types and forms of regulation have been developed. Some work better than others, and some work well for a time but lose their effectiveness. Thus regulation is an ever-changing system. In recent times, a major rethinking of U.S. and international regulation has occurred, and there is little doubt that government officials, business executives, and the public will continue to evaluate its effectiveness.

Key Questions and Chapter Objectives

- What are the major types of government regulation?
- How does the regulatory system work?
- Why has government increased in size and scope?
- What are the economic and social costs of government regulation?
- How is international regulation emerging, and how does it work?

In December 1990, the Interstate Commerce Commission voted unanimously to ban smoking on all regularly scheduled interstate buses in the United States. The commission's action occurred nine months after two intercity bus company trade associations requested a uniform policy. The ban affects 300 bus companies who carry 24 million passengers annually.

The Environmental Protection Agency sought to impose mandatory recycling laws on cities and counties that use incinerators to destroy solid waste. The agency's concern with air emissions from incinerators, and its belief that recycling must be used to reduce the volume of solid waste in all communities, led to the proposal. Upon reviewing the proposed regulation, however, the Competitiveness Council, a review body chaired by the Vice President of the United States, decided that the regulation was too costly to industry and communities. The EPA's proposed rule died.

All domestically produced peanuts must be inspected to ensure that they meet the same minimum requirements stipulated in an international marketing agreement that regulates imported peanuts. The U.S. Department of Agriculture established the rule after discussions with U.S. trade officials who had made a commitment to peanut producing nations to create a "level playing field" for foreign and U.S. producers in the U.S. market. According to a trade official, such evenhandedness is critical to building a market-oriented system of international trade.[1]

These actions or proposed actions of federal agencies highlight government's involvement in the day-to-day activities of business. Regulation is a primary way of accomplishing public policy and has direct impacts on business. No business can be successful without understanding and effectively managing its relationships with government.

Most governments rely on regulation as a primary means to achieve public policy objectives. This chapter concentrates on government regulation in the United States, including the purposes of business regulation, major problems and costs associated with regulation, and efforts to balance regulation with business's freedom to act. This discussion is related to some of the major ideas developed in earlier chapters, including the interactive model of business and society, corporate stakeholders, and emerging global business challenges.

AN OVERVIEW OF GOVERNMENT REGULATION

Government and business have long been closely entwined in the United States. Our earliest colonial governments depended on business for goods (e.g., military provisions) and services, and those businesses relied on government to make laws that encouraged economic development and prosperity. One of the main features of modern economies is the extensive involvement of business with government. Over several hundred years, many stakeholders, including business itself, have persuaded government to regulate business conduct in order to protect or promote their interests. Government has also used regulation as a way to reinforce the efforts of business to meet major current challenges such as exports, equal employment, energy development, and environmental cleanups.

Implementing Social Choices

Government regulation of business, in its most basic sense, is a mechanism for implementing social choices. In other words, when a society has chosen to pursue a certain goal—such as free competition in the marketplace—it may then decide

[1] These situations are based on news stories in the *New York Times* and *Wall Street Journal* during December 1990.

that the goal can be reached by preventing the growth of monopolies. It may further decide that monopolies can be curbed by making them illegal and by creating a government watchdog agency to monitor all business practices that may lead to monopoly. A definite sequence occurs: first, a social choice is made, then one or more laws are passed, and an agency is empowered to implement the choice. This sequence leads to government regulation, not just of business alone but also of hospitals, public schools, labor unions, and others.

When we discussed alternative socioeconomic systems in Chapter 7, government regulation was mentioned as one mechanism through which a society may choose to approach some of its social problems. In all countries of the world today, the government has significant powers to curb and guide enterprise. Governments often constitute the single most important decision-making body for a business to take into account.[2]

In the United States, many different types of problems are approached through regulation. The history of regulation is long; it dates back to the very earliest actions of government. The powers of government that define regulation are derived from English common law and involve traditional government authority to establish and disestablish economic activity.[3] As we shall point out later, much controversy surrounds this development, and many people question the wisdom of depending upon regulation to so great an extent. However, neither the controversial character of regulation nor its inherent complexity should be allowed to obscure the essential nature of government regulation. Basically, it is a method of carrying out certain social choices made by a society through its political and legal system.

Types of Regulation

Government regulations come in several different varieties. Some are directly imposed; others are more indirectly felt. Some are aimed at a specific industry such as banking, while others such as those dealing with job discrimination apply across the board to all industries. Some have been in existence for a long time—the Interstate Commerce Commission (ICC) was created in 1887—while others, such as the Consumer Product Safety Commission, originated in the 1970s. Economic objectives characterize some government activities, while social goals are paramount in others.

Industry-specific economic regulations

Our oldest form of regulation by government agency is directed at specific industries such as the railroads, telephone companies, and merchant shipping lines. Regulations of this type are primarily economic in nature and are delib-

[2] See George C. Lodge, *Comparative Business-Government Relations*, Englewood Cliffs, NJ: Prentice-Hall, 1990.

[3] Richard H. K. Vietor, *Strategic Management in the Regulatory Environment*, Englewood Cliffs, NJ: Prentice-Hall, 1989, pp. 23–39.

erately intended to modify the normal operation of the free market and the forces of supply and demand. Such modification may come about because the free market is distorted by the size or monopoly power of companies, or because the social side effects or consequences of actions in the marketplace are thought to be undesirable. Under such conditions, government regulators make a conscious effort to substitute their judgment for that of the marketplace in such matters as price setting, capital expansion, quality of services, and entry conditions for new competitors. For example, railroads were not permitted to raise most rates to shippers without permission from the Interstate Commerce Commission, nor could they abandon a red-ink line as a free market firm would do. Nor could telephone companies increase their charges, expand into related lines of business, or deny service to customers without first getting approval of various local, state, and federal agencies.

In these and other public utilities, a regulatory agency asserts control over the fundamental business matters facing an industry—prices, capital investments, services offered, customers served, and profits. Although a company is privately owned and managed, the scope of its decision making is severely restricted by government regulations. Public utility regulation is direct and close, bringing government officials and business executives into close working contact.

Some critics claim that the working relationships between regulatory officials and business executives breed a "you scratch my back and I'll scratch yours" attitude that injures the public interest. In some instances, regulatory officials may become more interested in seeing the industry prosper and grow than in ensuring that the original goals of regulation are achieved. In other instances, regulatory agencies may be asked to both regulate and promote an industry, a situation that often has proved difficult or impossible to manage effectively. This was the case, for example, facing the Atomic Energy Commission in the 1950s and 1960s, and the Civil Aeronautics Board from the 1930s to the 1970s. Both agencies were reorganized because of problems that developed.[4]

As Figure 10–1 illustrates, many industries have undergone extensive and shifting regulation throughout the twentieth century. Airlines, natural gas, telecommunications, banking and many others have gone through periods of rising regulation designed to correct abuses and problems, followed by periods of consolidation and implementation of regulation. When regulatory programs become ineffective, as command-type regulations often do, pressures to deregulate or otherwise reform the industry arise. Views change regarding how much regulation, and of what type, is required. For example, petroleum was regulated in the 1930s to stabilize a volatile oil marketplace. This approach was followed until the 1970s, when oil prices rose sharply. New regulatory controls were tried but by the 1980s, reformers concluded that deregulation of petroleum prices was needed to encourage exploration and development. Industry-specific regulation always faces problems of staying current with other factors that shape the dynamics of an industry.

[4] Alfred A. Marcus, Jr., *The Adversary Economy*, Westport, CT: Quorum Books, 1985, chap. 1.

FIGURE 10–1
Patterns of industry-specific regulation in the United States in the twentieth century.

SOURCE: Based on Richard H. K. Vietor, *Strategic Management in the Regulatory Environment*, Englewood Cliffs, NJ: Prentice-Hall, 1989, p. 25.

	Phase	Time
Airlines	preregulation	pre-1930s
	regulation	1930s
	breakdown	1960s and 1970s
	reform	Late 1970s (deregulation)
Railroads	preregulation	mid-1800s
	regulation	1880s, 1940s, 1970s
	breakdown	1970s
	reform	1980s (deregulation)
Petroleum	preregulation	1860–1920s
	regulation	1930s
	breakdown	1970s
	reform	1980s
Telecommunications	preregulation	1920s
	regulation	1930s
	breakdown	1970s
	reform	1980s (deregulation)

All-industry social regulations

Most all-industry regulations are aimed at four major social goals: environmental protection, workplace safety and health, consumer protection, and equal employment opportunities. Unlike the economic regulations mentioned above, social regulations are not limited to one type of business or industry. Laws concerning pollution, safety and health, and job discrimination apply to all major institutions, including business; and consumer protection laws apply to all relevant businesses producing and selling consumer goods.

Social regulations typically benefit large segments of society. Critics complain that the costs are shared by a narrow segment of society, business, and its customers. If the agencies that enforce social regulations do not consider the overall financial impact of their actions on firms or industries, businesses may experience losses and even be forced to close, leaving workers without jobs and customers without products. This type of argument does not excuse socially irresponsible conduct however. In recent years, more political leaders have recognized that disregarding the effect of regulation on an industry's economic health is potentially harmful to the public interest.[5]

Functional regulations

Certain operations or functions of business have been singled out for special attention by government regulators. Labor practices, for example, are no longer left to the operation of free market forces, since government sets minimum wages, regulates overtime pay, allows unions to determine the supply of workers if they

[5] Murray L. Weidenbaum, *Business, Government, and the Public*, Englewood Cliffs, NJ: Prentice-Hall, 1986, chap. 2.

can do so, and often intervenes to settle troublesome and serious labor-management disputes that threaten national well-being.

Competition is another business function strongly affected by regulation. Antitrust laws and rules, discussed in Chapter 11, attempt to prevent monopolies, preserve competitive pricing, and protect consumers against unfair practices.

Functional regulations, like social regulations, may cut across industry lines and apply generally to all enterprises, as they do in the case of antitrust and labor practices. Or they may—as with regulations governing the functioning of the stock exchanges and the issuance of corporate securities—be confined to specific institutions such as the stock markets or the companies whose stocks are listed on those exchanges.

Figure 10–2 depicts these three types of regulations—economic, social, and functional—along with the major regulatory agencies responsible for enforcing the rules. Only the most prominent federal agencies are included in the chart. Omitted are many other federal departments, as well as similar agencies in each state and in many cities.

How Regulation Works

In spite of the complexity of government regulation, it is possible to grasp the essentials. We want to emphasize here (1) the legal basis of regulation, (2) the primary regulatory organs or mechanisms used, and (3) the major steps involved in making regulation a reality. Knowing each of these components provides a sound basis for understanding how government regulates business and many other aspects of our lives.

The legal basis

A person who wonders about so much government intrusion into the private sector may well ask: Where does the government get its regulatory authority? The answer is: From two sources—the common law and the Constitution.

The common law is a body of legal precedents and customs built up over many years as a result of experience, trial and error, and court rulings. It contains many commonly accepted principles, such as trial by jury, the protection of property, and the enforcement of contracts. English common law, the original basis of the U.S. legal system, gave government the right to regulate human affairs in order to achieve fairness and justice.

The United States Constitution, which embodies several common law principles, is now the primary legal foundation for government regulatory activities. In one way or another, all government regulation must be justified in constitutional terms or it is not allowed to stand.

Most U.S. federal regulations today are based on four constitutional powers: (1) the power to regulate interstate and foreign commerce, (2) the power to tax and spend, (3) the power to borrow, and (4) the power to promote the general welfare.[6] These powers have been used to justify all the direct and indirect

[6] James Q. Wilson, *American Government: Institutions and Policies*, 2d ed., Lexington, MA: D. C. Heath, 1983, chap. 15.

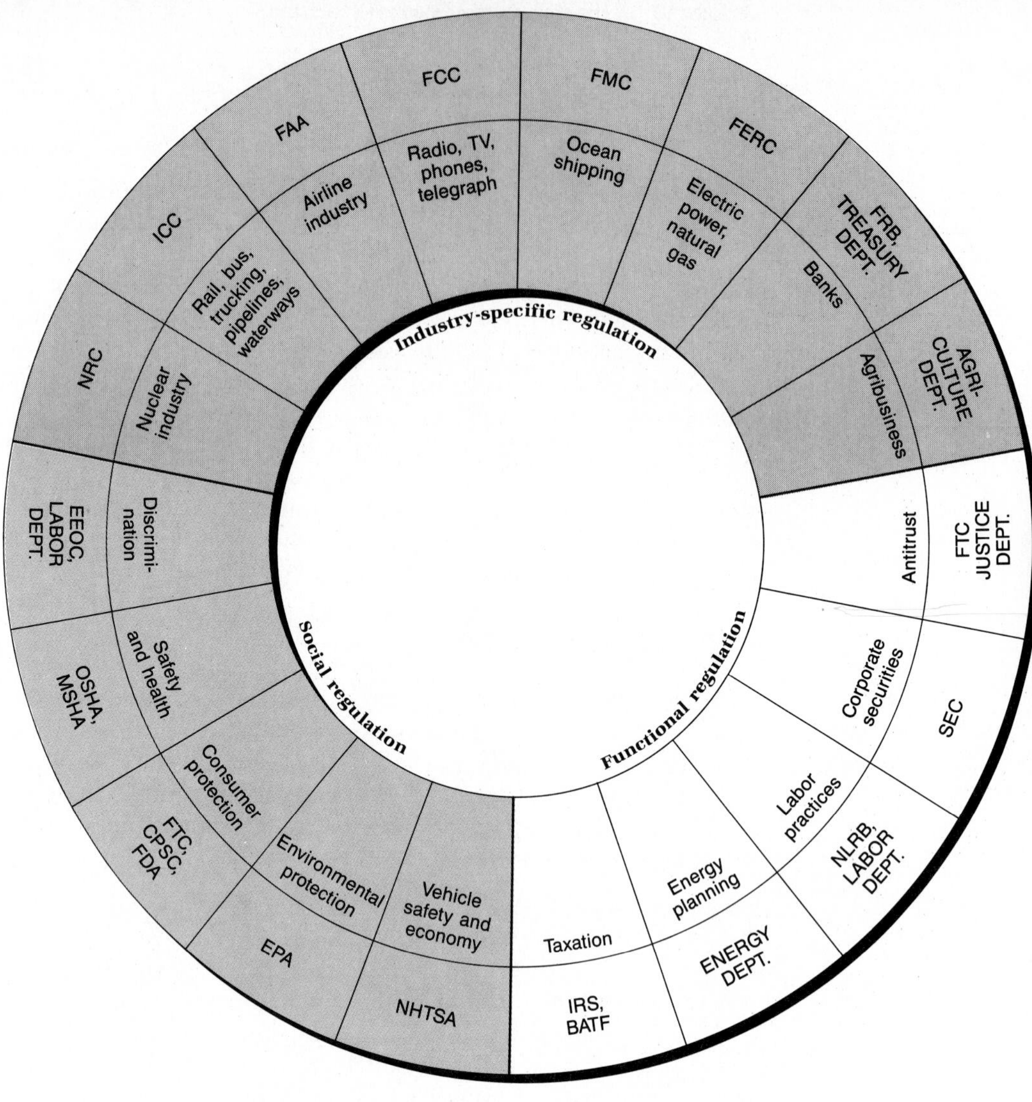

Industry-specific regulatory agencies

NRC	Nuclear Regulatory Commission
ICC	Interstate Commerce Commission
FAA	Federal Aviation Administration
FCC	Federal Communications Commission
FMC	Federal Maritime Commission
FERC	Federal Energy Regulatory Commission
FRB	Federal Reserve Board

Social regulatory agencies

EEOC	Equal Employment Opportunity Commission
OSHA	Occupational Safety and Health Administration
MSHA	Mine Safety and Health Administration
FTC	Federal Trade Commission
CPSC	Consumer Product Safety Commission
FDA	Food and Drug Administration
EPA	Environmental Protection Agency
NHTSA	National Highway Traffic Safety Administration

Functional regulatory agencies

IRS	Internal Revenue Service
BATF	Bureau of Alcohol, Tobacco, and Firearms
NLRB	National Labor Relations Board
SEC	Securities and Exchange Commission
FTC	Federal Trade Commission

FIGURE 10–2
Major federal regulatory agencies arranged by type of regulation.

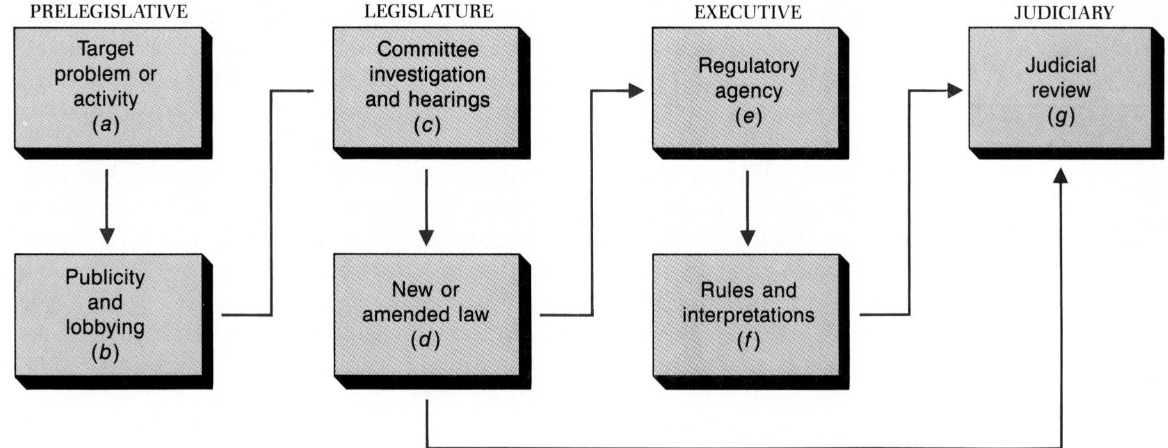

FIGURE 10–3
Major steps in federal regulation taken by the three branches of government.

regulations shown in Figure 10–2. The courts have generally upheld the right of the federal government to use its powers in these ways, although court interpretations are subject to modifications as society and the members of the judiciary change.

Several other constitutional provisions—for example, the implied powers, the war powers, the due-process-of-law provisions, the equal-protection clauses, and others—are used as a legal basis of government regulation. We leave the details of these to legal experts. The main point to remember is that government regulation rests securely on a foundation of common law and constitutional authority.

The regulatory mechanism

The main lines of regulation follow closely the three branches of government—the legislature, the executive, and the judiciary, as shown in Figure 10–3. Each branch has certain responsibilities where regulation is concerned. The legislative branch—Congress at the federal level; state legislatures, county commissions, and city councils at other levels—is empowered to enact new regulatory laws or amend old ones.

> For example, in 1970 Congress passed the Clean Air Act; it was amended in 1973, 1974, and 1977 (twice), and a major revision was made in 1990. The Superfund Act was passed in 1980 in the last days of the Carter administration. A 1986 revision of the law dealt with problems discovered since the initial bill was enacted by Congress. It was revised again in 1991. Such a process of revision and amendment is normal, as legislatures respond to the various interest groups in society that have a stake in the new regulations. These may include consumer advocates, environmentalists, and the affected business groups.

Once a law is enacted, the executive branch of government becomes officially involved. It may already have been unofficially involved by lobbying for or against the legislation. A regulatory agency—one like the Environmental Protection Agency or the Occupational Safety and Health Administration—may be created by the new law. Its task—as part of the executive branch—is to see that the provisions of a law are carried out, something it accomplishes by issuing rules and regulations that embody its interpretation of the law's intent.

The judiciary branch becomes active if serious disagreement arises between the regulators and those being regulated. The courts may be asked to judge the fairness or legality of the regulatory agency's rules and interpretations, or the entire law may be challenged as being unconstitutional. For example, a plumbing and heating contractor filed suit against OSHA, claiming that the agency was violating constitutional safeguards against unreasonable search when, for purposes of safety inspections, it entered a company's premises without advance notice. The courts agreed and required OSHA to obtain a court order before entering a company's property.

Our aim here is to outline the structure and main steps in the U.S. regulatory system. For the most part, business executives are involved with the task of adapting to the regulations affecting their industry or firm. But executives also can anticipate regulatory trends and be proactive or interactive in the shaping of regulations. To strategically manage regulation, one must recognize that its development includes many factors, some of them rational and others irrational. Proponents of a new regulation may exaggerate their case, particularly to persuade or affect a television audience. People's fears—of nuclear accidents, toxic waste sites, or insider trading abuses—may be highlighted by those people urging new regulations, while the businesses or other affected institutions issue defensive reassurances to the public. Politics is always present, as interest group influence is felt by legislators, and even by the courts, whose judges are not entirely isolated from social and political currents.[7]

THE SIZE OF GOVERNMENT

In U.S. history, there has never been a real question of whether there would be government participation in the business system. The Constitution itself provides for certain government participation. Throughout the development of the U.S. social system, the question has persisted: What kind of government intervention is appropriate, and how much should there be? In light of today's complex social demands, the roles and responsibilities of government and other major social institutions are being reexamined.

Compared with the government in the early days of the republic, or even with the one 100 years ago, today's government is gargantuan. The government at all levels in the United States employs over 17 million people, a figure that is about equal to every man, woman, and child in the greater New York City area. These government workers outnumber the total population of Australia, Switzerland,

[7] Vietor, op. cit.

FIGURE 10–4
Growth of government expenditures, 1980–1987, in current dollars.

SOURCE: *U.S. Statistical Abstract,* 1990, table 455.

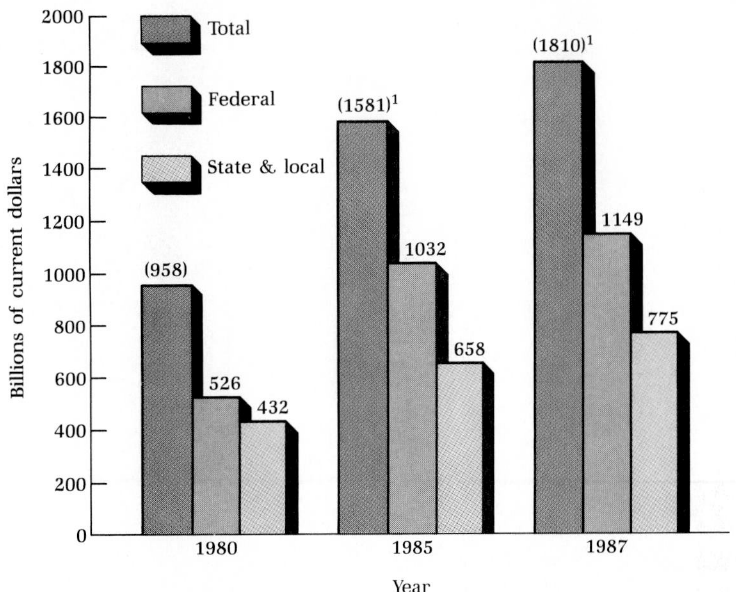

(In billions of current dollars)

	1980	1985	1987
Total government spending	$958.7 *	$1581.0	$1810.0
Federal	526.3	1032.0	1149.0
State & local	432.3	658.0	775.0

* Total varies due to rounding.

1. The 1985 and 1987 totals exclude government transactions with other government agencies. Federal, state, and local spending subtotals actually sum to a larger amount than that reported in the official government statistics.

or Iraq and exceed the combined number of employees of the 200 largest United States industrial corporations.

Government spending is equally impressive. In 1987, federal, state, and local governments in the United States spent a total of $1.8 trillion, an amount that exceeds the entire industrial output of some nations. With that amount of money, you could buy more than 2 billion color television sets, 75 million luxury automobiles, or 18 thousand houses costing $1 million each!

Not only is government big, but it has been expanding in recent decades. For example, expenditures of the federal government increased thirteenfold between 1950 and 1980, then nearly doubled between 1980 and 1987! (See Figure 10–4.) Government spending also is growing faster than the population. Between 1950 and 1983, per capita spending increased from $464 per person to $5,400; from

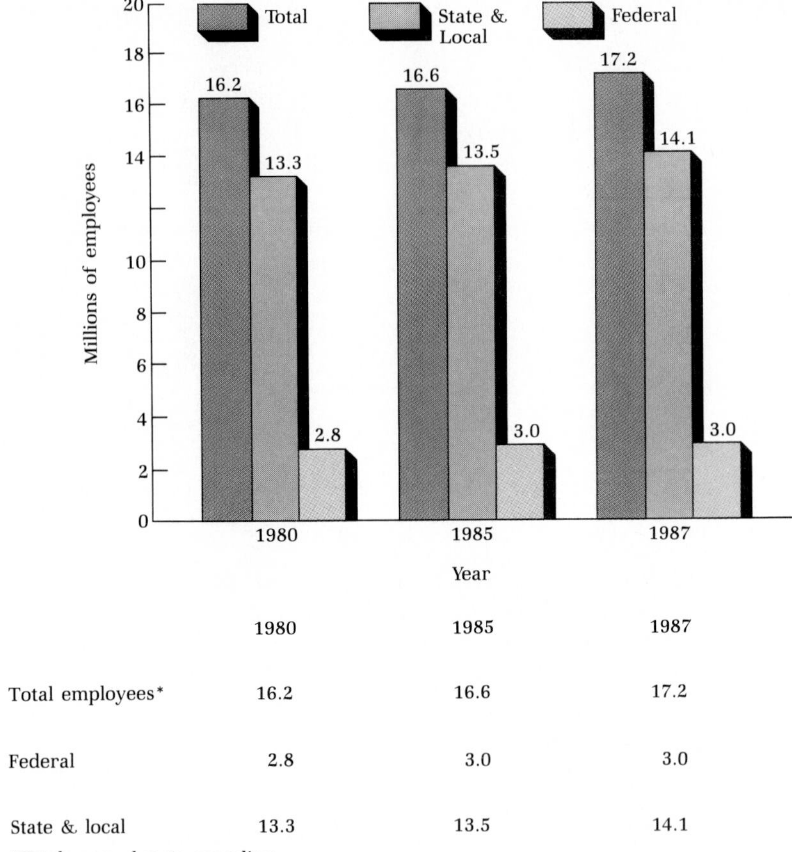

	1980	1985	1987
Total employees*	16.2	16.6	17.2
Federal	2.8	3.0	3.0
State & local	13.3	13.5	14.1

*Totals vary due to rounding.

FIGURE 10–5
Government civilian employees, full- and part-time.

SOURCE: *U.S. Statistical Abstract,* 1990, table 487.

1983 to 1987 per capita spending increased to $7,900, nearly a 50 percent increase.

There is a very complex relationship between the spending of federal, state, and local governments. In the quarter century between 1965 and 1990, federal spending increased eight times beyond the 1965 level while state and local government spending increased ten times over the 1965 levels. Some of this is predictable growth that stems from growth in government programs as population grows and public needs change. Other increases come from crises the government is asked to solve. The savings and loan failures of the 1980s, for example, were expected to cost the U.S. government—and U.S. taxpayers—more than $200 billion. That expense alone would add $800 to per capita government spending in the United States. State and local governments were among the strong advocates of federal government involvement to stabilize the financial system by taking action to close insolvent S&Ls.

Federal, state, and local government employment increases, which are illustrated in Figure 10–5, are also highly interdependent. For example, a local school may receive federal funds and hire personnel to teach handicapped children. It also may be obligated by a federal statute to initiate a dual-language program for students or support transportation for the purpose of desegregating a school system under a federal court order. Such situations are but a small example of the policy interactions between federal, state, and local governments.

During the 1980s, the Reagan administration consciously sought to control federal government spending by shifting many program-funding responsibilities to state and local governments. These efforts encountered resistance from advocates for federal funding of programs such as welfare assistance, but they have generally forced state governments to assume more financial responsibility for assistance programs. The effort produced a shift in spending by the federal government but did not produce any absolute reductions. The 1988, 1989, 1990, and 1991 federal budgets sent to Congress each set new records as the largest in the nation's history.

THE GROWTH OF REGULATION

Historians generally agree that regulation has been used to perform many tasks and to serve many different ends and purposes. Some have been economic, others political, legal, and cultural. The shapes and forms of U.S. regulation are so numerous and diverse that inconsistencies sometimes appear. Regulation is a tool of government, a tool that government policymakers have used to help solve important problems throughout U.S. history. Other nations also design regulatory systems in response to their own unique problems.

The 1990s appear to be a period of revived regulatory activity. The 1980s were mostly an era of reduced regulatory activity in response to the great growth of social regulation that occurred in the 1960s and 1970s. In fact, as we point out later in this chapter, government in the late 1970s and early 1980s relaxed some of its tighter economic regulations in such industries as air transportation, trucking, telecommunications, banking, and the railroads. But for two decades, the tide of social regulations rose higher and higher.

From 1962 to 1982, more than fifty major regulatory laws were enacted by Congress, each one imposing some type of limitation on the behavior of business. The focus of these laws reflects the major political issues of the times: consumer protection, pollution control, job discrimination, worker safety and health, financial security, energy conservation, and political contributions. As Congress defines new problem areas and responds to the public call for action (e.g., cleanup of toxic waste sites), specific regulatory systems are developed to deal with the problems (e.g., the Toxic Substances Control Act). The same process occurred with the financial collapse of savings and loan institutions in the 1990s. Congressional hearings were scheduled and more than a dozen new laws were proposed in less than two years. Exhibit 10–A highlights some of the many facts about one federal regulatory agency, EPA, as it reached its twentieth anniversary in 1990. In these facts are the elements of an answer to the question of how regulation grows.

EXHIBIT 10–A

"FACTS TO REFLECT ON"

EPA workforce in 1970: 5,500
EPA workforce in 1990: 17,170

EPA budget in fiscal year (FY) 1971: $1,289,000,000
EPA budget in FY 1990: $5,145,000,000

Percent of EPA's budget allocated to regional offices in 1981: 15
Percent allocated to regional offices in 1991: 43

Increase in U.S. population from 1970 to 1990: 48 million
Present ratio of increase in cars to increase in U.S. population: 2:1
Major federal environmental statutes EPA administers: 11
Pages of EPA statutes (1989): 670
Total number of EPA regulations in 1989: 9,000

Money awarded EPA in civil and criminal penalties in 1989: $45,300,000
Times EPA officials testified before congressional oversight committees in 1989: 168
Letters to EPA's Administrator and Deputy Administrator in 1989: 49,052
Freedom of information requests submitted to EPA in 1989: 35,205

SOURCE: Excerpted from Ross Ettlin, "Facts to Reflect On," *EPA Journal* ("EPA: The First Twenty Years"), September–October 1990, p. 29.

Why does society turn to more and more regulation as a way to solve some of its problems?

Part of the explanation lies in broad trends that have occurred, not just in U.S. society but worldwide. Science and technology have helped the industrial societies to meet many of their basic economic needs, allowing social concerns to receive more attention. Smokestacks that once signaled jobs and prosperity became negative symbols of environmental damage as society shifted its sights from economic growth to more social awareness.

Critics doubtful of free market philosophy charged business with using the environment to dispose of its wastes without regard for public health or aesthetic considerations. Minorities and women believed that equal opportunity depended upon government intervention rather than upon market forces to hire, reward, and promote them. Consumers, led by such champions as Ralph Nader, demanded regulatory curbs on business to enhance the quality and safety of its products. Workers, too, especially those employed in hazardous occupations, spurred organized labor to lobby for a government agency to safeguard employees on the job.

Media attention to environmental disasters, protest marches, and civil rights confrontations helped convince the general public that free market solutions were inadequate. Such coverage assisted interest groups—representing environmentalists, consumers, women, minorities, older people, the handicapped, and others—to develop political muscle and push through new regulatory laws. U.S.

history contained many precedents to guide these social activists, since farmers, small business, labor, public utilities, banks, and others had relied on government regulation to bail them out of difficulties in earlier times.

THE COSTS OF GOVERNMENT REGULATION

All social choices, including those made with the aid of government regulation, involve costs as well as benefits. An economic adage says, "There is no free lunch." Someone eventually has to pay for it. This inevitability of costs can be called the **Rule of Cost.** Simply stated, the Rule of Cost says that all actions generate costs. This cost rule applies in all types of socioeconomic systems, whether private enterprise or central state control.

Cost-Benefit Analysis

Since the Rule of Cost cannot be avoided, all societies try to make the benefits they want outrun the costs they must pay. This goal requires (1) well-organized and efficient institutions that can produce a steady stream of benefits at low cost and (2) a reliable method of identifying and measuring benefits and costs.

Cost-benefit analysis is a method of calculating the costs and benefits of a project or activity intended to produce benefits. If the potential costs outweigh the potential benefits, it might make sense not to undertake the project. For example, when a city thinks it should upgrade its health care facilities by building a new hospital and increasing the number of doctors and nurses working there, the expected benefits must be compared with the costs that will be incurred. A cost-benefit analysis attempts to identify all possible benefits and compares them with potential costs. (This is a form of utilitarian analysis, which was discussed in Chapter 4.)

Economic benefits and costs can be measured with greater ease than social benefits and costs. In business, money is the yardstick that measures business success. A cost-benefit analysis in business estimates whether monetary benefits do, or are expected to, exceed monetary costs. A company knows how much it pays its employees, the amounts it pays for materials, and how much interest is charged by lenders. Revenue from sales also is stated in dollar terms. If the firm's revenues exceed its costs, it makes a "bottom line" profit. This kind of cost-benefit analysis is usually made by a business before it launches a new product or makes a new investment.

On the other hand, social costs and benefits are more difficult to calculate because many of them cannot be measured in dollar terms alone. Consider the following situation:

> An urban housing authority decides to build a low-income housing project (a social benefit) by using recreational park land noted for its picnic areas,

lakes, and wooded lanes. The park adjoins a residential area (a social benefit) where luxurious homes are built on large, well-tended lots. Picnickers, boaters, and environmentalists object to losing recreational space (a social cost) for housing (a social benefit). Wealthy residents fear traffic congestion and a loss of privacy (social costs) and a decline in property values of their homes (an economic cost).

How can these conflicting and overlapping social benefits and costs be measured? Surely not in monetary terms alone. What is the "true value" of the relaxation and fun people have when using public parks? How much is neighborhood privacy "worth"? Is improved housing for the poor worth more? Social costs and benefits are indeed difficult to calculate with precision. For that reason, cost-benefit analysis is usually supplemented with less precise and more politically oriented methods.

The Cost Problem

An industrial society such as ours can "afford" almost anything, including social regulations, if it is willing to pay the price. Sometimes, the benefits are worth the costs. At other times, a more cautious—or different—approach to society's problems may provide a better payoff. We pay for the benefits of social regulation in the following ways.

Administrative and compliance costs

Regulatory costs take several different forms. Most obvious are the direct costs of running the regulatory agencies, including salaries of government employees, office equipment and supplies, utility bills, and other such items. The burden of regulatory costs was attacked in the 1980s by the Reagan administration. As Figure 10–6 illustrates, many areas of administrative costs and staffing were reduced but are now increasing.

But these administrative costs are only the tip of the iceberg. It costs money to comply with government's rules. Pollution control equipment must be bought, installed, and maintained in good working order; new hiring and training practices for disadvantaged employees have to be developed; many reports must be made to the regulatory agencies, consuming much time and many employee hours. By industry estimates, compliance costs total over $200 billion per year, about $800 for every person in the United States.

Paperwork

The sheer volume of paperwork involved in regulation is astounding. It has been estimated that federal agencies require U.S. businesses to fill out 4,400 different types of forms each year, costing 143 million hours of management and clerical time! More than 2 billion pieces of paper flow to government agencies from those firms and organizations being regulated. Only in recent times has it been possible to electronically file some of these reports and forms.[8] Paperwork requirements

[8] Robert Reich, "The Regulation Wars," *Business Month,* March 1988, pp. 61–63.

FIGURE 10–6
Percentage changes in federal regulatory costs and staffing, 1980–1990.

SOURCE: Melinda Warren and Kenneth Chilton, *The Regulatory Legacy of the Reagan Revolution: An Analysis of 1990 Federal Regulatory Budget and Staffing*, St. Louis, MO: Center for the Study of American Business, Washington University, 1990, p. 10.

Area of Regulation	% Change 1980–85		% Change 1985–90	
	Administrative Costs	Staffing	Administrative Costs	Staffing
Consumer safety and health	−12	−19	+5	+1
Job safety and other working conditions	−12	−20	−2	0
Environment and energy	+5	−6	+32	+17
Finance & banking	+33	+2	+40	+14
Industry-specific regulation	−20	−1	−4	−1

also slow business decision making, and long delays in getting permits can kill projects. An oil company building a pipeline from California to Texas had to obtain 700 environmental and construction permits before proceeding. It finally abandoned the entire project!

Higher prices and taxes

Business and nonprofit organizations can "afford" such cost burdens if they have a way to offset them. But in doing so, they often pass the costs along as higher prices to others. These "hidden taxes" constitute another way the public pays for government regulations.

Taxes, too, are sometimes raised when regulations force cities to build improved water treatment systems, military posts to clean up toxic waste disposal sites, and county governments to upgrade hospitals to care for the aged. The EPA's proposal to require recycling programs, described at the beginning of this chapter, was stopped because of the costs it would impose on communities and on industry.

Opportunity costs

Almost everyone, sometimes with considerable regret, sooner or later faces the question: What could I have done with that money if I hadn't spent it in that particular way? This is the meaning of an **opportunity cost:** What opportunity did I forego by spending money one way rather than another.

Social regulations cost money, sometimes huge sums. How might society have spent its money if it had chosen to have fewer social regulations? What are the opportunity costs to society for having extensive social regulations? The answers are almost as numerous as one's imagination permits. We might have more hospitals, better and safer highways, more urban renewal, an expanded national park system, a rebuilding of deteriorating bridges, more business investment in modernizing industrial plants in order to meet foreign competition, more research on life-threatening diseases, greater aid to the poorer nations of the world, and on and on through a long list of possible ways to budget society's money.

Or if society simply chose not to spend these sums on anything, consumers might enjoy lower prices, stockholders higher dividends, workers more jobs and higher take-home pay, and taxpayers lower tax bills. The existence of opportunity costs virtually guarantees that public debate will continue about how much regulation the nation can afford.

Unintended impacts of regulations

Some costs of government regulation are partially or totally unforeseen when the regulation is adopted.

One of the most serious impacts of government regulation is on the use of capital to modernize and expand the nation's industrial base. Without capital to reinvest, plants become obsolete and productivity falls. Both outmoded plants and lowered productivity put U.S. industry at a competitive disadvantage in world trade.

Other links in the chain of unintended consequences of regulation have been suggested. Compliance expenditures tend to favor big business over small business and sometimes create barriers to entry of new competitors into an industry. Unemployment may be raised by well-intended regulators. When the legal minimum wage was raised, for example, 320,000 fewer teenagers were hired by businesses that could not afford to pay the higher wages.[9]

Figure 10–7 depicts the "tree of regulatory costs," whose branches reach higher and higher into successive cost realms.

Economic and Social Trade-offs

Economic and social trade-offs occur when society discovers that its social goals involve economic costs and that its economic goals incur social costs. Figure 10–8 gives some examples. If we want cleaner and safer electric power plants (a social goal), then the added costs of installing safe, clean generators will increase utility bills (an economic cost). Society has to decide how much in economic terms it is willing to pay for this desirable social goal. Or in other words, how much cleanliness and safety will it trade away in order to avoid higher electric bills? Some families may not be concerned enough about safe working conditions or pollution to pay higher prices for electricity; others who live close to the plant or work there may feel differently.

The same kind of dilemma occurs when the pursuit of economic goals causes social costs.

> A classic example is found in the history of the SST aircraft. Sales of the Concorde supersonic airliner resulted in economic gain for its builders, cre-

[9] An excellent discussion of the consequences of regulation is found in Robert Leone, *Who Profits? How Regulation Creates Winners and Losers,* New York: Free Press, 1987.

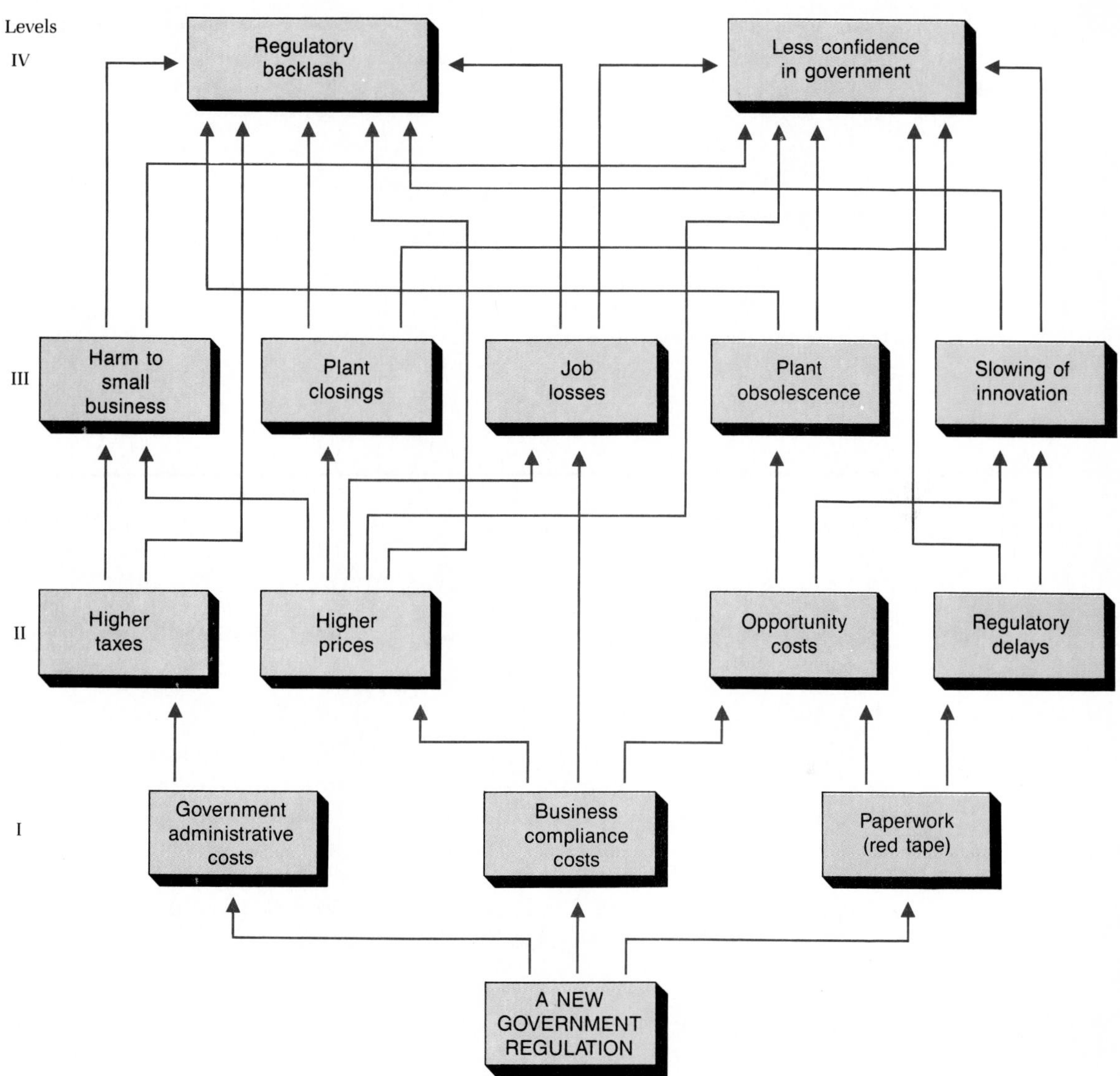

FIGURE 10–7
The "tree of regulatory costs."

ated jobs for French and English workers, and made swift trips possible for some people. But these economic goals were achieved at a social cost: high noise levels, air pollution, and discomfort for those living near airports. Interestingly, in France the trade-off was made in favor of the economic benefits. In the United States, however, the social costs of producing a supersonic plane were considered too high for the economic gains, and the trade-offs favored the social side when Congress failed to provide development funds. A new generation of SST aircraft is being proposed for development in the 1990s by European sponsors. The debate seems certain to continue.[10]

[10] Mel Horwitch, *Clipped Wings: The American SST Conflict*, Cambridge, MA: MIT Press, 1982.

FIGURE 10–8
Economic and social trade-offs.

Social Goal		Economic Cost
Clean air and water in a local community	vs.	Jobs lost when a marginal plant closes
Safe, tested pharmaceutical drugs	vs.	Slowdown in drug production, marketing, and R&D
Cleaner, safer electric power plants	vs.	Higher home heating and cooling bills
More job opportunities for women and minorities	vs.	Higher training costs for business
Safe noise levels in factories	vs.	Cost of installing noise abatement equipment
Economic Goal		**Social Cost**
1 billion tons of coal per year	vs.	Increased coal-related deaths
Fast supersonic trans-Atlantic air travel	vs.	Increased noise and air pollution
Industrial production costs and prices kept low	vs.	More job-related injuries and deaths per year

There is no single or simple solution to the trade-off problem because we have no socially acceptable way to equate human lives and social values with monetary values. Money can measure economic costs and benefits, but we have no generally acceptable, single yardstick for calculating social costs and benefits. In the United States, the trade-off answers are usually reached by working through the political system, which allows both social and economic inputs to be made by all interested parties who enjoy the benefits and pay the costs.

DEREGULATION AND RECENT TRENDS

Government regulation reached a high-water mark in the 1980s. Federal regulatory agencies spent $7.1 billion in 1985. The peak year for employent was 1980, with over 90,000 regulators working for the federal government.[11] After two decades of steady growth in government regulation, the public was ready for a change. Instead of regulation, society supported deregulation. **Deregulation** is the removal or scaling down of regulatory authority and regulatory activities of government.

[11] Melinda Warren and Kenneth Chilton, *The Regulatory Legacy of the Reagan Revolution: An Analysis of 1990 Federal Regulatory Budget and Staffing*, St. Louis, MO: Center for Study of American Business, Washington University, 1990; also, Murray L. Weidenbaum, "Regulatory Reform: A Report Card for the Reagan Administration," *California Management Review*, Fall 1983, pp. 8–24.

For many, President Ronald Reagan symbolized the public's revolt against government regulation, and he promised to "get government off the back of people." However, deregulation began even before President Reagan's election. Major deregulatory laws were enacted beginning in 1975 when Gerald Ford was president and continued through the administrations of Jimmy Carter and Ronald Reagan. These laws loosened the grip of the federal government on several industries and markets, in the following ways:

> In the petroleum industry, all price controls on domestic oil were abolished in 1981. Prices of natural gas were gradually decontrolled until all controls ended in 1987. A phased regulation of commercial airlines gradually removed government supervision of rates charged, allowed airlines to enter new domestic routes without government permission, and made mergers and acquisitions easier. The Civil Aeronautics Board, the chief airline regulator, was abolished in 1985.
>
> Intercity trucking companies were permitted to charge lower prices and provide wider services. More competitors were allowed into the industry. Even among the nation's railroads—which had been tightly regulated for nearly a century—greater competition was encouraged, with some shipping rates completely deregulated. Financial institutions were granted more leeway in setting interest rates on certain types of savings deposits; thrift institutions could establish a type of checking deposit for savers and invest savers' deposits in nontraditional projects; banks were required to pay interest on checking accounts; and the way was paved for interstate banking.

The sheer volume of paperwork involved in regulation is astounding. It has been decontrol other parts of the business system. Commercial radio broadcasting was deregulated in early 1981, and Congress relaxed the licensing process for radio and television stations. Steps were planned to promote more competition in the entire telecommunications industry—telephone service, electronic information transfer, and local and regional television broadcasting. International competition was making some regulations obsolete as new competitors were challenging once-powerful industries. More reliance on the marketplace and less on government guidance also characterized financial services, health care delivery, workplace safety, and environmental protection. Similar policies toward antitrust regulation were developed and are discussed in Chapter 11.

Deregulation can be achieved in several ways. In addition to changing or repealing regulatory laws, staff and budget cuts were made in the regulatory agencies; at the federal level, both were reduced in the early 1980s. Some people have, in fact, argued that financial cutbacks are the most effective method for effecting regulatory change and reform.

Other deregulation experts have emphasized the importance of personnel selections. The opportunity to appoint or designate new agency heads and senior regulatory staff officials is a primary tool for placing the administration's imprint on regulatory policy.

One very effective deregulatory tool was created by President Reagan in Executive order 12291, issued in early 1981. This directive requires federal agencies to submit proposed new regulations to the Office of Management and Budget for a thorough cost-benefit analysis. Rules whose costs outweigh their benefits are sent back to the agency. A similar regulatory impact analysis must be made for existing rules that might cause an increase in costs or prices, whose overall impact is $100 million or more, or that might be particularly burdensome for some specific industry or the economy in general. The EPA proposal to require mandatory recycling described at the beginning of this chapter was reviewed on this basis. The impact of this new system was dramatic: in one year, the number of proposed new rules dropped by 38 percent, the number of final rules approved went down by 27 percent, and the number of pages in the *Federal Register* describing new rules declined by 33 percent.[12]

Another interesting type of deregulation is the "sunset law." These laws, first adopted by a number of states in the mid-1970s, provide for a periodic review and sometimes a termination of government agencies unless they can justify their existence. A number of states have used sunset laws with success. Similar legislation has repeatedly been proposed in Congress but not adopted.

In spite of deregulation's general popularity during the 1980s, public sentiment has tended to support an increasing amount of government reregulation in the last few years. These included tougher job safety rules, new environmental protection laws, curbs on insider trading and corporate takeovers, requirements for airline collision avoidance equipment, and proposed drug testing of train engineers, airline pilots, and others.[13]

INTERNATIONAL REGULATION

International trade has tied people and businesses together in new and complicated ways. U.S. consumers regularly buy food, automobiles, VCRs, and clothing from companies located in Europe, Canada, Latin America, Australia, Africa, and Asia. Citizens of other nations do the same. As these patterns of international commerce grow more complicated, governments see the need to establish rules that protect and serve the public interest of their own citizens. No nation wants to accept dangerous products manufactured elsewhere that will injure local citizens. No national government wants to see its economy damaged by unfair competition from foreign competitors. These concerns are the reasons for a rapidly growing set of international regulatory agreements and actions. Three types of such regulation are discussed below and illustrated in Figure 10-9.

[12] Marvin H. Kosters and Jeffrey A. Eisenach, "Is Regulatory Relief Enough?" *Regulation*, March–April 1982, p. 24.

[13] Laurie McGinley, "Hands On: Federal Regulation Rises Anew in Matters That Worry the Public," *Wall Street Journal*, Apr. 21, 1987, pp. 1, 26; Kenneth Labich, "Should Airlines Be ReRegulated?" *Fortune*, June 19, 1989, pp. 82–89.

FIGURE 10–9
Forms of international regulation.

FORMS OF INTERNATIONAL REGULATION

Unilateral Regulation

COUNTRY A NATIONAL GOVERNMENT	regulates	■ All companies doing business in Country A. ■ Country–A companies doing business in any other nation.
COUNTRY B NATIONAL GOVERNMENT	regulates	■ All companies doing business in Country B. ■ Country–B companies doing business in any other nation.

Bilateral Regulation

COUNTRY A AND COUNTRY B	Agree to mutually accepted rules of doing business in both nations (e.g., no government subsidies for certain agricultural products).

Multilateral Regulation

COUNTRY A COUNTRY B COUNTRY C	Agree to common rules governing use of common resources (e.g., oceans, earth's atmosphere) or to impose sanctions on Country D which fails to comply with international standards (e.g., apartheid, genocide).

Regulation of Imported Products

When a U.S. child receives a Christmas toy that is made in Taiwan, that toy has met the product safety standard set by the Consumer Product Safety Commission, an agency of the U.S. government. Every nation has the power to set standards for products that meet its own health, safety, and quality standards. This requirement is a legitimate use of governmental authority. However, there can be a temptation for policymakers to set standards for foreign products that may be unjustifiably higher or more difficult to meet than for locally produced goods. If the Consumer Product Safety Commission set one standard for U.S. companies and a more demanding standard for foreign toy companies, the result would help the U.S. companies and hurt foreign competitors. Such a step might also hurt U.S. consumers, who would lose the chance to purchase the innovative or less expensive (but perhaps unsafe) toys made elsewhere. Because competition tends to favor the consumer, and because international competition is increasingly common, governments should encourage uniform standards of quality and safety for all competitors.

Governments, however, are under pressure from other interests, including local companies, labor organizations, and communities, not to open local markets to foreign sellers. These stakeholders may feel threatened by foreign competitors and seek to block them from selling to a "safe" market of customers. U.S. peanut growers would certainly prefer not to have imported peanuts competing for American sales. If the U.S. peanut growers mentioned at the beginning of this chapter are to have a chance to sell in other countries, however, those countries must know that the U.S. market is open to their companies and products.

As discussed in Chapters 7 and 8, political and economic arrangements, such as the European Economic Community, tend to favor greater free trade and discourage protective regulation. This trend is growing but is not easy to achieve. The desire to expand competition, improve consumer choices, and build healthy economies places pressures on governments and business to use regulation to promote and protect a broad spectrum of stakeholders.

Regulation of Exported Products

Governments have a real interest in knowing what types of products their businesses are exporting to the rest of the world. The federal government is understandably concerned that products that say "Made in America" are of good quality. U.S. companies have sometimes exported products to other nations that were banned from sale at home because of safety concerns. In addition, the government is concerned that U.S. companies not sell military technology to unfriendly nations. In the 1980s, a number of cases arose in which U.S. and West German businesses illegally sold sophisticated technology with potential military applications to Libya, Iran, and Iraq. These transactions violated U.S. laws that restrict the sale of classified military technology to only those customers approved by the Defense Department. For example, EG&G, a U.S. manufacturer of specialized electronic equipment for military uses, discovered that some of the triggering devices it manufactured for nuclear weapons were being sold to Iraq. The company cooperated with U.S. officials, and a shipment of such devices was traced through a series of intermediaries to a destination in Europe from which they were to go to Baghdad. With the cooperation of foreign officials, the illegal exporters were caught and arrested.

Industrialized nations such as the United States, Japan, Germany, and Britain all impose some controls on what products can be sold to customers around the world. During the mid-1980s when Libya was involved in hostile military action and alleged to be supporting international terrorist activity, West German officials discovered that a West German chemical company had worked with the Libyan government to build a chemical plant capable of manufacturing internationally banned chemical weapons. The West German managers were fired from their jobs, charges of "industrial treason" were filed, and the government threatened to close the company permanently. Similar examples were discovered in 1991 after Iraq was defeated in the Persian Gulf war.

Regulation of International Business Behavior

Nations also have sought to standardize trade practices through various international organizations. United Nations agencies such as the World Health Organization have worked with the pharmaceutical industry to create data bases on the side effects of drug product characteristics, establish quality standards, and resolve conflicting manufacturing and marketing practices that might harm the public. Elaborate processes of consultation between leaders of business, governmental, and nongovernmental organizations (e.g., consumer groups) are required to make such changes because of the vast number of stakeholders involved. The World Health Organization's international marketing code for infant formula products, for example, required nearly three years of meetings and consultations before a suitable code was ready for adoption by national governments.

National governments sometimes create special organizations to keep the discussions moving forward. For example, the General Agreement on Tariffs and Trade (GATT) is a set of international agreements among nations on acceptable trade practices. Periodically, nations agree to another "round" of negotiations to be hosted in a particular nation. In the early 1990s, the "Uruguay Round" of talks focused on such issues as government subsidies to agriculture that prevent fair competition from occurring. Japan, for example, had long subsidized its rice farmers. Rice prices in Japan were kept above the world market price and the market was closed to foreign suppliers. Negotiations of agriculture subsidies continued for several years during this round of talks. Japanese national political leaders wrestled with domestic interests in an effort to create internationally acceptable compromises. A compromise that reconciled domestic and international trade concerns took years to achieve.

At other times, nations work together to establish standards for the use of resources that are not owned by any nation. In recent years, international agreements have been reached to govern ocean fishing, the protection of sea mammals such as dolphins and whales, the ozone layer of the earth's atmosphere, and the dumping of hazardous chemicals and wastes in the oceans. In each instance national governments recognize the need to address a problem that could not be solved through the actions of one nation alone. The result is an emerging framework of international understandings and standards that, like national or state-level regulation, attempt to harmonize business activity and the public interest.[14]

THE FUTURE

Government regulation of business has been an important feature of the U.S. socioeconomic system for more than a century. Sharp increases in government

[14] William C. Frederick, "The Moral Authority of Transnational Corporate Codes," *Journal of Business Ethics*, Vol. 10, 1991, pp. 165–177.

regulation occurred during the depression decade of the 1930s, the war years of the 1940s, and the years of increasing social demands during the 1960s and 1970s. By the mid-1970s and throughout the 1980s, the pendulum swung in the other direction, toward greater reliance on free market solutions to social and economic problems. The 1990s are likely to see a continuation of this seesawing between government regulation and free market approaches. Eastern European nations in particular face long periods of adjustment as they move from central state control toward freer markets and less regulation. In the United States, and internationally, business and society seek an optimum solution to major problems along with the preservation of freedoms and social justice. Regulation is a primary means of achieving this balance.

SUMMARY POINTS OF THIS CHAPTER

- Government regulation of business is a mechanism for implementing social choices. Three types of U.S. business regulation are common: industry-specific economic regulation, all-industry social regulation, and functional regulation.
- U.S. government regulation is based on constitutional powers. Legislation usually creates a regulatory agency empowered to set standards. The executive branch administers the law and the judicial branch reviews the law and its implementation.
- The role of government has grown because society demands and expects more of government. Size, social complexity, and new needs have contributed to the growth of government.
- Government regulation is costly in several ways. Businesses find it burdensome to comply with paperwork, filing requirements, and the approval process of government. Society sometimes pays these costs in the form of higher prices, slowed product innovation, higher taxes, and other ways. Thus regulation requires a careful assessment of both benefits and costs.
- International regulation is emerging as global economic activity creates problems that cannot be solved by any one nation's government. Governments regulate imports, exports, and business practices. Agreements among national governments are the key to developing effective international standards.

KEY TERMS AND CONCEPTS USED IN THIS CHAPTER

- Industry-specific, social, functional regulation
- Regulatory mechanism
- Rule of Cost

- Cost-benefit analysis
- Opportunity cost
- Economic and social tradeoffs
- Deregulation
- International regulation

DISCUSSION CASE

SAVING THE BANKING SYSTEM

It was a bad start to the New Year. Within three hours of being sworn in as the new governor of Rhode Island on January 1, 1991, Governor Bruce G. Sundlun made an announcement that would shake the state's business community and citizenry: he was declaring an immediate "bank holiday" and closing 45 state-chartered Rhode Island financial institutions. Depositors could not get their funds, automatic teller machines would not function, and no date was set for reopening the institutions. The action was needed, according to Governor Sundlun, to preserve the solvency and integrity of the state's financial system. An entire week would pass before any of the closed institutions were permitted to reopen.

Less than a week after the Rhode Island announcement, the Federal Deposit Insurance Corporation (FDIC) announced that it had taken over the Bank of New England (BNE), headquartered in Boston. The federal agency had decided to close the third largest national bank in the entire New England region because of enormous losses that threatened to eat up all of the bank's capital. The action followed nearly two years' efforts by banking regulators, a new management team, and local government officials to save the bank from insolvency.

There were different underlying problems in the Rhode Island and Bank of New England cases. In Rhode Island, the 45 banks and credit unions were insured by a private insurer, the Rhode Island Share and Deposit Indemnity Corporation. The corporation turned to state government officials for help when they discovered that they had insufficient capital to meet the needs of their client financial institutions. The problem, it appeared, was that the private insurance fund had been defrauded of about $13 million by the president of one of its clients, Heritage Loan and Investment Corporation.

In most parts of the United States, banks and credit unions are protected by federal deposit insurance administered by the FDIC for banks and the National Credit Union Administration (NCUA). Both are U.S. government agencies. One out of every four Americans is a member of one of the more than 14,000 credit unions in the United States. About 10 percent of the credit unions—more than 1,400 with $18.6 billion of deposits—have chosen to create their own insurance programs rather than use the federal insurance available through NCUA. Nine other private groups continued to insure state-chartered credit unions after the Rhode Island Share and Deposit Indemnity Corporation was closed. Experts argued, however, that private credit union insurers were in jeopardy because they tended to have less strict capital requirements than NCUA. Private insurers tend to set lower reserve levels, which gives the credit union more funds to invest. When the economy slips into recession, or real estate values decline as happened in New England, loan failures increase. The fraudulent loans added to the underlying weakness and served as the "trigger" that led to the Rhode Island collapse.

Governor Sundlun's order required that credit unions apply for and receive federal credit union insurance before they could reopen. Meanwhile, depositors with funds in the closed credit unions were unable to get their funds. Indeed, because the insurer was insolvent, it was unclear whether depositors would get all of their deposit money back. Within days, 22 of the closed institutions applied for federal insurance. Seven credit unions received insurance quickly and reopened one week after the governor's order. Others took longer to reopen and at least a half-dozen were expected to close permanently, with depositors getting back only a small fraction of their savings.

When the FDIC moved to seize Bank of New England's assets, it recognized the potential ripple effects of taking over such a large financial institution. FDIC officials announced the takeover on a Sunday when all banks are closed for business, and indicated that all Bank of New England branches would be open for business as usual on Monday morning. Banking authorities also feared that depositors would withdraw deposits quickly from other major banks in the region in what is called a "run on the bank."

To avoid the financial panic that could result, FDIC officials announced that they would guarantee all of the deposits in the bank, including those which were above the usual $100,000 ceiling for FDIC guaranteed deposits. Businesses and government agencies often have bank accounts totaling millions of dollars. Modern banking makes it possible for those funds to be deposited in financial institutions all around the country and world. If BNE's large depositors were not guaranteed the safety of their deposits, they and other large depositors would prudently move funds out of the region to banks in other locations.

The FDIC was forced to step in and take over Bank of New England because of the withdrawal of $1 billion on the bank's last two days of business. The bank's management had asked the U.S. Comptroller of the Currency to provide assistance. Government officials concluded, however, that insolvency could not be forestalled. By taking over the bank, government officials hoped to stabilize the situation, restore confidence in the region's banking system, and find a buyer for the Bank of New England's assets. Within days it was rumored that Bank of America, headquartered in San Francisco, and BancOne, headquartered in Columbus, Ohio, were interested in acquiring BNE.

As talk of a buyer surfaced, members of the Organization for a New Equality demanded that federal regulators make minority needs a major consideration while negotiating the sale of BNE. Headed by Reverend Charles Stith, a leader of Boston's minority community, the group sent letters to FDIC officials and three potential acquirers. Reverend Stith said that "if BNE is too big to fail, the black community is too big to ignore. If BNE is going to be thrown a lifeline, the new bank must be required to extend a credit line to our communities." Regulators had the power to make such commitments a part of the requirements for buyers.[15]

[15] This case is based on news stories appearing in the *Wall Street Journal, New York Times,* and the *Boston Globe,* during January 1991.

Discussion Questions

1. Analyze the actions of Governor Sundlun and the federal credit union officials. Is it proper for a government agency to put private companies out of business? Why? Should Rhode Island permit private insurers to continue to exist?
2. Should the Rhode Island and federal officials who were studying the credit unions in the weeks before Governor Sundlun's action have warned depositors that they would be unable to get their funds? If you worked for one of these agencies, would you have warned your parents if they had funds in one of these credit unions?
3. Do you agree with the Federal Deposit Insurance Corporation officials who decided to cover deposits in excess of $100,000 at Bank of New England? Are some financial institutions too big to fail? Is this fair to smaller, local banks favored by many depositors?
4. Should the FDIC acknowledge the request of Reverend Stith's group and require the new owner of BNE to make commitments to the black community?
5. Consider the roles of state and federal officials who regulate financial institutions such as credit unions and banks. Would it make more sense to have just one level of regulation? If so, should it be federal or state? Why?

11

Competition, Antitrust, and Global Business

All socioeconomic systems face the problem of deciding how much power should be held by leading enterprises, whether they are privately owned or controlled by the state. In the United States, antitrust laws have long been used to curb corporate power, to preserve competition, and to achieve various social goals. As the economy has changed, however, new factors have raised policy issues concerning business competitiveness. These trends have presented public policymakers and corporate leaders with a need to reconcile corporate power, shareholders' interests, and social responsibility with new realities.

Key Questions and Chapter Objectives

This chapter focuses on these key questions and objectives:

- What dilemma does corporate power present in a democratic society?
- What are the objectives of the antitrust laws, and how are they enforced?
- Why does business criticize U.S. antitrust policy?
- What have been recent major trends in antitrust policy?
- How has the merger movement of the past fifteen years affected business-society relations?
- Why are intellectual property issues so important to competition policy?

The state of Texas sent out a request for bids that solicited proposals from infant formula companies to supply the state's needs for the Women, Infants, and Children (WIC) feeding program. Officials were surprised when companies' bids were more costly than had been expected. One of the industry's leading companies, Mead-Johnson, had sent a letter to WIC directors, which also reached its competitors, specifying the maximum refund it would offer on future bids. The Texas attorney general's office concluded that the letter was an attempt to "signal"

Mead-Johnson's intentions to its competitors in violation of the antitrust laws. A lawsuit was filed.

Prime Computer, Inc., had been facing vigorous competition in the hardware and software business. With profit margins on computer hardware being quite low, Prime—like many other computer firms—attempted to maximize its software sales and hardware maintenance businesses. The company began requiring that its hardware customers purchase computer maintenance from Prime, not from independent maintenance firms. Virtual Maintenance, Inc., a small Michigan computer maintenance firm, sued Prime for wrongfully "tying" its software updating services to the maintenance services required by its hardware purchasers. A Detroit jury agreed with Virtual Maintenance and found Prime guilty of unfair competition. The $8.4 million damage award was tripled as the law permits. With interest and attorneys' fees added, the court judgment totaled $30 million.

Go-Video, Inc., a small Scottsdale, Arizona, electronics company, had a better idea. It developed a dual-deck videocassette recorder. The machine can play one tape while recording another or tape two shows at once. Japanese companies dominate the VCR market and were slow to sell and deliver VCR components to Go-Video. The company charged fourteen Japanese and three Korean companies with conspiring to deprive it of parts while developing their own dual-deck systems. If proved, this action would violate U.S. antitrust and patent protection laws.[1]

These examples of competitive conflicts—between business and government, in the first instance, and between two companies in the second and third—illustrate how anticompetitive practices can arise in the free market system. This chapter looks at how the United States has traditionally sought to preserve and enhance competition. The 1990s present new challenges to traditional approaches according to some observers. As U.S. business competes in global markets, as services outgrow manufacturing, and as research and development become more vital to industry, antitrust and related competition policies are being reexamined.

CORPORATE POWER AND LEGITIMACY

By almost any measure used, the world's largest business enterprises are impressively big, as shown in Figures 11–1 and 11–2. Size can be measured in several ways—by annual sales, assets, profits, and employees—and a company's rank will vary depending on the measurement used. By most measures, the "big five" in 1990 were General Motors, Ford, Exxon, IBM, and General Electric. Among the biggest non-United States companies listed in Figure 11–2, oil companies, electronics, and automobile manufacturers dominate the top levels.

[1] "Prime Computer Broke Antitrust Law, Federal Jury Rules in Detroit Trial," *Wall Street Journal,* Oct. 10, 1990, p. B-5. "Go-Video Fails to Get Anti-Takeover Move Approved by Holders," *Wall Street Journal,* Jan. 24, 1991, p. B-3; "The Little Company That Could—Sue, That Is," *Business Week,* Apr. 8, 1991, p. 25.

FIGURE 11–1 The ten largest U.S. industrial and service corporations, 1988–1989.

SOURCE: *Fortune,* Apr. 23, 1990, pp. 338–392; *Fortune,* June 4, 1990, pp. 298–336. Fortune and Service 500, Copyright 1990, Time, Inc. All rights reserved.

Rank	By Sales (billions)	By Assets (billions)	By Profits (billions)	By Employees
1.	General Motors $126.9	General Motors $173.2	General Motors $4.2	General Motors 775,000
2.	Ford Motor 96.9	Ford Motor 160.9	General Electric 3.9	Sears 520,000
3.	Exxon 86.6	General Electric 128.3	Ford Motor 3.8	IBM 383,000
4.	IBM 63.4	Exxon 83.2	IBM 3.7	Ford Motor 366,000
5.	General Electric 55.2	Sears 77.9	Exxon 3.5	K-Mart 355,000
6.	Mobil 50.9	IBM 77.7	Philip Morris 2.9	General Electric 292,000
7.	Sears 50.2	Chrysler 51.0	AT&T 2.7	AT&T 283,000
8.	Philip Morris 39.0	Mobil 39.0	Dow Chemical 2.5	Pepsico 266,000
9.	Du Pont 35.2	Philip Morris 38.5	Du Pont 2.4	Marriott 229,000
10.	AT&T 35.2	AT&T 37.6	Texaco 2.4	Walmart 223,000

FIGURE 11–2 The ten largest industrial corporations outside the United States (ranked by 1989 sales).

SOURCE: *Fortune,* July 30, 1990, pp. 264–328. Copyright, 1990, Time, Inc. All rights reserved.

Company	Home Nation(s)	Sales (Billions)	Employees
1. Royal Dutch/Shell Group	Britain/Netherlands	$85.5	135,000
2. Toyota	Japan	60.4	91,700
3. Hitachi	Japan	50.8	274,000
4. British Petroleum	Britain	49.4	119,000
5. IRI	Italy	49.0	416,000
6. Matsushita	Japan	43.0	193,000
7. Daimler Benz	Germany	40.6	368,000
8. Fiat	Italy	36.7	286,000
9. Nissan Motors	Japan	36.0	117,000
10. Unilever	Britain/Netherlands	35.2	300,000

The ten United States corporations shown in Figure 11–1 generate more sales annually than the entire national output of Australia, Brazil, Canada, China, India, Italy, Mexico, or Nigeria. The employees of these same ten companies, if living together in one location, would make up the seventh or eighth largest metropolitan area in the United States—about the size of greater Boston or greater Washington, D.C. Some of the world's largest corporations are banks (Dai Ichi Kangyo of Japan and Citicorp of New York), insurance companies (Prudential), and other financial institutions (Merrill Lynch), which are not shown in Figure 11–1 or 11–2 but were previously identified in Figure 6–2.

These giant enterprises are not completely representative of business in the United States or other nations. The overwhelming number of business firms are owned by individual proprietors or by small groups of partners, as revealed in Figure 11–3. Only one of every five business firms in the United States is a corporation, and many of these corporations are small. For example, in 1990, the five hundredth largest industrial corporation in the United States (ranked by sales) employed only 3,060 people, and several higher-ranking companies had fewer than 2,000 employees. The largest firms at the top of the business pyramid are the focus of so much attention because of their size, power, and influence, not because they represent the entire business community.

Corporate Economic Power

Sheer size alone does not account for the economic significance of large corporations. Corporate power arises from the critical tasks society expects these organizations to perform. These functions as performed in the United States were described by one expert in the following way:

> Large American business corporations, although "private" enterprises, perform the great majority of essential economic tasks, which, due to their very essentiality, are in many countries undertaken by the state, either directly or through closely affiliated "public" entities. In this country, business corporations produce and distribute all forms of energy, process all ferrous and nonferrous metals and derivative products, provide air, sea, motor, and for the most part, intra-urban and inter-city rail transportation, maintain radio, television, telephone, and intercontinental satellite broad-

FIGURE 11–3 Major types and numbers of business firms in the United States.

SOURCE: Bureau of the Census, *Statistical Abstract of the United States, 1990*, Washington, DC, 1990, Table 859.

Type of Business Firm	1970	1975	1980	1985	1986
			(number in millions)		
Proprietorships (owned by one person)	5.7	7.2	8.9	11.9	12.4
Partnerships (owned by two or more persons)	0.9	1.0	1.3	1.7	1.7
Corporations (owned by stockholders)	1.6	2.0	2.7	3.2	3.4

> casting services, and, finally, service virtually all of the essential financial needs of the nation.[2]

By entrusting large private corporations with these central economic functions, society has granted business much economic influence. By amassing physical assets, employing and training thousands of persons, attracting huge pools of capital, engaging in research and development on a large scale, and reaching throughout the world for resources and markets, the largest corporations are the central economic institutions of industrial nations.

Corporate Political Power

The political influence of business, discussed in Chapter 9, tends to increase with the size of the business firm. One experienced observer of the corporate world confirms this relationship:

> Large corporations . . . have . . . moved a long way toward rivaling or surpassing the power of government on issues that are of special importance to them. . . . [In a sense,] the large corporation becomes a piece of government. This is the real character of the large companies that constitute a major part of the economic base of this country [the United States], a nation that still contains the greatest concentration of economic power in the world. In the real economy, where companies are unrecognized parts of the government, we must consider how such companies are governed and how they relate to the political structure within which they move and exercise their enormous capacity.[3]

Corporate Social Power

A corporation's social influence is felt in two kinds of ways: one is external and the other is internal.

Externally, a company's actions can influence how clean the community's air is, how adequate the local tax base is for civic improvement, whether voluntary nonprofit community agencies will be well funded, and the general tone of community relations, including local pride in community accomplishments.

A corporation's internal social influence is felt by employees who spend most of their waking hours in the service of their employer. The result, in the words of one expert, is that:

> The large corporation generally—and the megacorporation in particular—has become a social institution which embraces the thousands of human beings whose lives are affected by it and which provides an important focus for the employees' social relationships. In the more complex society, with greater mobility, the loosening of com-

[2] Edwin M. Epstein, "Societal, Managerial, and Legal Perspectives on Corporate Social Responsibility: Product and Process," in S. Prakash Sethi and Carl L. Swanson, *Private Enterprise and Public Purpose,* New York: Wiley, 1981, p. 84. Originally published in *The Hastings Law Journal,* May 1979.

[3] Alfred C. Neal, *Business Power and Public Policy,* New York: 1981, p. 126.

munity ties, and urban anonymity, the neighborhood social unit has lost its cohesion and the corporation has assumed some of its role.[4]

The Dilemma of Corporate Power

Neither size nor power alone is bad, when it comes to corporate performance. A big company may have definite advantages over a small one. It can command more resources, often produce at a lower cost, plan further into the future, and weather business fluctuations somewhat better. Big companies make tougher competitors against foreign firms. Many communities have benefited from the social initiatives and influence of large firms.[5]

Most questions of corporate power concern how business uses its influence, not whether it should have power in the first place. Most people want to know if business power is being used to affirm broad public-purpose goals, values, and traditions considered to be important to the nation as a whole. If so, then corporate power is considered to be legitimate, and the public accepts large size as just another normal characteristic of modern business. As we have stated earlier, organizations are legitimate to the extent that their activities are congruent with the goals and values of the society in which they function. The loss of public confidence is destructive to any organization, and legitimacy is perhaps the major element in the long-term survival of all social institutions.[6] Therefore, the crucial questions about corporate power are the following:

- First, will corporate economic power be used to promote the interests of the general public, including small business competitors and local communities? For example, large-scale computer systems may increase the productivity of big banks, but will this development jeopardize smaller banks? Or a cost-saving relocation of a plant from a New England town to Southeast Asia may bring severe economic distress to the community that is left behind.
- Second, will corporate political power be used wisely so as not to upset the pluralistic balance of power among a society's interest groups? Where large corporations have rivaled or surpassed the power of some governments concern is justified that corporate influence may be abused.[7]
- Third, will corporate social power respect the integrity and dignity of individuals, as well as the traditions and needs of the corporation's host communities? For example, corporate drug-testing programs and sudden plant shutdowns, while considered important for business purposes, may be seen as unacceptable and socially undesirable by those affected.

[4] Phillip I. Blumberg, *The Megacorporation in American Society,* Englewood Cliffs, NJ: Prentice-Hall, 1975, pp. 2–3.

[5] For several examples, see *1990 Social Report of the Life and Health Insurance Business: The Record of Corporate Public Involvement,* Washington, DC: Center for Corporate Public Involvement, 1990.

[6] See Edwin M. Epstein and Dow Votaw (eds.), *Rationality, Legitimacy, Responsibility: Search for New Directions in Business and Society,* Santa Monica, CA: Goodyear, 1978, p. 72.

[7] Neal, op cit., p. 136.

These three basic questions assume special meaning in Western societies with democratic traditions, representative political institutions, and a strong respect for the individual. In such nations, concentrated power of any kind—whether corporate, governmental, religious, scientific, or military—seems out of place. Reconciling corporate power with an open, free way of life is the crux of the problem. If large corporations can be made to fit into the webbing of an open, pluralistic society, their legitimacy—that is, their public acceptance—will be assured.

United States antitrust laws, highly controversial and far from perfect, stand as a monument to our society's efforts to cope with the various dilemmas of corporate power. For more than a century, since the first federal antitrust law was enacted, U.S. public policy has sought to balance economic power with social control. As antitrust policy enters its second century, the new realities of global competition and global economic power are forcing a reexamination of how power and social control are best balanced. We examine those issues after outlining antitrust goals and major federal laws.

ANTITRUST REGULATION

Someone once remarked that antitrust is as American as apple pie. Certainly it is an article of faith deeply embedded in the minds of many people. The U.S. antitrust laws originated in the late nineteenth century in the wake of some spectacular competitive abuses by big business leaders and their companies. An aroused public feared the uncontrolled growth of big business. The first antitrust laws were passed in this climate of fear and mistrust of big business. Since those early years, other antitrust laws have been enacted, and the first laws have been amended. The result is a formidable tangle of laws, regulations, guidelines, and judicial interpretations that present business with a need to carefully manage relationships with competitors and government antitrust officials.

Objectives of Antitrust

Antitrust laws serve multiple goals. Some of these goals—such as preserving competition or protecting consumers against deceptive advertising—are primarily economic in character. As one authoritative source states: "The U.S. antitrust laws are the legal embodiment of our nation's commitment to a free market economy."[8] Others, though, are more concerned with social and philosophical matters, such as a desire to curb the power of large corporations or even a nostalgic wish to return to the old Jeffersonian ideal of a nation of small-scale farmers and businesses. The result is multiple, overlapping, changing, and sometimes contradictory goals.

[8] Bureau of National Affairs (BNA), *Antitrust and Trade Regulation Report,* vol. 55, Washington: Bureau of National Affairs, 1988, p. 5–4.

The most important economic objectives of antitrust laws are the following:

First, the protection and preservation of competition is the central goal. This is done by outlawing monopolies, prohibiting unfair competition, and eliminating price discrimination and collusion. The reasoning is that customers will be best and most economically served if business firms compete vigorously for the consumer's dollar. Prices should fluctuate according to supply and demand, with no collusion between competitors, whether behind the scenes or out in the open. An important case from the 1980s illustrates this feature of antitrust regulation.[9]

> Du Pont Company and Ethyl Corporation, producers of 70 percent of lead-based gasoline additives, were determined by the Federal Trade Commission to be in violation of antitrust laws, not because they secretly agreed to artificially fix prices of the additives but because they managed to "signal' each other informally about the prices they planned to charge customers. The price-signaling scheme had several features: Advance announcements were made to customers of planned price increases, with an extra period granted that permitted uniform prices to develop between the two producers; contract clauses discouraged price discounts by promising each customer the lowest price given to any customer nationwide; and a uniform pricing system ignored transportation cost differences for customers in different parts of the nation. According to the FTC, this system caused artificially high prices and profits and a stifling of competition between the two producers. One antitrust expert said, "This case is about modern ways of influencing prices." He implied that today's managers "are too smart to get caught" actually agreeing to fix prices.

A second goal of antitrust policy is to protect the consumer's welfare by prohibiting deceptive and unfair business practices. The original antitrust laws were aimed primarily at preserving competition, assuming that consumers would be safeguarded as long as competition was strong. Later, though, it was realized that some business methods could be used to exploit or mislead consumers, regardless of the amount of competition. Consider the following examples of unfair practices:

> A company supplying plastic parts for electrical appliances bribed the purchasing agent for the appliance maker to buy the company's parts, even though they were priced higher than those made by a competitor. As a result, the consumer paid more for the appliances. This type of commercial bribery is forbidden by the antitrust laws because it takes unfair advantage of innocent consumers.
>
> In another case, a distributor of phonograph records sent record-club members more records than they had ordered and then demanded payment, substituted one record for another in some orders, and delayed prepaid orders of some customers for several months. Such practices are considered to be unfair by antitrust authorities.

[9] "The FTC Redefines Price-Fixing," *Business Week*, Apr. 18, 1983, pp. 37, 41; "Congress Moves on Price Fixing," *New York Times*, May 16, 1991, p. D-2.

A third goal of antitrust regulation is to protect small, independent business firms from the economic pressures exerted by big business competition.

For example, for forty years, Congress authorized states to have "fair trade laws." These laws permitted a manufacturer of toasters, for example, to set a minimum price on its toasters sold by all retailers in a given state. Large chain stores and discount centers could not charge lower prices, even though their overall costs of operation might enable them to price the toasters lower and still make a profit. In these cases, Congress was trying to protect small retail outlets from the more efficient competition of large stores. But in the late 1970s, Congress outlawed such restrictive trade practices.

In other cases, small business may be undersold by larger ones because manufacturers are willing to give price discounts to large volume buyers. For example, a tire maker wanted to sell automobile and truck tires to a large retail chain at a lower price than it offered to a small gasoline station. The antitrust laws prohibit such discounts to be given exclusively to large buyers unless it can be proved that there is a genuine economic saving in dealing with the larger firm.

In promoting the interests of small business over large business in these ways, antitrust regulations disregard both competition—because big businesses are not permitted to compete freely—and consumer welfare—because big firms could sell at a lower price than small firms. This inconsistency occurs because these laws serve the multiple and sometimes contradictory goals of many different groups.

A fourth goal of antitrust policy has more to do with social and political factors than with business and economics. A strong populist philosophy has been part of the antitrust movement from its beginning. Populists favored small town life, neighborly relations among people, a democratic political system, family-operated farms, and small business firms. They believed that concentrated wealth poses a threat to democracy, that big business would drive small local companies out of business, and that hometown merchants and neighboring farmers might be replaced by large impersonal corporations headquartered in distant cities. Populists advocated antitrust restrictions on business to preserve the values and customs of small-town America. One hundred years later, however, these social and political goals are beginning to conflict with business views of what is required in a world of global competition.[10]

The Major Antitrust Laws

Today's antitrust laws are the outcome of many years of attempting to make American business fit the model of free market competition. Many people have

[10] Lucid historical accounts may be found in Richard Hofstadter, "What Happened to the Antitrust Movement?" in Earl F. Cheit (ed.), *The Business Establishment*, New York: Wiley, 1964, pp. 113–151; and Louis Galambos and Joseph Pratt, *The Rise of the Corporate Commonwealth: Business and Public Policy in the Twentieth Century*, New York: Basic Books, 1988.

pointed out how unrealistic it is to expect a modern, high-technology, diversified, worldwide corporation to conform to conditions that may have been considered ideal a century ago when both business and society were simpler. The challenge of applying existing antitrust legislation to the technological, financial, political, and social environment of the late twentieth century begins with an understanding of the major antitrust laws.

Rather than trying to present all of the many detailed provisions of these laws and the history of each one, we concentrate here on the four main federal antitrust statutes and give a brief summary of each. Figure 11–4 identifies the purpose of these four laws and the major components of the enforcement process. States also have antitrust laws with similar goals and purposes.

The Sherman Act

Although several states enacted antitrust laws before the federal government did, the Sherman Act of 1890 is considered to be the foundation of antitrust regulation in the United States. This law:

- Prohibits contracts, combinations, or conspiracies that restrain trade and commerce

FIGURE 11–4
Antitrust laws and enforcement at the federal level.

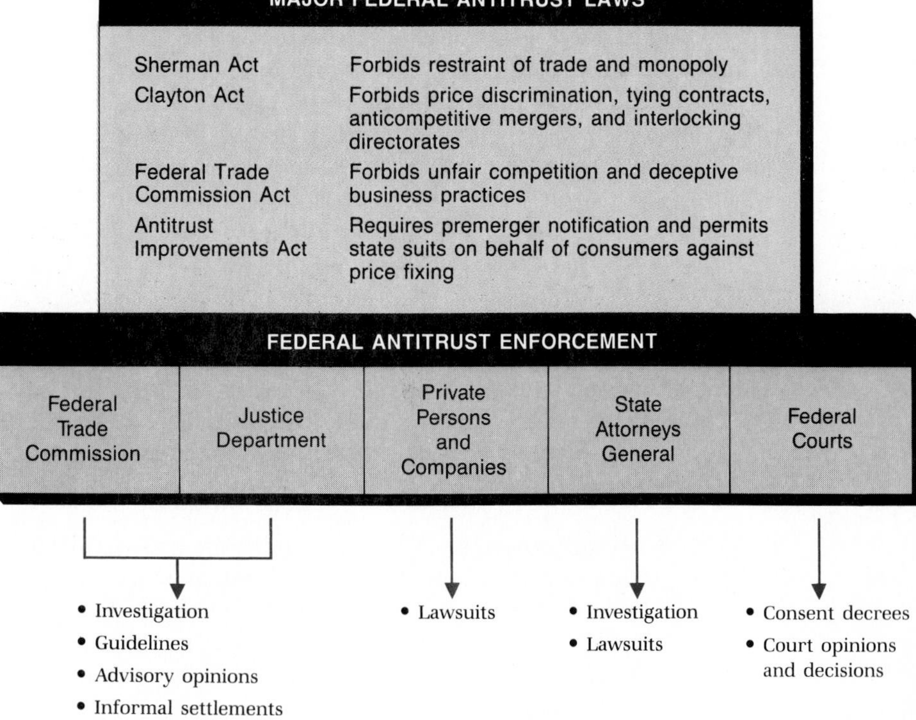

- Prohibits monopolies and all attempts to monopolize trade and commerce
- Provides for enforcement by the Justice Department, and authorizes penalties, including fines and jail terms, for violations

The Clayton Act

Originally passed in 1914 to clarify some of the ambiguities and uncertainties of the Sherman Act, the Clayton Act, as amended, now:

- Prohibits price discrimination by sellers (as illustrated by the tire maker who was forbidden to sell lower-priced tires to a chain store while selling at a higher price to a smaller independent store)
- Forbids tying contracts that require someone to buy a related and perhaps unwanted product in order to get another one produced by the same company (for example, Prime Computer was trying to force hardware purchasers to accept an unwanted maintenance contract as a condition of sale)
- Prohibits companies from merging through purchase of shares or assets if competition is lessened or a monopoly is created
- Outlaws interlocking directorates in large competing corporations (for example, Chevron and Mobil Oil would not be permitted to have a single person serve as a member of the board of directors of both companies at the same time)

The Federal Trade Commission Act

This act, too, became law in 1914 during a period when populist sentiment against big business was very strong. In addition to creating the Federal Trade Commission to help enforce the antitrust laws, it prohibited all unfair methods of competition (without defining them in specific terms). In later years, the act was amended to give more protection to consumers by forbidding unfair and deceptive business practices, such as misleading advertising, bait-and-switch merchandising, and other consumer abuses.

The Antitrust Improvements Act

All of the important additions made to the antitrust laws during the 1930s and 1950s (for example, the Robinson-Patman Act and the Celler Anti-merger Act) were incorporated into the three major laws as summarized above. But in 1976, Congress put a new and separate law on the books. The Antitrust Improvements Act strengthens government's hand in enforcing the other three laws. This law:

- Requires large corporations to notify the Justice Department and the Federal Trade Commission about impending mergers and acquisitions so that the regulators can study any possible violations of the law that may be caused by the merger (for example, the merger of two large steel companies was delayed by the Justice Department until two of the steel mills were sold in order to preserve competition)
- Expands the Justice Department's antitrust investigatory powers

- Authorizes the attorneys general of all fifty states to bring suits against companies that fix prices and to recover damages for consumers

Exemptions

Not all organizations are subject to these four antitrust laws. Congress has exempted labor unions that attempt to monopolize the supply of labor; agricultural cooperatives that sometimes engage in anticompetitive behavior; insurance companies, which are regulated by state, not federal, laws; and some business transactions related to national defense and cooperative research and development efforts.

One of the most important of these exemptions is the National Cooperative Research Act of 1984. This law clarifies the application of U.S. antitrust laws to joint research and development (R&D) activities. When companies collaborate on research and technology development, the collaboration may have anticompetitive impacts on others in the industry. Congress sought to balance the positive effects of cooperative R&D with a preservation of competition by instructing the courts to use a "rule of reason" in assessing individual cases. Companies that wish to form joint R&D activities that may have anticompetitive effects are required to submit notice of their plans to the U.S. Attorney General and Federal Trade Commission. If approved, the companies may share information and cooperate in ways that would otherwise violate antitrust standards.

Enforcing the Antitrust Laws

The two main antitrust enforcement agencies shown in Figure 11–4 are the Antitrust Division of the U.S. Department of Justice and the Federal Trade Commission. Both agencies may bring suits against companies they believe to be guilty of violating antitrust laws. They also may investigate possible violations, issue guidelines and advisory opinions for firms planning mergers or acquisitions, identify specific practices considered to be illegal, and negotiate informal settlements out of court. Figure 11–5 highlights some of the Justice Department's antitrust activity during the late 1970s and 1980s, including the number of major investigations begun, merger reviews, and lawsuits actually filed. Each activity includes hundreds, even thousands, of hours of work by government officials.

Antitrust suits also can be initiated by private persons or companies who believe themselves to have been damaged by the anticompetitive actions of a business firm. Nearly 95 percent of all antitrust enforcement actions are initiated by private parties, not government officials. The possibility of receiving triple damages also can be an incentive for companies, such as Go-Video Inc., which is mentioned at the beginning of this chapter, to initiate private antitrust lawsuits against the firms that have injured them.[11]

[11] Betty Bock et al., *Antitrust in the Competitive World of the 1980s: Exploring Options,* Research Bulletin 112, New York: The Conference Board, 1982, p. 18; and Betty Bock et al., *Antitrust Issues: Are We Investing in the Future of Competition?* Information Bulletin 94, New York: The Conference Board, 1981, p. 19.

	Year									
	1978	1979	1980	1981	1982	1983	1984	1985	1986	1987
Investigations										
Sherman Act Cases	183	245	284	203	160	142	157	134	180	128
Clayton Act Cases	98	155	66	86	96	80	117	103	120	132
Premerger Notifications Received	147	859	824	993	1204	1101	1339	1604	1949	2533
District Court Antitrust Cases Filed	27	31	28	25	18	10	14	11	6	15

FIGURE 11–5
Antitrust enforcement activity by Justice Department, 1978–1987.

SOURCE: Department of Justice, Antitrust Division, for Subcommittee on Antitrust, Monopolies, and Business Restraints, Senate Judiciary Committee, 1989. Reprinted in Bureau of National Affairs, *Antitrust and Trade Regulation Report,* Special Supplement, vol. 57, no. 1425, July 20, 1989.

Attorneys general of the various states also may take action against antitrust violators, not only to protect consumers from price fixing (under the Antitrust Improvements Act) but also by enforcing the antitrust laws of their own states. The National Association of Attorneys General has a special section on antitrust laws, and state officials often cooperate in the investigation and prosecution of cases.

For example, in the infant formula WIC program case, mentioned at the beginning of this chapter, the attorneys general of Florida, Texas, and California investigated and took legal action against specific companies, alleging various forms of unfair competition. In addition, a hearing by the U.S. Senate Antitrust Subcommittee led to a Federal Trade Commission investigation into alleged price fixing and other anticompetitive behavior. The U.S. Department of Agriculture, which administers the federal WIC program, also conducted a study of the cost and pricing factors affecting the price of infant formula.[12]

Finally, the courts usually have the last word in enforcement, and the outcome is never certain. Cases are sometimes tried before a jury; in one extremely complex case against U.S. Steel Corporation none of the jury members had completed high school. Sometimes a panel of judges will hear an appeal. At other times, a single judge will preside over a case that may last for years; the Justice Department's case against IBM was begun in 1969 and was finally dropped by government prosecutors in 1982. The Supreme Court is the court of final appeal, and its opinions carry great weight. Antitrust regulators and businesses alike often appeal their cases to this final forum because the stakes are so high and the judicial precedents created by the high court are so important in the long-run development of antitrust regulation.

[12] Kathleen Day, "A New Activism on Antitrust Policy," *Washington Post,* Jan. 13, 1991, pp. H-1, H-5; Barry Meier, "What Prompted Investigation into Pricing of Infant Formula?" *New York Times,* Jan. 19, 1991, p. 54.

Key Antitrust Issues

The business community, government policymakers, and the general public have to seek answers to several key issues if the nation's antitrust laws and regulations are to serve both business and society well. Some of the most important ones are briefly discussed.

Corporate size

The key question here is: Is large size evidence of monopoly or a threat to competition? In general, the courts have said that absolute size by itself is not a violation of the antitrust laws. If, however, a firm uses its larger size to take advantage of rivals through price discrimination, collusion with others, or other specific actions banned by the antitrust laws, then it may be found guilty. Corporations have increased in size for over a century, and the antitrust laws neither prevented nor have they significantly slowed their growth.

Economic concentration

The key question here is: Does domination of an industry or a market by a few large corporations violate the antitrust laws? Or, as some ask: Should the biggest firms in each industry be broken up? Many major industries and markets are dominated by a handful of mammoth companies—examples are automobiles, tires, computers, chemicals, insurance, steel, some food products, paper, and others. Where this kind of concentration exists, competition changes. Companies tend to compete less by underpricing their rivals and more by making their products appear distinctive, by servicing their customers, by building reliability into products and parts, by developing brand-name loyalty in customers, and by advertising.

Critics claim that economic concentration eliminates effective price competition, reduces consumer choices, causes firms to grow too large to be efficient, inhibits innovation, and concentrates profits in too few hands. The best solution, they say, is to break up the giants into smaller units. Others counter by claiming that big firms have become dominant because they are more efficient; that price competition still occurs along with other types mentioned above; that today's firms give consumers more, not fewer, choices of goods and services; that large companies can finance more innovation than small business; and that profits are distributed widely to an increasing number of stockholders. Breaking up large corporations would deprive society of these benefits, say the defenders, and should not be done.

Efficiency versus competition

Another antitrust issue is efficiency versus competition. The key question here is: Is big business efficiency more important than preserving competition? Many big companies claim that their large size makes possible many operating economies. Today's complex technology, far-flung markets, complicated financial systems, and transnational competition make bigness essential for survival and efficient operation. Some bigness is required to compete successfully against state-owned and state-subsidized foreign companies. Placing restrictions on today's corporate growth just to preserve a competitive ideal formed during the eighteenth and nineteenth centuries seems to make little economic sense. On the other hand, others point out that competition stands at the heart of private enterprise ideology and that small businesses, consumers, and workers should be protected against big business expansion even though it may mean a loss of efficiency.

Foreign competition

The emergence of competitors from nations including Japan, Germany, South Korea, and Brazil among many has forced U.S. policymakers to reassess traditional antitrust approaches. Many of the nations mentioned permit businesses to co-operate in ways that are illegal under U.S. antitrust laws. U.S. companies sometimes claim to be disadvantaged in their ability to compete against such firms. In industries such as consumer electronics, where foreign competitors already dominate the market, U.S. companies like Go-Video, mentioned at the beginning of this chapter, are trying to use antitrust law to break into the marketplace. In other industries, such as computers, semiconductors, and automobiles, however, U.S. firms seek opportunities to cooperate with domestic rivals in order to be more effective competitors in international markets. Other nations have their own version of antitrust laws, often referred to as "competition policies." European firms, for example, have long been guided by the Treaty of Rome, which established competitive guidelines for European businesses. In 1992, the European Economic Community will have an updated set of competition policies that reflect the newly integrated European economy.[13]

CORPORATE MERGERS

The 1980s were a decade of astonishing corporate merger activity as revealed in Figure 11–6. More than 26,000 major mergers occurred between 1980 and 1988, with a value of more than $1 trillion. The average size of these mergers also grew. By decade's end, it was common for acquisitions in excess of $1 billion or more to occur. A number of $5 billion mergers occurred as well, and it seemed that no company—whatever its size—could be completely immune to being acquired. Many questions were raised about the social and economic impact of such corporate consolidation. Not surprisingly, antitrust officials were deeply involved in deciding which mergers were acceptable and which were not.

Corporate mergers seem to occur in waves at different periods of history. The 1950s and 1960s saw much activity which culminated in 6,000 mergers during 1969. Most observers seem to agree that one factor stimulating the 1980s surge was the government's general philosophy of deregulation and a more relaxed attitude toward enforcement of the nation's antitrust laws. This philosophy and approach placed a greater degree of faith in the private enterprise system to

[13] See Daniel Oliver, "Antitrust as a 1992 Fortress," *Wall Street Journal,* Apr. 24, 1989, p. 28; "Swiss Put Pressure on Price-Fixing Cartels," *Wall Street Journal,* Jan. 29, 1990, p. 7A.

FIGURE 11–6
Mergers and acquisitions, 1980–1988.

SOURCE: Bureau of the Census, Statistical Abstract of the United States, 1990. Washington, DC, 1990, Table 883.

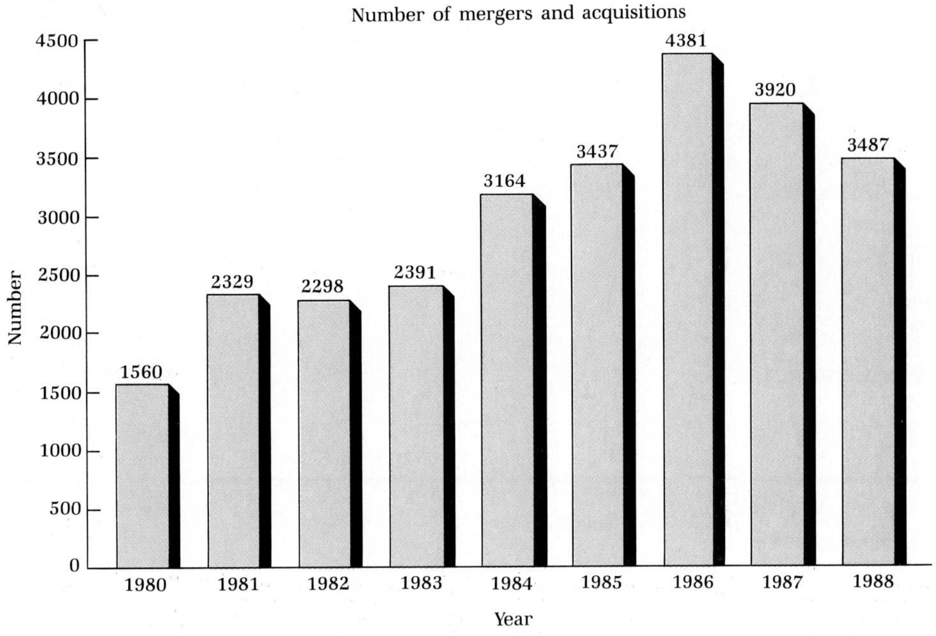

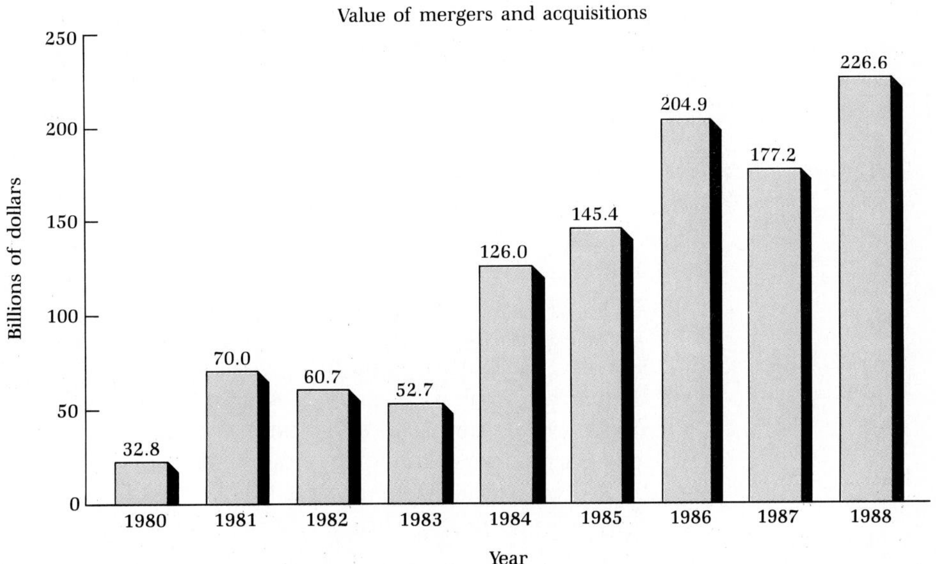

preserve competition, protect consumers, and ensure high levels of productivity than the opposite philosophy of curbing corporate power by strong antitrust regulations. In this general climate of greater permissiveness, the number of corporate mergers ballooned.

Students of corporate mergers usually distinguish between three different

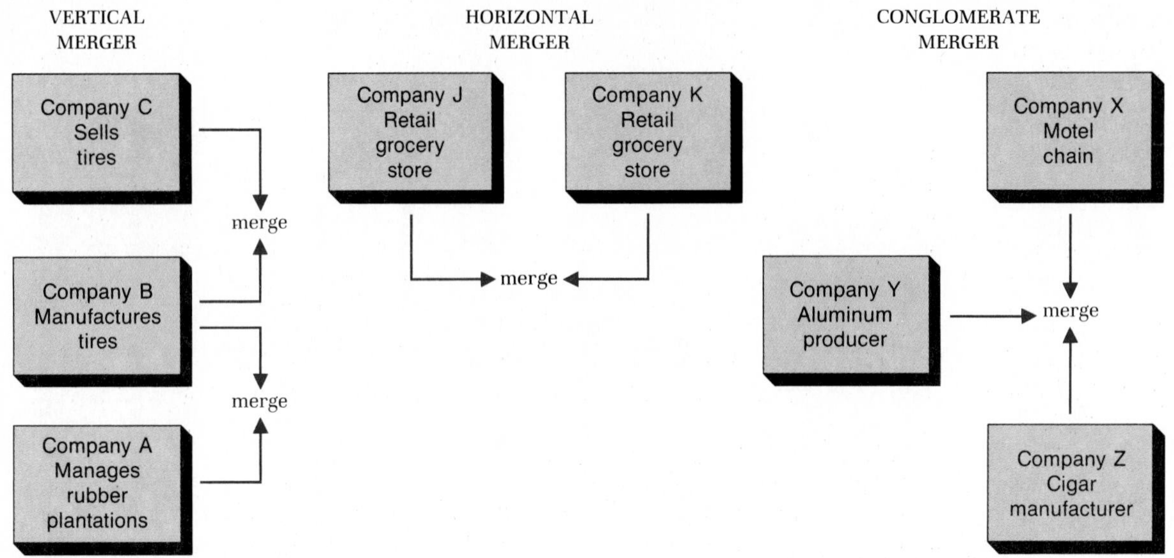

FIGURE 11–7
Three different types of corporate mergers.

types of business combinations, as depicted in Figure 11–7. Vertical mergers occur when the combining companies are at different stages of production in the same general line of business. For example, a rubber tire manufacturer may combine with a company owning rubber plantations and with a chain of auto parts dealers that sells the tires. Production "from the ground up" is then brought under a single management umbrella, so it is referred to as a vertical combination. Horizontal mergers occur when the combining companies are at the same stage or level of production or sales. For example, if two retail grocery chains in an urban market tried to combine, antitrust regulators probably would not permit the merger if the combined firms' resultant market share appeared to lessen competition in that area.

A conglomerate merger occurs when firms that are in totally unrelated lines of business are combined. Such companies as ITT and Textron grew rapidly in the 1960s and 1970s by combining diverse businesses under one corporate financial umbrella. Gulf & Western (G&W), a well-known conglomerate, merged under its corporate umbrella firms that manufactured pipeline equipment, auto and truck parts, cigars, chocolate candy, steel mill equipment, pantyhose, and paperback books; other units ran racetracks, distributed educational films, and staged the Miss Universe and Miss USA beauty pageants! Such diversity was thought to be a key to financial balance and success.

Critics say that conglomerate mergers give a smaller acquired company an unfair advantage over its rivals because it can draw on the superior financial and marketing resources of the big company. Others claim that a conglomerate has the power to "subsidize" one division by allowing it to cut prices and drive its competitors out of the market, only to raise prices once the struggle is won. Various other charges have been leveled at conglomerate mergers which suggest that they violate the spirit of the antitrust laws. Defenders suggest a conglomerate's pooled resources make it more capable of responding to the ups and downs of the business cycle than one based on a single product or service, and enable it to provide many centralized managerial, technical, and financial services to small business units that otherwise would be unable to afford them. Ironically, the 1980s saw the breakup of many conglomerates in a search to refocus attention on less diverse activities.

Mergers of the 1980s

The 1980s brought large numbers of all types of mergers. Some were designed to improve a company's share of market in particular industries, while others emphasized vertical integration or financial diversity. Much of the activity in the late 1980s and early 1990s has emphasized breaking up conglomerates created in the past that did not achieve hoped-for results. Many business leaders have concluded that it is important for a company to be more carefully focused on those activities where it performs well. Then by selling parts of the business that are performing poorly or are not related to the core capability of the firm, money can be raised to invest in the core business.

One of the important social policy implications of this selling of American business is the identity of the buyers. According to U.S. government statistics, as shown in Figure 11–8, of the 3,487 mergers occurring in 1988, 2,882, or 82 percent, involved U.S. companies acquiring other U.S. companies. Only 447 acquisitions (13 percent) of U.S. companies were initiated by foreign buyers, although these were relatively larger purchases, accounting for 27 percent of total value. However, there were relatively few (158) acquisitions of foreign companies by U.S. buyers. To some, this situation confirms the declining fortunes of U.S. firms in the world economy: Many U.S. companies are reorganizing, and nearly three times as many U.S. firms were bought by foreigners as were foreign firms acquired by U.S. companies.

FIGURE 11–8
U.S. and foreign mergers and acquisitions: Who acquires whom?

SOURCE: Bureau of the Census, U.S. Statistical Abstract, 1990, Washington, DC, 1990, Table 884.

MERGERS AND ACQUISITIONS

(Total Number: 3,487, Value (Billions) $226.6)				
U.S. companies acquiring U.S. companies	2,882	82.6%*	$159.3	70.3%*
Foreign companies acquiring U.S. companies	447	12.8	60.8	26.8
U.S. companies acquiring foreign companies	158	4.5	6.5	2.8

* Totals may not sum to 100 percent because of rounding.

The Consequences of Corporate Mergers

When the smoke has cleared from the wave of corporate mergers that began in the 1980s, what will the results be? No one knows the final story, but some preliminary results are already observable. The megamergers created enormously larger corporations, thus continuing a trend toward bigger and bigger business units. Employees often lose their jobs when companies combine, as duplicate staffs are joined, and local communities suffer when a large company moves out or shifts its activities to other regions. A surprising number of mergers simply do not work out as planned, which results finally in a breakup of the newly formed company after the expenditure of immense sums of money on a failed effort. Some acquired companies, often called "cash cows," are milked of their cash by the parent corporation, thus weakening that part of the newly formed company or preventing it from plowing the money back into modernization and growth.

One unfortunate result of mergers, particularly among those companies that end up with huge debt loads, is a management focus on short-run profits in order to pay the debt's interest charges. This often means that long-run investments in improving productivity are sacrificed. Other observers have criticized the multimillion-dollar fees charged by financial advisers who actively encourage megamergers, as well as huge profits taken by corporate raiders. These issues are discussed further in Chapter 12.

The results are mixed for stockholders. Share values often are driven up when a takeover struggle begins. The implication is that the company is not being managed to yield maximum value for the stockholders. In that case, shareholders would gain from a takeover.

A permissive approach to mergers was favored by federal officials in the 1980s as a means of strengthening U.S. business for global competition. Administration officials frequently spoke of the mistakes of interfering with "efficient markets." "Bigness doesn't necessarily mean badness," said the U.S. Attorney General in the early 1980s, and the U.S. Secretary of Commerce said, "Trade patterns have changed, but the antitrust laws have not. It is not that some parts of those laws are irrelevant today; it is the fact that they place additional and unnecessary burdens on the ability of U.S. firms to compete."[14]

Some business leaders, especially those at top levels of corporate management, strongly criticized the "anything goes" mentality that characterized the frenzied merger activity. For example, Rand Araskog, ITT chairman, noted that the 1980s merger mania "has more to do with self-fulfilling prophecies of some egomaniacal financiers and overwhelming ambition of some investment houses than with business efficiencies. Too many deals are being done because of the ability to do them—not because they have sound economic logic or business validity."[15]

As the merger movement grew, and the economic logic of mergers gave way to highly speculative financial deals, stock prices soared. Wall Street scandals

[14] Quoted in Walter Adams and James W. Brock, "Mergeritis: Another American Addiction," *Challenge*, March–April, 1990, pp. 47–49.
[15] Ibid.

involving such figures as Dennis Levine, Ivan Boesky, and Michael Milken led to criminal and civil lawsuits. When the stock market crashed in 1987, a sober realism returned to the merger business. In the early 1990s, a recession and the collapse of dozens of savings and loan institutions suggested that the wild atmosphere of the previous decade was far away.

Mergers, Antitrust, and Global Competitiveness

The application of antitrust law is part of the broader debate over how to improve the **national competitiveness** of the United States in the world economy. The past ten years have demonstrated that a company's market share in the United States is neither safe from foreign competitors nor even as important as in the past. For many products, such as automobiles, televisions, videocassette recorders, and dozens of others, global competition may better protect consumers than antitrust activity.

The U.S. Justice Department has tried to loosen the rules that affect how companies cooperate on research and development, and increasingly, on joint production agreements where there may be important economies of scale.[16] Joint manufacturing and marketing deals appear to be an area where future changes may be made. Potential antitrust prosecution deters some U.S. companies from "partnering" with other firms.[17] Instead, strategic alliances are formed with foreign companies, often with no antitrust questions being raised by government. Hewlett Packard, for example, has formed strategic alliances with Samsung (Korea), Northern Telecom (Canada), and Japanese firms including Sony, Hitachi, Canon, and Yokogawa. The joint manufacturing plant set up by General Motors and Toyota in California also was approved by antitrust authorities. Such a joint venture between GM and either Ford or Chrysler surely would have drawn antitrust objections on traditional grounds.[18]

As shown in Exhibit 11–A, government leaders are assessing how to harmonize antitrust protection with business needs in a global economy. According to one expert, the real objective should be to permit U.S. companies such as Zenith to cooperate with foreign companies such as SONY, Philips, and Thomson in joint ventures like the consortium to build high-definition television (HDTV), a frontier technology. Since those "foreign" companies have manufacturing facilities in the United States, American employees, suppliers, local communities, and customers sometimes benefit. Thus, in terms of the nation's economic future, a "partnered" company that is located in the United States is "one of us."[19] Not everyone agrees, because the management of a non-U.S. firm may be far less sensitive to social and political impacts, and it may be more difficult to control because it is more remote.

Antitrust policymakers are wrestling with the new realities of global business

[16] Robert B. Reich, "Who Is Us?" *Harvard Business Review,* January–February 1990, pp. 53–64.

[17] Michael Porter, *The Competitive Advantage of Nations,* New York: Basic Books, 1990.

[18] "Trust the Trust, or Bust the Trust?" *The Economist,* Sept. 2, 1989, pp. 63–64.

[19] Reich, op. cit.

EXHIBIT 11–A

"[In considering the international dimensions of the nation's antitrust laws] we must accomplish a difficult balancing act, since our government must provide protection to U.S. consumers by promoting healthy competition within this country, while at the same time allowing for legitimate efforts that will enable American companies to compete effectively in the global marketplace.

"Consequently, regulations which made good sense and worked well years ago, today may no longer strike the important balance we are constantly struggling to achieve.

"Let me give you one example. U.S. firms today face unprecedented challenges in the global marketplace. Innovations in many fields, such as superconductivity, high-definition television, robotics and computer-aided design and manufacturing, are being developed by our major trading partners as well as by U.S. firms.

"The costs of developing these technologies and bringing them to market often exceed the resources of any single firm. . . . This new economics features increasingly short product life-cycles, continuous incremental modification of products as experience indicates new areas for improvement, and rapid response to customer demands for variety and customization.

"Foreign firms keep pace with these competitive challenges in part by entering into cooperative production ventures. U.S. firms generally have not done so—and one reason is the fear of an antitrust challenge. To ensure that the federal government's antitrust enforcement policy does not inhibit legitimate international ventures, the Justice Department recently reformed and spelled out its policy in a set of guidelines designed to 'recognize the realities of a global economy' and to promote more effective global competition by U.S. companies."

SOURCE: Address by Attorney General Dick Thornburgh to the Economic Club of New York, Feb. 22, 1989.

competition. The days of the self-contained U.S. economy are gone. Virtually all businesses are touched, directly or indirectly, by the world marketplace. But the need for some form of social control on the excesses of business behavior has not disappeared. Temptations for anticompetitive behavior still exist. Thus, the optimal "fit" between antitrust protection and the global marketplace is not easily achieved.

There will remain a need for economic restructuring in the decades ahead, so mergers and acquisitions will continue. They can serve as a dynamic stimulus, producing gains for shareholders and the entire economy from improved efficiency and market pressure. When carried to excess, however, experience has shown that such business combinations can be costly in economic and social terms.[20] Social control, expressed through antitrust policy, will continue to seek the best balance between competition and other social goals.

[20] J. Fred Weston and Kwang S. Chung, "Takeovers and Corporate Restructuring: An Overview," *Business Economics*, April 1990, pp. 6–11. See also J. Fred Weston et al., *Mergers, Restructuring and Corporate Control*, Englewood Cliffs, NJ: Prentice-Hall, 1990.

COMPETITION POLICY AND A CHANGING U.S. ECONOMY

The foundations of U.S. antitrust policy were created in the late nineteenth century when railroads were the leading technology of the day and when control of natural resources—land, oil, minerals—was the surest way to wealth. More than 100 years later, the foundations of the U.S. economy are quite different. Services now equal or exceed manufacturing of consumer and industrial goods as an employer of workers and as a source of economic growth. Manufacturing itself is highly dependent on new technologies and innovation to remain competitive in world markets. According to one observer, "The most valuable resource in the modern economy is the human mind." The point is that innovation, research and development, and global competitiveness depend greatly on new ideas. These ideas are often referred to as **intellectual property,** and the protection of ideas is one of the most central issues for business, government, and society in designing competition policies for the 1990s.

The dilemma that intellectual property presents for antitrust and competition has three parts:

- First, the creator of an idea or invention should be entitled to the benefits that flow from that original creation if it can be proved that they came from that person or organization.
- Second, the right to get special economic advantage from such inventions should not exist forever. At some point, ideas enter the public domain and can be used by others. Thomas Edison was entitled to get some advantage from inventing the electric light bulb, but this advantage should not require everyone who has ever used a light bulb to pay something to Edison or his heirs.
- Third, the right of a person or organization to withhold new ideas or inventions for the purpose of injuring a competitor can be anticompetitive and damaging to the public interest.

In the Prime Computer case discussed at the beginning of this chapter, a small maintenance company was injured because Prime used its leverage in ways that damaged competition. Interestingly, computer hardware companies have long been able to require buyers to use special software for that equipment. Companies such as Apple Computer and IBM have been especially effective at creating configurations of hardware and software that appealed to buyers but which were not interchangeable. The Justice Department has long studied all aspects of the computer industry because of its size and allegations of anticompetitive behavior involving intellectual property. This encouraged Apple and IBM to license their technology to other firms. The development of hardware and software producers whose products were linked to either Apple or IBM helped expand consumer choices and lower prices for products.

The challenge for business and government leaders is to balance protection of new ideas with competitive conduct that benefits the public. For example, Go-Video, Inc. has been unable to bring its product to market because of an inability to secure parts from Japanese producers of VCRs. It has charged these suppliers with anticompetitive conduct designed to suppress Go-Video's patented dual track technology until they too are able to produce a dual track VCR. Go-Video has said it would consider licensing or selling its patented design to others, but without an ability to produce its products, it is unable to take advantage of its new technological idea. Ultimately, a court may have to decide the issues in the lawsuit. The problem has also been raised by U.S. trade officials in discussions with Japanese trade officials.

Protecting Ideas

Intellectual property is protected through a number of special laws and public policies including copyright and patent laws. A society that is scientifically and artistically creative has a big stake in such laws. In a global economy where information and knowledge are valuable resources, these forms of intellectual property are economically valuable. Global competition will soon alter the shape of the arts and sciences as well as the manufacture of products. A number of U.S. entertainment companies were bought by foreign businesses in the early 1990s for the purpose of acquiring copyrighted and trademarked property such as films, recordings, and books.

Business and political leaders will have to think carefully about how best to protect legitimate property interests, preserve competition in important industries, and serve the social and economic interests of many stakeholders. Exhibit 11–B presents one business leader's point of view on the importance of knowledge, information, and innovation. But the taking of other people's ideas has a high commercial value and a high legal cost when wrongfully done. Business, government, and society all have a very large stake in developing a balanced approach to these issues.

Many temptations can arise for businesses and individuals to use other people's ideas without permission. Patents, copyrights, and other intellectual property are sometimes "infringed"—or wrongfully used—by those who see an opportunity for quick profit. For example, Levi Strauss discovered that many imitation "Levi's" were being manufactured in the Far East, imported into the United States, and sold to unsuspecting buyers. Of course, the buyers were paying for the "Levi's" name and the quality it represents. To protect its reputation for quality, Levi Strauss had to aggressively pursue the "pirate" businesses that wrongfully used the Levi's name. Many lawsuits and governmental actions were required before the pirates halted their practice.

A great deal of "pirating" occurs in industries such as computer software and hardware, industrial machinery, printing and publishing, and designer clothing. Because some governments do not curb such practices, businesses who create ideas are injured. One estimate is that U.S. companies lose more than $60 billion of sales each year because of infringement by non-U.S. competitors. The United

EXHIBIT 11–B

"If you want to keep this industry as vibrant and successful as it's been, then a properly constructed intellectual property policy will respect protection but give preference to innovation. Over-protection of intellectual property is as pernicious as under-protection in its stifling effects on innovation and consequent loss to society.

"There is no question, as I look at my industry, that there has been an unsteady but stubborn march to extend the scope of copyright. But it is possible to go too far, and I'm concerned where the line ultimately gets drawn. . . .

"It's the nature of software for ideas to flow back and forth between competitors, companies and industries. Like architecture and the movies, software is a medium for ideas. We should not extend copyright protection to ideas, but confine it narrowly, essentially to literal expression. . . .

"America's software industry happens to be the best in the world—and that isn't due to intellectual property lawsuits. The challenge is, what regime is going to continue to support our ability to do well? If our policy comes out of court battles, then we're going to have an industry that looks like it was shaped by lawyers and judges—not by technically innovative and market-sensitive entrepreneurs."

SOURCE: Mitchell D. Kapor, founder of Lotus Development Corporation and chief executive officer of ON Technology, Inc., from testimony to the U.S. Congress. *Bulletin of the American Society for Information*, June–July 1990, pp. 19–21.

States government has made such intellectual property issues part of its international trade negotiating position.

The 1990s are a decade when many new ideas will be developed and lead to new commercial development in such fields as bioengineering, software programs, fiber optics, and medicine to name but a few. Such developments can affect the competitiveness of particular firms, industries, and nations.[21] The employees who work for those companies have an important stake in the fair use of ideas, as do customers who license the technology or buy the products. And issues of ethics, public policy, and business strategy can arise over the use of other people's ideas.

SUMMARY POINTS OF THIS CHAPTER

- The world's largest corporations are capable of wielding much influence because of the central functions they perform in their respective societies and throughout the world. Their economic, political, and social power raises questions about the largest corporations' legitimacy, especially in societies with strong democratic traditions.

[21] Susan S. Samuelson and Thomas A. Balmer, "Antitrust Revisited—Implications for Competitive Strategy," *Sloan Management Review*, Fall 1988, pp. 79–87. See also Thomas A. Stewart, "Brainpower: How Intellectual Capital Is Becoming America's Most Valuable Asset," *Fortune*, June 3, 1991, pp. 44–60.

- In the United States, the antitrust laws have been used to curb the influence of corporations and to protect consumers, small business competitors, and others affected unfairly by noncompetitive practices.
- The emergence of global competition in many industries has led business and political leaders to question the traditional goals of antitrust policy. They believe antitrust rules should be adjusted to help the U.S. better compete in the world economy.
- The merger movement of the 1980s consisted of a wave of mergers, acquisitions, and takeover attempts unprecedented in the number and size of corporate combinations. Some believed that it was good for stockholders, while others expressed concern about the long-run effects such mergers would have on both business and society.
- As services and more knowledge-based manufacturing have grown in economic importance, efforts have expanded to protect intellectual property. There are important economic and social issues associated with the ownership of ideas. Copyright and patent policies are being balanced and integrated with antitrust considerations by business and political leaders in the 1990s.

KEY TERMS AND CONCEPTS USED IN THIS CHAPTER

- Corporate power: economic, political, social
- Corporate mergers
- National competitiveness
- Intellectual property

DISCUSSION CASE

EASTMAN KODAK: A QUESTION OF COMPETITION

Eastman Kodak is one of America's leading corporations. Founded in the early 1900s, the company has been a leader in photography throughout the twentieth century. The list of Kodak inventions and innovations in camera technology, film, and processing is lengthy and impressive. In many of these segments, and for many years, Kodak has been the leading firm.

Naturally, Kodak has responded when new competitors have entered markets which it dominated. For example, Kodak's control of special coated paper for photographs was a source of market power in the 1960s. Berkey Photo attempted to enter the market and was defeated by Kodak. Berkey sued under the antitrust laws (Sherman Act), charging that Kodak had monopolized the amateur film and color paper markets and that it had unlawfully restrained trade in cooperation with General Electric and General Telephone and Electronics' (GTE) Sylvania unit, and finally, that it had (in violation of the Clayton Act) received unlawful price discounts from those companies in purchasing flash units. The case took years to work its way through the courts, with a federal court jury finding Kodak guilty and imposing a fine of $37.6 million for damages to Berkey. This amount was then trebled to $112.8 million because the laws provide for a recovery of triple damages for antitrust violations. An appeals court later modified the judgment and reduced the amount of damages awarded to Berkey.

For 30 years, one of Kodak's principal competitors has been Polaroid Corporation. In 1972, Polaroid Corporation launched a new product known as the SX-70 instant camera. The company, founded by Dr. Edwin Land, one of the premier U.S. inventors of the twentieth century, had earlier developed and perfected instant photography. The word "Polaroid" became synonymous with instant photography. The launch of the SX-70 opened a new era of instant photos by making it possible to develop instant pictures in color. Within a few years, black and white Polaroid cameras would become antiques.

To develop the color negatives for the SX-70, Polaroid collaborated with Kodak. Kodak was not in the instant photography business at the time of the SX-70 development. In April 1976, however, Kodak introduced its first instant camera directly in competition with the Polaroid SX-70. Polaroid filed suit six days later, charging that Kodak had infringed 10 patents, most involving the technology developed for the SX-70. Kodak denied the charges.

It took more than nine years for the case to reach trial. Polaroid claimed that it lost $4 billion as a result of Kodak's entry into the instant camera business. Kodak claimed that its people had been independently developing the technology used in its instant cameras. In 1986, after a long trial, Kodak was found guilty of infringing on Polaroid's patents.

Kodak was ordered to remove its instant cameras from the market immediately, and separate hearings were held on the size of the damages to be paid to Polaroid. Polaroid argued that Kodak had willfully stolen the technology and should therefore pay treble damages of $12 billion. Kodak contended that it never intended to use Polaroid's ideas. Meanwhile, Kodak had to stop selling instant film and was forced to buy back cameras it had once sold.

On October 12, 1990, a federal judge awarded Polaroid $909.4 million in damages for the patent infringement. Because Kodak's infringement was found to be "not willful," the judge turned down Polaroid's request that damages be tripled.

While Polaroid and Kodak slugged it out in court, Japanese photography giants aggressively moved into the U.S. market. Canon, Minolta, and others dominated the 35-millimeter camera market, and Fuji established a significant position in the film-processing business. As one-hour film processing became more widely available, the uniqueness and consumer appeal of instant photography was diminished.[22]

[22] This case is based on the following sources: "Polaroid's Patent-Case Award, Smaller Than Anticipated, Is a Relief for Kodak," *Wall Street Journal,* Oct. 15, 1990, p. A-3; "Polaroid Wins $909 million Award from Kodak," *Boston Globe,* Oct. 13, 1990, p. 1; "Kodak Told It Must Pay $909 Million," *New York Times,* Oct. 13, 1990, p. 33; and "Damages Voted against Kodak of $37.6 Million," *Wall Street Journal,* Mar. 23, 1978, p. 5.

Discussion Questions

1. Using the concepts of economic and social power discussed in this chapter, discuss Kodak's behavior in the Berkey and Polaroid situations. Alternatively, defend Kodak's position in each of these instances.
2. The Justice Department chose not to enter either of these cases. What were the private interests that led Berkey and Polaroid to sue Kodak? What public interests were involved, if any?
3. In the original decision in the Polaroid case, the judge ruled that Kodak must stop manufacturing or marketing its instant cameras. Does this ruling really put the company out of the instant camera business? How can such extreme action be justified?
4. Assume you worked for Polaroid in the mid-1970s when Kodak was trying to create an instant camera. If Kodak had been willing to pay a royalty for the use of the idea contained in the instant camera technology, should Polaroid have agreed? If not, why not? If not, would Polaroid itself have been engaged in anticompetitive behavior by trying to keep out potential competitors?

PART FOUR

Responding to Corporate Stakeholders

12

Stockholders and Corporate Governance

Stockholders occupy a position of central importance in the corporation because they are the company's legal owners and because they expect high levels of economic performance. But the corporation is not always run solely for their benefit, so they contend with management and the board of directors for control of company policies. Recent changes in corporate governance have affected stockholders' interests and increased the managerial attention given to this stakeholder group.

Key Questions and Chapter Objectives

This chapter focuses on these key questions and objectives:

- Who are stockholders and what are their goals and legal rights?
- What is the governance system of corporations?
- How can a corporation increase its responsiveness to its stockholders?
- What are the pros and cons of employee ownership of corporations?
- How are stockholders affected by insider trading and corporate takeovers?

In early 1991, General Motors Corp. bowed to a request from one of its largest shareholders, California Public Employees Retirement System (Calpers), to change its corporate bylaws and require that a majority of its board of directors consist of independent or nonemployee members. Calpers had threatened to file a proposal for shareholders to vote on at the annual meeting that would have required a majority of GM's board to be independent. By agreeing to the bylaw change, GM's top management avoided a shareholder battle and preserved good relations with one of the company's largest shareholders.

Calpers, which has $57 billion to invest, also has holdings in Japanese companies. In November 1989, Calpers wrote to 43 Japanese companies asking them to consider altering proxy voting practices to make it easier for overseas investors to cast ballots. The fund asked that the 14-day lead time between release of the proxy statement and the shareholder meeting be doubled and that the companies provide English-language summaries of their proxy statements. Translation of Japanese proxy statements often takes much of the current 14-day period. After many months, Calpers had received no response from any of the companies.

T. Boone Pickens, a well-known American investor and takeover specialist, also encountered problems in Japan. Despite being the single largest shareholder of the Koito Manufacturing Company with 26 percent of the outstanding stock, Pickens has been repeatedly refused a position on Koito's board of directors. Traditional Japanese investors, including a company's lenders, suppliers, customers, and insurers, have voted against allowing Pickens to select a member of the board. Pickens, in turn, sued the company, its management, and other investors for conspiring to deprive him of ownership rights. He even persuaded the U.S. government to make foreign ownership and board representation a discussion item in trade talks with the Japanese.

In Scottsdale, Arizona, the shareholders of Go-Video, Inc. refused to approve a staggered-term provision for corporate directors that would have made the company less vulnerable to an unwanted takeover. Go-Video's management said that the company was undervalued because its main product had just been introduced and an antitrust lawsuit was pending that could provide it with many millions of dollars of damages. Shareholders did approve a new stock offering by the company despite the complaint of some shareholders that to do so when the company had not earned a profit diluted the value of their shares.[1]

Why do corporate managers pay attention to the wishes of investors such as Calpers? What accounts for the cold-shoulder responses of the Japanese firms to which Calpers has written? Are its requests unreasonable? Why would Go-Video's shareholders not approve management's request for an antitakeover provision? Each of these examples and the questions they raise involve the complex relationship between the corporation and its legal owners, the stockholders. Management faces very difficult issues in responding to corporate owners and balancing their demands with other company goals. This chapter addresses this important set of issues and relationships.

STOCKHOLDERS

Stockholders (or shareholders, as they also are called) are the legal owners of business corporations. By purchasing a "share" of the company's stock, they become part owners of the company. For this reason, stockholder-owners have a big stake in how well their company performs. The firm's managers must pay close attention to their needs and assign a high priority to their interests in the company.

[1] These examples are drawn from "GM Bows to California Pension Fund by Adopting Bylaw on Board's Makeup," *Wall Street Journal,* Jan. 31, 1991, p. A-6; "Shareholders Seek Role in Japan," *IRRC Global Shareholder,* August 1990, pp. 1–6; "Go-Video Fails to Get Anti-Takeover Move Approved by Holders," *Wall Street Journal,* Jan. 24, 1991, p. B-3.

FIGURE 12–1 Numbers of individual stockholders in the United States and ratio of stockholders to adult population.

SOURCE: New York Stock Exchange and Securities and Exchange Commission.

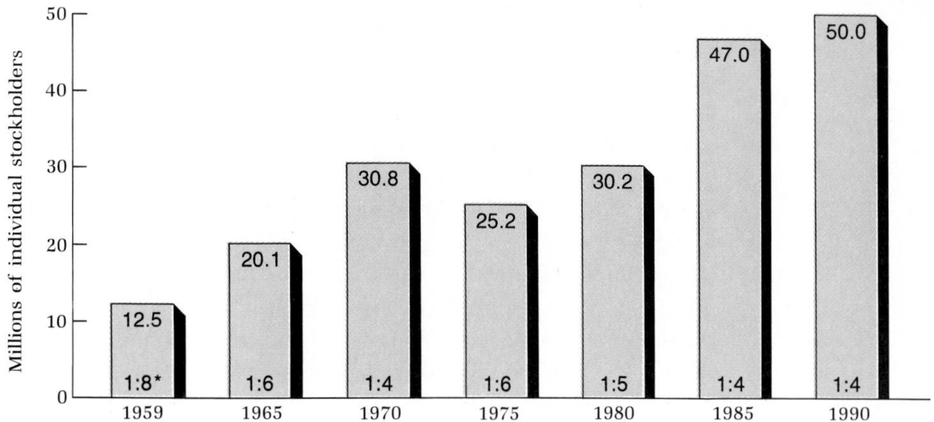

*This ratio means that 1 person out of every 8 adults is a stockholder.

Who Are Stockholders?

Two types of stockholders own shares of stock in United States corporations: individual people, and institutions.

Individual investors

As early as the 1920s, the public at large became significant owners of corporate stock. By 1970, their numbers had grown to over 30 million individuals, representing one of every four adults in the general population. Figure 12–1 charts the rise in stockholders from the late 1950s to the late 1980s, when the total approached 50 million people. People from practically every occupational group own stock: professionals, managers, clerks, craft workers, farmers, retired persons, women who work in the home, and even unemployed adults. Almost an equal number of women and men are shareholders.

Institutional investors

In addition to the 50 million individuals who have direct ownership in corporations, millions more are indirect owners through personal savings and investments in insurance companies, pension funds, mutual funds, churches, and university endowments. These institutions then invest their funds by buying shares of stock in corporations. Like individual shareholders, the institutions then become direct owners, and the individual savers are indirect owners. The New York Stock Exchange estimates that over one-half of the United States population has an indirect ownership interest in corporations. Generally, anyone who owns a life insurance policy, participates in a pension or deferred profit-sharing plan, has an account in a mutual savings bank, or receives a scholarship from a college endowment fund may be considered an indirect shareowner. Thus, many millions of people have a direct or indirect stake in the performance of business corporations.

Since the 1960s, the growth of institutional investors has been phenomenal because more and more people have purchased insurance policies, invested in mutual funds, and joined pension funds for their retirement years. In 1985, these institutions held nearly one-half of the value of all corporate stocks sold on the New York Stock Exchange. Studies by the securities industry revealed that institutional investors also are responsible for more than one-half of all trading activity on the New York Stock Exchange. Pointing out that "pension funds now own a third of the equity of all publicly traded companies in the U.S. and 50% or more of the equity of the big ones," one well-known management expert concluded that "Stock ownership has thus become more concentrated than probably ever before in U.S. history. Therefore, any business that needs money—every business sooner or later—has to be managed to live up to the expectations of the pension-fund managers."[2]

Purpose of Stock Ownership

Individuals and institutions own corporate stock for a number of reasons.

Economic purpose

Foremost among these reasons is the goal of receiving an economic gain or return on investment. Since such money could have been placed in a bank where interest would be earned with relatively little risk, investors choose stocks because they believe stocks will produce a gain greater than could be had from placing the funds in a bank. Different types of corporate ownership produce varying levels of return through dividends and an increase in the stock price. A company that pays a relatively high dividend (7 to 8 percent) is not likely to have rapid price appreciation. Conversely, a company whose stock is a "high flier" and likely to appreciate in price can choose to pay a lower dividend, if any at all, and still attract investors. Investors are thereby free to choose companies that are less speculative (high dividends) or more speculative depending on their personal goals and willingness to assume risk.

Corporate control

There are other reasons for investing in corporate stock. Some investors—including corporate raiders—are interested in gaining control of the corporation. This may be for the purpose of merging it with another firm or selling its assets to buyers who will pay more for the parts than for the whole company. Many of the takeovers of the 1980s were of this type. Such investments also may have a long-term economic purpose, but the immediate objective is to take control of the company and its assets.

[2] The quotation is from Peter Drucker, "A Crisis of Capitalism," *Wall Street Journal,* Sept. 30, 1986, p. 32.

Social purpose
Some investors purchase shares of stock to achieve a social purpose through their ownership. For example, a number of environmental groups and individuals purchased Exxon stock after the oil spill in Prince William Sound, Alaska, in order to have a right to question Exxon's top management about its actions at the annual meeting. Since only stockholders are entitled to attend and vote during such meetings, it was necessary to buy shares of Exxon in order to have a voice. According to one study, by 1990 investments of more than $450 billion went to companies that met various social criteria. Thus, some mutual funds and pension funds invested in companies with a good economic outlook and that worked to clean up the environment and refused to purchase shares of tobacco companies and firms manufacturing military weapons.[3]

Mixed purposes
Many investors, whether individuals or institutions, invest with both economic and social objectives in mind. They are interested in receiving a good return but do not want their money to be placed in companies that harm the environment, disregard human rights, or manufacture dangerous or destructive products. Such investors use various "investment screens" and require their stockbrokers or investment advisers to apply the social and economic criteria they regard as important to the purchase and sale of stock.

Investor Power to Achieve Social Goals

Historically, an individual's holdings of stock in any one company have been small, and individual investors have had little inclination to interfere with the management of a firm. They consider themselves to be investors seeking a return rather than owners trying to control the company. However, with purchases of large blocks of stock by institutional investors comes potential power to influence corporate policies, as illustrated by the Calpers example at the beginning of this chapter. These large institutional investors have significant voting strength in many of the nation's largest companies and are therefore in a position to influence policies and decisions of the corporations whose stock they hold.

Because of the large influence of institutional investors in the securities markets, the Securities and Exchange Commission requires institutions with major holdings of securities to disclose annually the names, types, and amounts of securities they hold and whether they can exercise the voting authority of those stocks. University endowment funds and state pension funds—two different types of institutional investors—normally invest large sums in the stocks of "blue-chip" or high-grade corporations. Beginning in the late 1970s, the managers of these funds came under increasing pressure from students, faculty members, churches, religious orders, state legislators, and social activist groups to stop investing in the stock of any company doing business in South Africa. By the late 1980s, more

[3] Sana Siwolop,"Ethical Investing?" *Financial World,* June 27, 1989, pp. 86–87.

than one hundred colleges and universities had "divested," or sold, $500 million of the stock of companies operating in South Africa as a way of protesting that nation's system of racial separation. The total amount of stocks held in some of these endowment funds was very large and potentially influential on corporate policy toward South African operations.

The amounts were even larger in some state and city funds. A 1984 New Jersey law directed the manager of that state's $13 billion employee pension fund to sell all securities of companies with South African ties. The total value to be sold was $3.5 billion. Was it good for New Jersey's pensioners who were the indirect owners of these stocks? The fund's director reported a $6 million loss on the sale of some securities, increased sales expenses of $5 million, and perhaps a loss of $25 million per year by not being able to buy blue-chip stocks of leading companies. California took similar action in 1986, divesting approximately $9.5 billion of South Africa–related stocks.[4]

The basic problem faced by institutional managers is one of getting the highest possible return on the stocks they purchase—for example, to maximize the future retirement pensions of employees—while at the same time being responsive to public pressures for social change. As institutional stockholders, these funds and their managers are in a unique position to exercise their ownership rights for both economic and social goals. They face the same public expectation that all businesses do—to balance their desire to make a profit with the need to show ethical concern.

STOCKHOLDERS' LEGAL RIGHTS AND SAFEGUARDS

In order to protect their financial stake in the companies whose stocks they hold, stockholders have several legal safeguards. Specific rights of stockholders are established by law. Legally, stockholders can influence corporate policy through the voting mechanism or, if necessary, by challenging actions of corporate officers in the courts. Stockholders have the following legal rights, and these vary somewhat among states: They have the right to share in the profits of the enterprise if dividends are declared by directors. They have the right to receive annual reports of company earnings and company activities, and they have the right to inspect the corporate books, provided they have a legitimate business purpose for doing so and that it will not be disruptive of business operations. They have the right to elect directors and to hold those directors and the officers of the corporation responsible for their acts, by lawsuit if they want to go that far. Furthermore, they usually have the right to vote on mergers, some acquisitions, and changes in the charter and bylaws, and to bring other proposals before the

[4] "Why Divesting Isn't Always That Easy," *Business Week,* Mar. 17, 1986, pp. 71–72; and "California's Legislature Votes to Force Sale of Holdings Linked to South Africa," *Wall Street Journal,* Aug. 28, 1986, p. 38.

FIGURE 12–2
Major legal rights of stockholders.

- To receive dividends, if declared
- To vote on: Members of board of directors
  Major mergers and acquisitions
  Charter and bylaw changes
  Proposals by stockholders
- To receive annual reports on company's financial condition
- To bring shareholder suits against the company and officers
- To sell their own shares of stock to others

stockholders. And finally, they have the right to sell their stock. Figure 12–2 summarizes the major legal rights of stockholders.

Stockholder Lawsuits

If stockholders think that they or their company have been damaged by actions of company officers or directors, they have the right to bring lawsuits in the courts. These stockholder suits can be of two kinds.

If stockholders are directly and personally damaged by actions of the company's officers, they can sue in court to recover their losses. For example, if they have lost money because of insider trading by company officers or directors, they have a right to sue. Such **individual shareholder lawsuits** are intended to reimburse stockholders directly and personally. The stockholder personally recovers the monetary damages.

On the other hand, in a **shareholder's derivative lawsuit** damages are awarded to the corporation. In these lawsuits, disgruntled stockholders are trying to protect the corporation's assets and not just their own personal investments, as shown in the following example.

> A shareholder of Allegheny International filed a derivative, class-action lawsuit against the company's directors, saying that they had wasted corporate assets and made improper business decisions. The shareholder alleged that the company maintained five corporate jets, had loaned over $32 million at 2 percent interest to some company officers and directors, and had paid excessive salaries and bonuses to executives including the CEO who allegedly received $1 million in compensation when the company had earned only $14.9 million and was in serious financial trouble. The lawsuit was filed after the board of directors of Allegheny International had refused to sue the CEO to recover some of these corporate funds. "We gave the board the opportunity to take action itself and, by not doing so, that triggered the right of the shareholder to sue the board in the name of the company," said the suing shareholder.[5]

[5] "Allegheny International Holder Sues Directors, Charging Breach of Duties," *Wall Street Journal*, Aug. 5, 1986, p. 13.

Shareholder suits are initiated to check many abuses, including insider trading, an inadequate price obtained for the company's stock in a buyout or takeover, lush executive pension benefits, or fraud committed by company officials.[6]

Corporate Disclosures

Giving stockholders more and better company information is one of the best ways to safeguard their interests. The theory behind the move for greater disclosure of company information is that the stockholder, as an investor, should be as fully informed as possible in order to make sound investments. By law, stockholders have a right to know about the affairs of the corporations in which they hold ownership shares. Those who attend annual meetings learn about past performance and future goals through speeches made by corporate officers and documents such as the company's annual report. Those who do not attend meetings must depend primarily on annual reports issued by the company and the opinions of independent financial analysts.

Historically, management has tended to provide stockholders with minimum information. But prompted by the Securities and Exchange Commission and by professional accounting groups, companies now disclose more about their affairs, in spite of the complicated nature of some information. A few corporations go further than required and publish financial information from the detailed "10-K" section of their official reports to the SEC. Stockholders therefore can learn about sales and earnings, assets, capital expenditures and depreciation by line of business, and details of foreign operations.

Corporations also are required to disclose detailed information about directors, how they are chosen, their compensation, conflicts of interest, and their reasons for resigning in policy disputes with management.

> For example, IBM's announcement of its 1991 annual meeting gave detailed information about the members of its board of directors, including their directorships in other corporations, the number of IBM shares they held, the salaries of board members who also were top managers of IBM, the amount and value of their stock options (a right to purchase additional shares of IBM stock), and details about their retirement benefits. To guard against charges of favoritism, the announcement also reported the amounts spent by IBM on purchases from other companies in which board members had a financial interest. Giving stockholders this kind of information reduces suspicions about how company funds are being spent and allows them to make up their own minds about the integrity of IBM's board of directors.[7]

[6] See Thomas M. Jones, "Corporate Board Structure and Performance: Variations in the Incidence of Shareholder Suits," in James E. Post (ed.), *Research in Corporate Social Performance and Policy,* vol. 8, Greenwich, CT: JAI Press, 1986.

[7] The information is from "Notice of 1991 Annual Meeting and Proxy Statement," IBM Corporation, 1991.

CORPORATE GOVERNANCE

Who will govern the corporation internally is a central issue facing business. There is no easy answer to the question: Who's in charge? As Figure 12–3 reveals, several key stakeholder groups are involved. Managers occupy a strategic position because of their knowledge and day-to-day decision making. The board of directors exercises formal legal authority over company policy. Stockholders, whether individuals or institutions, have a vital stake in the company. Employees, particularly those represented by unions, can affect some policies. Government, through laws and regulations, also is involved, as are creditors who hold corporate debt.[8] Importantly, these issues exist in major industrial nations of Europe and in Japan as the examples at the beginning of the chapter highlight.

The following discussion concentrates on the three groups that traditionally govern the corporation: the board of directors, top management, and stockholders. Creditors, a newly powerful group, are also discussed. While this discussion is based on U.S. laws, the basic concepts are applicable to corporations in several other countries, although important variations also occur.

The Board of Directors

The board of directors is a central factor in corporate governance because corporation laws place legal responsibility for the affairs of a company on the directors. The board of directors is legally responsible for establishing corporate objectives, developing broad policies, and selecting top-level personnel to carry out these objectives and policies. The board also reviews management's performance to be sure that the company is well run and stockholders' interests are protected.

Corporate boards are legally permitted to vary in size, composition, and structure so as to best serve the interests of the corporation and the shareholders who elect directors. A number of patterns do exist, however, thereby permitting some general statements about these factors. In general, large companies whose stock is publicly held, especially by institutional investors, tend to have relatively large boards of directors (average: 13 members). Of these members, it is likely that about two-thirds will be outside directors, including chief executives of other companies, retired executives of other firms, women, ethnic minority members, investment bankers, academics, and attorneys. A recent study highlighted the growing tendency of companies whose business is increasingly global to have internationally experienced executives among its outside directors. As Exhibit 12–A illustrates, the composition of the board makes a difference in the independence it brings to corporate policy decisions.

[8] For a discussion of modern corporate governance concepts, see Michael C. Jensen, "Eclipse of the Public Corporation," *Harvard Business Review*, September–October, 1989, pp. 61–74. See also Deborah A. Demott (ed.), *Corporations at the Crossroads: Governance and Reform*, New York: McGraw-Hill, 1980; and Thomas M. Jones, "Corporate Control and the Limits to Managerial Power," *Business Forum*, Winter 1985, pp. 16–21.

FIGURE 12–3
Major stakeholders involved in corporate governance.

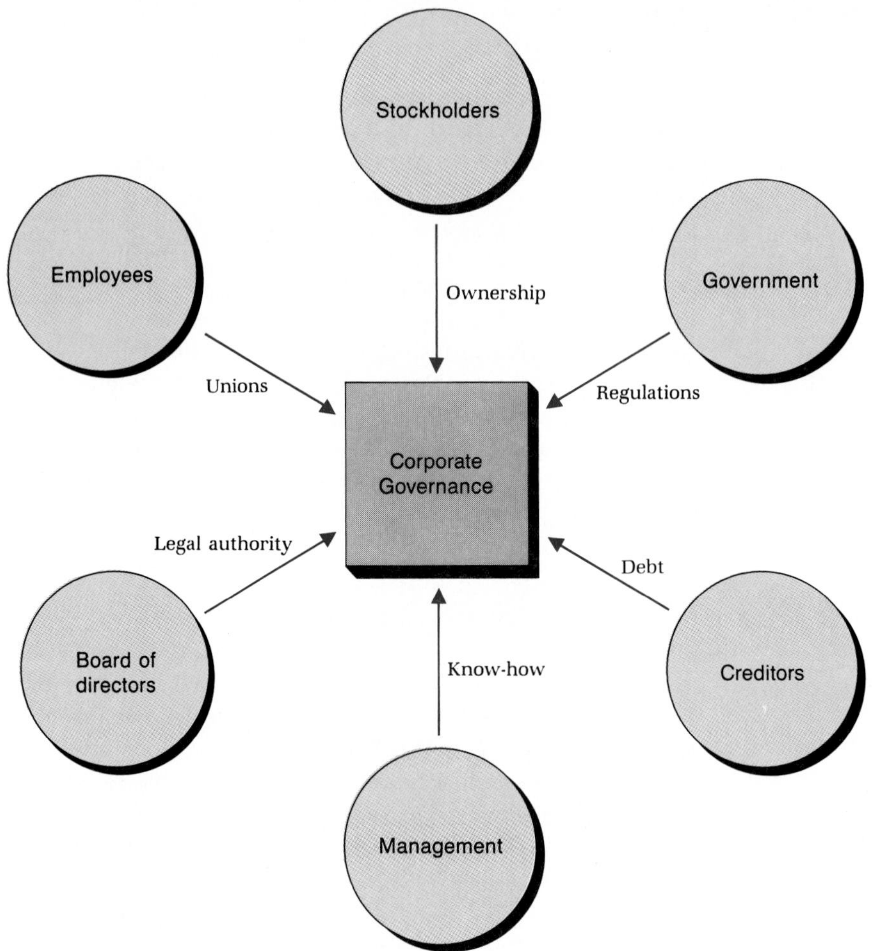

EXHIBIT 12–A

TRENDS AMONG CORPORATE BOARDS OF DIRECTORS

"U.S. boards of directors have come under repeated fire for what some observers call a lackluster record in corporate governance. The body of evidence collected in the last decade, however, suggests otherwise. U.S. corporations have emerged from a decade of drastic economic change and widespread corporate restructuring. And their boards matured during those years, gaining more power and greater independence in the face of these challenges.

"Clearly, the balance of power between the CEO and the board has shifted. The CEO no longer reigns as an absolute monarch, expecting corporate policy to be rubber-stamped. Rather, directors, have become stronger and more independent partners in corporate leadership."

Source: Korn/Ferry International, *Board of Directors: Seventeenth Annual Study, 1990,* Introduction, p. 1.

Most corporate boards perform their work through committees. The executive committee (present in 73 percent of corporate boards) works closely with top managers on important business matters.[9] The audit committee (present in 97 percent) is normally composed entirely of outside directors; it reviews the company's financial reports, recommends the appointment of outside auditors, and oversees the integrity of internal financial controls. The compensation committee (91 percent), also having a majority of outside directors, administers and approves salaries and other benefits of high-level managers in the company. The nominating committee (57 percent) is charged with finding and recommending candidates for officers and directors, especially those to be elected at the annual stockholders' meeting. Since the 1980s, a significant number of corporations have created an ethics committee (7 percent) or public affairs committee (11 percent) that gives special attention to ethical issues and social responsibility problems. For example, Dow Chemical Company has a Safety and Environment Committee consisting of five inside and two outside directors. The committee reviews the company's environmental, health, safety, and risk policies and performance. Its concerns are communicated to Dow's top management and the full board of directors.

These committees, which may meet several times each year, give an active board of directors very important powers in controlling the company's affairs. In addition, when the entire board meets, it hears directly from top-level managers and has an opportunity to influence their decisions and policies. As a direct result of these important powers, the board can no longer play a passive role in corporate governance. Today, more than ever, the board must assume an active role that is protective of shareholder rights, sensitive to communities in which the company operates, responsive to the needs of company vendors and customers, and fair to its employees. If directors are not willing to initiate appropriate action, we have seen from recent experience that corporate shareholders will take action to protect their interests.[10]

Top Managers

Professional managers generally take the leading role in large corporations. These managers might have backgrounds in marketing and sales, or in engineering design and production, or in various aspects of financial analysis. The expanding scale and complexity of national and international business calls for management specialists to guide the affairs of most big companies. The source of their power is a combination of their managerial expertise and simply being given organizational responsibility for carrying out the needed work.

Managers increasingly tend to consider their responsibilities as being primarily to the company, rather than just to the stockholders. They perceive themselves

[9] The figures in this section are based on data presented in Korn/Ferry International, *Board of Directors: Seventeenth Annual Study*, 1990.

[10] See "A Landmark Ruling That Puts Board Members in Peril," *Business Week*, Mar. 18, 1985, pp. 56–57; and "The Job Nobody Wants," *Business Week*, Sept. 8, 1986, pp. 56–61.

to be responsible for (1) the economic survival of the firm; (2) extending its life into the future through product innovation, management development, market expansion, and other means; and (3) balancing the demands of all groups in such a way that the company can achieve its objectives. This viewpoint considers shareholders to be just one of several stakeholder groups that must be given attention. Concerning their specific responsibilities to owners, managers today often express the belief that "what is good for the company in the long run is good for the stockholder."

Stockholders

According to the theory of corporation law, the stockholders of a company have ultimate control over its policies and actions. It is easy to see why this should be true. After all, the owners have put their money into the firm and they expect to receive a return from a well-managed operation. It is therefore reasonable to believe that they should have an important voice in what the company does. As the following discussion shows, sometimes they do and sometimes they do not.

Stockholders' annual meetings

Stockholders' annual meetings are held for the purpose of discussing business, and to offer an opportunity for shareholders to approve or disapprove of management. Approval is generally expressed by reelecting incumbent directors, and disapproval may be shown by attempting to replace them with new ones. Where corporations are small and local, annual meetings work reasonably well. It is relatively easy to assemble most of the stockholders, and corporate business is considered and acted upon personally by at least a majority of them. But for the large corporation with thousands of owners, annual meetings are not satisfactory. The number and wide geographical dispersion of stockholders have altered the character of annual meetings. Typically, only a small portion of stockholders attend to vote in person. Those not attending are given an opportunity to vote by absentee ballot (called a "proxy"). Most stockholders vote as management recommends by signing and sending their proxies back to the corporation, and this allows management to outvote dissident stockholders in most cases. Opposing votes seldom add up to much more than 10 percent, if that much.

> As the introductory example of T. Boone Pickens' investment in Japan illustrates, practices in the United States are more open than in other nations. In Japan, more than 80 percent of all stockholders' annual meetings in 1989 concluded in 30 minutes or less! Japanese companies sometimes pay "sokaiya," or professional shareholders, to ensure that no disruptions occur.[11]

Even if they were so disposed, few small stockholders are equipped financially to initiate and wage a fight for control with existing management. To unseat

[11] John Taylor, "Shareholders Seek Role in Japan," *IRRC Global Shareholder*, August 1990, p. 7.

present management requires gathering enough voting power by proxy to outvote the incumbents. In proxy fights, the odds for success are heavily weighted in favor of present management. It is not easy to stir a group of apathetic stockholders to join the opposition. Lack of knowledge concerning issues typically leads small, uninterested stockholders to cast their lot on the side of management. Financially, too, management has the upper hand. It may, and typically does, use both corporate personnel and corporate funds to ask stockholders to send their proxies to management. Challengers must use their own resources to wage the fight. The combination of voting strength held by the board and by top management often allows them to perpetuate themselves and continue their policies against the wishes of some stockholders.

Shareholder resolutions

The Securities and Exchange Commission (SEC) allows stockholders to place resolutions concerning appropriate economic and social issues in proxy statements sent out by the company. Originally the SEC rules prohibited proposals that dealt with religious, political, or social issues. These rules were designed to protect management against harassment by nuisance proposals submitted by social reformers. This change of rules seemed to reflect a spreading belief by society that stockholders should be allowed to vote on social as well as economic questions that are related to the business of the corporation.

The SEC has tried to minimize harassment by requiring a resolution to receive minimum support in order to be resubmitted in following years—5 percent of votes cast the first year, 8 percent the second year, and 10 percent the third year. Resolutions cannot deal with a company's "ordinary business," since that would constitute unjustified interference with management's decisions in running the company. Business initially favored the rule changes because they weeded out nuisance resolutions, reduced paperwork, and eliminated disorderly debates at some annual meetings. In recent years, however, the number of shareholder resolutions has soared.

Shareholder activists in 1991 sponsored more than 300 resolutions dealing with twenty major social issues at meetings of more than 100 corporations. Over one hundred church groups were joined by individual shareholders and a growing number of pension funds. Figure 12–4 summarizes the leading social policy resolutions in 1991.

Since shareholder resolutions not favored by management scarcely ever garner enough votes to be adopted, what is their point? There are several answers. The annual meetings provide a forum for debating social issues. Stockholders have a legal right to raise such issues and to ask questions about how "their" company is responding to them. Management is questioned about controversial issues and has to justify its policies in public. In order to avoid the glare of publicity, an increasing number of corporations have met with dissident groups prior to the annual meeting and agreed to take action on an issue if the groups' proposed resolutions are withdrawn. As the General Motors example at the beginning of the chapter points out, discussions between top managements and organized shareholders are sometimes held. Although these limited responses may amount

FIGURE 12–4
Major social policy shareholder resolutions, 1991.

SOURCE: Data collected by Investor Responsibility Research Center and reported in various Center reports.

Area of Resolution	Number of Shareholder Resolutions Filed
■ **Environmental responsibility** (Valdez Principles—code of conduct)	53
■ **Tobacco—Smoking and Health Effects** (Sales of, investment in tobacco companies)	15
■ **Mexican plants ("Maquiladoras")** (Environmental and employment conditions)	11
■ **Military Issues** (War toys, foreign sales, and criteria for military weapons contracts)	23
■ **Northern Ireland** (Recognition of human rights violations and commitment to action)	33
■ **Equal Employment Opportunity** (Reporting of data and special efforts to expand opportunities)	4
■ **South Africa** (Withdraw or change business operations)	52
■ **Infant Formula** (Halt advertising practices)	2
■ **Animal Testing** (Report on use of animals and halt unnecessary testing)	6
■ **Corporate Contributions** (Restrictions on corporate support for controversial organizations and issues)	3

to small victories, shareholder resolutions are one way for stockholders to make their influence felt in the executive suite.[12]

Creditors

Since the mid-1980s, creditors have become a powerful influence in the governance of corporations. Traditionally, creditors have lent money to businesses to help them finance the purchase of new buildings, equipment, or the expansion of a business into new areas of activity. In the 1980s, a number of financiers—led by Michael Milken—persuaded corporate executives that issuing high-risk, high-yield bonds, known as "junk bonds," could enable them to acquire other

[12] For further discussion, see Lauren Talner, *The Origins of Shareholder Activism*, Washington, DC: Investor Responsibility Research Center, 1983; and David Vogel, *Lobbying the Corporation: Citizen Challenges to Business Authority*, New York: Basic Books, 1978.

firms, reorganize them, sell off unwanted portions, and both meet the debt payments and improve total corporate financial performance.

The idea was appealing, and dozens of companies used such financing to build larger and larger corporate empires. The threat of unwanted takeover bids became so serious that many managements sought to find ways of making their companies "private"—i.e., eliminate the public stockholders. This led, in turn, to further use of debt in a series of **leveraged buyouts** (LBOs). An LBO uses debt financing to purchase the outstanding shares of stock from shareholders. For management, this arrangement replaces impatient shareholders, who are ready to sell their stock to the highest bidder, with a creditor whose view is longer-term. As long as the company can continue to pay the high yield on the bonds, management is relatively well protected from hostile takeover action. During the 1990–1991 recession, however, many users of debt financing such as Donald Trump, Frank Lorenzo, Eastern Airlines, and Pan American Airways found that revenues were insufficient to pay bond interest. The result was often bankruptcy, and in Eastern's case, a complete dissolution of the company. This course of action was forced by the creditors, who wanted some return—albeit less than full value—on the money they had loaned. Dealing with creditors has therefore become a major corporate governance issue for companies.[13]

INCREASING CORPORATE RESPONSIVENESS TO STOCKHOLDERS

Since a corporation's stockholders are one of its most important stakeholder groups, managers must find ways to respond to their needs and interests. Some of the most important possibilities are the following ones.

Reforming the Board

There is a growing public concern, shared by some directors themselves, that boards of directors are no longer meeting the requirements of a rapidly changing society. Critics demand that directors monitor both the social and economic performance of the companies they direct in order to promote long-range stockholder interests. A variety of suggestions have emerged to make boards of directors more effective and able to function better in serving stockholder interests. Figure 12–5 charts the following four proposed reforms:

- *Stakeholder directors:* One popular proposal among corporate reformers is to appoint special-interest directors to represent the company's major stakeholder groups, including consumers, minorities, women, environmentalists, employees, and the general public. The objective is to broaden the corporate

[13] Michael Jensen's article, "Eclipse of the Public Corporation," op. cit., discusses the role of creditors in corporate governance.

FIGURE 12–5
Proposed reforms of the board of directors.

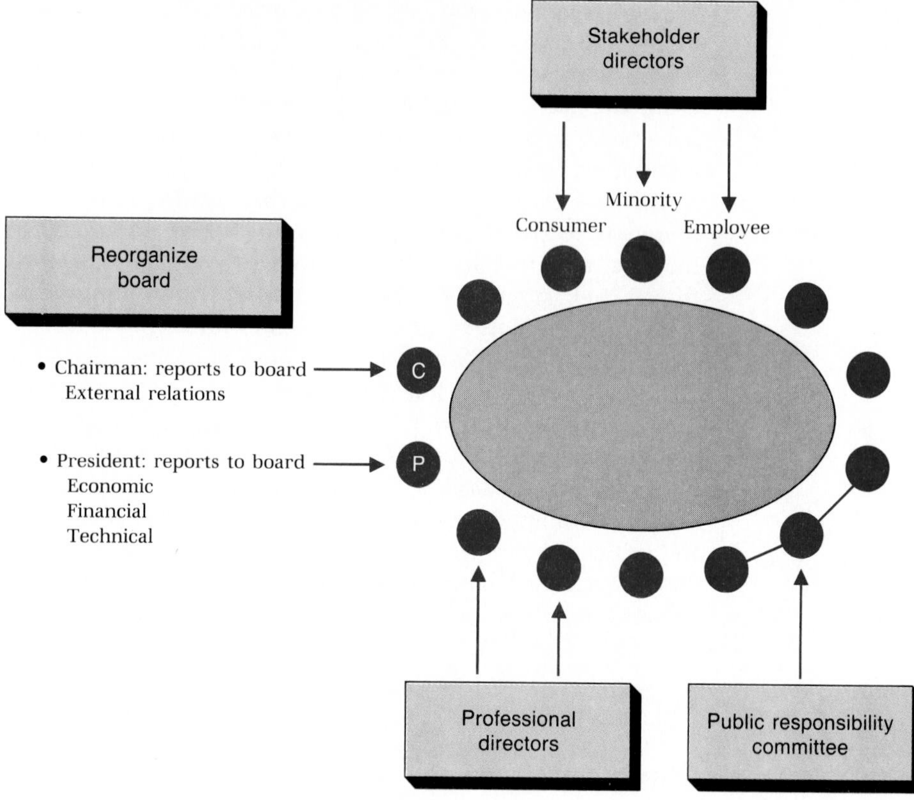

point of view and allow affected groups to participate significantly in corporate decision making. Business is generally opposed to stakeholder directors on grounds that directors need to put the general welfare of the company before the special interests of any one group.[14]

- *Professional directors:* These directors, unlike most, would serve on a full-time basis, continuously monitoring the performance of a company's managers to ensure that policies and actions are economically effective and in compliance with the law. More than one in four large corporations has at least one professional director on its board, and the trend is growing.
- *Ethics committees or public affairs committees:* A number of experts think that these committees can be a useful way of alerting a company to external pressure and social issues. By scanning the social environment and feeding such information into the corporate decision-making process, these committees can enhance the social sophistication of a company's operations.
- *Separating the board chairman and the president:* Some have recommended making a clear distinction between the duties of the board chairman and

[14] For a discussion, see Thomas M. Jones and Leonard D. Goldberg, "Governing the Large Corporation: More Arguments for Public Directors," *Academy of Management Review,* October 1982, pp. 603–611.

those of the chief executive or the chief operating officer, rather than combining the two in one person as is done in many corporations. Under this plan, the chairman gives primary allegiance to the board and is responsible for overseeing external relations. The company's president also reports directly to the entire board of directors, and not to the chairman, as usually occurs. The chief executive is responsible for internal affairs, such as the economic, financial, and technical operations of the company. With this split in responsibilities, a board has an improved chance of receiving completely candid reports about the company's external and internal affairs. By 1990, this idea had gained little headway since about 80 percent of large corporations had combined the roles of chairman and chief executive officer.

Federal Chartering and Codetermination

Two additional modifications in the way corporations make decisions have been advocated. **Federal chartering** would have the federal government replace state governments as the chartering agent for corporations. Advocates say that federally issued charters could specify tighter controls over corporate boards and management, for the benefit of shareholders and others. State chartering has been criticized for the different standards that exist from state to state, allowing companies to incorporate in states with the least restrictive provisions and encouraging states to lower incorporation rules to attract many companies. Opponents of federal chartering say that it would extend the power of the federal government over an already overregulated private business sector. The banking industry, for example, has long had a dual system of federally chartered and state chartered banks.

Labor-management **codetermination** would have U.S. corporations follow the example of some western European nations in requiring labor representation on the boards of major companies. This system is called labor-management codetermination. Supporters say that this arrangement promotes a greater degree of worker loyalty to a company by giving labor an opportunity to be directly involved in decision making. Detractors doubt that the system will work in the United States, where labor-management relations have traditionally relied on a strong adversarial system to work out differences. The first significant breakthrough toward labor representation on a corporate board in the United States occurred in 1980 when the president of the United Automobile Workers union became a director of Chrysler Corporation. The appointment was tied to Chrysler's request for federal assistance. Few companies have followed this example, and in 1991 Chrysler announced its intention to eliminate this position from its board.

EMPLOYEE STOCK OWNERSHIP

One interesting form of stock ownership occurs when the employees of a company become its owners. **Employee stock ownership plans** (ESOPs) encourage employees to invest some of their wage and salary earnings in the stock of the company where they work. The idea is to give employees direct profit-sharing interest in addition to their wage and salary income. ESOP advocates claim that this kind of share ownership benefits the company by increasing worker productivity, reducing job absenteeism, and drawing management and employees closer together into a common effort to make the company a success. Not only do ESOP participants receive regular dividends on the stock they own, but retiring workers either take their stock from the fund or sell their shares back to the company at retirement time. A major financial benefit to an ESOP company is the reduction of company taxes that occurs when employees purchase company stock and the company is able to deduct from its income the dividends paid to these stockholders. Other companies have created ESOPs as a way to fend off a hostile takeover, because employees are unlikely to vote for an acquisition that endangers their jobs or their community even if there is a short-term advantage to the ESOP's stock holdings.

> For example, Chevron Corp. created an employee stock ownership plan in 1989 that purchased $1 billion of company stock, raising employee ownership to more than 15 percent. The company had been a rumored takeover target but Chevron management was opposed to either a merger or a breakup of the company's business operations. The ESOP was apparently designed to take advantage of a Delaware law that allows holders of 15 percent or more of a company's stock to block a hostile merger for three years. Chevron is incorporated in Delaware.[15]

Beginning in the mid-1970s, ESOPs grew at an explosive pace, mainly because of new federal and state laws that encouraged their formation. From less than 500 in 1975, ESOPs grew to more than 10,000 before the 1987 stock market crash. Their annual growth rate exceeded 10 percent, in part because Congress passed sixteen laws promoting ESOPs from 1974 to 1985 and thirteen states added laws of their own.[16] The growth of ESOPs has slowed in the 1990s, in part because the stock market crash of 1987 and the 1990 recession showed how vulnerable these investments can be. The value of employees' stock can decline as well as increase, and that risk has important financial consequences for employees.

PROTECTING AND PROMOTING STOCKHOLDER INTERESTS

Stockholders can be damaged at times by abusive practices. On other occasions, they suffer losses because management is inefficient or careless or puts its own

[15] "Chevron Creates ESOP to Buy $1 Billion Stake," *Wall Street Journal*, Nov. 28, 1989, pp. A3, 8.

[16] Corey M. Rosen, Katherine J. Klein, and Karen M. Young, *Employee Ownership in America: The Equity Solution*, Lexington, MA: Lexington, 1986, pp. 2, 15; and "ESOPs: Revolution or Ripoff?" *Business Week*, Apr. 15, 1985, p. 94. The Rosen, Klein, and Young book is an excellent source of information on this subject, and it contains capsule accounts of many different types of ESOPs.

needs ahead of stockholder interests. Two areas calling for special efforts to protect and promote stockholder interests are insider trading and corporate mergers.

Insider Trading

Insider trading occurs when a person gains access to confidential information about a company's financial condition and then uses that information, before it becomes public knowledge, to buy or sell the company's stock. Since others do not know what an inside trader knows, it is possible to make advantageous investments or sell stock well in advance of other stockholders. If the secret information reveals that the company's stock is liable to go up when the information becomes public, then it is smart to buy the stock ahead of everyone else when its price is low. If the inside information says that the company is in trouble, then its stock price is liable to drop. In that case, it is a good time to sell the stock before the bad news becomes generally known.

The most spectacular insider-trading scandal in Wall Street history occurred in 1986 when several individual investors and a few officers of investment banking firms were revealed to have made millions of dollars illegally through secret insider trading. By sharing confidential information about forthcoming mergers of large corporations, they were able to buy and sell stocks before the mergers were announced to the public. The leading investor in this scandal netted an estimated profit of $203 million in 1985 and 1986. In a settlement with the Securities and Exchange Commission, he paid a $50 million fine, returned $50 million in illegal profits, was barred from the securities industry for life, and served a jail term. Several other involved investors were arrested for fraud, conspiracy, and violations of the securities laws. A Justice Department attorney who helped direct the investigation said: "Insider trading is not a complex crime. It's theft. These guys are thieves. They steal information and then they fence it. It's no different than if they were stealing ice skates."[17]

Insider trading not only is illegal but also is contrary to the logic underlying the stock markets: all stockholders ought to have access to the same information about companies. None should have special privileges or gain unfair advantages over others. Only in that way can investors have full confidence in the fairness of the stock markets. If they think that some investors can use inside knowledge for their own personal gain while others are excluded from such information, the system of stock buying might break down because of lack of trust.

Some financial authorities think that insider trading increases the efficiency of the stock markets by getting information out quickly. Although some insiders gain an advantage over other investors, good or bad news about a corporation spreads quickly through the entire market. In that way, the real value of the stock becomes apparent as soon as the word is disseminated. Despite this view, the courts have strongly upheld the ban on insider trading.

[17] See Dennis B. Levine, "The Inside Story of an Inside Trader," *Fortune,* May 21, 1990, pp. 80–89. The quotation is from *Wall Street Journal,* Dec. 24, 1986, p. 13.

TAKEOVERS AND CORPORATE CONTROL

Mergers and acquisitions are, as discussed in Chapter 11, an important way for business to keep reinventing itself to meet new competitive conditions. The takeover of another company can be either friendly or hostile but usually involves the need of the acquiring firm to get control of the target company through ownership.

Corporate Takeovers—Friendly and Hostile

People favoring corporate takeovers say that they are good for business (by increasing efficiency and making companies stronger competitors), for consumers (by delivering more and better goods at fair prices), and for stockholders (by producing maximum value for their shares of stock in the merged companies). A certain "synergy"—or favorable multiplier effect—is thought to occur when two companies get together under one corporate umbrella.[18]

Takeover tactics

When two companies combine, their stock (shares of ownership) and assets (physical, financial, managerial, and employees) are merged into one corporate identity, usually but not always with a new corporate name. For example, when Nabisco and Standard Brands merged in the early 1980s, the newly formed company's name was changed to Nabisco Brands. Later, when R. J. Reynolds acquired Nabisco Brands, the name was changed to RJR Nabisco.

"Friendly" mergers occur when both companies agree to combine, and these stock and asset transactions normally cause no problem or controversy. "Hostile" mergers, on the other hand, can create spectacular fights for control, with both sides resorting to a wide range of takeover tactics such as the following ones:

- *Proxy fights:* A corporate "raider" or takeover specialist sometimes wages a fight for control of a corporation's board of directors and seeks one or more seats on the board. To be successful, the raider has to convince stockholders to vote for the raider's candidates. If enough stockholders cast their votes for those candidates, or if they send their proxy to the raider, the raider may be successful in putting enough supporters on the board to influence company policies without buying the company's assets or stock. In this case, an actual merger need not take place since control of the target corporation is achieved in other ways.
- *Cumulative voting:* One technique for winning seats on the board of directors is to concentrate all of one's votes on just one or two candidates instead of voting for all of those up for election. Some states permit this practice, while others do not. For example, when T. Boone Pickens attempted to take over Pennsylvania-based Gulf Oil, he threatened to use this tactic to win

[18] "Do Mergers Really Work?" *Business Week,* June 3, 1985, pp. 90–91.

seats on Gulf's board. Gulf's board of directors responded by reincorporating in Delaware, whose laws forbid cumulative voting.

- *Tender offers:* Most takeovers, especially hostile ones, involve offers by the takeover specialist to buy shares of stock in the target corporation. In the language of Wall Street, shareholders are asked to "tender," or formally offer, their shares of stock for sale at a price the raider is willing to pay. These tender offers can become furiously competitive, and stockholders often see the price of their stock bid higher and higher as raiders compete to win a majority of the company stock. In 1990, AT&T attempted to acquire NCR. The opening bid was $62 per share of NCR stock. As the battle dragged on, the price rose to more than $100 per share.
- *Two-tier offers:* Another much-criticized technique used in corporate takeovers involves a two-tier tender offer. A corporate raider may offer to buy just over half of a company's stock at a cash price of, say, $40 per share, thereby giving the raider enough stock to control the company. Any stockholders who do not take advantage of this initial offer may then be offered a lower price, for example, $30 per share, for their stock or they may get other types of securities in a swap that is not always as favorable financially. As a counter to this tactic, some corporations have put a "fair price" amendment in their charters that requires tender offers to pay the same price to all shareholders.

Takeover defenses

Corporate managers usually resist takeover efforts for three basic reasons. Takeover battles can divert a company's top managers and planners from their important tasks of planning strategically for the company's future. When so much energy has to go into defending the company from outsiders, the day-to-day business decisions as well as the long-run strategic ones may suffer neglect. As long as managers serve in top-level posts, they have an obligation to run the company and carry out plans approved by the board of directors. Having to fight off takeover efforts only complicates an already complex job.

A second reason why top managers resist corporate takeovers is fear of losing their jobs after the merger occurs unless they are given a "golden parachute," which guarantees their financial benefits for a number of years if they are dismissed. It stands to reason in most cases that fewer managers and other professionals and specialists will be needed when two companies are merged to form one company.

In addition to their own personal interests, a corporation's managers have a fiduciary or legal responsibility to the company's stockholders to make decisions in the owners' interests. A chief executive officer may therefore believe that a raider's tender offer is too low and that stockholders would not receive fair market value if they accepted such an offer. In these cases, it is best to resist.

A number of takeover defenses, often called "shark repellents," are available:

- *Staggered board terms:* One way to fight off an attempt to gain seats on the board of directors is to stagger the terms of board members so that fewer than a majority of the seats are up for election in any one year. Used successfully, this tactic may stretch out over several years a raider's attempt to gain a majority of the seats.

- *Supermajorities:* Another way to fend off a potential takeover is to amend the corporation's bylaws to require that any offer to buy the company be approved by a very large majority, perhaps from 65 to 80 percent, of the stockholders. It is difficult for raiders to accumulate enough votes on their own or through proxies to achieve such a supermajority vote.
- *Nonvoting or supervoting stock:* Normally, each share of common stock issued is entitled to one vote. Some corporations have created special classes of stock with no voting rights at all or with more than one vote per share. By allocating voting shares carefully, a company's management could lock up most of the votes in ways that would favor its own position on merger attempts.
- *Greenmail:* If desperate enough, a management with its back to the wall and faced with a persistent raider might be willing to pay "greenmail," which is an agreement to buy back a big block of the company's stock at a premium. The offer is unfair to other company stockholders who are not paid such a premium or who may actually lose money when the company's stock falls after the raider agrees to go away.
- *Increasing the company's debt:* Another last-ditch tactic is to load the company up with so much new debt that it becomes a less attractive takeover target. This might be done by borrowing huge sums of money to buy another company. It seems hard to justify this maneuver as anything more than a selfish effort by an entrenched management to protect itself, since the bloated debt must be serviced before any dividends can be paid to stockholders.
- *Selling off profitable units:* One way to defeat a raider is to sell off the corporation's profitable units to another company, leaving behind a corporate shell containing only unprofitable businesses for the raider to inherit. In some antitakeover plans, these sales are triggered only when a raider acquires enough stock to control the target company.
- *Poison pills:* These plans discourage a hostile raider by allowing all shareholders in the target company to purchase stock or other securities in the proposed merged companies at a sharp discount. Some pills also permit stockholders to sell their shares to the acquired company at a premium. The poison pill is normally activated only when a raider acquires over 50 percent of the stock of the target company. Thus, a raider may succeed in taking over a company but only after paying a premium price for the controlling block of stock, while other stockholders buy or sell stock at a bargain price.
- *White knights:* If all else fails and a company is practically in the grasp of a hostile raider, the threatened company might be able to find a friendly buyer, known as a "white knight." This tactic was used by Gulf Oil when it seemed as if T. Boone Pickens was about to succeed in his offer to buy a majority of Gulf's stock. Gulf's board of directors made an agreement with

Chevron to sell the company to Chevron for $80 per share. Gulf's top managers then bailed out in their "golden parachutes" (the CEO collected around $7 million in stock options and other benefits) and the company they had managed lost its identity and disappeared from America's corporate rolls.

- *State antitakeover laws:* Worried that corporate takeovers might harm their industrial base, several states have laws that restrict hostile tender offers. In a landmark case, the U.S. Supreme Court in 1987 upheld an Indiana law that prevents a bidder who buys 20 percent or more of a company's stock from voting those shares until a majority of the other shareholders approve. The effect is to delay—and perhaps eventually to scuttle—a raider's takeover attempt. Pennsylvania and Minnesota have adopted particularly strong protective antitakeover laws since the Supreme Court decision.

STAKEHOLDER MANAGEMENT AND THE STOCKHOLDER

Shareholders have become an increasingly powerful and vocal stakeholder group in corporations. Management dominance of boards of directors has weakened, and shareholders—especially institutional investors—are pressing directors and management more forcefully to serve stockholder interests. Institutional investors also have acquired new power as creditors, using their purchases of corporate bonds, including junk bonds, as an additional form of leverage on corporate management.

In order to guard against abuses of stockholder interests, T. Boone Pickens proposed in 1986 to establish a nationwide shareholder-rights lobbying group. Among other provisions, he favored secret ballots for stockholders voting their stock, on grounds that some institutional stockholders as well as employee-owners might be afraid to vote against entrenched management. If they did, employee-owners might lose their jobs, and pension-fund managers might lose a corporation's pension account. Others disagreed, saying that a vote "in the open sunshine" would increase the public accountability of institutional stockholders.

Another effort to protect the rights of institutional stockholders was the creation in 1985 of the Council of Institutional Investors. The Council's thirty members represent institutions and pension funds with corporate investments totaling more than $200 billion. Its "Shareholder Bill of Rights" favors equal voting rights for common stockholders; favors requiring majority shareholder approval of greenmail, poison pills, and golden parachutes; and advocates fair and equal treatment of shareholders regarding tender offers.[19]

Investors also are organizing new types of coalitions to advance their economic and social interests. A coalition of institutional investors concerned about environmental practices of companies has led a campaign to have corporations com-

[19] James E. Heard, "Pension Funds and Contests for Corporate Control," *California Management Review*, Winter 1987, pp. 89–100; and "Shareholders Aren't Just Rolling over Anymore," *Business Week*, Apr. 27, 1987, pp. 32–33.

EXHIBIT 12–B

MERGERS AND ACQUISITIONS: EUROPE'S FUTURE

"During the past five years, an extraordinary volume of mergers and acquisitions has taken place in Europe. Corporations there, inspired by a major change of direction toward free-market economics, have begun a period of industrial restructuring very similar to that which U.S. companies went through in the 1980s. The activity likely has many years yet to run, during which an active and competitive market for corporate control, along the lines of those already operating in the United States and United Kingdom, can be expected to emerge in continental Europe. This market will do much to aid the strategic restructuring and efficiency enchancement of European industry. It will also help generate opportunistic behavior by a new breed of European corporate raiders and financial entreprenuers in the 1990s."

(SOURCE: Roy C. Smith and Ingo Walter, "The First European Merger Boom Has Begun," Publication No. 103, Center for the Study of American Business, January, 1991, p. 1.)

mit to a set of environmental principles known as the "Valdez Principles" created in the aftermath of the Exxon Valdez oil spill. Among the principles is one calling for an environmental representative on the board of directors. A number of small companies have already made such a commitment. (See Chapter 19 for additional information.)

The 1990s seem certain to see an expansion of these shareholders' efforts in the United States and other nations. As the opening examples suggest, Japan may become one of the corporate governance battlegrounds in this decade. Europe also faces such issues as Exhibit 12–B suggests.

Clearly, stockholders are a critically important stakeholder group. By providing capital, monitoring corporate performance, assuring the effective operation of stock markets, and bringing new issues to the attention of management, stockholders play a very important role in making the business system work. Corporate leaders have an obligation to manage their companies in ways that promote and protect a variety of stakeholders. Balancing these various interests is a prime requirement of modern management. While stockholders are no longer considered to be the only important stakeholder group, their interests and needs remain central to the successful operation of corporate business.

SUMMARY POINTS OF THIS CHAPTER

- Individuals and institutions own shares of corporations as a means of economic gain. Social purposes sometimes guide investors, as when certain businesses are avoided because of their negative social impacts. Shareholders are entitled to vote, receive information, select directors, and attempt to shape corporate policies and action.

- The governance system is the relationship among directors, officers, and shareholders. It determines who has legitimate power and how this power can be exercised. Creditors have become an important new factor in this relationship.
- Corporate responsiveness to shareholders can be achieved through reform of the board of directors, including a more diverse group of directors.
- Employee stock ownership programs (ESOPs) give employees a stake in the financial success of a company and may enhance worker commitment and productivity. Such ownership also leaves employees vulnerable to declining stock prices and negative economic conditions.
- Insider trading is illegal and unethical. It benefits those with illicitly acquired information at the expense of those who do not have it. Ultimately, it undermines fairness in the marketplace.
- Corporate takeovers are a legitimate and important business activity that raises issues of ethical conduct and corporate responsibility to stakeholders. Recent history has demonstrated that business and society have a large stake in curbing excesses and abuses in this area. Business and government leaders are involved in voluntary and public policy initiatives to do so.

KEY TERMS AND CONCEPTS USED IN THIS CHAPTER

- Stockholders
- Institutional investors
- Individual shareholders' lawsuits
- Shareholders' derivative lawsuits
- Corporate governance
- Shareholder resolutions
- Leveraged buyouts (LBO)
- Federal chartering
- Codetermination
- Employee stock ownership plan (ESOP)
- Insider trading

DISCUSSION CASE

BATTLE IN THE BOARDROOM: THE FORD MOTOR STORY

In what *Fortune* described as the "odd eclipse of a star CEO," Ford Motor Company chief executive Donald Petersen stepped aside in 1990 one and a half years before he reached the company's mandatory retirement age. Originally announced as a personal decision that would allow him to "repot himself," stories soon emerged that indicated that Ford's board of directors, including eleven outside members who were chief executives of other large, well-known companies, were dissatisfied with the succession plan Petersen had designed.

Petersen had been chief executive of Ford during a period of great business success. The company's Taurus design had been warmly accepted by customers in the United States. In Europe, Ford continued to enjoy prosperity from a well-developed market position. In 1989, the company acquired Jaguar, makers of the British luxury car of the same name. The acquisition was seen as an important step to broaden the upper end of Ford's product line, which had long been dominated by Lincoln and its Continental automobiles.

Why, in the midst of such business success, would a board of directors want to change horses? The explanation seemed to rest on the directors' assessment of the company, its near-term future, and Petersen's interests. It was widely expected that the automobile industry would suffer during the recession that was predicted for 1990 and beyond. Thus, one question dealt with Ford's preparedness for such a downturn. The second question involved Petersen's plans for a successor. Several executives seemed qualified, but their age and experience were of concern to some directors. They had hoped to see a more careful grooming of Petersen's successor than had occurred. Although Petersen was prepared to stay on as chief executive for a time, some directors concluded that there would be insufficient time for a successor to emerge before Petersen reached the company's mandatory retirement age of 65. Finally, Petersen apparently resisted any attempt to force him to change his highly visible public role as an industry leader. He clearly believed that it was more important, and more interesting, to be speaking on issues of public importance such as education, the environment, and national priorities. The impasse between the board of directors and Petersen could not be allowed to affect the business, so a pressure emerged to bring the issue to an end.

Ultimately, the board forced Petersen to resign in order to create a stronger management team for the recession they anticipated. Harold ("Red") Polling, a senior Ford executive, was named to replace Petersen.[20]

Discussion Questions

1. Was the board of directors acting within its powers when it tried to get Petersen to resign? How can a shareholder know if the board was acting in the shareholders' interest?
2. As a shareholder of Ford Motor Company, would you have been pleased with the board's action? If not, what could you do about it?
3. Ford's stock had dropped from a price of about $50 per share to about $26 per share during the twelve months before Petersen's resignation. How might this have affected your answer to the previous question?
4. Are the shareholders of Ford Motor Company entitled to know the "full story" of Petersen's dealings with the board of directors? Should the company's directors feel a responsibility to explain their behavior to shareholders at the annual meeting if asked?

[20] See Alex Taylor III, "The Odd Eclipse of a Star CEO," *Fortune*, Feb. 11, 1991, pp. 86–96.

13

Employees: The Human Factor in the Workplace

Employees have a big stake in corporate decisions and policies, so managers must give careful attention to their workplace needs and rights. Management decisions may support, as well as endanger, employee job opportunity, privacy, and well-being. Assigning high priority to the human factor in the workplace can produce benefits for both business and society.

Key Questions and Chapter Objectives

This chapter focuses on these key questions and objectives:

- How has greater diversity in the labor force affected business's obligations to its employees?
- What are the challenges for business in providing equal job opportunities for employees?
- Are employee safety and health adequately protected by government regulations and corporate safety programs?
- To what extent does a firm have a right to probe into an employee's personal activities?
- Do employees have a duty to blow the whistle on corporate misconduct or should employees always be loyal to their employer?

In March 1989 an Exxon oil tanker, the Valdez, hit a reef and spilled 240,000 barrels of Alaskan crude oil in the pristine Prince William Sound off the coast of Alaska. After the accident, the tanker captain allegedly tested positive for blood alcohol, and it was reported that he previously had been treated for alcoholism. This episode caused big oil companies to consider revising their policies on crew members' drinking. Although most U.S. oil companies prohibit alcohol on their U.S.-flag vessels, alcohol is available aboard some foreign tankers as part of a ship crew's labor agreement. Over half of the tankers owned by U.S. oil companies fly foreign flags, where cultural customs approve serving beer and wine at mealtime. Wanting to avoid other environmental disasters linked to alcohol use, but wanting also to keep tanker crews satisfied with working conditions, oil-company officials faced a tricky situation.[1]

Flour-mill operators confronted another knotty problem affecting their employees. Research revealed a much higher rate of lymph cancer in flour-mill workers than among others in the grain industry, leading to a tentative belief that chemicals used to combat insect infestations in the grain elevators may be carcinogenic. Workers most exposed to these chemicals seemed to contract cancer from three to eight times more frequently than coworkers. Flour-mill managers faced the prospects of having to give up the chemical fumigants that had been widely used since the 1960s. Doing so might greatly increase flour-mill operating costs and result in lower-quality flour for bakers and other consumers.[2]

Yet another kind of workplace issue arose when the space shuttle Challenger exploded in 1986, killing all seven astronauts. Engineers from Morton Thiokol, the manufacturer of the booster rockets, charged that defective sealing rings had been used with the knowledge of company managers and NASA officials. The engineers claimed to have blown the whistle internally to company supervisors prior to the shuttle launch, believing that the rings would fail under the exceptionally cold weather conditions prevailing at launch time. According to the engineers, Morton Thiokol managers overruled their protests. They and NASA officials were under pressure to meet the launch date to stay on schedule. This tragic episode posed the classic issue of loyalty to one's employer: Should employees follow the boss's orders when doubt exists, or do they have a duty that goes beyond the company's boundaries?

These three issues—substance abuse, job safety, and whistle-blowing—are just a few of many issues that are critical to the employer-employee relationship. This chapter identifies and explores these three problems plus equal job opportunities and the privacy rights of employees.

WORKPLACE DIVERSITY IN THE 1990S

The sheer diversity of the U.S. workforce spawns many new employee issues and problems. Women, blacks, Hispanics, Asians, and other new entrants are changing the nation's labor pool in dramatic ways. According to the Hudson Institute, 85 percent of the growth expected in the U.S. workforce by the year 2000 will come from white and nonwhite women, nonwhite men, and immigrants of both sexes and various races. As the large group of white men now dominant in the labor force ages and retires, they will occupy a smaller share of the total labor pool—only about 39 percent by the year 2000, according to the U.S. Department of Labor.

[1] "Firms Debate Hard Line on Alcoholics," *Wall Street Journal,* Apr. 13, 1989, p. B1; and "Oil Concerns Revising Rules on Drinking Aboard Tankers in Aftermath of Valdez," *Wall Street Journal,* Feb. 23, 1990, p. A7A.

[2] "Flour-Mill Workers Face Increased Risk of Lymph Cancer, Federal Study Shows," *Wall Street Journal,* May 16, 1990, p. B4.

Business firms will have important adjustments to make as a result of these trends.[3]

Immigration

Immigration alone has complicated the management jobs of many companies. The Immigration Reform and Control Act, passed in 1986, was intended to reduce the flow of *illegal* immigrants into the United States by forbidding their employment. Hiring illegal aliens, or failure of a business firm to keep accurate records of its employees' immigration status, can result in fines and jail sentences. This legal pressure has caused some employers to go beyond the law and refuse to hire anyone who looks or sounds like a foreigner. This kind of job bias against foreigners, or against those merely imagined to be illegal immigrants, is on the increase, according to the General Accounting Office. Job seekers object to this kind of job discrimination, while employers complain that they are made to act as immigration officers for the government.[4]

Language in the Workplace

About one in five new workers seeking jobs in the 1990s is expected to be an immigrant. That often means relying on employees whose limited knowledge of English can interfere with their work. Motorola confronted the problem in the following way.[5]

> For most of Motorola's 60-year history, Poles, Greeks and Hispanics clustered on the shop floor, remaining cocooned in their native tongues. Their work didn't change much and didn't require much communication. If a supervisor needed to get a message across, he would find someone who could interpret.
>
> Today, there are fewer managers and little time to translate; an order for a circuit board that took days to fill just last year now takes [only a few] hours. And Motorola plants overflow with words. Even employees at the lowest level are now expected to read blueprints, respond to computer commands and speak up at staff meetings.
>
> But Motorola will "meet employees halfway," says a training supervisor. Classes are at company expense, and increasingly on company time. By 1992, the company expects to have spent up to $30 million on the program, begun in 1986, which includes basic literacy for English speakers. Motorola says about 6,000 employees will get language training.

The push for on-the-job language efficiency can lead to problems, though, if a company decides that all of its rules and regulations must be exclusively in

[3] "Firms Address Workers' Cultural Variety," *Wall Street Journal,* Feb. 10, 1989, p. B4; "Firms Grapple with Language Barriers," *Wall Street Journal,* Nov. 7, 1989, p. B1; and "As Cultural Diversity of Workers Grows, Experts Urge Appreciation of Differences," *Wall Street Journal,* Sept. 12, 1990, p. B1.

[4] "Wide Bias in Hiring Blamed on Immigration Sanctions," *Wall Street Journal,* Mar. 8, 1990, pp. B1, B5.

[5] "Firms Grapple . . . ," op. cit., p. B1.

English. Such English-only rules, according to the U.S. Equal Employment Opportunity Commission, can be used to discriminate against certain groups at work, thereby heightening ethnic tensions. Where non-English-speaking employees make up a large bulk of a company's workforce, employers need to demonstrate a commitment to fairness by adopting a flexible language policy.

Managing a Culturally Diverse Workforce

Managers have many new lessons to learn if they are to be effective in motivating and directing their multicultural employees. One lesson is to listen—to hear the distinct and often subtle ways of speaking and communicating that are routinely used by various ethnic groups, to hear the often submerged voices of women employees, Hispanics, Native Americans, African Americans, Asian Americans, and others. Just as important is the lesson of tolerance and understanding, which means knowing about and showing respect for the diverse values that employees bring to the workplace. When employees believe they are respected, rather than ridiculed, for the way they talk, or for the way they approach business problems, or for their gender or their ethnic background, their morale is higher and a company's productivity tends to be higher. When managers work with culturally diverse employees, "The hope in cross-cultural communication . . . is not to decide 'who's rational and who's irrational' but to understand both perspectives and become comfortable with them."[6]

This is only another way of saying what other chapters in this book say: Business operations always occur within a social and cultural setting, and the best managers are those who recognize this relationship and learn to make their decisions on that basis. A later chapter in this book focuses on the workplace issues that occur as greater numbers of women seek jobs.

EQUAL JOB OPPORTUNITY

Working to ensure **equal job opportunity** continues to be a socially desirable goal for U.S. business. This area of employee relations calls for positive responses and initiatives if business is to continue its evolution toward social responsiveness and public approval.

Government Policies and Regulations

Beginning on a major scale in the 1960s, U.S. presidents issued directives and Congress enacted laws intended to improve equal treatment of employees. The most important ones are shown in Figure 13–1. These government rules apply to most businesses in the following ways:

[6] "As Cultural Diversity . . . ," op. cit., p. B1.

- Discrimination based on race, color, religion, sex, national origin, physical or mental handicap, or age is prohibited in all employment practices. This includes hiring, firing, promotion, job classification and assignment, compensation, and other conditions of work.
- Government contractors must have written affirmative action plans detailing how they are working positively to overcome past and present effects of discrimination in their workforce.
- Women and men must receive equal pay for performing equal work.

The major agencies charged with enforcing federal equal employment opportunity laws and executive orders are the Equal Employment Opportunity Commission (EEOC) and the Office of Federal Contract Compliance Programs

FIGURE 13–1 Major federal equal job opportunity laws and executive orders.

LAWS	
Equal Pay Act Requires equal pay for equal work.	1963
Civil Rights Act Created EEOC. Forbids job discrimination by race, color, religion, and national origin.	1964
Age Discrimination in Employment Act Forbids job discrimination against persons forty to sixty-five years of age.	1967
Equal Employment Opportunity Act Strengthened enforcement powers and expanded jurisdiction of EEOC. Forbids sex discrimination.	1972
Vocational Rehabilitation Act Requires affirmative action for handicapped persons by government contractors and other companies.	1973
Americans with Disabilities Act Bans discrimination against disabled people in employment, public accommodations, transportation, and telecommunications. Provides protection for AIDS-infected workers.	1990
EXECUTIVE ORDERS AND GUIDELINES	
Executive order 10925, President Kennedy Prohibits job discrimination by government contractors.	1961
Executive Order 11246 and 11375, President Johnson Requires written affirmative action programs by most government contractors.	1965, 1967
Revised Order No. 4, OFCCP, Department of Labor Requires results-oriented affirmative action, with goals, timetables, and statistical analysis.	1970

(OFCCP). The EEOC was created in 1964 and given added enforcement powers in 1972. This agency is primarily responsible for enforcing provisions of the Civil Rights Act, the Equal Employment Opportunity Act, the Equal Pay Act, the Age Discrimination in Employment Act, and the Americans with Disabilities Act. The OFCCP in the Department of Labor monitors compliance of government contractors.

During the 1970s and early 1980s, regulators and courts used a results-oriented approach to these laws. In other words, a company would be considered in violation of the law if a statistical analysis revealed that its jobs were out of line with the proportions of whites and blacks or men and women potentially available for such work. In most cases, the courts said that good intentions were not enough and that business must produce tangible results in overcoming discriminatory employment patterns.

In the 1980s, other judicial interpretations were handed down. In 1982, the Supreme Court ruled that an actual intention to discriminate must be proved. In 1984, the Supreme Court also ruled that job seniority could not be set aside just to protect the jobs of minorities or women during layoffs or bad economic times. These decisions were seen as "gains" for business because companies were less vulnerable to discrimination lawsuits and freer to make personnel decisions on their own. Yet in 1989 the Supreme Court ruled that employers in sex discrimination suits have the burden of proving that they would have reached the same employment decision even if there had been no charge of bias. Firms would then have to be sure that job decisions were based on justifiable business reasons and not on bias.[7]

As the 1990s began, Congress enacted a new job discrimination law intended to overturn the effects of U.S Supreme Court decisions that had made it more difficult for minority employees to bring and win lawsuits alleging job bias. President George Bush objected to parts of the bill and vetoed it, saying that it would have placed unfair burdens on employers. Congress then failed to override his veto. However, these developments among the three main branches of the federal government—judiciary, executive, and legislature—indicated that government efforts to ensure equal job opportunities were likely to remain high on the public policy agenda.

A Supreme Court decision in early 1991 held that U.S. laws that promote and protect equal job opportunities in the United States do not apply to a corporation's business operations in other nations. This ruling therefore gives flexibility and managerial discretion to U.S. companies operating abroad, permitting them to adhere to local host-country job laws but also allowing the application of U.S.-based standards where management believes it to be feasible.

Corporate Responses

Business approaches to curbing discrimination and equalizing employment opportunities are shown in Figure 13–2.

[7] "High Court Shifts Burden to Firms in Sex-Bias Cases," *Wall Street Journal,* May 2, 1989, pp. B1, B6.

FIGURE 13–2
Alternative methods for reducing job discrimination and promoting greater job equality for excluded groups.

- **Passive Nondiscrimination:** all company hiring and promotion decisions are made without regard to race, sex, age, color, religion, national origin, or handicap
- **Affirmative Action:** company efforts to ensure employment opportunities are highly visible and firm seeks minorities, women, and other excluded groups for employment
- **Preferential Hiring:** company gives preference to minorities, women, and other excluded groups in hiring and promotion decisions
- **Employment Quotas:** company establishes specific numbers or proportions as goals for minorities, women, and other excluded groups to be hired or promoted

One of the most successful approaches has been affirmative action programs. Since the mid-1960s, major government contractors have been required by Presidential executive order to adopt written affirmative action plans specifying goals, actions, and timetables for promoting greater on-the-job equality. Their purpose is to reduce job discrimination by encouraging companies to take positive (that is, affirmative) steps to overcome past employment practices and traditions that may have been discriminatory. Affirmative action plans are monitored by the OFCCP in the Department of Labor. In addition, the EEOC may require companies to take affirmative steps to achieve equal job opportunities. Both agencies may seek court orders to enforce compliance with the executive orders and equal opportunity laws.

Companies that have not responded affirmatively to equal employment opportunity laws often find themselves faced with expensive back-pay settlements, as shown by these examples:

> In 1983 General Motors agreed, after pressure from government regulators, to begin a $42.5 million program to hire more women and minorities over a five-year period. Only six years later GM agreed again to pay $3 million to 3,000 former and current employees for back pay and pay adjustments due to alleged racial discrimination against salaried black employees. Another prominent company, State Farm Insurance, settled a 1988 sex discrimination suit in California for $200 million, compensating 1,113 women who had been denied jobs as insurance agents. Sexual and racial discrimination are not the whole story. Malcolm Anderson, 59, sued Lykes Pasco Inc. for age discrimination when he was fired after 30 years of service; he received 10 times his final annual salary in the settlement.

On the other hand, some large corporations have found that legally required affirmative action programs are helpful in monitoring the company's progress in providing equal job opportunity. General Electric, AT&T, and IBM have said that they would continue to use affirmative action goals and timetables even if they were not required by law.

Reverse Discrimination

Reverse discrimination describes the unintended negative impact suffered by an individual or group as a result of legal efforts to overcome discrimination against another individual or group. For example, reverse discrimination occurs if granting job rights to an individual who is a member of a religious or racial group that is legally protected against discrimination directly causes others to be denied such rights and privileges. Reverse discrimination can occur regarding preferential treatment in hiring, training, layoffs, promotions, and other job opportunities.

Title VII of the Civil Rights Act prohibits reverse discrimination, but Supreme Court rulings have varied, as shown in the following court decisions.

> In a 1979 landmark case, *United Steelworkers of America v. Weber,* the court ruled that Brian Weber, a white employee, could be excluded from a voluntary joint union-management training program at Kaiser Aluminum, even though, to achieve a 50-50 racial balance, less qualified black employees were included in the program. However, in another 1979 ruling in *Teamsters v. United States,* the court allowed the use of job seniority that tended to protect white employees in deciding layoffs. Then in the mid-1980s, the Supreme Court again ruled against reverse discrimination in *Firefighters Local Union No. 1784 v. Stotts* (1984). In this case, the court emphasized that Title VII of the Civil Rights Act protects the seniority system and that it is inappropriate to deny any employee the benefits of seniority even if it adversely affects minority employees.[8]

JOB SAFETY AND HEALTH

Much industrial and service work is inherently hazardous because of the extensive use of high-speed and noisy machinery, production processes requiring high temperatures, an increasing reliance on sophisticated chemical compounds, and the nature of such work as construction, underground and undersea tunneling, drilling, and mining. Accidents, injuries, and illnesses are likely to occur under these circumstances.

An aroused and alarmed union labor movement mounted a campaign in the late 1960s for stronger federal legislation to protect employees at work. The resulting new laws and government agencies thrust the issue of employee safety and health into the forefront of social problems facing employers.

[8] See Paul S. Greenlaw, "Affirmative Action or Reverse Discrimination?" *Personnel Journal,* September 1985, p. 84.

Occupational Safety and Health Administration

The Occupational Safety and Health Administration (OSHA), created by Congress in 1970, quickly became one of the most controversial of all the government agencies established in the great wave of social legislation during the 1970s. Congress gave OSHA important powers over employers, requiring them to provide for each employee a job "free from recognized hazards that are causing or likely to cause death or serious physical harm." Employers found in violation of OSHA safety and health standards can be fined and, in the case of a willful violation causing the death of an employee, can be jailed and fined.

OSHA in the early 1980s

OSHA's relations with business in the early 1980s reflected the Reagan administration's deregulatory philosophy. During this time OSHA proposed to exempt nearly three-fourths of all U.S. manufacturing companies from routine safety inspections. A year later, OSHA proposed a year-long experimental program of self-inspection where companies would take over the agency's job-safety-and-health inspections.[9] However, these changes were never made, and labor and other groups continued to call for stricter safety regulations, as they have done for decades. In 1987, for example, the National Safe Workplace Institute claimed that nearly 6,000 workers in manufacturing, mining, construction, and agricultural jobs died needlessly in the first half of the 1980s. According to the institute's executive director, "Although overall workplace fatalities have declined, deaths among workers in high-risk occupations have risen inordinately. . . . We don't feel OSHA has done a good job of standard setting, targeting or imposing penalties, particularly criminal penalties."[10]

OSHA in the late 1980s

As a response to its critics, OSHA demonstrated renewed vigor as a government watchdog.

> For example, Chrysler was fined $910,000 (later reduced to $295,000) for failing to report serious injuries at its Belvedere, Illinois, auto assembly plant. A year later Chrysler agreed to pay $1.6 million to settle OSHA charges of worker overexposure to lead and arsenic and other alleged health and safety violations. Another example was Union Carbide's agreement to pay a $408,500 fine to settle hundreds of contested health and safety violations, including allegations that it exposed unprotected workers to toxic gases at two chemical plants in West Virginia. Also, OSHA's largest-ever fines during the 1980s were levied against two meat-packing companies—IBP ($5.7 million) and John Mor-

[9] "OSHA Plans to End Routine Safety Checks for 75% of Manufacturers After Oct. 15," *Wall Street Journal,* Sept. 24, 1981, p. 17; and "OSHA Is Reducing Inspections Based on Complaints," *Wall Street Journal,* Feb. 2, 1982, p. 33.

[10] "Federal Commitment to Worker Safety Criticized," *Los Angeles Times,* Sept. 7, 1987.

rell ($4.3 million)—for job-safety hazards and record-keeping violations. IBP agreed to establish a three-year safety program in all of its U.S. plants.[11]

These tougher regulatory actions were accompanied by new workplace exposure standards intended to protect employees from hazardous substances. The agency declared 376 potentially toxic chemicals dangerous enough to justify greater engineering controls to limit worker exposures. OSHA also expanded its requirement that employers inform workers who are exposed, or face possible exposure, to hazardous substances. These new rules were expected to reduce on-the-job hazards for over 21 million employees, especially the 4.5 million who were working in environments where exposure levels were higher than the new rules permit.[12]

OSHA's efforts at the federal level are frequently supplemented by both state and local job-safety regulations. For example, San Francisco adopted a law regulating the use of video display terminals, after widespread concerns were expressed about their possible health effects on users.

Management's Responses

Although some praised OSHA's renewed posture as an aggressive government watchdog, business has generally criticized OSHA as being too costly a way to safeguard employees. Small businesses in particular have a difficult time carrying the paperwork burden required by OSHA's rules. Other companies object to the high cost of redesigning machinery and production processes, saying that these expenses would far outweigh any tangible or marginal benefit in increased safety and health for workers. Employees themselves have refused to wear required safety goggles, earplugs, respirators, and other special equipment to protect them from harm, but if they were to be injured while not wearing such items, the employer, not the employee, would be subject to penalty.

Many businesses are actively developing programs, sometimes in cooperation with OSHA, to ensure the safety and health of their workers. For example, the United Auto Workers and Chrysler Corporation have worked jointly to minimize repetitive-motion disorders among workers at five assembly plants. This workplace injury occurs frequently when employees perform the same tasks repeatedly—on production lines, in meat-packing plants, and at video display terminals (VDTs). As many as 5 million employees in the United States may suffer from this on-the-job injury. Another job-related concern has centered on electromagnetic emissions from the 40 million VDTs used throughout industry. Responding to this concern, IBM introduced new models with lower emission rates.[13]

[11] "Chrysler to Pay Record Penalty in OSHA Case," *Wall Street Journal,* Feb. 2, 1987, p. 20; "Union Carbide Agrees to Pay Record Fine," *San Francisco Examiner,* July 24, 1987; and "OSHA Asks $2.6 Million Fine, Says Major Injuries Unreported," *Washington Post,* July 22, 1987; and *Wall Street Journal,* Nov. 23, 1988, p. A7.

[12] "OSHA Adopts a Set of Limits on 376 Toxins," *Wall Street Journal,* Jan. 16, 1989, p. B2.

[13] "An Invisible Workplace Hazard Gets Harder to Ignore," *Business Week,* Jan. 30, 1989, pp. 92–93; and "IBM to Reduce Radiation from Future VDT Models," *Wall Street Journal,* Nov. 22, 1989, pp. B1, B4.

Businesses seem to be responding with cautious cooperation to renewed federal, state, and local involvement to protect employees. Some appear to be complying only with the letter of the law; others are exceeding government standards to avoid regulatory investigation. In spite of these mixed results, many firms accept their social responsibility toward their employees and recognize them as a valuable corporate asset and an integral stakeholder.

PRIVACY

Privacy rights in the business context refer primarily to protecting a person's private life from intrusive and unwarranted business actions. The employees and customers of business, along with the general public, believe that their religious, political, and social beliefs, as well as personal life-styles and health condition, are private matters and should be safeguarded from snooping or analysis. The same view applies to personal acts and conversations in locations such as company lavatories and private homes. Exceptions are permitted grudgingly only when job involvement is clearly proved. For example, it may be appropriate to know that an automobile assembly worker is taking cocaine while on the job or that a job applicant is carrying a fatal communicable disease. Other behaviors are not so clear-cut. For example, should employers be permitted to deny jobs to smokers and even fire those who smoke secretly when not at work?[14] Or what protective action, if any, is justified when an employer learns that a key employee who possesses highly confidential information is dating an employee in a competing firm? At what point do company interests weigh more heavily than an employee's right to freedom and privacy?

The major areas where privacy is involved are summarized in Figure 13–3 and are discussed next.

Computer Data Banks

The development of computers with massive capacity to store and recall information has caused concern about the potential for improper storage and release of personal information. Companies need information about people in order to conduct business, but rights of privacy must be judiciously balanced against the firm's right to know. Policies to handle these rights are typically based on three principles reported by the federal Privacy Study Commission in 1977:[15]

- Minimize intrusiveness on the individual by seeking only information that is necessary for the activity involved.
- Maximize fairness by allowing people to see records about themselves and to challenge inaccurate records.

[14] "The Job Is Yours—Unless You Smoke," *Wall Street Journal*, Apr. 21, 1989, p. B1.
[15] W. Lee Burge, "Privacy in the Information Society," *Business*, January–March 1982, pp. 52–54.

FIGURE 13–3
Selected business activities that involve employee privacy rights.

- Computer data banks
- Employee monitoring
- Control of drug abuse
- Control of alcohol abuse
- Genetic testing
- AIDS testing
- Polygraph testing
- Honesty testing

- Maintain a high level of confidentiality by utilizing stringent corporate policies and government laws in releasing information.

Several federal privacy laws govern the dissemination of information: the Fair Credit Reporting Act (1970), the Privacy Act (1974), the Right to Financial Privacy Act (1978), the Video Privacy Protection Act (1988), and the Computer Matching and Privacy Protection Act (1988). Unfortunately, each of these laws has loopholes. For example, under the Fair Credit Reporting Act, anyone with a "legitimate business need" can gain access to personal information in credit files. The Right to Financial Privacy Act is intended to forbid access to individuals' bank accounts; however, the act makes exceptions for state agencies, law enforcement officials, and private employers.[16]

Monitoring Employee Activity

Besides the collection and storage of employee information, corporations are actively involved in observing workers' activities. Hidden surveillance devices in employee locker rooms and lavatories have been used by employers to detect worker theft. These actions are usually considered invasions of one's privacy but often are defended because there may be a criminal act in progress and it may cause a financial loss to the corporation. Advanced technology has made corporate monitoring more frequent and more accurate, as the following examples illustrate.[17]

> General Electric Co. says it uses tiny, fish-eye lenses installed behind pinholes in walls and ceilings to watch employees suspected of crimes. Du Pont Co. says it uses hidden, long distance cameras to monitor its loading docks around the clock. At airlines such as Delta, computers track who writes the most reservations. And Management Recruiters Inc. in Chicago says its bosses surreptitiously watch computerized schedules to see who interviews the most job candidates.

Management justifies the increase in employee monitoring, citing the need to protect the company from employee theft and employee negligence (which

[16] "Is Nothing Private?" *Business Week*, Sept. 4, 1989, p. 77.

[17] "Is Your Boss Spying on You?" *Business Week*, Jan. 15, 1990, pp. 74–75.

could lead to the company's legal liability). Yet employees are becoming more aware of corporate monitoring and are challenging it in court as an invasion of privacy. Judges have ruled that workers must prove that their reasonable expectations for privacy outweigh the company's reasons for secretive monitoring. Employers sometimes satisfy the court's demands by simply informing workers of the company's surveillance policies. Others require job applicants to sign a privacy waiver before being hired.

Drug Abuse and Drug Testing

Abuse of drugs, particularly hard drugs such as heroin and cocaine, has become an epidemic problem for employers. In 1986, 75 percent of drug users reported that they had used drugs on the job, and 64 percent said they had sold drugs on the job. Eighteen percent of drug users had drug-related job accidents and 60 percent reported impaired job performance. Nearly one in five said they stole from their employer to pay for drugs.[18]

One way business has dealt with on-the-job drug abuse is through **drug testing.** Company drug testing increased from 5 percent in 1982 to almost 50 percent in 1988. Some of this increase may be attributed to the Drug-Free Workplace Act of 1988, which requires federal contractors to establish and maintain a workplace free of drugs. Tests of job applicants in several different industries revealed that approximately 12 percent tested positive for drug use.[19]

Typically drug testing is used on three different occasions.

- *In preemployment screening.* Some companies test all job applicants or selected applicants before hiring, usually as part of a physical examination, often informing the applicant ahead of time that there will be a drug screen.
- *Random testing of employees.* This type of screening may occur at various times throughout the year. In many companies, a member of a particular job category (for example, an operator of heavy machinery) or job level (for example, a supervisor) is eligible for screening at any time.
- *Testing for cause.* This test occurs when an employee is believed to be impaired by drugs and unfit for work. It is commonly used after an accident or some observable change in behavior.[20]

Small businesses also are becoming more involved in employee drug testing. "The word on the street is that people with drug problems are going to small companies because they know that the IBMs and the Xeroxes and the GTEs are drug screening and have been for years," said an operations vice president at

[18] George E. Stevens, Carol D. Surles, and Faith W. Stevens, "A Better Approach by Management to Drug Testing," *Employee Responsibilities and Rights Journal,* 1989, pp. 61–71.

[19] "Evidence Is Skimpy That Drug Testing Works, but Employers Embrace Practice," *Wall Street Journal,* Sept. 7, 1989, p. B1.

[20] Stevens et al., op. cit., p. 63.

FIGURE 13–4
Pros and cons of employee drug testing.

Arguments Favoring Employee Drug Testing

- Business cooperation with U.S. "War on Drugs" campaign
- Improves employee productivity
- Promotes safety in the workplace
- Decreases employee theft and absenteeism
- Reduces health and insurance costs

Arguments Opposing Employee Drug Testing

- Invades an employee's privacy
- Violates an employee's right to due process
- May be unrelated to job performance
- May be used as a method of employee discrimination
- Lowers employee morale
- Conflicts with company values of honesty and trust
- May yield unreliable test results
- Ignores effects of prescription drugs, alcohol, and over-the-counter drugs
- Drug use an insignificant problem for some companies

Corporate Wellness, a drug counseling firm. So, employers at small businesses see a growing need to protect themselves from drug abusers. As an example, Chamberlain Contractors "pays $70 to $100 a year per worker for a program that includes preemployment drug tests, random tests twice a year, quarterly training sessions for all workers, and an employee assistance program that offers counseling on divorce, rebellious teenagers, finances, and other topics that may be troubling employees in addition to drugs and alcohol."[21]

The debate over employee drug testing is summarized in Figure 13–4. In general, proponents of testing emphasize the need to control the potential harm to others and the cost to business and society attributable to drug use on the job. Opponents of drug testing challenge either the effectiveness of drug testing or its intrusion on individual privacy.

Alcohol Abuse

Company programs for drug abusers and alcohol abusers are often combined. Throughout the 1980s an increasing number of firms recognized that they had a role to play in helping alcoholics control or break their habit. As with drug rehabilitation programs, most alcoholism programs work through employee assistance programs that offer counseling and follow-up. United Airlines' EAP reported dramatic reductions of absenteeism plus excellent recovery rates during a ten-year period, and it was considered to be a model for other firms interested in managing the problems of alcohol abuse at work. The importance of controlling workplace alcoholism was emphasized by the Exxon Valdez oil spill, as mentioned at the beginning of this chapter, and again in 1990 when two Northwest Airlines pilots were found guilty of flying too soon after a night of heavy drinking. The

[21] "Small Companies Move to Increase Anti-Drug Programs," *Wall Street Journal*, Nov. 6, 1990, p. B-2.

same potential problems can affect personnel in a wide range of sensitive jobs, such as train crews, nuclear power station operators, flight controllers, and many others.

Genetic Testing

Two developments have presented employers and employees with yet another issue where business necessity and employee privacy can come into conflict. One development is newly acquired knowledge of genetics—the hereditary components of our physical makeup. This new knowledge has appeared at a time when workers in all kinds of businesses are increasingly concerned about the health effects of hazardous substances present in the work environment. This second development—a heightened health awareness—has combined with the first development—genetic knowledge—to thrust genetic testing into the limelight.

Genetic testing is any attempt to use the science of genetics to understand the links between our inherited makeup and certain illnesses. Genetic testing can occur in two different forms: genetic screening and genetic monitoring. *Genetic screening* is used to identify *persons* who are susceptible to certain genetically based illnesses. The goal of genetic screening is to single out individual persons or groups of people who have certain genetic traits. *Genetic monitoring*, on the other hand, is used to identify *substances* that are capable of causing damage to the genetic makeup of people. The goal of genetic monitoring is to single out, not people, but harmful substances.[22]

Critics fear that the widespread use of genetic screening could result in discrimination against employees with certain inborn tendencies to illness. By screening out these persons, companies could save considerable sums of money on health costs and could reduce absenteeism caused by illness.

Genetic monitoring tends to be less threatening to employees' rights to privacy and to jobs because it acts as an early warning system for any group of employees exposed to a potentially dangerous chemical. However, an employer who discovers a genetically damaging substance in the workplace environment may then bar some employees from holding jobs there. For example, women who have been denied or fired from jobs in work environments that have high levels of lead have sued employers for unequal and discriminatory treatment. In 1991, the U.S. Supreme Court ruled that such job restrictions are illegal.

In another case, though, all employees benefited from genetic monitoring. When Johnson & Johnson discovered that ethylene oxide, a gas used to sterilize medical supplies and equipment, may have caused genetic damage in some of its workers, it discontinued all use of the chemical at one of its plants. The U.S. Occupational Safety and Health Administration also tightened up exposure stan-

[22] Thomas H. Murray, "Genetic Testing at Work: How Should It Be Used?" *Personnel Administrator*, September 1985, pp. 91–102; and Anne E. Libbin, Susan R. Mendelsohn, and Dennis P. Duffy, "Employee Medical and Honesty Testing," *Personnel*, November 1988, pp. 38–48.

dards after tests in a number of companies confirmed that genetic harm was being done by the chemical.

AIDS Testing

The disease known as acquired immune deficiency syndrome (AIDS) became a major public health problem in the United States during the 1980s. Its rapid spread and its resistance to treatment or a permanent cure raised many questions of an ethical nature, especially since initial infection is largely a matter of personal life-style. Among those questions was the issue of mandatory **AIDS testing** of employees whose work activities were thought to carry some potential risk of infecting coworkers or customers.

By the early 1990s, companies had begun to focus on certain key principles in dealing with AIDS when it appears among employees.

- *Legal status.* Legal experts believe that those with AIDS qualify as handicapped persons under the Vocational Rehabilitation Act of 1973, which requires government contractors and recipients of federal funds to make "reasonable accommodations" for workers with handicaps. Accepting this legal interpretation, some companies take the position that AIDS victims have a right to their jobs as long their illness does not interfere with job performance. The states have been more active than the federal government in responding to this issue. California, for example, bars job discrimination against people with AIDS. More than 30 states have similar antidiscrimination rulings.[23]
- *Testing is not recommended.* Employees should not be tested for the presence of the AIDS virus, partly because it would be an invasion of privacy, partly because the available tests are frequently inaccurate, and partly because the tests do not reveal whether a person having AIDS antibodies will ever develop the disease.
- *No workplace restrictions.* According to guidelines issued in 1985 by the U.S. Department of Health and Human Services, since AIDS cannot be contracted by casual and normal workplace contacts, employees with the illness should not be segregated from others nor should they be restricted in performing jobs for which they are qualified.

Many firms believe that information is the best defense against AIDS, and the benefits that may result are listed in Figure 13–5. Even so, AIDS imposes costs on companies, especially through their health benefit programs. Insurance companies favor trying to isolate high-risk applicants by means of AIDS antibody tests, fighting off attempts by some states to ban such blood tests, and using substitutes for tests where they are banned. Insurers also favor denying new policies on grounds of the enormous costs to society and aggressively fighting existing policyholders' claims in court.[24]

[23] "AIDS Is Ruled Handicap by California Commission," *Wall Street Journal,* Feb. 11, 1987, p. 25.

[24] "How Insurers Succeed in Limiting Their Losses Related to the Disease," *Wall Street Journal,* May 18, 1987, p. 12; and "Who Will Pay the AIDS Bill?" *Business Week,* Apr. 11, 1988, p. 71.

FIGURE 13–5
Advantages of an AIDS information program.

- Minimizes disruption in the workplace
- Decreases chances of costly litigation
- Establishes consistent company guidelines
- Reduces health care costs
- Enhances employee-employer relations
- Provides up-to-date AIDS information to employees
- Promotes a responsible corporate public image

Polygraph and Honesty Testing

Polygraph testing has been used by many companies as a preemployment screening procedure or upon discovery of employee theft. Its use has long been considered an invasion of privacy and a coercive procedure. In 1988, the Employee Polygraph Protection Act became law. This law severely limits polygraph testing by employers and is expected to prohibit approximately 85 percent of all such tests previously administered in the United States. Employers are required to post a notice of the prohibition in the workplace.

Some organizations are exempt from the act: all government agencies, businesses engaged in intelligence and counterintelligence functions, private security services, and pharmaceutical companies. Employers are permitted to use polygraphs in an ongoing investigation of economic loss or injury to the employer's business arising from theft, embezzlement, or misappropriation of funds.

In addition to the 1988 federal law, more than 20 states and the District of Columbia regulate or restrict the use of polygraphs, and the federal law does not preempt any state or local law that is more restrictive.

In response to the federal ban on polygraphs, many corporations have switched to written psychological tests that seek to predict employee honesty on the job. These pen-and-paper tests rely on answers to a series of questions that are designed to identify undesirable qualities in the test taker. Developed for the military in the 1940s, such tests have been used in the private sector since the 1960s, but their use has increased markedly since 1988.

The tests' defenders—mainly companies that design and administer them for private industry—say they will identify potentially dishonest people about 85 percent of the time. However, critics emphasize the harm done by poor or incorrect assessment in the other 15 percent of the cases. Critics also argue that the tests intrude upon a person's privacy and discriminate disproportionately against minorities.[25] The American Psychological Association in a 1991 report said some of the tests help predict integrity, and it urged employers to use care in interpreting test results.

[25] "Integrity-Test Firms Fear Report Card by Congress," *Wall Street Journal*, Sept. 20, 1990, p. B7; and "Prominent Psychologists Group Gives Qualified Support to Integrity Tests," *Wall Street Journal*, Mar. 7, 1991, p. B8. For a thorough discussion of both kinds of tests, see Paul R. Sackett, "Honesty Testing for Personnel Selection," *Personnel Administrator*, September 1985, pp. 67–76; and Anthony Gale (ed.), *The Polygraph Test: Lies, Truth and Science*, London: SAGE, 1988.

WHISTLE-BLOWING

Sometimes the loyal bonds between a company and an employee are strained to the breaking point, especially when a worker thinks the company is doing something wrong or harmful to the public. When that occurs, the employee "blows the whistle" by reporting alleged organizational misconduct to the public or to high-level company officials.

Whistle-blowing has both defenders and detractors. Generally, employees are not free to speak out against their employer because there is a public interest in allowing companies to operate without harassment from insiders. Company information is generally considered to be proprietary and private. If employees, based on their personal points of view, are freely allowed to expose issues to the public and allege misconduct, the company may be thrown into turmoil and be unable to operate effectively.

On the other hand, there may be situations in which society's interests override those of the company, so an employee may feel an obligation to blow the whistle. According to one expert, certain conditions must be satisfied to morally justify blowing the whistle to outsiders (for example, by informing the media or government officials):

- An unreported act would do serious and considerable harm to the public.
- Once such an act has been identified, an employee has reported the act to his or her immediate supervisor and has made the moral concern known.
- If the immediate supervisor does nothing, the employee tries other internal pathways for reporting the problem.[26]

Only after each of these conditions has been met should the whistle-blower "go public."

Government protection for the whistle-blower has increased at federal and state levels. A 1989 federal law protects federal employees from retaliation by their supervisors when they expose government waste or fraud. Similar laws were adopted by several states to protect workers in the private sector. Legislation also may guarantee back pay if the whistle-blower was wrongly fired, and some states assist the whistle-blower with their legal expenses by providing free legal advice.[27]

Financial rewards for whistle-blowers are becoming more common. The federal False Claims Act allows employees to sue companies suspected of defrauding the government and then to share in any financial restitution. Whistle-blowers received 22 percent of the $3.5 million General Electric settlement with the federal government, after blowing the whistle on a timecard-altering scheme that allegedly cheated the government out of millions of dollars.[28]

[26] Richard DeGeorge, *Business Ethics*, 3d ed., New York: Macmillan, 1990, pp. 208–211.

[27] "States Begin to Protect Employees Who Blew Whistle on Their Firms," *Wall Street Journal*, Dec. 31, 1984, p. 11.

[28] "GE Will Pay $3.5 Million to Settle Suits Brought by Whistle-Blowers," *Wall Street Journal*, Feb. 24, 1989, p. B6.

EMPLOYEES AS CORPORATE STAKEHOLDERS

The issues discussed in this chapter illustrate forcefully that today's business corporation is open to a wide range of social forces. Its borders are very porous, letting in a constant flow of external influences. Many of these social factors are brought inside by employees whose personal values, life-styles, and social attitudes become a vital part of the workplace.

Managers and other business professionals need to be aware of these employee-imported features of today's workforce. The human factor is central to getting a corporation's work done, as well as to helping satisfy the aspirations of those who contribute their skills and talents to the workplace. The task of the corporate manager is to help reconcile potential clashes between employees' human needs and the requirements of corporate economic production. Acknowledging the important stake that employees have in the successful pursuit of the corporation's economic mission enables business leaders to cope more effectively with the many issues that concern employees.

SUMMARY POINTS OF THIS CHAPTER

- An increasingly diverse workforce requires corporate managers to respect and be able to deal effectively with a wide range of cultures and social attitudes among today's employees.
- Equal job opportunity remains a high priority in U.S. society and calls for positive responses by corporations to assure that legal and ethical responsibilities are met.
- After a period of relative neglect in the early 1980s, job safety and health have been the focus of renewed attention by both government and business during the late 1980s and early 1990s.
- Employee privacy rights are frequently challenged by employers' needs to have information about their health, their work activities, and even their off-the-job life-style. When these issues arise, management has a responsibility to act ethically toward employees while continuing to work for a high level of economic performance.
- Blowing the whistle on one's employer is often a last-resort way to protest company actions considered to be harmful to others; it can usually be avoided if corporate managers encourage open communication and show a willingness to listen to their employees.

KEY TERMS AND CONCEPTS USED IN THIS CHAPTER

- Equal job opportunity
- Reverse discrimination
- Privacy rights
- Drug testing
- Genetic testing
- AIDS testing
- Polygraph testing
- Whistle-blowing

DISCUSSION CASE

RESPONDING TO AIDS IN THE WORKPLACE

Tim, a service support manager for San Francisco–based Wells Fargo Bank, had been an exemplary employee for several years. A strong leader who had a good reputation, 32-year-old Tim was well liked by upper management and the 15 employees he supervised.[29]

This up-and-coming individual also had a medical condition that was beginning to wear down his body's immune system. Infected with the human immunodeficiency virus (HIV), Tim had developed a form of acquired immune deficiency syndrome (AIDS) known as AIDS-related complex (ARC). Although not as severe as AIDS, ARC can result in such symptoms as shortness of breath, a lingering dry cough, skin rashes, extreme fatigue, and lightheadedness. Symptoms never surface in many people who are infected, and others develop conditions years after infection.

Extreme fatigue became part of Tim's daily life and was a detriment to his usual top-notch performance. As his health deteriorated, he began to realize his physical limitations. About 15 months earlier, Tim revealed the information about his health to his middle management supervisor, Sandra. He asked her to keep the news confidential. Tim was aware of his condition several months before he informed his manager. Because HIV is not contagious through casual contact, this individual was not a health risk to other bank employees and therefore was under no obligation to share such personal information with his employer. Because he could not keep up with his workload, however, Tim wanted to inform Sandra that the problem was medical. Knowing that Wells Fargo's policy on HIV ensured his confidentiality, Tim believed that the company would accommodate him by not disclosing his illness.

After her discussion with Tim, Sandra consulted Bryan Lawton, the bank's employee assistance director and a clinical psychologist. She asked how to respond to managers and employees who have questions about workers who have HIV. "Sandra was distressed because she was concerned about Tim's health,"

[29] This case was adapted from an actual incident reported in Jennifer J. Laabs, "Wells Fargo's and IBM's HIV Policies Help Protect Employees' Rights," copyright April 1990, p. 40. Reprinted with the permission of PERSONNEL JOURNAL, Costa Mesa, CA. All rights reserved. The names of employees have been disguised.

says Lawton. Tim was showing signs of fatigue and was missing work. His co-workers began to wonder if he was ill. "Sandra was afraid that Tim was wearing himself down," Lawton adds. "She also was concerned about the impact the illness was having on the people he supervised—people who had suspicions about him being infected with the disease, but who didn't know what to say or do."

Sandra was aware of the company's four-point policy:

- Keep confidential all information about the medical condition and medical records of an employee who has AIDS, ARC, or another HIV condition.
- Consult Employee Assistance Services (EAS) immediately after learning that an employee has been diagnosed with AIDS, ARC, or another HIV condition.
- Work with EAS and your personnel officer to arrange job accommodations that are deemed medically necessary for the employee with one of these conditions.
- Help employees learn about AIDS by asking EAS for the AIDS Education Program.

Yet, even though Sandra was aware of the policy, she had never had to implement it or manage its effects. She had several questions and needed assistance in how to implement company policy on Tim's behalf. She also wanted to demonstrate concern and compassion for her fellow employee while staying within the legal boundaries of confidentiality. One particular point of interest for Sandra was possible job-based adjustments that Tim might need in the months ahead. Because Tim was a valued employee, Sandra wanted to minimize his concerns while maximizing his tenure.

Discussion Questions

1. In your opinion, does the bank's AIDS policy adequately protect the rights of all Wells Fargo employees?
2. Is the protection of Tim's privacy rights more important than, less important than, or equally as important as the bank's need to be efficient in getting its day-to-day work done? Should Tim be removed from his job?
3. If Tim is given special job privileges because of his illness, would other bank employees have a right to complain about unequal and discriminatory treatment?

14

Consumer Protection

Safeguarding consumers while continuing to supply them with the goods and services they want is a prime social responsibility of business. Consumers in the 1990s have become increasingly aware of the impact that consumption can have on the environment, on nutrition and health, on the values acquired by children, and on the images of women and ethnic groups that are projected through consumer advertising. Government agencies serve as watchdogs for consumers, supplementing the actions taken by socially responsive corporations.

Key Questions and Chapter Objectives

This chapter focuses on these key questions and objectives:

- Why did a consumer movement develop in the United States?
- What are the environmental impacts of a high-consumption society?
- Why has advertising become a target of consumer activists and government regulators?
- In what ways do government regulatory agencies protect consumers?
- How have socially responsible corporations responded to consumer needs?

Knowing that she had a potentially defective heart valve implanted in her chest "has made living a nightmare," declared one of the estimated 60,000 recipients of a Shiley Convexo-Concave heart valve. Her fears stemmed from awareness that 389 similar valves had broken, killing 248 of the recipients. She also had been told that surgery to replace her valve was riskier than leaving it in place. Her peace of mind was not improved by knowing that the U.S. Food and Drug Administration (FDA) had approved sale of the valve in 1979, seeing it as an improvement over earlier models. After repeated valve failures, the manufacturer withdrew it from the market in 1986 when strong pressure was exerted by FDA regulators. By early 1990, the company had settled an estimated 180 lawsuits brought by patients or their survivors.[1]

[1] "Heart Trouble at Pfizer," *Business Week*, Feb. 26, 1990; and "FDA Says Pfizer Inadequately Warned Heart-Valve Recipients of Risk of Death," *Wall Street Journal*, Dec. 10, 1990, p. B4.

"You can bet your last dollar this is going to be a tough year for fur retailers," said an animal rights activist in 1989. They were protesting the use of furs for making coats, jackets, gloves, and hats. Demonstrations were staged across the nation, including parades during the Christmas shopping season and sit-ins at stores selling fur products. "Sit-ins are a form of civil disobedience in the spirit of people like Martin Luther King and Mahatma Gandhi," claimed another activist. "Profits are plunging. As people realize this is a business of cruelty and greed, furs will go out of fashion." Furriers did not agree, saying "The animal rights groups aren't a factor [in lower profits]. The real issue is warm weather and over-production." Another retailer said, "Show a woman a nice mink, and she'll never turn you down." But in London, Harrod's closed its 150-year-old fur salon after a nationwide campaign by activists that included broken windows and firebombing of fur shops. One store owner declared, "It's giving in to terrorists."[2]

When a controversy developed over the introduction of milk from cows that had been given a genetically engineered hormone to boost milk production, a Kraft vice president told reporters, "We're going to follow our consumers' concerns on this." Kraft was joined by other well-known companies in rejecting use of the BGH (bovine growth hormone) milk in their products. Four of the nation's largest supermarket chains also balked at handling such milk. A Safeway representative said, "We don't want our customers or stores being used as guinea pigs."[3]

These three episodes demonstrate some of the complexities of serving consumers in the 1990s. New standards of business performance are being demanded. Today's consumers are increasingly aware of the broad impact that consumption can have not only on themselves but on society generally. This chapter examines these issues and the various ways that consumers, government regulators, and business firms have dealt with them.

PRESSURES TO PROMOTE CONSUMER INTERESTS

As long as business has existed—since the ancient beginnings of commerce and trade—consumers have tried to protect their interests when they go to the marketplace to buy goods and services. They have haggled over prices, taken a careful look at the goods they are buying, compared the quality and prices of products offered by other sellers, and complained loudly when they feel cheated by shoddy products. So, consumer self-reliance has always been one form of consumer protection. The Latin phrase, *caveat emptor*—meaning "let the buyer beware"—has put consumers on the alert to look after their own interests. This form of individual self-reliance is still very much in existence today.

However, the increasing complexity of economic life in the twentieth century, especially in the more advanced industrial nations, has led to organized, collective

[2] "Fur Industry Braces for a Rough Season," *Wall Street Journal*, Nov. 6, 1989, p. B1; and "Never Mind, Ladies, They'll Still Have Cashmere Sweaters," *Wall Street Journal*, Jan. 15, 1990, p. B8.

[3] "Sour Reception Greets Milk Hormone" *Wall Street Journal*, Sept. 15, 1989, p. B1.

efforts to safeguard consumers. These organized activities are usually called **consumerism** or the consumer movement.

The Anatomy of Consumerism

At the heart of consumerism in the United States is an attempt to expand the rights and powers of consumers. The goal of the movement is to make consumer power an effective counterbalance to the rights and powers of business firms that sell goods and services.

Within an advanced, industrialized, free enterprise nation, business firms tend to grow to a very large size. They acquire much power and influence. Frequently, they can dictate prices. Typically, their advertisements sway consumers to buy one product or service rather than another. If large enough, they may share the market with only a few equally large competitors, thereby weakening some of the competitive protections enjoyed by consumers where business firms are smaller and more numerous. The economic influence and power of business firms may therefore become a problem for consumers unless ways can be found to promote an equal amount of consumer power.

Most consumers would feel well-protected if their fundamental rights to fair play in the marketplace could be guaranteed. In the early 1960s, when the consumer movement in the United States was in its early stages, President John F. Kennedy told Congress that consumers were entitled to four different kinds of protections:

1. *The right to safety:* to be protected against the marketing of goods which are hazardous to health or life.
2. *The right to be informed:* to be protected against fraudulent, deceitful, or grossly misleading information, advertising, labeling, or other practices, and to be given the facts to make an informed choice.
3. *The right to choose:* to be assured, wherever possible, access to a variety of products and services at competitive prices and in those industries in which competition is not workable and government regulation is substituted, to be assured satisfactory quality and service at fair prices.
4. *The right to be heard:* to be assured that consumer interests will receive full and sympathetic consideration in the formulation of government policy, and fair and expeditious treatment in its administrative tribunals.

The **consumer bill of rights,** as it was called, became the guiding philosophy of the consumer movement. If those rights could be guaranteed, consumers would feel more confident in dealing with well-organized and influential corporations in the marketplace.

Reasons for the Consumer Movement

The **consumer movement** exists because consumers believe that there is an unfair use of business power. The balance between business power and business responsibility is uneven, which results in consumer abuses such as unfairly high prices, unreliable and unsafe products, excessive advertising claims for the effectiveness of some consumer goods and services, and the promotion of some products (such as cigarettes, fatty foods, and farm products contaminated with pesticides) known to be harmful to human health.

Additional reasons for the existence of the consumer movement are the following:

- Complex products have enormously complicated the choices consumers need to make when they go shopping. For this reason, consumers today are more dependent on business for product quality than ever before. Because many products are so complex—a personal computer or a television set, for example—most consumers have no way to judge at the time of purchase whether their quality is satisfactory. Many of the component parts of such products are not visible to consumers who, therefore, cannot inspect them even if they have the technical competence to do so. Instructions for use or care of products often are so complicated and detailed that buyers cannot understand or remember what to do. First-time computer users may spend weeks or months learning even the simplest software package—and then discover that it is not adequate for their needs. Consumers find that they are almost entirely dependent on business to deliver the quality promised. In these circumstances, business power can be used responsibly or it can be used unfairly to take advantage of uninformed consumers.
- Services, as well as products, have become more specialized and difficult to judge. When choosing lawyers, dentists, colleges, or hospitals, most consumers do not have adequate guides for evaluating whether they are good or bad. They can rely on word-of-mouth experiences of others, but this information may not be entirely reliable. Or when purchasing expensive items such as refrigerators, householders have not only to judge how well the items will perform but also to know what to do when they break down. The consumer faces a two-tier judgment problem in making purchases: First, is the product a good one? Then, what will good service cost? The uninformed or badly informed consumer is frequently no match for the seller who is in the superior position.
- When business tries to sell both products and services through advertising, claims may be inflated or they may appeal to emotions having little to do with how the product is expected to perform. An example was a television ad for designer jeans featuring the film star Brooke Shields, who teased viewers by asking, "Do you want to know what comes between me and my Calvins? Nothing." Another ad for fashion clothes was described this way: "A tousled blond beauty stands in the corner of a cattle pen, one finger caught between her lips, her denim bodice unbuttoned. In the next photograph she is lying down, and a man's hand is opening her shirt to reveal ample cleavage. In another shot she is dancing with a cowboy, her jean skirt ripped and her bra exposed. The jumbled black-and-white photo mon-

tage—part of a series of print-advertising campaigns for Guess fashions—is one of the latest entries in the fashion industry's era of provocation."[4] Ad-industry critics have frequently found fault with advertisements during children's television programs that feature violence, that sell sweetened cereals, or that promote toys—for example, Nintendo or foods such as California raisins—by building program plots around these products, thus taking advantage of young children unable to differentiate between a fictional program and a commercial advertisement.[5] Beer commercials that feature "good old boys" relaxing after work, cigarette advertisements that hint at freedom and pleasure for users, or auto advertisements that link male virility with horsepower and speed have come under attack for ignoring the negative impacts of alcohol abuse, tobacco use, and high-speed automobile deaths and injuries.

- Product safety has often been ignored. The symbolic beginning of consumerism in the United States was Ralph Nader's well-publicized charges about the hazards of driving the Corvair.[6] As public interest in health and nutrition grew during the 1960s and 1970s, many consumers worried about food additives, preservatives, pesticide residues left on fruits and vegetables, diet patterns that contributed to obesity, and the devastating health effects of long-term tobacco use. If the public could not count on business to screen out these possible dangers to consumers, who could they turn to for help? This question was raised more and more often, which led eventually to organized collective efforts to redress the imbalance of power between sellers and consumers.

Consumer Advocacy Groups

One of the impressive features of the consumer movement in the United States is the many organized groups that actively promote and speak for the interests of millions of consumers. One organization alone—the Consumer Federation of America—brings together over 200 nonprofit groups to espouse the consumer viewpoint; they represent some 30 million Americans. Two nonprofit organizations—Consumers' Research and Consumers Union—conduct extensive tests on selected consumer products and services and publish the results, with ratings on a brand-name basis, in widely circulated magazines. (*Consumer Reports* is the best known of these magazines.) Consumer cooperatives, credit unions, and consumer education programs in schools and universities and on television and radio round out a very extensive network of activities aimed at promoting consumer interests.

The most-publicized consumer advocate is Ralph Nader, who with his associates formed the organizations shown in Figure 14–1. Public Citizen, founded

[4] "Sexy Does It," *Newsweek*, Sept. 15, 1986, p. 62.

[5] "Watch What Your Kids Watch," *Business Week*, Jan. 8, 1990, pp. 50–52.

[6] Ralph Nader, *Unsafe at Any Speed: The Designed-in Dangers of the American Automobile*, New York: Grossman, 1972.

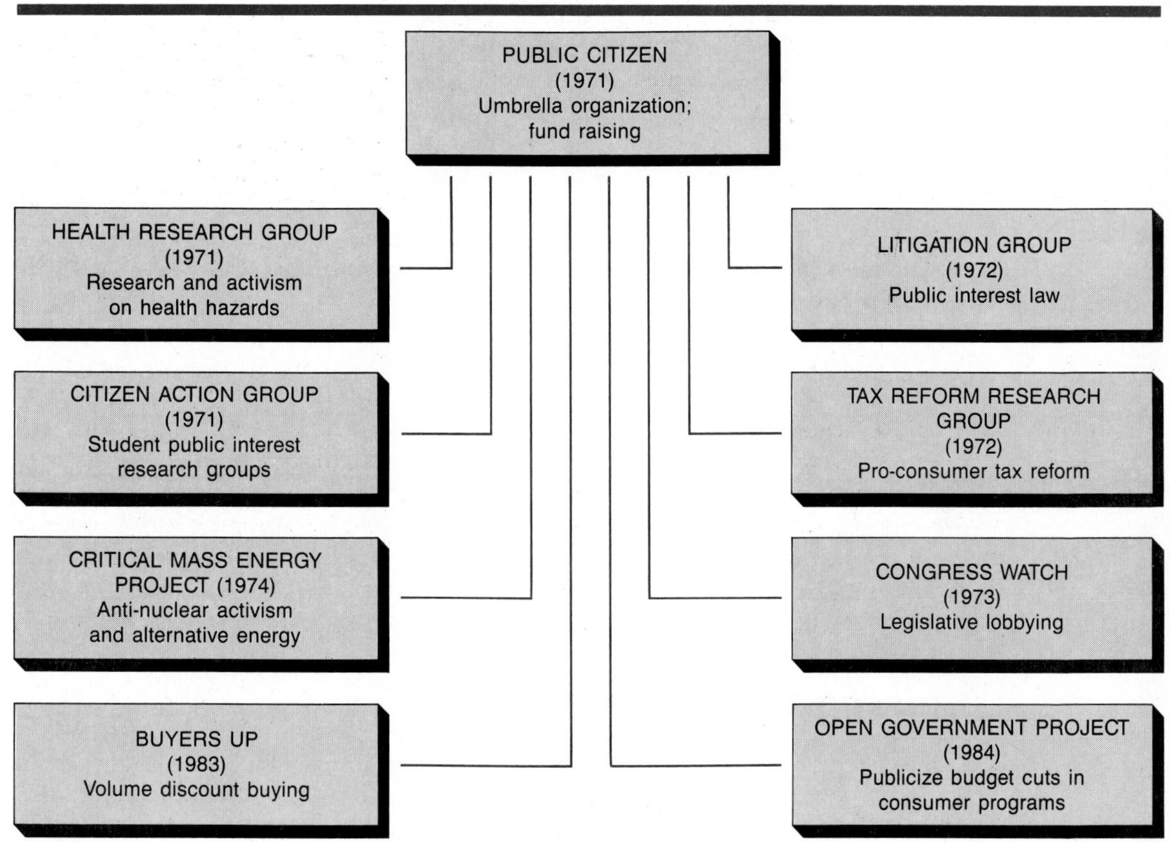

FIGURE 14–1
Ralph Nader's consumer protection network.
SOURCE: Adapted from David Bollier, "15 Years," *Public Citizen*, October 1986, pp. 20–24, 32.

in 1971, became the umbrella organization for specialized units, the main fund-raising organization, and a publishing arm for consumer publications. The Health Research Group took the lead in urging a ban on harmful color dyes used in various foods, putting warning labels on dangerous products, setting exposure limits on hazardous substances, helping consumers victimized by harmful medicines to bring lawsuits against drug companies, alerting the public to possibly dangerous medical products on the market, and publishing an exposé of more than 600 prescription drugs whose ingredients were shown not to be effective.

The Litigation Group, formed in 1972, gives legal assistance to people who have difficulty in gaining adequate access to the court system. Consumers harmed by cancer-causing food additives, homeowners exposed to the harmful effects of insulation in their homes, or airline travelers with reservations who have been bumped from their flights have been helped by the Litigation Group. Congress Watch came into being in 1973 as a citizens' watch group to keep an eye on Congress. It lobbied against subsidies to various industry groups and has sought curbs on pesticides, unfair banking practices, and rising telephone rates. Other Nader inspired efforts include the Tax Reform Research Group that promotes tax legislation intended to be more fair to consumers; the Critical Mass Energy Project that opposes nuclear energy and favors a conservationist approach to national energy problems; and Buyers Up, started in 1983, which negotiates volume discount prices for consumer goods and services.

Nader's network of state and local activist groups has campaigned effectively to reduce car insurance rates in California. It also pressures state legislatures to restrict the use of ozone-depleting materials and to make it easier for consumers to sue corporations for wrongdoing. Nader himself does not hesitate to compliment some corporations for acting in socially responsible ways, and he expresses admiration for some of corporate America's top executives.[7]

LEADING CONSUMER ISSUES OF THE 1990s

After three decades of consumer activism, the consumer movement in the early 1990s had begun to concern itself with more than just protecting consumers against poorly made, overpriced goods and services. A broader range of social issues emerged. Three of these issues were (a) the ecological impacts of high consumption; (b) nutritional and safety concerns; and (c) the value-shaping and image-making force of advertising. Each of these issues is discussed next.

Ecological Impacts of Consumption

According to national surveys conducted in the late 1980s and early 1990s, four out of every five U.S. consumers said that a company's environmental reputation would affect whether they would buy its products. Even larger numbers said they would be willing to pay more for products or packaging with environmental benefits. This intersection of environmentalism and consumerism is called **green consumerism** or "green marketing," which one observer said "may be the most powerful new environmental force to emerge in the past decade."[8]

"Green consumers" focus public attention on the ecological impacts brought on by a high-consumption society. "Each year Americans throw away 16 billion disposable diapers, 1.6 billion pens, 2 billion razors and blades, and 220 million tires. They discard enough aluminum to rebuild the entire U.S. commerical airline fleet every three months."[9] As a result of this mountain of disposable waste, municipal landfills began reaching capacity limits in many parts of the nation.

Products made of plastics, paper, and cardboard, which account for over half of municipal solid waste, have been targeted for special attention. Suffolk County,

[7] David Bollier, "15 Years," *Public Citizen*, October 1986, pp. 20–24; "The Second Coming of Ralph Nader," *Business Week*, Mar. 6, 1989, p. 28; and Ralph Nader and William Taylor, *The Big Boys: Power and Position in American Business*, New York: Pantheon, 1986.

[8] Denis Hayes, "Harnessing Market Forces to Protect the Earth," *Issues in Science and Technology*, Winter 1990–1991, p. 50. Survey data are from *Fortune*, Feb. 12, 1990, p. 50; "So, What Is 'Environmentally Friendly'?" *New York Times*, Jan. 26, 1991, p. 50; and Hayes, op. cit., pp. 46–47.

[9] *Time*, Jan. 2, 1989, p. 45.

New York, banned styrofoam and other types of plastics used by fast-food restaurants. Berkeley, California, Portland, Oregon, and Minneapolis adopted similar laws. In addition to reducing the bulk of solid wastes, these actions also lowered the amount of ozone-destroying chemical compounds released into the atmosphere.

Another goal of these ordinances is to encourage recycling by manufacturers and to spur a search for biodegradable materials that will break down and be absorbed into the environment over time. Some of the nation's biggest plastics makers responded by beginning pilot programs to test the feasibility of recycling. Union Carbide planned to recycle plastic wrapping, film, and bags; Du Pont and Waste Management joined to build recycling plants for soda bottles and milk jugs that were estimated to increase the amount of these reclaimed plastics by 70 percent over current rates. Dow Chemical organized a consortium of companies whose plants would eventually recycle 250 million pounds of polystyrene annually, a major material used by fast-food chains. Dow's director of styrene production said, "We hope this effort will stop further bans [of our product]."[10]

Leading producers of consumer goods also have felt the pressures of consumers' ecological concerns, as illustrated by the following examples.

> Procter & Gamble produces and sells $21 billion worth of consumer goods each year. Its disposable diapers, plastic bottles, and packaging have been targets for both consumer and environmental protests. P&G's chairman, saying he wanted "to make our products environmentally friendly," directed the company's operating managers to treat environmental concerns just like they would approach any other consumer demand. The company quit using inks and pigments that might contaminate landfills when containers and packaging were discarded. It redesigned plastic bottles, changed production processes, reduced the size of packages, and encouraged consumers to accept reusable containers for some of its products. P&G also became a stronger supporter of recycling by increasing the amount of recycled bottles it uses for soft drinks and detergents. As a very large user of plastics, the company's actions were considered to be a significant boost for the recycling movement.[11]

> In another encouraging move prompted by consumer pressures, McDonald's agreed to work with the Environmental Defense Fund to reduce the tons of trash it generates daily while serving 22 million customers. Greater use of recycled materials for napkins and boxes, reducing the amount of packaging, relying less on polystyrene plastic, greater use of unbleached paper, and using food wastes and packaging for composting were aims of the partnership.[12]

[10] "Minneapolis, Providing a Model, Prods Industry to Bury Hatchet on Recycling," *Wall Street Journal*, Jan. 2, 1990, pp. B1, B2.

[11] "P&G Tries Hauling Itself Out of America's Trash Heap," *Business Week*, Apr. 23, 1990, p. 101.

[12] "Big Mac Joins with Big Critic to Cut Trash," *Wall Street Journal*, Aug. 2, 1990, p. B1.

Mobil and Sunoco Products initiated programs to recycle the 12 billion plastic grocery bags used each year. They hoped to convince environmentally conscious consumers and lawmakers that recycling would be preferable to a ban on the bags, which now account for 60 percent of grocery bags used in the United States. Mobil earlier had been pressured by attorneys general from several states to stop claiming that its plastic garbage bags were biodegradable. Although the company had added a chemical to the bags that permitted them to decompose when exposed to sunlight, rain, and wind, they would not disintegrate when buried in a sealed landfill.[13]

Consumer advocates in several nations have begun programs that label products and packaging considered to be environmentally friendly. In 1977, the Federal Republic of Germany started the world's first environmental labeling program. Canada's Environmental Choice labeling began about the same time, Japan followed in 1988, and Norway, Sweden, France, the Netherlands, Great Britain, and Spain have similar efforts under way. Leaders of the German program claimed that improvements required of producers who use the "Blue Angel" label reduced emissions from oil and gas heaters and also lowered paint solvents entering that nation's waste stream. In the United States, consumer advocates and environmentalists proposed a "Green Seal" label to be awarded to products considered to be environmentally acceptable.[14]

Nutritional and Safety Concerns

Consumers in Western industrial nations tend to favor diets high in protein, animal fats, salt, and sugar. Processed foods that often are low in nutritional quality also are popular, as are the so-called convenience foods and fast foods that match the lifestyles of busy people. As greater nutritional awareness and education have spread throughout the general public, food manufacturers have heard increasing demands from their customers who want to know more about the content of the foods they buy. Oversugared and oversalted foods and fatty meats have been at the center of nutritional concern, because too much of these items can contribute to long-term health problems. Many food experts have urged people to rely more heavily on grains, fresh unprocessed vegetables, and diets high in fiber.

To provide better information for consumers, Congress in 1990 tightened food-labeling requirements. A new law requires food manufacturers to adopt a uniform nutrition label, specifying the amount of calories, fat, salt, and other nutrients contained in packaged, canned, and bottled foods. The same kind of information about fresh fruits and vegetables, as well as fish, must be posted in supermarkets. Manufacturers' claims about the health benefits of their food products are to be

[13] "Mobil to Recycle the Plastic Bags from Groceries," *Wall Street Journal,* May, 16, 1990, p. B1; and "Mobil Unit to Face Suit on Hefty Bags," *Wall Street Journal,* June 12, 1990, pp. B1, B8.

[14] Hayes, op. cit., pp. 46–51.

regulated by the Food and Drug Administration. Consumer activists favored the legislation because it provides uniform labeling information for consumers. Because the federal law did not override food labeling regulations of the states, food industry officials feared that they would be faced with a proliferation of varying standards throughout the nation.[15]

As consumers heeded the advice of food experts and began to eat more fresh vegetables and fruit, they confronted yet another problem—pesticide and herbicide residues left on farm products. Some of these chemicals cause nerve damage if consumed in large quantities, others have produced cancers in test animals, while some consumers have serious allergic reactions to vegetables or fruit treated with chemicals to preserve freshness or color. Children are thought to be especially at risk because they eat proportionately more vegetables and fruit per body weight than adults consume, and the chemicals are thought to do serious damage to developing nerve, digestive, and other systems.

Some companies have been quick to respond to these perceived risks. Over 1,200 supermarkets—but only a small segment of the national market—agreed to stop selling produce that has been treated with suspected cancer-causing pesticides. Three leading producers of EBDC, a popular fungicide used to combat infestation of food crops, agreed to voluntarily reduce its use on several farm products, while continuing to use it on others. The companies said they wanted "to maintain public confidence in the safety of fruits and vegetables" but pointed out that normal processing removes much of the residue before the products get to the consumer.[16]

Exhibit 14-A describes one of the more publicized episodes of pesticide contamination in recent years.

Advertising's Social Dimension

"There's a great deal of social consciousness building up among consumers that is to some extent putting restrictions on advertisers. In the '90s, people are going to politicize consumer products. Companies that aren't socially responsible are going to be hearing from consumers."[17] This statement by the head of an advertising agency summed up a new awareness among advertisers and consumers that advertisements do more than simply attempt to sell products. Many advertisements and advertised products carry strong, sometimes controversial social messages, as well. A vivid example is the uproar over explicit sexual terms used by rock music groups, which led to voluntary labeling of records and videotapes containing potentially offensive language. Advertising's social influence is seen also in the pictures and images of people depicted in ads, in the health claims

[15] "Food-Label Bill Clears House Panel," *Wall Street Journal,* May 17, 1990, p. B1.

[16] "Grocers Plan Their Own Ban on Pesticides," *Wall Street Journal,* Sept. 11, 1989, p. B1, B11; and "Cancer Findings Prompt Curb on Fungicide," *Wall Street Journal,* Sept. 7, 1989, p. B1.

[17] "Critics Use New Soapbox to Assail Ads for Infant Formulas, Tobacco," *Wall Street Journal,* Mar. 15, 1990, p. B6.

EXHIBIT 14-A

ALAR

Alar is a trade name used by Uniroyal Chemical Company for daminozide, a growth regulator. It is used by apple growers to keep ripening apples on the tree and by apple processors to keep the fruit firm and red and to prolong storage life. Until a few years ago, Alar was sprayed on about 40 percent of the apples consumed in the United States, including some of the most popular brands.

In the mid-1980s, the Environmental Protection Agency (EPA) reported that Alar might cause cancer. Also implicated was a related compound called UDMH that was produced when Alar-treated apples were cooked to make sauce and juice. When EPA proposed to ban Alar, experts discovered that the animal tests used to detect Alar's possible danger were not done properly. EPA then required Uniroyal to conduct a series of further animal tests and to measure levels of the suspected agents in the food supply.

The publicity created by these developments caused widespread alarm among consumers, especially parents, because children generally consume more apple juice, apple sauce, and raw apples than adults do. Some school cafeterias stopped serving apples. Some supermarkets refused to stock apples treated with Alar and apple processors shunned fruit sprayed with it. Uniroyal's sales of the product dropped 75 percent in a three-year period.

When the new test results came in, Alar was not found to be a cancer agent, but the derivative compound UDMH was suspected of causing tumors in laboratory mice. Since these results exceeded EPA's established safety guidelines, that agency moved to ban Alar in February 1989.

Within a few months, Uniroyal announced that it was voluntarily ending sales of Alar in the United States but would continue marketing it in more than seventy other nations. Consumer activists worried that this action was insufficient to protect U.S. consumers because they claimed that 50 percent of apple juice concentrate used in the U.S. is imported and the real danger comes from UDMH which is created when apples are processed. Consumer Reports, a national testing organization, reported in mid-1989 that it found Alar in apples and apple products, in spite of the earlier pledges of processors and grocery chains to stop buying Alar-treated fruit. Other observers questioned the wisdom of sales in foreign countries when doubt existed about the product's safety.

SOURCE: "Alar: Not Gone, Not Forgotten," *Consumer Reports,* May 1989, pp. 288–292; and "Avery's Uniroyal Ends Alar Sales in U.S.; Apple Product Imports Still Worry Critics," *Wall Street Journal,* June 5, 1989, p. B2.

made for some products, and in the promotion of alcohol and tobacco products. Some of these broader social dimensions of advertising are discussed next.

Advertising images

It is natural for almost any group in society to want to be fairly and accurately represented when appearing in advertisements. Advertising images, because they are sent out to so many viewers, have the potential to influence the way people think about other people, as well as about the product being advertised. Some advertisers have learned this lesson the hard way, as shown in the following illustrations.

Advertisements by Quaker Oats Company featured a well-known cartoon character called Popeye the Sailor. Popeye had always been known to comics-page readers as a tough fighter who was strong because he ate spinach. However, the Quaker ads showed the sailor eating instant Quaker Oatmeal and then using his legendary strength to batter his enemies, sharks, and other targets. Following these deeds, he would proclaim, "I'm Popeye the Quaker Man!" Quakers, who are members of the religious order known as the Society of Friends, and who have long been known for their peaceful, nonviolent approach to life, objected. Some Quaker school children wrote the company, saying, "We think anyone calling himself a Quaker should act like one and stick with Quaker philosophy." Others called the advertisements "totally offensive." Following these complaints, the company modified the ads, and a company official said, "Try as we might, we sometimes unwittingly offend particular groups."[18]

How to depict women in advertisements has become another puzzling problem for advertisers. To feature them exclusively in homemaking settings—waxing floors, preparing meals, tending children—runs the risk of offending women who prefer to emphasize the newer professional and working roles being filled by more and more women. Advertisers cannot ignore the two-thirds of all U.S. mothers, and over half of those with very young children, who now work outside the home. How to appeal to women consumers who now fill a variety of social and professional roles challenges advertisers to recognize the opinion-shaping influence of their advertising images. "You can't talk to all women in the same way. By targeting one group, you alienate the other," said the editor of one women's magazine.[19]

Health-related claims

Even more serious impacts can occur when companies make excessive health claims for their products.

U.S. aspirin makers came under pressure from the Food and Drug Administration to stop promoting aspirin as reducing the risk of a first heart attack. Their claims were based on a scientific study that said taking an aspirin every other day had lowered the risk of heart attacks in middle-aged men. The FDA said that the study's findings were preliminary, were restricted to the test group, and could not be recommended for the general population. After meeting with FDA officials, the companies voluntarily stopped their advertising claims.

A more dramatic corrective was ordered for the makers of Accutane, a drug used to treat acute cases of acne. After the drug was linked to birth defects,

[18] "Will Quaker Oats Bow to Friendly Persuasion?" *Business Week,* Mar. 12, 1990, p. 46.

[19] "Grappling with Women's Evolving Roles," *Wall Street Journal,* Sept. 5, 1990, p. B1. A later chapter in this book discusses other business changes brought about by the entry of women into the nation's workforce.

government regulators ordered Hoffman-LaRoche, Accutane's manufacturers, to include an image of a deformed baby in the packages sold to consumers, to warn against improper use of the drug.

Carnation, a subsidiary of Nestle, labeled its baby formula food "hypoallergenic" but was forced to change the label after some babies suffered serious allergic reactions upon being fed the formula. The company claimed that "hypoallergenic" did not mean "nonallergenic," but the label created widespread confusion among mothers and doctors. After strenuous objections by the Food and Drug Administration and the American Pediatric Association, Carnation agreed to relabel the formula.

Leading food companies, too, have found it desirable to limit the health claims of their products. Kellogg, Campbell Soup, Sara Lee, General Mills, and other companies have had their advertising claims challenged.

Curbing tobacco and alcohol promotions

Tobacco and alcoholic beverages carry health risks, not just for users but for others as well. For that reason, when tobacco and beverage companies advertise their products, they are having an impact on public health that goes beyond a company's goal of persuading smokers and drinkers to use a particular brand.

Awareness of this public health problem is widespread. A survey commissioned by the *Wall Street Journal* found that almost half of U.S. consumers favor banning all television ads for beer and wine, and over half approve bans of cigarette ads in magazines and newspapers. Several other nations, including Italy, Portugal, Norway, Sweden, Canada, Singapore, Kuwait, and Thailand, have already banished tobacco ads from television and the print media. The 12-nation European Economic Community (EEC), as it moved toward more complete economic integration in 1992, planned to clamp tight restrictions on tobacco advertising. An EEC official said, "We are talking about a product which every year kills 440,000 people in the Community." California, often a leader in social legislation in the United States, financed an antismoking advertising campaign by imposing an excise tax on cigarette companies. A 1988 federal law requires health-warning labels on alcoholic beverages.[20]

In all of these ways, consumers and their government representatives were sending a strong signal to the manufacturers and their advertising agencies that tobacco and alcohol promotions should be strictly curbed. It is another example, among many mentioned in this book, that business operates within a web of social values and social attitudes that can have a vital impact on how business should be conducted.

[20] For the survey data, see "Rebelling against Alcohol, Tobacco Ads," *Wall Street Journal*, Jan. 14, 1989, pp. B1, B11. The EEC quotation is from "EC May Chase Tobacco Symbols Like Marlboro Man into Sunset," *Wall Street Journal*, Oct. 10, 1989, p. B7.

HOW GOVERNMENT PROTECTS CONSUMERS

The federal government's involvement in consumer affairs is extensive. During the 1960s and 1970s, Congress passed important laws to protect consumers, created new regulatory agencies, and strengthened older consumer protection agencies. These developments meant that consumers, rather than relying solely on free market competition to safeguard their interests, could turn to government for protection.

During most of the 1980s, a deregulatory attitude by the federal government tended to blunt federal initiatives in behalf of consumers. However, state governments became more active, particularly regarding price-fixing, car insurance rates, and corporate takeovers that threatened jobs and consumer incomes.

Goals of Consumer Laws

Figure 14–2 lists some of the safeguards provided by **consumer protection laws.** Taken together, these safeguards reflect three goals of government policymakers and regulators.

First, some laws were intended to provide consumers with better information when making purchases. Consumers can make more rational choices when they have a maximum amount of information about the product, thereby making comparison with competing products easier. For example, the Truth in Lending Act requires lenders to inform borrowers of the annual rate of interest to be charged, plus related fees and service charges. The laws requiring health warnings on cigarettes and alcoholic beverages broaden the information consumers have about these items. Knowing the relative energy efficiency of household appliances, which must be posted by retailers, permits improved choices.

A second aim of consumer legislation is to protect consumers against possible hazards from products they may purchase. Required warnings about possible side effects of pharmaceutical drugs, limits placed on flammable fabrics, inspections to eliminate contaminated or spoiled meats, and the banning of lead-based paints are examples of these safeguards.

A third goal of consumer laws is to encourage competitive pricing. When competitors secretly agree to divide up markets among themselves, or to rig bidding so that it appears to be competitive, or to fix prices of goods and services at a noncompetitive, artificially high level, they are taking unfair advantage of consumers. Both federal and state laws forbid these practices. Competitive pricing also was promoted by deregulation of railroads, airlines, intercity bus lines, trucking, telephones, and various financial institutions. Prior to deregulation, government agencies frequently held prices artificially high and, by limiting the number of new competitors, shielded existing businesses from competition.

Major Consumer Protection Agencies

Figure 14–3 depicts the principal consumer protection agencies that operate at the federal level, along with their major areas of responsibility. The oldest of the

FIGURE 14–2
Major consumer protections specified by consumer laws.

Informational Protections

Hazardous home appliances must carry a warning label

Home products must carry a label detailing contents

Automobiles must carry a label showing detailed breakdown of price and all related costs

Credit loans require lender to disclose all relevant credit information about rate of interest, penalties, etc.

Tobacco advertisements must carry a health warning label

Alcoholic beverages must carry a health warning label

All costs related to real estate transactions must be disclosed

Warranties must specify the terms of the guarantee and the buyer's rights

False and deceptive advertising can be prohibited

Direct Hazard Protections

Hazardous toys and games for children are banned from sale

Safety standards for motor vehicles are required

National and state speed limits are specified

Hazardous, defective, and ineffective products can be recalled under pressure from EPA, CPSC, NHTSA, and FDA

Foods contaminated by pesticides and other farm chemicals can be banned from sale

Pricing Protections

Unfair pricing, monopolistic practices, and noncompetitive acts are regulated by FTC and Justice Department and by states

Liability Protections

When injured by a product, consumers can seek legal redress

Other Protections

Equal opportunity must govern the extension of credit

five is the Food and Drug Administration and its predecessors which, along with the Department of Agriculture's meat and poultry inspection programs, date back to the first decade of the twentieth century. The Federal Trade Commission was established in 1914 and has been given additional powers to protect consumers over the years. Two of the agencies—the Consumer Product Safety Commission and the National Highway Traffic Safety Administration—were created during the great wave of consumer regulations in the early 1970s. Not pictured in Figure 14–3 is the Antitrust Division of the Department of Justice, which indirectly

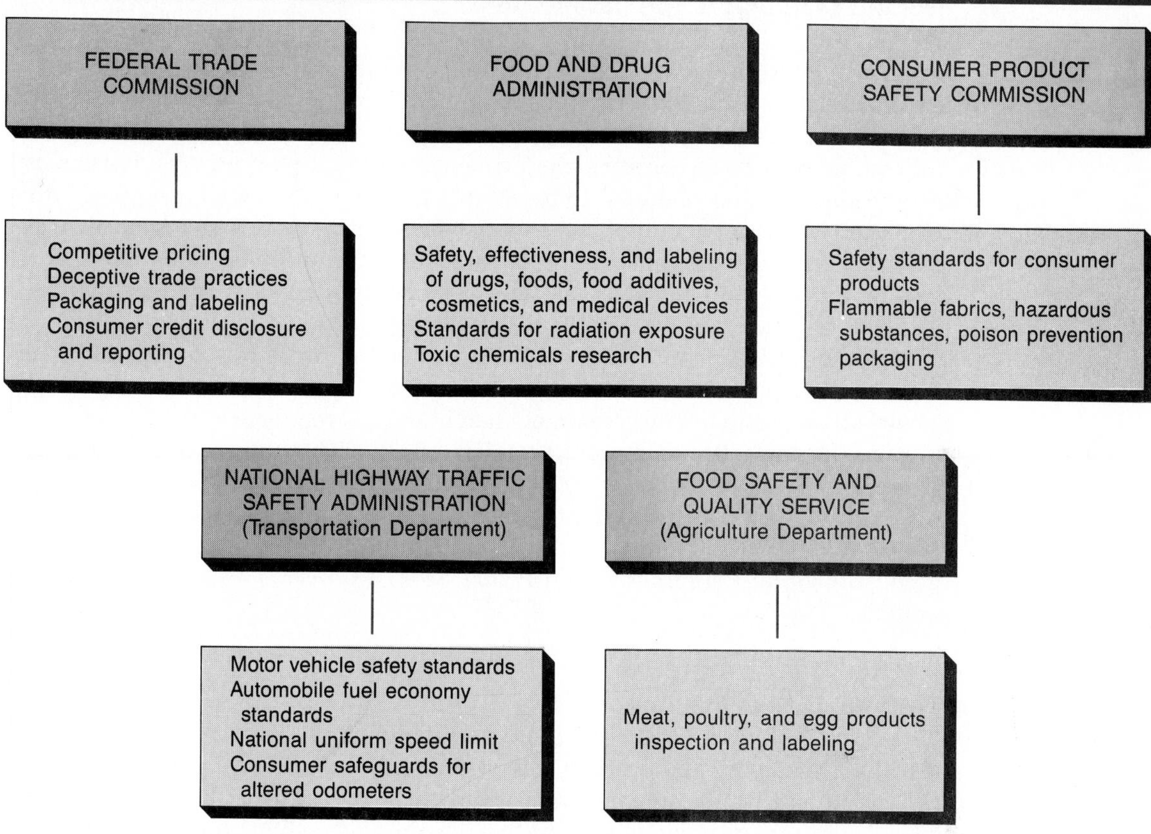

FIGURE 14–3 Major federal consumer protection agencies and their main responsibilities.

protects consumers by policing monopolistic and anticompetitive practices of business firms.

Of these government agencies, the Consumer Product Safety Commission was affected the most by the deregulatory policies of the 1980s. Appointees to the five-member commission relied less on legal enforcement, favoring voluntary safety programs and cooperation with industry. The agency's budgets were reduced by almost half during the decade, and by the end of 1988 the commission had no chairman and only two members, fewer than necessary to make agency decisions. A new chairman was appointed by President Bush in 1989, and she pledged to reinvigorate the agency.[21]

These government regulatory agencies are authorized by law to intervene directly into the very center of free market activities, if that is considered necessary to protect consumers. In other words, consumer protection laws and agencies substitute government-mandated standards and the decisions of government officials for decision making by private buyers and sellers.

[21] "Troubles of a Safety Agency: A Battle to Keep Functioning," *New York Times,* Mar. 18, 1989, p. 52; and "Consumer Advocate No. 1," *Washington Post,* July 5, 1990, p. MD1.

Product Liability: A Special Problem

In today's complicated economy, consumers' relationships with products they use and relationships with producers of those products are much more complicated and abstract. It is no longer reasonable to expect consumers to share the responsibilities for product performance as they once did. The burden of responsibility has been shifted to the producer. Although many businesses have attempted to assume much of the responsibility through money-back guarantees and other similar policies, consumers have thought that this is not enough and have demanded that business assume a larger burden of responsibility. The result has been a strengthening of product liability laws and more favorable court attitudes toward consumer claims. Walls protecting producers from consumer lawsuits have crumbled, and there has been a dramatic increase in product liability suits. Traditionally consumers had little legal recourse against producers of faulty products. The common legal defenses available to producers were the doctrine of privity of contract, warranties, and the doctrine of strict liability in tort. Each of these tended to limit the legal liability of manufacturers or to place the burden of proving injury on the consumer. All three, now modified in favor of consumers and summarized in Figure 14–4, are discussed in the following sections.

Privity of contract

The doctrine of privity of contract stressed direct contractual relationships and held that producers could avoid responsibility for product failure if a product was purchased from someone other than the manufacturer. This meant that injured consumers could sue only the person from whom they purchased a defective product—not the producer. The dealer could then sue the wholesaler and so on up to the manufacturer. In the economy of the early 1800s, this doctrine probably made a great deal of sense. But as the distance between consumer and producer widened and as products passed through longer and more complex channels of distribution, the strength of this defense has been dissipated through court decisions. The landmark decision was rendered in 1916.

FIGURE 14–4
Three types of legal liability to consumers.

MacPherson purchased a new Buick from a local automobile dealer. Shortly thereafter defective wooden spokes in a wheel collapsed, and MacPherson was injured as a result. He sued Buick. The company claimed that MacPherson had purchased the car from a dealer and not from Buick and therefore Buick had no obligation to him. The judge ruled that Buick had been negligent because the wheel had not been inspected before it was put on the car. He further ruled that Buick was responsible for defects resulting from negligence, regardless of how many distributive firms were in between.

This legal philosophy has been expanded since the MacPherson decision. Today an injured consumer can sue any or all people in the chain of distribution. In general, the courts have reasoned that through advertising and labeling, manufacturers make a variety of representations about a product. The manufacturer intends and expects the product to be purchased and used in accordance with representations of performance and assurances of quality. Therefore, when a consumer purchases the product and that product fails to live up to express or implied representations and thereby causes injury to the purchaser, that purchaser has the right to be reimbursed for the injury.

Warranties

There are two kinds of warranties—express and implied. When a product is offered for sale, the seller makes claims for its characteristics. Claims that are explicitly stated by the seller are express warranties. Representations on a warranty card that the parts of a product will not fail within ninety days from the time of purchase are examples of express warranties. Not all express warranties are on the warranty card. Statements on labels, wrappers, packages, and in advertising also are express warranties.

More troublesome for sellers is the question of implied warranties. Courts have held that simply by selling a product to a customer the seller implies that the product is fit for the ordinary use for which it is likely to be used. The landmark case in the area of implied warranty occurred in 1960.

In this case, Claus Henningsen purchased a new automobile that he and his wife drove around town for several days. Then, when driving out of town, the steering mechanism failed, and Mrs. Henningsen crashed into a highway sign and then into a brick wall. She sustained injuries and the car was a total loss. Henningsen went to court. The automobile company claimed that Henningsen had signed a disclaimer when he bought the car and this limited the liability of the company to replacement of defective parts. The court held that the company could not avoid its legal responsibility to make automobiles good enough to serve the purpose for which they were intended.

Congress attempted to clarify warranty provisions by passing the Magnuson-Moss Warranty Act in 1975. The law, administered by the FTC, requires manufacturers, retailers, and importers to specify whether warranties they voluntarily issue are full or limited, says the terms must be spelled out in clear language, and gives consumers the right to sue if warranties are not honored.

Strict tort liability

A tort is a civil wrong that sometimes results in injury to a person. Within the last few years courts have increasingly taken the position that manufacturers are responsible for injuries resulting from use of their products. One result has been a rapid rise in the number of personal injury and product liability lawsuits—from about 20,000 in 1960 to over 40,000 in 1986.[22] The trend is not confined to the United States; member nations of the European Economic Community have tried to establish uniform standards and limits on product liability claims. Small companies are especially vulnerable to lawsuits and may be driven out of business by sky-high liability insurance rates.

Under existing court interpretations, it is not necessary for consumers to prove either negligence or breach of warranty by the producer. Nor is the consumer's contributory negligence an acceptable defense by the manufacturer. If a product is judged to be inherently dangerous, manufacturers can be held liable for injuries caused from use of the product. And strict liability extends to all who were involved in the final product—suppliers, sellers, contractors, assemblers, and manufacturers of component parts.

The following case illustrates the extent to which manufacturers can be held liable today:

> Ford Motor Company and Goodyear Tire & Rubber Company were sued by the mother of a driver killed in the crash of a Mercury Cougar automobile that had been traveling more than 100 miles per hour when a tire failed. Court records established that the driver's blood tested far in excess of the established standards for intoxication. However, a federal district court, later upheld by an appeals court, ruled that both companies were liable for the death and must pay damages to the mother. Ford had argued that it had no duty to warn the owner against tire failure, that it had not manufactured the tire, and that the car's driver was guilty of contributory negligence by being intoxicated.
>
> The appellate court said:
>
> The sports car involved here was marketed with an intended and recognized appeal to youthful drivers. The 425 horsepower engine with which Ford had equipped it proved a capability of speeds over 100 miles per hour, and the car's allure, no doubt exploited in its marketing, lay in no small measure in this power and potential speed. . . . It was to be readily expected that the Cougar would, on occasion, be driven in excess of the 85 miles per hour proven maximum safe operating speed of its Goodyear tires. . . . Consequently, Ford cannot escape its duty either to provide an adequate warning of the specific danger of tread separation at such high speeds or to ameliorate the danger in some other way.

[22] *Wall Street Journal,* Oct. 17, 1988, p. B1.

EXHIBIT 14-B

NISSAN'S POWER-AND-SPEED MACHINE

The Nissan 300ZX Turbo automobile was featured in a television commercial during the 1990 Super Bowl game. "It shows the redesigned 300ZX racing a motorcycle, a race car, and finally, a jet fighter. The chase reaches an estimated 150 mph in the final moments of the 60 second advertisement as the car becomes airborne."

The president of the Insurance Institute for Highway Safety (IIHS), a research group supported by insurance companies, privately asked Nissan to withdraw the commercial because "the only message in the commercial is look how fast this car can go." Nissan refused to cancel the advertisement, saying that the ad "is so fanciful and far-fetched that we see no confusion or connection with real-world driving situations."

Following Nissan's refusal, eighteen medical, insurance, and law enforcement groups then publicly requested that the ad be recalled. Nissan again refused.

The IIHS president referred to two recent fatal crashes of the 300ZX and said: "Nissan claims this ad is a fantasy. But what isn't a fantasy at all—what is all too real—is that people are dying in high speed crashes involving this car." He also pointed out that unlike nearly all cars in this class, the 300ZX was not equipped with air bags and displayed "vastly inferior" automatic seat belts that could be easily disconnected. "Where are Nissan's safety ads? We can't find any—none at all . . . . We challenge Nissan to start engineering air bags into all of its cars and begin promoting safety instead of speed."

A Washington, D.C., trauma surgeon, who joined in the appeal for a recall of the advertisement, said, "They come into trauma units dismembered, many paralyzed or injured for life. It is quite unconscionable that these cars are offered without air bags."

According to an IIHS study, 1985–1987 300ZX models had the fifth highest fatality rate among 103 of the most popular cars on the road during 1986 through 1988.

Among the groups supporting the advertisement's recall were the Epilepsy Foundation, the Consumer Federation of America, the National Head Injury Foundation, the American Academy of Pediatrics, the American Trauma Society, the International Association of Chiefs of Police, and the Center for Auto Safety.

SOURCE: *Status Report,* vol. 25, no. 3, Mar. 3, 1990, pp. 1–2. Published by the Insurance Institute for Highway Safety, Arlington, Virginia.

In this case, a company (Ford) was held liable for damages caused by use of a product (the Goodyear tire) it did not even manufacture and where the user was clearly irresponsible due to intoxication. However, the court went on to point out that the car itself was potentially hazardous and that Ford had a responsibility "for its own active role in the assembly of the unreasonably dangerous composite product, the Cougar automobile."[23]

Consumer safety advocates and insurance companies continue to be concerned about the emphasis that automakers put on power and speed. An example of this concern is shown in Exhibit 14-B.

[23] Insurance Institute for Highway Safety, *Status Report,* Sept. 17, 1980, p. 6.

Business efforts to reform the product liability laws

Faced with an increasing flood of liability suits, business has lobbied for changes in laws and court proceedings. Since the early 1980s, bills have been introduced in Congress that would establish the following principles in liability suits:

- Set up uniform federal standards for determining liability. This would reduce a company's exposure to repeated trials on the same charges in many different states, and it would lower legal costs for companies and help them develop a uniform legal strategy for confronting liability charges in court.
- Shift the burden of proving liability to consumers. They would have to prove that a manufacturer knew or should have known that a product design was defective before it began producing the item for consumption. Under present law and judicial interpretations, a company is considered to be negligent if a product injures the user, and it is up to the company to prove otherwise.
- Eliminate some bases for liability claims. Products not measuring up to a manufacturer's own specifications—for example, poorly made tires that blow out at normal speeds—could be the basis for a liability claim, but the vast majority of liability cases go further and blame poorly designed products or a failure of the manufacturer to warn of dangers.
- Severely curb the expanded privity of contract adopted by court rulings. No longer could consumers seek compensation for their injuries by suing retailers, distributors, or others unless it could be proved that they, along with the manufacturer, also were negligent.
- Allow judges, not juries, to determine punitive damages. Currently, the size of damage awards is commonly determined by the jury that hears the testimony during the trial, and these jury awards may be very large. Proposed laws would have judges, not juries, determine the amount of punitive damages, which would greatly reduce these awards. Attempts by several state legislatures to put an upper limit on punitive awards granted by juries have been only partially successful, since some of these laws have been declared unconstitutional on grounds that they interfere with the constitutional right to trial by jury. In 1989, juries showed little inclination to reduce the size of damages awarded in product-liability cases. The ten largest awards totaled $475 million in 1989, and the number of damage awards of $1 million or more rose from 398 in 1987 to 474 in 1988. However, a study by the Rand Corporation pointed out that most of these multimillion dollar awards by juries are reduced an average of 40 percent by judges.[24]

POSITIVE BUSINESS RESPONSES TO CONSUMERISM

The consumer movement has demonstrated to business that it is expected to perform at high levels of efficiency and reliability in order to satisfy the consuming

[24] "Juries Rule against 'Tort Reform' with Huge Awards," *Wall Street Journal,* Feb. 9, 1990, p. B1, B6.

public. Because business has not always responded quickly or fully enough, consumer advocates and their organizations have turned to government for protection. On the other hand, much effort has been devoted by individual business firms and by entire industries to encourage voluntary responses to consumer demands. Some of the more prominent positive responses are discussed next.

Consumer Affairs Departments

Many large corporations have created consumer affairs departments, often placing a vice president in charge. These centralized departments normally handle consumer inquiries and complaints about a company's products and services, particularly in cases where a consumer has not been able to resolve differences with local dealers. Some companies have installed consumer "hot lines" for dissatisfied customers to place telephone calls directly to the manufacturer. Experienced companies are aware that consumer complaints received internally by a consumer affairs department can be handled more quickly, at lower cost, and with less risk of losing goodwill than if customers take a legal route or if their complaints receive widespread media publicity.

Arbitration

Some companies have established arbitration panels that are given authority to settle disputes between customers and the company. In these cases, specially appointed arbitrators who are not related to either party in the dispute make final decisions.

General Motors, Ford, Chrysler, and many foreign auto importers "now sponsor some kind of local umpire system that will handle knotty warranty, product, service, or sales problems when the customer cannot get satisfactory redress from the company or dealer."[25] Automakers find that many complaints—from 40 to 85 percent—can be resolved without going to an arbitration panel. They also have learned that these referee programs reduce consumer dissatisfaction and improve the industry's image.

Consumer Action Panels

Consumer Action Panels (CAPs) have been formed by some industries, and they go one step beyond Better Business Bureaus in resolving consumer complaints. Dissatisfied customers are encouraged to work out the problem at the local level first, then by writing to the manufacturer, and finally by contacting a CAP. Those who work with CAPs claim a large measure of success for the system; the Major-Appliance Consumer Action Panel, for example, reported that 90 percent of complaints were resolved before the CAP was involved. CAPs have been organized by

[25] "Detroit's Tonic for Lemon Buyers," *Business Week*, Apr. 4, 1983, pp. 54–55; and Leslie Maitland, "Arbitration Plan Set for Defects in G.M. Cars," *New York Times*, Apr. 27, 1983, p. 1.

carpet and rug manufacturers, the furniture industry, automakers, and insurance companies.

Product Recalls

Beginning in the mid-1970s, **product recalls** by companies become a more frequent way of dealing with consumer dissatisfaction. A product recall occurs when a company, either voluntarily or under an agreement with a government agency, takes back all items found to be dangerously defective. Sometimes these products are in the hands of consumers; at other times they may be in the factory, in wholesale warehouses, or on the shelves of retail stores. Wherever they are in the chain of distribution or use, the manufacturer tries to notify consumers or potential users about the defect so that they will return the items. A recalled product may be repaired or replaced or destroyed, depending upon the problem.

The four major government agencies responsible for most mandatory recalls are the Food and Drug Administration, the National Highway Traffic Safety Administration, the Environmental Protection Agency (which can recall polluting motor vehicles), and the Consumer Product Safety Commission.

Figure 14–5 lists some of the most important and well-publicized recalls through early 1991. Some of these recalls were the result of allegedly defective and unsafe products, while others were necessary because corporations and their

FIGURE 14–5
Some major product recalls.

Company	Item	Estimated Cost (in millions)	Year
Recalls Involving Alleged Defective Products			
Firestone Tire	Radial 500 tire	$135	1978
Parker Brothers	Riviton construction set	$ 10	1978
Procter & Gamble	Rely tampon	$ 75	1980
Volkswagen AG	Audi-5000 automobile	n/a	1987
Recalls Involving Tampering and Contamination			
Johnson & Johnson	Tylenol capsules	$100	1982
Johnson & Johnson	Tylenol capsules	$150	1986
Smith-Kline-Beckman	Contac, Teldrin, and Dietac capsules	$8–10	1986
Bristol Myers	Excedrin, Datril, and Bufferin capsules	n/a	1986
Burroughs Wellcome	Sudafed capsules	n/a	1991
Other Recalls			
Source Perrier	Bottled water	$70–75	1990

customers were victimized by individuals who held grudges or were deranged mentally.

Not all recalled products are actually found to be defective. Over 250,000 Audi-5000 autos were recalled in early 1987 after some of the cars suddenly and unexpectedly accelerated because of an alleged defect in the automatic transmission. However, extensive tests performed later by the company and by independent experts failed to find a design flaw that might have contributed to the problem. The publicity and the recall badly tarnished Audi's reputation and was partly responsible for a drastic drop in U.S. Audi sales from 74,000 in 1985 to 21,000 in 1989.[26]

CONSUMERISM'S ACHIEVEMENTS

After thirty years of the consumer movement, its leaders could point to some important gains for U.S. consumers. Consumers in the 1990s are better informed about the goods and services they purchase, are more aware of their rights when something goes wrong, and are better protected against inflated advertising claims, hazardous or ineffective products, and unfair pricing. Several consumer organizations serve as watchdogs of buyers' interests, and a network of federal and state regulatory agencies acts for the consuming public.

Some businesses, too, have heard the consumer message and have reacted positively. They have learned to assign high priority to the things consumers expect—high-quality goods and services, reliable and effective products, safety in the items they buy, fair prices, and marketing practices (such as advertising) that do not threaten important human and social values.

All of these achievements, in spite of negative episodes that occasionally occur, bring the U.S. consuming public closer to realizing former President John F. Kennedy's four consumer rights: to be safe, to be informed, to have choices, and to be heard.

SUMMARY POINTS OF THIS CHAPTER

- The U.S. consumer movement that began in the 1960s represents an attempt to promote the interests of consumers by balancing the amount of market power held by sellers and buyers.
- By the 1980s the consuming public was aware that many consumer products and services, whose production and distribution generate much solid waste and hazardous substances, can be harmful to the environment. Public pres-

[26] "Audi Problems with Sudden Acceleration May Not Be Over," *Wall Street Journal*, Jan. 20, 1987, p. 31; and "Audi Is Picking Up but Has Miles to Go," *Wall Street Journal*, Aug. 23, 1990, pp. B1, B4.

sures have been exerted on business to correct some of these environmental impacts.

- The general public's growing interest in nutrition and safety, plus the ability of advertising to exert widespread social influence, brought new demands for business to be socially responsible in serving consumers.
- Consumer protection laws and regulatory agencies attempt to assure that consumers are treated fairly, receive adequate information, are protected against potential hazards, have free choices in the market, and have legal recourse when problems develop.
- Socially responsible companies have responded to the consumer movement by giving serious consideration to consumer problems, by increasing channels of communication with customers, and by recalling defective products.

KEY TERMS AND CONCEPTS USED IN THIS CHAPTER

- Consumerism
- Consumer movement
- Consumer bill of rights
- Green consumerism
- Consumer protection laws
- Product liability
- Product recalls

DISCUSSION CASE

BIG MAC STRIKES BACK

"This ad is reckless, misleading, and intended to scare rather than inform," declared a McDonald's executive.

The full-page ad, which had appeared in several major U.S. newspapers in early April 1990, was entitled "The Poisoning of America!" It singled out the well-known hamburger chain, saying, "McDonald's, Your Hamburgers Have Too Much Fat!" Showing the familiar Big Mac and french fries, it claimed that this popular combination contained 25 grams of saturated fat, with the fat content of the meat alone being 21.5 percent. The ad went on to point out that the firm's french fries were cooked in beef tallow, which is high in cholesterol, while other fast food chains used "heart healthy oils." The widely circulated ad, which listed McDonald's' telephone number and address, urged readers to call or write the company, demanding a reduction of the fat content of their hamburger meat by 10 percent "as their contribution to lowering cholesterol levels for Americans."

The ads, which cost $500,000, were placed by Phil Sokolof, an Omaha industrialist and founder of the nonprofit National Heart Savers Association. It was not the first time Sokolof had attacked food companies. In earlier ads, he criticized food processors for using saturated oils in making cookies, cereals, TV dinners, candies, and other food products. Following those widely publicized charges, several leading companies reformulated their ingredients to reduce cholesterol and fat. Consumers also were listening, according to Sokolof. "A Gallup Poll showed 31 percent of the public had heard our message and 38 percent of them had decreased their visits to fast-food restaurants as a result."

With this kind of publicity threatening to damage its first-place grip on the highly competitive fast-food business, McDonald's struck back. Executives claimed their hamburgers contained only an average of 19.5 percent fat and that efforts had been made to reduce fats in other products. McDonald's attorney warned newspapers not to reprint the ads, saying, "Now they know the facts, now they are all on notice. . . . To publish anything like that ad would be a malicious act." On a more positive note, the company said it was already beginning to phase out beef tallow as a frying agent and was reformulating its shakes with a low-fat mix. Two months later, it announced it would put up wall posters in its restaurants showing nutritional data for its products. A year after Sokolof's ad first ran, McDonald's introduced a new low-fat hamburger that was said to contain only 9 percent fat.

Industry observers were not convinced that the new lean hamburger would be a success. According to one food industry representative, "People may talk healthy, but they don't buy healthy." Another said, "Customers are unwilling to trade flavor for lower calories." As for the nutritional posters, even McDonald's' president said, "The people who are really interested in this already have the information." Other food chains, including Pizza Hut and Wendy's, had little luck when they introduced health-conscious menus. "We spent a whole year and about $10 million advertising this menu and nobody would bite," said a Wendy's spokesperson.

In the meantime, Phil Sokolof was undeterred in his efforts to convince consumers and food companies to adopt healthier diets. A victim of a cholesterol-induced heart attack, he had founded the Heart Savers association in 1985. He pressured Congress to pass a food-labeling bill by running four national advertisements asking voters to write to their senators and representatives. Sokolof said, "The American people passed that bill. They made their wishes known to lawmakers and will be rewarded next year with the identification of cholesterol, saturated fat, sodium, calories and other important nutritional information, on all packaged foods. The public does not realize the dramatic power it wields. The consumer's wish is big business's command."

In a final comment that might draw uncomfortable frowns in McDonald's' executive suite, Sokolof stated, "McDonald's and I are now working the same territory. The public's nutritional needs make for strange bedfellows."[1]

[1] Based on news accounts appearing in the *Wall Street Journal, New York Times,* and Reuters and Associated Press stories during April and June 1990 and March 1991. The Sokolof quotations are from "Taking the Fast-Food Chains to Task," *New York Times,* Mar. 24, 1991, p. F9.

Discussion Questions

1. Do you agree with Phil Sokolof that "The consumer's wish is big business's command"? Does Sokolof's campaign prove his point? Why or why not?
2. Comment on McDonald's' reactions to the Sokolof ads. Did the company react in socially responsible and socially responsive ways?
3. Using the Sokolof-McDonald's episode as background information, tell who you believe should be mainly responsible for consumer well-being. Should it be the individual consumer, the companies that serve consumers, or consumer-protection agencies of the government?

15

The Community and the Corporation

When business has a good relationship with its community, it can make an important difference in the quality of that community's life and in the successful operation of the company. Communities look to business for civic leadership and for help in coping with urban problems, while business expects to be treated fairly and in supportive ways by the local community. In the 1990s, corporate restructuring is creating special problems to be solved through joint efforts of business and community groups.

Key Questions and Chapter Objectives

This chapter focuses on these key questions and objectives:

- What are the links between business and the community?
- How does business respond to community problems and needs?
- What are the community impacts of plant closings, and what are some strategies used for coping with such problems?
- What are some goals, strategies, and benefits of business contributions to the community?
- How are social partnerships between business and the community created to resolve today's community problems?

IBM announced that it would spend $3 million in 1991 to build five child care centers near its offices and plants around the United States to serve 530 preschool children. It said it would also spend an additional $500,000 in communities that had large IBM employee populations to improve existing day care centers and to recruit and train people who care for children in their homes. J. T. Childs, Jr., director of the company's Work/Life Program, noted that the number of male employees at IBM had declined by 20 percent over the last 30 years while the number of female employees had tripled, so child care had become a vital program to keep women in the workforce. Childs also noted that although IBM is building child care centers to help its own employees, at least half of the enrollment at most centers will be open to the public.

In Houston, Texas, employees at the Shell Oil Co. participate in an all-volunteer good works program called SERVE (Shell Employees and Retirees Volunteerism Effort). In 1990, more than 1,500 volunteers took part in a wide variety of community involvement activities. According to Shell's coordinator, "what we do is match individual volunteers with the community's needs." More than 300 local organizations provide information to a community data bank; volunteers are then matched with groups that can use their skills. Shell also uses a monthly want ad style employee publication, called "SERVE Classified," to inform employees of volunteer opportunities at its eight Houston locations. The jobs are varied: a Shell attorney tapes broadcast readings for the blind; a safety technologist serves as a mediator in landlord-tenant disputes; a husband and wife team conducts guided tours at Houston's Women's hospital for expectant grandparents. The program began when Shell moved from New York in the mid-1970s and sought ways for its transferred employees to get oriented to their new communities. Fifteen years later, Shell employees had donated more than one million hours of volunteer time to the Houston communities in which they live and work.

Jameshedpur is one of the best-run cities in India. A city of more than a half-million residents, Jameshedpur has good public transportation, health facilities, and public services. It is also a company town. The Tata Iron and Steel Co., India's largest private firm, owns and controls Jameshedpur. Company executives write the laws, arbitrate disputes, and determine who can do what and where within the city limits. According to one local business operator, Jameshedpur is like George Orwell's novel, *1984*, "Big Brother watches over you all the time." Tata's 77-year-old chairman does not disagree: "From time to time we're authoritarian, but certainly not cruel. . . . Here, things work. Take Tata Iron away and in three years things will be like anywhere else in India." One-third of Jameshedpur's population is directly supported by the steel mill, and nearly all are economically dependent on it. The prosperity that is associated with the company thereby benefits nearly everyone. Tata is willing to assume many community responsibilities so that its workforce is happy, well-cared-for, and supportive of the company.

In Jameshedpur, there is disagreement about what makes for a sound company-community relationship. Democratic government does not exist in Jameshedpur. To Tata leaders, it would interfere with good community management; to others, the absence of self-government is too high a price to pay for prosperity. They long for the freedom to criticize the company, its leaders, and their policies.[1]

These three situations illustrate the range of issues that arise between a company and the communities in which it operates. This chapter identifies and explores how companies balance their concern for the community with their financial goals and objectives.

[1] These situations are described in Carol Lawson, "Like Growing Numbers of Companies, I.B.M. Is Building Child-Care Centers," *New York Times*, Dec. 12, 1990, p. A-20; John A. Conway, "Shell Volunteer Program Serves Needs of Community and Employees," *Wall Street Journal*, Dec. 27, 1990, p. B-2; Sudeep Chakravarti, "A Prosperous Company Town in India Pays a Price for Corporate Pampering," *Wall Street Journal*, Nov. 4, 1988, p. A-8.

COMMUNITY RELATIONS

The **community** discussed in this chapter is an organization's area of local business influence. It often includes more than one geographic or political community, for such boundaries do not necessarily follow economic and social impacts. A bank in a large metropolitan area may have as its community the central city and numerous satellite towns and cities. A local merchant's community may comprise several surrounding cities or towns. A multinational firm may have a separate community for each of the local areas it serves around the world. In all cases, both company and community have a mutual dependence that is significant economically and socially.

The involvement of business with the community is called **community relations.** Community relations in the 1990s are quite different from those of 50 or 100 years ago. Technological advances and massive population shifts in the United States and much of the industrialized world are putting great pressures on both business and the community. Community relationships in the United States and abroad are entwined with cultural norms. Business decisions have become more complex, and the impact of those decisions has loomed larger in the life of communities. Keeping their community ties alive, well, and relevant is a major task for today's businesses.

Many corporations have established community relations offices to cope with their numerous, complex communities. Community relations offices coordinate community programs such as those described at Shell, manage donations of goods and services, and encourage employee volunteerism in nonprofit and civic organizations.[2] Companies have increasingly become involved with local communities on diverse issues including school improvement, solid waste management, local taxes, and improving the lives of the homeless. Their aims are to improve local conditions that produce or attract a workforce qualified to meet the company's needs and to build a positive relationship between the firm and important local groups. Community relations officers work closely with other corporate offices that link the corporation to the external world, such as the employee relations, public relations, or public affairs offices. These linkages form a bridge between the corporation and important community groups.[3]

Limited Resources Face Unlimited Community Needs

Every community has many social needs requiring far more resources than are available. Choices must be made and priorities established. In some instances, the community decides the priorities, but in other instances, such as Jamesheddpur, business influences community priorities very directly. Further, in all cases,

[2] See Lee Burke et al., "Corporate Community Involvement in the San Francisco Bay Area," *California Management Review*, Spring 1986, pp. 122–141.

[3] Boston College Center for Corporate Community Relations, "1988 Profile of the Community Relations Profession," *Community Relations Letter*, March 1989, Chestnut Hill, MA: Boston College Center for Corporate Community Relations.

once management has decided to help serve a need, it still must decide how its resources can best be applied to that need. This means that any action management takes will result in some dissatisfaction from those who get no help and from those who do not get as much help as they want. It is impossible for business always to fully satisfy everyone's expectations.

Figure 15–1 illustrates the large variety of expectations that communities have of business. The figure reports some of the major requests made of a large manufacturer in a Midwestern U.S. city. There are artistic, educational, and charitable requests serving both special groups and the community as a whole. The company agreed to support all of these requests, and its work with them consumed hundreds of days of employee time and thousands of dollars of company resources. Meanwhile, the company was required to meet its primary obligation of serving customers competitively throughout the nation.

Community Involvement and Firm Size

Community involvement has become a part of most corporate life-styles. Studies show that both large and small businesses, whether they are local firms or branches of national firms, tend to be active in community affairs.[4] Business leaders bring knowledge and ability to civic and community matters. Much of this activity involves participation in groups such as local business councils and

FIGURE 15–1
Community requests made of a manufacturer during a year.

REQUESTS MADE

- Assistance for less-advantaged people
- Support for air and water pollution control
- Support for artistic and cultural activities
- Employment and advancement of minorities and women
- Assistance in urban planning and development
- Support of local health care program
- Donation of equipment to local school system
- Support of local bond issues for public improvements
- Aid to community hospital drive
- Support of local program for recycling to conserve scarce resourcs and prevent pollution
- Executive aid for local United Fund
- Company participation in "get out the vote" campaign

[4] Center for Corporate Public Involvement, *1990 Social Report of the Life and Health Insurance Business*, Washington, DC: American Council of Life Insurance and Health Insurance Association of America, 1990.

roundtables, leadership civic task forces, and regional public affairs councils. Through such activities executives become familiar with local needs and issues and the ways in which businesses and communities affect each other.

Large companies usually have more public visibility in community affairs. These firms are more established and help to characterize their surrounding towns.[5] Executives, often acting as board members and consultants, tend to participate more actively in philanthropy, volunteerism, and community issues when the headquarters is located in the community.[6]

When a company has numerous branches, its interests extend into those communities. Like IBM in the opening example, an effective corporate policy has to be implemented in differing local situations. An effective policy has to recognize the unique needs of each community in which the firm is involved. This makes it desirable for corporate headquarters to give local managers broad leeway to make community-related decisions. One study found that nearly 60 percent of firms have delegated community relations responsibilities to managers in local plants, branch offices, and service branches.[7]

Small business participation in community activities is just as important as large business involvement. Small business representatives, such as appliance service people, automobile dealers, and retail merchants, significantly influence the quality of community life. They tend to be both personally and professionally involved in community affairs, often expressing a deep commitment to the community based on many years of residence.[8] When all businesses, large and small, work with local city and town councils to support civic improvements, the quality of community life tends to improve.

Community Support of Business

The relationship of business and community is one of mutual interdependence. Each has obligations to the other because each has social power to affect the other. This power-responsibility equation applies to both parties to remind them that success is a matter of mutual support, rather than opposition.

Types of support that business normally expects from a community are shown in Figure 15–2. In general, business expects fair treatment, and it expects to be accepted as a participant in community affairs because it is an important part of the community. It also expects community services such as a dependable water supply and police protection. It will be encouraged to remain in the community and grow if there are appropriate cultural, educational, and recreational facilities for its employees. Businesses also have come to recognize that they rely heavily

[5] Ibid.

[6] See Burke et al., op. cit., for a discussion of those involvements.

[7] Boston College Center for Corporate Community Relations, "1987 Profile of the Profession," *Community Relations Newsletter*, Chestnut Hill, MA: Boston College Center for Corporate Community Relations, 1988.

[8] For a discussion see Daniel J. Brown and Jonathan B. King, "Small Business Ethics, Influences, and Perceptions," *Journal of Small Business Management*, January 1982, pp. 11–18.

FIGURE 15–2
Areas of desirable community service and support for business.

COMMUNITY SERVICES DESIRED BY BUSINESS

- A cultural and educational environment that supports a balanced quality of life for employees
- Adequate family recreational facilities
- Complete public services, such as police and fire protection and sewage, water, and electric services
- Taxes that are equitable and do not discriminate for or against business
- Open acceptance of business participation in community affairs
- A fair and open public press
- An adequate transportation system to business and residential areas (for example, suitable public transportation and well-maintained streets)
- Public officials, customers, and citizens who are fair and honest in their involvement with business
- In general, a cooperative problem-solving approach in working with mutual problems

on the public school system and other local services, so that they can run their businesses efficiently.

If community citizens, labor organizations, or the government abuse business or take advantage of it, then success for both business and the community becomes more difficult. This lack of support may take many forms. For instance, one city required a proposed new factory in the city limits to install its own water main for a mile along city streets. The management declined and built in a neighboring city. Another city harassed a retail store with parking and beautification requirements, which took months of public hearings. The publicity generated community opposition to the store, sales deteriorated, the store closed, and a proposed new department store declined to enter the community.

The desirable combination of business-community mutual support is shown in Figure 15–3. As shown by point C and the shaded area in the figure, both business and community leaders need to develop attitudes that support each other's interests as well as their own. Often they think primarily of their own needs, as represented by point A for business and point B for the community. The result is that they fail to understand each other's problems and fail to develop adequate cooperation for problem solving. In the long run in this kind of situation, both business and community are likely to lose.

CORPORATE RESTRUCTURING, PLANT CLOSINGS, AND COMMUNITY RELATIONS

Throughout the 1980s, corporate restructurings and reorganizations became a serious and disruptive fact of life for communities throughout the United States and in other industrial nations. **Corporate restructuring** means that companies are reshaping their business activities in some fundamental way so as to become

FIGURE 15–3
Business and communities need high levels of support from each other.

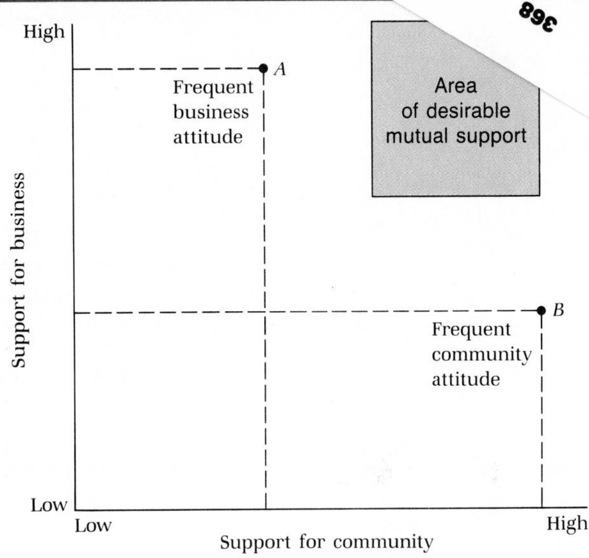

more competitive. Restructured companies often close down older, less productive facilities, thereby improving the firm's ability to produce goods more efficiently. Sometimes they sell off assets to other corporations who may not have the same relationship to the local community as the previous owner. Restructurings may be voluntarily undertaken by management to avoid being taken over by a hostile corporate "raider" or simply to meet the forces of global competition by introducing new laborsaving technology, moving production facilities to low-wage regions of the world, or substituting new materials for old (such as plastic and ceramic auto parts for steel parts).

Whatever the reasons for the restructuring, the effects on the community are similar: local plants close, workers are laid off, jobs are lost, individuals are relocated. Research shows that displaced workers seldom manage to find new jobs as good or as well paying as the ones they lose when a plant closes. Single-income families may be so hard hit that home mortgage payments cannot be met, and homes may be sold to meet back taxes. Sometimes pension benefits and health care insurance are lost. Older workers, minorities, and women suffer more than other groups of displaced workers, taking longer to find new jobs and receiving lower pay when they do. Family tensions build up: divorce rates increase, depression and mental illness increase, suicides become more frequent, alcoholism and drug abuse grow, child abuse and spouse abuse occur more readily.[9]

Some communities, especially one-company or one-industry towns, may be unable to provide basic services.

[9] Angelo J. Kinicki, "Toward Socially Responsible Plant Closing," *Personnel Administrator*, June 1987, pp. 116–128.

Akron, Ohio, in the heart of what has come to be called the "Rustbelt" because of the decaying dominance of heavy manufacturing industries, was for many years known as the Rubber Capital. Millions of tires and inner tubes were produced in Akron's massive tire factories until more than 10,000 jobs were lost in the intense global competition that took place in the early 1980s. Struggling to recover from these devastating losses, Akron's city government worked hard to attract and develop smaller and mid-sized businesses in the city to replace some of the jobs that were lost. While Akron has begun to recover, the massive factories of earlier times are gone and the new industries require more active cooperation between public and private sector executives in order to succeed.[10]

The human and community problems created by restructuring are not confined to the midwestern United States. California's Silicon Valley and Massachusetts' high technology belt also have been squeezed by foreign competition in the 1990s. Texas, Louisiana, and other oil-producing states faced falling oil prices in the mid-1980s, resulting in dramatic and well-publicized failures of savings and loan institutions and a decline in the local housing market. This led to job losses and all of the associated negative impacts on people and communities. In the United States, each year during the 1980s, plant closings displaced about 500,000 workers who had more than three years on the job. These job losses primarily affected lower-paid and lower-skilled workers, with minorities suffering above-average rates of displacement and those longer on the job suffering greater earnings losses.[11]

Available research identifies five major stakeholder groups affected by these restructuring activities: (1) local, state, and federal governments, (2) company management, (3) affected employees, (4) labor unions, and (5) the local community.[12]

Local, State, and Federal Governments

As the impacts of plant closings have become better known over the last decade, federal and state governments have stepped up their efforts to protect workers and communities. Local governments generally mirror the concerns and activities of the communities they serve. Legislatures have adopted numerous **plant closing laws** requiring a company to give advance notice—anywhere from 60 days to 1 or 2 years—before a plant closes. In 1988, the U.S. Congress enacted the Workers Adjustment Retraining Notification Act (WARN legislation), which went

[10] See John Case, "Back to the Future," *Inc.*, October 1989, pp. 33–34.

[11] See Daniel S. Hamermesh, "What Do We Know about Worker Displacement in the U.S.?" *Industrial Relations*, Winter 1989, pp. 51–59.

[12] Jeanne P. Gordus, Paul Jarley, and Louis A. Ferman, *Plant Closings and Economic Dislocation*, Kalamazoo, MI: W. E. Upjohn Institute for Employment Research, 1981. See also U.S. Department of Labor, *Plant Closings: What Can Be Learned from Best Practice*, Washington, DC: Government Printing Office, 1982.

into effect in 1989. WARN requires employers to give 60 days' advance notice of plant closings and major layoffs that result in permanent job losses. The legislation applies to all businesses employing 100 or more full-time employees.

Such laws are controversial because it is believed that they affect smaller businesses more than larger ones, who can more easily afford the cost incurred. There is research evidence to suggest, however, that most of the negative impacts on business resulting from these laws are temporary.[13] Nonetheless, lawmakers have to carefully weigh the potential costs and benefits of such legislation for smaller businesses, which account for half of nonfarm, nongovernmental employment in the United States, creating millions of new jobs each year.[14]

Much of the current U.S. worker legislation is modeled on western European government requirements that employers provide notice to employees, job training, and job search assistance when layoffs are necessary.[15] European laws often require compensation payments to the community as well. Business has tended to oppose these protective laws because they restrict the freedom of managers to redirect company resources to their most efficient uses in the competitive marketplace.

Company Management

Managerial policies and attitudes vary from company to company. In some cases, advance notice is given and management makes an effort to find new jobs for displaced workers and to work with local citizens' groups and municipal officials to ease the impact of a closing. At other times, only the minimum legal requirements are met by a company that does not want to be pressured to reverse its decision. Such a company may offer little aid to employees, the union, and community groups.

> For example, when Brown & Williamson's planned to close one of its facilities, it did so in phases over a three-year period. The company provided more than eighteen months' advance notice, relocated workers, and provided separation pay, health and insurance benefits, and vocational training to laid-off workers. On the other hand, National Car Rental gave its workers only three weeks' notice of an indefinite closing. The company did not inform employees until one year later that the closing was permanent.[16]

[13] Ronald G. Ehrenberg and George H. Jakubson, "Advance Notification of Plant Closing: Does It Matter?" *Industrial Relations,* Winter 1989, pp. 60–71.

[14] See Thomas A. Gray, "Let Small Business Do What It Does Best—Create Jobs," *Journal of Labor Research,* vol. 10, Winter 1989, pp. 78–81.

[15] "Europeans Take Plant-Closing Notice for Granted," *Pittsburgh Post-Gazette,* May 2, 1988, p. 11.

[16] Kinicki, op.cit.

Sometimes companies discover after the fact that poor planning cost them their most skilled managers and workers. Such treatment can result in lack of loyalty and low morale among remaining employees, making it even more difficult for the company to respond effectively to the competitive pressures that forced the restructuring in the first place.[17]

Affected Employees

Employees faced with job loss suffer a variety of fates. Some may move to another job with the same company but in a different location. Some are retrained and enter a new skill or craft. Others hang on to false hopes: one mill worker with 20 years of experience at one job for one company simply refused to accept reality, saying, "I think it's going to open again." Even those who find new jobs often end up with lower pay, have less desirable jobs, and lose their seniority.

Labor Unions

Labor union reactions may vary considerably. In the past, very few labor union contracts contained provisions protecting workers in case of a plant closure. As restructuring became more common, many unions began seeking guarantees against plant closings or loss of benefits should layoffs become necessary. In some cases, unions have been willing to make concessions on pay and work rules in order to secure plant closing benefits. In general, a union's first response to an announced plant closing is to try to reverse management's decision to relocate or to close; if that fails, the union may pressure the company to delay its decision, transfer workers to other plants, and grant generous layoff payments. Eventually, the union will work with a variety of community groups to deal with the effects of the plant closing.

Some unions have also created employee stock ownership plans (ESOPs) to acquire ownership of plants that were in danger of closing. (ESOPs are discussed in Chapter 12.) Employees then become owners as well as workers at the plant, although such approaches rarely save a plant that is too old or too inefficient to compete in the marketplace.

The Local Community

Research demonstrates that many communities need help in responding to problems caused by plant shutdowns.

[17] Thomas J. Murray, "For Downsizers, the Real Misery Is Yet to Come," *Business Month,* vol. 133, February 1989, pp. 71–72.

> Bethlehem Steel's closing of its Lackawanna, New York, plant in 1983 crippled the city. After the plant closed, Lackawanna was faced with staggering budget deficits and an increase in unemployment cases from 23,000 to 38,000. The city also suffered a significant decline in its population and an inability to replace the lost jobs with new industry.[18]

As can be seen in the Lackawanna case, the effects of corporate restructurings touch many community groups. The most successful strategies for coping with these new pressures on community life involve a well-coordinated program to counsel employees about their future prospects combined with a training program for those losing their jobs. The most successful communities, as shown in the Akron, Ohio, case, bring together a coalition of community groups, government, and businesses to work closely in developing new industries and job opportunities that help ease the pain of the old ones closing down.

OTHER BUSINESS RESPONSES TO COMMUNITY NEEDS

Business initiatives have helped improve the quality of life in communities in a number of ways, some of which are shown in Figure 15–4. These community concerns challenge management to reapply their talent to the changing needs in the local towns.

Improving Economic Development

Frequently businesses are involved in local or regional economic development, which is intended to bring new businesses into an area or to otherwise improve local conditions.[19] Central business districts, unlike older and often neglected poorer residential areas, have benefited from businesses during recent decades. Business has helped transform these business areas in major U.S. cities into a collection of shining office buildings, entertainment facilities, fashionable shopping malls, conference centers, and similar urban amenities. In spite of these developments, many urban areas have become forbidding and inhospitable places, lacking diversity, coherence, and human touch and experiencing high crime rates.

Through extensive cooperative efforts, planners are trying to control development so that the central business districts will again become attractive to all citizens. Some of the ingredients needed are open spaces devoted to fountains, small plots of green grass, trees, outdoor sitting areas, arcades, a variety of attractive stores, outdoor cafes, theaters, and encouraging more people to live in the city.[20]

[18] See John Strohmeyer, "The Agonizing Ordeal of a One-Company Town," *Business and Society Review,* Summer 1985, pp. 45–49.

[19] Patricia Sellers, "The Best Cities for Business," *Fortune,* Oct. 22, 1990, pp. 48–57.

[20] Clarke Thomas, "New Bustle in Toledo at Its Old Waterfront," *Pittsburgh Post-Gazette,* Jan. 10, 1986, pp. 1, 6.

FIGURE 15–4 Community projects of 180 insurance companies.

SOURCE: Center for Corporate Public Involvement, *1990 Report of the Life and Health Insurance Business*, Washington, DC, Center for Corporate Public Involvement, 1990.

Types of Projects	Percentage of Reporting Companies Supporting Projects in Each Area
Education	86
Arts and Culture	81
Local Health Programs	73
Youth Activities	69
Neighborhood Improvement Programs	68
AIDS Education and Treatment	54
Drug or Alcohol Abuse Programs	53
Minority Affairs	51
Programs for Handicapped	50
Programs for Hunger and Homeless	49
Activities for Senior Citizens and Retired Persons	45
Safety Programs	38
Housing Programs	33
Hard-to-Employ Programs	32
Crime Prevention	25
Day-Care Programs	25
Environmental Programs	24
Transportation Programs	13
Prenatal Programs	12
Other	9

Sometimes the rush of business development can be a problem as well as an opportunity for a community. For example, when Toyota announced in December 1985 that it would build an automobile manufacturing facility in Georgetown, Kentucky, residents were both pleased and anxious. The plant was expected to add as many as 3,500 jobs, but local people worried abut how the community would be able to absorb the influx of outsiders and how their tightly knit community would be affected. Acknowledging its responsibility for the expected changes, Toyota gave Georgetown $1 million to build a community center. By working closely with local government officials, acknowledging their responsibility, and communicating openly about expected problems, Toyota helped the community become a more dynamic place to live while expanding its business presence.[21]

The congestion and other problems that accompany metropolitan growth are not limited to the biggest cities. Office building has mushroomed in many suburban areas; almost two-thirds of new office space built in the late 1980s was in the suburbs. Technological changes related to computers permit some operations to be shifted away from central headquarters, sometimes causing community backlash in the suburbs. In the San Francisco suburb of Walnut Creek, local

[21] See "Toyota in Bluegrass Country," *Industry Week*, June 5, 1989, pp. 30–33; "As U.S. Car Makers Cut Back, Toyota Is Expanding Briskly," *New York Times*, Jan. 1, 1991, p. A-1.

citizens voted to bar large-scale office buildings and retail projects until traffic congestion was relieved. Still, suburbs appeal to business because of the generally less crowded conditions.

To avoid community backlash and an antigrowth public attitude, business leaders need to work with community groups in balancing business growth with a high quality of community life. Neighborhood housing efforts by municipal governments in cooperation with private industry represent one of the steps that business can take to achieve this balance.

> Life and health insurance companies have taken the lead in programs to revitalize neighborhood housing through organizations such as Neighborhood Housing Services (NHS) of America. NHS, which is locally controlled, locally funded, nonprofit, and tax-exempt, offers housing rehabilitation and financial services to neighborhood residents.
>
> Similar efforts are being made to house the homeless. Transamerica Life Companies was a founding partner for the Greater Los Angeles Partnership for the Homeless. The company has provided money and sent trained people to assist the partnership's efforts.

Environmental Concerns

The positive impacts of business on the community are balanced by a number of negative effects, including environmental problems. As local landfills near capacity, for example, communities have become concerned about the disposal of solid wastes. Citizen groups using slogans like NIMBY ("not in my back yard") or GOOMBY ("get out of my back yard") have resisted development of additional landfills to handle solid waste disposal, to which businesses contribute in great quantities. So concerned with the disposal problem were Seattle, Washington, citizens that Procter & Gamble began a pilot project there to collect and recycle disposable diapers. The company recognized that success of its own products is uncertain when communities raise concerns about their environmental effects.

Workforce Improvement

The aging of the post World War II "baby boom" generation and the subsequent decline in the number of entry-level workers have forced businesses to pay attention to the quality of the workforce. In assessing how the available workforce can be improved, many businesses have recognized that local public schools are a critical resource. Much criticism has been aimed at deficiencies in public schools in the United States for not preparing the average worker.

Thousands of local school-business partnerships sprang up throughout the 1980s.[22] Many of these collaborations are called "adopt-a-school" partnerships

[22] See Sandra A. Waddock, "Understanding Social Partnership: An Evolutionary Model of Partnership Organizations," *Administration and Society,* vol. 21, May 1989, pp. 78–100. The National Alliance of Business project is described in National Alliance of Business, *The Compact Project: School–Business Partnerships for Improving Education,* Washington, D.C.: National Alliance of Business, 1989.

in which businesses work to help schools to teach. Business leaders often participate on school boards and work as advisers to schools and government officials who may need business-specific training.

The National Alliance of Business (NAB) has, for example, developed a social "compact" project in which local businesses pledge their assistance and support to local schools. Demonstration projects in twelve cities led to an improved understanding of the factors required for successful business–education collaboration.

Other efforts at workforce improvement involve direct business participation in worker training and retraining, especially efforts to train the disadvantaged. Much of this participation has come about as a result of federal job legislation, which requires that public sector job training programs be supervised by private sector managers. Business has welcomed this chance to participate as a way to better match school and community efforts with business workforce opportunities and needs.

Technical Assistance to Municipal Government

In a number of cities, business has spearheaded programs to upgrade the quality of local government. It provides special advice and technical expertise on budgeting, financial controls, and other management techniques. Business know-how in these matters can inject vitality and efficiency into government systems that often are overburdened, underfinanced, and obsolete.

Aid to Minority Enterprise

In addition to programs to hire and train urban minorities for jobs in industry, private enterprise has extended assistance to minority-owned small businesses that must struggle for existence in the inner cities. These businesses are often at a great economic disadvantage: they do business in economic locations where high crime rates, congestion, poor transportation, low-quality public services, and a low-income clientele combine to produce a high rate of business failure.[23] Large corporations, sometimes in cooperation with universities, have provided financial and technical advice to minority entrepreneurs and have helped launch programs to teach managerial, marketing, and financial skills. They also have financed the building of minority-managed inner-city plants and sponsored special programs to purchase services and supplies from minority firms. In sum, private sector efforts have significantly helped some minority entrepreneurs who otherwise might have failed.[24]

[23] "St. Louis Blues: A Blighted Inner City Bespeaks the Sad State of Black Commerce," *Wall Street Journal,* May 10, 1988, pp. 1, 22; "Black Entrepreneurs Face Hugh Hurdles in Places Like Miami," *Wall Street Journal,* May 17, 1988, pp. 1, 18.

[24] For a discussion of the problems encountered by some of these inner-city plants, see "Why Few Ghetto Factories Are Making It," *Business Week,* Feb. 16, 1987, pp. 86, 89.

CORPORATE GIVING

One of the most visible ways in which business helps a community is through gifts of money, property, and employee service. This corporate philanthropy, or **corporate giving,** demonstrates the commitment of business to assist the community by supporting such nonprofit organizations as United Way, Community Chest, and individual hospitals, schools, homeless shelters, and other providers of important community services.

Since 1936, the federal government has encouraged corporate giving for educational, charitable, scientific and religious purposes. An incentive for such giving is the current Internal Revenue Service rule permitting corporations to deduct from their taxable income all such gifts that do not exceed 10 percent of the company's before-tax income. In other words, a company with a before-tax income of $1 million might contribute up to $100,000 to nonprofit community organizations devoted to education, charity, science, or religion. The $100,000 in contributions would then reduce the income to be taxed from $1 million to $900,000, thus saving the company money on its tax bill while providing a source of income to the community agencies. Of course, there is nothing to prevent a corporation from giving more than 10 percent of its income for philanthropic purposes, but it would not be given a tax break above the 10 percent level.

As shown in Figure 15–5, average corporate giving in the United States typically has been far below the 10 percent deduction now permitted. Though it varies from year to year it has been closer to 1 percent of before-tax income since the early 1960s but increased sharply in the early 1980s, reaching a peak in 1985. Some large corporations, many of them headquartered in the Minneapolis–St.

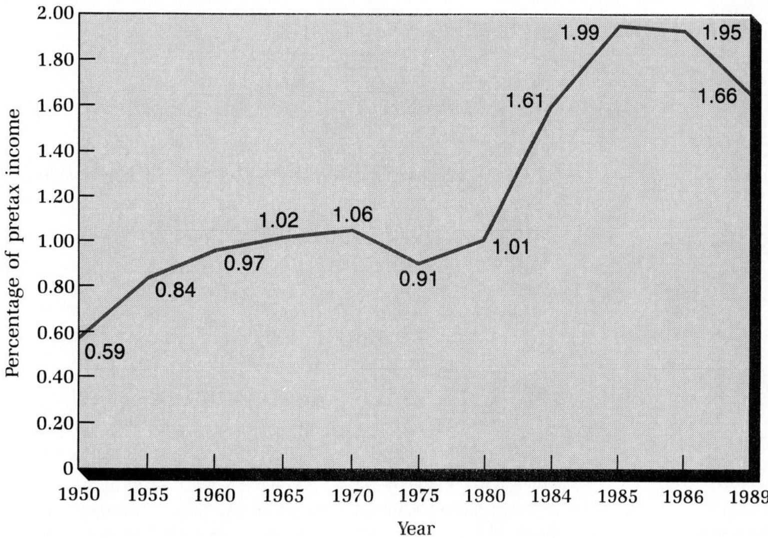

FIGURE 15–5 Corporate contributions as a percentage of pretax net income for selected years.
SOURCE: Linda Cardillo Platzer and Maureen Nevin Duffy, *Annual Survey of Corporate Contributions*, 1989 Edition (for calendar year 1987), New York, NY: The Conference Board, p. 35.

Paul metropolitan area, have pledged 5 percent of their pretax income.[25] Even at the national average of 1 percent giving, substantial amounts of money are channeled to community organizations, totaling in 1988 more than $5 billion.[26]

The courts have ruled that charitable contributions fall within the legal and fiduciary powers of the corporation's policymakers. Some opponents have argued that corporate managers have no right to give away company money that does not belong to them. According to this line of reasoning, any income earned by the company should be either reinvested in the firm or distributed to the stockholders who are the legal owners. But the courts have taken the position that corporate contributions are one additional way in which companies link themselves to the broader interests of the community, thereby advancing and strengthening the company rather than weakening it.

Another way a company helps local communities is through the substantial number of business gifts donated but not recorded in these figures because they are handled separately. Several examples are as follows:

- Routine gifts of products and services for local use often are recorded as advertising expenses.
- Gifts of employee time for charity drives and similar purposes usually are not recorded.
- Costs of soliciting and processing employee gifts, such as payroll deductions for the United Way, usually are not recorded.
- Recorded gifts of depreciated property and equipment may substantially understate its value to the organization that receives it.

A large number of businesses (38 percent of those surveyed in one study) have established nonprofit foundations to handle their contributions. This approach permits them to administer their giving programs more uniformly and provides a central group of professionals that handles all requests, especially large grant requests.

Corporate Giving in a Strategic Context

One way to stretch the corporate contributions dollar is to make sure that it is being allocated and used strategically to meet the needs of both recipient and donor. A strategy of mutual benefits for business and society is one of the major themes of this book. More companies are thinking about their giving in this way.

> Chevron Corporation tries to allocate its annual $25 million in contributions along strategic lines. The company sets a limited number of specific target agencies to receive the bulk of its gifts, usually donating to education, environmental concerns, economically and socially disadvantaged groups, youth,

[25] Katherine Troy, *The Corporate Contributions Function,* New York: The Conference Board, 1982.

[26] Conference Board, *Survey of Corporate Contributions, 1990 Edition,* New York: The Conference Board, 1990.

> and the elderly. Contributions to these groups are part of Chevron's program to stay in touch with grass-roots developments likely to affect the company's operations. Links are made also to the corporation's business plans for operations around the world. For example, when a new facility is to be built, the managers in charge of corporate contributions identify how the new operation will affect the local community and what the company might require from the community. Contributions are then allocated to improve the company's image and acceptance by the community.[27]

One group of scholars pointed out that strategic philanthropy occurs in two forms. One, called "strategic process giving," applies a professional business approach to determine the goals, budgets, and criteria for specific grants. The second approach, called "strategic outcome giving," emphasizes the links between corporate contributions and certain business-oriented goals (such as introducing a new product) or providing needed services to employees (such as child-care centers) or maintaining positive contacts with external stakeholder groups (such as Asian-Americans). Chevron's attempts to stay in touch with grass-roots organizations are an example of this approach. The most popular of these two approaches among companies surveyed was strategic process—in other words, the one that treats corporate giving in a businesslike manner.[28]

Priorities in Corporate Giving

The distribution of corporate contributions reflects how the business community views major community needs. As shown in Figure 15–6, corporate giving in 1984, 1986, and 1988 varied somewhat among categories, but the "pie" was divided in approximately the same way. These percentages are not identical among different companies and industries, and Figure 15–7 illustrates the variations among leading industries.

The actual contributions of an individual company may differ from these patterns, based on company goals and priorities. Corporate giving is often justified as a social investment that benefits business in the long run by improving the community, its labor force, the climate for business, or other conditions affecting business. An alternative view is that routine local gifts are a normal business expense of operating in the community and are treated like other public relations expenses. Another view holds that the corporation is a citizen and, as such, has the same duty of giving without regard to self-interest. Yet another view is that

[27] "Thinking Strategically: Chevron Sets the Pace in Corporate Giving," *Business International*, Jan. 18, 1985, pp. 17, 22–23; "Corporate Giving: Who Spends Most, and For What," *Across The Board*, May 1990, pp. 30–33.

[28] Jeanne M. Logsdon, Martha Reiner, and Lee Burke "Corporate Philanthropy: Strategic Responses to the Firm's Stakeholders," *Nonprofit and Voluntary Sector Quarterly*, vol. 19, no. 2, Summer 1990, pp. 93–109. For a similar view, see Timothy S. Mescon and Donn J. Tilson, "Corporate Philanthropy: A Strategic Approach to the Bottom-Line," *California Management Review*, Winter 1987, pp. 49–61.

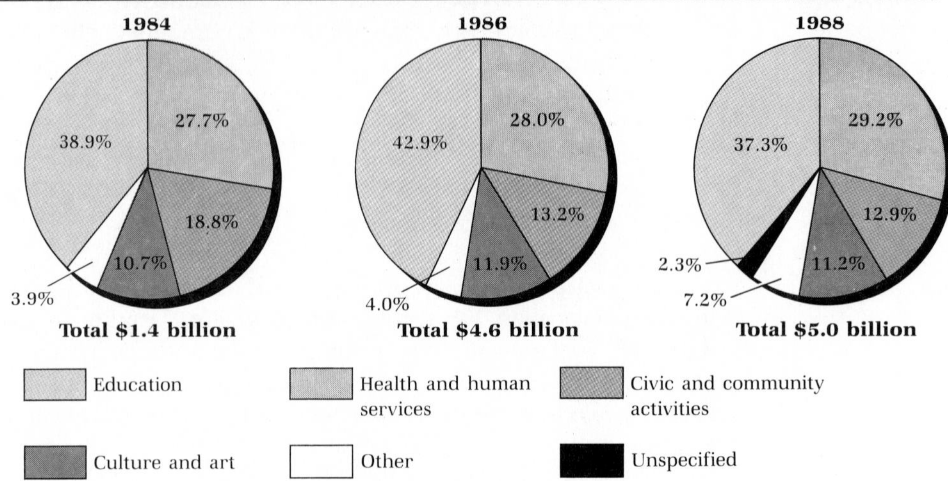

FIGURE 15–6 Distribution of corporate contributions dollars, 1984, 1986, 1988.

SOURCES: Linda Cardillo Platzer and Maureen Nevin Duffy, *Annual Survey of Corporate Contributions, 1989 edition,* New York: The Conference Board, 1989, p. 21; also, "Corporate Giving, 1988," *The Chronicle of Philanthropy,* Sept. 18, 1990, p. 14.

giving should be linked to business purposes as exemplified in cause-related marketing pioneered by American Express. This technique involves contributions to a local charity each time a company's product is purchased or used. The customer gains the benefit of the product or service, the charity receives a contribution, and the company increases sales.

Another assumption is that some corporate gifts take on the characteristics of taxes. Since it is widely believed that corporations should be good citizens, helpful neighbors, and human institutions, the community's expectations come close to imposing some types of gift giving on the corporation as a form of unofficial tax. The gifts are given to retain public approval.

Regardless of whether gifts are considered to be an investment, an expense, philanthropy, or a tax, most of their costs are probably passed on to consumers, because giving in the long run becomes a cost of doing business. Business is then acting partly as agent and trustee for the community, receiving funds and distributing them according to perceived and expressed community needs. In its trusteeship role, business responds to various stakeholder claims in its community, and one of these responses is gifts to those whose claims are perceived as being either legitimate or so powerful that they threaten the business if not satisfied. Thus, both legitimacy of claim and power of claimants are considered when making a decision concerning corporate giving.

THE NEED FOR PARTNERSHIP

In few areas of society is the need for a **public-private partnership** between business and government more apparent than in dealing with community problems. As one leading group of business executives has said:

> Whether growing or contracting, young or old, large or small, in the Frost Belt or Sun Belt, America's urban communities possess the resources of an advanced and affluent society: highly educated and skilled individuals, productive social and economic in-

stitutions, sophisticated technology, physical infrastructure, transportation and communications networks, and access to capital. Developing this potential will require cooperation. . . . Public-private partnerships are a source of energy and vitality for America's urban communities.[29]

FIGURE 15–7 Industry leaders by area of corporate contributions.

SOURCE: "Corporate Giving, 1988," *Chronicle of Philanthropy*, Sept. 18, 1990, p. 14.

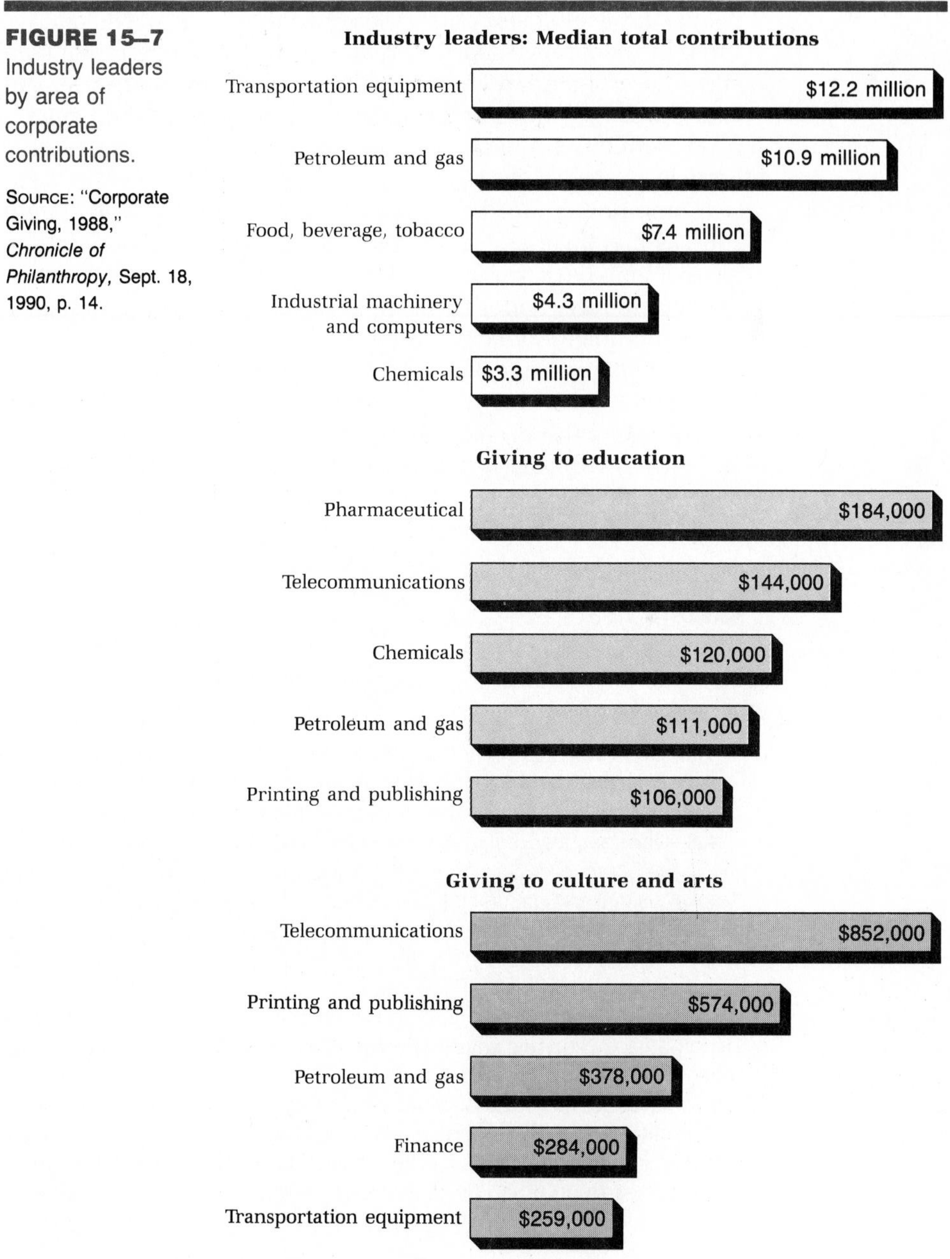

[29] Committee for Economic Development, *Public-Private Partnership: An Opportunity for Urban Communities*, New York, 1982, p. 1.

This last point is worth emphasizing. Many community problems are "people problems" involving hopes, attitudes, sentiments, and expectations for better human conditions. Neither government nor business can simply impose solutions or be expected to find quick and easy answers to problems so long in the making and so vast in their complications. Grass-roots involvement is needed, where people are willing and able to confront their own needs and work to fulfill them through cooperative efforts and intelligent planning. In that community-oriented effort, government and business can be partners, contributing aid and assistance where feasible and being socially responsive to legitimately expressed human needs. Exhibit 15-A describes such an effort in communities along the U.S.-Mexico border.

Communities need jobs, specialized skills, executive talents, and other resources that business can provide. Business needs cooperative attitudes in local government, basic public services, and a feeling that it is a welcome member of the community. Under these circumstances, much can be accomplished to upgrade the quality of community life. The range of specific business-community involvements is extensive, giving business many opportunities to be socially responsible. Careful handling of plant closings, planning operations to minimize urban and suburban congestion, and strategically placing corporate contributions are a few of the ways business can have a positive impact on the quality of community life.

EXHIBIT 15-A

MAQUILADORA BLUES

The South Texas border with Mexico is not the usual hotbed of corporate community affairs. It is, however, a hotbed of commercial expansion as dozens of companies from all over the world establish manufacturing and assembly operations called "machiladoras." Inexpensive Mexican labor and easy access to American markets make the machiladoras the vehicle for boom town development.

The boom towns are growing in areas where social problems—including no schools, no housing, and no social infrastructure to hold together the community—abound. Patricia Fogerty, a former NYNEX community affairs officer who lives in McAllen, Texas, says: "Some (companies) are finding they have to develop the entire social infrastructure in the towns."

A model for doing so is being developed by the El Paso Community Foundation. It organizes Hispanic wives of workers to do community work and serves as a bridge between employers and social problems in the border communities. Among the leadership companies that have "partnered up" with community groups are Levi Strauss, General Electric, Sierra West, and Alcoa. Yet the "machiladora blues" are so serious that many church groups in the United States are engaged in a campaign to press companies to do much more in dealing with these poor and needy communities.

(Source: "Machiladora Blues," in Craig Smith (ed.), *Corporate Philanthropy Report,* vol. 5, no. 1, August–September, 1989, p. 12.) Used with permission.

SUMMARY POINTS OF THIS CHAPTER

- Business and the community have a mutual dependence that is both economically and socially significant. Thus, business works to be accepted as a participant in community affairs by developing attitudes that support community interests as well as their own.
- Many corporations have established a community relations office which links the company's activities to local needs and important community groups.
- Impacts of plant closings can affect many community groups—merchants, employees, school systems, local government, and charitable organizations. Successful strategies for coping with these new pressures on community life involve business, government, employees, labor unions, and community organizations.
- Corporate contributions to educational, charitable, scientific, and community purposes help sustain vital community institutions as well as benefiting business in a variety of ways.
- Partnerships between business and community organizations are effective ways to tackle serious community problems such as education, economic development, and social service needs.

KEY TERMS AND CONCEPTS USED IN THIS CHAPTER

- Community
- Community relations
- Corporate restructuring
- Plant closing laws
- Corporate giving
- Public-private partnerships

DISCUSSION CASE

THIS LAND IS YOUR LAND, THIS LAND IS MY LAND?

"This is not a third-world country. This is the panhandle of Texas." "Corporate Phillips," meaning Phillips Petroleum Company, should not be allowed to "push Texas Americans around." So said a Houston lawyer hired by a group of citizens of Phillips, Texas, to help them fight an eviction order to leave their homes.

The tiny town with a current population of 1,500 was established some 65 years ago by the company to house its refinery workers. In the intervening years, the refinery expanded until the residents were living in the shadow of the huge refinery with its tanks of volatile liquids. In 1980, a huge explosion at the refinery leveled the town's two churches and damaged most houses in town. A company official declared, "If the refinery were being built today, houses would not be built there." The company admitted, though, that safety was not the only reason it wanted the houses vacated—it might need the land for future expansion of the refinery.

Although homeowners owned their houses, Phillips Petroleum owned the land on which they stood. In earlier times, the company owned the entire town, including the houses, had built a park and a swimming pool, and even repaired the streets. In the 1950s, it sold the houses but not the land to its workers. Each homeowner paid Phillips Petroleum $18 land rent each month plus $9 for trash collection. A local cattle company also owned some of the lots and had been negotiating with the homeowners to sell them the land where their houses stood. But the oil company bought the cattle company and wanted to reclaim all the land and had ordered all homeowners to leave.

Townspeople were upset about the deal offered them by the company. Fewer than half had accepted the corporation's plan to give each homeowner a free plot of land in a neighboring town plus paying them $3 to $4 per square foot to help defray the cost of moving their houses to the new location. Opponents said it was not enough and that many families could not afford the additional cost of moving. Others said that they did not want to move regardless of what the company would pay because they liked small-town living and had lived nowhere else for their entire lives. For them, the company had no right to force people to give up their birthplace.

Faced with losing their homes, a group of citizens formed the Phillips Homeowners Association. It was this group that called in a colorful lawyer from Houston known as Racehorse Haynes. He told the group, "They might whup us fair and square, but they better bring lunch." Townspeople were split on what to do. Those who favored accepting the company's offer were called "company men," while those opposed were labeled "radicals."[30]

Discussion Questions

1. Compare the situation in Phillips, Texas, with the one described at the beginning of this chapter concerning Jameshedpur, India. Which town illustrates the better relationships between the company and community? How do you account for the differences?
2. Using Figure 15–3, plot the position of business-community relationships in Phillips, Texas, at three different times: at the town's founding 65 years ago; during the 1950s when workers bought their homes; and at the time the company sent eviction notices to the homeowners.
3. What solution do you recommend in Phillips, Texas? Assume that the company wants to act in a socially responsible way and would prefer to avoid a costly legal battle that might damage its public image.

[30] Robert Reinhold, "Oil Company Town, Facing Eviction, Digs in for Legal Battles," *New York Times*, Feb. 23, 1986, p. 22.

PART FIVE

Social Issues in Management

16

Women, Men, and the Family: Workplace Issues

Developing opportunities for women who work in business has become a major social challenge for corporations. Barriers to women's equal participation in the workplace are yielding to the forces of economic change, greater need for skilled people in all categories, the demands of women to be treated equally, and equal opportunity laws. Achieving full workplace parity remains a goal to be reached. Women's greater participation in the nation's labor force has brought adjustments in family life and social values, requiring changes in corporate practices and policies.

Key Questions and Chapter Objectives

This chapter focuses on these key questions and objectives:

- Why have women entered the workforce in such large numbers?
- What major problems do working women face?
- How do social customs and traditions affect the job status of working women?
- What changes are needed in corporate policies and practices to promote women's workplace opportunities?

> [My opportunities are] still very open-ended. There are two possibilities, probably in the next couple of months—a move up in human resources or a line job. My dream is executive management, to be in the core of fifty managers where my boss is. I don't care if I'm the first woman. I think a woman will be there within the next year or two. Maybe it will be me a couple of years from now. There are no limits unless I decide to put them on. Even if I have children, there are ways to combine things.[1]

This optimistic view of one high-level U.S. corporate manager was not unusual in the early 1990s. Nearly half of all U.S. workers—and four of every ten managers—are women. For a half century, women have been entering the workforce in larger and larger numbers, finding jobs formerly denied to them.

[1] Quoted in Ann M. Morrison, Randall P. White, and Ellen Van Velsor, *Breaking the Glass Ceiling: Can Women Reach the Top of America's Largest Corporations?* Reading, MA: Addison-Wesley, 1987, p. 140.

This enormous demographic transition has improved women's economic standing, has given them new professional goals to achieve, and has provided them with a larger range of self-actualizing experiences. It also has improved the quality of the nation's labor force at a time when global competition poses tough challenges for U.S. business.

A broad-scale change of this magnitude, while carrying advantages, also produces new social challenges. In this chapter, we discuss these changes and the challenges they present to business. Understanding the historical background is a key to seeing what business can do today to meet these challenges.

THE STATUS OF WOMEN IN SOCIETY: HISTORICAL BACKGROUND

The status of both women and men in society is largely a product of social custom and tradition. These customs evolve over extremely long periods of time, and they resist change. In all societies, it is customary for men to perform certain tasks and for women to perform others. This sexual division of labor is usually based on more than functional factors alone—that is, who is stronger, more dextrous, has keener eyesight, is quicker mentally, etc. Once established, these distinctions between women's tasks and men's tasks tend to be accepted as proper and are reinforced over time by habit and custom. The sexual division of labor exerts a strong influence on the relative amounts of power and influence possessed by men and women within the family, clan, tribe, or larger society. Societies around the world and throughout history have varied greatly in how they arrange this basic division of labor.

Most societies in human history have been both patriarchal—men serving as head of the family or clan—and patrilineal—tracing family lineage through the father's ancestors. Because these men-centered social customs allocate power and privileges mainly to male members, women have generally found themselves with relatively less social standing than men. Matriarchal societies—where women are politically, economically, and socially dominant—have occasionally existed but not as frequently. Generally, it has been patriarchs, rather than women, who become chiefs, clan heads, tribal elders, shamans and priests, monarchs, presidents, prime ministers, generals, and corporate executives. Women's social standing in these patriarchal societies has been tied closely to childbearing and family sustenance.[2]

This general pattern of male-female relations continues in modern societies. Sex segregation based on custom has meant that today's women in general possess less economic and political power than men. Until quite recently, leadership positions in politics, government, business, religion, trade unions, sports, engineering, university teaching, military service, space exploration, science, and others have been considered off-limits to women. Although today's research

[2] For a discussion of the history of patriarchy, see Gerda Lerner, *The Creation of Patriarchy*, New York: Oxford University Press, 1986.

EXHIBIT 16–A

THE LONG SHADOW OF SEX SEGREGATION

"The explicit policies to segregate the workplace and to fire married women that I have uncovered in the historical records of hundreds of firms would be clearly illegal today. . . . Many of these discriminatory policies, at least as the written procedures of firms, were abandoned sometime after 1950. Some were changed in the 1950s as a response to tighter labor supply conditions, while others were altered only later when the policies became clearly illegal. *But their impact remained long after.* If few women worked for extensive periods of time, even fewer would remain when jobs were dead end and when women were barred from promotional ladders. When virtually no woman was an accountant, for example, few would train to be accountants. And if women's work was defined in one way and men's in another, few individuals would choose to be the deviant, for deviance might cost one dearly outside the workplace. Thus change in the economic sphere is slowed not only by the necessity for cohorts (age groups) to effect change, but also by the institutionalization of various barriers and by the existence of social norms maintained by strong sanctions."

SOURCE: From *Understanding the Gender Gap: An Economic History of American Women*, by Claudia Goldin. Copyright © 1990 by Oxford University Press, Inc. Reprinted by permission. Emphasis added.

demonstrates that women are as qualified as men to hold these high-level positions, sex discrimination based on custom, social habit, and gender bias has limited their opportunities.

Exhibit 16–A provides a striking example of how these persistent, gender-based customs can affect the jobs women hold, even long after explicit sex discrimination has been outlawed.

The Women's Movement

The women's movement of the 1960s, 1970s, and 1980s is the most recent phase of women's efforts to redress the unequal balance that cultural history has left on contemporary society's doorstep. The fight for equal rights for women in modern times began over a century earlier in England as women sought the right to vote. In the United States, that same right was finally secured in 1920 with the passage of the 19th amendment to the U.S. Constitution.

The women's movement that renewed itself among middle-class American women in the 1960s proved to be a watershed. On one side lay history's customs that cast most women in their traditional roles of homemaker and helpmate to their male companions—loyal sister, dutiful daughter, faithful wife, nurturing mother. On the other side of the watershed, events ran rapidly toward a new kind of attitude toward women's place in society. This attitude supported the liberation of women from customary restraints and stressed the importance of greater choice and personal control. Without rejecting the vital social contributions women had long made, leaders of the movement nevertheless advocated greater independence for women and a reexamination of long-accepted social habits and attitudes. In this climate, women began to question their roles, their lives, their relationships, and where it all was leading them.[3]

This questioning ran deeper than had earlier struggles of women to gain the right to vote, to own and control property, and to regulate family size. None of those earlier campaigns, even when successful, had seriously challenged society's prevailing distribution of power, privileges, and jobs that favored men. Women now were seeking equal rights, equal privileges, and the kind of liberty that would permit them to pursue lives determined largely by options of their own choosing. Their aims were self-determination and social justice, which meant having an equal claim on human rights and an equal standing with others around them. After a quarter century, these goals remained strong; two-thirds of U.S. women were reported in 1989 to believe that the United States "continues to need a strong women's movement to push for changes that benefit women."[4]

WHY WOMEN HAVE ENTERED THE WORKPLACE

Women want jobs for the same reasons that men do. They need income to support themselves, their children, their aging, retired, or sick parents or other close relatives, and their nonworking marital partner, and to enjoy a satisfying life-style. A paycheck is a ticket to economic freedom, a symbol of freeing oneself from having to ask others for money to pursue one's own interests.

Having a job with pay also gives a woman psychological independence and security. It can open up new vistas of opportunity, permitting and encouraging higher degrees of self-actualization. Being economically productive and contributing to society through paid work contributes as much to women's as to men's sense of self-esteem.

When marriages terminate, through either divorce or the death of one partner, the remaining person usually needs a paying job. Many women who choose not to work outside the home during their married life confront this necessity when joint savings or life insurance are inadequate for their postmarriage life. Research reveals that most women, even those with jobs, suffer a decline in their living standard following divorce. During the 1980s when many corporate takeovers and mergers, along with increased global competition, resulted in massive job layoffs, working women often found themselves the sole breadwinner in their family. Inflation also puts financial pressure on families, frequently pushing women into the labor force just to sustain an accustomed standard of living or

[3] The classic statement of the U.S. women's movement is Betty Friedan's *The Feminine Mystique*, first published in 1963. For her views of what the movement had accomplished after twenty years, see the Foreword of *The Feminine Mystique*, 20th anniversary edition, New York: Norton, 1983.

[4] "Struggle for Work and Family Fueling Women's Movement," *New York Times*, Aug. 22, 1989, p. A1. For international aspects, see Arvonne S. Fraser, "Women and International Development: The Road to Nairobi and Back," in Sara E. Rix, *The American Woman 1990–91: A Status Report*, New York: Norton, 1990, pp. 287–300; and Nancy Adler and Dafna N. Izraeli (eds.), *Women in Management Worldwide*, Armonk, NY: Sharpe, 1988.

to put children through college or to care for aging parents. The inadequacies and uncertainties of retirement plans and health-care programs frequently mean that women, as well as men, need to save, invest, and plan for the future.

Women have always "worked," whether paid or not. As homemakers, their workday typically has exceeded the hours of those who do paid work outside the home. Most homemaking tasks call for both physical labor and managerial skills. A typical day means being on one's feet much of the time, lifting and carrying, stooping and bending, pushing and pulling, climbing and reaching, traveling to the marketplace and hauling products home, and (in some homes with children) delivering children to school and picking them up. More complex responsibilities involve planning, scheduling, communicating, delegating, coordinating, mediating, overseeing, and motivating others. In some ways, running a home is very much like running a business. It has to be kept on an even keel because it will not run itself. A homemaker is a type of manager. The managerial skills used there are typically needed in the business world.

In a family with two married parents, two or three children, all living together in one home, and with only the man working for pay, the homemaker's job clearly undergirds the man's job and profession. Social traditions produced a division of labor between men and women in which the homemaker-woman relieves the breadwinner-man from the burdens of keeping house and attending to many of the children's needs. In return, she expects to share in the man's income which her home labor makes possible. Even in two-income families, this pattern of homemaker subsidy tends to prevail. In what has been called the "executive family," the stay-at-home wife acquires still other duties associated with her mate's job, such as playing social hostess to her husband's business associates, showing up for company social functions, and generally projecting the kind of traditional homemaker's image considered to be proper for a rising executive.[5]

The strain on or rupture of some of these deep-seated family arrangements, as more and more women have entered the labor force, has been responsible for much of the criticism directed toward women who work for pay. It also has focused attention on the numbers and types of jobs actually held by women, which we examine next.

WHERE WOMEN WORK AND WHAT THEY ARE PAID

Figure 16–1 gives some of the salient facts about working women in the United States. Highlights about working women include the following:[6]

[5] For a discussion, see Arlie Hochschild, *The Second Shift: Working Parents and the Revolution at Home,* New York: Viking, 1989.

[6] Rix, op. cit., pp. 349–397; "Women in Management," *Facts on Working Women,* Washington, DC: Women's Bureau, Department of Labor, December 1989; Korn/Ferry International, Demographic Profile of Senior Executives, August 1990; and "More Women Head Off to the Workplace," *Wall Street Journal,* Mar. 5, 1991, p. B1.

FIGURE 16–1
Comparing working women and working men.

	Women	Men
U.S. population	51%	49%
U.S. labor force	45%	55%
Doing paid work (total of each)	58%	76%
Total management jobs	39%	61%
Top corporate executives	3%	97%
Personnel managers	49%	51%

- Over half (58 percent) of all women are employed.
- Women make up nearly half (45 percent) of the entire labor force.
- Most working women (73 percent) have full-time jobs.
- Over half (57 percent) of the jobs held by women are year-round jobs rather than seasonal ones.
- A large proportion (56 percent) of married women with young children hold jobs outside the home.
- The main jobs held by women are administrative and clerical work (28 percent of all women's jobs) and service work (16 percent). Only one of every ten working women is a manager.
- Women hold 39 percent of all executive, administrative, and managerial posts, but most of these are at low and middle levels of organizations.
- Only 3 percent of top corporate executives are women.

It is apparent that women have become major participants in doing the paid work of United States society. To work outside the home is now the standard for most American women. Having children does not exclude women from the job market, although only about one-third of women with young children hold full-time jobs. In two-fifths of U.S. married households—26 million families in all—both husband and wife work, far outnumbering the family with husband working while wife remains at home with the children (only 13 percent or 8.4 million families are of this type).

Women owning their own businesses also expanded during the 1980s, according to the U.S. Census Bureau. Their numbers increased by 58 percent from 1982 to 1987 to more than 4 million firms, a rate of growth four times faster than business in general. In 1990, women owned 30 percent of all U.S. companies; however, most of them were small firms, with only 15 percent having paid employees. These women-owned enterprises are concentrated in retail trade and finance, insurance, and real estate. Contrary to popular belief, women entrepreneurs are just as successful as men, according to a mid-1980s study of over 400 midwestern small firms. The study's researchers reported that "the determinants of survival and success operated in much the same way for men and women. . . . Despite the widely shared assumption that women are less apt than men to innovate, for example, we found no evidence of women's being less likely to do

FIGURE 16–2
The gender pay gap, 1955–1988.

SOURCE: Claudia Goldin, *Understanding the Gender Gap,* New York: Oxford University Press, 1990, pp. 60–61; and "Women Still Earn Less, But They've Come a Long Way," *Business Week,* Dec. 24, 1990, p. 14.

Year	Women's Earnings as Percent of Men's Median Year-Round Earnings (Full-time Employees)
1955	64
1965	60
1975	59
1981	59
1982	62
1983	64
1984	64
1985	65
1986	64
1987	66
1988	68

this in their businesses. Moreover, we found no evidence that men were more confident of their business abilities."[7]

Although women hold more jobs than formerly, their distribution among jobs and industries is lopsided. They have found more places in the service industries than in manufacturing, mining, or agriculture. They serve more as clerks and low-level administrative helpers than as high-level leaders in organizational life, and as staff workers more than holding line jobs with central authority over policies and practices.

One persistent feature of the average working woman's world is receiving lower pay than men. This **gender pay gap** narrowed during the 1980s but Figure 16–2 shows that women as a group earned only 68 percent of men's pay in 1988. Different measures reveal slightly different results, and the gap tends to become narrower in some jobs that call for more education or among younger workers or where the experience of men and women is more balanced. Black women and Hispanic women received even smaller shares than white women.

Most observers believe that the pay gap persists because of what is called **occupational segregation.** Because so many women hold low-paying jobs as secretary, waitress, or clerk or because they take jobs in the relatively low-paying retail and service industries, women's average income is pulled down below the average wages of men. The labor market produces this kind of occupational segregation, partly because women find these jobs the most accessible to them when they look for work and partly because employers are eager to find people who will take the jobs at the prevailing pay rates. In some cases, an entire occupational category such as bank teller or clerical office worker will shift from employing all men to hiring virtually all women, as men move on to more attractive

[7] Arne L. Kalleberg and Kevin T. Leicht, "Gender and Organizational Performance: Determinants of Small Business Survival and Success," *Academy of Management Journal,* March 1991, pp. 157–158; and *Wall Street Journal,* Oct. 17, 1990, p. B2.

and high-paying job opportunities. Occupational segregation frequently means that women do not land the jobs or obtain the career openings that could break the cycle of relatively low pay.[8]

WOMEN IN MANAGEMENT

The most prestigious and highest-paid jobs in a corporation are in top management. Because corporations are organized hierarchically, top management jobs are few in number. For that reason, only a minority of either men or women can hope to reach the upper levels of management. Men have traditionally filled most of these desirable spots. Business's challenge now is to broaden these high-level leadership opportunities for women.

Where Women Manage

Over 5 million U.S. women were managers by the late 1980s, doubling their numbers in one decade. In 1988, as Figure 16–3 reveals, four out of every ten managers were women, and every tenth working woman was a manager. Clearly, women had broken into the management ranks. Women are more likely to be managers, though, in occupational areas where women are more numerous at lower levels, including medicine and health care, personnel, labor relations, and education. They also are concentrated in service industries and in finance, insurance, real estate, and retail businesses.

Where women managers are scarce is in the executive suites of large corporations. Rarely do they represent more than 1 to 3 percent of these top jobs. Occasional exceptions do occur, as in Avon Products, where women hold 81 percent of managerial positions.[9]

Access to management jobs is restricted in most areas of the world, according to a study of women managers in several nations.

> In country after country, the proportion of women holding managerial positions falls short of that of men. Corporations, it appears, have systematically ignored women as a potential resource. In all countries, the higher the rank within the organization, the fewer the women found there. In some countries, the percentages, though small, have increased over the last decade; but in none have they approached equality. This pattern prevails in oriental and occidental cultures, communist, socialist, and capitalist systems, and [in] both economically developed and developing countries.[10]

[8] For two examples, see Myra H. Strober and Carolyn L. Arnold, "The Dynamics of Occupational Segregation among Bank Tellers," in Clair Brown and Joseph A. Pechman, *Gender in the Workplace*, Washington, DC: Brookings, 1987, pp. 107–148; and Sharon Hartman Strom, " 'Light Manufacturing': The Feminization of American Office Work, 1900–1930," *Industrial and Labor Relations Review*, October 1989, pp. 53–71.

[9] "Best Employers for Women and Parents," *Wall Street Journal*, Nov. 30, 1987, p. 21.

[10] Adler and Izraeli, op. cit., pp. 7–8.

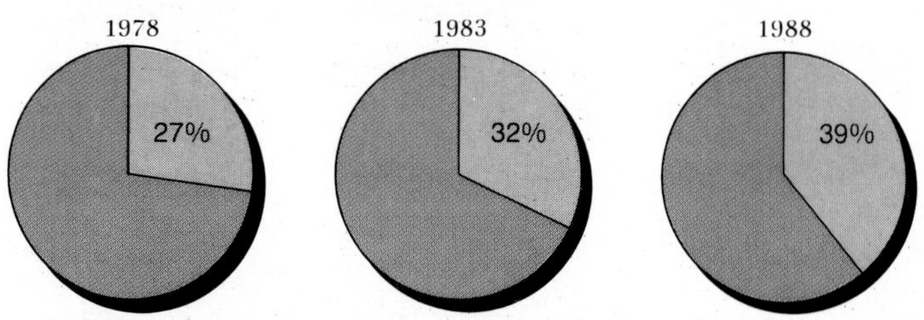

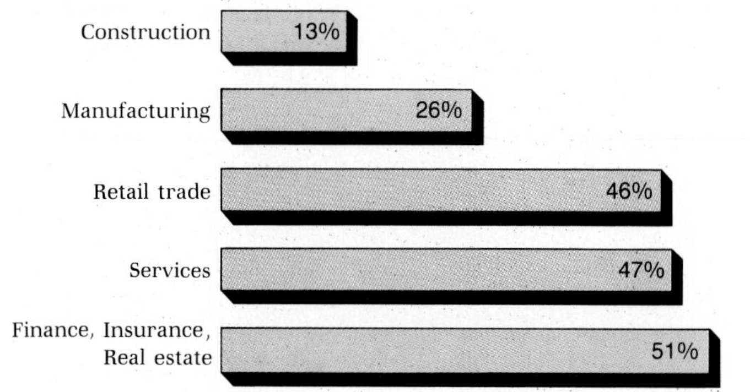

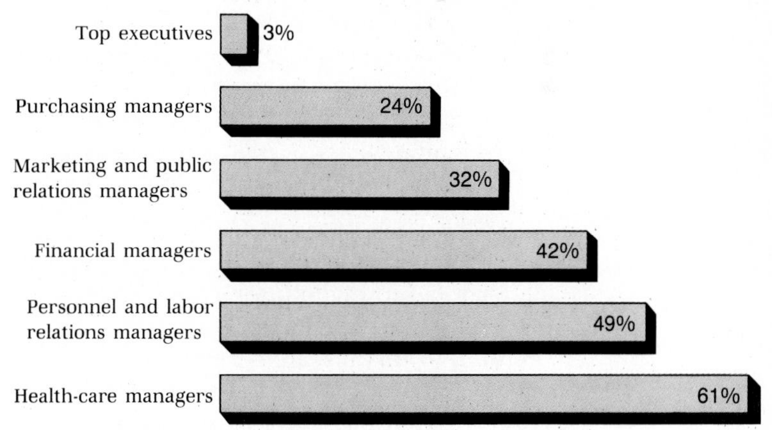

FIGURE 16–3
Where women manage.

SOURCE: Women's Bureau, U.S. Department of Labor, "Facts on Working Women," December 1989.

Do Women and Men Managers Manage Differently?

When women do become managers, do they bring a different style and different skills to the job? Are they better, or worse, managers than men? Are women more highly motivated and committed than male managers? Are they accepted by

FIGURE 16–4
Sex similarities and differences in management.

SOURCE: Gary N. Powell, "One More Time: Do Female and Male Managers Differ?" *Academy of Management Executive*, August 1990, p. 69. Reprinted by permission of the publisher and author.

SEX DIFFERENCES IN MANAGEMENT: SELECTED RESULTS

Dimension	Results
BEHAVIOR	
Task-oriented	No difference
People-oriented	No difference
Effectiveness ratings	Stereotypical difference in evaluations of managers in laboratory studies: Males favored No difference in evaluations of actual managers
Response to poor performer	Stereotypical difference: Males use norm of equity, whereas females use norm of equality.
Influence strategies	Stereotypical difference: Males use a wider range of strategies, more positive strategies, and less negative strategies. This difference diminishes when women managers have high self-confidence.
MOTIVATION	No difference in some studies Nonstereotypical difference in other studies: Female motivational profile is closer to that associated with successful managers.
COMMITMENT	Inconsistent evidence regarding difference
SUBORDINATES' RESPONSES	Stereotypical difference in responses to managers in laboratory studies: Managers using style that matches sex role stereotype are favored. No difference in responses to actual managers

those they manage, or do customary ways of thinking cause both men and women to react negatively to having female managers?

The research evidence strongly favors the no-difference point of view. According to this research, managers of both sexes do not seem to differ in any significant way in performing their tasks. These results are summarized in Figure 16–4. Women managers do not appear to be more people-oriented than men, nor do they tackle task-oriented jobs less effectively than their male counterparts. Men managers and women managers score about the same on motivation tests, but one study of 2,000 managers, cited by Gary N. Powell, seemed to demonstrate that "female managers were more concerned with opportunities for growth, autonomy, and challenge" and exhibited a "more mature and higher-achieving motivational profile" than the men in the study.

Commitment studies show mixed results, with women sometimes more job-committed and men at other times registering stronger commitment. For both sexes, commitment is always stronger when people have satisfying jobs, believe their work is meaningful, and when their skills are used and appreciated. On-the-job sex discrimination can contribute to lowered job commitment by making the workplace less attractive for women. The amount of time and commitment that anyone brings to a job and career is also affected by the amount of home-based support one receives. Women who bear a disproportionately large share of household tasks and family care may be unable to make as full a commitment to job and career as they would prefer.

Reaction of subordinates to women managers varies, but "once subordinates have worked for both female and male managers, the effects of [traditional sex-role] stereotypes disappear and managers are treated as individuals rather than representatives of their sex."[11]

Some research supports the idea that women bring different attitudes and skills to management jobs, such as greater cooperativeness, an emphasis on affiliation and attachment, nurturance, and a willingness to bring emotional factors to bear in making workplace decisions. These differences are seen to carry advantages for companies, because they expand the range of techniques that can be used to help the company manage its workforce effectively.[12]

A study commissioned by the International Women's Forum discovered a management style used by some women managers (and also by some men) that differs from the command-and-control style traditionally used by male managers. Using this "interactive leadership" approach, "women encourage participation, share power and information, enhance other people's self-worth, and get others excited about their work. All these things reflect their belief that allowing employees to contribute and to feel powerful and important is a win-win situation—good for the employees and the organization." The study's director predicted that "interactive leadership may emerge as the management style of choice for many organizations."[13]

The Glass Ceiling

Although women are as competent as men in managing people and organizations, they still do not attain the highest positions in corporations. Their ascent seems to be blocked by an invisible barrier. At some point, they bump into what is called "the glass ceiling."

Failure to attain the topmost jobs in some cases is due to lack of experience or inadequate education. Because gender bias has kept women out of management until recent years, they have not had time to acquire the years of experience

[11] Gary N. Powell, "One More Time: Do Female and Male Managers Differ?" *Academy of Management Executive,* August 1990, pp. 68–75. For a discussion of similarities and differences among men and women managers, see Powell's book *Women and Men in Management,* Newbury Park, CA: Sage, 1988; and Morrison et al., op. cit., pp. 48–54.

[12] Jan Grant, "Women as Managers: What They Can Offer to Organizations," *Organizational Dynamics,* Winter 1988, pp. 56–63.

[13] Judy B. Rosener, "Ways Women Lead," *Harvard Business Review,* November–December 1990, pp. 120, 125.

that are typical of most high-ranking executives. Also in earlier years, women were discouraged from entering graduate schools of engineering, science, business, and law which have been pathways to corporate management. Even as those barriers have been lowered, though, women remain underrepresented at executive levels. As a group, they have not yet broken through the glass ceiling to become chief executive officers, presidents, or board chairpersons. Something continues to hold them back.

In one authoritative study, women executives identified three kinds of pressures that complicated their professional advancement: (a) the day-to-day, year-in-year-out demands and hectic pace of executive work (which men also feel); (b) their pioneering role as "first woman executive" and the special need to prove themselves to others; and (c) the strain of meeting family obligations.[14] In other words, these women managers faced all of the normal demands of executive work that men experience plus two additional requirements traceable to their customary roles in society. Having proven managerial talent was not enough. Psychologically, they had to prove themselves the equal of men (or even better). Socially, they found themselves carrying a disproportionate share of family obligations and homemaking responsibilities. These psychological and social brakes can hold back the most skilled and dedicated manager, even in companies where gender bias is at a minimum.

The glass ceiling blocks the rise of women managers, not because they are personally deficient in managing organizations. Their progress is retarded because patriarchical organizational systems, and the discriminatory attitudes they sometimes encourage, tend to favor men over women.[15]

WHAT BUSINESS CAN DO: POLICIES AND STRATEGIES

When women enter the labor force in large numbers, seeking permanent, well-paid, full-time jobs, aspiring to lifelong business careers, and being unwilling to accept a discriminatory double standard that puts and keeps them at a workplace disadvantage, some changes are bound to take place in the way business organizes and conducts its affairs. The three types of changes most needed in business are (a) reforming personnel policies and production policies to assure equal opportunities, (b) providing support programs that make a working life and a family life possible and rewarding for both men and women, and (c) removing sexist attitudes toward working women. Gender bias occurs throughout society, and not just in the workplace, so these business reforms represent only those steps that business itself can take to provide equal workplace opportunities for women.

[14] Morrison et al., op. cit., pp. 15–20.

[15] For an analysis of the glass ceiling problem, see Glenis Joyce, "Training and Women: Some Thoughts from the Grassroots," *Journal of Business Ethics*, vol. 9, 1990, pp. 407–415.

Reforming Personnel Policies and Production Policies

If women are to be treated equally in the workplace, all jobs and occupations must be open to them so that they may compete on the same terms as all others. A company's recruiters need to seek out qualified workers and not assume that women are unqualified. Rates of pay and benefits need to be matched to the work to be done, not to the gender of the jobholder. Pay raises for doing one's present job well, along with promotions to more attractive jobs, also rate equal treatment. Job assignments should be made on the basis of skills, experience, competence, capability, and reliability—in other words, proven ability to get the job done, not whether women have traditionally worked at one task rather than another. Since past gender bias has sometimes prevented women from acquiring as much job experience as men, special training and mentoring support can be provided to offset this temporary disadvantage. All employees—and not just women—need to learn how to cope with and correct on-the-job sex discrimination, so special sensitivity training programs are desirable. Exhibit 16–B describes a company that fits this pattern remarkably well.

EXHIBIT 16–B

HEWITT ASSOCIATES

Hewitt Associates is a leading employee benefits consulting firm, serving an extensive network of corporate clients, including over 70 percent of the *Fortune*-500 companies. Headquartered in a Chicago suburb, Hewitt has a reputation as a desirable place to work. According to *The Best Companies for Women,* sexual harassment and sex discrimination appear to be nonexistent in the company. Of Hewitt's 2,000 employees, 60 percent are women, 10 percent of upper-level managers are women, and women make up 15 percent of the firm's senior partners. About half of those interviewed and hired are female, and the firm is pledged to equal pay for women and men. Family needs of its employees rank high, as shown by the following major benefits:

- Reimbursement for child or parent care when overnight work or travel requires absence from home
- Financial assistance when an employee adopts a child
- Financial support for child care centers near the company's offices
- Information and counseling for expectant parents
- Workshops to help employees balance work and family responsibilities
- Private on-the-job facilities for nursing mothers
- Maternity leave plus two additional weeks beyond
- Up to two years extended maternity leave of absence, with equivalent job guaranteed on return
- Part-time work arrangements and job sharing available
- A consultant to help working parents solve work-and-family problems
- A resource library stocked with books, audio- and videotapes, magazines, and other materials on parenting, child development, child care, elder care, and related family issues

SOURCE: Baila Zeitz and Lorraine Dusky, *The Best Companies for Women,* New York: Simon & Schuster, 1988; and Hewitt Associates newsletters.

Career ladders, whether short ones going only a few steps or longer ones leading into the higher reaches of corporate authority, should be placed so that both men and women can climb them as high as their abilities can carry them.

Providing Support Programs for Work and Family

No other area of business illustrates the basic theme of this book better than the close connection between work and family life. *Our basic theme is that business and society—in this case the family symbolizes society—are closely and unavoidably intertwined, so that what affects one also has an impact on the other.* When large numbers of women began to enter the ranks of business in the 1940s, 1950s, and 1960s, they did not shed their usual roles in society. Women continued to marry and bear children. The customary roles of wife, homemaker, and child-caretaker did not disappear. Women were still expected to be "feminine" even as they filled what had formerly been "masculine" jobs. So when women came to work, they carried more than a lunch pail or a briefcase; they also bundled their customary family roles on their backs.

Study after study has demonstrated that women continue to do more housework than their male partners. Child care, preparing meals, cleaning house, shopping, and other household functions are still seen to be the responsibility of the mother more than the father, even when both parents work full-time. Many women thus work what has been called a "second shift" before and after their paid job. In the 1960s and 1970s women worked a month longer each year in combined job and housework than men did, and later studies show a continuation of the general pattern. A 1989 opinion poll found that the majority of wives and husbands agreed that the wife does most cooking, most housecleaning, and most food shopping. Single women, especially those with young children, enjoy even less home support than those who live with marital partners.[16]

In other words, many women work within a surrounding network of social obligations imposed by tradition. For them and for their employers, business and the family are inseparably intertwined. Men, too, are part of this family-society-business network, being assigned their own distinctive roles to play. But persistent social practices cause women to assume a larger share of work—occurring partly in the workplace and partly at home. This close relationship between family and work presents business with new kinds of challenges and requires changes in customary routines. Some of these are discussed next.

Child care and elder care

The demand for **child care** is enormous and growing. Some 24 million children need daily care, especially the six out of every ten children whose mothers hold jobs. A major source of workplace stress for working parents is concern about their children; for example, almost half of American Express employees who were

[16] See Hochschild, op. cit., especially the Appendix, "Research on Who Does the Housework and Childcare"; and "Women's Gains on the Job: Not Without a Heavy Toll," *New York Times*, Aug. 21, 1989, p. A14.

surveyed admitted that this kind of worry affected their work, and over one-third were absent from their jobs because of child-care problems.[17]

Business has found that child-care programs, in addition to raising employee morale, reducing absenteeism, and improving productivity, also aid recruiting by improving the company's image and helping to retain talented employees. Some socially aware business firms have begun to take needed steps to provide child care for their employees, but they represent only about 14 percent of all U.S. companies. The options include company-operated child-care centers, support for community centers, and participation with other companies in child-care consortia.

Some companies have begun to take an interest in parents-to-be by establishing prenatal-care programs for pregnant employees. Their motive is to lower the company's health-care costs. Sunbeam Appliance Company's prenatal program reduced its employee maternity- and nursery-care medical costs 84 percent in a three-year period; three years earlier just four premature babies born to Sunbeam employees ran up half of the $1 million in health-care costs incurred by all Sunbeam employees.[18]

Other companies have combined child care with **elder care,** since many of today's families must find ways to care for aging parents and other older relatives. Stride Rite Corporation began one of the nation's first intergenerational day-care centers in 1990, saying that "People caring for elder relatives lose as many days of work, four or five a year, as people with young children."[19]

Parental leaves

What was once called a maternity leave has become a **parental leave** or, where care of elderly parents is involved, it is called a **family leave.** Whatever name is used, both parents need time off from work when children are born and during the important early months of the child's physical and emotional development. Many large companies give pregnant employees a paid leave of six to eight weeks, and some of them grant additional unpaid time off and guarantee that the employee will get her job back upon returning to work. Smaller companies do much less for mothers-to-be.

Even fewer companies give the same unpaid job-protection leave to men who become parents, and several studies have demonstrated that men are reluctant to take advantage of parental leave programs. Because men typically make more money than their spouse, taking a long unpaid job leave may work greater financial hardships on a family. Men also fear that being away from the job will interfere with their career. As a result, among married couples, child care and elder care continue to fall mainly on the wife. Reducing salary inequities and breaking down

[17] Richard Levine, "Childcare Inching Up the Corporate Agenda," *Management Review,* January 1989, p. 44. For a status report, see Fern Marx and Michelle Seligson, "Child Care in the United States," in Rix, op. cit., pp. 132–169.

[18] "Corporate Prenatal-Care Plans Multiply, Benefiting Both Mothers and Employers," *Wall Street Journal,* June 24, 1988, p. 17.

[19] *Wall Street Journal,* Feb. 2, 1990, p. A1.

occupational segregation would change this situation and allow family-care responsibilities to be more evenly distributed.[20]

Flextime and part-time employment

Aetna Life & Casualty, one of America's biggest insurance companies, demonstrates the benefits of flexible work scheduling for both company and employees.[21]

> Women make up 70 percent of Aetna's 45,000 employees and nearly two out of every ten Aetna managers, so company officials realized that flexible scheduling would meet the needs of many women employees. In some departments, 40 percent of employees work "flextime" schedules, beginning and quitting at different times of the day. Others share jobs, with each working half a week. Many jobs are held on a part-time basis, leaving the worker time to be at home with children or elderly parents. Several hundred Aetna employees "telecommute"—work with computers—from their homes. Six-week unpaid family leaves are available to expectant mothers. These work patterns help meet family needs without seriously disrupting company routines. As one Aetna official said, "We're not doing it to be nice, but because it makes business sense." The company's family leave program cut employment attrition rates of new mothers in half after just one year.

Aetna was only one corporation introducing these practices. A survey of over 250 corporations revealed that 42 percent had flextime schedules, 36 percent offered part-time work, and 17 percent permitted job sharing.[22]

Two-track career plans

One proposed solution to the stalled executive careers of women calls for companies to create two distinct career paths for its women managers.[23] The "career-primary" path would be for women who put their careers first, who are willing to work an executive's long hours, make the personal sacrifices in their lives, and forego a major role in parenting. These women executives would be treated the same as men executives and given every opportunity to reach the top rungs of the corporate ladder.

The company's "career-and-family" path would be reserved for women "who want to pursue serious careers while participating actively in the rearing of children." This path would not take women into the highest reaches of the corporate chain of command, but, according to its advocates, it would enable many women to lead satisfying professional lives while accepting responsibilities as parents. Companies, too, would benefit by retaining large numbers of highly

[20] Margaret E. Meiers, "The Progress of Parental Leave Policy," *Management Review*, January 1989, pp. 15–17; and Tarl O'Carolan, "Parenting Time: Whose Problem Is It?" *Personnel Administrator*, August 1987, pp. 58–63.

[21] "As Aetna Adds Flextime, Bosses Learn to Cope," *Wall Street Journal*, June 18, 1990, pp. B1, B5.

[22] "Careers Start Giving In to Family Needs," *Wall Street Journal*, June 18, 1990, p. B1.

[23] Felice N. Schwartz, "Management Women and the New Facts of Life," *Harvard Business Review*, January–February 1989, pp. 65–76. For reactions to the original article, see "Management Women: Debating the Facts of Life," *Harvard Business Review*, May–June 1989, pp. 182ff.

talented women managers who might otherwise decide to drop out of the corporate world. Having a career-and-family path would require companies to install the family-support programs, especially child-care centers, flexible work schedules, parental leaves, and others discussed earlier.

Opponents of these "two-track" plans say that they would create an inferior class of women managers, would reinforce the idea that women and not men should have primary responsibility for child care and homemaking, and, by reducing the overall pool of women managers who have potential to reach the top, would leave the executive suite largely in male hands.

Reforming Attitudes in the Workplace

The largest obstacle to equity for working women is conventional attitudes about the place of women in society. Both men and women hold these attitudes. Such views contribute to continued occupational segregation, unequal pay and job opportunities, stymied career paths, and failure of society to draw fully on all of its human resources for productivity and higher living standards. A key problem that symbolizes the need for changed workplace attitudes is **sexual harassment,** which is discussed next.

Sexual harassment

Sexual harassment at work occurs when any employee—woman or man—experiences unwanted and uninvited sexual attention, or when on-the-job conditions are hostile or threatening in a sexual way. It includes both physical conduct—for example, suggestive touching—as well as verbal harassment, such as sexual innuendoes, jokes, or propositions. Women are the target of most sexual harassment. Guidelines issued by the U.S. Equal Employment Opportunity Commission give legal protection to employees.

Harassment can occur whether the targeted employee cooperates or refuses to cooperate. Jobs can be lost or gained by sexual conduct; if such behavior is treated as a requirement or strong expectation for holding a job or getting a promotion, it is clearly a case of unlawful sexual harassment. This kind of sex discrimination is not limited to overt acts of individual coworkers or supervisors; if a company's work climate is blatantly and offensively sexual or intimidating to employees—through prevailing attitudes, bantering, manner of addressing coworkers, lewd photographs, or suggestive behavior—then sexual harassment exists.[24]

Women employees regularly report that sexual harassment is common. From 40 to 90 percent of working women have told researchers that they have been sexually harassed on the job. Managers and supervisors are the most frequent offenders, and female office workers and clerical workers are the main targets.[25]

[24] John P. Kohl and David B. Stephens, "Expanding the Legal Rights of Working Women," *Personnel,* May 1987, p. 48.

[25] The results of several studies are reported in Robert C. Ford and Frank S. McLaughlin, "Sexual Harassment at Work," *Business Horizons,* November–December 1988, p. 17.

EXHIBIT 16–C

CONTROLLING SEXUAL HARASSMENT

Barbara Gutek, an authority on sexual harassment in the workplace, advocates that companies adopt a four-point action program to curb sexual harassment.

1. *Adopt a companywide policy forbidding sexual harassment and communicate it to all employees and others who deal with the company.* Specific actions include orientation of new employees, training films and seminars, posters, a personal statement by top management, and designation of a neutral third party to hear complaints and field questions from employees.

2. *Vigorously investigate all complaints and act on the findings.* Specific actions include giving investigative responsibility to a qualified person who understands the psychological and organizational dimensions of sexual harassment. Follow-up based on the findings is required if the policy is to have meaning for everyone in the company.

3. *Include sexual harassment in performance appraisals of all employees, punishing those who violate company policy.* Treat sexual harassment as a form of unprofessional conduct that lowers the victim's job satisfaction, affects her progress and career in the company, and lowers overall company performance and productivity. Promoting or otherwise rewarding a harasser sends the wrong message about sexual harassment.

4. *Create and reinforce a climate of professional behavior that discourages sexual harassment.* Specific steps include frequent reminders of the importance of acting professionally, alerting employees to professional forms of addressing one another (avoiding "girlie," "doll," and "sweetie," for example), and striving for sex-neutral interchanges when men and women work together.

SOURCE: Adapted from Barbara A. Gutek, *Sex and the Workplace: The Impact of Sexual Behavior and Harassment on Women, Men, and Organizations,* San Francisco, CA: Jossey-Bass, 1985, pp. 173–178.

Like most other problems that confront women in the workplace, sexual harassment stems from customary attitudes about women's functions in society. One expert explains these attitudes as **sex role spillover,** meaning that many men continue to think of women mainly as performing their traditionally defined roles as sex partners, homemakers, and childbearers—and only secondarily as coworkers and qualified professionals. These attitudes "spill over" into the workplace, leading to improper behavior that has no relation to the work to be done. This kind of conduct is most likely to occur where jobs and occupations are sex-segregated and where most supervisors and managers are men.[26]

What can companies do to combat sexual harassment? Exhibit 16–C summarizes four major steps recommended by one authority. The twin keys to success are (a) strong and visible support by a company's top management and (b) making sex-neutral behavior part of the company's reward structure. Only then is there a chance that the company's culture and work climate will begin to encourage attitudes that welcome women as full and equal workers and professionals.

[26] Barbara A. Gutek, *Sex and the Workplace,* San Francisco, CA: Jossey-Bass, 1985, chap. 8.

GOVERNMENT'S ROLE IN SECURING WOMEN'S WORKPLACE RIGHTS

From early in the twentieth century, government laws and regulations—nearly all of them enacted at the state level—were used to protect women from some of the harsh and risky conditions found in factories, mines, construction sites, and other forms of business. These protective laws were adopted on grounds that women were weaker physically than men, that their childbearing powers should be shielded from workplace harms, and that whatever work they performed was generally to supplement family income rather than to be the main breadwinner. However, "protection" often meant being excluded from certain jobs and occupations, thus contributing to occupational segregation and unequal pay. Protective laws, however well-intentioned, put women at a competitive disadvantage in the labor market.

Equal Pay and Equal Opportunity

The idea that women should be paid the same as men has been around for a long time. In the 1860s, for example, male printers demanded that female printers should receive "equal pay for equal work"—mainly so that their own wages would not be depressed by competition from lower-paid women. The same fear that women workers would lower all wage rates was observed during the First and Second World Wars when women took over jobs formerly held by men who were in the armed forces. It was not until 1945 that an Equal Pay Act was introduced in Congress; even then, it was a tactic to defeat or forestall a more comprehensive Equal Rights Amendment to the U.S. Constitution. The Equal Pay Act finally become law in 1963.

One year later, Congress adopted the Civil Rights Act, which prohibits employment discrimination on the basis of race, color, religion, sex, or national origin. When the Civil Rights Law was strengthened in 1972, working women—along with minorities—finally had legal machinery that was more responsive to their quest for workplace equality.[27]

Figure 16–5 outlines the major laws that are intended to promote women's on-the-job opportunities. Executive orders issued by the President require government contractors to take affirmative action to correct workplace discrimination against women and other groups. These equal opportunity laws and regulations are discussed in more detail in Chapter 13.

For more than half a century, an Equal Rights Amendment to the U.S. Constitution has been advocated but never ratified by the necessary number of states. The proposed amendment declares: "Equality of rights under the law shall not be denied or abridged by the United States or any state on account of sex." Congress also has debated (but through early 1991 had failed to enact) the Family

[27] Claudia Goldin, *Understanding the Gender Gap: An Economic History of American Women*, New York: Oxford University Press, 1990, pp. 201–202. The word "sex" was inserted in the 1964 Civil Rights bill, just one day before Congress voted on it, by a congressional opponent who was said to believe that its inclusion would help defeat the bill.

FIGURE 16–5
Major federal laws to protect women's workplace rights.

EQUAL PAY ACT (1963)
Mandates equal pay for equal work

CIVIL RIGHTS ACT (1964)
Forbids sex discrimination in employment

EQUAL EMPLOYMENT OPPORTUNITY ACT (1972)
Increased power of Equal Employment Opportunity Commission to combat sex (and other types of) discrimination

PREGNANCY DISCRIMINATION ACT (1978)
Forbids employers to discharge, fail to hire, or otherwise discriminate against pregnant women

and Medical Leave Act, which would require employers of more than 50 persons to grant up to 12 weeks of unpaid, job-protected leave to employees faced with serious family problems such as the birth or adoption of a child or crisis situations involving child care and elder care.

Comparable Worth

Equal pay for equal work combats pay discrimination within the same job categories within the same firm—for example, providing equal pay rates for men and women carpenters and equal salaries for men and women managers performing identical work. However, it does little to reduce pay inequities when men and women hold different jobs that require approximately equal skills but are paid at unequal rates. Much of the gender pay gap—women earning about two-thirds of men's income on average—occurs because many women are grouped in jobs and occupational categories that are lower-paid than those held by men. Equalizing pay levels in the same job category does nothing about the unequal rates paid to different jobs or occupations. The problem is especially unfair when these different jobs call for about the same degree of skill, effort, and responsibility.

Comparable worth is an attempt to overcome this kind of pay inequity. Jobs are matched with each other in terms of skills, effort, responsibility, and working conditions, and pay is made equal when these factors for the two jobs are about equal or comparable with one another. Figure 16–6 charts the fairness relationships between work and pay, and compares equal pay with comparable worth. As of the early 1990s, pay equity based on comparable worth had been rejected by U.S. federal courts, but some states have laws authorizing comparable worth plans. Both Canada and Great Britain have comparable worth laws that appear to be effective in lessening pay discrimination.[28]

[28] For a description and analysis of Canada's comparable worth laws, see Kenneth A. Kovach and Peter E. Millspaugh, "Comparable Worth: Canada Legislates Pay Equity," *Academy of Management Executive*, May 1990, pp. 92–101. Britain's experience is described in Zafiris Tzannatos, "Narrowing the Gap—Equal Pay in Britain 1970–1986," *Long Range Planning*, April 1987, pp. 69–75.

FIGURE 16–6
Fairness of equal pay and comparable worth.

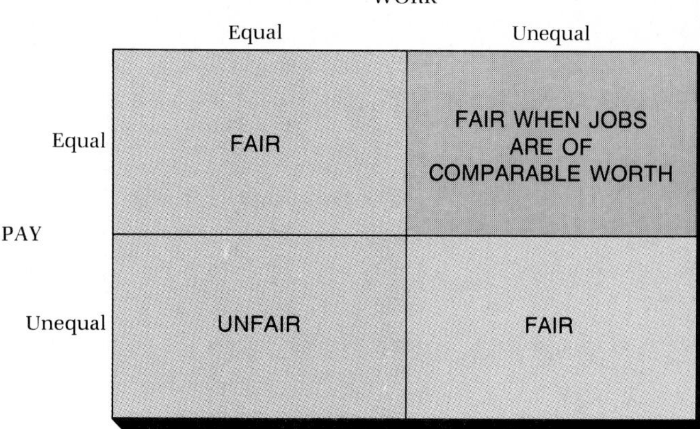

THE GENDER-NEUTRAL CORPORATION

As a desirable goal for both business and society, a gender-neutral corporation would be one that had removed sex discrimination from all aspects of its operations. Job advantages would not be earned or granted on the basis of gender. People would be hired, paid, evaluated, promoted, and extended benefits on the basis of their qualifications and ability to do the tasks assigned. The route to the top, or to satisfaction in any occupational category, would be open to anyone with the talent to reach it. The company's stakeholders, regardless of their gender, would be treated in a bias-free manner. All laws forbidding sex discrimination would be fully obeyed. Where persistent social customs and traditional attitudes outside the workplace continue to burden working women with unequal shares of homemaking, corporate policies and support programs would attempt to compensate for these imbalances. Corporations themselves would then experience a much-desired and much-needed boost in productivity, as the nation's entire range of potential managerial and professional skills—provided by both men and women—becomes available for use.

By adopting these gender-neutral policies, this kind of corporation would embody such ethical principles as social justice and respect for human rights, would express the social responsibilities of enlightened corporate self-interest, would demonstrate the kind of social responsiveness that serves the corporation's stakeholders, and would align itself with currents of social change that have brought the issue of women's rights to the fore in the late twentieth century.

SUMMARY POINTS OF THIS CHAPTER

- Women have entered the workforce in large numbers to gain economic security, to find satisfying work, and to achieve psychological independence.

- Working women encounter job discrimination, including unequal pay, occupational segregation, and negative attitudes, but some gains have been registered in the last half of the twentieth century.
- Traditional attitudes about the place of women in society and in family life exert a persistent negative influence on women who work for pay.
- To provide equal opportunity, corporations need to reform their personnel and production policies, provide family-support programs for their employees, and create positive workplace attitudes about working women.

KEY TERMS AND CONCEPTS USED IN THIS CHAPTER

- Gender pay gap
- Occupational segregation
- The glass ceiling
- Child care and elder care
- Parental leave and family leave
- Sexual harassment
- Sex-role spillover
- Comparable worth

DISCUSSION CASE

REPRODUCTIVE RISK AND EQUAL OPPORTUNITY

"The foreman came up while I was pouring and asked if I could still have children, and I said yes. He had a man right there to take my place." A female worker who poured iron into molds that were turned into engine blocks for General Motors was describing how she was transferred to a lower-paying job at GM's Ohio foundry. She filed grievances through her union representative, claiming job discrimination, and later earned a license to operate a hot-metal crane, only to be barred from holding that job also. Eventually, she was permitted to operate the crane, but the threat of being transferred remained.[29]

The reason for her transfer was a General Motors policy that barred women from working in areas where exposure to lead may endanger health. Lead is known to cause serious problems if absorbed into the body; it can damage the central nervous system, kidneys, the body's immune system, and the reproductive systems of both men and women. A human embryo is especially prone to risk, suffering brain damage that may show up later as behavioral or learning deficits.

GM was not the only company with such a policy. Chemical manufacturers, hospitals, laboratories, tire makers, photographic processors, semiconductor manufacturers, and others—industries using large amounts of toxic compounds—have had similar policies that bar women from working in areas where exposure has potential health consequences. Government agencies estimate that

[29] "Workplace Debate: Businesses and Women Anxiously Watch Suit on 'Fetal Protection,' " *Wall Street Journal,* Oct. 8, 1990, pp. A1, A10.

15 to 20 million jobs in the United States expose workers of both sexes to chemicals that might cause reproductive injury. Some of these compounds are capable of damaging human sperm and causing male infertility and genetic damage.

More than concern for workers' health is involved. Employers fear lawsuits filed by employees claiming health damage either to themselves or to their children.

Two early cases raising these issues occurred in the mid-1970s.[30] American Cyanamid, a lead-based-paint manufacturer in West Virginia, issued a policy giving women of childbearing potential three choices: transfer out of the paint department to jobs with lower pay and loss of job seniority, quit, or be sterilized. At the time, it was believed that eight women could be transferred to other jobs but nine would have to be laid off. Five women chose sterilization. Three months after the policy went into effect, the paint plant closed.

The other firm was Bunker Hill Company, an Idaho mining company that operated a zinc refinery, lead smelter, and fertilizer plant. It barred fertile women employees from working around toxic substances unless they could provide proof of sterilization. At least three women chose sterilization in order to save their jobs. Other women were moved to other departments, causing them to lose their job seniority.

To protest these corporate policies, lawsuits were filed on grounds of sex discrimination. Since only women are targeted by the exclusionary policies and since transfers sometimes result in lost job opportunities, less chance for overtime work, and lower wages, women appear to be treated unequally. Title VII of the Civil Rights Act forbids unequal job treatment. EEOC guidelines issued in 1988 declare that a policy that denies employment opportunities to one sex because of a reproductive hazard, without barring the other sex, is unlawful. Only "business necessity" can justify such a policy; even then, if reasonable alternatives to exclusion exist, a company must use them instead of barring members of just one sex from jobs. In other words, a company's policy must consider reproductive risks to both men and women.[31] To most business firms, "business necessity" has come to mean reducing the company's risk from lawsuits based on workplace injury.

Some women who have been affected by these policies make another point. They say that their privacy has been violated by having very personal matters discussed and made part of the public record. Sterilized women have been harassed by male coworkers who have seen sterilization as a license for promiscuity. Others feel that their employer is being paternalistic and is taking away their autonomy, as well as interfering with a family's right to make its own decisions concerning childbearing.

When Johnson Controls of Milwaukee in 1982 barred women employees from lead-exposure jobs in its fifteen battery plants, the United Automobile Workers

[30] See Donna M. Randall, "An Eclipse of Justice: Policies Regulating Reproductive Health in the Work Place," unpublished manuscript, Washington State University, n.d., and "Fetal Protection Policies: A Threat to Employee Rights?" *Employee Responsibilities and Rights Journal*, vol. 1, 1988, pp. 121–128.

[31] Michael W. Sculnick, "Key Court Cases," *Employment Relations Today*, Spring 1989, pp. 75–79.

union sued, saying that the policy was discriminatory. This lawsuit, which eventually worked its way up to the Supreme Court, became the landmark case that would test the legality of reproductive risk policies in business. In a rare unanimous decision, the high court declared these policies to be a violation of the Civil Rights Act of 1964, as amended. The court's majority opinion said, "Decisions about the welfare of future children must be left to the parents who conceive, bear, support and raise them rather than to the employers who hire those parents. . . . Women as capable of doing their jobs as their male counterparts may not be forced to choose between having a child and having a job." Some of the justices thought that the costs of workplace protections should be considered, along with employers' concerns about fetal safety, and one justice pointed out that other workplace hazards should get as much corrective attention as those endangering reproductive functions.

Following the Johnson Controls decision, businesses were faced with other ways to handle this kind of workplace risk. They could reduce the total amount of the dangerous substances in the workplace instead of removing a few employees from their jobs, thereby giving greater protection to all workers. Substitute materials might used in some but not all industrial applications. Employees could be required to use safety devices, such as breathing masks and protective clothing, to lower the risks. What employers could no longer do legally was to bar women or men from these jobs. The most they could do was to warn employees of the potential risks to themselves and their families.

Discussion Questions

1. Identify the ethical issues that arise in cases like those that have occurred in American Cyanamid, Bunker Hill, and Johnson Controls. How can conflicting rights be reconciled? How can social justice be attained? How can privacy be preserved while also protecting people's on-the-job health?
2. What would be the socially responsible course of action for companies that use hazardous materials and also employ workers who may be at risk from those toxic compounds? Refer to the principles of social responsibility discussed earlier in this book.
3. Was the Supreme Court's decision in the Johnson Controls case fair to business? Should the court have given more weight to the high costs involved in making the workplace safer?
4. Should U.S. corporations with operations in other countries apply this new reasoning about the workplace rights of women to those foreign settings, even though U.S. civil rights laws do not officially apply there (as the Supreme Court ruled in early 1991)? What would be the ethical and socially responsible thing for business to do?

17

Business and Media Relations

Media institutions—television, videocassettes, radio, newspapers, magazines, films, recordings, and books—have become enormously important elements affecting the relationships between business and the general public. Business frequently complains that the media give an inaccurate and unfair view of business, thereby complicating its task of establishing good relationships with its many stakeholders. The media's great powers of communication focus special attention on their social responsibilities to business and the general public.

Key Questions and Chapter Objectives

This chapter focuses on these key questions and objectives:

- In what ways are media institutions critically important to business and society relations?
- What basic economic and financial factors determine the behavior of media in the United States?
- Why is government regulation of the media limited?
- What major social issues are raised by media operations?
- How can corporations develop effective relations with the media?
- What are the social and ethical responsibilities of the media?

"It is a toy, but it it more than a toy: it is a whole new medium, an immensely powerful agent for the dissemination of culture. Eleven million of them have been sold in the United States in just over three years, and by the end of the year they are expected to be in nearly 20 million American homes. Nearly 50 million of the indispensable game cartridges are expected to be sold [in 1989] alone." Most Nintendo players are boys between 8 and 15 years old, who get a steady diet of combat and violence as the Super Mario Brothers bludgeon, karate chop, mace, and slash their way through their enemies. One young player said, "You just want to play it and play it until you beat it. You just get so nervous near the end. You perspire. Your heart rate is way up. Afterwards you just want to drop dead." Many

"Nintendo parents" have set special limitations on the hours their children are exposed to this "powerful agent for the dissemination of culture."[1]

Another kind of image was projected by a Boston television station. A 30-second commercial showed blood oozing from an overturned coffee mug. Urging viewers to boycott Folgers Coffee, actor Ed Asner said, "What it brews is misery and death." The ad's sponsor was Neighbor to Neighbor, a political group, which claimed that Folgers' purchases of coffee beans from El Salvador helped support that nation's bloody civil war. Procter & Gamble (P&G), Folgers' owner, calling the spot "defamatory and destructive," canceled advertisements for all of its products at the television station, and allegedly instructed its advertising agencies it would do the same for other stations that ran the commercial. The cancellation was estimated to cost the Boston station nearly $1 million in lost revenue. The president of the American Association of Advertising Agencies said, "Normally, we deplore an advertiser's effort to use their clout to influence television content. But this advertising was exaggerated and hysterical." A former television executive, referring to P&G's huge advertising outlays, said, "If you spend a billion and a half on advertising, you shouldn't use that as a lever. It's a misuse of power."[2]

Other television images are positive. Speaking as a paraplegic, an editor of magazines for disabled people said, "It's really only come into its own this last year or two." He was referring to an increasing number of televised advertisements featuring the disabled, adding, "I think there's a lot of room for improvement." Nike was spending 20 percent of its fall 1989 advertising money on commercials showing an Olympic bronze medalist working out and shooting baskets—from a wheelchair. Levi Strauss, McDonald's, Apple Computer, IBM, Citicorp, and other blue-chip corporations have put handicapped people in their television ads. They were following the lead of some popular television shows that have included a retarded person and a person with Down's syndrome. A McDonald's representative said, "People who are physically or mentally challenged are part of life. All those folks are our customers, and we're happy to have them."[3]

These three episodes demonstrate what is meant when people say that the media have great power to influence their audiences. Nintendo is a constant companion to many children, repeatedly exposing them to violent ways of accomplishing their goals. P&G reacted quickly to the damage it believed the coffee ad would do to its corporate reputation—and then demonstrated how its own advertising budget could be used to influence the offending station. And corporate advertisers, by featuring disabled people in their television advertisements, were sending a needed message to the general public that handicapped people are, as McDonald's said, "part of life."

This chapter takes a deeper look at the media, what role they play in shaping the public's view of life, why these particular forms of business have such special social and ethical responsibilities, and how corporations can develop policies

[1] "The Nintendo Kid," *Newsweek*, Mar. 6, 1989, pp. 64–68.

[2] Zachary Schiller and Mark Landler, "P&G Can Get Mad, Sure, but Does It Have to Get Even?" *Business Week*, June 4, 1990, p. 65.

[3] "Disabled People Featured in More Ads," *Wall Street Journal*, Sept. 7, 1989, p. B4.

and strategies that improve their interactions with the media and with a society that is so strongly influenced by media messages.

An overview of the major media institutions, their goals, and how they are regulated is followed by a discussion of the most important social and ethical issues raised by media operations. Because of television's central importance, the discussion emphasizes its role.

THE MEDIA—AN OVERVIEW

The **media,** taken together, create a vast communication network responsible for sending millions of messages to the public on a daily basis. The media assume many forms, as shown in Figure 17–1. Most people have multiple, overlapping media exposure because they view television, read daily newspapers, listen to the radio, view videotapes, subscribe to magazines, read books, attend the theater, see films, and enjoy listening to a wide range of musical recordings.

Television broadcasting on a commercial scale in the United States began shortly after the Second World War. It became enormously popular during the 1950s and is now the premier medium of mass communication in the United States and throughout much of the world. By the early 1990s, 98 percent of U.S. homes—a total of 92 million "TV homes"—had at least one television set, and over 56 million had two or more sets.[4] Television sets outnumber refrigerators and bathrooms in these homes.

Figure 17–2 shows average television viewing time. The average U.S. citizen sees about twenty hours of television programming each week, and the television set in an average home was on for seven hours each day in 1988.

Popular television programs reach into millions of homes. Figure 17–3 lists the ten most watched television programs over a 30-year period, plus the ten favorite programs in 1988. While viewing these programs, millions of people are simultaneously sharing the images, viewpoints, and emotions—whether fictional, factual, or commercial—projected onto their television screens. Television's ability to touch the lives of its viewers, perhaps briefly through a single program or through sustained average viewing time, is of great significance in the media world. Media researchers have known from early in the television age that intertwining sight and sound in the convenience of one's home reaches and affects more people more effectively and more lastingly than other media forms. Extended widely enough throughout the world, television may be potentially capable of creating a "global village" based on widely shared understandings and common perceptions.[5]

[4] *World Almanac, 1990,* New York: Newspaper Enterprise Association, 1990, p. 368; and *Standard & Poor's Industry Survey,* October 1990, p. L27.

[5] This point was first made by Marshall McLuhan, *Understanding Media: The Extensions of Man,* 2d ed., New York: McGraw-Hill, 1964.

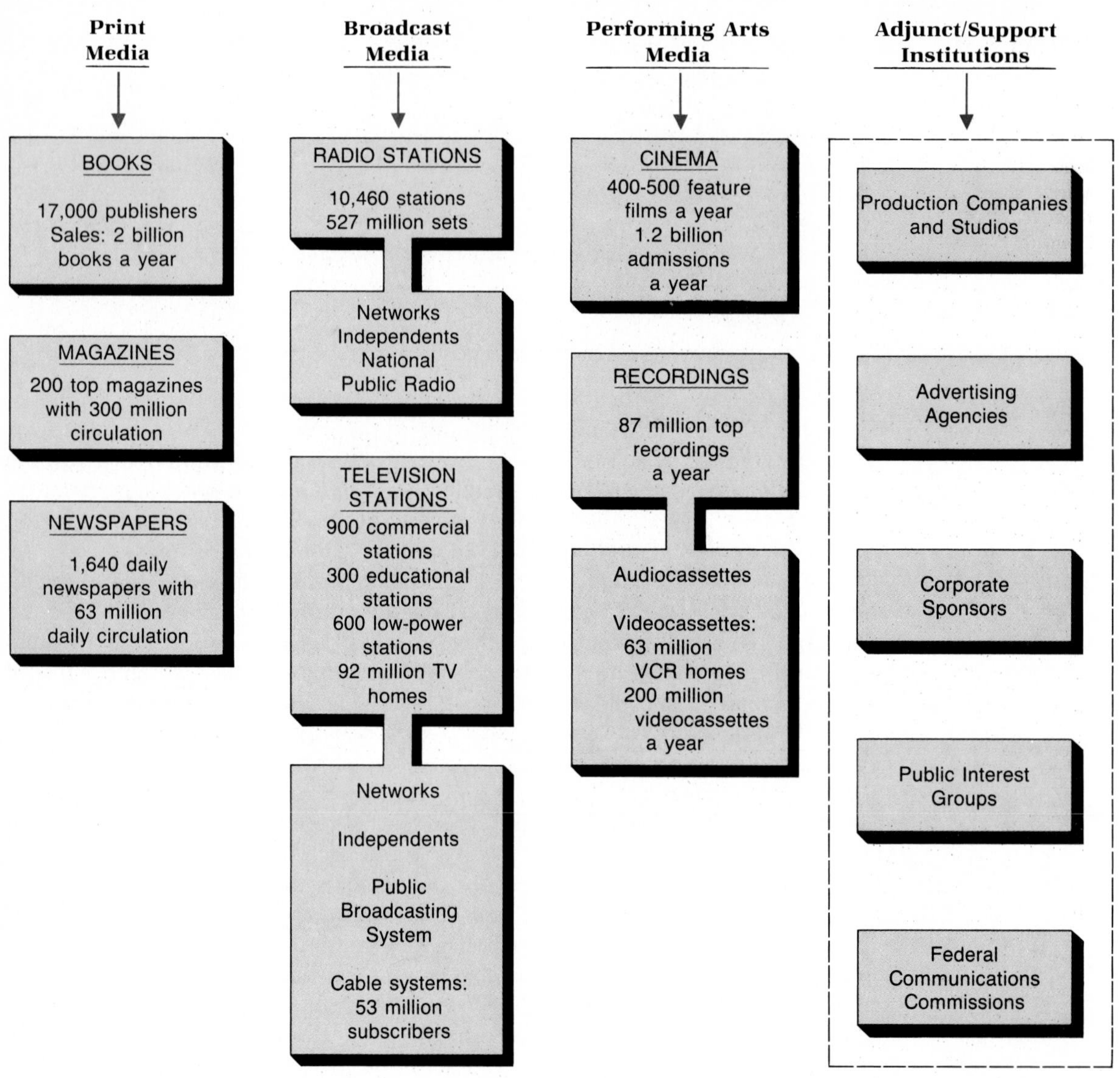

FIGURE 17–1
Major types of media in the United States.

MEDIA BUSINESS IN THE UNITED STATES

Media operations and behavior can best be understood by realizing that they are private businesses pursuing profit goals. To make a profit, they must find and serve an audience that is willing and able to buy and receive the media's messages. Without such a receptive market, no media business can make a profit or continue to operate. As Forrest Sawyer, a network news correspondent, stated, "A central

FIGURE 17–2
Average television viewing time in the United States.

SOURCE: *World Almanac, 1990,* New York: Newspaper Enterprise Association, 1989, p. 369.

Viewing Group	Hours, Minutes per Week
Average, all persons	19:53
Women, 18 years and older	24:02
Men, 18 years and older	18:52
Teenagers, female, ages 12 to 17	15:14
Teenagers, male, ages 12 to 17	15:08
Children, ages 2 to 5 years	20:42
Children, ages 6 to 11 years	16:23

fact about television is that, except for public broadcasting, which exists through charitable contributions, television is a money-making business. This is a fact with which we have to live. Television is a profit center, and it is shaped by the bottom line."[6]

The ways of finding and keeping that audience vary among the media.

- Book publishers, record companies, and video- and audiocassette makers generally sell to the customer through retail outlets and through book and record clubs. The source of their income is the sales price of the product.
- Other media—radio, television, newspapers, and magazines—rely heavily on advertising revenues for their income, and that tends to be the key to finding and keeping an audience. *Their programs or the content of their magazines and newspapers must attract and hold an audience long enough for advertisers to get their commercial messages across to potential customers.* Newspapers and some magazines receive significant revenues from subscriptions and newsstand sales but remain heavily dependent on advertising for their financial stability.

Media enterprises tend to be large, with lucrative earnings, as shown in Figure 17–4. Several of these U.S. companies are among the largest in the nation. Their earnings run into billions of dollars. The electronic media—especially radio and television—are capable of reaching far beyond regional and national boundaries. Media ownership is increasingly global in scope, reflecting both technological capability and the financial goals of media companies. Australian-born Rupert Murdoch's News Corp, consisting of several television stations, newspapers, and magazines, is perhaps the best example of media ownership extending across national boundaries. Similar developments are predicted for the media in European Common Market nations as they draw closer together economically. Even though the globalization of the media industry spotlights large companies, not all media companies are big. Some of them, such as local newspapers or specialized magazines, serve relatively small markets or audiences.

[6] "Realities of Television Programming," in Stuart Oskamp (ed.), *Television as a Social Issue,* Newbury Park, CA: Sage, 1988, p. 30.

FIGURE 17–3
Most popular U.S. television programs.

SOURCE: *World Almanac, 1990,* New York: Newspaper Enterprise Association, 1989, pp. 368–369.

THE TEN MOST POPULAR TELEVISION PROGRAMS 1960–1989

	Year	Network	Households
M*A*S*H Special	1983	CBS	50,150,000
Super Bowl XX	1986	NBC	41,490,000
Dallas	1980	CBS	41,470,000
Super Bowl XVII	1983	NBC	40,480,000
Super Bowl XXI	1987	CBS	40,030,000
Super Bowl XVI	1982	CBS	40,020,000
Super Bowl XIX	1985	ABC	39,390,000
Super Bowl XXIII	1989	NBC	39,320,000
Super Bowl XVIII	1984	CBS	38,800,000
ABC Theater (The Day After)	1983	ABC	38,550,000

TOP TEN REGULARLY SCHEDULED NETWORK PROGRAMS, 1988		TOP TEN SYNDICATED PROGRAMS 1988	
Show	Percent TV Households	Show	Percent TV Households
Bill Cosby Show	27.2	Wheel of Fortune	17.0
A Different World	24.7	Jeopardy	14.3
Roseanne	24.0	Cosby Show	12.1
60 Minutes	23.8	Oprah Winfrey Show	11.8
Cheers	23.2	Star Trek Next Generation	10.4
Murder, She Wrote	23.1	PM Magazine	9.3
Golden Girls	23.0	Current Affairs	8.5
Who's the Boss?	21.7	Entertainment Tonight	8.0
Empty Nest	20.2	Donahue	7.9
CBS Sunday Movie	19.5	Family Feud	7.9

Television as a Business

Television advertising has made the commercial sponsor—usually a business firm—an inevitable and unavoidable fact of television life, as noted by one experienced industry participant:

> "The television sponsor has become semi-mythical. He is remote and unseen, but omnipresent. Dramas, football games, press conferences pause for a 'word' from him.

FIGURE 17–4
Selected media companies, cable channels, and cable system operators.

SOURCE: *Fortune*, June 4, 1990, pp. 304, 386; *Standard & Poor's, Industry Survey*, Leisure Section, October 1990, p. L27, and Media Section, p. M32.

SELECTED U.S. MEDIA COMPANIES

Company	Types of Media	1989 Sales (billions)
Time Warner	Magazines, books, films, cable TV, records, home video, TV programming	$7.6
Paramount	Films, TV, home video, books	5.9
Capital Cities/ABC	Network TV and radio, TV and radio stations, cable TV programming, newspapers, books, periodicals, data bases	5.1
Walt Disney	Motion pictures, home video, Disney Channel	4.7
Gannett	Newspapers, TV and radio stations, outdoor advertising	3.5
MCA	Films and programs for TV, home video, theater, books	3.5
Times Mirror	Newspapers, books, cable TV	3.5
CBS	Network TV and radio, TV and radio stations, records, music video, magazines, books, software, data bases	2.9

TOP FIVE CABLE CHANNELS, 1989–1990
Number of Subscribers

Basic Service		Pay Service	
ESPN	54.8 million	HBO	17.0 million
CNN	52.6 million	Showtime	6.6 million
TBS	51.0 million	Cinemax	6.6 million
USA	50.8 million	Disney Channel	4.3 million
C-Span	47.5 million	The Movie Channel	2.7 million

TOP FIVE CABLE SYSTEM OPERATORS, 1989
Numbers of Subscribers

TCI	6.2 million
ATC	4.1 million
UA Entertainment	2.6 million
Continental	2.4 million
Warner	1.6 million

> He 'makes possible' concerts and public affairs broadcasts. His 'underwriting grants' bring you folk festivals and classic films. Interviews with visiting statesmen are interrupted for him, to continue 'in a moment.' . . .
>
> "A vast industry has grown up around the needs and wishes of sponsors. Its program formulas, business practices, ratings, demographic surveys have all evolved in ways to satisfy sponsor requirements.
>
> ". . . sponsorship is basic to American television."[7]

Advertisers spend about $27 billion annually for television commercials. The programs they underwrite must attract a large viewing audience if these expenditures are to be justified. This necessity puts television stations and production companies on notice. If they wish to sell advertising time, their presentations must appeal to the broadest range of desires and interests to be found in the general consuming public. Attracting mass audiences requires a mass appeal. Programs that cater to highly specialized interests run the risk of being turned off by most viewers. A CBS vice president made the point this way: "[T]elevision being a mass medium, [we] need to search for creative concepts that cut across demographic boundaries. . . . [A] mass medium cannot possibly satisfy all the audience's tastes all of the time. In this age of diversity and competition among media, the role of fully satisfying narrower interests must fall mainly to other media."[8] Some critics of the television industry say that the unfortunate result of commercial sponsorship is programming that caters to the widest and lowest common denominator of public taste.

Figure 17–5 graphically depicts the flow of advertising through the main segments of the U.S. television system. Broadcasting stations depend very largely on production companies to create the kinds of programs listed in Figure 17–3. Other production firms may design and produce commercials. As they develop programs and ad ideas, these production companies work directly with advertising agencies who provide ideas and general themes they want to feature in their clients' ads. The ad agencies, in turn, identify the type of audience suitable for the advertiser's product and encourage the creation of programs and commercials that will attract that kind of viewer. In effect, the ad agency is the channel of influence from the corporate advertiser to the program and ad designers. This influence is possible because it is the corporate client whose money is the ultimate source of funding for the programs and the advertisements produced. The commercial broadcasting station earns revenues by selling time slots for the presentation of these advertisements. The final step occurs when the programs and commercials are beamed to the viewing public.

The financial payoff is very large for successful programming that effectively targets the desired audience. A one-point increase in a television network's prime-time rating scale can add from $75 million to $100 million in pretax profits to the broadcaster.[9]

[7] Erik Barnouw, *The Sponsor: Notes on a Modern Potentate*, New York: Oxford University Press, 1978, pp. 3, 4.

[8] Donald D. Wear, Jr., "Constraints on the Television Industry," in Oskamp, op. cit., pp. 53, 54.

[9] "CBS Cancels Half of New Shows as Network Remains in Last Place," *Wall Street Journal*, Dec. 14, 1988, p. B6.

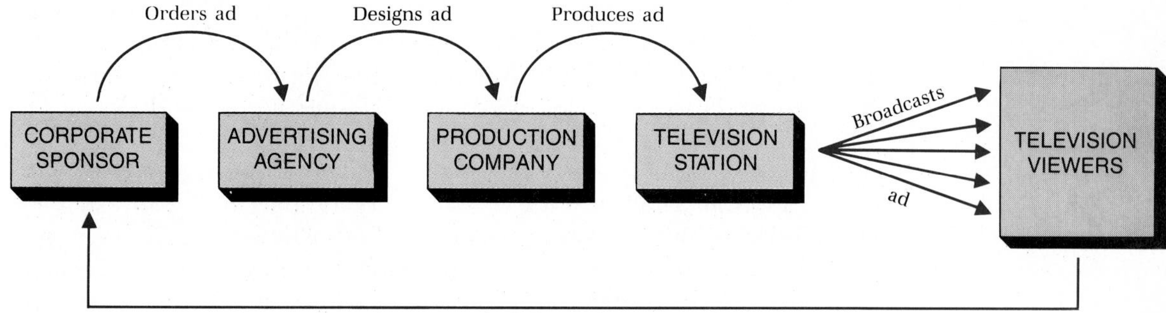

FIGURE 17–5
Flow of advertising through the U.S. commercial television system.

Cable television depends less on advertising revenue than the major networks do, because so much of its revenue comes from viewer subscriptions. In 1988, cable generated less than 5 percent of television advertising dollars, although the volume increased sharply during the 1980s.[10]

Government Regulation of Television

U.S. Constitutional guarantees of free speech and a free press, which are discussed later in this chapter, place important limits on government regulation of television. The main regulatory agency is the Federal Communications Commission.

Federal Communications Commission

This agency (FCC) was created in 1934 to regulate radio broadcasting, and its powers were extended later to include television broadcasting. However, the FCC was specifically forbidden by the Federal Communications Act of 1934 to censor broadcast programs. While it cannot dictate program content, the FCC does have some power over the orderly day-to-day operation of stations; it makes certain that they operate in accordance with "public interest, convenience, and necessity." Since broadcast channel space is limited in any given geographic region, the FCC oversees the granting of broadcast licenses and supervises the renewal or revocation of these licenses. Additional FCC powers do exist, such as the following ones.

Programming control

- Restrictions are placed upon broadcast programs that are considered to be indecent, obscene, or profane. For example, the use of profane four-letter words or the description of explicit sexual functions or activities has been restricted by the FCC. Much controversy occurs when these regulations are imposed because broadcasters usually argue that their constitutional rights of free speech are threatened or denied by such restrictions.

[10] *Standard & Poor's Industry Surveys*, Media Section, Jan. 11, 1990, p. M-15.

- The "prime-time access rule" was adopted by the FCC in the 1970s. It requires network stations in the fifty largest TV markets to allow one hour of programming to originate from local stations. During early evening hours the intention is to encourage creative local programming and to give independent producers a market for their programs.
- Another programming regulation governs broadcast time devoted to candidates for political office. If the views of one candidate are broadcast, then all competing candidates must be permitted equal time to reply. Newscasts and news interviews are exempted from this rule, as are political debates between candidates. Broadcast stations also must allow candidates running for federal elective offices—the Senate, the House of Representatives, and the Presidency—the right to purchase time to broadcast their political messages. (Contrast this requirement with the situation found in some totalitarian nations where government-owned media monopolize the airwaves and do not permit opposition political candidates any access to the media.)
- The fairness doctrine that deals with on-air presentations of controversial issues of public importance is discussed later in this chapter.
- The Children's Television Act of 1990 limits the amount of commercial advertising shown during children's television programs to no more than 10.5 minutes per hour on weekends and no more than 12 minutes per hour on weekdays. This law was adopted to protect impressionable young viewers from excessive exposure to advertising. The legislation also created a National Endowment for Children's Educational Television to encourage the development of more educational television programs for children.

Competitive and ownership safeguards

- Major television networks may not own cable systems but can invest in cable channels. The goal is to reduce the potential for media control by a few large networks.
- No person, group, or company may own more than 12 commercial television stations, and those stations' programs may not reach more than 25 percent of U.S. viewers. The idea is to encourage competition among larger numbers of media firms.
- No company is permitted to own both a newspaper and a television station or radio station in the same city. The goal of this cross-ownership rule is to protect the people in one city against monopoly control of media information. Critics of the rule argue that the proliferation of cable channels, independent television stations, satellite dishes, and electronic data services makes it impossible for a single company to dominate news coverage.
- Foreign ownership of U.S. broadcast facilities is prohibited. This rule caused Rupert Murdoch, the Australian media magnate, to obtain U.S. citizenship so that his News Corp firm could purchase a group of U.S. television stations.
- Following widespread complaints about rising cable television rates and unresponsive service, congressional committees in 1990 initiated legislation

to reregulate some aspects of cable broadcasting and encourage greater competition in the industry.

CRITICAL MEDIA ISSUES

The nature, size, and influence of the media have created several pivotal and highly controversial issues. All of these issues raise questions about business's social and ethical responsibilities. They do so in two ways. As discussed earlier, the media themselves are businesses, and they are expected to adhere to the same social responsibility principles that apply to all other businesses. The same is true of companies that buy advertising time in the media for their commercial messages and the advertising agencies and production companies that design and produce the ads. They are not exempt from social and ethical obligations to the general public. Perhaps in no other area of business and society relationships does it become so clear that business actions and policies can have such an enduring and significant impact on the quality of life and on a society's fundamental values. Four of the most critical media issues are discussed next.

The Image Issue

The **image issue** is about the way people and social groups, including business, are depicted by the media.

Although all media are capable of projecting false or misleading images of people and social groups, much of the criticism is directed at television. As one authority said of television entertainment, "These shows are registries of symbols, central bulletin boards on which the looks of social types get posted."[11] The following examples illustrate some of the problems.

Media images of business

One of business's strongest complaints about the media is that business activities and business people frequently are portrayed in unflattering, negative ways. For example, the Media Institute studied 200 episodes from the top fifty entertainment programs during the 1979–1980 television season and reported that two out of three TV businesspeople were portrayed as foolish, greedy, or criminal. Over half of all corporate chiefs in these programs committed illegal acts ranging from fraud to murder.[12]

Prime-time television programs such as *Dallas* present business executives as ruthless, greedy, and self-centered with little or no social conscience. Only rarely

[11] Todd Gitlin, "The Image of Business on Prime Time Television," *California Management Review*, Winter 1984, p. 64.

[12] Leonard J. Theberge (ed.), *Crooks, Conmen and Clowns: Businessmen in TV Entertainment*, Washington, DC: The Media Institute, 1981.

are business leaders shown to be engaged in socially useful or economically productive activities.

Ironically, the media images of business that appear in entertainment programs are designed and produced by business, paid for by other businesses whose ads make the programs possible, and broadcast by media companies that are themselves businesses.

Some companies have fought back when shown in a negative light by media presentations.

> Illinois Power was one such company. It was featured in a *60 Minutes* program that emphasized cost overruns in the construction of nuclear power plants, especially in a plant being built by Illinois Power. The company claimed that the *60 Minutes* presentation was grossly unfair and damaging to the company's reputation. A public affairs official said, "The show was simply devastating to us. . . . We began getting hate telephone calls minutes after the broadcast. The next day, Monday, more than three times as many shares of our stock were traded in a single day than ever before, and the stock price dropped by more than one dollar. And our employee morale hit rock bottom. We knew we had to do something, and fast."[13]
>
> Fortunately, the company had made its own videotapes as *60 Minutes* interviewed its executives. It used these tapes and additional facts taken from official government records to answer the *60 Minutes* charges. Entitled "60 Minutes/Our Reply," it compared what was shown on network television with the actual films made of the interviews. One *60 Minutes* interview that lasted ninety minutes was edited to show only two-and-one-half minutes that told Illinois Power's side of the story. Several statements *60 Minutes* made about the company and its cost structure were revealed by the full videotape to be false and misleading. The Illinois Power videotape was widely distributed and became a well-known symbol of corporate efforts to offset negative and unfavorable media images of business.

Media images of other groups

Numerous research studies have shown that U.S. women are numerically underrepresented in television programming, are shown mainly in roles as wives and/or parents more than as professionals, are depicted as more emotional than men, subordinated to men, and less likely to control events in their lives than men are. A United Nations survey of television content in 95 countries concluded that "the media's portrayal of women . . . is narrow, at worst it is unrealistic, demeaning and damaging."[14]

African-Americans have long criticized films, radio, and television for ignoring blacks almost entirely or for presenting negative images of black behavior. During the 1950s and 1960s, black people were rarely seen on television and practically

[13] Quoted in Frank M. Corrado, *Media for Managers: Communications Strategy for the Eighties*, Englewood Cliffs, NJ: Prentice-Hall, 1984, p. 86.

[14] Bradley S. Greenberg, "Some Uncommon Television Images and the Drench Hypothesis," Oskamp, op. cit., pp. 88–93.

never in commercials. Later, when they began to appear, the characters they played tended to reflect traditional racial stereotypes. Black actors appeared less frequently than whites, and the roles they played were minor and involved less time on screen than others. Only in the 1980s did black superstars—such as Michael Jackson, Bill Cosby, Oprah Winfrey, and Tina Turner—emerge in significant numbers.

Hispanic Americans, the fastest-growing ethnic group in the United States, are only marginally visible to national television audiences, and one study said Hispanic men were usually "cast as funny, crooked, or cops."[15] Helping to offset this negative image are the several Spanish-language television stations in large urban centers whose programming includes Hispanic cultural content and truer and more positive images.

Most observers agree that the greatest harm done by negative social stereotypes and images is their influence on children, whose values, attitudes, and understanding of life are significantly influenced by television, films, and radio. A study sponsored by Action for Children's Television made the following observation: "As a representation of some of the real changes taking place in the status of women in society, children's television provides a distorted mirror, with outdated models for young children. Commercial children's television can only be seen as a major barrier in the battle for recognition of and respect for ethnic groups in this country.[16]

The Values Issue

The **values issue** is about the power of the media to shape social attitudes and values.

The values issue is closely related to the image issue just discussed, but more is involved because values are one of the basic determinants of human behavior and social attitudes. Most of us acquire our values from early family experiences, from observing and imitating the behavior of friends and authority figures (parents, teachers, and other role models), and from the trial-and-error process of growing up and learning to live with other people. The media, especially records, tapes, radio, films, and television, are now recognized as new value-shaping forces in society. That gives them an importance that goes far beyond their ability to inform, to entertain, and to promote the sale of goods and services. As a value source, the electronic media tend to act as parent, school, church, peers, and Ann Landers all rolled into one. In the Television Age, that little screen defines for millions of viewers "what life is all about."[17]

Materialism is one value that gets a big boost from the media. Commercial messages bombard listeners, viewers, and readers with opportunities to live "the

[15] Ibid., pp. 94–97.

[16] F. Earle Barcus, *Images of Life on Children's Television: Sex Roles, Minorities, and Families,* New York: Praeger, 1983, pp. xiii, 65, 114, 115.

[17] See Richard Collins et al. (eds.), *Media, Culture and Society: A Critical Reader,* Newbury Park, CA: Sage, 1986.

good life" if only they will buy the advertised products. As one television beer ad put it, "It doesn't get any better than this." Another one urged the audience to hurry and buy its brand of beer because "You only go around once." A dazzling array of goods and services, including luxury cars, exotic vacation trips, stylish clothing, expensive appliances, and cash prizes, are regularly shown and won during contest shows. The effect (and purpose) of this steady drumbeat of material display is to attract a viewing audience and to stimulate consumer demand for these and similar goods and services. While the media do not necessarily *initiate* or *begin* the cycle of consumer materialism—which, as noted previously, is probably a combination of family influence, peer pressure to conform, and learning the traditional pathways to adulthood in our society—the media surely encourage and support the value of material consumption. Their programs, films, and commercial images show materialism to be a desirable social value, embraced by those who have succeeded in life.[18]

But more than materialism is involved. It is possible that other values can be inculcated or reinforced through the media. Violence as a way of solving a problem is one. The relationship between televised violence and behavior remains a controversial subject, but most studies report a connection between viewing television violence and acting out aggressive behavior. Not all children are susceptible to this kind of influence; researchers have concluded that TV violence has a large effect on a small percentage of child viewers but only a small effect on a large percentage of children. Some cases have been recorded of children and adults committing crimes of violence after seeing similar acts in television shows. Studies also have revealed that the rate of teenage suicides increases following television presentations about suicide, even when the programs are an attempt to prevent such suicides by encouraging public discussion of the issue.[19]

Since the media apparently can influence the acceptance and acting out of aggression, as well as other values that are objectionable as well as desirable, what can or should business do about it? Some business executives and their companies take a very strong stand on this issue.

> An example is Mars, the candy manufacturer, that was reported in 1989 to have given its ad agencies a list of some 50 television shows and told them not to run ads on them. The company apparently believed the programs were offensive and in bad taste. A Mars spokesperson said the company "will associate itself only with advertising vehicles which reflect the corporation's principles and our responsibilities as a good corporate citizen." The unacceptable areas were ethnic, racial, and other stereotypes, superfluous violence, explicit sexual behavior, drug abuse, and endorsement of "anti-family, anti-religious, or anti-social behavior." Other companies, including Hardee's Food Systems, have taken similar stands.[20]

Aware of the value-shaping power of television, some educational groups have experimented with programs that teach socially acceptable "prosocial" values

[18] Gitlin, op. cit., pp. 64–73.

[19] For a survey of current research, see Oskamp, op. cit., part III, Television Violence, chaps. 14–18.

[20] "Advertisers Draw Up TV Boycott Lists," *Wall Street Journal*, June 21, 1989, p. B4.

and attitudes. The popular children's programs *Sesame Street* and *Mr. Rogers' Neighborhood* are examples. However, some critics argue that television should not be used deliberately to socialize children because the "systematic use of television entertainment to influence children is undoubtedly a subtle but effective type of brainwashing. Now that we *can* harness the potential power of television to influence children, the question of whether we *will* remains." On the other hand, it can be argued that commercial television already does shape values, and since it is not possible to be neutral about values, the real question is *which* values should be promoted.[21]

The Fairness and Balance Issue

The **fairness and balance issue** is about how the news media report events, particularly business activities that are being discussed in this chapter.

The Media Institute, a probusiness organization that analyzes media treatment of the news, has charged that television coverage of business news is generally unfair to business and does not give viewers enough information to make rational decisions about controversial issues such as nuclear power, oil spills, and product recalls. An example was described by another observer when a Senate subcommittee held hearings on the oil industry and oil imports:

> For seven days the committee heard what a Texaco spokesman termed "anti-industry" witnesses. These witnesses were extensively covered by the [*Washington*] *Post*. [Then] the pro-industry witnesses were heard. Not a single line of their testimony was reported. The score for the *Washington Post* was: anti-industry days, 300 lines; pro-industry days, 0. The business newspaper, *The Wall Street Journal*, ran only one story on the entire hearing, which covered thirteen days.[22]

One reason for inadequate media business reports, which is acknowledged by many media people, is that few reporters are well trained in financial and business matters.

Another reason sometimes given is that most journalists tend to be liberal in their social and political outlook, although this point is disputed by others. One national survey of journalists and business executives found that half of the journalists identified themselves as liberal while 70 percent of the executives classified themselves as conservative. Sixty-one percent of journalists expressed a preference for the Democratic Party, and 87 percent of executives preferred the Republican Party. In the presidential elections of 1972, 1976, and 1980, large majorities of journalists voted for Democratic candidates, while business executives voted overwhelmingly for the Republican candidates.[23]

[21] The quotation is from Robert E. Liebert et al., *The Early Window: Effects of Television on Children and Youth*, 2d ed., New York: Pergamon, 1982, chap. 7. Another good discussion is Oskamp, Part IV: Prosocial Values and Television, op. cit., pp. 215–280.

[22] Scott M. Cutlip, "The Media and the Corporation: A Matter of Perception and Performance," in Craig E. Aronoff (ed.), *Business and the Media*, Santa Monica, CA: Goodyear, 1979, p. 139.

[23] Fred J. Evans, "Management and the Media: Is Accord in Sight?" *Business Forum*, Spring 1984, p. 18. A thoughtful discussion of this kind of media bias is Ronald Berman, *How Television Sees Its Audience*, Newbury Park, CA: Sage, 1987, chap. 5, National News.

However, the question of media bias is a complex one. One well-respected study of representative households in the United States demonstrated that three out of five people believe the news media are biased in their treatment of business. But of those who thought the media are biased, half said the media are biased *in favor* of business and half believed the media are biased *against* business. People who were already favorably disposed toward business tended to see media bias against business, while those seeing bias in favor of business began with an unfavorable attitude toward business.[24]

Corporate lawbreaking, which encourages people to hold negative views of business, is given much attention by network television news programs. For example, 40 percent of a representative sample of news broadcasts from 1974 to 1984 included at least one story on corporate crime. Some studies have revealed that "television broadcasts give greater emphasis to bad news than neutral or positive news about business." Research on media coverage of wrongdoing by large oil companies showed that the seriousness of the crime determined whether it would be reported, not simply whether the company was large or had a previous record of lawbreaking. Not surprisingly, the *Wall Street Journal* gave proportionately less coverage to oil companies' illegal behavior than network newscasts, but this leading business newspaper published a greater number of articles on corporate wrongdoing than either magazines or broadcast stations did.[25]

Even though media representatives may square off against business on specific issues, they do not question the fundamental principles of free enterprise. As noted in one study of newspaper business editors:

> The newspaper business editors surveyed are not only positively disposed toward capitalism in an absolute sense; as a group they are more favorably disposed toward capitalism than is the general public. . . . [T]he generalized perception that the news media are biased against business (and capitalism) is probably too simplistic and requires further research and refinement.[26]

The Fairness Doctrine

As one way of trying to assure that all sides of an issue are made available to the public, the FCC developed the **fairness doctrine.** Its rules required broadcasters who air controversial topics of broad public interest to give opponents an opportunity to respond. It also permitted a person who is attacked or criticized in the media an opportunity to reply. This rule is not the same as the "equal access" rule discussed earlier, which requires political candidates to be given equal media time to promote their views to the voting public.

[24] Robert A. Peterson et al., "Perceptions of Media Bias toward Business," *Journalism Quarterly,* Autumn 1982, pp. 461–464.

[25] Donna M. Randall, "The Portrayal of Corporate Crime in Network Television Newscasts," *Journalism Quarterly,* vol. 64, no. 1, pp. 150–153, 250; and Donna Randall and Robert DeFillippi, "Media Coverage of Corporate Malfeasance in the Oil Industry," *Social Science Journal,* vol. 24, no. 1, 1987, pp. 31–42.

[26] Robert A. Peterson et al., "Attitudes of Newspaper Business Editors and the General Public toward Capitalism," *Journalism Quarterly,* Spring 1984, p. 65.

The fairness doctrine has been used by opponents of nuclear power to tell their side of the story after programs favorable to nuclear power plants have been broadcast. Stations also have been required to provide broadcast time to consumer groups who opposed media-advertised rate increases for public utilities. The idea in all such cases is to give the listening or viewing public both sides of an issue of public importance so they can make up their minds without unbalanced influence from the interested parties.

The broadcasting industry has opposed the fairness doctrine as an unwarranted restriction of their First Amendment free-speech rights of expression. The original reason for the doctrine was the need to prevent a handful of licensed stations from abusing their power to influence the public. But opponents say that this condition no longer exists, because greater numbers of stations and an increasing diversity of broadcast technology now bring many diverse points of view of the public. As one veteran observer of the industry said, "Just count the number of newspapers in your city and compare it to the number of cable channels on your TV set. . . . If a broad exchange of views is your goal, it had better be done on television."[27] Still others say that the doctrine actually diminishes the amount of broadcast time devoted to important public issues because stations know they will be forced to provide opponents an opportunity to reply.

In the deregulation climate of the 1980s, the head of the FCC advocated elimination of the fairness doctrine, and a 1986 federal court ruling stated that the doctrine was not required by law but was only a discretionary power of the FCC. In August 1987, the FCC voted to abolish the fairness doctrine, but the doctrine's supporters hoped that Congress would reinstate the rule by making it a law.

The Free Speech Issue

The **free speech issue** is about how to find a balance between the media's constitutional right to free expression and business's desire to be fairly and accurately depicted in media presentations, as well as to present its views on controversial public issues. (Of course, the free speech issue also affects other groups in society, but our discussion focuses on business.)

The press in the United States is a "free press," meaning that it operates under explicit constitutional protections. The First Amendment to the Constitution says, in part, "Congress shall make no law . . . abridging the freedom of speech, or of the press. . . ." State governments also are prohibited, under the due process clause of the Fourteenth Amendment, from passing laws that impair free speech or interfere with a free press. Although these Constitutional provisions are subject to continual interpretation and reinterpretation by government regulators, by the courts, and by general public opinion, their fundamental meaning does not change through time. Constitutional free-press guarantees mean that the privately owned, profit-seeking media are free to print, broadcast, and distribute messages to the general public without getting authorization from government officials.

[27] Thomas Garbett, "The Issue of Issue Ads," *Public Relations Journal*, October 1986, p. 33.

Defenders of the media say that freedom of expression, even when the result is negative or unfavorable to business, is a vital part of maintaining a free and open society.

> If business could conduct its affairs in a society that had a controlled press, the only news that would be made public would be that presently found in house organs, annual reports, company brochures, and speeches by executives. Management could comfortably go about its business without revealing anything that might in any way be legally damaging. But the qualities of our society and the protection of public interest which all of us—business executives as well as reporters—hold especially dear would be jeopardized.[28]

The contrasting business point of view is that the media's right to free speech is not the same as an ordinary citizen's right of expression. The media are enormously influential in shaping public attitudes toward business. When the media disseminate messages to the public, those messages cannot be called back. They enter the public domain where they create impressions, encourage certain attitudes, and inculcate various values. Therefore, business says, the media have an overarching responsibility to be fair, balanced, and accurate in their portrayals of business if they are to be justified in retaining their constitutional rights to freedom of expression.

Another free-speech issue occurs when corporations try to express their opinions on controversial questions of public policy, such as the size of the national debt or impending environmental regulations. Since the mid-1970s, the U.S. Supreme Court has held that "commercial speech"—that is, the kind that appears in commercial advertisements—is partially protected by the First Amendment's guarantee of free speech. But occasional high-court rulings demonstrate that some curbs are still permitted. That is one reason why the three major television networks have usually refused during the prime-time viewing period to run "public issue" advertisements sponsored by corporations. Television executives also feared that the more controversial ads might offend their biggest advertisers (as in the P&G episode mentioned at the beginning of this chapter) or that the networks would be accused of favoring only those groups who could afford the high cost of these ads. By 1990, though, the networks had begun to accept a few issue ads. As one station manager said, in referring to the weakened fairness doctrine, "We don't have to worry about absolute balance [now]."[29] Many of the networks' competitors, including cable television, independent broadcasters, radio stations, newspapers, and magazines, regularly accept public-issue advertisements.

CORPORATE MEDIA STRATEGIES

To be effective in communicating with the public—which means getting the corporation's viewpoint across to key stakeholders—companies can take action on three fronts.

[28] David Finn, "The Media as Monitor of Corporate Behavior," in Aronoff, op. cit., p. 125.
[29] "TV Networks Gingerly Lift Prohibition on 'Issue Ads,' " *Wall Street Journal,* Oct. 15, 1990, p. B1.

Managing Public Affairs and Public Relations

The most fundamental **media strategy** for any corporation is to design and manage an effective public affairs and public relations program. Chapter 5 in this book describes the major features of the public affairs function in today's socially responsive corporations. Briefly, a good public affairs program sends a constant stream of information from the company to stakeholders, and the company keeps its doors open for dialogue with stakeholders whose lives are affected by company operations. Public affairs should be proactive, not reactive. Channels of communication with the media should be established on a continuing basis, not just after a problem has arisen. Once this step has been taken, a company can then view the media as a positive force that can help the company communicate with the public.

Advocacy advertising—another term for "issue ads" discussed earlier—is another way to get a corporate viewpoint into the media. The best-known example is Mobil Corporation's vigorous and sometimes provocative advocacy ads on a broad range of public issues; they appear in national-circulation newspapers as statements of the company's views which frequently are at odds with editorial opinions and government policies.[30]

Media Relations during Crisis Management

Media relations are a vital part of crisis management. Crisis management occurs during any period when a company faces a serious disruption in its operations, such as a massive oil spill or a large-scale industrial accident. A specially chosen crisis management task force devotes full time to coping with the problem and trying to find solutions. In the best-managed companies, a media-contact person is a key member of this group, and contingency plans are made beforehand on how media relations are to be handled during any emergency period. In highly visible emergencies, an outside public relations firm may be called in to develop an ongoing plan for dealing with the media and assuring that the company's point of view is included in media presentations.

A good example of the effective use of media relations during crisis management is Johnson & Johnson's handling of the Tylenol poisoning episodes in 1982 and 1986. After initiating a swift recall, a leading public relations firm was hired, company executives made themselves available for numerous media interviews, and the company launched a vigorous campaign to keep the public fully informed.

On the other hand, some emergencies are handled very ineptly by well-known corporations. Examples are Union Carbide's sluggish media response to the chemical leak that killed thousands of people in Bhopal, India; Perrier's failure to be forthright and prompt about the source of contamination in its bottled water;

[30] See "Mobil Oil Corporation: Advocacy Advertising," in Rogene A. Buchholz, William D. Evans, and Robert A. Wagley, *Management Response to Public Issues,* Englewood Cliffs, NJ: Prentice-Hall, 1985, pp. 186–199. For another comprehensive case study, including many examples of advocacy ads, see "Bethlehem Steel Corporation: Advocacy or Idea/Issue Advertising Campaign," in S. Prakash Sethi, *Up against the Corporate Wall,* 4th ed., Englewood Cliffs, NJ: Prentice-Hall, 1982, pp. 162–205.

and Exxon's delay in providing reliable public information about the massive Alaskan oil spill. In each case, the media were given confusing and unclear information about the causes and consequences of the emergencies. All three companies suffered a loss of credibility as a result.[31]

Media Training for Employees

A third step corporations can take to develop successful relations with the media is to give media training to executives and others in the company who are likely to have contact with the media.

Media training is necessary because communicating with the media is not the same as talking with friends or coworkers. As a company representative, an employee is normally assumed to be speaking for the company or is expected to have special knowledge of company activities. Under these circumstances, the words one speaks take on a special, "official" meaning. In addition, news reporters sometimes "ambush" an executive, asking penetrating or embarrassing questions and expecting instant answers. Even in more deliberate news interviews, the time available for responding to questions is limited to a few seconds. Moreover, facial expressions, the tone of one's voice, and "body language" can convey both positive and negative impressions.

Many large corporations, such as Mobil, General Motors, and Bank of America, routinely send a broad range of their employees to special courses to improve their media skills. Media communication experts generally give their clients the following advice:

- Resist the temptation to see reporters and journalists as an enemy. It is better and more accurate to accept them as professionals with a job to do. Most of the time, their main interest is to get information that will help them write a news report.
- Resist the temptation to avoid the media. It is better, even in the most difficult situations, to establish positive contacts with media representatives. Withdrawing into a shell of silence tends to generate suspicion that the company has something to hide.
- "Honesty is the best policy" tends to be the wisest long-run media strategy. Not only does this attitude create a positive impression but it avoids embarrassment at a later time if new and different information becomes available to the company or the media.
- Employees facing the media should be well informed about company actions and policies and determined to put that point of view across, rather than falling victim to a reporter's or an interviewer's own agenda.[32]

[31] For Exxon's media ordeal, see Stratford P. Sherman, "Smart Ways to Handle the Press," *Fortune*, June 19, 1989, pp. 69–75.

[32] Mary Munter, "Managing Public Affairs: How to Conduct a Successful Media Interview," *California Management Review*, Summer 1983, pp. 143–150; and "Learning to Shine in the Limelight," *Business Week*, July 7, 1986, pp. 88–89.

SOCIAL RESPONSIBILITY GUIDELINES FOR THE MEDIA AND MEDIA SPONSORS

The public expects the media to exhibit a high level of social responsibility for two basic reasons.

The first reason is the awesome power of the media to influence culture, politics, business, social groups, and individual behavior. Media technology reaches into every corner of society and into the inner recesses of human consciousness. No other form of technology is so subtle and insidious in influencing human affairs.

Social and ethical responsibilities also arise from the potential clash of commercial motives and society's traditional values. The media's need for high ratings and large circulation figures may at times allow cherished human and social values to be overridden, ignored, or diminished.

The media's great potential for being a positive force in society is most likely to be realized if the media and their commercial sponsors try to observe the following social responsibility guidelines.

- Balance media power with an equal amount of responsibility in all presentations because the media wield such potentially great influence on social values and individual behavior.
- Seek and present the truth accurately and professionally, while striving for a balanced view of controversial issues and events.
- Protect and preserve the privacy and dignity of individuals who are the subject of media coverage. The public's "right to know" needs to be balanced against the price paid by individuals whose privacy and personal dignity may be threatened by media presentations.
- Portray professional, social, and ethnic groups accurately, avoiding unfavorable stereotypical images that damage such groups' social acceptability. This principle applies to media images of business, as well as to those of ethnic minorities, religious groups, and others.
- Present the full spectrum of human values typical of a society, rather than emphasizing a narrow band of values that tends to distort social reality. Choices among a society's values can then be made with greater intelligence by the people themselves, instead of allowing the media to substitute their judgment for the public will.

SUMMARY POINTS OF THIS CHAPTER

- Media institutions exert great influence on public opinion, other institutions, and the behavior of individuals and groups. Media messages condition public attitudes toward business, shaping both positive and negative feelings about business's goals and operations.

- Media in the United States are private businesses, organized to make a profit by attracting a large audience of readers, viewers, or listeners. This goal greatly affects the content of media presentations.
- U.S. constitutional guarantees of free speech and a free press restrict the amount and type of government regulations placed on the media. Some media content can be legally restricted, and competitive safeguards are imposed.
- The most important social issues involved in media operations are the kinds of images of people and institutions projected by the media, the values emphasized by media presentations, whether fairness and balance characterize media programming, and the balance that must be found between free speech and social responsibility.
- Corporations that are the most successful in dealing with the media possess comprehensive public affairs departments, make media relations a key part of crisis management, and provide media training for their personnel.
- Social responsibility guidelines for the media emphasize accuracy, fairness, and balance, recognizing the widespread influence that media messages have on business and society.

KEY TERMS AND CONCEPTS USED IN THIS CHAPTER

- Media
- Image issue
- Values issue
- Fairness and balance issue
- Fairness doctrine
- Free speech issue
- Media strategy

DISCUSSION CASE

MEDIA WOES

Burroughs Wellcome's Sudafed

Burroughs Wellcome, maker of a decongestant product called Sudafed 12-Hour Capsules, recalled the product nationwide in March 1991 when two people died and a third become gravely ill after taking cyanide-contaminated Sudafed Capsules. The company acted less than 24 hours after learning of the two deaths. Network television, radio, and national newspapers carried the recall announcement. Notices were sent to pharmacies, doctors, retailers, wholesalers, and warehouses. Worried customers could call a toll-free number for information. Burroughs Wellcome's CEO held a news conference four days after the recall to offer a reward for information about the tampering. A week later, he appeared in a nationally televised 60-second commercial, alerting viewers to the problem and explaining the company's actions to avoid further deaths and illness.

In spite of these prompt steps, Burroughs Wellcome came under fire for not doing enough soon enough. Speaking of the ten-day delay in airing the CEO's TV spot, one public relations official said, "The basic rule of crisis communication is to tell it all and tell it fast. Sudafed is awfully late. They have a big-time communication problem." A marketing expert faulted the company for not reassuring customers earlier and arranging exchanges and refunds for capsules they had purchased prior to the recall. He said, "It's important to have thought through your strategy. Not two weeks later. By this time, people have found alternatives. It's much too late to wait." And a corporate image consultant, aware that Burroughs Wellcome had been widely criticized earlier for the high price it charged for AZT, an AIDS drug, added, "Who is Burroughs Welcome? They haven't attended to their image concerns. . . . when a tragedy happens to a company that hasn't maintained its image as a high priority, you've got a problem."[33]

Source Perrier's Bottled Water

Another company that stumbled in its media relations was Source Perrier, the French company that sells Perrier bottled water. As noted in another chapter of this book, Perrier was recalled from world markets when U.S. government officials found traces of benzene—three times the amount allowed under U.S. law—in bottles of the famous spring water. As one source said, "Perrier's explanation for the recall has changed as quickly as a trendy Yuppie's drink of choice." Perrier's officials first said that a worker had contaminated a bottling line when cleaning it with a benzene-based fluid and that only bottles sold in the U.S. had been affected. Then, to everyone's astonishment, the company admitted that benzene is a naturally occurring ingredient of the spring water, which had always been promoted for its purity. Workers, according to the company, had failed to clean the filters often enough, which allowed small amounts of the toxic chemical to remain in the bottled product. A month later, it was reported by Perrier consultants that the *real* problem was failure to change gas filters in a special holding tank used to boost the natural bubble content of the spring water. This latter disclosure only added to the company's image problems because Perrier water had always been advertised as "naturally sparkling," a designation that the U.S. Food and Drug Administration said would now have to be removed since some of the carbonation was artificial.

In what was described as "a raucous news conference in Paris," Perrier's president declared that "all this publicity helps build the brand's renown," a remark that dumbfounded some marketing experts. "That's unbelievable," said one. "No publicity is a lot better than bad publicity. It's extraordinarily hard to believe that benzene will be good for the brand."[34]

[33] The quotations are from the *Wall Street Journal*, Mar. 12, 1991, p. B6.

[34] The quotations are from *Newsweek*, Feb. 26, 1990, p. 53, and the *Wall Street Journal*, Feb. 15, 1990, pp. B1, B8.

Exxon's Alaskan Oil Spill

Ten days after Exxon's oil tanker ran aground in Alaska's Prince William Sound, spilling 240,000 gallons of crude oil in one of the world's biggest environmental disasters, the company ran a full-page ad in national newspapers. Signed by the company's CEO, the ad asserted that Exxon had acted "swiftly and competently" to clean up the spill. Even though the company then apologized for the accident, the ad was not convincing in light of much evidence that the cleanup had not been handled quickly or skillfully enough to avoid extensive environmental damage. Exxon's CEO also was faulted for not going to the spill's site—he was reported to feel that the technical experts there could handle the problem without his presence—and for letting a low-level company manager tell the company's side of the story to the media in the first few crucial days of the disaster. Once out of his media shell and appearing on national news programs, the CEO claimed it was not his job to know technical details of the cleanup, and he argued defensively that the cleanup was being slowed by Coast Guard and government officials. A company public relations representative said later, in a statement that was perhaps only half true, "In the first few days, we dealt with the problem, not the perception." A writer for *Fortune* magazine said, "Certainly trying to convey perceptions through the filters of reporters, editors, and producers is risky. But it is less risky, on balance, than not trying."[35]

Discussion Questions

1. For each of the three companies, identify the central media problem that led to poor public relations and a tarnished image for the firm. What aspects of media strategy were overlooked in each company? In discussing the issues, draw upon relevant concepts discussed in this chapter.
2. What social and ethical responsibilities did the media have in each one of these episodes? Did they have an obligation beyond merely getting the facts and reporting them to their readers?
3. When a company's image is threatened or damaged by media stories, do the media bear any of the responsibility? Should media reporters and editors soften the impact of their news stories in order to protect business's image?

[35] Stratford P. Sherman, "Smart Ways to Handle the Press," *Fortune*, June 19, 1989, p. 75. For a general discussion, see Dieudonee Ten Berge, *The First 24 Hours: A Comprehensive Guide to Successful Crisis Communications*, Cambridge, MA: Basil Blackwell, 1990.

18

Science, Technology, and Business

Business is one of the major institutions through which new forms of science and technology are introduced into society. As we prepare to enter the twenty-first century, civilization is in its greatest age of technological change. Both business and society are in the midst of the massive task of absorbing technology on a scale never before experienced. Modern technology has given business new powers but also the responsibility to use technology in a way that enhances the quality of life.

Key Questions and Chapter Objectives

This chapter focuses on these key questions and objectives:

- What are the major features of technology?
- How do societies move through the five major phases of technology and what are the social systems created with each move?
- What are the technological characteristics of a service and a knowledge society?
- What are the economic and social consequences of technological change?
- Why does business need to consider the restraints placed on technology and technological innovation?

Researchers have been isolating chemicals that naturally occur in the human body for the past two decades. The goal for this field of biotechnology has been to synthesize drugs that can overcome deficiencies of these compounds in the human chemical factory. These drugs, biological response modifiers (BRMs), have been developed through a process called gene splicing. While these "magic bullets" have been effective in curing their target diseases in some cases, they have been equally disappointing in other cases. Often serious side effects and misuse of the drugs have led to some failures. For example, since the human growth hormone (HGH) was first approved in 1985, the market for HGH has grown to $165 million on far more than the strength of the 15,000 children that have been treated for dwarfism. Since one of HGH's effects is to build lean muscle mass, an underground market has arisen among athletes.

Energy is essential to economic activity. In the United States, Japan, and much of Europe, petroleum and other fossil fuels dominate energy use. One consequence, of course, is noxious air emissions. This form of pollution has harmful health effects on people and other living organisms. Plentiful and relatively inexpensive fossil fuels enabled business to grow and prosper. The problems of such "dirty" fuels however are now stimulating research to develop "clean fuels."[1]

These examples show that science and technology are like a double-edged sword; often they present two sides to society. One side is highly beneficial and promising, and the other side is threatening to individuals and society. This chapter looks at the two sides of science and technology and the issues they present for business and society.

TECHNOLOGY AS A SOCIAL FORCE

Throughout history technology has pressed onward like a glacier, overturning everything in its way and grinding all opposition into dust. In early nineteenth century England, for example, a band of unhappy workers known as Luddites challenged the Industrial Revolution by roaming the countryside smashing machinery and burning factories. From their narrow viewpoint, machines were enemies taking away jobs and freedom and harming people. But the Luddites were soon overcome by the benefits brought by the same machinery they opposed. Their movement failed, much the same as their more modern successors did, such as the glassblowers who opposed glassmaking machinery. We know now that they were largely mistaken about the broader significance of industrial technology. Though the Industrial Revolution created new and serious human problems for some people in society, it was a great advance in the history of civilization.

Technology continues to grow because of people themselves. Human beings, having tasted the fruit of knowledge, cannot suppress their desire for it. They forever seek to expand knowledge of their environment, probably because of the excitement of learning and their belief that more knowledge will help them control their environment.

Features of Technology

The dominant feature of technology is change and then more change. Technology forces change on people whether they are prepared for it or not. In modern society it has brought so much change that it creates what is called future shock, which means that change comes so fast and furiously that it approaches the limits of human tolerance and people lose their ability to cope with it successfully.

[1] Joan O'C. Hamilton, "The Many Personalities of Gene-Spliced Drugs," *Business Week,* July 30, 1990, p. 68; and "The Greening of Detroit," *Business Week,* Apr. 8, 1991, pp. 54–60.

Although technology is not the only cause of change, it is the primary cause. It is either directly or indirectly involved in most changes that occur in society.

Some years ago, right after the start of the personal computer revolution, industry experts observed that if automobiles had developed at the same rate as the computer business, a Rolls-Royce would cost $2.75 and go three million miles on a gallon of gasoline. Today's microcomputers cost no more than those of 1983 and offer ten times the power and many more times the speed of their predecessors.[2]

Another feature of technology is that its effects are widespread, reaching far beyond the immediate point of technological impact. Technology ripples through society until every community is affected by it. The shock waves push their way into even the most isolated places. People cannot escape it. Even if they travel to remote places like the Grand Canyon, technology is still represented by vapor trails from airplanes flying overhead, microwave communication signals from satellites moving at the speed of light, and a haze from air pollution often preventing a view of the other side.

An additional feature of technology is that it is self-reinforcing. As stated by Alvin Toffler, "Technology feeds on itself. Technology makes more technology possible."[3] This self-reinforcing feature means that technology acts as a multiplier to encourage its own faster development. It acts with other parts of society so that an invention in one place leads to a sequence of inventions in other places. Thus, invention of the wheel led rather quickly to perhaps a dozen or more applications. These applications, in turn, may have affected fifty other parts of the system and led to several additional inventions that similarly influenced society as technology multipliers.

> The automobile serves as an example. It could not have been invented much earlier because hundreds of inventions had to precede it, such as improvements in metallurgy, vulcanization of rubber, electrical generation for spark plugs, and refining of crude oil. Once these inventions existed, the automobile almost had to be invented, because there was a market for faster transportation than horses and bicycles and for more individualized transportation than trains offered. Today, automakers are using advances in areas of science and technology such as polymer chemistry and microcomputers to develop a fuel-efficient car. Prototypes of these automobiles weigh 30 percent less than current models and computers supervise most of the operational aspects of the engine.
>
> When the technological breakthrough of the automobile did occur, its effects were pervasive throughout society. It changed the living habits of people, including their buying habits, the location of their homes, their independence, and even their patterns of courtship. It increased the number of supermarkets and helped create drive-in movies. It expanded land areas allocated to roads, increased traffic to wilderness areas, and added pollution

[2] Mark Alpert, "Tremors from the Computer Quake," *Fortune*, Aug. 1, 1988, p. 44.

[3] Alvin Toffler, *Future Shock*, New York: Bantam, 1971, p. 26.

to the air. By means of the truck, it altered shipping patterns and manufacturing locations. Hardly any area of society remained untouched by the automobile.

The same principle holds for the computer, for television, for organ transplant technology, for genetic engineering, and for many other forms of modern science and technology. Once started, they spread their effects widely and persistently throughout society.

Business Applies Technology

As soon as new knowledge exists, people want to apply it in order to reap its benefits. At this point business becomes important, because business is the principal institution that translates discovery into application for public use. Printing, manufacturing, housing, education, and television are all dependent on business activities to make them work productively. Society depends on business to keep the stream of discovery flowing into useful goods and services for all people. Less-developed nations have learned that scientific discoveries mean very little to them unless they have competent business systems to produce for their people what science has discovered. In a similar manner, developed nations have learned that an innovative business system helps translate technological developments into useful goods and services for their people.

Phases of Technology and the Social Systems They Create

Looking at technology in a very general way, five broad **phases of technology** have developed, as shown in Figure 18–1. One phase at a time tends to dominate

FIGURE 18–1
Phases in the development of technology in the United States.

Technology Level	Phases in the Development of Technology	Approximate Period of Dominance in U.S.	Activity	Primary Skill Used
1	Nomadic-Agrarian	Until 1650	Harvests	Manual
2	Agrarian	1650–1900	Plants and harvests	Manual
3	Industrial	1900–1960	Builds material goods	Manual and machine
4	Service	1960–1975	Focuses on providing services	Manual and intellectual
5	Knowledge	1975–1990s	Abstract work	Intellectual and electronic

the work of a nation, and in so doing it has a major influence on that nation and creates its own distinct type of social system. In history, nations have tended to move sequentially through each phase, beginning with the lowest technology and moving higher with each step, so the five phases of technology roughly represent the progress of civilization throughout history. Although one phase of technology tends to dominate a nation's activities at a particular time, other phases often will be practiced at the same time. The five phases are discussed in the following paragraphs.

Nomadic society

In a nomadic society people live primarily by hunting, fishing, picking berries, digging roots, and otherwise taking what nature has provided. Rather than producing more by planting and cultivating, they merely take what is available. Their technology of spears, fishing hooks, digging tools, and baskets, while ingenious, is poorly developed. Often they move as nomads to wherever a good natural harvest is available.

Agrarian society

An agrarian society is one in which agricultural activities dominate work and employ the largest proportion of the labor force. Eventually, an agrarian society may develop in which people domesticate plants and animals for specific uses. Many nations in the modern world are still primarily agrarian. More than 50 percent of their labor force is busy providing food for the population. These nations tend to remain at an agrarian level until they can develop enough productivity to release many of their labor force from the farm and employ them in other productive occupations.

Industrial society

In the 1800s the United States began a mechanical revolution that transformed it into an industrial society by the early 1900s. An industrial society is one in which the building and processing of material goods dominates work and employs the largest proportion of the labor force. It is the natural result of the great Industrial Revolution, which originated in Britain, and it symbolically represents the materialism that social critics sometimes condemn.

When a nation progresses from an agrarian to an industrial technology, dramatic changes usually occur, as they did in the United States. Large factories develop because of economies of scale, and the tasks of the labor force become specialized. This new type of enterprise also makes management more necessary and important. People move off the farms and into the cities for higher wages, and congestion and pollution develop. Both the factories and the cities require large amounts of new capital, which leads to emphasis on capital formation. In addition, the changed living conditions, greater affluence, and new material goods produce new life-styles. Indeed, the move from an agrarian to an industrial society substantially changes a social system.

Service society

Business was so successful in applying technology in factories that by the 1960s the United States became the world's first service society, sometimes called a postindustrial society. The United States made remarkable technological progress by moving, in less than one century, from an agrarian to an industrial to a service society.[4]

A service society is one in which the majority of the labor force is employed in service industries, such as retailing, banking, health care, and insurance, that provide nonproduct values (service), rather than in direct production work, such as manufacturing, farming, and construction. In the United States, 70 percent of the working population works to provide services of one type or another, and services account for approximately one-half of gross national product and each family dollar spent.[5] In a service society the production of material goods is no longer the primary user of labor or the central economic and social problem.

Although no one can be sure what long-run changes a service society will bring, some possible changes can be mentioned based on preliminary experience with it. Until recently, it was thought that a service society's productivity would decline because much service work is labor-intensive and difficult to mechanize. During the 1980s, however, business poured millions of dollars into high-tech investments in the service sector, which boosted productivity sharply. As we prepare to enter the twenty-first century, the high-tech investment that has begun to have the greatest payoff for the service industry is in the area of communications. Building an electronic communication infrastructure with radio, telephone, television, and computers has gone on for most of the twentieth century. By the mid 1990s technology will make it possible to link up all of these communication devices.

Once signals from phones, television and information services are translated into digital form, they are, technically speaking, identical. The only difference between the bursts of 0's and 1's that bring you a rock concert on a compact disk, your phone call home, and an episode of *Cheers* will be whether the digital code represses sounds, pictures, words, or a combination. That makes it possible for it all to be sent over a signal line and even decoded by a single machine.[6]

Knowledge society

Knowledge is such a distinct phase of technology that, when it dominates a nation's activities, it creates a different type of social system. A **knowledge society** is one in which the use and transfer of knowledge and information, rather than manual skill, dominates work and employs the largest proportion of the labor force. Work becomes abstract, the electronic manipulation of symbols.[7] Examples

[4] This development was first discussed comprehensively by Daniel Bell, *The Coming of Post-Industrial Society*, New York: Basic Books, 1973, chap. 2. For a later analysis see Alvin Toffler, *The Third Wave*, New York: Bantam, 1981.

[5] Daniel Bell, "The Third Technological Revolution," *Business Quarterly*, August 1982, pp. 33–37; and James D. Robinson III, "A Full Partnership for Services," *Business Week*, June 29, 1982, p. 15.

[6] "Idea for 1991: Communication," *Fortune*, Jan. 14, 1991, p. 35.

[7] Shoshanah Zuboff, *In the Age of the Smart Machine*, New York: Basic Books, 1988. See also Ronald Henkoff, "Make Your Office More Productive," *Fortune*, Feb. 25, 1991, pp. 72–84.

of people in knowledge jobs are news editors, accountants, computer programmers, and teachers. Even a transplant surgeon, who must use a delicate manual skill, is primarily working from a knowledge or intellectual base. Examples of knowledge industries are newspaper publishing, television, education, book publishing, telecommunications, and consulting.

It is estimated that the United States became the world's first knowledge society sometime in the 1970s. Since no nation had ever reached this technological goal before, there were no specific guidelines learned from the experiences of others, but its effects were massive. As people moved from manual work to information processing and intellectual work, there were substantial changes in life-styles, education, recreation, and living conditions. Today, many nations in addition to the United States have significant portions of their economic activity tied to knowledge and are witnessing similar social and cultural consequences.

A knowledge society's technology is primarily electronic in nature and is heavily dependent on the computer and the semiconductor silicon chip. The power of these devices rests on their ability to process, store, and retrieve large amounts of information with very great speed. By the early 1980s technical advances ushered in a new generation of computers called the second generation. This second generation was made possible by the development of the microprocessor—called a computer on a chip—that has vastly greater computing power than those that were first developed in the early 1970s.

However, despite the fact that computer technology is still so primitive in its ability to integrate with the average person's daily tasks, the second generation has made its mark and paved the way for the third. With the arrival of the 1990s, the third generation soon will be fully with us. The third generation will be better educated and more "affluent" than its predecessors. Some believe it will be literate, articulate, and completely integrated with its human partners in every arena of human endeavor.[8]

In the early 1980s it was forecast that by 1990 people in the knowledge society would work, shop, and bank from their homes. This development has not occurred the way many people envisioned. It is not for lack of technical capability, since many professionals do work from their homes. Instead, portable computers and cellular telephones have allowed us to work while we are mobile. One reason why widespread working at home has been slow to develop is that people need to have face-to-face contact with others; they need to feel part of an organization by being physically present.

The technological innovations of a knowledge society are only a small part of a broad and revolutionary social transformation occurring in many institutions throughout the postindustrial world. Alvin Toffler has called this period of broad-scale social change "The Third Wave." The First Wave of social change came with the rise and dominance of agriculture in several parts of the world, a period that lasted from 8000 B.C. to A.D. 1650–1750. The rise of industrial civilization signaled the beginning of the Second Wave, which reached a peak in the mid-1950s, according to Toffler. The Third Wave is typical of all high-technology, service-

[8] Robert M. Price, "Computers in the '90s'," *Vital Speeches*, Feb. 13, 1990, pp. 530–531.

oriented, information-based societies. In each of these three major eras, human institutions and values have been shaped by underlying technological systems. The movement of society from one major period to another is painful and confusing, owing to the lag that occurs between people's accustomed ways of thinking and acting and the new conditions created by new forms of technology. We examine some of the economic and social effects of Third Wave technology in the following sections.[9]

SOME ECONOMIC EFFECTS OF TECHNOLOGY

Higher Productivity

Perhaps the most fundamental effect of technology is greater productivity in terms of quality and quantity. Productive gain is the main reason that most technology is adopted. In a hospital the objective may be qualitative, such as maintaining a life with electronic monitoring equipment regardless of costs. In a factory the goal may be quantitative in terms of more production for less cost. While great strides have been made we are still in the experimental stage of introducing new electronic technologies into the factory.

> In Japan, at Fanuc, one of the largest and most modern manufacturers of industrial robots, it seems to be a script out of a science fiction movie as robots are making robots.
>
> The factory has an eerie, futuristic air to it. On a floor the size of two football fields, the fewer than 90 workers look like ants, lost among the yellow robots and complicated machinery. Most of the robots are in the work cells, loading or unloading the parts that will make their comrades. But, because they cycle (or move) only as needed, it seems at first glance that little is happening. Much of the actual grinding, drilling, and boring is done by machine tools that are partially enclosed and make little noise. At night, human workers disappear from the floor, manual and testing operations cease, and the machining operations in the cells continue automatically, with a solitary worker monitoring progress from gauges and terminals in the central control room.[10]

U.S. manufacturing, faced with increasing competition from abroad, is aggressively investing in the technology needed for these factories of the future. By developing their technology base, Japanese and western European companies

[9] Toffler, op. cit. For a similar view of social trends increasingly typical of advanced societies see John Naisbitt and Patricia Aburdene, *Megatrends 2000,* New York: Morrow, 1990.

[10] Frederick L. Schodt, "In The Land of Robots," *Business Month,* November 1988, pp. 67–75.

have made dramatic gains in their factory productivity. This has led to increased competition that challenges the United States' leadership in world and domestic markets. Even though for each unit of input the United States still produces more output than any other nation, U.S. productivity is not growing as fast as formerly, or as fast as productivity growth elsewhere, most notably in Japan.[11]

More Emphasis on Research and Development

As technology has advanced, **research and development** (R&D) has become a giant new activity in organizations. Research concerns the creation of new ideas, and development concerns their useful application. Effective management of R&D is important because it brings social benefits through increased productivity. With the world's exploding population and the needs of less-developed nations, society requires the material and social gains that R&D can provide. Society also depends on R&D to find ways to reduce pollution and otherwise improve the quality of life.

In the past twenty years, the United States' commitment to research and development has grown dramatically. As shown in Figure 18–2, R&D spending has grown from $26 billion in 1970 to more than $150 billion in 1990, a six hundred percent increase! The federal government, industry, and universities are important participants as both providers of research money and, as also shown in Figure 18–2, the users of such funds. Government, business, and universities have a strong working relationship in the R&D area.

Money alone does not guarantee success in research and development. The United States has 5.5 million scientists and engineers, double the number in Japan, and spends nearly twice the amount of Japan and Germany combined. Yet there are many criticisms of the comparative results achieved for this large investment. As Figure 18–3 illustrates, the majority of R&D funds spent in the United States go to "development" rather than basic or applied research. This means that activities such as the creation of prototypes (e.g., "automobiles of the future") receive much more money than basic scientific and engineering research. Many foreign nations, including Japan, have focused more of their spending on applied research that allows them to improve manufacturing processes that lead to greater productivity and to the continuous improvement of products.

Invention and innovation are not synonymous, nor does one necessarily flow from the other. Invention refers to the creation of new ideas, products, and machinery; innovation refers to improvement of existing products, processes, and methods. Japanese manufacturers have tended to emphasize production-oriented innovation, often copying and improving upon products first invented in the United States. This approach is now widely seen as one of the keys to Japan's competitive success in world markets. This, in turn, has led many experts in business and government to press U.S. industry to emphasize more transfer of technology from ideas to applications. Invention without innovation is not suf-

[11] Michael L. Dertouzos, Richard K. Lester, and Robert M. Solow, *Made in America*, Cambridge, MA: MIT Press, 1989, p. 26.

FIGURE 18–2
Sources of R&D spending in the United States.

SOURCE: Derived from data presented in National Science Foundation, *National Patterns of R&D Resources,* Surveys of Science Resources Series, Washington, DC: Government Printing Office, 1990.

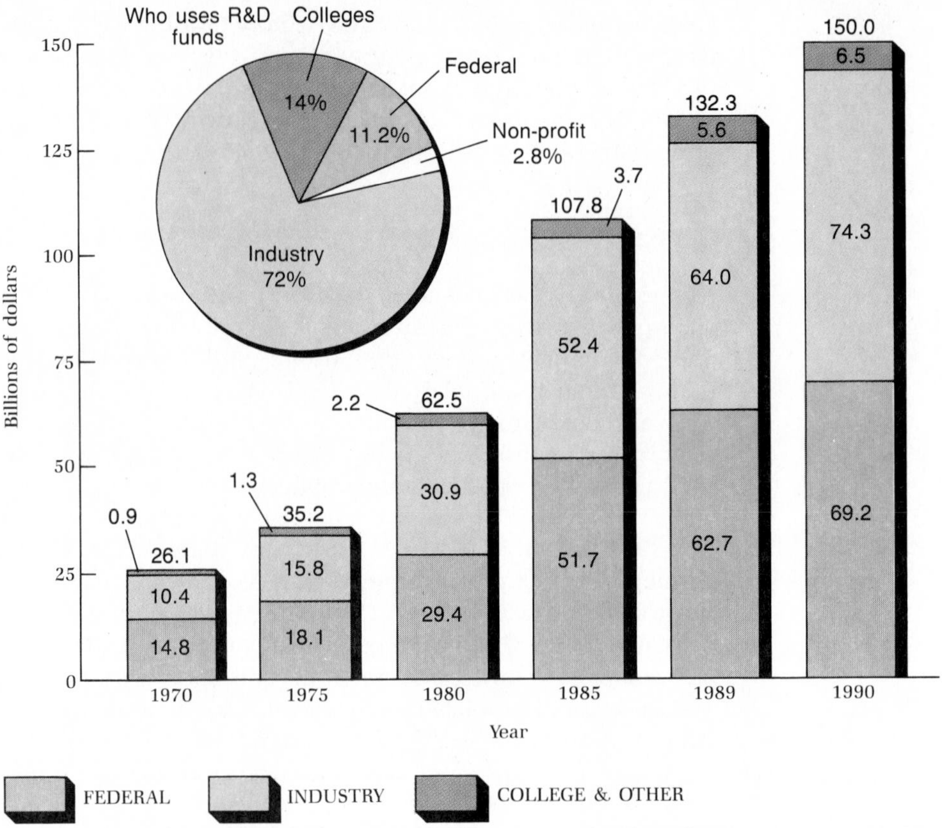

Who uses R&D funds
Colleges 14%
Federal 11.2%
Non-profit 2.8%
Industry 72%

Billions of dollars
150
125
100
75
50
25
0

1970: 26.1 (14.8, 10.4, 0.9)
1975: 35.2 (18.1, 15.8, 1.3)
1980: 62.5 (29.4, 30.9, 2.2)
1985: 107.8 (51.7, 52.4, 3.7)
1989: 132.3 (62.7, 64.0, 5.6)
1990: 150.0 (69.2, 74.3, 6.5)

Year

FEDERAL INDUSTRY COLLEGE & OTHER

FIGURE 18–3
Type of R&D conducted in the United States.

SOURCE: "Funding Research: An Overview," *Wall Street Journal,* Nov. 10, 1986, p. D–5.

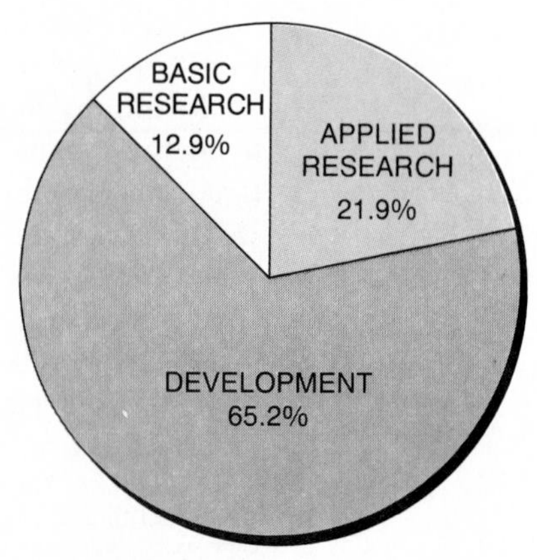

ficient in markets where competition is able to quickly copy and improve upon others' ideas.[12]

R&D has become so important in some companies that it is ranked along with production and sales as a primary activity. With accelerated technology, many companies now develop goods, as well as produce and sell them. A number of companies can show that 25 to 50 percent of their revenues today are from products not even produced ten years ago. Research and development in such firms becomes a major department, sometimes having as many employees as either production or sales. Its salary budget is similarly large, and it assumes an active voice in the councils of top management. Within such a company, influence on decision making may shift from production to R&D. As business continues to move to a global marketplace, R&D has become a national priority. During the 1980s, several laws were passed in the United States to encourage more cooperative efforts between government and industry. The goal of these alliances is to better commercialize innovation to ensure that the United States can continue to compete globally.[13]

Upgraded Job Skills

With the advance of technology, jobs tend to become more intellectual and otherwise upgraded. The job that once required several day laborers now requires a skilled crane operator, and the job that was done by a clerk now calls for a computer expert. A generation ago the typical factory had a range of skills approaching curve A shown in Figure 18–4. This curve was shaped like the normal curve of intelligence among people. Being matched to people, it suggested that an adequate supply of labor would be available at all levels of business in the long run.

In modern business the curve has moved toward the right, higher in skill, as shown in curve B. And in many organizations the skill distribution has become bimodal, as shown by the second top on the curve. Many scientific and professional people are required in research, development, planning, and other specialized work, creating the secondary bulge toward the skilled end of the scale.

Curve C represents the skill distribution that is developing in firms oriented toward research and development. Even though these firms manufacture products for sale, much of their effort is devoted to development and to building a small number of complex products. In some of these firms the number of engineers, scientists, and college graduate specialists exceeds the total number of other employees.

The nature of technology is that it creates jobs that many people are not yet prepared to fill. The bargain that technology strikes with workers is to take away one job and offer them another one, usually requiring higher ability, for which they may not be qualified. It places a burden of training and education on the

[12] Otis Port, "Back to Basics," *Business Week*, Special Edition: Innovation in America, 1989, pp. 15–17.

[13] Alan Schriesheim, "Toward a Golden Age for Technology Transfer," *Issues in Science and Technology*, Winter 1990–1991, pp. 52–58.

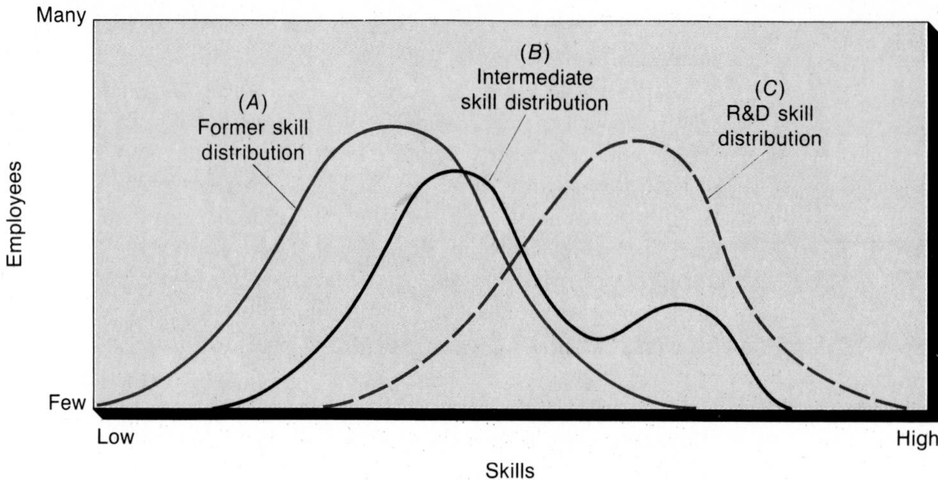

FIGURE 18–4 Changes in the skill distribution in a business required by advances in technology.

employee, the firm, and the nation. The poorly educated, the aged, and other marginal employees are the first to be dislocated, and they usually are the ones least able to adjust. Society faces the immense task of motivating and aiding these persons, for without help they become the long-term unemployed and the "untrainables."

More Scientific and Professional Workers

The increased number of intellectual workers represented by curves *B* and *C* in Figure 18–4 has placed new responsibilities on business for managing the creative spirit, which is sometimes called "maverick management." Historically, scientists have worked in small laboratories at their own pace, usually in an academic setting, but more and more they are working for big organizations, both private and public. Most certainly they perform best in a work culture different from that of the assembly line.

Creative and intellectual workers—sometimes referred to as "individual contributors"—expect relatively high job freedom. They are motivated by opportunities that offer change, growth, and achievement. They are often less motivated by expectations of higher formal authority than by their own professional interests and perceptions of opportunities. Their orientation, toward their profession and the world outside their organization, is cosmopolitan rather than local. Although they are a part of the company work culture, they are just as much a part of a separate scientific culture operating beyond their organization's boundaries. Under these conditions they may have an organizational rootlessness that tends to increase job mobility.

Business is adjusting its supervisory practices to meet the needs of such knowledge-based workers. Some companies have established dual promotion ladders so that distinguished technical people can rise to ranks and receive salaries that are equivalent to those of upper level executives. Flexible work schedules are allowed. Profit sharing is provided to give creative persons a financial stake in the ideas they create and to discourage rootlessness. Attendance at professional meetings and writing professional articles is supported. In further response to intellectual workers' cosmopolitan interests, they are allowed to teach part time or are given special assignments with schools, colleges, and universities.

Greater Capital Requirements

Another effect of technology is its insatiable demand for capital. Large amounts of capital are required to build the enormous production systems that save labor time and provide other benefits of technology. At the turn of the century, an investment of $1,000 for each worker often was adequate in a factory, but modern investments in pipelines and petroleum refining exceed $200,000 for each worker.

Technology is costly but essential for business, thereby creating a problem for managers. The failure to maintain current, up-to-date technology can mean a loss of competitiveness. Both productivity and product quality can suffer. Such expenditures do not tell the entire story however. New technology requires other expenditures to keep the labor force up to date with the machinery and technological changes. This in turn requires managers to select their technology carefully, train people properly, and encourage the continuous improvement of employees' understanding about the best ways to make use of technological capability. These demands also require business to generate large amounts of capital and engage in more long-range planning and budgeting for capital use. It also is desirable for government to establish public policies that encourage business to generate capital for needed jobs.[14]

SOCIAL CONSEQUENCES OF TECHNOLOGICAL CHANGE

Technological advances bring both benefits and costs to society. Over long historical epochs, civilization has been carried to supreme heights of material progress and accomplishment by technology and science. The five phases of technological development summarized in Figure 18–1 illustrate the progressive steps toward material betterment that human society has taken. Economic growth—driven by the engine of technological progress—has conferred wide benefits on humankind: supporting large populations at higher levels of living, extending expected life spans, and expanding a whole range of human potentialities that were the subject of science fiction novels not too long ago.

Social Costs

However, in the same way that a lifesaving engineered gene may have side effects, technology also has had social side effects. When they are negative, they become

[14] See, for example, Dertouzos et al., *Made in America*, op. cit., which was influential in this discussion in the early 1990s.

social costs. While a nation's political infrastructure lacks the capability to monitor and pass judgment on the overall good or bad impact of every scientific advancement, societal values may provide mechanisms that evaluate new technologies. On the political front, courts and legislatures can regulate the use of certain technologies. This power was dramatically illustrated in 1990 when a Michigan doctor used a device to help a patient commit suicide. The machine was banned by court order and the doctor was barred from using it again. When coupled with a mobilization of public constituencies, similar political forces have checked and curbed the use of technology in business.

Technology assessment is a useful technique that seeks to provide feedback about technology's effects and to anticipate the unintended, indirect, and possibly harmful effects of new technology. The Office of Technology Assessment was created by Congress to undertake studies of this type in projects involving government funding. Since its creation in 1972, it has conducted thousands of studies of all types of technologies.

A fact that is frequently overlooked is that technology can be used to correct side effects of other technologies. For instance, cancer-fighting drugs often have serious side effects for patients which other medicines can correct. As scientific advances in medicine have enabled doctors to artificially support human life in ways that were not possible before, our society has been forced to confront the moral dilemmas that accompany such capabilities. Individually and collectively our society has begun to address quality-of-life questions such as whether to keep comatose patients alive on life support machines when there is no hope of recovery. The challenge is one that technological advancement has put squarely on both business leaders' shoulders and on each of us as individuals.

There are other social costs to technology as well. Pollution, congestion, depleted natural resources, overpopulation, and the use of technology in settings such as developing nations where conditions for safe use may not exist all raise serious questions about the balance between technology and society. Business is an important actor in creating and resolving these dilemmas. Production, marketing, and strategic planning decisions should not be made in a vacuum that ignores such social costs. The responsibility of business to current and future stakeholders in society requires careful attention to these costs.

Biotechnology—A New Frontier

Another good example of the problems and opportunities associated with new scientific and technological breakthroughs is the modern era of **genetic engineering,** also called **biotechnology.** Genetic engineering has a history over a century old, rooted in agriculture. In the nineteenth century the botanist, Gregor Mendel, pioneered the science of genetics. Ever since, genetic scientists have cloned and propagated crops that have helped farmers produce more food per acre that is of better quality and less labor-intensive.

The new era of genetic engineering includes new techniques that enable scientists to combine knowledge from various areas of science, such as biochemistry, genetics, microbiology, and ecology. Scientists can now identify and manipulate molecules in genetic material with revolutionary applications in agriculture, medicine, and industry. Some of the results are truly startling, as the following examples illustrate.

- Newly engineered forms of bacteria have been introduced into experimental crops. This development may reduce the need for many pesticides that are now used to control insect damage but which damage groundwater.
- Growth hormones are used to promote animal growth and production; one estimate claims that this technique might increase United States milk production by 20 percent. By stimulating growth by these artificial means, commercial farmers could save vast sums of money on feed costs.
- Perhaps the most heralded and controversial biotechnology breakthroughs are in medicine. Gene-sleuthing scientists are discovering the flaws in DNA that cause hereditary diseases. Eventually, scientists want to inject the correct copy of a gene into a patient with a genetic flaw. The gene will find diseased cells and insert itself into them, thus curing the disease. Billions of dollars will be invested by business in these efforts. Pharmaceutical, chemical, and biotechnology companies, along with venture capitalists and institutional investors, will thereby have a stake in these activities.[15]

No one doubts the end-use benefits of these new scientific and technological advances. The trouble comes when the economic, ethical, and social consequences are considered. Boosting milk production by using growth hormones is fine, but it may force from 10 to 25 percent of dairy farmers out of business since fewer farms will be able to produce all the milk needed. The Congressional Office of Technology Assessment predicted in 1986 that about 1 million farms, in other words, nearly half of the total in the United States, would disappear by the end of the century, leaving only 50,000 large farms to produce three-quarters of the foodstuffs. So the small farmer may vanish from the social scene, the victim of a scientific revolution intended to improve the quality of life for all.

Other fears involve environmental dangers. While herbicide-resistant crops promise higher yields by clearing weeds, their availability may lead to showering the land with an even greater load of chemicals. Pesticide runoff and seepage into the groundwater is threatening to contaminate the drinking water supply in many farming regions. In Kansas, pesticides were detected in 11 percent of the wells tested in 1972. Their quantity rose to 72 to 78 percent of the same wells in 1984.[16]

One of the biggest worries surrounding biotechnology and genetic engineering is the uncontrolled escape of synthetically developed materials. For example, an engineered bacterium intended to build disease immunity into a plant might also accidentally kill off a beneficial insect. History proves that this effect is a real possibility since many of the insects that currently damage crops in the United

[15] The Genetic Age," *Business Week,* May 28, 1990, pp. 69–83.

[16] Fund for Renewable Energy and the Environment: Renew America Project, *State of the States* (Washington, DC, 1989), p. 15.

States are accidentally released pests that have been imported during this past century. Some people fear that nature's sometimes tightly knit ecological systems could possibly be upset and irreversibly damaged by infiltrating them with human-engineered genetic units. Although the bulk of United States scientists appear to favor continued experiments and carefully controlled environmental uses of genetically engineered materials, the controversy is likely to continue. Public opinion polls show that the general public also is on the side of pushing ahead with genetic engineering but that it wants strong curbs on the possible uses of these new techniques.

The biotechnology revolution has produced activists strongly opposed to many of the innovations favored by business. One of the best known is Jeremy Rifkin, who has successfully delayed a number of proposed experiments by bringing lawsuits against government regulators and genetic engineering firms. He and others have formed coalitions of various stakeholder groups, ranging from members of the Humane Society who oppose genetic engineering on animal genes, to religious leaders who object to using human reproductive cells for such experiments. Rifkin answers his critics by saying, "I'm asking the fundamental economic, social and ethical questions that should be asked first, rather than waiting for the damage."[17]

Restraints on Technological Growth

Students of technology have identified three major factors that may limit technology's ability to contribute to society in a positive way as depicted in Figure 18–5.

Pollution

Pollution is an unavoidable consequence of industrial production since waste by-products are produced along with useful things. In addition, many useful consumer products (e.g., automobiles) are themselves responsible for much pollution; and sooner or later, all manufactured goods wear out and are discarded as useless.

The biosphere—the land, air, water, and natural conditions on which all life on earth depends—can absorb and break down many of these industrial contaminants without harm to people, animals, or plants. But the biosphere is not an infinite sponge, and the buildup of harmful chemicals in the ecosystem poses a threat to all life and the planet itself. The earth's absorptive capacity is especially limited when a single society concentrates its industrial technology and industrial products too densely in a single region. The Los Angeles urban area is particularly susceptible to this kind of environmental overloading when industrial operations and automobile emissions clog the air. A critical issue today is society's capability to raise the standard of living everywhere as less-developed countries industrialize without causing irreparable damage to the earth's biosphere. Part of the answer

[17] "Rifkin's Vow: 'We Will Not Be Cloned,'" *Business Week*, May 26, 1986, p. 56. See also "The Genetic Age," *Business Week*, May 28, 1990, pp. 69–83, for a discussion of the pros and cons of biotechnology.

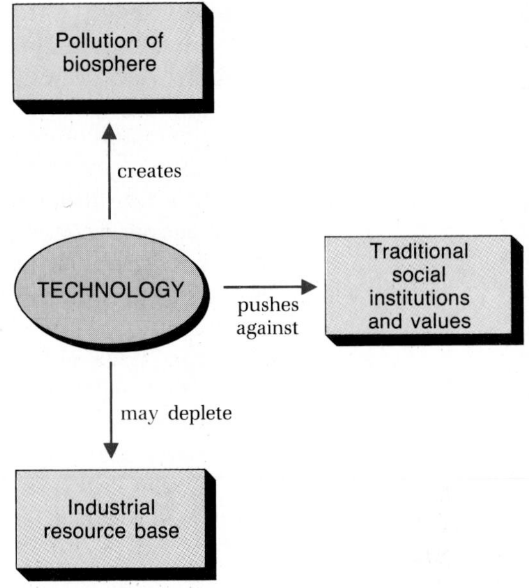

FIGURE 18–5
Three major factors capable of limiting technological development.

to this potential obstacle to further technological development is to invent and use new and less polluting forms of technology and energy.

The Industrial Resource Base

A second, closely related factor limiting technological growth is the possible depletion of the world's industrial resource base. This base is composed mainly of minerals, various forms of energy, water supplies, a skilled labor force, and human knowledge. Some studies have questioned whether the globe's supplies of reasonably priced minerals, energy, and water are sufficient to support unlimited industrial and technological expansion.

There are several offsetting forces that encourage a more positive view of the future. Technological ingenuity keeps making it possible for humans to dig deeper, explore more surely, retrieve minerals more economically, and use what is found more efficiently. Human knowledge also continues to expand, growing both broader and deeper. As our knowledge broadens, it is possible to see interconnections and relationships not previously understood. And as we learn more about the specific ways in which the natural and human-created worlds behave, alone and in conjunction with one another, we become better able to create imaginative ways to harness new and more economical technology to meet human needs. The difficulty of designing and successfully marketing light, fuel efficient automobiles, for example, illustrates how technology and human behavior both need to be adjusted in order to meet current energy and environmental requirements.[18]

[18] See "The Greening of Detroit," op. cit. The argument for better understanding of how technology and people interact is also made in Dertouzas et al., op. cit.

Social institutions

A third factor limiting technology is social values and institutions that may be inconsistent with the full productive potential that is present in technology.

> An example is seen in western Australia, where aborigines prevented two international mining companies from drilling for oil at a spot considered sacred by the tribal group. According to their tribal legends, the spirit of a giant sacred serpent lies sleeping under the ground where the oil was discovered. Australian labor unions supported the aboriginal demands to halt drilling by boycotting the site and threatening to blacklist all other mining operations of the two companies. Anthropologists estimate that western Australia may have as many as 200,000 sacred sites like this one, thereby posing a considerable problem for mining and drilling operations there.[19]

Many societies, perhaps most of those that adopt modern technology, encounter similar but less dramatic problems in arriving at a fit between their traditional social institutions and the new trends of technological development.

BUSINESS RESPONSIBILITY FOR TECHNOLOGICAL CHANGE

In a broad general sense, business has served as society's designated agent responsible for developing new technology. Whether one thinks of Henry Ford's Model–T car or today's microprocessor chip, private enterprise has led the way in introducing new technology for human use. In the United States, the public has expected and wanted business to perform this function; and it has praised business for enriching and elevating human life and experience in all the material ways made possible by technology: higher living standards, the creation of jobs, greater leisure time, and an apparently inexhaustible cornucopia of new products and services. For taking the technological lead, business has been rewarded with profits, growth, and general social approval.

In one important sense, business has only responded to expressed or potential public demands for more and better technology. In a private enterprise society, people register their wants through the marketplace, voting with their purchasing dollars. These free market demands have encouraged business to push for ever greater technological growth through the introduction of new products and services. The enormous popularity and demand for today's many electronic inventions—whether video games, videocassettes, pocket calculators, laptop computers, or digital recordings—illustrate the powerful dynamics of combining modern technology with a private enterprise system.

At times, these technological advances have occurred pell-mell and with little foresight for long-term consequences. For example, when technologically superior

[19] "The Spirit of a Serpent Stalls a Mining Project," *Business Week*, Oct. 27, 1980, pp. 69, 73. For a similar episode, see Geraldine Brooks, "Giant Mining Project in Papua New Guinea Is Beset by Calamities," *Wall Street Journal*, Apr. 24, 1985, pp. 1, 27.

trucks, buses, and airlines cut deeply into the freight and passenger business of railroads, entire towns such as Altoona, Pennsylvania—a large rail center—suffered severe economic decline. Or when new surface mining equipment made coal recovery in the western regions of the United States more profitable than the deep mining that was typical in the southern and eastern regions, many parts of Appalachia were thrust into deeper poverty than they had ever known. At the same time, helter-skelter, unplanned urban sprawl can accompany rapid economic buildup brought on by the newer forms of electronic technology. California's Silicon Valley, home of the revolutionary computer chip, is a good example of headlong economic development that presses hard on environmental resources and brings on many serious urban problems.

These problems may seem unique to today's technological age but they are not. Adjusting society's institutions and people to new technology is an ancient problem. Long ago, many farmers resisted the use of iron plows instead of wooden ones, believing that the metal would contaminate the soil and ruin the crops. The Luddites resisted factory machinery. The automobile was once considered by some persons to be a less genteel and refined mode of transportation than the horse and buggy; the same snobbish attitude developed toward ready-to-wear clothes when compared with tailor-made ones. Many people have expressed fear and hostility concerning the computer, just as others did years ago when telephone companies switched home dialing systems to digits from a combination of letters and digits. Not only were people forced to change their habits; they also feared a loss of individual identity and being regimented to an impersonal technological system.

The major difference today in adjusting technology and institutions is in the scale, magnitude, and speed of needed adjustments. Worldwide competition and enormous productivity gains pose the possibility of massive unemployment in industrial nations. The need for retraining programs for workers whose skills are outdated is far greater today than formerly. The economic and social dislocations appear to be more painful, more long-lasting, and more resistant to satisfactory solution.

What are business's responsibilities in a time of rapid and sometimes disruptive technological change? Now that the Pandora's box of technology has been opened, it cannot be closed again. There is no turning the technological clock back to a more serene era. Instead, society seems to be sending three kinds of signals to the business community.

- One message is that society wants new technology to be introduced with greater care and more foresight. For example, premarket testing of drugs, safety guidelines for genetic engineering projects, and government regulation of chemical waste disposal can safeguard individuals and society.
- Another emerging development is the idea of a compensatory payment or other type of support by business that would help individuals, groups, or communities readjust their lives when damaged by technological changes. Examples of such help include industrial retraining programs for technologically displaced employees; advance notification to employees and local

communities when plants are to be closed; compensation payments to communities and severance pay to laid-off employees; and acceptance by multinational firms of some sacrifice in economic efficiency in order to strengthen national security and preserve jobs at home instead of shifting operations to the lowest-cost foreign location. When business firms take these kinds of steps, they build confidence in society that the social costs of new technology will be widely shared rather than resting on just a few persons or groups.

- Perhaps less clearly perceived—but vitally necessary—is an emerging understanding that technology is far too central, far too important, and far too complex in its consequences to be entrusted to any single institution in society. Business has pioneered the creative development of much technology, just as government has led the way in sponsoring the technology of national defense. Society has much to gain from both, as well as much to think about in terms of their respective social costs. Universities, labor unions, nonprofit institutions, professional groups, and many local communities have made distinctive contributions to technological advance. All of these groups and institutions are technological stakeholders, each with an interest in the outcome of society's great adventure in technological achievement.

The idea of a broad institutional partnership for humane technological advance belongs in the thinking of business leaders, as well as in the minds and actions of all those in society who have a stake in the technological future.

CONCLUSION

The rate of technological change during the past century has been greater than all of the technological advances made in the previous two thousand years. As technology marches on into the twenty-first century, business is presented with the opportunity to capitalize on these innovations and the challenge to utilize technology in a way that reflects society's moral standards. Society must weigh the benefits of technology against its negative side effects to ensure that the mistakes of the past are not repeated so that innovation will continue to improve the quality of life.

SUMMARY POINTS OF THIS CHAPTER

- Technological advances produce change at a geometric rate. Forces of change are widespread as technology affects relationships with other institutions in a huge societal ripple effect.
- Historically, a society's technology has advanced along five broad phases

of development. Even though this development is not homogeneous throughout society each phase will dominate a society's work and will create a distinct social system.

- The manufacture of products is complemented by the creation of services in a modern knowledge-based society. A premium is placed on intelligent, well-educated people who can bring imagination and innovation to business.
- Technology results in both beneficial and potentially harmful effects on a society and its economy. Adjustments to technological change can take years to accomplish.
- Business faces physical and social restraints on its continued use of technology. The earth is limited in its capability to both absorb pollution and provide the natural resources that fuel the application of technology. Also, social institutions sometimes prevent full realization of technological development.

KEY TERMS AND CONCEPTS USED IN THIS CHAPTER

- Phases of technology
- Knowledge society
- Research and development (R&D)
- Technology's social impacts
- Technology assessment
- Genetic engineering and biotechnology
- Restraints on technology

DISCUSSION CASE

GENES VERSUS GENETIC ENGINEERING

As president of a hypothetical genetic engineering firm, imagine that you have just received the following letter:[20]

"Dear Ms. President:

"I represent a group known as the Group to Eliminate New Experiments in Science (GENES), which has a number of chapters in the United States and a rapidly growing membership from all walks of life, including science. At our recent national convention, a resolution was adopted that opposes all types of genetic engineering, including the kind of work your firm is doing.

"We believe that you and your scientific staff cannot improve on nature and

[20] Although hypothetical as presented here, the letter is an adaptation of an actual incident.

should not try to do so. To us, you are tampering with and trying unsuccessfully to imitate Divine intelligence. Human beings are not prepared either psychologically or morally to handle the kind of power conferred by this brand of science. We fear also that "engineered" microorganisms will escape from your laboratories into the environment and possibly cause unfortunate and irreversible damage to healthy living things, including ourselves and our children. The same bad effects may well occur when the altered genetic materials you use in industrial applications come into contact with employees, customers, and the general public. Overall, we think you are using the biosphere in unwise ways, just for the sake of making a profit for your stockholders.

"GENES recently purchased 10 shares of stock in your company and plans to offer some suggestions at the next annual stockholders' meeting for restricting your work in genetic engineering. I would be pleased to hear from you before that time. As stockholders, we believe you have an obligation to respond to our viewpoints. As members of the public, we think you should consider the risks your firm is creating through this new form of technology."

The letter was signed by someone identifying himself as a professor of biochemistry at a leading university.

Discussion Questions

1. As president of the firm, how would you respond to this letter? Would you answer it, ignore it, or wait to see what happens at the annual stockholders' meeting? What corporate strategy could be developed for dealing with GENES?
2. In your own personal opinion, are the members of GENES just another version of the nineteenth century Luddites (described in this chapter), who are opposed to new technology because it threatens society's traditional ways of doing things?
3. What can business firms like this one do to reduce public concerns and fears about the new technological and scientific advances that occur in a knowledge society?

19

Ecology and Environmental Policy

The 1990s are being called the decade of the environment. Strong public interest in preserving nature's ecological balance and a clean, healthy environment means that business must constantly strive to achieve these goals for society. At the same time, business is expected to produce needed goods and services at reasonable prices. The task for corporate and public policy makers is to find socially acceptable ways to meet both environmental and economic goals.

Key Questions and Chapter Objectives

This chapter focuses on these key questions and objectives:

- How are business and environmental concerns related to each other?
- How, and why, has environmental damage become a major national and global issue?
- What are the main features of United States environmental laws?
- How has environmentalism changed in the 1990s?
- What are the major environmental challenges for business in the 1990s?

It rises out of the Arizona desert like a giant greenhouse, a beacon of light against the dark, star-filled sky. Inside, eight human beings are living and working in eight climatological zones including rainforest, ocean, savannah, and desert. Living in each zone are appropriate animals and plants, balanced in the best self-sustaining ways that human beings can imagine. This environment will be sealed tightly for two years, during which time the people, animals, plants, and other living creatures will try to survive. It is called "Biosphere 2," and it is a $30 million experiment to test how much we know about ecological interdependencies. The scientists who developed Biosphere 2 say it will inform us about what must happen if humans are ever to build space colonies on Mars. More importantly, it will teach us more about our own relationship with Biosphere 1, the planet Earth.[1]

Thousands of miles away, crews of workers toil on the oily shores of the Persian Gulf. They are trying to clean up the remains of one of the world's worst oil spills, the intentional dumping of oil by Iraqi military officials during the 1990–1991 war. Environmental experts watched helplessly as the spill killed thousands of sea birds, turtles, fish, and other living organisms. Some experts concluded that the spill would leave the Persian Gulf a "dead sea." Others concluded that it would take years or decades for the shores of the Gulf to become pollution-free.

People living near Prince William Sound, Alaska, the Rhine River that flows through Switzerland and Germany, and the Russian city of Kiev, a few miles north of Chernobyl, understand the importance of the biosphere and the terrible consequences of human damage to the environment. The Exxon Valdez oil spill, the explosion at a Sandoz AG factory in Basel, Switzerland, and the nuclear reactor fire at Chernobyl are tragic milestones in recent environmental history. Today, the world is more aware than ever of the limited ability of earth to accept such ecological shocks. There is a new urgency to halting environmental damage, cleaning up the effects of past practices, and creating a new relationship between economic activity and environmental concerns.

Tragic events symbolize the major collision between industrial technology and nature's ecological systems. Agricultural chemicals, nuclear power, and the many other advances made possible by modern science and technology bring enormous benefits to humankind. But the human price and the pressures on the earth's ecological systems are sometimes unacceptably high. Finding a balance between industrial benefits and life-sustaining ecological systems is a major challenge facing business managers, government policymakers, and society. The work of the "biospherians" in Biosphere 2 is intended to advance our scientific understanding of humans and the environment. The work of business and government leaders, and society generally, is critical to meeting what has been called the challenge of "managing planet earth."[2]

ECOLOGICAL CHALLENGES

Ecology is the study of how living things—plants and animals—interact with one another and with their environment. The ecological challenge occurs when wastes created by human productive activities cannot be readily absorbed into the environment without causing harm. These wastes—for example, strip mining wastes or the emissions from power plants—are produced directly by industrial

[1] John Allen, *Biosphere 2: The Human Experiment*, New York: Penguin Books, 1991. See also "Noah's Ark—The Sequel," *Time*, Sept. 24, 1990, p. 72, and "Planet in a Bottle: The Making of Biosphere 2," *Washington Post Magazine*, Jan. 21, 1990, pp. 10–26.

[2] "Managing Planet Earth," *Scientific American*, Special Issue, September 1989.

operations. Other wastes—for example, automobile exhausts and discarded rubbish—are created by using the goods and services produced by industry. When these wastes are injected into the air, water, open spaces, and human communities, they can upset the long-established natural rhythms, cycles, and interrelationships that support plant, animal, and human life.

The ecological challenge requires business to formulate strategies, for the present and the future, that (a) make the most efficient use of scarce resources, (b) reduce wastes that pollute the environment, and (c) keep industrial production within the limits set by nature's ecological systems. In the 1990s, this challenge is more formidable and more critical than at any time in human history. For this reason, many leaders believe this to be the "decade of the environment."

The Global Commons

Throughout history, communities of people have created "commons." A commons is shared land on which, for example, a herder can graze as many animals as he or she wishes. The limited carrying capacity or ability to sustain population on a given quantity of land of the commons is strained as each individual herder adds more animals to the grazing land. If short-term decisions dominate, the commons will be destroyed because each herder gets a near-term advantage from grazing the maximum number of his or her animals. In the long term, of course, all herders lose. The only solution in the near term is restraint, either voluntarily or through some mutual coercion such as a law that would limit animals to a maximum number. As the author of "Tragedy of the Commons" writes, "Freedom in a commons brings ruin to all."[3]

We live on a **global commons.** Recent scientific evidence has demonstrated that the earth's ecological systems are endangered by the short-term activity that has harmful long-term consequences for the environment. These dangers exist at two levels: (1) local environmental damage, such as toxic waste dumping, leaves areas of the earth unable to support life; and (2) global systems of climate, atmospheric protection, and food resources are breaking down from the cumulative effects of pollution. Depletion of the ozone layer, destruction of rainforests, and desertification of land from topsoil loss are but a few of the ominous global environmental processes now underway. These environmental systems cannot be destroyed without affecting everyone. The deliberate spilling of oil into the Persian Gulf mentioned at the beginning of the chapter damaged not only Iraq's enemies but others in the region.[4] Such events and the outrage they provoke, only reinforce the message that preservation of the global commons is a new imperative for governments, business, and society.

[3] See Garrett Hardin, "Tragedy of the Commons," *Science,* Dec. 13, 1968, pp. 1243–1248. Also, Peter Stillman, "The Tragedy of the Commons: A Re-analysis," *Alternatives: Perspectives on Society and Environment,* 4 (Winter 1975), p. 12.

[4] "A Fragile Ecosystem off Bahrain Faces Ravages of Oil Slick," *Wall Street Journal,* Feb. 13, 1991, p. A–1.

Sustainable Development

The World Commission on Environment and Development, including leaders from many industrialized and developing nations, has described the need for balance between economic and environmental considerations as **sustainable development**—"development that meets the needs of the present without compromising the ability of future generations to meet their own needs."[5] There are two concepts within this idea that bear directly on business and society.

- First, the concept of "needs," in particular the essential needs of the world's population, rich and poor, to survive
- Second, the concept of "limitation" imposed by the state of technology or social organization on the environment's ability to meet present and future needs

Reconciling human needs, which are met through economic activity, with limitations imposed by our environment is the practical challenge that now confronts all businesses. As the views expressed in Exhibit 19A suggest, protection of the global commons through environmental management is a vital step toward sustainable development.

HISTORICAL PERSPECTIVE ON POLLUTION

Pollution needs to be seen in its historical perspective in order for it to be understood with a balanced view. It is not something new to the twentieth century. People have dumped their trash into the soil and water since the beginning of civilization. Archeological excavations show the trash of several civilizations (not generations) dumped one on top of the other. Smoke from household fires has polluted the air since the Stone Age. Citizens of early Rome complained that soot from fires dirtied their clothes, and London was described in 1660 as covered with "clouds of smoke and sulphur."

Natural Pollution

Nature itself pollutes the air. Dust storms toss dirt and debris into the air, natural forest fires cast a pall of smoke over mountain valleys, and lightning creates certain chemical compounds. The pollution from volcanoes is phenomenal and puts modern pollution clearly in perspective. The 1980 eruption of Mount St. Helens in the state of Washington spewed 1.3 billion cubic yards of ash and rock into the air, which was enough material to fill 162.5 million dump trucks. One hundred square miles of forestland were burned or polluted, as were fisheries, streams, and lakes.

[5] The World Commission on Environment and Development, *Our Common Future,* New York: Oxford University Press, 1987, p. 43.

EXHIBIT 19–A

Three Views of the Ecological Challenge

"The conflict between environmental protection and economic competitiveness is a false dichotomy based on a narrow view of the sources of prosperity and a static view of competition. Strict environmental regulations do not inevitably hinder competitive advantage against foreign rivals; indeed, they often enhance it.

Michael Porter, "America's Green Strategy"

"Although efforts to manage the interactions between people and their environments are as old as human civilization, the management problem has been transformed today by unprecedented increases in the rate, scale and complexity of those interactions. What were once local incidents of pollution now involve several nations. . . . What were once acute episodes of relatively reversible damage now affect multiple generations. . . . What were once relatively straightforward confrontations between ecological preservation and economic growth now involve multiple linkages—witness the feedbacks among energy consumption, agriculture and climatic change that are thought to enter into the greenhouse effect."

William Clark, "Managing Planet Earth"

"Thanks to all of us the planet is in trouble. From the factory owner who spills poison into our drinking water, to the teen-ager who swills soda from a disposable bottle, to the primitive hunter who kills rhinoceroses, we are all guilty of contributing to the world's growing environmental problems. But something new has been added in recent years to this striving for a better life. What we used to call progress is being interrupted by a worldwide revolution. In this case, the revolutionaries are consumers, and their battle cry is for products and services that will preserve a cleaner, healthier, richer environment for themselves and their children."

Joe Cappo, *Advertising Age*

SOURCE: Michael E. Porter, "Green Competitiveness," *Scientific American*, Apr. 1991, p. 168; William Clark, "Managing Planet Earth," *Scientific American*, Sep. 1989, p. 47; Joe Cappo, "To Our Readers," *Advertising Age*, Jan. 29, 1991, p. 3.

Although pollution has existed for many centuries, it was of minor significance. Since 1700, however, three additional causes have arisen that have fundamentally altered the seriousness of pollution. They have upset the delicate balance of nature that allowed people to live comfortably in their environment. They are the industrial revolution, a higher standard of living, and the population explosion. All of these have contributed to a related problem, the excessive use of polluting forms of energy. In more recent years, a fourth factor—social value changes associated with technologically advanced societies—has focused greater attention on environmental issues.

The Industrial Revolution

A primary cause of air and water pollution has been the industrial revolution. Its factories spread first across Britain and then the rest of the world, with smokestacks belching contaminants into the air. Industry requires energy, much of which is secured from incomplete combustion that releases pollutants of various types. The complex chemical processes of industry produce undesirable by-products and wastes that pollute land, water, and air. Its mechanical processes often create dust, grime, and unsightly refuse. More recently, the agricultural revolution as an adjunct of the industrial revolution had produced overkill with pesticides, herbicides, chemical fertilizers, refuse from cattle-feeding "factories," and other unpleasant conditions.

One major result of the Industrial Revolution is production of manufactured chemicals that biodegrade slowly or that have cancer-causing potential. As long as nature can biodegrade waste, such as a fallen tree trunk, the waste does not create a long-run problem. However, modern science has created complicated wastes that may take years to biodegrade, so the accumulated waste becomes a burden on the environment. Nuclear wastes also can be dangerous, because they degrade slowly for decades or centuries.

Other chemicals are shown to increase the rate of cancer when the chemicals contact the human system in high concentrations or for prolonged periods of time. In addition, laboratory experiments have shown that some chemicals cause cell mutations, so they are suspected as cancer agents. The result is that business and government must be extremely careful to verify the safety of these products before releasing them for general use.

A Higher Standard of Living

Industrialization has raised the standard of living enormously. As people consume more, their consumption tends to create more wastes. The more they buy, the more paper and packaging are required, most of which becomes refuse. When they buy a car, they travel more and the cars they use leave more airborne pollution.

It is a fact that the real economic output of the United States grew about as much from 1950 to 1980 as it did in the three centuries from the time the pilgrims landed in 1620 until 1950! And pollution tended to increase at somewhat the same pace. Meanwhile the earth's capacity to recycle wastes remained substantially unchanged. The result is that normal and moderate increases in the standard of living in the last few decades have helped create an ecological crisis.

The Population Explosion

The ultimate time bomb in pollution is a speedup in population growth. Population growth is not simply the result of a higher birth rate, because the birth rate is declining in many parts of the world. Instead, population is expanding because people live longer, primarily as a result of economic and medical progress.

Each additional person adds pollutants to land, air, and water. The result is more intensive pollution of these existing resources, unless people take steps to reduce pollution or learn to recycle renewable resources. In the year 1900 in the United States, for example, about 3 million square miles accommodated less than 80 million people. By the 1990s, this area, and the air and water that go with it, had to accommodate over 250 million persons. It should therefore not be surprising that the environment is becoming more polluted.

Changes in Social Values

High-consumption, technologically advanced societies tend to undergo important shifts in social values. With a more secure economic foundation and rising standards of material living for most people, such societies turn their attention to other matters. Leisure time is available for recreation, hobbies, creative expression, and related outlets. Freed from around-the-clock work routines, people can be more concerned about health, nutrition, exercise, and outdoor enjoyment generally. They also may give more attention to voluntary work in their own communities and may join a variety of groups that promote a higher quality of life locally and regionally. Their political interest and involvement tends to be highest, too, particularly where community life is concerned.

These subtle shifts in behavior and attitude probably are symbolic of underlying value changes occurring in society. In turn, the changes have a powerful effect on people's attitudes toward the environment. More concern is expressed about industrial pressures on the natural environment; wilderness areas and open spaces are considered worth preserving; and all kinds of actual or potential threats to ecological balance and human health get more attention. These new attitudes and values have powered the environmental movement and raised the public's consciousness about the importance of their natural surroundings.

ROLE OF GOVERNMENT

Pollution is an external effect, or **environmental externality,** of production. Firms have limited incentive to minimize their externalities, and incur costs, if their competitors do not. Government has the power and capability to require all firms to minimize the external effects of production and thereby has a major role to play in pollution control. It has mechanisms for setting priorities, general policies, and minimum standards for environmental quality. It also can provide economic incentives to encourage businesses, communities, and regions to reduce pollution, and it can offer legal and administrative systems for resolving disputes about pollution.

Often business firms favor government standards because they realize that a cleaner environment can be accomplished only by joint action of all firms. If only one company acts to reduce pollution, the environmental improvement may not be evident, and the remaining pollution will continue to give even the nonpolluting firm a poor public image. Clearly, this situation requires government standards.

FIGURE 19–1
Leading U.S. environmental protection laws.

Year	Law	Description
1969	National Environmental Policy Act	Created Council on Environmental Quality to oversee quality of the nation's environment.
1970	Clean Air Act	Established national air quality standards and timetables.
1972	Noise Pollution and Control Act	Defined noise limits and standards for certain equipment.
1972	Water Pollution Control Act	Established national goals and timetables for clean waterways.
1972	Pesticide Control Act	Required registration of and restrictions on pesticide use.
1974	Safe Drinking Water Act	Authorized national standards for drinking water.
1974	Hazardous Materials Transport Act	Regulated shipment of hazardous materials.
1976	Resource Conservation and Recovery Act	Regulated hazardous materials from production to disposal.
1976	Toxic Substances Control Act	Established national policy to regulate, restrict, and (if necessary) ban toxic chemicals.
1977	Clean Air Act Amendments	Revised air standards.
1977	Surface Mining Control and Reclamation Act	Established standards for strip-mining and land restoration.
1980 & 1988	Comprehensive Environmental Response Compensation and Liability Act (Superfund)	Established superfund and procedures to clean up hazardous waste sites.
1987	Clean Water Act amendments	Authorized funds for sewage treatment plants and waterways cleanup.
1990	Clean Air Act	Required cuts in urban smog, acid rain, greenhouse gas emissions; promoted alternative fuels.

Major Environmental Laws and Agencies

Figure 19–1 summarizes the growth in federal environmental laws enacted by Congress. These command-and-control techniques represented movement away from an unregulated market system. In adopting these laws, Congress was responding to strong public concerns and pressures to save the environment from further damage. Public opinion polls taken regularly show that a strong majority of the public favors environmental protection, so these new laws expressed the general public's preference for environmental action.

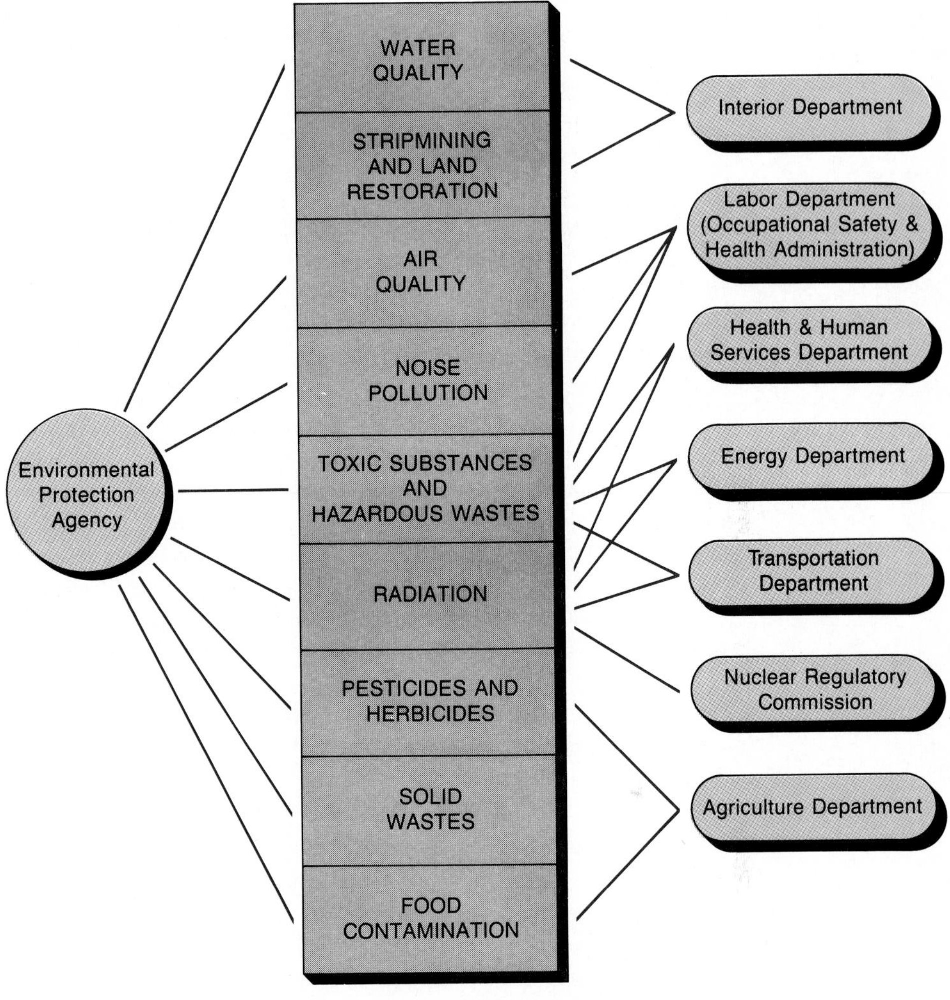

FIGURE 19–2 Regulatory and monitoring jurisdiction of major federal pollution control agencies.

Accompanying these laws were new regulatory agencies and a strengthening of the powers of some existing government departments. Figure 19–2 diagrams the jurisdictional authority of several major federal agencies and departments relative to different types of environmental problems.[6]

Environmental Protection Agency (EPA)

As shown by Figure 19–2, EPA is obviously the nation's main pollution control agency. It was created in 1970 to coordinate most of the government's efforts to protect the environment. It sets standards for air and water quality, controls the use of toxic substances including pesticides, monitors radiation levels, oversees solid-waste and noise-control programs, and even becomes involved in safe-

[6] A fuller description of these and other federal agencies can be found in the *United States Government Manual*, 1990–1991, Office of Federal Register, Washington, DC: Government Printing Office, 1990.

guarding food through its pesticide and toxic substances controls. The EPA also is responsible for conducting cost/benefit analyses to determine what levels of environmental protection are going to be promulgated. These studies compare the benefits to society with the costs for environmental protection that will be incurred. In 1991, EPA became a cabinet-level agency of the federal government.

Nuclear Regulatory Commission (NRC)

Created in 1974 as a successor to the Atomic Energy Commission, NRC licenses and regulates nuclear facilities and materials, including their possible impacts on the environment. It is often a target of groups protesting the licensing and building of nuclear power plants.

Occupational Safety and Health Administration (OSHA)

OSHA, created in 1970, enters into the pollution picture when it attempts to make the work environment safer for employees by controlling emissions from production processes and chemicals used by workers. It has, for example, opposed the use of coke oven sheds intended to reduce external air pollution because they increase pollution inside the plant where the workers are. OSHA also has clashed with EPA concerning dust controls in grain elevators; EPA opposes venting the dust outside, while OSHA wants it reduced inside to protect workers and to reduce the risk of dust-induced explosions. Continuing the historical thread between environmental protection and human health concerns, recent worker and community right-to-know legislation has focused on the use of toxic chemicals by business.

Other government departments

Several other government departments house various research or regulatory organizations responsible for a portion of the federal government's environmental watchdog role. The Department of Health and Human Services has a special mission of monitoring the health effects of toxic substances and radiation exposure. The Interior Department polices water quality and surface mining, including restoration of strip-mined areas, and it administers the endangered species program to protect wildlife. The Transportation Department has regulatory powers regarding the transport of hazardous materials. Nuclear waste problems and issues fall within the jurisdiction of the Energy Department. And the Department of Labor, in addition to housing OSHA, also oversees operation of the Mine Safety and Health Administration.

Council on Environmental Quality (CEQ)

CEQ does not appear in Figure 19–2 because it is not, strictly speaking, a regulatory agency, although it does play an important role. It was established in 1969 to formulate and recommend national policies regarding environmental improvement. Its annual reports to the President contain a wealth of environmental information, and the council has been a strong advocate of continued progress in cleaning up the environment. Perhaps its most important and controversial function is to oversee the environmental impact statements required when federally assisted projects pose a potential threat to the environment.

Regional, State, and Local Agencies

Under the United States system of federalism, state and local governments share pollution control powers with the federal government, although federal regulations and laws are paramount in case of disagreements among regulators. In a typical state, there is a state department of environmental control; some counties have special bureaus to monitor and enforce controls; and many cities have ordinances regulating solid-waste disposal, noise, and other kinds of pollution. Where special pollution problems occur across state lines, regional authorities are sometimes created to encourage cooperation and effective regulation.

State governments have taken the lead since the late 1980s in dealing with environmental problems such as solid waste, environmental labeling, and air quality standards. For business, the varying standards from state to state have a negative effect; many products which are designed and manufactured for a national marketplace must be adapted to individual state markets. The result is costly and has led some business leaders to call for uniform federal standards.

Ways of Applying Government Controls

Government can apply pollution controls in a variety of ways even though the most widely used method of regulation is to impose standards based on the implementation of best available technology. This is intended to bring state-of-art technology to bear on pollution problems. In order to cover different pollutants, pollution sources, economic conditions, and technological features, government needs to use alternative approaches. Some of the alternative approaches that have been employed on a limited basis with good results are incentives, environmental standards, pollution charges, and buying and selling pollution rights.

Incentives for environmental improvement

The government may offer various types of incentives to firms who reduce their pollution. Sometimes these incentives work toward standards that may eventually be required. At other times they work for any improvement. For example, the government may decide to purchase only from those firms that meet certain pollution standards, or it may offer aid to those that install pollution control equipment. Tax incentives, such as faster depreciation for pollution control equipment, also may be used.

The major advantage of incentives is that they encourage voluntary improvement without the stigma of governmental force. They allow different industries and businesses to proceed at a pace that is best for their individual situation. Further, some businesses may be encouraged by incentives to go beyond the minimum standards of compliance that a regulation would have been able to achieve.

The main disadvantage of incentives is that what is voluntary may not be accomplished at all. The incentive may be too small, or there may be side effects, such as expensive product or process redesign, that reduce the appeal of such action for the companies. In such instances, a better incentive can be offered or government can use its regulatory powers to require compliance.

Environmental standards

Another type of pollution control is **environmental standards.** These standards are established by legislative action and applied by administrative agencies and courts. One type of standard is an *environmental-quality standard.* In this instance the specified environment is permitted to have only a certain amount or proportion of pollution, such as a certain proportion of sulfur dioxide in the air. Polluters then are required to control their emissions to maintain the area's standard of air quality. EPA has legal authority to set this type of ambient air quality standard for several different kinds of pollutants considered dangerous to public health and property, as well as similar water quality standards.

A second type of standard is an *emission standard.* For example, the law may specify that the permissible release of fly ash from a smokestack is 1 percent of the ash generated by the plant. Each business is then required to install fly-ash-control equipment that removes at least 99 percent of the fly ash. Emission standards, with some exceptions, are usually set by state and local regulators who are familiar with local industry and special problems caused by topography and weather conditions.

To sum up, federal regulators decide how clean the air and water should be by establishing environmental-quality standards. Local regulators then impose direct emission controls on polluting sources in order to achieve the federally mandated standards.

An advantage of environmental standards is that they are enforceable in the courts; therefore, there is greater assurance that their requirements will be met than through the use of incentives, which are voluntary. Further, they are usually across-the-board standards applicable to all, and so general compliance in society is their goal. A disadvantage is that in order to apply the standard to all businesses fairly, the lawmakers may so water down the standard and fill it with exceptions that it is not effective. A further disadvantage is that the law is only as good as the administrative agency enforcing it. A number of sound laws have been weakened by poor administration. Another disadvantage is that across-the-board standards may cause inequity and suffering because each business faces a different pollution control problem. Older, less efficient plants especially face problems because it is costly to renovate them, and building a new nonpolluting plant may not be justified because of capital costs or market conditions.

The bubble concept. In order to ease compliance with environmental rules while still protecting the public, government regulators in 1979 introduced the "bubble concept." A large industrial plant has many potential sources of pollution from numerous smokestacks, manufacturing processes, and pipes that discharge liquid by-products. At one time, environmental rules required that each one of these pollution sources conform to mandated standards. However, under the bubble concept, regulators treat an entire plant as if it were surrounded by an invisible plastic bubble and they measure only the total pollution coming out of the top of the bubble. This approach means that one or more smokestacks or discharge pipes may actually emit more pollutants than the law allows, as long as the entire plant's total emissions do not violate air and water quality standards.

> An example of how this system works and how much it can save in pollution costs comes from a manufacturer of pressure-sensitive tapes and labels. Pollutants are given off in several stages of manufacturing, particularly in the coating and drying processes. An EPA-approved bubble plan allowed the company to restrict these emissions at some points but not at each and every point in the production run. Total emissions were kept within legal bounds, and the company saved $500,000 per coating line.

Environmental groups sometimes express concern that concepts such as the bubble give business too much discretion and flexibility. They argue that government agencies should not relinquish their responsibility to enforce environmental standards without a guarantee that business will meet the overall pollution reduction goals of the law.

Pollution Charges

Another type of pollution control is establishment of **pollution charges.** Each business pays fees for the quantity of undesirable waste that it releases, and the fee varies with the amount of waste released. The result is, "The more you pollute, the more you pay." A pollution charge can be set high enough to accomplish any desired degree of pollution removal. Pollution charges are based on the proposition that market mechanisms are a better form of control than extensive standards that specify precisely what companies are to do. Sufficiently high charges must be put on pollution to discourage its release. Then each firm is allowed to work out its own least-cost relationship for waste release or abatement according to its own special set of circumstances.

The principal disadvantage of pollution charges is expressed by critics as "a license to pollute." It does not seem consistent with environmental philosophy to allow people to pollute even when they pay a charge for doing so. Further, some critics fear that charges will be so low that present polluters will continue. Another disadvantage is that for some types of pollutants it may be difficult to compute charges, and so this approach may not be effective.

Buying and selling pollution rights

A fourth regulatory approach allows pollution to be controlled by applying the free market principle of buying and selling the right to pollute. Although it sounds contradictory to environmental goals to allow someone to buy the right to pollute, this approach may work as well as other methods and save money at the same time.

The 1990 Clean Air Act incorporated the concept of tradeable rights as a key part of its approach to pollution reduction. The law established emission levels and permitted companies whose emissions were below the standard to sell their "rights" to the remaining permissible amount to another firm whose emissions were above the standard, and hence faced a penalty. The entire "system" would thereby meet the emissions reduction objective but encourage the most economic responses from industry. Interestingly, Minnesota Mining and Manufacturing (3M), which had exceeded emissions standards and thereby had pollution credits to sell, announced that it would not do so because it believed all companies should meet the new standards.

> A similar principle guides a "mitigation banking" project of Tenneco LaTerre, an oil and gas producer in Louisiana's coastal wetlands. Saltwater intrusion threatens the delicate ecological balance of this area, which also is a prime region for energy resources. Oil and gas production requires the building of canals, but these canals permit saltwater to invade freshwater areas. Working with federal and state regulators and private conservationists, Tenneco LaTerre agreed to a plan of protecting and improving the swamplands in advance of canal dredging and filling operations. It then "banks" these ecological improvement credits and uses them to offset future damage caused by its search for energy in the wetlands. For this innovative plan, Tenneco received an Environmental Achievement Award from the National Wildlife Federation's Corporate Conservation Council.

This offset policy operates on a barter or trading principle, rather than actual buying and selling, but the basic idea of swapping pollution debits and credits is the same. Supporters claim that all of these market-oriented policies—bubbles, sales of pollution rights, air pollution banks, offsets—can accomplish government-supervised environmental goals more efficiently, at greater savings, and with less government red tape than other methods.

The trend toward using more flexible, market-oriented approaches to achieve environmental objectives can only be successful if accompanied by a commitment from managers to meet environmental goals. As in other areas of market activity, people have to believe in the "system" for the system to be effective. One can cheat in the environmental marketplace just as one can cheat in the product marketplace. The result is the same: business and society are injured in both circumstances.

COSTS OF A CLEAN ENVIRONMENT

One of the central issues of pollution control and environmental protection is its cost. In the past, the question was whether the nation could afford to clean up its environment and keep it clean. In the twenty years of the modern environmental era that began in the 1970s, the United States has invested heavily in

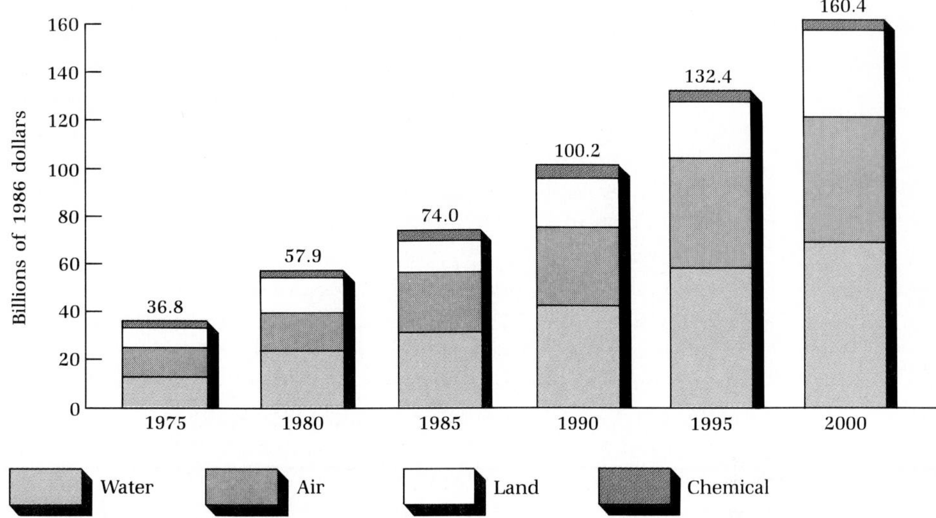

FIGURE 19–3 How much has been spent on pollution control in the United States and how much will be spent in the year 2000.

SOURCE: EPA. *Environmental Investments: The Cost of a Clean Environment,* 1990.

cleaning up the environment. Figure 19–3 shows how much has been spent on pollution control in the United States in recent times. According to a study by the Environmental Protection Agency, environmental spending exceeded $100 billion in 1990, or 2 percent of the nation's gross national product.[7] The report cites three critical facts:

- Spending on environmental problems is rising significantly for governments at all levels and for industry. If the upward trend continues, it could affect U.S. competitiveness in world markets.
- The allocation of resources also is changing. The amount of money spent on land protection will be rising during the 1990s relative to spending on air and water protection.
- The costs of pollution control are rising at a time when unmet needs remain quite large. Public expectations continue to rise, creating pressure for more environmental improvement. But that cannot be achieved without recognition of the price involved.

During the early days of the environmental movement, pollution control expenditures by some companies were punishingly high. Hardest hit were the older "smokestack" industries such as steel, coal, paper manufacturers, chemical companies, and electric utilities. Some of these industries spent from 10 to nearly 20 percent of their total plant and equipment budgets on pollution controls. Industry leaders argued that these large expenditures did not contribute anything to a company's output or to its overall productivity. Money spent on pollution control might create cleaner air and water but it did not help the "bottom line" where profits are measured. When such expenses were imposed on older, marginal

[7] Environmental Protection Agency, *Environmental Investments: The Cost of a Clean Environment,* December 1990, p. iii.

plants, the result was often to close the plant and lay off employees. In the mid-1970s, the Council on Environmental Quality reported that 107 plants employing over 20,000 people had named pollution control as a significant factor leading to their closing. Some experts believed the number was as much as ten times higher!

Looking back, the 1970s were a period of coming to grips with years of environmental neglect. The huge expenses, plant closings, and layoffs were part of the "bitter medicine" business and society had to take to reclaim the environment. At the beginning of the 1970s, a few rivers were so full of toxins that they actually burned.

As the cost issues loomed larger and larger, in the late 1970s and 1980s, business leaders began to fight back against overzealous environmentalists who were ready to accept the benefits of pollution control but seemed to ignore or downplay the costs involved. The result was a blunting—a slowing down, not a halt—of the drive to clean up the environment during the 1980s. Advocates of the slowdown asserted that society should take stock of what it was spending each year and think about whether that money could be spent better on other public purposes or be returned to the taxpaying public in the form of lower taxes. This view was sufficiently widespread to be one of the contributing factors to the development of market-oriented approaches for achieving environmental goals. By the end of the 1980s, political and environmental leaders were exploring many incentive approaches.

By 1990, twenty years of environmental commitment had produced impressive progress in dealing with the worst forms of air and water pollution. This decade presents many other serious problems, of course. Population has increased, and with it comes inevitable pollution. Problems that were not recognized in the past, such as radon and global warming, are now discussed seriously by the general public and government leaders. Moreover, the public has set its sights higher than in the past. Where once it was enough to clean up the burning river, communities now are anxious to remove toxic waste sites and restore environmental features such as the scenic vistas of the Grand Canyon. Meeting all of these environmental objectives requires resources. Figure 19–4 shows that private industry and individuals pay the bulk of the nation's pollution bill. Major industries such as automobiles, utilities, chemicals, and petroleum continue to bear a larger part of this expense.

ENVIRONMENTALISM TODAY

The environmental movement rests on two basic building blocks: conservation and pollution control.[8] The historic roots of the conservation movement sprang forth in mid-nineteenth century America with writers such as Henry David Thoreau, who asserted that "in Wilderness is the preservation of the World." Through

[8] Robert C. Paehlke, *Environmentalism and the Future of Progressive Politics,* New Haven, CT: Yale University Press, 1989, chap. 1.

FIGURE 19–4
Who paid the $1.167 billion for pollution control in the United States in 1990.

SOURCE: EPA, *Environmental Investments*, 1990. BEA, *Pollution Abatement and Control Expenditures*. DRI McGraw-Hill, *22nd Annual Survey of Pollution Control Expenditures, 1988–1990.*

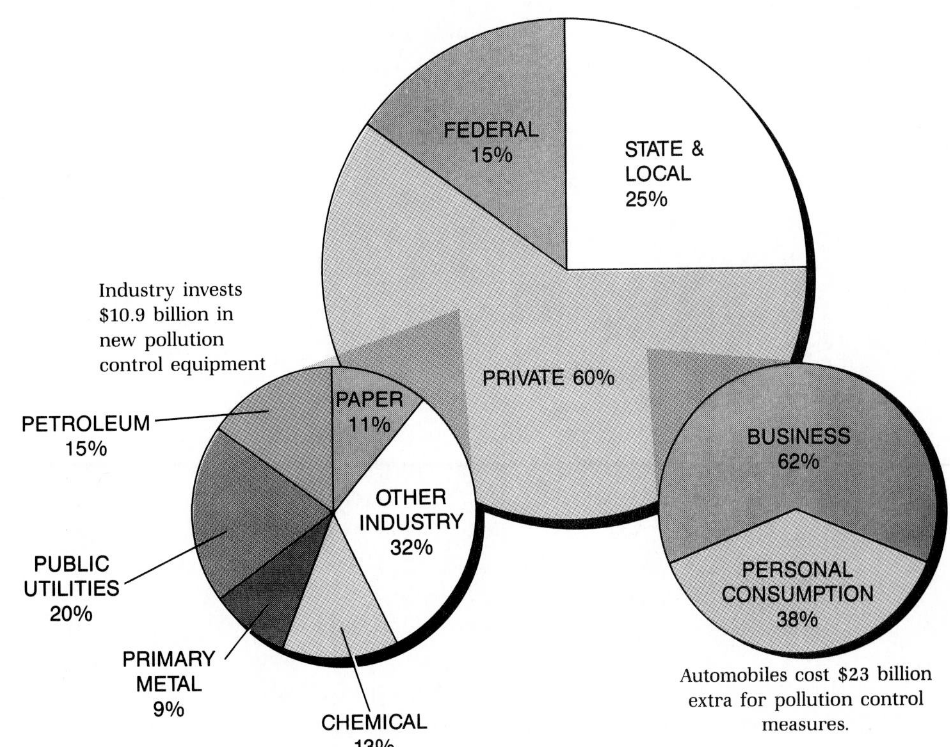

the early 1900s, at the time of President Theodore Roosevelt, conservationist thinking flourished. It became a less prominent strain of public policy for several decades, until it once again arose in the modern environmental movement. Preservation of wilderness, habitat, and biodiversity are major elements of the modern environmental agenda.

The concern about pollution has taken new forms today. First, scientific understanding of the risks to human health and natural resources is more refined than in the past. New risks, such as depletion of the ozone layer, are better understood in terms of causes and effects. Moreover, scientific ability to measure exposures and risks is far greater than in the past. Where scientists once referred to "parts per million" in discussing toxics in water or air, it is now possible to state those exposures in parts per billion or parts per quadrillion! Whether such minute exposures are meaningful to humans is a question provoking great debate even among scientists. But as public fear of toxic exposure grows, great political pressure is exerted on government to reduce or eliminate such environmental risks.

A complex set of scientific, social, and political values also has made environmentalism a powerful political philosophy today. "Green politics" describes a basic view of the world that is politically important in many European countries, including Germany and Holland, where "green" political parties have won seats in the national legislature. Hedrick Smith, author of *The New Russians*, has noted that if a green party were permitted in the Soviet Union, it would almost surely be a significant political power, given public concern in the aftermath of the Chernobyl nuclear accident.[9]

Global Issues

Among the global issues are three that will have major consequences for business and society. They are ozone depletion, global warming, and biodiversity. Each is discussed briefly.

Ozone depletion

Since the 1970s, scientists have warned about the depletion of stratospheric ozone. The ozone layer of the earth's atmosphere provides a shield against harmful ultraviolet rays from the sun. A number of gases used in industry, especially chlorofluorocarbons, or CFCs, react with ozone when they are released into the atmosphere. In the 1970s, CFCs were used as propellants in spray cans and were banned by the United States as research showed the harm being done. However, CFCs are also used in refrigerants and have other industrial uses for which adequate substitutes are not readily available. After years of discussion, an international agreement, known as the Montreal Protocol, was signed by more than 100 nations to eliminate CFC production and use by the end of the 1990s. Companies such as Du Pont, the largest manufacturer of CFCs in the world, were faced with serious ethical and strategic dilemmas as the scientific evidence unfolded. Despite uncertainty, they chose to comply with the international political agreement and began to phase out production and use of CFCs.

Global warming

The earth's atmosphere is warming, according to many scientists. There is some disagreement about the rate at which this is happening, but business and governments are beginning to respond. The release of carbon dioxide is a primary contributor to global warming, along with various other "greenhouse gases" used by industry. Today, international organizations are trying to develop an agreement like the Montreal Protocol that will limit greenhouse gas emissions and slow the pace of warming. If this is not done, experts fear that the polar ice caps will begin to melt, raising sea levels and flooding coastal plain areas such as Bangladesh and threatening many other coastal areas. The human and habitat costs of such climate change could be devastating to many of the world's economies.

Biodiversity

Human beings depend on a great number of species of plant and animal life. Genetic diversity of plants, animals, and people is vital to each species' ability to survive. By destroying this biological diversity, we are actually undermining our survivability as a species and as a planet inhabited by living organisms. Like the

[9] Hedrick Smith, *The New Russians*, New York: Random House, 1990.

Biosphere 2 example discussed at the beginning of the chapter, habitats must be carefully balanced if they are to survive. As natural resources such as the Amazon rainforest are destroyed, many species of plant and animal life are eliminated. This process has serious environmental balancing effects and has high human costs as well. The pharmaceutical industry, for example, each year develops new medicines based on newly discovered plants from rainforest areas. As they are destroyed, so too is this potential for new medicines.

A Paradigm Shift?

For over twenty years, the United States has been grappling with the environmental consequences of economic activity. We have become accustomed to viewing the relationship between economic activity and environmental pollution as tradeoffs, with the latter being the price we must pay for the former. In the view of some experts, that view is about to change. They describe a radical rethinking of the relationship between the economy and the environment. Lester Brown writes, for example:

> Throughout our lifetimes, economic trends have shaped environmental trends, often altering the earth's natural resources and systems in ways not obvious at the time. Now, as we enter the nineties, the reverse is also beginning to happen: environmental trends are beginning to shape economic trends.[10]

The destruction of global resources requires global solutions. The urgency of these problems adds a dramatic new dimension to the environmental debate. It is forcing governmental and business leaders to embrace some radical new ideas about preserving environmental resources. The paradigm, or model, of environmental protection that managers and policymakers have relied upon may be in the process of major change. No one can yet say with certainty where environmental concerns and issues will lead us in this decade. Yet it seems clear that business and government will be responding more seriously, and more creatively, to these problems. Corporate policies and public policies have shifted considerably in recent years, and the foundation of a "green economy" is being created. It is an economy that relies on efficient use of renewable resources, clean technologies, and products that minimize harmful environmental impacts, conservation through waste minimization and recycling, and significant investment of gross national product to clean up environmental problems in communities and nations (e.g., eastern Europe) that are burdened with serious risks. Building such an economy will require many years of effort, but the forces that are driving these trends are powerful. Managing in an economy that integrates environmental considerations and economic decisions will be a major challenge in the years immediately ahead.

[10] Lester R. Brown, "The Illusion of Progress," in L. Brown et al., *State of the World, 1990,* Washington, DC: Worldwatch Institute and W. W. Norton, Inc., 1990, p. 3.

FIGURE 19–5
Environmental issues affect many business functions.

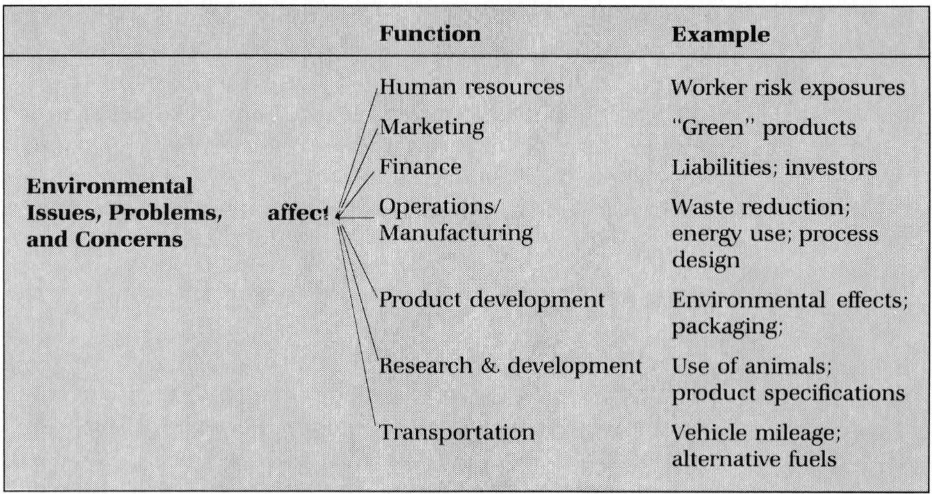

Environmental Issues, Problems, and Concerns **affect**

Function	Example
Human resources	Worker risk exposures
Marketing	"Green" products
Finance	Liabilities; investors
Operations/ Manufacturing	Waste reduction; energy use; process design
Product development	Environmental effects; packaging;
Research & development	Use of animals; product specifications
Transportation	Vehicle mileage; alternative fuels

THE GREENING OF MANAGEMENT

Environmental issues are forcing businesses to manage in new ways.[11] For example, the idea that "waste" gasses could be freely vented to the atmosphere, or waste water could be carelessly dumped into sewer systems, is no longer appropriate. Managers must now think in terms of "closed systems" and must have accounting and information systems that show where these "wastes" have gone. This approach is the practical way in which sustainable development can occur.

If such a policy approach is widely adopted, governments will increasingly work to impose "full costs" and "true costs" of production on business. The company that releases waste into the air and water would then have to pay for the damage to those resources; the business whose products are "overpackaged," thereby contributing to solid waste problems, would have to pay for that extra demand on scarce landfill resources. Such penalties would create incentives for business to make decisions that are not environmentally harmful.

Impact of Environmental Issues

Environmental considerations touch all aspects of a business's operations. As illustrated in Figure 19–5, modern environmental problems affect the management of a company's operations, marketing, human resources, and other activities. Even areas such as finance and accounting are directly influenced by these issues. For example, federal rules now require a company to account for its toxic materials with an elaborate system of reports and an internal audit of environmental com-

[11] See James E. Post, "The Greening of Management," *Issues in Science and Technology*, Summer 1990, pp. 64–72. Also, John Davis, *Greening Business: Managing for Sustainable Development*, Cambridge, MA: Basil Blackwell, 1991.

pliance. Financial officers recognize the increasing power of institutional investors that use environmental criteria in selecting companies for investment. Environmental mutual funds have grown rapidly since the 1980s. Courts also have ruled that the purchaser of real estate assumes the full environmental liability for that property. Companies that merge or acquire other businesses are thus buying potential environmental liabilities as well as assets.

Strategic and operational decisions are both affected. Management decisions about where to locate facilities, what product lines to develop, and environmental, health, and safety standards in all of the firm's facilities are major decisions. How a firm fuels its fleet of cars and trucks (gasoline or alternative fuels), designs energy efficiency into its facilities, organizes employee transportation services, minimizes toxics in manufacturing, and communicates about all of these to communities and government officials affect its environmental profile. In an era when media, government officials, and the general public are interested in these matters, environmental performance has become a focal point for management. Several examples illustrate these effects:

- **Biodegradable trash bags.** Mobil introduced a "degradable" trash bag in June 1989. Within months, a major controversy erupted over the meaning of the term. Environmental concern about the "plastics are forever" threat that trash bags represent had first led Mobil to improve the photodegradability of its bags. Environmentalists were not satisfied that the new bags were any improvement, however, and lawsuits by private and governmental organizations against the claims being made for them quickly followed. Eventually, Mobil withdrew the bags and stopped its advertising. The problem of defining terms such as "reusable," "recycled," and "recyclable" led a coalition of industry trade associations to ask the Federal Trade Commission to develop standards for the use of such terms.[12]
- **Disposable diapers.** Disposable diapers have become a lightning rod of public sentiment on solid waste in the United States; 1 to 2 percent of all solid waste in landfills comes from disposable diapers. Landfill space is increasingly limited and expensive, and many people believe acceptable alternatives (cloth diapers) are readily available. The plastic components of each disposable diaper do not readily decompose, thereby making the landfill problem still worse. Procter & Gamble, the leading manufacturer of disposable diapers, has responded by decreasing the amount of plastic in each diaper from 80 to less than 20 percent and by cooperating with experiments to recycle diapers.
- **Packaging.** McDonald's, the world's largest fast food restaurant chain, has used polystyrene—a form of plastic—to package its foods since the early 1980s. Coffee cups, hamburger boxes, and tray liners create enormous amounts of solid waste. Some communities have acted to ban such pack-

[12] John Holusha, "U.S. Guidelines Sought for Environmental Ads," *New York Times*, Feb. 15, 1991, p. D–2; "Coming Clean on Products: Ecological Claims Faulted," *New York Times*, Mar. 12, 1991, p. D–1.

aging. McDonald's began working with plastics recyclers to develop processes that would enable the company to spend most of its $100 million annual packaging budget on recycled materials. Public criticism eventually led the company to announce a return to paper packaging, a decision that worried the fledgling plastics recycling industry.

- **New products.** During 1990, as war threats in the Persian Gulf pushed oil prices higher, ARCO announced a reformulated gasoline that would improve gas mileage and reduce air pollutants. Although the reformulated gasoline was more expensive than regular unleaded fuel, consumers quickly began using the new product.
- **Environmental leverage.** U.S. retailer Wal-Mart, and Canadian grocery chain, Loblaws, introduced special "green lines" of products in their stores. Suppliers were told to meet new criteria or risk loss of shelf space. Customers were informed that each retailer had selected products that were environmentally safe for the special green tags or labels. Wal-Mart also set up recycling centers in the parking lots of its stores, thereby enabling customers to "get into the recycling habit." The retailers drew favorable consumer responses for their efforts to create environmentally safe choices.
- **Removing environmentally harmful products.** Wisconsin Electric received the National Wildlife Federation's Corporate Conservation Council Environmental Achievement Award in 1991 for a program that recycled refrigerators. Because old refrigerators have large quantities of chlorofluorocarbons (CFCs) in their refrigerants, they pose a danger to the ozone layer if released into the atmosphere. Wisconsin Electric picks up old refrigerators at no charge to its customers, recycles the CFC refrigerant, and thereby prevents environmental damage. The utility was the first in the nation to start such a program, and its success has led other utilities to begin similar programs.
- **Green Seal Programs.** As discussed in Chapter 14, two U.S. groups have begun programs to certify environmental qualifications of products through seal programs. These efforts follow the lead of several European programs which began in the 1980s and developed substantial consumer support. The U.S. programs are called "Green Seal" and "Green Cross," and each has a distinctive label which a certified product can use on its package. Program officials test the products for their environmental effects. Green Seal also analyzes the entire manufacturing process that produced the product to determine how effective the company has been in minimizing environmental side effects. Sponsors believe that several hundred products will be reviewed for seals by 1995.[13]

Consumer support for environmentally safe products does not seem to be a fad. As shown in Figure 19–6, consumers have strong opinions about the industries

[13] See Denis Hayes, "Harnessing Market Forces to Protect the Earth," *Issues in Science and Technology*, Winter 1990–1991, pp. 46–51. See also D. Hayes, "Feeling Green about 'Green'," *Advertising Age*, Jan. 29, 1991, p. 46.

FIGURE 19–6 Public assessment of the environmental concern of ten leading consumer product industries.

SOURCE: Derived from information presented in *Advertising Age,* "The Green Marketing Revolution," Jan. 29, 1991.

Overall Rank	Industry	Industry Mean Score	Best Company Score	(name)
7	Automobiles	2.82	2.85	(Ford Motor Co.)
6	Beer	2.83	2.85	(Anheuser Busch)
1	Cereals	3.13	3.14	(General Mills)
9	Cosmetics	2.55	2.59	(Revlon Group)
10	Diapers	2.46	2.50	(Procter & Gamble—Pampers)
8	Fast food	2.80	2.94	(McDonald's)
5	Laundry soap	2.87	3.00	(Procter & Gamble—Tide)
3	Retail	2.93	3.12	(Wal-Mart)
2	Soft drinks	3.01	3.02	(Pepsi Cola)
4	Toothpaste	2.92	2.98	(Procter & Gamble—Crest)

rating scale: 4 = very concerned; 3 = somewhat concerned; 2 = somewhat unconcerned; 1 = very unconcerned;

and companies that are environmentally aware and responsive. In a public poll, consumers indicated that cereal manufacturers rank highest as an industry in being very concerned about the environment. Diaper manufacturers ranked lowest among the ten industries, finishing below cosmetics, fast food, and automobiles. Do these rankings make a difference? When understood as a part of a pattern of public concern and changing buyer behavior, they seem to reinforce a basic message to business: Behave as if the environment matters, because we believe it does!

SUMMARY POINTS OF THIS CHAPTER

- Business, through its production of goods and services, and consumers by using them, unavoidably create pollution. These by-products of economic activity can have negative effects on the environment. It is a price we pay for growth and development.
- The cumulative effects of economic activity have reached proportions never before achieved. Despite two decades of cleanup, some forms of pollution are worse than ever. Global problems, such as ozone depletion, global warming, and rainforest destruction, are relatively new crises that affect everyone.
- Environmental laws in the United States have traditionally been of the

"command and control" variety, specifying standards and results. New laws are adding a layer of incentives to encourage environmentally sound behavior.

- Environmentalism today is a global phenomenon. Scientific knowledge is more precise, "green politics" has emerged in Europe and the United States, and international organizations are actively working to create global standards for industry.
- All business functions are affected by environmental issues, especially manufacturing, marketing, and product development. Corporations are especially sensitive to environmentally concerned customers who have sparked a broad "green revolution." The primary challenge for business is to act in ways that are environmentally sustainable.

KEY TERMS AND CONCEPTS USED IN THIS CHAPTER

- Ecology
- Global commons
- Sustainable development
- Environmental externality
- Environmental incentives
- Environmental standards
- Pollution charges
- Pollution rights
- Green management

DISCUSSION CASE

THE VALDEZ PRINCIPLES

Investors have exerted pressure on companies to address environmental problems. For example, a group of institutional investors known as the Coalition for Environmentally Responsible Economies, or CERES, developed a statement of principles of environmental conduct. Named the Valdez Principles, in recognition of the Alaskan oil spill tragedy, CERES has communicated with more than four hundred companies and urged them to sign the principles. By 1991, seventeen small specialty companies had agreed to do so. Most large companies have objected to one or another of the principles, however. According to a number of corporate environmental officers, the principles dealing with restoration of past environmental damage, disclosure of potential hazards, creating environmental positions on management teams and boards of directors, and conducting annual audits are the most difficult to accept. CERES members have pressed companies to discuss the problems openly, and if necessary, adopt their own statements. The real goal is to get the corporations to pay attention to these issues. With billions of investor dollars behind the effort, it seems unlikely that business will be able to ignore the pressure. The principles are:

1. *Protection of the biosphere:* Minimize and seek to eliminate the release of pollutants that cause damage to the air, water or earth or its inhabitants. Safeguard habitats in rivers, lakes, wetlands, coastal zones and oceans and minimize contributing to the greenhouse effect, depletion of the ozone layer, acid rain or smog.

2. *Sustainable use of natural resources:* Make sustainable use of renewable resources, such as water, soils and forests. Conserve nonrenewable natural resources through efficient use and careful planning. Protect wildlife habitat, open spaces and wilderness, while preserving biodiversity.

3. *Reduction and disposal of wastes:* Minimize the creation of waste, especially hazardous waste, and wherever possible recycle material. Dispose of wastes through safe and responsible methods.

4. *Wise use of energy:* Make every effort to use environmentally safe and sustainable energy sources to meet our needs. Invest in improved energy efficiency and conservation in our operations. Maximize energy efficiency of products we produce and sell.

5. *Risk reduction:* Minimize environmental, health and safety risks to employees and communities in which we operate by employing safe technologies and operating procedures and by being constantly prepared for emergencies.

6. *Marketing of safe products and services:* Sell products or services that minimize environmental impacts and are safe as consumers use them. Inform consumers of environmental impacts of products or services.

7. *Damage compensation:* Take responsibility for harm we cause to the environment by making every effort to fully restore the environment and to compensate persons adversely affected.

8. *Disclosure:* Disclose to employees and to the public incidents relating to operations that cause environmental harm or pose health and safety hazards. Disclose potential environmental, health or safety hazards posed by operations and take no action against employees who report conditions that create a danger to the environment or pose health and safety hazards.

9. *Environmental directors and managers:* Commit management resources to implement these principles, monitor and report on implementation, and ensure that the board and CEO are kept informed of and fully responsible for environmental interests.

10. *Assessment and annual audit:* Conduct and make public an annual self-evaluation of progress in implementing these principles and in complying with all applicable laws and regulations throughout worldwide operations. Work toward the timely creation of independent environmental audit procedures completed annually and made available to the public.[14]

[14] Coalition for Environmentally Responsible Economies (CERES).

Discussion Questions

1. Analyze the ten points of the Valdez Principles. Do these seem reasonable to you? Why or why not?
2. Read the annual reports of large companies such as Dow Chemical, Eastman Kodak, General Motors, or Monsanto. Do they seem to be addressing the issues in the principles?
3. Why would large companies object to these principles? What advantage could a company gain by agreeing to the principles? What benefits could a small company get by signing?

Case Studies in Corporate Social Policy

CASE STUDY THE TYLENOL RECALLS[1]

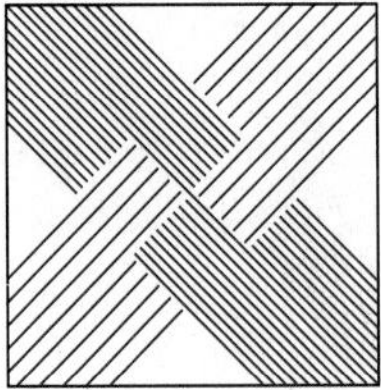

Twice within a four-year period, one or more poisoners placed cyanide in capsules of Extra-Strength Tylenol sold as over-the-counter (o-t-c) medications for pain relief. These tainted capsules killed seven persons in 1982 and one person in 1986. Tylenol's manufacturer, Johnson & Johnson, is a leading health care products firm, and at the time of both poisonings Tylenol was one of the company's major and most successful products.

When these two poisoning episodes occurred, the company faced crises of enormous ethical and financial proportions. With human lives at stake, swift decisions were needed to prevent further deaths. But with millions of dollars also at stake, company officials realized that a false step or a bad judgment could jeopardize not only Tylenol but also the company's financial future and the jobs of its employees. Few management challenges have been so filled with frightening possibilities as the ones that unfolded in Chicago in September 1982 and in New York's Westchester County in February 1986.

When it was all over, most observers praised Johnson & Johnson officials for the way they handled the two crises. Their actions were widely accepted as "the way to do it."

Johnson & Johnson: A Brief History

Johnson & Johnson began operations in 1886 in New Brunswick, New Jersey, and was incorporated in 1887. The company pioneered the concept of an antiseptic surgical dressing, based on the work of Sir Joseph Lister, an English surgeon. Over the years the company grew in size by broadening its array of products for the health care market. BAND-AID, one of its best known and most widely used products, was introduced in 1921.

The company pursued a vigorous strategy of growth by acquisition as well as internal development of new products and businesses. New product lines included baby care, feminine protection, birth control, ethical surgical products, hypodermic needles and syringes, prescription drugs, veterinary drugs, kidney dialysis products, and other health care items.

Simultaneously with product line expansion and diversification, the company began to expand internationally. Johnson & Johnson in 1982 was a worldwide group of 150 companies, based in 50 countries, whose products were sold in 149 nations.

[1] Prepared with the assistance of Vasudevan Ramanujam. Sources include articles in the *Wall Street Journal,* the *New York Times, Advertising Age, Chemical Week, Business Week, Newsweek, Fortune,* and *Chemical Marketing Reporter* during October and November 1982 and several months in 1986. These sources are cited in the case narrative only when used for verifying specific figures or quotations, company information, and similar items. Two Johnson & Johnson publications were used: "Brief History of Johnson & Johnson" and "The Tylenol Comeback," both available from the company.

In 1959, the company acquired McNeil Laboratories, a producer of prescription pharmaceuticals. In keeping with the spirit of decentralization generally prevalent in the company, McNeil was operated as an autonomous division. McNeil was the manufacturer of the Tylenol line of o-t-c analgesics.

The parent company was known as a maker of quality products serving the needs of society. Its commitment to quality products and its strong consumer orientation were handed down from the company's early founders. The following legend appears on a large bronze plaque in the company's New Brunswick headquarters:

> We believe our first responsibility is to the doctors, nurses, and patients, to mothers and all others who use our products and services. In meeting their needs, everything we do must be of high quality.

The above quotation was a part of what the company called its "credo" philosophy. In looking back over their own conduct in the face of the Tylenol tragedy, company officials credited this "credo" for guiding their actions and decisions during the 1982 crisis.[2]

The First Tylenol Crisis: 1982

The first five Tylenol-related deaths occurred on Thursday, September 30, 1982, in three Chicago suburbs. That morning Johnson & Johnson learned of three of the deaths from a reporter of the *Chicago Sun-Times*, who, in turn, had heard about them from the Cook County (Illinois) medical examiner's office. Within forty-eight hours, the roster of victims rose to seven, all from the Chicago area.

The Company's Response

Johnson & Johnson's response to the bad news was swift and direct. Within hours of learning of the Chicago deaths, the company announced a recall of all 93,400 bottles of Extra-Strength Tylenol in the implicated MC2880 lot, which had been manufactured in McNeil's Fort Washington, Pennsylvania, plant and distributed to thirty-one Eastern and Midwestern states. This decision was made quickly, even though tests on samples of the same lot did not reveal any contamination, suggesting that the poisoning may not have occurred in manufacture. By noon that day, the firm had dispatched nearly half a million mailgrams to physicians, hospitals, and wholesalers, alerting them to the danger. A press staff member and several scientific and security people were flown to Chicago by corporate jet to assist in the investigations. A laboratory was set up outside Chicago and staffed with thirty chemists to help the authorities analyze samples of Extra-Strength Tylenol.[3] It placed an additional 500 salespersons from two of its phar-

[2] "The Tylenol Comeback," New Brunswick, NJ: Johnson & Johnson, p. 4.

[3] However, local authorities appeared to have been reluctant to release the suspected samples to the company, leading to one of the few skirmishes between the company and the investigators. In another instance, an attorney for McNeil objected when Chicago authorities broadened the recall to include other forms of Tylenol in addition to extra-strength capsules. See the *Wall Street Journal*, Oct. 4, 1982, pp. 3, 16.

maceutical divisions on call to help recall the Tylenol shipments. By late evening the company also offered a $100,000 reward to anyone who could give information leading to the arrest and conviction of "the person or persons responsible for the murders." All advertising and promotion of Tylenol was suspended. One of the company's two plants that manufactured Tylenol capsules was idled.

The recall was expanded by the following day to include one more batch of 171,000 bottles that had been manufactured in Round Rock, Texas, since the death of the latest victim was traced to a capsule from that batch. However, the worst was yet to come. An apparently unrelated case of strychnine-contaminated Tylenol that almost killed a man in Oroville, California, prompted the company to extend the recall to *all* Tylenol capsules, both regular and extra-strength. Production of the capsules was temporarily halted. On October 5, 1982, within a week of the first of the Tylenol deaths, the company was beginning to pull back the product and was considering destroying the entire stock. Some 31 million bottles with an estimated retail value of $100 million were involved. The decision to recall all Tylenol was considered by the company for four days and was no doubt hastened by the California incident. The after-tax impact was expected to be approximately $50 million. On the following morning, cyanide was discovered in Tylenol capsules in the apartment of a Philadelphia student who was thought to have committed suicide some seven months earlier.

The company stated that its first reaction was to protect the public and inform them about rapidly unfolding developments. The recalls seem to have been decided on almost as a matter of course. In fact, according to *Fortune,* James E. Burke, the chairman of Johnson & Johnson, had wanted to announce a total recall of all Extra-Strength Tylenol from the very beginning, but, surprisingly, the FBI and the Food and Drug Administration (FDA) had advised him against premature recall on the grounds that such an action might "cause more public anxiety than it would relieve."[4] Early during the crisis, Burke said, "It's important that we demonstrate that we've taken every single step possible to protect the public, and that there's simply nothing else we can do."[5] At that point, the company said they were not thinking about the future of the brand. Another Johnson & Johnson executive declared, "We've been trying to put out the fire. We really haven't thought about how to rebuild the house."

In its effort to protect and inform the public, the company undertook a number of other voluntary steps. A conscious decision was made not to place any warning ads in newspapers but to respond only to press calls. In the first week of the crisis, toll-free lines were established to respond to inquiries concerning the safety of Tylenol. Through November, more than 30,000 phone calls had been handled through this medium. The company made it a policy to respond to every letter from consumers about Tylenol. By late November, some 3,000 responses had been sent.

[4] "The Fight to Save Tylenol," *Fortune,* Nov. 29, 1982, p. 48.

[5] *Wall Street Journal,* Oct. 4, 1982, p. 16.

FIGURE 1 **Estimated Market Shares of the Over-the-Counter Analgesic Industry Prior to the Tylenol Crisis**

Company	Product	Market Share (%)
Johnson & Johnson (McNeil Consumer Products Company Division)	Tylenol	37
American Home Products	Anacin	13
	Anacin-3	1
Sterling Drug	Bayer Aspirin	11
Bristol-Myers	Excedrin	10
	Bufferin	9
	Datril	1
All others		18

SOURCE: *Chemical Week,* Nov. 3, 1982, p. 30.

Rebuilding the Tylenol name

While the above steps were of a firefighting nature, the company soon began to plot a strategy for reestablishing the embattled Tylenol name. A seven-member crisis management team of key Johnson & Johnson and McNeil executives began to meet twice daily to make decisions on rapidly developing events and to coordinate companywide efforts.

At the time of the crisis, Tylenol was the leading o-t-c analgesic, with an estimated 37 percent share of the $1.2 billion a year market. From modest beginnings in the mid-seventies, when it held a 10 percent share of a much smaller market, Tylenol was carefully nurtured to its dominant position by shrewd and sometimes hard-hitting marketing techniques. By 1982 Tylenol had far outdistanced its nearest competing brands. Figure 1 gives estimated market share data for those brands.

Tylenol had been positioned as a safe and effective alternative to aspirin, and the company claimed it to be free of the unpleasant side effects that some aspirin users experienced. For many years it was promoted heavily among doctors and hospitals before a concerted program of advertising and promotion directly aimed at the end user was begun. This change of approach was mainly in response to the heavy advertising and promotion campaigns launched by competitor Bristol-Myers for its own nonaspirin painkiller, Datril. In the marketing battle that ensued, Tylenol emerged the clear winner. Tylenol's spectacular success over the years was attributed to its image as a safe and effective product and to the trust and support it received from the medical community, the retail trade, and, of course, the final consumer. Advertising had clearly played a major role in the process of building up this overwhelming level of trust and support. In 1981, Tylenol alone accounted for an estimated $43 million of advertising expenditures, the largest in the analgesics field.[6]

[6] *Chemical Week,* Nov. 3, 1982, p. 33.

The critical question facing Johnson & Johnson and McNeil in the days immediately following the crisis was, "To what extent had the Chicago incidents damaged the product's image, and how long would it take to repair that damage, if it was at all possible to do so?" To many experts the brand's prospects appeared very dim, in view of its association with death. But the company remained strongly committed to the Tylenol name. The options of dropping the line or reintroducing it under another name were never seriously considered.

To gauge the shifting public perceptions in the weeks following the crisis, the company commissioned a series of opinion polls. The polls revealed that both the brand and the company were getting a lot of potentially negative publicity, the effects of which could not be estimated with confidence. However, a large proportion of the respondents did not appear to be blaming the company for the poisonings, and as time passed, more and more of the regular users were expressing a willingness to return to the fold. By the fifth week after the tragedy, this figure rose to 59 percent. When asked if they would buy Tylenol in a tamper-resistant package, as many as 77 percent of regular Tylenol users answered positively.[7]

In the wake of the crisis, sales of Tylenol fell sharply, by as much as 80 percent, according to some estimates. At the same time, sales of aspirin and other competing brands of nonaspirin pain relievers were beginning to surge. In the face of such adverse circumstances, the company mounted a carefully planned campaign of communication and packaging modifications in an effort to win back the public trust it was losing. It began by sending some 2 million pieces of literature to doctors, dentists, nurses, and pharmacists, the groups that had most contributed to making Tylenol the success it was. The fact that the company had not been the source of the poisonings was strongly emphasized in the communications.

Throughout the crisis, employees of the company had shown a strong sense of commitment and high morale. Hundreds of them volunteered to work around the clock without extra pay, and many were staffing the phone lines to answer as many calls as possible. To help maintain that morale, the company also undertook an internal communications program. This included writing letters to all employees and retirees, keeping them updated on important information and thanking them for their continued support and assistance. Four videotaped special reports were prepared and distributed or shown to employees.

Before the crisis, the company had generally been known for its low-key profile and tight-lipped approach to dealing with press and public inquiries. The crisis changed that policy. The press became a close ally of the company, especially in the first frenzied days, providing the company with its most accurate information on various developments. The company praised the efforts of the broadcast community, which had been instrumental in getting Tylenol commercials off the air in a matter of hours after news of the first deaths.[8] In a reversal of the company's traditional policy, company executives made several appearances on television,

[7] See *Advertising Age,* Nov. 15, 1982, p. 78, and Oct. 11, 1982, p. 78.

[8] *Advertising Age,* Oct. 11, 1982, p. 78.

including *60 Minutes, The Phil Donahue Show, ABC Nightline, Live at Five,* and others. Interviews were freely granted to business journals and periodicals, such as *Fortune* and the *Wall Street Journal.* In short, every effort was made to "get the word out," to use the company's own phrase.

The press praised Johnson & Johnson's quick action, citing it as an example of corporate responsibility. The *Wall Street Journal* declared:

> Johnson & Johnson, the parent company that makes Tylenol, set the pattern of industry response. Without being asked, it quickly withdrew Extra-Strength TYLENOL from the market at a very considerable expense . . . the company chose to take a large loss rather than expose anyone to further risk. The anticorporation movement may have trouble squaring that with the devil theories it purveys.

The *Washington Post* equally admired the company's actions in the face of adversity:

> Johnson & Johnson has efficiently demonstrated how a major business ought to handle a disaster. From the day the deaths were linked to the poisoned TYLENOL . . . Johnson & Johnson has succeeded in portraying itself to the public as a company willing to do what's right regardless of cost.[9]

While Tylenol advertising still remained off the air, Johnson & Johnson beamed a series of trust-building messages to the American public during October and early November. These sixty-second messages featured Dr. Thomas Gates, medical director of McNeil, who assured consumers that the company would do everything possible to maintain the trust and support of the public, and it also alerted them to the fact that the company planned to reintroduce Tylenol capsules in new tamper-resistant packaging.

The company hastened to be the first in the market with improved tamper-resistant packaging for its Tylenol products, even though new regulations on the packaging of o-t-c products were still being debated by the Food and Drug Administration (FDA) and the Proprietary Association, the trade association of the o-t-c products industry. On November 11, 1982, a new safety package, with three separate safety seals, was demonstrated at a video conference, broadcast via satellite, and simultaneously aimed at thirty cities and attended by some 1,000 reporters and news media representatives. In that conference the chairman of Johnson & Johnson reaffirmed his company's continuing commitment to the Tylenol name, referring to the commitment as a "moral imperative."

The company's polls had revealed that 35 percent of Tylenol users had thrown away their supplies of the product when news of the crisis broke. To make good their loss and to help overcome their reluctance to use the product again, the company placed special coupons in newspapers nationally that could be exchanged for a free bottle of any Tylenol product. A toll-free number also was established for this purpose. Consumers could call and a coupon would be sent in the mail for a free bottle of Tylenol.

[9] Both press passages are quoted in Johnson & Johnson, "The Tylenol Comeback," p. 8.

The company was fully aware that while a beginning had been made, restoring Tylenol's market share to its precrisis level of 37 percent was still a formidable task. In one interview, the chairman of McNeil stated that he expected Tylenol's share for the next reporting period to be in the 5 to 10 percent range.[10] In that interview, it also was revealed that in a four-city survey where Tylenol had a 27 percent market share before the tragedy, grocery scanning data showed that the brand's share fell to 6.5 percent the week after the poisonings but had rebounded to 18 percent. By the end of 1982, Tylenol had regained first place among analgesics, with 29 percent market share.

The cost impact

In addition to the toll of human lives, the Tylenol tragedy had a profound cost impact on the company in the short term. Just prior to the crisis, Johnson & Johnson's stock had been trading on the market at $46.125. Immediately following the crisis, it fell by as many as 7 points before eventually stabilizing in the mid-40s.

The costs directly associated with the recall of the capsules translated into a $50 million write-off against the company's third-quarter profits. In percentage terms, this represented a 26 percent drop in net income. Fourth-quarter domestic income declined by more than $25 million compared with the same period in 1981, and industry observers believed the drop was due to the Tylenol incident.

The company decided to absorb the costs of the improved packaging, estimated to be 2.4 cents a bottle. Since price increases were ruled out as a matter of company policy and may not have been practical anyway, these costs would continue indefinitely. The costs of the coupon campaign were estimated between $20 million and $40 million. The dealer discount program also added to the overall costs. Johnson & Johnson estimated that the cost of all these actions could run as high as $140 million.

The company also was faced with three lawsuits shortly after the deaths in Chicago. However, some observers believed that since it appeared that the company was not responsible for the poisonings and could not reasonably have foreseen them, no damages could be won in court.[11]

Other intangible costs to the company were difficult to estimate. For many weeks the Tylenol crisis occupied the key executives of the company on a full-time basis. The day-to-day operations of the other divisions of the company were left to others. What effect this had on their performance, if any, remains uncertain.

Government regulatory responses

The first actions of a regulatory nature were taken by local and state officials, who issued warnings and orders of their own. Stores began to remove stocks of Tylenol in response to these warnings. At first the FDA issued a warning related only to the first implicated lot, but as news of more deaths followed, implicating other lots, the warnings were extended to Tylenol capsules in general. The FDA

[10] *Advertising Age,* Nov. 15, 1982, p. 78.

[11] *New York Times,* Oct. 7, 1982, p. B-12; and *Chemical Week,* Oct. 13, 1982, p. 17.

also sent its inspectors to McNeil's Fort Washington, Pennsylvania, plant, to collect samples, review batch records, and to investigate manufacturing processes. The agency's nineteen laboratories began collecting and testing some 40,000 Tylenol samples. It was expected at that time that some 2,100 FDA employees would assist in the testing. Over the weeks that followed, some 8 million capsules were analyzed, of which 75 were found to contain cyanide. The major question for the agency was to determine quickly if the cyanide had been introduced into the capsules during the manufacturing process, at a later point in the distribution chain, or at retail stores.

Chicago's mayor went on the air to urge citizens not to take any Tylenol. The sale of Tylenol was banned in the state of North Dakota, and Colorado ordered stores to withdraw all Tylenol capsules, while Massachusetts retailers were directed to remove all Tylenol products. Warnings also were issued by health officials in New York. Similar actions were taken in foreign countries as well.[12]

Soon initiatives for regulating safety packaging of all o-t-c products were taken. On October 4, the Cook County Board voted unanimously to require all o-t-c drugs and medicines to carry manufacturers' seals. The ordinance was to take effect in ninety days, and required a seal of plastic, paper, metal, or cellophane, which restricts air into the product, and when broken, would be evident to an observer or consumer. Mayor Byrne also proposed an ordinance to the City Council that would, after hearings, require protective sealings on all o-t-c products.

There was some concern that piecemeal local and state regulations would proliferate. The federal government was irked by the precipitate actions of local authorities in Chicago, which some believed had been politically motivated because county legislators were facing reelection soon. The FDA was ordered to enact an emergency packaging code that would require manufacturers to introduce interim bottle seals within ninety days. Industry and government officials had announced earlier that they would work together to develop federal regulations requiring tamper-resistant packaging for all drugs sold without a prescription. It was anticipated that such regulation would take time to draft and implement, since no single, simple solution would be uniformly applicable to all products. Also, the industry association believed that individual companies should have sufficient flexibility in choosing packaging methods or options. A later meeting of industry representatives concluded that tamper-resistant packaging was feasible for drug items. As a first step, a tamper-resistant package was defined as "one that can reasonably be expected to provide visible evidence to consumers if the package is tampered with or opened."[13]

While the industry association and the FDA both appeared to favor some form of packaging regulation, one economist expressed doubts about the costs and benefits of such regulation. In an article in the *New York Times*, he argued that the costs of such regulation would far exceed the benefits, and the consumer

[12] *New York Times*, Oct. 2, 1982, p. 21, and Oct. 6, 1982, p. A-24.

[13] *Chemical Week*, Oct. 13, 1982, p. 16; *New York Times*, Oct. 6, 1982, p. A-1; *Wall Street Journal*, Oct. 8, 1982, p. 17.

would pay more for drugs.[14] Some expressed more pragmatic concerns, namely, that seals and other elaborate protective measures might render the package harder to open by arthritics, who were among the major users of pain relievers.

Competitor and industry responses

Competitive reactions varied. Many competitors asserted that they had no intentions of exploiting the company's misfortunes. However, the actions of some told a different story. Major retail chains such as Walgreen in Chicago were approached by the representatives of Johnson & Johnson's competitors with offers to fill the shelf space vacated by Tylenol.[15] American Home Products, maker of Anacin, Anacin-3, and Arthritis Pain Formula, and normally low-key and press-shy, called a rare press conference to announce plans for increased production of its nonaspirin pain relievers. The company also announced plans for newer formulations of its Anacin-3 brand.[16] Although American Home Products declined to disclose whether it planned to step up advertising support for its products, one report alleged that the company was trying to pick up the air time released by Tylenol. The company responded with a statement that it was not AHP's policy to capitalize on the misfortunes of its competitors.[17]

At Bristol-Myers, whose Datril had suffered badly when Johnson & Johnson battled it head-on with heavy advertising of Tylenol, company officials would not discuss any plans. It acknowledged a surge in demand for Datril and stated that the company was looking into new packaging for all its analgesic products. The company ran coupons for Bufferin and Excedrin in a number of national newspapers during the first week of the Tylenol crisis. What made these advertisements unusual was their placement on late-news pages, not in the usual food-shopping sections. A company representative claimed that the company was simply doing "business as usual."[18] Seemingly opportunistic moves also were made by Richardson-Vicks, which ran consumer ads for the first time for its newly acquired Percogesic brand.

The search for the killer

Finding the Tylenol poisoner was not easy. One suspect was convicted and given a ten-year jail term for trying to extort $1 million from Johnson & Johnson after the poisonings took place; his wife had formerly worked for Tylenol's maker. Another person who had been employed in a store where some of the poisoned capsules were found was imprisoned for the 1983 slaying of a man he believed had identified him to the police as a Tylenol suspect. Authorities were not convinced that either of these suspects was the actual Tylenol killer. A police official

[14] Paul W. MacAvoy, "F.D.A. Regulation—At What Price?" *New York Times,* Nov. 21, 1982, p. F-3.

[15] *Wall Street Journal,* Oct. 5, 1982, p. 22; *Chemical Week,* Nov. 3, 1982, p. 30.

[16] *Advertising Age,* Oct. 18, 1982, p. 82.

[17] *Advertising Age,* Oct. 11, 1982, p. 78; *Chemical Week,* Nov. 3, 1982, p. 30; and *Fortune,* Nov. 29, 1982, p. 49.

[18] *Advertising Age,* Oct. 11, 1982, p. 78.

said, "This is an unusually tough case. There's little physical evidence. The victims and the tainted bottles show no pattern. And the motive is unclear. It's enormously frustrating."[19]

The Second Tylenol Crisis: 1986

By early 1986, Tylenol was once again the premier over-the-counter (o-t-c) pain reliever, with a 35 percent share of the annual $1.5-billion market. It was Johnson & Johnson's most profitable single brand, bringing in $525 million in revenues. Extra-Strength Tylenol, the type that had been involved in the Chicago killings, accounted for about one-third of those revenues. Overall, the company's recovery had been remarkable.

The poisoning and early management response

On the evening of February 8, 1986, a 23-year-old woman living in Yonkers, New York, took two Extra-Strength Tylenol capsules from a brand-new package and went to bed. When she did not appear for breakfast and lunch the next day, relatives went to her room and found her dead. The cause of death was cyanide poisoning. Investigating police found three other cyanide-tainted Tylenol capsules in the same bottle. The bottle had been purchased at a nearby A&P grocery store.

The first public reaction was, How could this have happened again, since all Tylenol containers had been triple-sealed after the Chicago experience? The mystery only deepened when it was learned that the Yonkers bottle had indeed been triple-sealed in the approved manner. The finding led to an early theory that the poison had been put in the capsules during the manufacturing process, but this theory apparently would not hold up under more careful investigation that was to come later.

When the cause of death was announced on February 10, Johnson & Johnson's chairman, James Burke, who had guided the company through the 1982 crisis, ordered continuous monitoring of consumer sentiment about Tylenol products. He also cancelled all Tylenol capsule advertising after seeing an ad for the capsules on the same newscast that announced the cause of the victim's death. Although shocked by the reappearance of poison, this time in the safety-sealed packages, company officials tended to believe that it was an isolated incident.

Then came the real shocker. On February 13, Frank Young, head of the Food and Drug Administration (FDA), whose staff had been examining Tylenol that was pulled from stores in the Yonkers area, told Burke that a second container of cyanide-laced Extra-Strength Tylenol had been found in a Woolworth's store only two blocks from the A&P store where the first bottle had been bought. Burke replied, "Frank, that is the worst news you could give us."[20] The poisoned capsules in the second container showed evidence of tampering—the logo printed on the capsule halves was misaligned—but the outer and inner seals appeared to be

[19] *New York Times*, Feb. 21, 1986, p. A-11.
[20] *Newsweek*, Mar. 3, 1986, p. 52.

intact. Again, it seemed that the cyanide must have been introduced during manufacture before the safety seals were secured.

To make things even more complicated, investigators discovered that the two containers were produced in different locations at different times. After the safety seals were affixed, the two bottles had been stored at the some storage facility but at different times. Within a day, the FDA revealed that the cyanide in both of the contaminated bottles appeared to have come from the same source, but it did not match the cyanide found in Tylenol capsules during the 1982 crisis.

The recall

Spreading public alarm caused the FDA to warn consumers not to use Tylenol capsules for the time being, and ten states banned their sale. Inside Johnson & Johnson, officials were reading the results of polls showing that customer loyalty was beginning to fade as the "single local incident" theory looked less plausible. Other market research revealed that 36 percent of the public believed the tampering came from inside the company, which was a contrast with the 1982 episode when the vast majority concluded that an outsider had been to blame.

Burke created a six-member crisis management team. It included the two top managers from Johnson & Johnson and from McNeil Consumer Products Company (the maker of Tylenol) plus Johnson & Johnson's general counsel and its vice president for public relations. The team was advised by the public relations firm of Burson Marsteller.

The day following the FDA chief's phone call to Burke, the crisis management team decided to suspend production of Tylenol capsules. Saying that "[t]his is an act of terrorism, pure and simple," Burke offered a $100,000 reward for information leading to the arrest and conviction of the poisoner. The company also announced that it would give a refund or a new bottle of Tylenol tablets or caplets to customers wishing to exchange their Tylenol capsules. More than 200,000 people responded to the offer. Simultaneously, Johnson & Johnson's stock price fell $4 per share to $47.75.

With capsule advertising and production suspended and public confidence waning, a spirited debate broke out among top company officials about next steps to take. Burke himself told reporters later that some of the meetings were punctuated with "yelling and screaming." Managers from McNeil Consumer Products Company, the maker of Tylenol, argued that the company should try to ride out the storm since only two tainted bottles had been found and since surveys showed that 52 percent of capsule users wanted the company to keep producing them. They also feared the financial impact on the McNeil division if more drastic action were taken. However, Burke concluded that "there is no tamperproof package [and there] is never going to be a tamperproof package." If a third poisoned package were to turn up, "Not only do we risk Tylenol, we risk Johnson & Johnson."[21]

Eight days after the Yonkers death, on February 16, the company decided to recall all Tylenol capsule products and to abandon the use of capsules entirely

[21] Ibid.

for all of its o-t-c products. The decision was announced to the public the next day. These actions would cost the company an estimated $150 million in 1986.

The case took another puzzling turn in late February when the Federal Bureau of Investigation (FBI) reversed an earlier opinion that the tampering probably occurred in the manufacturing process. An FBI official said, "Previously undetected signs of tampering have now been discovered using sophisticated scientific examinations. Our examinations have further determined it was possible to invade the bottles after packaging was complete without detection through conventional means of examination." This finding applied to both bottles containing the poisoned capsules.[22]

Tylenol's recovery

"To date [mid-1986], our recovery looks very strong," said McNeil's vice president of marketing. Just five months after the second tampering, Tylenol had recovered 90 percent of its previous market share. In fact, discontinuing the capsule form apparently had not damaged the company as much as some had feared. Immediately after the poisoning death, Tylenol sales dropped by $128 million, but $48 million of these sales had been regained by late April. One reason for the quick recovery was the availability of caplets as an alternative to capsules. Johnson & Johnson's caplets had been on the market since 1984 and already accounted for nearly one-fourth of all Tylenol sales. When the capsules were recalled, McNeil's plants went on a crash program to increase production of caplets, spending $20 million for new equipment. In the switchover from capsules to caplets, which caused the encapsulating machinery to be idled, no McNeil employees were furloughed.

Doctors and hospitals continued to recommend Tylenol to their patients, and McNeil's sales force managed to convince 97 percent of their top accounts to maintain shelf space for Tylenol products. One year after the Yonkers poisoning, Johnson & Johnson claimed it was once again the leading seller of o-t-c analgesics.[23]

Copycat tampering

A major reason why public authorities are wary of nationwide recalls of suspect drugs is the fear of encouraging further tampering and creating consumer panic. It did not take long for "copycat" episodes to emerge.

A Nashville, Tennessee, man was found dead on February 23 of a massive dose of cyanide. A bottle of Extra-Strength Tylenol containing one capsule was found under his bed. Investigators said the bottle and capsule revealed traces of cyanide, but they were unwilling to say that his death was caused by taking poisoned Tylenol.

One of the most bizarre episodes occurred in March when Smithkline Beckman Corporation withdrew Contac, Teldrin, and Dietac capsules from the market after

[22] *New York Times*, Feb. 27, 1986, p. 20.

[23] "Tylenol Begins Making a 'Solid Recovery,'" New Brunswick, N. J.: Johnson & Johnson, 1986; and *New York Times*, Feb. 8, 1987, p. 35.

rat poison was found in some of these products. Police then arrested a former stock brokerage clerk who allegedly hoped that the poisoning threat would force down the price of Smithkline stock, thus enabling him to make a profit by trading in stock options. He was convicted and jailed in October.

Other copycats followed. In May, the Walgreen drugstore chain removed all Anacin-3 capsules from its shelves, following the death of an Austin, Texas, man whose body contained cyanide. An opened bottle of Anacin-3 that had been bought at Walgreen's Austin store showed signs of tampering. Bristol-Myers ordered a nationwide recall of Excedrin capsules after two deaths in the Seattle area were linked to the cyanide-tainted painkiller. Like Johnson & Johnson, Bristol-Myers was expected to replace capsules with caplets at an estimated cost of $10 million.

The tampering was not limited to drugs. IC Industries' Accent flavor enhancer had to be removed from Texas stores after someone claimed that he had placed cyanide in six cans. A similar call forced General Foods to clear the shelves of sugar-free Jello in four supermarket chains in four states.

Nor was tampering confined to the United States. In Japan eight people had died in 1985 after drinking juice that had been mixed with weedkiller, and boxes of chocolate had to be recalled after being dusted with cyanide. The previous year, animal-rights activists in Britain who were opposed to using animals for tooth-decay research forced a recall of Mars candy bars after claiming some were poisoned.[24]

Gerber Foods dug in its heels and refused to recall baby food after receiving a rash of reports that glass shards were found in over 200 bottles in at least thirty states. In fact, Gerber sued the state of Maryland for ordering retailers in that state to withdraw Gerber's strained peaches from sale. As with Johnson & Johnson, it was Gerber's second contamination crisis; in 1984, it had voluntarily recalled over a half million bottles of juice at a considerable financial loss. Believing the company was being victimized by fraudulent claims of contamination, Gerber's CEO said, "When we tried to quiet the press with an unjustified recall [in 1984], it didn't work. So why should we do it again? It's our decision not to keep this media event going. We have found no reason to suspect our product. I suppose we could get on television and make that statement every day. But generally, the sensational gets covered, and the unsensational does not."[25]

The industry response

Where capsules were concerned, sentiment throughout the o-t-c analgesic industry tended to favor Gerber's hard-nosed stand rather than Johnson & Johnson's more cautious approach of banning capsules. American Home Products, maker of Anacin-3, decided to stick with capsules. So did Smithkline Beckman, whose Contac cold capsules had been contaminated with rat poison. Smithkline's consumer products division president said, "We looked for a way to improve the relative safety of the capsule and found one; the others decided they couldn't.

[24] *Fortune,* Mar. 31, 1986, p. 62.

[25] *Business Week,* Mar. 17, 1986, p. 50.

One of us could be wrong, or we could both be right. It will be interesting to watch. We take our responsibility for public safety very seriously," However, the company also offered Contac customers a choice of caplets or capsules.[26]

Both the FDA and the Proprietary Association, a trade association for nonprescription drug makers, opposed a general ban on capsules. The FDA's chief officer said, "If we banned capsules the problem of tampering wouldn't go away. It would probably occur in other product forms which are just as vulnerable."[27] Some consumerists disagreed, citing the spate of capsule contamination cases already on the record as evidence of the need for even greater caution. They wondered if the FDA, as one of the federal government's main consumer protection agencies, might be working too closely with an industry that it was supposed to be regulating in the public interest.

The issue arose again in early 1991 when two people died and another became gravely ill after taking cyanide-contaminated capsules of Sudafed 12-Hour Capsules, manufactured by Burroughs-Wellcome. The triple-sealed packages had been opened, and cyanide had been placed in some of the capsules. A Burroughs-Wellcome official said, "Nobody would put their hand on their heart and say that any package was tamper-proof." The CEO of a consumer consulting firm added, "This proves once more that no consumer product is tamper-resistant. The over-the-counter health products makers have done more than any other consumer category to make tamper-resistant packages, and yet it is their products that people bent on poisoning take on as a challenge."[28]

One defensive tactic favored by the Proprietary Association was to offer rewards for information about tamperers. More than $1 million was set aside for this purpose, and it paid a $200,000 reward to a stockbroker who reported the trading activities of the clerk who had put rat poison in Contac capsules.

Federal antitampering laws were strengthened after the 1982 Tylenol episode; tampering with food, drugs, or cosmetics can lead to a maximum penalty of life imprisonment and a $250,000 fine, and a hoax can land a person in jail for five years. However, of more than 100 tampering investigations undertaken by the FBI from 1984 to early 1986, only four convictions were obtained; sentences were relatively light, ranging from five years' probation to five years in jail.[29]

In May 1991, Tylenol's manufacturer reached a confidential out-of-court settlement with the families of the 1982 victims. Some observers speculated that the company feared more bad publicity and additional copycat poisonings if the case had gone to trial. A company official said, "Though there is no way we could have anticipated a criminal tampering with our product or prevented it, we wanted to do something for the families and finally get this tragic event behind us."[30]

[26] *Wall Street Journal,* July 31, 1986, p. 23.
[27] *Wall Street Journal,* May 30, 1986, p. 2.
[28] *Wall Street Journal,* Mar. 5, 1991, p. B1.
[29] *Fortune,* Mar. 31, 1986, p. 62.
[30] *Wall Street Journal,* May 14, 1991, p. B5; and *New York Times* News Service, May 14, 1991.

DISCUSSION QUESTIONS

1. Do you consider Johnson & Johnson's voluntary recall decisions to be acts of corporate social responsibility? Why or why not?
2. Product tampering has been called "corporate terrorism." What corporate strategies can you recommend for reducing this kind of terrorist attack?
3. Identify the ethical issues involved in product-tampering episodes. To what extent are companies such as Johnson & Johnson obligated to take ethical actions to protect their customers, even if doing so causes financial losses to stockholders or threatens employees' jobs?
4. What is the role for public policy in the area of product tampering? Assess the actions of government authorities—local, state, and federal—in the Tylenol poisonings, and tell whether you believe they acted properly and in the public interest.
5. Relations between the news media and business corporations are not always congenial, but they were in both Tylenol episodes. What factors produced this good relationship? Do those factors provide a basis for improving media-and-business relationships in general? Discuss the possibilities. Gerber Foods seemed to blame the media for the problems it had with complaints of broken glass in some of its products. Evaluate the contrasting media attitudes and media strategies of these two companies.

CASE STUDY THE ZEEBRUGGE CAR FERRY DISASTER

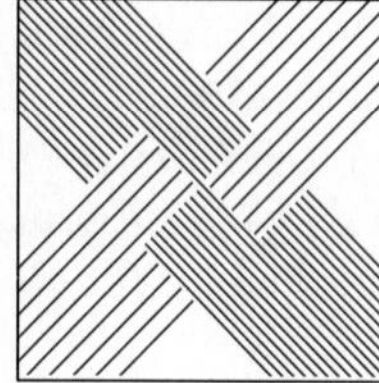

by **Colin Boyd** *College of Commerce, University of Saskatchewan*

"It is with profound sadness that I must introduce this report with the tragic loss of the "Herald of Free Enterprise" off the Belgian coast. The Herald is a Townsend Thoresen ship and, as you know, Townsend Thoresen became part of P&O in January. At the time of writing the precise cause of the disaster is unknown. We have instituted an immediate investigation and of course both the British and Belgian governments are conducting enquiries. Whatever the outcome of these you may be assured that the safety of our ships and those who man them and travel in them is our overriding priority."

So began the somber letter by chairman Jeffrey Sterling introducing the 1986 P&O annual report, published in April 1987. The roll-on/roll-off passenger car ferry *Herald of Free Enterprise* capsized in the approaches to the Belgian port of Zeebrugge en route to Dover in England at 7.05 P.M. local time on March 6, 1987. There was a light easterly breeze and the sea was calm. The ship had a crew of 80 and carried 459 passengers, 81 cars, 3 buses, and 47 trucks. She capsized in about 90 seconds soon after leaving the harbor, ending on her side half-submerged in shallow water. Only a fortuitous turn to starboard in her last moments prevented her from sinking completely in deeper water.

Following the capsize a heroic search and rescue operation was mounted. At least 150 passengers and 38 members of the crew lost their lives, most inside the ship, from hypothermia, in the frigid water. Many others were injured. It soon became apparent to the rescuers that the *Herald of Free Enterprise* had left the port of Zeebrugge with her bow doors open. The death toll was the worst for a British vessel in peacetime since the sinking of the *Titanic* in 1912.

The Cross-Channel Transport Market

The English Channel between England and the continent of Europe is one of the most heavily traveled waterways in the world. In 1985, a total of 20,056,000 passengers and 3,387,200 cars, buses, trucks, and unaccompanied trailers crossed the Channel by ferry. The most popular crossing is the shortest one, between Dover and Calais in France, a 22-mile trip that takes 90 minutes.

The mixture of demand for channel ferry services was changing. Passenger travel had remained stable since 1982, but freight traffic was increasing. Part of this increase was due to increased trade (particularly since Britain became a member of the European Economic Community), and part was due to the technological advance represented by the introduction of roll-on/roll-off (ro-ro) ships. These ships, essentially flat pontoons covered by a superstructure, have bow and stern doors which enable vehicles to drive on and off via adjustable ramps at the

© Colin Boyd 1988, 1990. All rights reserved. This case study was prepared from public source materials.

dock. The speed of ferry loading and unloading is vastly improved for a ro-ro ship, reducing the unproductive time a ship spends in port.

Competition on cross-channel ferry services was influenced by the British government's July 1984 privatization of Sealink UK Ltd., previously a subsidiary of government-owned British Rail. At that time Sealink UK, its European state-owned counterparts, and Townsend Thoresen dominated the industry. Historically, channel ferry services had functioned mainly as the sea link between rail terminus points at channel ports.

Other changes in the ferry industry included the introduction of high-capacity mixed freight and passenger "jumbo" ferries; reductions in crew levels, despite the strong opposition of the maritime unions; the modernization of dock-side facilities to help speed ferry turnaround time; the introduction of special freight-only ro-ro ferries; and the promotion of a wider range of fares, especially for day trippers and off-peak travel. These changes were similar to trends in other transport sectors, notably the airline industry.

The Channel Tunnel poses an extreme threat to the ferry industry. In 1986, after 100 years of aborted attempts to initiate a tunnel project, and against the bitter opposition of the ferry operators, the French and British governments finally gave the go-ahead to the project. The 30-mile-long dual railway tunnels underneath the Channel would commence operations in 1994.

Townsend Thoresen

Under the marketing name Townsend Thoresen, European Ferries is the major ferry operator in Europe, with services from the United Kingdom to destinations in France, Belgium, Holland, and Northern Ireland. The origins of European Ferries can be tracked back nearly 60 years to when Captain Stuart Townsend pioneered the first specialist car ferry service between Dover and Calais.

In the 1970s, the European Ferries Group diversified into harbor operations and into real estate, first in the southeast of England and later in the United States, Spain, and Germany. In 1985, European Ferries made £48 million in profits before tax ($86 million) on revenue of £403 million ($725 million). The Townsend Thoresen shipping division produced £19 million in profits ($34 million) from sales of £280 million ($504 million).

In 1986, the Peninsular and Oriental Steam Navigation Company (P&O) acquired a minority interest in European Ferries. Sir Jeffrey Sterling, the chairman of P&O, was invited to join the board of directors of European Ferries on January 21, 1986. Founded originally as a cargo and passenger shipping firm, P&O had diversified into road transportation, house building and property construction, and property management. In 1985, profits before tax of the P&O Group were £126 million ($240 million) on sales of £1,629 million ($2,932 million).

In December 1986, the boards of European Ferries and P&O jointly announced a £340 million ($612 million) takeover offer for the shares of European Ferries by P&O. European Ferries' financial performance had been severely hurt by losses in the Houston property market, caused by a severe fall in the price of oil, and by losses from a 10-week-long strike within Townsend Thoresen. The majority of European Ferries' shareholders accepted the P&O offer by the deadline of 3.00 P.M. January 16, 1987.

European Ferries had experienced a prior disaster in 1982 when the Townsend Thoresen ferry *European Gateway* capsized with the loss of 6 lives after a collision with a Sealink ship in the approaches to the port of Harwich. The speed of the capsize drew speculation on the lack of stability of ro-ro ferries when water enters the main vehicle deck.[1] Like the *Herald* after her, the *European Gateway* came to rest on her side half-submerged in shallow water, narrowly avoiding a deep-water sinking with heavy loss of life.

The Capsize of the *Herald of Free Enterprise*

The *Herald of Free Enterprise,* like her sister ships *Pride of Free Enterprise* and *Spirit of Free Enterprise,* was a modern ro-ro passenger/vehicle ferry designed for use on the high-volume short Dover-Calais ferry route. She could accelerate rapidly to her service speed of 22 knots. She was certificated to carry a maximum of 1,400 persons.

At 433 feet long and 7,950 gross tons, the *Herald* was of record size at her launching in 1980 and was one of the prides of the 22-ship Townsend Thoresen fleet. She had two main vehicle decks, and at Dover and Calais double-deck ramps connected to the ferry, allowing simultaneous vehicle access to both decks. At Zeebrugge there was only a single-level access ramp, which did not allow simultaneous deck loading. Ferry turnaround time was longer at this port. This single ramp could not quite reach the upper vehicle deck, and so water ballast was pumped into tanks in the bow of the *Herald* to facilitate loading.

When the *Herald* left Zeebrugge on March 6, 1987, not all the water had been pumped out of the bow ballast tanks, causing her to be some 3 feet down at the bow. Mr. Stanley, the assistant bosun, was responsible for closing the bow doors. He had opened the doors on arrival at Zeebrugge and then supervised some maintenance and cleaning activities. He was released from this work by Mr. Ayling, the bosun,[2] and went to his cabin. He fell asleep and was not awakened by the "harbor stations" public address call alerting crew to take their assigned positions for departure from the dock.

The bosun left the car deck at the "harbor stations" call to go to his assigned station. He later said, "It has never been part of my duties to close the doors or make sure that anyone is there to close the doors." The chief officer, Mr. Leslie Sabel, was in charge of loading vehicles. He stated that he remained on the car

[1] According to Lloyd's Register in London, over 30 accidents to ro-ro ferries had involved loss of life. The worst previous British accident was in 1953, when the *Princess Victoria* sank in the Irish Sea, killing 134. The world's worst disaster was in 1981, when 431 died on an Indonesian ferry which caught fire and sank in the Java Sea. In roughly two-thirds of the cases, the capsize took less than 5 minutes.

[2] The bosun (a variant spelling of the word boatswain) is responsible for ship maintenance. The rank is equivalent to sergeant; assistant bosun is equivalent to corporal.

deck until he saw—or thought he saw—Mr. Stanley threading his way through the parked cars toward the door control panel. He then went to the bridge, his assigned position for departure from dock.

The *Herald* backed out of the berth stern first. The *Herald* had a new design of clamshell doors which opened and closed horizontally. This design made it impossible for the ship's master, Captain David Lewry, to see from the bridge if the doors were opened or closed. As the ship increased speed, a bow wave began to build up under her prow. At 15 knots, with the bow down 3 feet lower than normal, water began to break over the main car deck through the open doors at the rate of 200 tons per minute.

In common with other ro-ro vessels, the *Herald's* main vehicle deck lacked subdividing bulkheads. If water entered the deck, it could flow from end to end or from side to side with ease. The flood of water through the bow doors quickly caused the vessel to become unstable. The *Herald* listed 30° to port almost instantaneously. Large quantities of water continued to pour in and fill the port wing of the vehicle deck, causing a capsize to port 40 seconds later. The *Herald* settled on the sea bed at slightly more than 90° with the starboard half of her hull above water. There had been no chance to launch any of the ship's lifeboats.

Under the 1894 Merchant Shipping Act, a Court of Formal Investigation of the capsize of the *Herald of Free Enterprise* was held in London between April and June 1987 before the Wreck Commissioner, the Hon. Mr. Justice Sheen, a respected judge. The court had investigative powers, the power to suspend or remove a Merchant Officer's Certificate of Competency, and the power to determine who should contribute to payment of the investigation's costs. The court had no other powers.

EXTRACTS FROM THE REPORT OF THE COURT OF FORMAL INVESTIGATION

Herald of Free Enterprise

The remainder of this case study consists of verbatim extracts from the Report of the Court of Formal Investigation written by the Hon. Mr. Justice Sheen, and released on July 25, 1987. Statements of opinion and interpretation of facts are his, not the case writer's. [Any comments or elaborations by the case writer are shown in square brackets.] Key personnel mentioned in the report are:

- Mr. Mark Stanley—Assistant Bosun
- Mr. Leslie Sabel—First Officer
- Captain David Lewry—Master of the *Herald of Free Enterprise*
- Captain John Kirby—Senior Master of the *Herald of Free Enterprise*
- Mr. John Alcindor—Deputy Chief Superintendent
- Mr. Jeffrey Develin—Director, and Chief Superintendent
- Mr. Wallace Ayers—Director, and Group Technical Director

The Manning [Staffing] of the *Herald* on the Zeebrugge Route

"On the Dover-Calais run these ships are manned [staffed] by a complement of a Master, two Chief Officers and a Second Officer. The officers are required to work 12 hours on and not less than 24 hours off. In contrast, each crew was on board for 24 hours and then had 48 hours ashore. . . . The sea passage to Zeebrugge takes 4.5 hours . . . which gives the officers more time to relax. For this reason the Company employed a Master and two deck officers [instead of three] on this run. . . .

"Captain Kirby was one of five masters who took it in turn to command the *Herald.* He was the Senior Master . . . a co-ordinator between all the masters and officers in order to ensure uniformity in the practices operated by different crews. As three different crews served with five different sets of officers, it was essential that there should be uniformity of practice. Furthermore there were frequent changes among the officers. Captain Kirby drew attention to this in an internal memo dated 22nd November 1986.

> The existing system of Deck Officer manning . . . is unsatisfactory. When *Herald* took up the Zeebrugge service our Deck Officers were reduced from 15 to 10. The surplus 5 were distributed around the fleet. On *Herald's* return to the Calais service, instead of our officers returning, we were and are being manned by officers from whatever ship is at refit. Due to this system, together with Trainee Master moves, *Herald* will have had a total of 30 different deck officers on the books during the period 29th September 1986 to 5th January 1987. . . .

"Captain Kirby returned to this theme with a further memorandum dated 28th January 1987:

> I wish to stress again that *Herald* badly needs a *permanent* complement of good deck officers. Our problem was outlined in my memo of 22nd November. Since then the throughput of officers has increased even further, partly because of sickness. During the period from 1st September to 28th January 1987 a total of 36 deck officers have been attached to the ship. We have also lost two masters and gained one. To make matters worse the vessel has had an unprecedented seven changes in sailing schedule. The result has been a serious loss of continuity. Shipboard maintenance, safety gear checks, crew training and the overall smooth running of the vessel have all suffered. . . .

Pressure to Leave the Berth

"Why could not the loading officer remain on deck until the doors were closed before going to his harbor station on the bridge? The operation could be completed in three minutes. But the officers always felt under pressure to leave after loading. . . .

"The "Bridge and Navigation Procedures" guide which was issued by the Company included the following:

Departure from Port

- O.O.W./Master should be on the Bridge approximately 15 minutes before the ship's sailing time; . . .

"That order does not make it clear whether it was the duty of the O.O.W.[3] or the Master to be on the bridge 15 minutes before sailing, or whether the officer was to remain on the bridge thereafter. If the O.O.W. was the loading officer, this order created a conflict in his duties. The conflict was brought to the attention of Mr. Develin by a memorandum dated 21st August 1982 from Captain Hackett, Senior Master of *Free Enterprise VIII* in which he said:

> It is impractical for the O.O.W. (either the Chief or the Second Officer) to be on the Bridge 15 minutes before sailing time. Both are fully committed to loading the ship. At sailing time, the Chief Officer stands by the bow or the stern door to see the ramp out and assure papers are on board etc. The Second Officer proceeds to his after mooring station to assure that the propellers are clear and report to the bridge.

"The order illustrates the lack of thought given by management to the organization of officers' duties. [On the Zeebrugge run this problem of the orders telling the O.O.W. to be in two places at once was exacerbated by the reduced number of officers. The loading officer's task was more complex at Zeebrugge because of the single-level loading ramp.]

"The sense of urgency to sail at the earliest possible moment was exemplified by an internal memorandum dated 18th August 1986 sent to assistant managers by the operations manager at Zeebrugge:

> . . . put pressure on the first officer if you don't think he is moving fast enough. . . . Let's put the record straight, sailing late out of Zeebrugge isn't on. It's 15 minutes early for us.

"Mr. A. P. Young [the Operations Manager] sought to explain away that memorandum on the basis that the language was used merely for the purpose of what he called "motivation." But it was entirely in keeping with his own thoughts at the time. . . . The Court was left in no doubt that deck officers felt that there was no time to be wasted. The Company sought to say that the disaster could have been avoided if the Chief Officer had waited on deck another 3 minutes. That is true. But the Company took no proper steps to ensure that the Chief Officer remained on deck until the bow doors were closed."

The Negative Reporting System

"The Company has issued a set of standing orders which include the following:

> *01.09 Ready for Sea*
> Heads of Departments are to report to the Master immediately they are aware of any deficiency which is likely to cause their departments to be unready for sea in any

[3] O.O.W. stands for Officer of the Watch, who is one of the deck officers and not the master.

respect at the due sailing time. In the absence of any such report the Master will assume, at the due sailing time, that the vessel is ready for sea in all respects.

"That order was unsatisfactory in many respects. . . . Masters came to rely upon the absence of any report at the time of sailing as satisfying them that their ship was ready for sea in all respects. That was, of course, a very dangerous assumption.

"On the 6th March, Captain Lewry saw the Chief Officer come to the Bridge. Captain Lewry did not ask him if the ship was all secure and the Chief Officer did not make any report. Captain Lewry was entitled to assume that the assistant bosun and the Chief Officer were qualified to perform their respective duties, but he should not have assumed they had done so. He should have insisted on a report to that effect.

"In mitigation of Captain Lewry's failure to ensure that his ship was in all respects ready for sea a number of points were made on his behalf, of which the three principal ones were as follows:

1. Captain Lewry merely followed a system which was operated by all the masters of the *Herald* and approved by the Senior Master, Captain Kirby.
2. The Court was reminded that the orders entitled "Ship's standing orders" issued by the Company make no reference, as they should have done, to opening and closing the bow and stern doors.
3. Before this disaster there had been no less than five occasions when one of the Company's ships had proceeded to sea with bow or stern doors open. Some of these incidents were known to management, who had not drawn them to the attention of other Masters. . . .

"The system . . . was defective. The fact that other Masters operated the same defective system does not relieve Captain Lewry of his personal responsibility for taking his ship to sea in an unsafe condition. In so doing he was seriously negligent in the discharge of his duties. That negligence was one of the causes contributing to the disaster. The Court is aware of the mental and emotional burden resulting from this disaster which has been and will be borne by Captain Lewry, but the Court would be failing in its duty if it did not suspend his Certificate of Competency."

The Management of Townsend Thoresen

". . . a full investigation into the circumstances of the disaster leads inexorably to the conclusion that the underlying or cardinal faults lay higher up in the Company. The Board of Directors did not appreciate their responsibility for the safe management of their ships. They did not apply their minds to the question: What orders should be given for the safety of our ships?

"The directors did not have any proper comprehension of what their duties were. There appears to have been a lack of thought about the way in which the

Herald ought to have been organized for the Dover-Zeebrugge run. All concerned in management, from the members of the Board of Directors down to the junior superintendents, were guilty of fault in that all must be regarded as sharing responsibility for the failure of management. From top to bottom the body corporate was infected with the disease of sloppiness. . . . It is only necessary to quote one example of how the standard of management fell short. . . . It reveals a staggering complacency.

"On 18th March 1986 there was a meeting of Senior Masters with management, at which Mr. Develin was in the Chair. One of the topics raised for discussion concerned the recognition of the Chief Officer as Head of Department and the roles of the Maintenance Master and Chief Officer. Mr. Develin said, although he was still considering writing definitions of these different roles, he felt 'it was more preferable not to define the roles but to allow them to evolve.' That attitude was described by Mr. Owen,[4] with justification, as an abject abdication of responsibility. It demonstrates an inability or unwillingness to give clear orders. Clear instructions are the foundation of a safe system of operation.

"It was the failure to give clear instructions about the duties of the Officers on the Zeebrugge run which contributed so greatly to the cause of this disaster. Mr. Clarke, [counsel] on behalf of the Company, said that it was not the responsibility of Mr. Develin to see that Company orders were properly drafted. In answer to the question, 'Who was responsible?' Mr. Clarke said, 'Well in truth, nobody, though there ought to have been.' The Board of Directors must accept a heavy responsibility for their lamentable lack of directions. Individually and collectively they lacked a sense of responsibility. This left, what Mr. Owen so aptly described as, 'a vacuum at the center.'

". . . Mr. Develin [Director and Chief Superintendent] was prepared to accept that he was responsible for the safe operation of the Company's ships. Another director, Mr. Ayers, told the Court that no director was solely responsible for safety. Mr. Develin thought that before he joined the Board, the safety of ships was a collective Board responsibility.

". . . as this Investigation progressed, it became clear that shore management took very little notice of what they were told by their Masters. The Masters met only intermittently. There was one period of two and a half years during which there was no formal meeting between Management and Senior Masters. Latterly there was an improvement. But the real complaint, which appears to the Court to be fully justified, was that the "Marine Department" did not listen to the complaints or suggestions or wishes of their Masters. The Court heard of four specific areas in which the voice of the Masters fell on deaf ears ashore [each detailed in separate sections below]."

Carriage of Excess Numbers of Passengers

"During the course of the evidence it became apparent from the documents that there were no less than seven different Masters, each of whom found that from

[4] Counsel for the National Union of Seamen, certain surviving crew, and the next of kin of deceased crew.

time to time his ship was carrying substantially in excess of the permitted number [1400]."

[The Report then details a series of memoranda between various Masters and Mr. A. P. Young, the Operations Manager, on the topic of excess passengers. These were exchanged in 1982, 1983, and 1984] ". . . . But the matter became really serious in 1986. The Court heard evidence from Captain de St. Croix, who was Master of the *Pride of Free Enterprise.* On the 1st August 1986 he sent a memorandum to Mr. Young. . . .

Passenger Numbers on 15.00 D/C, 1.8.86

On the above sailing from Dover, the first passenger total given to the RO [radio operator] by the Purser was 1228. A call from the manifest office then informed the RO to add on another 214. The RO queried this as the total then had been way over the top. After a short delay the manifest office came back with a figure of 1014 plus an add-on of 214 making a total of 1228.

As seeds of doubt had by then been sown in my mind I decided to have a head count as they went off at Calais. The following figures were revealed:

Total passengers	1587
Crew	95
Total on board	1682

This total is way over the life saving capacity of the vessel. The fine on the Master for this offence is £50,000 [$90,000] and probably confiscation of certificate. May I please know what steps the company intend to take to protect my career from mistakes of this nature.

"[The Report details 6 more memos sent to Mr. Young between August and October 1986 by various Masters complaining about overloading. In a memo sent on 31st October 1986, Mr. Develin attempted to arrange a meeting with Mr. Young to discuss the problem with a representative of the Senior Masters.] ". . . Mr. Young did not invite Mr. Develin to meet him to discuss the subject. Mr. Young took the view that this was not a marine matter and deliberately excluded Mr. Develin from further investigation of the problem.

". . . The Court reluctantly concluded that Mr. Young made no proper or sincere effort to solve the problem. The Court takes a most serious view of the fact that so many of the Company's ferries were carrying an excessive number of passengers on so many occasions. . . .

". . . After it became apparent that this Court was greatly interested in the system for checking the number of passengers carried on each ship further thought was given to the matter by the Company. On 29th May 1987 Mr. Young produced a memorandum containing some ideas for improving the system of counting the number of passengers."

Door Status Warning Lights for the Bridge

"On the 29th October 1983 the assistant bosun of the *Pride of Free Enterprise* neglected to close both the bow and the stern doors on sailing from No. 5 berth

Dover. It appears he had fallen asleep. . . . On 28th June 1985 Captain Blowers of the *Pride* wrote a sensible memorandum to Mr. Develin:

> In the hope that there might be one or two ideas worthy of consideration I am forwarding some points that have been suggested on this ship and with reference to any future new-building programme. Many of the items are mentioned because of the excessive amounts of maintenance, time and money spent on them.
>
> . . . Mimic Panel—There is no indication on the bridge as to whether the most important watertight doors are closed or not. That is the bow and stern doors. With the very short distance between the berth and the open sea on both sides of the Channel this can be a problem if the operator is delayed or having problems in closing the doors. Indicator lights on the very excellent mimic panel could enable the bridge team to monitor the situation in such circumstances.

"Mr. Develin circulated that memorandum amongst managers for comment. It was a serious memorandum that merited serious thought and attention, and called for a serious reply. The answers which Mr. Develin received will be set out verbatim. From Mr. Alcindor, a deputy chief superintendent: "Do they need an indicator to tell them whether the deck store-keeper is awake and sober? My goodness!!" From Mr. Reynolds: "Nice but don't we already pay someone!" From Mr. Ellison: "Assume the guy who shuts the doors tells the bridge if there is a problem." From Mr. Hamilton: "Nice!" It is hardly necessary for the Court to comment that these replies display an absence of any proper sense of responsibility. Moreover the comment of Mr. Alcindor on the deck store-keeper was either ominously prescient or showed an awareness of this type of incident in the past.

"If the sensible suggestion that indicator lights be installed had received, in 1985, the serious consideration which it deserved, it is at least possible that they would have been fitted in the early months of 1986 and this disaster might well have been prevented. [The Report details further requests for indicator lights made by two Masters in 1986, and also records their written rejection by Mr. King:]

> I cannot see the purpose or the need for the stern door to be monitored on the bridge, as the seaman in charge of closing the doors is standing by the control panel watching them close.

[The Report notes] ". . . that within a matter of days after the disaster indicator lights were installed in the remaining Spirit class ships and other ships of the fleet."

Ascertaining Draughts

[Following the loss of the passenger ferry *European Gateway* in 1982, Townsend Thoresen instituted an investigation into passenger safety] ". . . . As a result of that investigation, on the 10th February 1983, Captain Martin sent a report to Mr. Develin. That report was seen by Mr. Ayers. It begins with the words:

The Company and ships' Masters could be considered negligent on the following points, particularly when some are the result of "commercial interests."

- The ship's draught[5] is not read before sailing, and the draught entered into the Official Log Book is completely erroneous.
- It is not standard practice to inform the Master of his passenger figure before sailing;
- The tonnage of cargo is not declared to the Master before sailing;
- Full speed is maintained in dense fog.

". . . For the moment we are only concerned with the draught reading. Later in the report under the heading "recommendations" there is the statement "company to investigate installing draught recorders[6] on new tonnage." Mr. Ayers was asked if he did investigate. His answer was "somewhere in this period the answer was yes." In the light of later answers given by Mr. Ayers, that answer is not accepted by the Court.

". . . Mr. Ayers may be a competent Naval Architect, but the Court formed the view that he did not carry out his managerial duties, whatever they may have been. Mr. Ayers was asked whether each director of Townsend Car Ferries was given a specific area of responsibility. His answer was "No; there were not written guidelines for any director." When he was asked how each director knew what his responsibilities were his answer was "It was more a question of duplication as a result of not knowing than missing gaps. We were a team who had grown together." The amorphous phrasing of that answer is typical of much of the evidence of Mr. Ayers. He appeared to be incapable of expressing his thoughts with clarity.

[Mr. Ayers had previously not answered another Master's request for the installation of draught recorders. The draught of the *Herald* turned out to be a critical question. Research undertaken for the Court revealed that the *Pride* and the *Spirit* each weighed about 300 tons more than previously thought. The origin of most of this excess weight was a mystery. The *Herald* was probably 300 tons overweight also. Further loading miscalculations arose from the estimates of the tonnage of freight vehicles on the ship. No weigh scales were used, as the tonnage was calculated by using drivers' declarations of vehicle weights. Experiments revealed that these were frequently false. An average ferry load of trucks was found to weigh 13 percent more than the sum of drivers' declarations.]

"Captain Lewry told the Court quite frankly that no attempt had been made to read the draughts of his ship on a regular basis or indeed at all in regular service. Fictitious figures were entered in the Official Log which took no account of the trimming water ballast. . . .

"The difficulties faced by the Masters are exemplified by the attitude of Mr.

[5] [The depth of a loaded vessel in the water, taken from the level of the water line to the lowest point of the hull. Section 68(2) of the Merchant Shipping Act 1970 makes it a legal requirement for a master to know the draught of his ship and to enter this in the official log book each time the ship puts to sea.]

[6] [Such recorders enable anyone on the bridge to determine how low in the water the ship is. Without such devices the draught markings can only be read from outside the ship.]

Develin to a memorandum dated 24th October 1983 and sent to him by Captain Martin:

> For good order I feel I should acquaint you with some problems associated with one of the Spirit class ships operating to Zeebrugge using the single deck berths:
>
> - At full speed, or even reduced speed, the bow wave comes three quarters of the way up the bow door.
> - Ship does not respond so well with water ballast in the bow and problems have been found when maneuvering.
> - As you probably appreciate we never know how much cargo we are carrying, so that a situation could arise where not only are we overloaded by 400 tons but also trimmed down at the bow by 4.5 feet. I have not been able to work out how that would affect our damage stability.

"Mr. Develin was asked what he thought of that memorandum. His answer was: 'Initially I was not happy. When I studied it further, I decided that it was an operational difficulty report and Captain Martin was acquainting me of it.' Later he said: 'I think if he had been unhappy with the problem he would have come in and banged my desk.' When Mr. Develin was asked what he thought about the information concerning the effect of full speed he said: 'I believe he was exaggerating.' In subsequent answers he made it clear that he thought every complaint was an exaggeration. In reply to a further question Mr. Develin said: 'If he was concerned he would not have sailed. I do not believe there is anything wrong sailing with the vessel trimmed by the head.' "

The Need for a High-Capacity Ballast Pump

"On 28th February 1984 Mr. R. C. Crone, who was a chief engineer, sent a memorandum to Mr. Develin. . . .

> *Ballasting Spirit Class Ships on Zeebrugge Service*
>
> Normal ballasting requirements are for Nos. 1 and 14 tanks to be filled for arrival at Zeebrugge and emptied on completion of loading. Using one pump the time to fill or empty the two tanks is 1 hr. 55 mins. With two pumps the time can be reduced to 1 hr. 30 mins. Problems associated with the operation include—
>
> - Pumping time amounts to approximately half the normal passage time.
> - Ship down at the bow for prolonged periods causing bad steerage and high fuel consumption.
> - Continuous pressurizing of tanks to overflow/vent level.
> - Time consuming for staff.
> - Bow doors subjected to stress not normally to be expected, certainly having its effect on door locking gear equipment.
> - Dangerous complete blind operation that should not be carried out as normal service practice, i.e., no knowledge of tank capacity during operation, the tanks are pumped up until the overflow is noticed from the bridge, thereafter emptied until the pump amperage/pressure is noted to drop!

> Purely as a consideration realizing the expense compared with possible future double ramp berths. . . . I recommend fitting a high capacity ballast pump.

"Mr. Develin said that he did not agree with some of the contents. He appeared to think that the chief engineer was grossly exaggerating the problem. Mr. Develin said that Mr. Crone came to his department on several occasions to press for the implementation of his recommendations but that after discussion he must have been satisfied. In due course an estimate was obtained for the installation of a pump at a cost of £25,000 [$45,000]. This cost was regarded by the Company as prohibitive."

The Court's Conclusion

"The Court finds that the capsizing of the *Herald of Free Enterprise* was partly caused or contributed to by serious negligence in the discharge of their duties by Captain David Lewry (Master), Mr. Leslie Sabel (Chief Officer) and Mr. Mark Victor Stanley (assistant bosun), and partly caused or contributed to by the fault of Townsend Car Ferries. The Court suspends the certificate of the said Captain David Lewry for a period of one year and suspends the certificate of the said Mr. Leslie Sabel for a period of two years.

"There being no other way in which this court can mark its feelings about the conduct of Townsend Car Ferries Limited other than by an order that they should pay a substantial part of the costs of this investigation, I have ordered them to pay the sum of £350,000 [$630,000].[7] That seems to me to meet the justice of the case."

What Happened Subsequently?

A Coroner's inquest[8] into the deaths of 188 people on the *Herald of Free Enterprise* was held in October 1987. The jury returned a verdict of unlawful killing, an unusual and unexpected verdict which implied that a crime had been committed. The Director of Public Prosecutions then instructed the police to investigate the deaths.

In October 1987 P&O eliminated the name "Townsend Thoresen" and operated their ferry services under the new name "P&O European Ferries." They subsequently renamed all the ships in the P&O ferry fleet which had the words "Free

[7] [Townsend Thoresen had previously made some payments to the injured and to the relatives of the deceased. The final sum paid to each victim of the Zeebrugge disaster will probably average £80,000, or $144,000, with an unknown proportion paid from insurance coverage. Civil suits for additional damages are unlikely under English law.]

[8] In England a coroner is a judicial officer (not a medical examiner or a medical doctor) who enquires into the manner of death of any person who is slain or dies in suspicious circumstances. The inquest is held before a jury of from 7 to 12 members of the public. If the jury return a verdict of murder, or manslaughter or infanticide against any person by name, then the inquisition is equivalent to an indictment, and it is the duty of the coroner to commit the accused to trial.

Enterprise" or "Enterprise" in their names. In March 1988 P&O dismissed all its ferry employees, who had been on strike for seven weeks protesting plans to reduce staffing levels on cross-channel ferries. The strike was soon broken, and P&O was able to cut the number of ferry employees by 400.

In June 1989, after a 15-month police investigation, seven individuals were charged with manslaughter, and P&O European Ferries was charged with corporate manslaughter. It was the first time under English law that a company had faced this charge. The seven individuals charged were Mr. Stanley, Mr. Sabel, Captain Lewry, Captain Kirby, Mr. Alcindor, Mr. Develin, and Mr. Ayers.

On October 19th, 1990, after 27 days of a trial expected to last 5–6 months, the judge dismissed the case by instructing the jury to find the defendants not guilty of manslaughter. He considered that the prosecution had failed to prove, in the words of the charge, that the defendants should have perceived the possibility of the *Herald of Free Enterprise* sailing with its doors open to be "an obvious risk."

Discussion Questions

1. Assess the relative importance of mechanical problems versus managerial problems that are described in the case. In your opinion, was the primary failure leading to the disaster a technological or a managerial failure? Cite evidence from the case to support your view.
2. Who should bear the major portion of the blame for the sinking of the *Herald of Free Enterprise?* Should it be the ferry's officers and crew, the on-shore operational managers (the superintendent, etc.), the directors of P&O European Ferries, or Sir Jeffrey Sterling, the P&O chairman? How did the company's general culture contribute to the tragedy?
3. What remedy is appropriate to avoid a repetition of this accident? Drawing upon the major themes and concepts from the chapters in this book, outline a plan of action that would move P&O European Ferries toward social responsibility, social responsiveness, and ethical awareness in all of its operations.

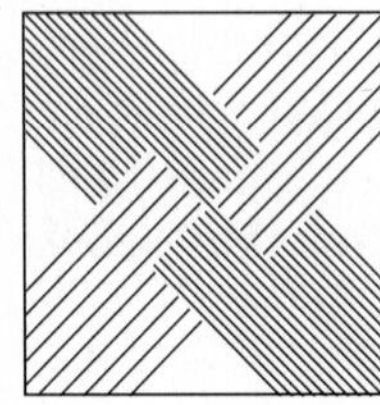

I STEVEN COHEN: AGENCY MANAGER

by **Robbin Derry** *The American College*

Steve Cohen sat at his desk late Monday afternoon looking over the sales figures for the prior month. It was early August, and July had been slow for his insurance agency. July was always a slow month, but this year Steve felt even greater anxiety. Word had filtered down from the home office about consolidation of less productive agencies, and Steve had no interest in being consolidated out of his job as agency head. He felt that he had not yet achieved his potential in running the agency that he took over six years ago.

Tuesday morning would be the weekly training session and Steve wanted to convey to his agents the urgency of meeting the production goals for August. He had broken down the target levels into weekly goals and established rewards for agents who consistently met or exceeded the weekly goals. Steve's main concern was how to convince or energize his agents in an inspiring way to get them out hustling for new prospects and closing more sales calls.

As Steve was struggling to find ways to translate his anxiety into motivating words for the training meeting, Art knocked on the open office door and walked in. Art had been with Steve's agency for eight months. He had scored high on the initial aptitude screening tests and quickly learned the sales techniques. For the first two months it seemed as if Art was great at finding good prospects and establishing trust with them quickly, but he had trouble in actually closing sales. Steve had paired him with another agent for a couple of months and had worked with him alone to determine just what the problem was. They had reviewed sales presentations, the timing of questions, and how to respond to clients' doubts. These contacts convinced Steve that Art had enormous potential, and he was eager to see his investment in training pay off both for the agency and for Art. Over the last six months Art's sales had been improving and Steve hoped that Art would stay through the long learning process and become one of his major producers.

"Hey, Steve, I've got a question. I'm not sure if you want to talk about it, and if you don't, just say so. But I've been thinking about it for a couple of weeks and I'm not quite sure what the right thing to do is. You know, back when I was working with Bill, he showed me more about using the company software to illustrate returns in ways that would really convince the client what a great investment we were offering. What he showed them were rates of return that were higher than the actual rates people were getting, but it wasn't too many years ago that interest rates were that high, and who's to say that they won't climb back up there? I mean it does seem to make a big difference in how the prospect responds to my sales pitch. When you talked about using the company software last year, you suggested using a pretty narrow range of rates. The way

Bill does it really gives them a better feel for the potential earnings of their investment. Besides, I've realized that most of the guys vary the rates of return depending on how sophisticated their clients are and what they think the client would like to hear."

As Art talked, Steve recalled the meeting where he had told his agents about the software packages that had been highly successful in increasing sales. The color graphics allowed the agent to lead a prospective client through a series of highly attractive illustrations that simplified what for many were baffling and confusing features of insurance. He also had become aware that some agents used interest rates in the range of 12 to 15 percent when prevailing rates were closer to 8 percent. As a result, the color graphics magnified the amount paid on the illustrated investment. When attending an industry luncheon not long ago, Steve was told that agents from one of his main competitors routinely followed this practice. His own home office provided the software to each agent but without any specific rates or numbers, leaving it to the agent to "fill in the blanks." Since interest rates tend to fluctuate regularly, it was important for the agent to update the software illustrations with current rates. When a sale was made, the insurance policy included a disclaimer about guaranteed and nonguaranteed rates, but customers tended to overlook these details, partly because they sounded more complex when put in writing than when shown in color graphics.

Art went on, "I'm just trying to get clear in my mind whether this approach is the best one. I've used it now for several months and my sales are definitely up. Everybody pretty much makes up his own illustrations and you haven't really said what the limits are. Are there any limits? As long as it increases our sales and the client is getting a policy that will meet his or her needs, does it matter what pictures we're showing them? I mean, everybody knows of course that it is completely impossible to predict what the interest rates are really going to do, so it's not like we're making any false promises."

Art's questions hit Steve hard. He knew that his agents used a range of rates in their presentations, and he hadn't wanted to set hard and fast rules about what range was appropriate. Even if he did make rules, how could he enforce them? But now that Art had put the matter so plainly, Steve needed to provide some guidelines. If he limited his agents to current rates or conservative projections, he wondered what that might do to their sales. As he pondered what to say to Art, he was interrupted by a phone call from the home office telling him that all agency heads were being called to a meeting the following week to discuss declining sales.

Discussion Questions

1. What kind of ethical problems, discussed in Chapter 3, are involved in this encounter between Steve and Art: face-to-face ethics? corporate policy ethics? functional-area ethics? Who should be responsible for finding solutions?
2. Which of Steve's ethical obligations is greater: to Art, his employee, in whom he has invested considerable time and genuine interest? to his agency's cus-

tomers, who depend on the agents for reliable information? to the home office, which expects him to maintain high sales? to his own family that depends on him for their livelihood?

3. Which of Art's ethical obligations is greater: to Steve, his boss, who has helped and encouraged him to succeed as an agent? to his clients, who are seeking secure and well-paying investments? to his coworkers, the other agents, whose own jobs might be jeopardized if they are not allowed to use "creative" rates of return in their software presentations?
4. What should Steve tell Art?

II RONALD HARRIS: DIVISION MANAGER

by **Barbara Ley Toffler** *Resources for Responsible Management*[1]

"Let me talk about the hardest ethical dilemma I've had, personally. It was early in my career. After I'd been here about two years, they gave me the responsibility for a test system development project. One of the things included in the development was a memory system involving a core memory. At that time we did not have a core memory manufacturing capability, so we bought our core plans from outside vendors and we built all the electronic circuitry around it. Typically, we were involved intimately in the design since what we bought was a customized product; it was not a generalized product sold to other people. So the design was ours, but a vendor would supply us a core stack that would go in our machine.

"A core stack is old technology; it's not used anymore. Nowadays, there are semiconductor devices that do the same thing, but at that time it was an important cost element in the machine.

"For our security, there were about six vendors, all of whom made core memory systems. There were a lot of manufacturing issues and a lot of design issues. In this program we wanted to go with multiple sources for the memory so we wouldn't be exposed. So we turned on four vendors, all of whom were designing their own solutions to our problem based on our specifications. The design would be ours when we were done. We evaluated the four vendors and from the four we selected a primary vendor and turned him on to 70% of our volume and a secondary vendor to 30% so that if the primary vendor stumbled we'd push harder on the secondary vendor. We would also qualify—to be held in the wings, so to speak—a third vendor and decide whether to bring him on or not.

"There was a company at the time who had no engineering capability, but they could manufacture memories. You'd give them the design and then they would give you a price on it and manufacture it. And because they had no engineering capability, they had no overhead. Consequently, they had a very low cost structure. The situation I found so tough was that our purchasing agent at the time had identified this vendor, but I didn't know anything about him until

[1] Excerpted from Barbara Ley Toffler, *Tough Choices: Managers Talk Ethics*, copyright © 1986 Barbara Lee Toffler, pp. 120–123. Reprinted by permission of the author and John Wiley & Sons, Inc. Ronald Harris is a pseudonym, but his company is real and the words are his own.

late in the program. We selected our two vendors and the third in the wings, and we were ready to go when this manufacturer came in with about a 15% cost savings on the manufacture of this very critical element, an estimate based on a verbal description of what we were looking for. He wanted the core stacks from one of the other vendors to take a look at so they could see if they could really manufacture it.

"And the problem I struggled with was: the design was *ours*. However, all those companies put their design effort into trying to get themselves qualified to manufacture our core memory. Was it fair to give this manufacturer one of these core stacks and let them look at it to give us an estimate? The property legally was ours. I had immediate reaction that I didn't want to do that because it wasn't fair. And the purchasing agent said, 'You ought to think about that. We're out here trying to get the lowest cost of production for the company.' That was one of the most agonizing factors. There were other engineering programs in parallel who did that. And that company was qualified to do the work. The reason I agonized over it was because there was a temptation. One of my goals was producing a product at low manufacturing cost, and I struggled with what was the right thing to do.

"The fundamental question for me had nothing to do with whether it was legal or not. It was. But the real question was, Is that the relationship I want to have with vendors and the reputation I want to have? I had worked very hard with these other vendors to get them qualified and they put a strong effort into the work, and was it fair to take that effort which they put in and hand the designs that came from them to someone else and let someone else build an absolute copy? I thought, 'Let's see, one of the things we could do is let them get a certain amount of volume and at that point say, 'OK, now we're sure you covered your engineering costs, we're going to take this stack and give it to other people and now you're going to have to compete with other manufacturers.'

"But the issue for me was, what was fair? And I just felt I couldn't do that. The criticism I got on the other side was people saying to me, 'Ron, I think you're crazy. These guys steal technology from each other all the time. There isn't anybody else in the business who would have that kind of concern.' They would say, 'Gee, I really respect you; you stick to your value system. But I don't relate to it. Why do you want to do that kind of thing?' Finally I said, 'The decision's clear. We're not going to do it.' I then agonized and reevaluated for a long time.

"That was probably the toughest one I've run across. And in looking back on it, maybe it was the toughest because there weren't sufficient external extenuating factors to pressure me, so it was all left up to me. There were no external influences strong enough to rationalize the decision. The pressure was self-made. You see, you usually rationalize after.

"The nub of the problem was: Is it right to take the technology of some other company who has worked hard with you in partnership, even though you have rights to it? You know it's legally right, but is it morally right to give that technology to someone else, and let them, through that technology, have an opportunity to be more competitive because they omit one step, the design, from their process? That was really the nub of the problem."

Discussion Questions

1. Is it ethical for Ronald Harris to express a loyalty to the vendors if it results in an increased cost to his employer? Since "stealing technology" is said to be common in this industry, why shouldn't Ronald Harris go along with the usual practice?
2. What does Ronald Harris mean when he says that giving away the technology to someone else is "legally right but not morally right?" What does he mean by "morally right?"
3. What steps could Ronald Harris's company have taken to make his decision an easier one? How do you evaluate the ethical climate in this company? Was it proper company policy that the decision, as Ronald Harris said, "was all left up to me?"

III WILLIAM ROBERTSON: VICE PRESIDENT

by **Barbara Ley Toffler** *Resources for Responsible Management*[2]

"I have a man working for me right now with whom I'm going through a bit of a trauma. This man is an officer and he has emphysema, which is a deteriorating illness. I feel we should let him keep working for as long as he wants to continue working, even though he is physically unable to give a full day's work, for the next eight or nine years he has until he retires. He's got 30 years in this bank. However, I can't go just by what I think I should do for this man. I have to consider the effect on the bank.

"If I did not have to think of the bank, I probably would go along with his doing whatever he was capable of doing—like come in a couple of days a week—and keep paying him because the guy still has expenses. But I can't go that route. I'm trying to work out the best way I can to get him the most money for the longest time the bank will go along with. The only thing I can work out under that premise is to put him on disability. He *is* disabled, and yet if I were making the decision outside of business, my decision would be to do whatever is best for him as an individual psychologically. Under the premise I have right now, I'm saying I can't do that because business says you have to get productive work out of a person *all* the time. If you don't, then you ought to be cutting down what you're paying for him. I realize the practicality of this, and I know I'm not really going to hurt this individual tremendously. I am hurting him a little psychologically because he'll have to make a decision that he doesn't really want to make, namely, to stop working.

"In terms of legality, there's nothing illegal about it. To *me,* it's immoral, but that doesn't mean it's immoral in terms of what big business does. Big business

[2] Excerpted from Barbara Ley Toffler, *Tough Choices: Managers Talk Ethics,* copyright © 1986 Barbara Lee Toffler, pp. 200–204. Reprinted by permission of the author and John Wiley & Sons, Inc. William Robertson is a pseudonym, but his company is real and the words are his own.

has to go on the premise that they should get a dollar's work out of a dollar's worth of pay. This man no longer is producing. And yet 30 years of this man's life was given to the bank. My values are different than the business values in this case. I have a tendency to believe we have to look towards the individual first and the company second. But when it comes to this decision, I have to look towards the company first and the individual second. I wonder if I am calling this an ethical decision as a way of letting out my unhappiness at the fact I cannot do what I think is right.

"It bothers me. Let me tell you a secret. After 30 years of running a human relations area, I still get into discussions as to why I think the bank should do something, 'humanly' versus practically. I run a big organization. I'm involved in the mechanics of it. But the majority of what I would call ethical decisions I face have had to do with my dealings with people, rather than what I have to do to get my job done. I assume there have been times when the bank has, in effect, asked me to do something that if I were outside I might refuse to do. But those times thankfully have been few and far between. I think that as far as the bank is concerned, I haven't run into too many situations where I've been asked to do something that was against my will or against my grain. I have to say, though, that in the last 20 years, when it came to dealing with people, there have been vast differences of opinion between what they have set as corporate policy and what I try to do in a lot of cases.

"The bank does offer disability. Most big businesses have what is called short-term disability. So, for six months this fellow will get his pay, but he will not be working, or he will be working very little. It requires that a doctor say he's not capable of working. At the end of the six months he will go on long-term disability. Long-term disability varies with different companies. In our case it means that 60% of his salary will be covered by an insurance company until he's 65 years old, at which time he will start getting his pension. This fellow is 56, 57 years old, so we're talking about a seven- or eight-year time frame.

"Part of the problem in this case is that I know too much about the individual. I know his home circumstances; I know his family. His wife used to work for me. So there's a whole array of things. If this were a common occurrence in the bank, then I would attack it. But I'm so personally involved, and know so much about what's going on with this individual, that I don't know if I could find other cases that would fit these circumstances.

"Maybe in this situation, because I'm so personally involved, I should not make a case. But I could use it for background. There are other types of medical conditions that should be considered. Maybe we should take another look at the medical side of all these things and not be so business-practical. After all, this bank, and most big businesses, like to be considered humane. I think that is something I may look into. Not the individual case, but the question of what the bank's practice is going to be in terms of illnesses where there is some productivity, although less than 100%. That's a cause I might be able to get into, because I'm not afraid to attack decisions of the bank, as long as I can convince myself I have some solid arguments and an opportunity to have some effect."

Discussion Questions

1. Is the situation described by Robertson an example of face-to-face ethics, corporate policy ethics, or functional-area ethics? What difference does it make?
2. Does Robertson, the vice president, face a genuine ethical dilemma, or is he merely letting his own personal views and values interfere with an ordinary personnel problem? On what grounds could he say that this is a "real" ethical issue?
3. In grappling with the older employee's situation, how much weight should Robertson give to the bank's need for high productivity, and how much weight should he give to the employee's personal desires and needs? What basic ethics principles can be used to decide?
4. Would it be fair to the bank's able-bodied employees if Robertson were to make an exception for the partially disabled older employee and allow him to receive full pay for part-time work? Would your answer apply to all disabled people who work for the bank?

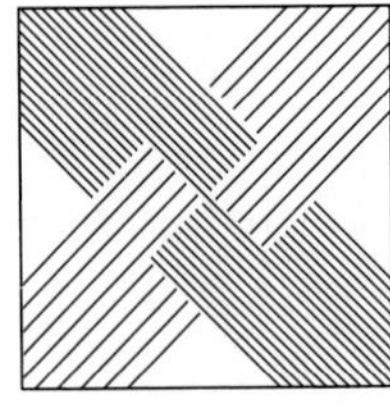

Northern Ireland: The "Troubles"

For more than two decades Northern Ireland has been embroiled in civil unrest. Since 1969 the "troubles" have led to almost 3,000 violent deaths. During these two decades of violence world attention has been drawn to the conflict with scenes of confrontation between patrolling British troops and protestors, sometimes erupting in street battles and guerrilla attacks between extremist Catholic and Protestant organizations. The conflict has created martyrs from both sides, focusing attention on the sectarian aspect of the conflict starting with "Bloody Sunday" in January 1972, when thirteen Catholic demonstrators were killed in the streets of Londonderry by British paratroopers, followed in 1979 by the terrorist murder of Britain's war folk hero Lord Mountbatten in Sligo; and the 1981 hunger strike by Bobby Sands, an imprisoned Provisional Irish Republican Army (PIRA) soldier, which resulted in his death.[1] The conflict, which has been mostly confined to Northern Ireland, was extended to London in 1990 when the London Stock Exchange was bombed by the IRA and later in 1991 when the War Cabinet building was damaged by a mortar attack.

Background

In 1921, after a protracted struggle for home rule, the southern two-thirds of Ireland gained independence from British rule, becoming the Free Irish Republic. This left six of the nine counties of the historic province of Ulster in Northern Ireland, which is about the size of Connecticut, to remain part of the United Kingdom. Even though sectarianism has been cited as the root of the differences between the two cultures, the conflict, which includes extensive dispute over language and history, is not solely about religion; rather, it is a clash between conflicting national identities of Irish-identified Catholic "nationalists" and British-identified Protestant "unionists." Because of their majority and a tradition of maintaining strong ties with Britain, the Protestants have dominated Northern Ireland politically, socially, and economically since the early seventeenth century, when they were encouraged by King James to emigrate from England and Scotland to the "plantation of Ulster."

Throughout most of the twentieth century the two cultures in Northern Ireland remained separate. In the late 1960s, however, a Catholic civil rights movement gained momentum. The civil rights movement focused on discrimination in housing and employment, and on a call for equity in voting rights for Catholics. Many Catholics have felt that the only effective solution is independence from Britain,

[1] Mendel-Viney Leslie, "Londonderry Air: A New Spirit," *U.S. News & World Report*, Sept. 3, 1990, p. 34.

thereby linking civil rights issues to sovereignty for Northern Ireland. Partly in response to the protests, the Northern Ireland prime minister attempted to reform the political system. This effort resulted in erosion of the support for the provisional government in his own unionist party, forcing him to resign. Once the provisional government collapsed, the British government was confronted with increasing sectarian violence. To restore order, the British government sent several thousand of its troops to the region, assuming authority over all security forces in Northern Ireland in August 1969.[2] Since then, there has been a broad pattern of continued conflict and violence.

Multinational Corporations in Northern Ireland

Subsidiaries and minority-owned affiliates of U.S. companies employ more than 11,000 people in Northern Ireland, accounting for about 10 percent of the region's manufacturing workers. Du Pont and American Brands are the largest U.S. multinational companies in Northern Ireland. Each employs about 1,700 workers. American Home Products, Baker Hughes, Data-Design Laboratories, Federal Express, Ford Motor Company, 3M, and Nynex also are major employers.[3]

Despite the domestic unrest and a recession that began in the early 1980s, Northern Ireland has been one of the most attractive European locations for U.S. companies. The Industrial Development Board for Northern Ireland (IDB), the agency responsible for attracting overseas manufacturers, offers some attractive financial incentives for investment: tariff-free access to the European marketplace, 30 percent grants toward the cost of building and equipping plants, generous training grants, and total exemption from real estate taxes.[4] In addition, Northern Ireland has a modern infrastructure including roads, ports, and communications. The country has a highly skilled, low-cost, readily available labor force with high levels of productivity. There is a positive attitude by the government toward the private sector.[5]

Proxy Voting for Human Rights

Shareholders' resolutions focusing on the position of U.S. multinational companies in foreign countries began in the 1970s when church organizations began to question U.S. corporate investment in South Africa, where the government's apartheid policies discriminated against blacks. The power of shareholder resolutions has rested less in individual proxy voting than in the leverage that large-block stockholders—most notably universities and pension fund managers—have with corporate boards of directors. In South Africa, U.S. companies were influ-

[2] Investor Responsibility Research Center, Inc., Social Issues Service, 1991 Background A, "U.S. Corporate Activity in Northern Ireland," Washington, D.C., 1990.

[3] Ibid., p. A-28.

[4] Ibid., p. A-29.

[5] Peter Ballinger, "Irish Economies Offer an Imaginative Mix of Investment Incentives," *Business America*, May 9, 1988, p. 36.

enced by the Sullivan Principles, a code of good practice for companies operating in that nation. Based on the success of institutional investors in influencing the human rights policies of South Africa, came the resolutions addressing the employment practices in Northern Ireland. Modeled after the Sullivan Principles, the MacBride Principles have pressured U.S. multinational firms to recognize the host country's human rights issues.

Fair Employment in Northern Ireland

Census statistics in 1982 indicated that young Catholic males were two and a half times more likely to be unemployed than their Protestant counterparts in Northern Ireland. To a certain degree this disparity was a result of "institutionalized" advantages for Protestants that were embedded in the political system and social structure. Much of the emotion surrounding the issue of discrimination centers around a history of bias against the Catholics that can be traced back to "penal laws" enacted in the 1700s. Traditionally, Protestants have received the technical training preparing them for top-management positions and skilled jobs in industry, while many Catholics have pursued less specialized liberal arts education. The entire situation has been exacerbated by a decline in the basic industries where Catholics have been employed. Added to all of this complexity has been an economic recession that besieged Northern Ireland's economy from the early 1980s. This recession fueled double-digit unemployment for the entire workforce.

The British Parliament acknowledged the problem of the employment disparity in 1976, passing the Fair Employment Act which outlawed discrimination based on religious grounds. Yet it quickly became apparent that the 1976 law was ineffective. As a 1985 British government report characterized it:

> . . . despite almost 10 years of anti-discrimination legislation and enforcement, the Catholic community remained at a serious disadvantage in employment in both quantitative and qualitative terms; that this obtained throughout the province (even in areas of relatively high employment); and that it persisted despite progressive convergence of education attainment between Protestant and Catholic communities.[6]

The MacBride Principles

Shareholders at thirty-three companies were asked in 1991 to vote on resolutions, called The MacBride Principles, related to fair employment in Northern Ireland. The MacBride Principles campaign, announced in late 1984, has been a U.S.-based effort to influence Northern Ireland employers—particularly U.S. corporations—to improve equal opportunity in employment without regard to religion.

The MacBride Principles were drafted by Father Sean McManus and sponsored by the now deceased Sean MacBride, who was a Nobel and Lenin Peace prize recipient for his founding of the human rights organization, Amnesty Interna-

[6] Ibid., p. A-8.

tional. The principles are not viewed as a product of one-sided sectarianism, however. Two prominent Protestant leaders have cosponsored them: Dr. John Robb, a highly regarded surgeon in Northern Ireland; and Inez McCormick, a trade unionist and former member of the Fair Employment Agency.

Since the beginning of the campaign for the MacBride Principles only one company has signed the principles. Belleek Pottery, Ltd., a Northern Irish company principally owned by California entrepreneur George Moore, agreed to become a signatory in November 1990. Yet five other companies agreed to implement the principles, though they did not formally sign or endorse them.[7] As of the beginning of 1991, twelve institutional investment organizations, led by the New York City Comptroller's Office, had subscribed to the principles, and the New York City system alone had filed twenty-five proxy resolutions with companies. Unlike the Sullivan Principles, institutional investors who support the MacBride Principles have not encouraged divestment as a form of leverage to change social policies in Northern Ireland. The focus has stayed on employment reform.

Pressure on multinational companies to adopt the shareholder resolutions also has come from fourteen states and a number of local governments that have passed laws endorsing the MacBride Principles. Several of these mandates included provisions authorizing fiduciaries for state funds to make investment decisions based in part on corporate conformance with the MacBride Principles. Even though divestiture was not encouraged in the principles, at least one state, Connecticut, passed legislation requiring divestiture of stock in companies that did not adopt and implement the MacBride Principles.[8]

The Debate

Emotionalism has surrounded the debate over the MacBride Principles. Advocates view the campaign for the principles as a method of waging peace and a modest assertion of basic civil rights. Proponents of the MacBride Principles also have asserted that, unlike the Sullivan Principles that were a catalyst for the exodus of multinational companies from South Africa, the MacBride Principles encourage foreign investment by stabilizing the employment situation. This argument has been strengthened by the pressure put on corporations by institutional investors to stay in Northern Ireland *and* ensure fair employment practices as good corporate citizens.

Opponents have seen the resolutions as another lever in support of the Irish Republican Army's (IRA) campaign to destabilize the government in Northern Ireland, linking the job discrimination issue to Northern Ireland's sovereignty. Their worst fears were confirmed when, in 1989, British Secretary of State Brooke initiated talks regarding political arrangements in Northern Ireland. Opponents also have maintained that companies adopting the MacBride Principles will be breaking the law by requiring reverse discrimination. This argument led to an important lawsuit challenging the right of an institutional investor to urge a

[7] Ibid., p. A-19.
[8] Ibid., p. A-27.

company to break local laws. A U.S. Federal District Court ruled, in 1986, that none of the principles would require any illegal action on the part of U.S. companies adopting them.[9]

Some of this controversy has been fueled by the legacy of Sean MacBride. Son of John MacBride, who was executed for his involvement with the IRA during the Irish uprisings in the 1920s, Sean MacBride had been chief of staff for the IRA in the early 1930s before he broke with the IRA, renouncing violence.

The Fair Employment Act of 1989: Change?

The MacBride Principles have drawn international attention to the disparity in Catholic and Protestant unemployment rates in Northern Ireland. The British government acknowledged that there was a problem, and as a result, the Fair Employment Act of 1989 was passed by the British Parliament. The major features of this new legislation provided for increased monitoring of discriminatory employment practices and a Code of Practice to serve as "the standards by which employers' practices will be judged."[10] Critics of the legislation were quick to point out that the new law did not have any specific affirmative action goals or penalties for those found guilty of discrimination. These critics believe that some of their concerns were confirmed when the Fair Employment Tribunal, in its first major ruling, decided that the act made it illegal for employers to reveal information about the religion of specific employees.[11] Mitchell McLaughlin, the economic spokesperson for Sinn Fein, the political wing of the IRA, reinforced this skepticism when he criticized the 1989 law as "fundamentally flawed and inadequate for the task publicly set for it by the British government."[12]

Baker Hughes Resolution

Baker Hughes, a U.S. corporation, has 283 employees in Northern Ireland. In 1991, the company received the following resolution asking that it implement the MacBride Principles.

Stockholder Proposal No. 2 on Implementation of the MacBride Principles in Northern Ireland

The following proposal was submitted to Baker Hughes by the Minnesota State Board of Investment which holds beneficially 91,120 shares of the Corporation's Common Stock, and is included in this Proxy Statement in compliance with the rules and regulations of the Commission.

WHEREAS, Baker Hughes Incorporated's subsidiary in Northern Ireland, is one of the largest foreign-owned firms in that country;

[9] Ibid., p. A-19.
[10] Ibid., p. A-12.
[11] Ibid., p. A-29.
[12] Ibid., p. A-25.

WHEREAS, employment discrimination in Northern Ireland has been cited by the International Commission of Jurists as being one of the major causes of the conflict in that country;

WHEREAS, the Fair Employment Agency for Northern Ireland has found that Baker Hughes "does not provide equality of opportunity" to Ulster's Catholic population;

WHEREAS Dr. Sean MacBride, founder of Amnesty International and Nobel Peace Laureate, has proposed several equal opportunity employment principles to serve as guidelines for corporations in Northern Ireland. These include:

1. Increasing the representation of individuals from under-represented religious groups in the workforce including managerial, supervisory, administrative, clerical and technical jobs.
2. Adequate security for the protection of minority employees both at the workplace and while traveling to and from work.
3. The banning of provocative religious or political emblems from the workplace.
4. All job openings should be publicly advertised and special recruitment efforts should be made to attract applicants from under-represented religious groups.
5. Layoff, recall and termination procedures should not in practice favor particular religious groupings.
6. The abolition of job reservations, apprenticeship restrictions and differential employment criteria which discriminate on the basis of religion or ethnic origin.
7. The development of training programs that will prepare substantial numbers of current minority employees for skilled jobs, including the expansion of existing programs and the creation of new programs to train, upgrade and improve the skills of minority employees.
8. The establishment of procedures to assess, identify and actively recruit minority employees with potential for further advancement.
9. The appointment of a senior management staff member to oversee the company's affirmative action efforts and the setting up of timetables to carry out affirmative action principles.

RESOLVED, Stockholders request the Board of Directors to:

Make all possible lawful efforts to implement and/or increase activity on each of the nine MacBride Principles.

Proponent's statement in support of proposal

- Continued discrimination and worsening employment opportunities have been cited as contributing to increasing support among Catholics for a violent solution to Northern Ireland's problems.
- In May, 1986, the United States District Court ruled in NYCERS vs American Brands, 86 Civ. 3188 Slip Op. (S.D.N.Y., May 12, 1986) that "all nine of the MacBride Principles could be legally implemented by management in its Northern Ireland facility."
- An endorsement of the MacBride Principles by Baker Hughes Incorporated will demonstrate its concern for human rights and equality of opportunity in its international operations. Please vote your proxy FOR these concerns.

Statement of the Board of Directors and Management in Opposition to Proposal No. 2

Baker Hughes has a long standing policy of being an equal opportunity employer worldwide. This policy requires managers to conduct their employment practices in such a manner as to eliminate discrimination on the basis of race, color, religion, sex, national origin, age, handicap or veteran's status. The Corporation's subsidiary in Northern Ireland, Hughes Tool Company Limited ("HTCL"), has subscribed to this policy. In addition, HTCL has signed a Declaration of Principle and Intent under the Fair Employment Act (Northern Ireland) of 1976 (the "Act") indicating its commitment to be an equal opportunity employer. That Act has as its purposes the promotion of equal opportunity and the elimination of discrimination in employment for persons of different religious and political beliefs.

Your Board of Directors believes HTCL's employment policies and practices ensure the Corporation does not discriminate in employment and that its hiring and promotion practices do not make it more difficult for persons of a given religious belief to obtain employment or advancement.

The MacBride Principles and the Northern Ireland Fair Employment Law both seek to eliminate employment discrimination in Northern Ireland. By adopting the MacBride Principles, HTCL would become unnecessarily accountable to two sets of similar but not identical fair employment guidelines. For these reasons, your Board of Directors believes that implementation of the MacBride Principles would be burdensome, superfluous and unnecessary, particularly in light of HTCL's own policies and its compliance with the requirements of the Northern Ireland Fair Employment Act.

Your directors have determined that HTCL's policies on equal employment opportunity are entirely consistent with the Corporation's obligations and goals to act as an ethical and responsible member of the business community. Your Board of Directors does not believe that endorsement of the MacBride Principles is necessary, appropriate or in the best interest of the Corporation and its employees.

Your Board of Directors recommends a vote AGAINST approval of Stockholder Proposal No. 2 on implementation of the MacBride Principles in Northern Ireland.

Discussion Questions

1. Assume that you are an owner of Baker Hughes stock. Would you vote for or against this resolution? Why or why not?
2. In what ways would the MacBride Principles be "burdensome" to companies doing business in Northern Ireland?
3. Can, or should, companies ignore the human rights issues raised in Northern Ireland and other nations? Do managers have an ethical obligation to speak out on these matters? Do they have an obligation to their company to keep quiet?

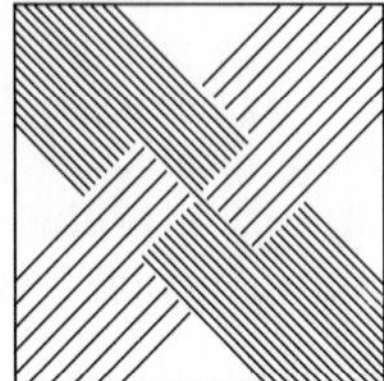

by **Jeanne M. Logsdon** *University of New Mexico*[1]

Lorraine Ross lived in Los Paseos, a neighborhood in San Jose, California. Her year-old daughter had been born with a heart defect, and she had heard of a high number of other birth defects, miscarriages, and serious illnesses suffered by neighbors living in the area. She wondered, as she read the *San Jose Mercury News* in early 1982, whether she might have discovered a clue to these health problems. The paper reported that hazardous chemicals were contaminating groundwater. A well had been closed six weeks earlier because of high concentrations of a potentially carcinogenic (cancer-causing) chemical, TCA (1,1,1-trichloroethane). The well provided drinking water to 16,500 residents of Los Paseos. The TCA had leaked from an underground chemical storage tank at the Fairchild Semiconductor plant, which was located about half a mile from the well.

Over the next few weeks, four other large high-technology companies announced that they had discovered leaking underground chemical tanks or pipes during the previous two years. These reports triggered public concerns and fears that tap water was dangerous. Since 50 percent of the drinking water in the region comes from deep underground aquifers, chemical contamination was potentially a very serious public health problem. The companies and local public officials were under pressure to insure that the water was safe and that no more leaks would occur.

High-Tech and Chemical Use

High-technology electronics firms provide many useful consumer and industrial products. Computers, compact disk players, calculators, video equipment, cars, and many other products contain semiconductor chips that process information at phenomenal speed and accuracy. In order to manufacture chips and high-tech products, companies use a wide variety and high quantity of hazardous chemicals. Some of these chemicals are known or suspected carcinogens or cause other serious health problems if stored or used improperly. For example, a widely used solvent, trichloroethylene (TCE), was phased out in the late 1970s because scientific studies found that it caused cancer in laboratory animals. Many firms switched voluntarily to a substitute solvent, TCA. TCA's carcinogenic status was not established, but it was considered to be much less hazardous.

Companies stored large quantities of chemicals in tanks located underground with connecting pipes to their plant facilities. Local fire codes required that the tanks be placed underground to protect against the danger of fires and explosions. During the 1960s and 1970s, companies complied with existing fire regulations

[1] This case study is based upon interviews with key participants and archival research, especially news reports by the *San Jose Mercury News*.

Black 526 ⊠ ⊗

when they installed the standard single-walled steel tanks. No one had foreseen that the tanks and pipes might corrode and leak the contents.

Early Discoveries of Tank Leaks

IBM was the first Silicon Valley electronics firm to discover that its underground storage tanks had leaked TCE and other chemicals into the soil. IBM was conducting a voluntary companywide survey after tank leaks had been found at one of its east coast facilities. When soil contamination was confirmed at the South San Jose plant in April 1980, IBM notified the regional office of the state agency responsible for regulating surface water quality. This agency had no formal jurisdiction over underground water or chemical tanks—no regulatory agency did at that time. But the agency had the closest connection to underground water quality, and it assumed an oversight role.

IBM recommended that it install monitoring wells to investigate whether any chemicals had migrated through the soil to reach water levels. After several months of monitoring, tests confirmed that some contamination in parts per billion was occurring at water levels near the surface, but it was not endangering any drinking water supplies that come from deep aquifers. Geological experts thought that the aquifers were protected from contamination by a clay layer that would stop the chemicals. Since there were no dangers to public health, IBM and the agency agreed that no public announcement was necessary. The company removed the leaking tanks, transported contaminated soil to approved hazardous waste sites, and installed more monitoring wells to continue investigating the extent of contamination.

Over the next year, Hewlett Packard, Intel, and Advanced Micro Devices also discovered leaking tanks and voluntarily notified the state agency. Each firm stopped using the tanks immediately, installed monitoring wells to identify the magnitude of contamination, and removed contaminated soil. As with the IBM leaks, no publicity accompanied these voluntary disclosures and cleanup efforts. The agency was satisfied that the companies were handling the leaks responsibly.

Fairchild Semiconductor discovered its tank leak in mid-November 1981. This time, however, the consequences were quite different. The company's environmental consultants conducted studies for several weeks and then informed Fairchild that the chemicals had migrated off-site into the drinking water well for the Los Paseos neighborhood. Fairchild, in turn, informed the water company in early December, and the well was closed immediately. Six weeks later, citizens read about the well closure in the local newspaper. The prevailing geological opinion had proved to be wrong—it had not taken into account the presence of abandoned agricultural wells that connected near-surface waters with deep aquifers. These old wells had punctured the clay layer long ago and became conduits for the chemical contaminants.

Public Fears and Demands

Lorraine Ross began to talk to her neighbors about her suspicions that the drinking water was causing medical problems. When this possible linkage was reported in the media along with the reports about the leaks found at the other large firms, citizens throughout the region became alarmed. Industry leaders shared their concerns. According to one knowledgeable manager, executives were as surprised as the general public at these announcements. Companies had not shared with each other the information about leaks they had discovered in their own tanks. Nor had any government agency told them that other companies were experiencing similar problems with chemical storage tanks. Since most leaks had occurred in tanks installed within the previous five years, each firm had believed that its leak was a fluke and each worked independently and quietly to handle the problem. But now it appeared that the leaking-tank problem might be more pervasive.

The high-tech firms, which had enjoyed a good public image and community support in the past, faced a suspicious and angry public for the first time. Many people were shocked when they learned about the hazardous nature of the chemicals that were routinely used by the industry. Previously, chipmakers were known for the surgical-operating-room cleanliness of their operations, and these new disclosures put them in a new unfavorable light. Since the companies had not disclosed these problems earlier, some citizens accused them of being negligent and irresponsible.

High-tech executives and public officials both were blamed for not protecting the public from contaminated water. Many angry public meetings were held over the next two months to force immediate action to clean up existing sites and prevent any future chemical leaks. Los Paseos residents attended meetings carrying signs that said, "Who's got the leak of the week?" and "Water, water, everywhere, not a drop we'd drink." The regional water quality agency took the lead role for the first task of investigation and cleanup. The second task of preventing future leaks was left to local governmental jurisdictions.

Over the next two years, 136 sites where chemicals had contaminated the soil or groundwater were reported to the agency. About 40 percent of the sites were operated by electronics firms. Firms in other industries, such as chemical processing and distribution, chemical waste recycling, metal plating, printing, and pharmaceuticals, found chemical tank leaks too.

The Model Ordinance Task Force

Santa Clara County, the center of the Silicon Valley, is composed of 15 cities, including San Jose, the locale of the Los Paseos neighborhood. These cities often zealously guard their independence, even when dealing with interdependent regional problems. Several cities aggressively compete with one another for industrial development. Other cities prefer to remain quiet residential areas and sometimes resent the costs of regional growth, including overcrowding, traffic congestion, air pollution, and noise. However, in the spring of 1982 it was widely perceived that prevention of chemical tank leaks was not just each industrial city's problem. Underground aquifers extend under political boundaries. Nor could each city solve the problem individually without incurring costs in lost economic base if less responsible firms sought out cities with weak regulations. In short, local government officials quickly identified the presence of a collective interest in establishing uniform standards throughout the county.

Most electronics firms also perceived a collective interest in addressing the prevention issue quickly. Negative publicity was threatening the relatively good rapport that these companies had developed with local governments and citizens. They needed a way to demonstrate responsiveness to public concerns. The risk of potential future liability for health and environmental damage was another incentive to support prudent prevention standards. In addition, certainly most if not all executives were genuinely concerned about the possible health risks to communities—after all, they and their families also drank the local water—and they supported reasonable prevention rules that would apply equally to all firms. Thus high-tech companies backed the concept of uniform storage tank standards.

The common interests of local government and industry stimulated the formation of a task force to develop a Model Hazardous Materials Storage Permit Ordinance. The goal of the task force was to create a uniform set of requirements and then convince each city council in the Silicon Valley to pass and implement them.

The convening group was the Santa Clara County Fire Chiefs' Association. This somewhat surprising choice for sponsorship of the task force was actually quite logical and even brilliant. The fire chief of the city of Santa Clara had sponsored a very innovative chemical hazards program in 1980 to inventory chemicals for fire safety protection. Palo Alto's fire department had copied Santa Clara's program. Thus some experience with chemicals, but not with storage tank leaks, had developed within two local fire departments. In addition, the fire chiefs' association was perceived as oriented toward public safety but neutral about the economic impacts of tank regulations on firms and cities. It was widely respected by all parties as fair and professional.

The process of collaboration began in spring 1982 when Lt. Charles Rice of the Sunnyvale Public Safety Department was appointed to head the Model Ordinance Task Force. He was advised to create a uniform ordinance that would satisfy everyone and to do it quickly. Rice recruited participants, eventually numbering one hundred, from both the public and private sectors. He believed that success depended on including as many groups and individuals as possible. While diverse membership would be difficult to manage, it would pay off in the long run with easier passage and implementation of new regulations. All cities in Santa Clara County, the county government, and appropriate state and local public agencies were represented. On the business side, high-technology firms were represented through the Industry Environmental Coordinating Committee (IECC).

The IECC was itself a collaborative group of five trade associations: the Semiconductor Industry Association, Santa Clara County Manufacturing Group, American Electronics Association, Electronics Association of California, and the Peninsula Industry and Business Association. The IECC was formed shortly after public disclosure of the Fairchild leak. Leaders of the Semiconductor Industry Association (SIA) and the Santa Clara County Manufacturing Group championed the formation of IECC in order to coordinate the public policy positions and activities of individual companies and trade associations.

Larry Borgman of Intel was selected to head IECC because he was then serving as chair of the Facilities and Buildings Standards Subcommittee of SIA's environment and health committee. His subcommittee was working on building and fire code recommendations for semiconductor manufacturing plants. Since trade association executives initially viewed the issue as a building or fire code problem, Borgman's experience with codes would be valuable. In addition, he had worked with public officials in many jurisdictions in his Intel assignment as the worldwide manager of facilities engineering and planning. He was widely regarded as not only technically knowledgeable but also politically astute.

Some high-tech companies felt apprehension in turning over responsibility for representing their individual interests to IECC. The firms and associations had not worked together before. In fact, many of the companies were very tough marketplace competitors with one another. In spite of these tensions, Borgman and leaders of the trade associations were effective in convincing individual companies of their collective interest in supporting reasonable tank standards, the necessity of a joint approach, and the competence of the managers who served on IECC. This trust was essential in creating a mechanism for collaborative industry participation.

Borgman quickly realized that the problem could not be solved through changes in building or fire codes. Codes were not automatically binding on cities, and environmental agencies did not recognize these codes as legitimate environmental regulations. Borgman evaluated several initiatives that were being suggested at various governmental levels for dealing with chemical tank standards. He decided that the Model Ordinance Task Force was the most likely to succeed and offered to have industry executives serve as members on all seven subcommittees that Lt. Rice had established.

The government-industry task force worked for three months on the first draft of the model ordinance. Weekly meetings of the central committee were held, with more frequent subcommittee meetings. Very little legal precedent was available for use by the task force. The only existing U.S. environmental regulations for tanks had been developed for fuel storage tanks in Suffolk County, New York, and Dade County, Florida. Many task force members initially believed that their task was to devise legal standards for each separate industry. But IECC representatives stressed that the issue was hazardous materials storage across all types of businesses. The ordinance should not target specific industries but should apply more generally to all chemical tanks. This view was quickly accepted by other task force members, and the subcommittees began their work on topics such as materials to be regulated, tank technology, disclosure issues, insurance requirements and availability, and legal wording.

The leadership role played by Lt. Rice was critical in establishing ground rules and keeping the process open for new participants. Rice made it clear that all information would be known by all participants and there would be "no dealing around people." He perceived his role as facilitator, peacekeeper, diplomat, and in a few instances decision maker. On several occasions when a point could not be resolved by consensus, Rice decided what the draft ordinance would state and indicated to the other side that they could take the issue to the next round of public debate if they felt strongly about their position.

IECC chair Borgman's style also helped the early discussions to be productive and lead quickly to consensus. He identified simple points that were irrefutable. For example, he continually said, "What goes into the tank is supposed to stay in the tank." This position established the principle that no leak, however small or slow-moving, was permissible. So the members did not have to get bogged down in deciding what levels of various chemical leaks might be safe. When enough of these simple points were accepted by the participants, consensus formed fairly easily around specific tank regulations.

The first draft of the ordinance was presented to the public in July 1982. The draft proposal reflected electronics industry support for generally strong and effective regulation. The draft's major provisions included the following requirements:

- Permits for using any underground chemical storage tank.
- A monitoring system for existing tanks and replacement of leaking tanks.
- Secondary containment (such as double-walled construction) and a monitoring system for new tanks.
- An inventory of chemicals used at each site and a comprehensive management plan for handling them.
- Insurance coverage for each firm to pay for cleanup in case of accidental leaks.
- Permit fees, set by each city, to cover regulatory costs.
- Fines for noncompliance up to $500 per day.
- Information that companies were to give to regulatory authorities to comply with the ordinance would be protected from public disclosure, and disclosure of this information would be penalized as a misdemeanor.

The response at the first public meeting was generally favorable. However, criticisms were voiced by several labor leaders and public interest activists. They focused on the lack of public disclosure and the anti-whistle-blower bias in the draft. An industry member of IECC defended the confidentiality provision, saying it would protect trade secrets and ensure security from thefts and terrorist attacks. However, the activists had identified and capitalized on an issue that captured public and media attention.

The Silicon Valley Toxics Coalition

Shortly after this public meeting, the Silicon Valley Toxics Coalition was formed as a focal organization for citizen concern. The coalition sought to become a party to the collaborative process in its call for membership: "Together we can work with the industry to ensure appropriate control of toxic substances. We all live and work in Silicon Valley and ultimately we all have the same survival interests." The Toxics Coalition was a collaboration of established environmental and labor organizations as well as individual citizens. Local attorney and activist Ted Smith became its director. Since Lt. Rice was committed to open participation, Smith and other members of the Toxics Coalition were invited to join in the second round of task force meetings. So now the task force was expanded beyond government and business to include public activists.

The next series of task force meetings was somewhat more discordant at first. Skeptical new public interest participants tested their ability to influence the process. However, an industry member notes that some tension had occurred each time any new participant joined because "it takes time to adjust norm states." On a number of issues, IECC and Toxics Coalition representatives agreed and worked together. The respect that developed among the participants helped to generate consensus on most of the issues, and it was crucial in sustaining the process when differences on other issues could not be resolved. With public concern accelerating throughout the period of task force meetings, participants were highly motivated to search for consensus. When conflicting positions could not be compromised, task force members did not resort to delaying tactics but chose instead to keep to the timetable and address conflicts in the appropriate forums for public debate.

The most controversial issue during this second drafting period involved public disclosure. Toxics Coalition members viewed it as the public's right to know about hazards and pushed for 100 percent disclosure of all chemical quantities. Industry members stressed the paperwork burden of including small quantities, as well as the trade secret problem. Manufacturing processes are an important source of competitive advantage, and knowledge of the exact quantities of particular chemicals used by a firm would reveal this proprietary secret. Task force participants could not reach a consensus about how to deal with this issue. Industry's argument about trade secret confidentiality was persuasive to Lt. Rice, who ultimately decided to retain limits on reporting and no public disclosure in the final draft.

Negotiating the Final Ordinance

The arena in which the final provisions of the model ordinance were to be negotiated was the Intergovernmental Council (IGC), a regional advisory group of city, county, and public agency representatives. Their review of the model ordinance took place from November 1982 to February 1983. IGC's main concern was to settle all major differences so that every city would adopt the model without modification. During this period, a series of public meetings was held to gather input from various constituencies. Members of the task force, now including the Toxics Coalition, attended these meetings to explain and speak in favor of a uniform countywide approach. The often large citizen attendance, in part the result of grassroots organizing by the Toxics Coalition, indicated continuing public concern and support for the ordinance. The meetings also gave opponents an opportunity to raise objections and provided the IGC with an indicator of the opposition's strength.

While favoring the uniform approach and most of the model provisions, the Toxics Coalition and the IECC tried to gain support for some changes in the ordinance. The coalition pushed for full public disclosure, protection of whistle-blowers, and an expanded list of chemicals for reporting. The key issues for IECC were to protect trade secrets against public disclosure and limiting required reports for stored chemicals to quantities over 55 gallons.

During the second round of public meetings, opposition to the ordinance was expressed by three individual high-tech firms, several local chambers of commerce, and one powerful industry, petroleum retailing. National Semiconductor, GTE Sylvania Systems, and Lockheed objected to the ordinance because of its high cost, red tape, and potential for delays that might disrupt important defense work. The major criticism made by the chambers of commerce was the cost and paperwork impact on small firms such as dry cleaners, auto repair shops, and gas stations.

Chevron, Shell Oil, and the petroleum retailers trade association concentrated on getting an exemption for fuel tanks. Petroleum interests had not participated significantly in the collaborative task force effort. While a number of petroleum executives had attended several meetings, they maintained no continuity of participation and did not work actively on the subcommittees. They only belatedly discovered that the ordinance would apply to fuel tanks. So they began their effort to influence the ordinance late in the process but with the use of considerable resources.

Their position was that gasoline was not a major groundwater contamination problem and that gasoline storage was already heavily regulated as a flammable material. Another argument they used was the absence of available technology for double containment of very large gasoline tanks, while promising future availability of stronger single-walled fiberglass tanks that would not leak. Some gas stations were already converting from steel to fiberglass tanks to reduce gasoline leaks caused by corrosion. The fundamental issue was cost. Industry representatives said that double containment would cost $30,000 per tank, raising gasoline prices by 4 to 5 cents a gallon.

The major threat to uniformity was the city of Santa Clara. A large number of high-technology firms are located there, and it already had developed a successful chemical hazards program. However, its program did not deal with underground chemical tank leaks but only with inventory reporting requirements and inspection visits. Other cities were watching carefully for Santa Clara's response. If it did not support the major provisions of the ordinance, prevention of groundwater contamination in the entire region was in jeopardy, and Santa Clara would continue to get a large portion of new electronics facilities. It was feared that the entire task force effort was at stake. Amidst extensive media coverage, the Santa Clara City Council indicated in late January 1983 that it would accept in principle almost all of the major provisions of the ordinance. Supporters claimed this was a major victory and a signal to the IGC that the drive for uniformity was working.

Final hearings before the IGC in early February 1983 provided one last opportunity to voice support and objections. Hundreds of people attended the hearings. By chance, a network television camera crew was in town and came to tape the proceedings, and its presence added to the feeling that this was a momentous event. Larry Borgman and other electronics industry representatives expressed firm support for the Model Ordinance in principle and for almost all of its provisions. They requested one change to exempt small quantities of chemicals from required reports. Ted Smith and Toxics Coalition members also expressed support for the ordinance but asked for three changes: full public disclosure, whistle-blower protection, and an expanded list of covered chemicals. High-tech executives opposed these changes. The petroleum industry made a particularly strong showing with representatives flown in from around the country. It pressed for a complete exemption from the ordinance.

The final wording of the Model Ordinance revealed the fine art of compromise. The electronics industry got limited trade secret protection through short-form reporting of competitively significant chemicals stored only in small quantities. More extensive public disclosure of large quantities of competitively neutral chemicals would be revealed in long-form reporting. Labor and public interest activists got full whistle-blower protection and public disclosure with restrictions when trade secrets were declared by a firm. The petroleum industry lost a motion to delete double containment for fuel tanks but did get agreement for an additional three-month study of its proposed substitute regulations. The unanimous vote by the IGC, while only advisory, signaled strong support for uniformity when the ordinance was submitted to each city council.

Passage and Implementation

Acceptance of the Model Ordinance was virtually unanimous by every city council in the county. Three large industrial cities acted almost immediately to incorporate the ordinance into their city regulations. By the end of 1983, the other cities, except for Santa Clara, had acted to pass the complete ordinance or have the county government administer the tank permit program.

The only exception to complete uniformity was taken by the city of Santa Clara. On the recommendation of the fire chief, it modified its existing chemical hazards program to incorporate the model's major provisions for secondary containment and monitoring. However, it did not support public disclosure. The fire chief explained later why he did not recommend the model's disclosure provisions. In 1980, he had received the cooperation of the Chamber of Commerce for the chemical hazards inventory and inspection program with the understanding that the information would remain confidential. He felt obliged to continue to honor that agreement. With this relatively minor exception in Santa Clara, the Model Ordinance quickly became the uniform standard throughout Silicon Valley.

Regarding implementation of the ordinance, some companies began to install monitoring systems and double-walled tanks even before final passage of the new ordinance. By February 1986, nearly 85 percent of the 5,546 covered facilities in the county had applied for permits, and 74 percent had received them. In addition, 22 percent of the single-walled tanks that were used in 1982 had been removed, and 618 double-walled tanks had been installed. By 1986, the major criticism of implementation was that city resource constraints had slowed permit processing and inspections.

The hazardous materials ordinance was never challenged by companies in court. In fact, the ordinance that was developed in Silicon Valley became the basis for California and eventually federal tank regulations. Thus high-tech firms and the Toxics Coalition influenced not only the local regulatory approach but set a precedent that affected many different industries all over the nation. While none of the participants claimed that the ordinance was the ideal solution from their group's perspective, they said after it was all over that the Model Ordinance was the best that could have been devised and passed under the circumstances.

Discussion Questions

1. Develop a stakeholder map for the participants in this episode, identifying both primary and secondary stakeholders, along with the major interests and powers of each stakeholder grouping. How could this kind of map contribute to the development and adoption of a Model Ordinance?
2. Assess the social responsibility of each of the corporations and industries involved. In your opinion, did these companies and industries demonstrate skills in social responsiveness? How would you characterize the corporate social strategies they used?
3. Government-business relations are rarely without tension and controversy, but in this case government officials, business representatives, and community activists seemed to get along remarkably well. What factors were responsible for the successful collaboration they achieved? Can those reasons be extended to other kinds of problems?

CASE STUDY THE LINCOLN SAVINGS AND LOAN SCANDAL[1]

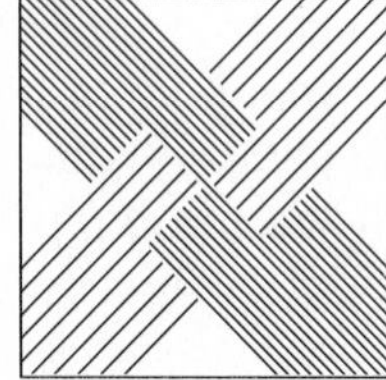

by **Anne T. Lawrence** *San Jose State University*

Shortly after two o'clock in the morning on November 16, 1989, sixty FBI agents, Federal Deposit Insurance Corporation officers, and other plainclothes police strode into the pink marble lobby of the opulent Phoenician resort hotel in Scottsdale, Arizona. Moving quickly and coordinating their actions by walkie-talkie, the agents informed the startled night clerks that the resort was being seized by order of the federal government. As proceedings were videotaped for possible later use in court, agents posted severance notices on the doors of some thirty managers and ushered on-duty employees out of the building. Across a walkway, agents quickly secured executive offices, including those of Charles H. Keating, Jr., the head of Lincoln Savings and Loan, majority owner of the Phoenician. By the time dawn broke, the 605-room, 130-acre luxury hotel in the Valley of the Sun, from its 18-hole golf course to its seven swimming pools, was firmly in the hands of the federal government.

The predawn raid on the Phoenician severed the final connection between Charles H. Keating, Jr., and Lincoln Savings and Loan, which seven months earlier had been put in receivership by the government. Of the 600 or so S&Ls seized by government regulators at that time in the growing savings and loan crisis, Lincoln was by far the most expensive. The *New York Times* called the Lincoln case a "microcosm—in the extreme to be sure—of the failure of hundreds of other thrift institutions," and an illustration of the forces that contributed to a financial scandal whose eventual cost to taxpayers could exceed $350 billion.

Some read into the Lincoln case a story of political influence and corruption in high places, others a story of deregulation out of control. Others saw simply the consequences of the decline of an overinflated sun belt real estate market, which threatened loans made by the thrift. As for Keating, some saw him as a villain, an immoral and even criminal "financial Blackbeard" who wantonly misused federally insured deposits of a thrift he controlled for his own enrichment. Others saw him as a morally upright, successful real estate developer and financier who was improperly harassed and driven out of business by overzealous and incompetent regulators. Whoever or whatever the villains were, the collapse of Lincoln Savings and Loan had many victims, from the U.S. taxpayers who will

[1] This case was prepared especially for this edition. Sources include articles appearing in the *Wall Street Journal*, the *New York Times*, the *Washington Post*, the *Los Angeles Times*, *Business Week*, *Barrons*, *Forbes*, the *San Francisco Examiner*, the *San Francisco Chronicle*, *Time*, *Newsweek*, and the *U.S. News and World Report* in 1989 and 1990. These sources are cited in the case narrative only to reference direct quotations by individuals or attributions of opinion. The history of the savings and loan industry is based primarily on Paul Zane Pilzer, *Other People's Money: The Inside Story of the S&L Mess* (New York: Simon and Schuster, 1989), and Stephen Pizzo, Mary Fricker, and Paul Muolo, *Inside Job: The Looting of America's Savings and Loans*, New York: McGraw-Hill, 1989.

pay for the $2.5 billion failure to the 23,000 savers, many of them elderly, who were left holding worthless paper when the company collapsed.

Charles H. Keating, Jr., Sun Belt Developer

Charles H. Keating, Jr., was born in 1923 into the family of a prominent industrialist in Cincinnati. He attended the University of Cincinnati, earned a law degree, and set up a business law practice in his home town with two associates. As a young attorney, he caught the eye of Cincinnati-based corporate financier Carl Lindner, who after a long informal association brought Keating on board as an executive vice president of his firm, American Financial, in 1972. In 1975, Keating moved to Phoenix, Arizona, to run Lindner's home construction subsidiary there. Two years later, Keating bought out Lindner's share in the company for $300,000 and pushed to develop American Continental Corporation (ACC) as a major real estate development firm. Within a decade, Keating had taken ACC to annual revenues of $857 million, developing a reputation both as a builder of upscale homes and commercial properties and as a financial operator with a penchant for creative financing.

By the early 1980s, Keating had established himself, by most measures, as a very successful sun belt real estate mogul. But already, a darker underside to his career had surfaced. In 1979, the Securities and Exchange Commission (SEC) issued a complaint against Keating, Lindner, and another associate based on their activities at American Financial. The complaint charged that the three men had caused several federally insured Ohio financial institutions they controlled to make loans on "wildly preferential terms" to various associates. Keating himself had borrowed $4.5 million, largely unsecured. In settlement of the SEC complaint, Keating "consented" to the charges (although without admitting guilt) and formally agreed to refrain from any further violations of securities laws.

It's a Wonderful Life

The savings and loan industry, as it evolved historically, seemed an odd match for a man of Charles Keating's temperament and business inclinations. For years, S&Ls were jokingly referred to as the "3-6-3" industry; its executives borrowed money from depositors at three percent, loaned it out for home mortgages at six percent, and arrived at the golf course at three P.M. The image of savings and loans as staid, "pillar of the community" institutions was perhaps best captured in Frank Capra's classic 1946 film, "It's a Wonderful Life," in which Hollywood star Jimmy Stewart played the part of an understanding S&L executive who stopped a run on the bank by reminding the community that the thrift had provided mortgage funds to a young couple just starting out.

Savings and loans, or thrifts as they are known, emerged historically in the early 1800s as voluntary associations designed to pool and safeguard their members' savings. Unlike commercial banks, which invest in commercial real estate and other business ventures, savings and loans historically have invested mainly in home mortgages and public bonds. During the Great Depression of the 1930s, many thrifts (as well as commercial banks) failed, and hundreds of thousands of Americans lost their life savings. As part of a larger program of depression-era New Deal banking reforms, Congress in the mid-1930s passed a series of laws governing the thrift industry. Legislators established the Federal Savings and Loan Insurance Corporation (FSLIC), funded by an assessment on deposits at insured institutions, that guaranteed each S&L deposit up to a maximum of $5,000. Over time, this limit was gradually increased; by the time of Lincoln's failure, the maximum stood at $100,000.[2]

In exchange for these guarantees, Congress also tightened up federal control of the industry. It authorized the Federal Home Loan Bank Board (FHLBB) to regulate thrifts and placed restrictions on their activities. Savings and loans were limited in the rate of interest they could pay depositors and could lend only for residential mortgages in their home communities. In effect, the U.S. government told the thrift industry: we will shore up public confidence by guaranteeing your depositors' savings; in exchange, you must act conservatively so as not to put taxpayer's money at risk. For almost half a century, this New Deal "deal" worked without a hitch. Public confidence returned, and at the industry's height one-third of Americans had their savings in their local S&Ls. Returning these funds to the communities they served in the form of residential mortgages, thrifts permitted many Americans to realize their dreams of home ownership.

Undoing the New Deal "Deal"

By the late 1970s, however, the New Deal "deal" had begun to unravel. The entire system rested on a base of stable, low rates of interest and a low inflation rate. When the Vietnam War, followed by the Arab oil embargo of 1973, set off an inflationary spiral, savers saw the value of their S&L fixed-rate accounts rapidly erode. Many depositors pulled out, moving their savings into money market accounts and other new financial vehicles paying higher rates. By 1980, fully 85 percent of thrifts were losing money.

Congress's response to the growing crisis was to ease government controls over savings and loans. This political reaction to the thrift industry's troubles was consistent, of course, with the broad movement toward economic deregulation in the 1970s and early 1980s. In the airline, trucking, telecommunications, and other industries, policymakers had moved to reduce government oversight and permit a freer play of market forces. Their objectives were to increase competition,

[2] The Federal Deposit Insurance Corporation (FDIC), the insurance fund covering commercial banks, is legally backed by the "full faith and credit" of the U.S. government. In other words, if the FDIC fails, the U.S. government and taxpayers are required to cover the shortfall. By contrast, the FSLIC does not provide such a guarantee; if it fails, deposits are insured only to the extent that Congress can be persuaded to appropriate funds. This is why the "bail-out" of the savings and loan industry in the late 1980s and early 1990s was not automatic but had to be debated by Congress. In practice, it is highly unlikely that Congress would permit savings and loan depositors to lose insured funds, since this would cause a massive loss of faith in the nation's banking system. (Pilzer, *Other People's Money*, pp. 52–53.)

improve efficiency and productivity, and lower prices to the consumer. Now, Congress reasoned, the same approach might help the faltering S&L industry by permitting thrifts to compete freely with other financial institutions.

The deregulation of savings and loans proceeded in several steps. First, the federal government permitted thrifts to pay higher interest rates on deposits. This cure was almost worse than the disease, however, for S&Ls still had their assets locked up in long-term, low-interest home loans and were therefore caught in a vicious "squeeze" between high rates paid to attract depositors and low rates on old loans. The solution, the lawmakers determined, was to allow S&Ls to move into more lucrative (and higher-risk) investments. In 1982, Congress passed the Garn–St. Germain Act, which permitted S&Ls not only to offer money market rates but also to invest up to 40 percent of their assets in nonresidential real estate loans. The federal government also eased accounting standards and lowered net worth requirements. During this period, several states also changed their rules (most thrifts are subject to both state and federal regulation). Texas, California, and Florida, in particular, moved to permit investment in a wide range of nontraditional areas.

At the same time that industry rules were loosened, the federal government reduced its support for regulatory agencies. The Reagan administration cut the frequency of field examinations and stabilized the number of bank board examiners just as the industry was deregulated. At the height of the savings and loan crisis, only 750 FHLBB examiners were charged with regulating the nation's 5,500 savings and loans. Critics have charged, moreover, that federal examiners, who earned an average salary of $25,000 and half of whom had been on the job for less than two years, were ill-equipped to understand the complex financial transactions typical of the high-flying thrift operators of the 1980s.

The regulation of the industry in the 1930s had rested on two foundations: federal deposit insurance and tight government controls. The deregulation of the 1980s effectively decoupled the two by loosening controls, while still retaining federal insurance. In this respect, the deregulation of S&Ls differed from that of other industries of the period, where no such insurance protected players from the downside of market competition. To its supporters, the deregulation of S&Ls was a formula for bailing out a faltering industry by permitting it to compete fairly with other financial institutions. To its critics, it was an invitation to the unscrupulous to speculate widely with the full backing of U.S. taxpayers.

Operating in a Nontraditional Manner

Many entrepreneurs previously unassociated with the savings and loan industry were quick to seize on the opportunities presented by deregulation. Among them was Charles Keating. In February 1984, American Continental purchased Lincoln Savings and Loan of Irvine, California, for $51 million. Keating and his associates found Lincoln attractive because California had recently changed its rules governing thrifts, for the first time permitting direct investment in real estate and securities. Apparently, regulators who approved the sale failed to notice Keating's prior entanglements with the SEC; they later said this "would have made a difference."[3] At the time, Lincoln was a traditional, 29-branch S&L with a loan portfolio consisting mainly of home mortages. Although the thrift earned $3 million the year before its purchase by ACC, many—including Keating's critics—agree with his assessment that Lincoln was fundamentally a troubled institution, caught like many S&Ls of that era in the squeeze between low-interest home loans and high-interest deposits.

Although he promised the bank board he would retain Lincoln's top-management team, Keating quickly fired the S&L's conservative lending officers and internal auditors and installed his son, Charles Keating III, then a 24-year-old college dropout most recently employed as a country-club busboy, as chairman of the board. "We declared from the beginning," Keating later said, "our intention to operate Lincoln in a nontraditional manner."[4] Lincoln quickly sold off its portfolios of home loans. In addition, the thrift moved to attract deposits. Like many other aggressive S&Ls in the deregulated 1980s, Lincoln sought out, in regulators' lingo, "hot money." By offering high interest rates, thrifts were able literally overnight to raise large sums by selling federally insured $100,000 certificates of deposit (CDs) through various fund brokers. Of course, this practice increased risk, since these deposits were fickle and often withdrawn in search of higher rates when the CDs expired.

Keating promptly moved to invest depositors' funds and the proceeds from the sale of home mortgages into a wide range of high-risk, speculative ventures. The S&L invested $100 million, for example, in Wall Street financier Ivan Boesky's arbitrage fund, $132 million in Gulf Broadcasting Corporation during a hostile takeover attempt, and $12 million in the "junk bonds" of Circus, Circus, a Las Vegas casino. Lincoln also made loans for the purchase of large tracts of undeveloped desert land and bankrolled several commercial real estate projects by ACC and other Keating associates, including the lavish Phoenician hotel. Between 1984, when Keating purchased Lincoln, and 1988, the thrift's assets (loans and other investments) increased fivefold from $1.1 billion to $5.5 billion. In defense of these investment practices, Keating and his attorneys later argued that he had done exactly what federal and state policymakers in the early 1980s had permitted—indeed, encouraged—thrift operators to do, namely, move their assets into highly risky but also potentially highly profitable ventures.[5]

Keating's investment practices, although highly speculative, were in some respects consistent with much other financial activity of the 1980s, a decade that celebrated the pursuit of money, even if by means of an unproductive exchange of assets and accumulation of debt. The deal making that characterized many of Keating's investments was reminiscent of that of many other "players" of the 1980s, including Michael Milken of Drexel Burnham, himself a Keating associate who

[3] *Wall Street Journal,* Nov. 20, 1989, p. 1.
[4] *New York Times,* Nov. 9, 1990, p. C6.
[5] *Washington Post,* Apr. 10, 1990, p. A23.

helped raise the funds to purchase Lincoln, and who was later indicted in a separate case for racketeering and securities fraud.[6]

Making Out Handsomely

Keating maintained that under his stewardship, these deposit and investment practices generated high profits. By his account, Lincoln earned $17 million in 1984, $100 million in 1985, $80 million in 1986, and $60 million in 1987. He attributed the falloff in earnings after 1985 to regulatory harassment. Even in the wake of government seizure, Keating continued to maintain that Lincoln was a phenomenally successful business. He testified in federal court in January 1990, that "if they [federal regulators] would have left us alone, we'd still be making $100 million a year."[7]

Lincoln did, in fact, earn some big windfalls on its unusual investments. The thrift earned $30 million on its Gulf Broadcasting stock; in effect, Lincoln used federally insured depositors' money to "greenmail" a private firm. Regulators later charged, however, that most, if not all, of the gains Keating cited were bogus, the result of intricate schemes to boost paper profits. In a typical transaction, Lincoln might purchase a tract of desert land. Keating would then arrange for its sale—at a much higher price—to an associate, with the purchase financed by a loan from Lincoln. On paper, the S&L would post a tidy profit on the sale. Eventually, of course, if the borrower defaulted, the loan would be worth much less than its book value, since the inflated price could not be supported on the open market. By the time government regulators seized Lincoln, it had millions of dollars' worth of such bad loans on its books.

In an arrangement that regulators later found particularly worrisome, Keating also siphoned federally insured Lincoln funds directly to American Continental. Under bank board rules, Lincoln was permitted to "upstream" to the parent firm funds for tax liabilities due on Lincoln's earnings. Keating apparently abused this rule, however, upstreaming to ACC some $95 million in funds that were never paid to the IRS. After ACC declared bankruptcy in April 1989, the government's only access to these funds was through the bankruptcy court, where it had no priority over other creditors.

Whether or not Lincoln was making or losing money—still a matter of dispute—it is clear that Keating and his associates were making out handsomely. In the three years before Lincoln was seized by regulators, Keating and members of his family received $34 million in salaries, bonuses, and payments for their stock in American Continental. As chairman of ACC, Charles Keating himself earned $1.7 million annually during the period ACC owned Lincoln. His son, Charles Keating III, in 1988 received a salary of $1.16 million as chairman of Lincoln S&L. Keating defended the young man's compensation on the grounds

[6] For more on the "money culture" of the 1980s, see John Taylor, *The Circus of Ambition* (New York: Warner Books, 1989) and Kevin Phillips, *The Politics of Rich and Poor: Wealth and the American Electorate in the Reagan Aftermath* (New York: Random House, 1990).

[7] *Los Angeles Times*, Jan. 6, 1990, p. D1.

that "my son ran an extraordinarily profitable real estate company, probably the largest in the United States."[8]

A Ticking Time Bomb

In 1984, around the time Keating took control of Lincoln, Edwin J. Gray, then chairman of the Federal Home Loan Bank Board, became increasingly concerned about aggressive lending practices some S&Ls had begun in the wake of deregulation. In May, he proposed a new "equity" rule, limiting direct investment in real estate to 10 percent of a thrift's assets. This rule, of course, conflicted directly with Keating's plans for Lincoln. Not long after, the bank board's San Francisco office, which had jurisdiction over Lincoln, began a routine audit of the Irvine thrift. Examiners found direct investments exceeding the 10 percent limit. Over the next three years, the San Francisco office continued to turn up irregular practices, including millions of dollars worth of loans made without proper appraisals or credit checks on borrowers and direct investments far over the mandated limits. Although, in retrospect, it is clear that the San Francisco regulators missed much—including the $95 million upstreamed to ACC—by 1987 they had seen enough. In May of that year William Black and Michael Patriarca of the San Francisco FHLBB sent their Washington superiors a 285-page report that recommended federal seizure of Lincoln and also made a "criminal referral," that is, recommended federal investigation for fraud.

Keating countered the mounting challenge from regulators with typical aggressiveness. One approach was simply to offer jobs at lucrative terms to regulators or their relatives. Keating actually offered to hire his nemesis at the bank board, Edwin Gray, at a salary of $300,000 a year. Gray refused. He also offered a position to Patriarca's wife, a banking attorney. She also turned him down. Taking another approach, Keating pushed for the nomination of Lee Henkel, a lawyer with whom he had close ties, to the three-member bank board, apparently to counter Gray's influence. Henkel received an interim appointment but withdrew his nomination in the face of intense criticism after he proposed a rule that would have exempted Lincoln from direct investment limits.

Keating also sought the support of prominent intellectuals. In 1985, he hired Alan Greenspan, then a well-respected private economist and later chairman of the Federal Reserve Board, to prepare an analysis of Lincoln. Greenspan provided a letter, which Keating widely distributed, that called Lincoln "a financially strong institution that presents no foreseeable risk." Greenspan later said that "I never anticipated the types of problems Lincoln would ultimately create."[9]

The Keating Five

Keating's most effective effort, by far, was his campaign to influence political figures to intervene on his behalf. In explaining his practice of making contri-

[8] *Time*, Apr. 9, 1990, p. 20.

[9] *U.S. News and Report*, Nov. 27, 1989, p. 20, and *Wall Street Journal*, Nov. 20, 1989, p. A8.

butions to politicians, Keating said, "We support and campaign for the political leaders we believe will represent the best of American virtues. In the contract between the voter and the politician, we have the right to seek their help when needed and demand it when justified. This I have done."[10]

In making contributions, Keating eschewed the use of political action committees (PACs), which are limited by law to donations of $5,000 per candidate per election. Instead, he preferred direct, individual gifts.[11] Federal election laws limit individual contributions to $1,000 per candidate per election and to a total of no more than $25,000 annually. Federal authorities believed Keating may have circumvented this limit by overpaying his employees with the expectation that they would contribute to designated candidates.[12] On a single day in March 1986, for example, 51 contributions were made to Senator John McCain by Keating, members of his family, and ACC employees. A second method of political influence favored by Keating was known as the "soft money channel": corporate contributions to political parties or other political organizations for nonpartisan activities, such as voter registration. Such indirect donations are not limited by law. During the mid-1980s, Keating and American Continental Corporation gave slightly over a million dollars to targeted political organizations.

Most favored as objects of Keating's largess were five U.S. senators—Alan Cranston (Democrat-California), John Glenn (Democrat-Ohio), John McCain (Republican-Arizona), Dennis DeConcini (Democrat-Arizona), and Donald W. Riegle, Jr. (Democrat-Michigan). The "Keating Five," as these senators later became known, received over $1.4 million in both direct and indirect contributions, as shown in Figure 1. Keating, personally an archconservative, had little in common politically with most of these senators, but they had potential influence on banking regulators. Riegle, for example, served as chairman of the powerful Senate Banking Committee; Cranston, senate whip, was next in line for the same post.

Of the Keating Five, Cranston received the most contributions, including $850,000 in 1987 and 1988 to three tax-exempt, nonpartisan political organizations he founded—USA Votes, Forum Institute, and the Center for Participation in Democracy (CPD). Although Cranston drew no salary from them, these groups paid for sixteen trips by him in 1988. They also provided his son Kim, who served as the unsalaried director of the CPD, with visibility in state political circles. In addition, all three organizations were involved in extensive voter registration

[10] *Los Angeles Times,* May 30, 1989, p. 11.

[11] Political action committees (PACs) are organizations of like-minded individuals who join together to raise money and donate it to candidates for public office. Under federal election law, companies may not donate directly to a PAC, but they may use corporate funds to create and administer a PAC and may solicit contributions from employees and stockholders. PAC contributions are limited to $5,000 per candidate per election. Although the companies controlled by Keating—American Continental Corporation and Lincoln Savings and Loan—did not use PACs as a vehicle for campaign contributions, many savings and loans during this period did. For example, in the 1988 congressional election, PACs affiliated with savings and loans gave $680,000 to members of the Senate and House Banking Committees, who helped oversee the federal government's regulatory policies. U.S. Representative Jim Leach (Republican-Iowa) has said that S&Ls "historically have gotten their way with Congress as much as any group on the hill." (*Los Angeles Times,* Feb. 15, 1989, p. 16.)

[12] *New York Times,* Nov. 9, 1989, p. C6.

FIGURE 1

Contributions by Charles Keating and Close Associates, and American Continental Corporation, to Five U.S. Senators

	Direct	Indirect	Total
Cranston	$ 47,000	$ 935,000*	$ 982,000
Glenn	34,000	200,000†	234,000
McCain	112,000	—	112,000
Riegle	76,000	—	76,000
DeConcini	55,000	—	55,000
TOTAL	$324,000	$1,135,000	$1,459,000

* To three political organizations controlled by Cranston and to the California Democratic Party.
† To a political organization controlled by Glenn.
SOURCE: *New York Times*, Nov. 18, 1989, p. 12.

activity, mostly aimed at such traditionally Democratic constituencies as minorities and the poor. In the final days of the close 1986 election—which Cranston won by a razor-thin 1 percent—Keating also gave $85,000 to a California Democratic Party get-out-the-vote drive that Cranston acknowledged helped put him over the top.

Both defenders and critics of the Keating Five agree that the high cost of running a senatorial campaign—which can top $10,000 per day for every day of a senator's six-year term in populous states—puts tremendous pressure on elected officials to accept contributions, even from those whose motives may be suspect. In defense of his acceptance of substantial sums from Keating, Cranston told an interviewer in February 1990 that "I have to think in large numbers because I have to raise so darn much money. I did not see anything wrong in doing it. In retrospect, I see how people can read things into that that are not there. That I regret."[13]

On Behalf of Their Friend and Contributor

On April 2, 1987, Senator Riegle summoned FHLBB chief Gray to a meeting with Senators DeConcini, Cranston, Glenn, and McCain. Participants later disagreed over what transpired. Gray recalled that the senators proposed a deal "on behalf of their friend and contributor," in which Lincoln would make more traditional home loans if regulators would withdraw restrictions on direct investments by the thrift. Gray reported that the senators "came at me like lawyers arguing for a client" and called their intervention "an attempt to subvert the regulatory process."[14]

The senators present at the meeting flatly denied this interpretation of events. DeConcini later wrote Gray that "your recollection of the meeting is so distorted

[13] *San Francisco Chronicle*, Feb. 22, 1990, p. A4.
[14] *Time*, Nov. 6, 1989, p. 27, and *Newsweek*, Nov. 6, 1989, p. 36.

as to bear no resemblance to fact." Cranston recalled that he and his colleagues had simply told Gray that "if a case could not be made against Lincoln, [regulators should] bring a halt to what appeared to be . . . harassment."[15]

A week later, all five senators convened again, this time to meet with examiners summoned from the FHLBB's San Francisco office. The content of the second meeting also is in dispute. James Cirona, a top regulator in the San Francisco office, informed the senators that Lincoln was a "ticking time bomb." He and the other examiners stated that Lincoln was "flying blind on all of their different loans and investments" and that their loan practices "violated the law, regulations, and common sense." One examiner later testified at a congressional hearing that "the meeting with five senators was an extraordinary example of political influence—the most extraordinary I've ever seen."[16]

Cranston, disputing this account, later told reporters that the senators met with federal regulators on April 9, 1987, simply to say: "What's going on here? Why don't you bring this to a conclusion one way or the other? That's one of the things a senator is expected to do. We were elected to write laws, but also to go to bat for constituents, at least if it seems they are getting the run-around from the government."[17] On another occasion, Cranston added that he also was motivated by concern that if Lincoln were seized by regulators several hundred Californians would lose their jobs and depositors would be "shaken up."[18]

When asked at a press conference after Lincoln was seized if his financial support had influenced political figures to take up his cause, Keating responded, "I want to say in the most forceful way I can: I certainly hope so."[19]

Cutting the Legs Out from Under the Troops

While the content of the meetings between regulators and the "Keating Five" is in dispute, what then happened is not. The seizure of Lincoln and criminal prosecution recommended by the San Francisco examiners several weeks later did not go forward. Instead, M. Danny Wall, a former aide to Senator Jake Garn (coauthor of the Garn–St. Germain Act that deregulated S&Ls), who succeeded Gray as head of the FHLB in the summer of 1987, transferred the Lincoln case from San Francisco to Washington, where it would be under his direct supervision. The San Francisco examiners interpreted this move as evidence that "political influence" had been used to prevent them from shutting down the savings and loan. Wall, however, strenously denied that politics played any part in his decision to transfer the case and later told a reporter that "my responsibility was to see that this was not a lynch mob after Keating. The San Francisco office [of the FHLBB] has a history of being hysterical, overzealous, swept away by smoke where there is no gun."[20] U.S. Representative Henry Gonzales (Democrat-Texas) later

[15] *Los Angeles Times,* Nov. 8, 1989, p. A15.

[16] *Time,* Nov. 6, 1989, p. 27, and *Newsweek,* Nov. 6, 1989, p. 36.

[17] *San Francisco Examiner,* Nov. 29, 1989, p. 2.

[18] *San Francisco Chronicle,* Feb. 22, 1990, p. A4.

[19] *Wall Street Journal,* Oct. 16, 1989, p. B10.

[20] *Time,* Nov. 27, 1989, p. 29.

offered a different interpretation, when he stated at a House hearing that Wall had "cut the legs out from under his . . . troops in the middle of battle."[21]

Rather than closing Lincoln down, as recommended by his local examiners, Wall entered into private negotiations with Lincoln that went on for almost two years, aimed at resolving the thrift's difficulties without a government takeover. Wall and his allies in the Washington FHLBB office were concerned that they lacked specific documentation of wrongdoing that would hold up to certain court challenge. Wall specifically said later that if he had known of the $95 million improperly upstreamed to ACC, he would have moved sooner.[22] Washington regulators also wanted to avoid the cost of shutting Lincoln down, hoping instead that the case might be resolved either through Keating's cooperation or by the sale of the thrift to a qualified buyer.

In delaying action against Lincoln, Wall and his associates said they were also influenced in part by reports filed by Lincoln's independent auditor, Arthur Young and Co., which gave the company a clean bill of health in 1986 and again in 1987. Keating later hired Jack Atchison, the Arthur Young & Co. partner who had headed these audits, at a salary of $900,000. Kenneth Leventhal and Co., an auditor later hired by regulators, reported that Lincoln had booked bogus gains for 1986 and 1987 by counting bad loans as profitable. Leventhal said that "seldom . . . have we encountered a more egregious example of the misapplication of generally accepted accounting principles."[23] Keating disagreed, later testifying in federal court that the government auditors simply did not understand complex real estate syndication procedures.

William Seidman, later chairman of the Federal Deposit Insurance Corporation, testified before House Banking Committee hearings in October 1989 that Lincoln should have been seized by regulators as early as 1986, based on his staff's retrospective study of the thrift's records. He estimated that between 1987, when the San Francisco examiners first recommended action, and the April 1989 shutdown, the cost of the Lincoln debacle to the taxpayers rose from approximately $1.3 billion to $2.5 billion, as the thrift continued to make bad loans and investments with depositors' insured funds.

The two-year delay was especially costly for 23,000 small investors, many of them retirees, who purchased uninsured bonds at Lincoln branch offices in the final months of the thrift's existence. In 1988, as regulators were closing in, American Continental sold through Lincoln's branch offices $250 million worth of its own high-yield, short-term subordinated debentures, or "junk bonds." Internal memos revealed that Lincoln employees were paid bonuses for convincing customers to invest, leading them to believe that the uninsured bonds were just as safe as federally insured CDs. The ACC bonds subsequently became worthless.

Finally, American Continental itself forced the government's hand. On April 13, 1989, ACC filed for bankruptcy, apparently to protect its assets from seizure by regulators should Lincoln be shut down. The following day, U.S. government

[21] *San Francisco Chronicle*, Oct. 27, 1989, back page.
[22] *Los Angeles Times*, Nov. 7, 1989, p. D9.
[23] *Wall Street Journal*, Nov. 20, 1989, p. A8.

agents seized Lincoln and ousted its top management. The bank board gave a terse reason for the takeover, saying that Lincoln's management "appeared to operate Lincoln mainly for the benefit of American Continental Corp. at the expense of the institution [and] has repeatedly violated regulations relating to transactions with affiliates, used poor underwriting and has refused to follow supervisory directives." Seven months later, in seizing the Phoenician hotel, the government severed Charles Keating's final relationship with Lincoln.

Four Miles of Legal Documents

The case of the Lincoln Savings and Loan quickly became mired in multiple lawsuits that promised to take years, if not decades, to resolve. At least 24 civil lawsuits were filed both by individuals and government agencies, and at least seven state and federal agencies launched investigations of criminal wrongdoing. By early 1990, a records depository in Phoenix had accumulated no less than 20 million pages of documents files in connection with Lincoln litigation—enough file boxes that, if set end to end, would stretch four miles.

Among the highlights of these lawsuits and investigations were the following ones:

- On September 15, 1989, the federal government filed a $1.1 billion civil racketeering lawsuit against Keating, charging that he engaged "in numerous fraudulent, illegal, and imprudent transactions [and] . . . used [Lincoln's] resources to promote his own personal, financial, political, ideological, and religious convictions."[24] The FBI also undertook a criminal investigation.
- On November 17, 1989, the Senate Ethics Committee initiated an investigation into allegations that the Keating Five improperly interfered with regulators' oversight of Lincoln Savings and Loan.
- Bondholders filed several class action suits, charging that Lincoln employees falsely represented ACC bonds as federally insured and seeking recompense from ACC, its auditors and attorneys, and the government.
- As for Keating, he in turn filed multiple lawsuits of his own, charging the government with illegally seizing his assets and blackening his reputation. He continued to maintain that taxpayers would be best served if the government returned Lincoln to him. "I'd love to have Lincoln back," Keating told an interviewer in April 1990. If I got Lincoln back, it would not cost the U.S. taxpayers one dollar, and all my bondholders would get paid off. . . . Give us our assets back and let us work them out, see what happens."[25]

Discussion Questions

1. Who or what in your view bears primary responsibility for the Lincoln Savings and Loan scandal: Keating and his associates, Keating's attorneys and ac-

[24] *Washington Post,* Mar. 5, 1990, p. D6.
[25] *Time,* Apr. 9, 1990, p. 20.

countants, federal regulatory agencies, Congress, the Keating Five, economic conditions, or the public? Tell why you think so.

2. What steps might the federal government, the thrift industry, or the public take to lessen the likelihood of a repetition of the Lincoln Savings and Loan debacle?
3. Do you believe political action committees (PACs) and contributions to candidates and political organizations played a role in the Lincoln Savings and Loan incident? What reforms in campaign financing laws, if any, would reduce the influence-peddling illustrated by this case?
4. Did deregulation cause the savings and loan crisis? What other steps might policymakers have taken in the early 1980s to address the impending crisis in the industry at that time?
5. Conduct a stakeholder analysis of this case. How were various stakeholders of Lincoln Savings and Loan (such as employees, depositors, stockholders, and taxpayers) affected by Keating's actions? Do you feel Keating acted ethically toward these stakeholder groups?

CASE STUDY ASHLAND OIL TANK COLLAPSE[1]

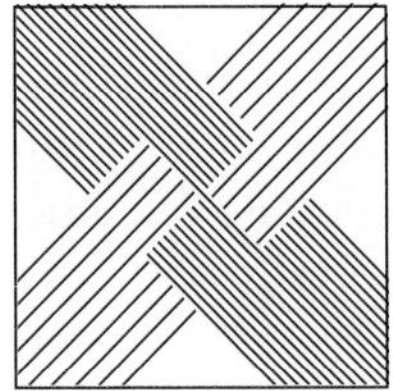

by **Deborah Crimmins** *Boston University*

Shortly after 5:00 P.M. on Saturday, January 2, 1988, the operator at Ashland Oil's Floreffe terminal heard a thunderlike sound and turned to see a four-million-gallon oil tank collapse. A 30-foot wave of diesel oil erupted from the tank, burst over the containment dike, and surged toward Pennsylvania's route 837 and the Monongahela river. In the days following the tank's collapse, Ashland responded to constant media attention, informed the public about the situation, and coordinated cleanup efforts with numerous federal, state, and local officials.

Ashland Oil

Ashland Refining Company was founded in Kentucky in 1924. In 1936, Ashland was consolidated with Swiss Oil Corporation and incorporated as the Ashland Oil and Refining Company. Ashland was primarily a regional refiner and marketer of oil until Orin E. Atkin's tenure as chairman and CEO. According to *Business Week,* "A voracious dealmaker, he (Atkin) took charge in 1965 and transformed Ashland from a regional refiner with $448 million in sales to a $9.5 billion powerhouse by the time he was ousted in 1981."[2] During this period Ashland acquired a number of oil and chemical companies.

Along with growth, Atkin brought controversy. In 1973, he was fined $1,000 for an illegal contribution to the Committee to Reelect the President [Nixon]. In 1975, the Securities & Exchange Commission (SEC) charged Ashland with illegal campaign contributions of nearly $800,000 between 1967 and 1973. Still later, SEC charged that Ashland had made $4 million in questionable overseas payments. Because 22 percent of its crude oil was imported from Iran, Ashland was hard hit during the 1979 oil crisis. Allegations were made that Ashland paid millions of dollars to preserve oil supplies from Abu Dhabi and Oman during this period. Ashland also was in a dispute with the National Iranian Oil Company over $283 million worth of oil the company received just before the embargo.

In May 1981, Ashland announced Atkin was retiring to pursue personal business interests, and John R. Hall was named chairman and CEO. Hall joined Ashland in 1957, was named president of Ashland Chemical in 1971 and executive vice president of Ashland Oil in 1984. Hall, who has been characterized as "unflamboyant, matter-of-fact, but knows where he wants to go,"[3] strengthened the core refining business by investing in the Catlettsburg refinery, closing some

[1] © Boston University Public Affairs Research Program, 1989. Used with permission. This case was prepared under the direction of Professors James E. Post and Susan S. Samuelson.

[2] Zachary Schiller, "Ashland Just Can't Seem to Leave Its Checkered Past Behind," *Business Week*, Oct. 31, 1988, p. 2.

[3] Seth H. Lubove, "Ashland Chief Seen Able to Handle Crisis by Belzbergs' Takeover Proposal," *Wall Street Journal*, Mar. 31, 1986, p.34.

operations, and slashing inventories. In 1984, Ashland sold a number of unrelated operations, including insurance and pollution control businesses.

Hall had dealt with a number of crises since 1981. These included charges by the SEC that Ashland made $28.7 million in illegal payments to foreign officials, a lawsuit by former employees who claimed they were fired for refusing to cover up those payments, and the arrest of former CEO Atkin for selling documents to the Iranians. Hall also guided Ashland through a takeover attempt. In March 1986, the Belzberg family of Canada revealed that they owned 9.2 percent, or 2.6 million shares, of Ashland's stock. They offered $1.8 billion for the company. One day after this bid, Kentucky's legislature passed an antitakeover law intended to prevent outsiders from "wrest(ing) control of the corporation from a board deeply committed to the well-being of Kentucky."[4] Since 1981, Ashland had contributed $10 million to Kentucky's educational institutions. Ashland settled with the Belzbergs by buying their shares for $134 million. Shortly afterward, Ashland's board authorized the repurchase of up to 27 percent of the company's outstanding shares and established an employee stock ownership plan.

In 1988, Ashland Oil was the largest of the "independent" oil companies. Unlike major national and international companies who integrate into every facet of the petroleum industry, independents traditionally focus on one segment of the business. Ashland concentrated on refining and marketing and ranked sixtieth in the Fortune 500 for fiscal 1987, fifteenth among oil companies in sales and twelfth in profits.

In 1988, Ashland consisted of seven groups: Petroleum, Superamerica, Valvoline, Chemical, Engineering and Construction, Exploration, and Coal. The largest group, Ashland Petroleum, ranked thirteenth in U.S. oil-refining capacity with 346,500 barrels per day out of the total U.S. capacity of 15,067,800 barrels per day. Ashland's three refineries, located at Catlettsburg, Kentucky, St. Paul Park, Minnesota, and Canton, Ohio, operated at 93 percent of capacity during fiscal 1988. Ashland maintained 23 terminals in 9 states, including 15 river terminals, and owned the largest private tank barge fleet on inland waterways.

Ashland's other groups included Superamerica, which operated 500 retail station/store combinations in 17 states and 1,500 gasoline outlets; Valvoline, which marketed the third-ranked branded motor oil and operated 175 oil-change outlets; Ashland Chemical, which was the largest distributor of thermoplastic resins and a petrochemical marketer; Engineering and Construction, which owned reserves of 2.4 million barrels of domestic crude, 212 billion cubic feet of natural gas, and foreign reserves of 45 million barrels; and a 46 percent ownership of Ashland Coal and 50 percent of Arch Mineral, both of which mined in four states.

Ashland's Safety and Environmental Record

After the tank's collapse, Ashland's environmental record came under scrutiny. J. Dan Lacy, Ashland's vice president of corporate communications, reported that

[4] Seth H. Lubove, "Kentucky Aid for Ashland Marks Power of Firm and Fears of Outside Ownership," *Wall Street Journal,* Apr. 1, 1986, p. 64.

the company had six small spills over the five years before the collapse, with the largest fine being $2,000. Richard Golub of World Information Systems commented, "On oil pollution, Ashland has no major black marks, no major accidents until now. It has had oil tank storage spills in the past, but any company involved in storing oil has too."[5]

In July 1986, Ashland agreed to pay a $762,500 penalty for water pollution that had occurred at its Catlettsburg refinery over a six-year period. The company attributed these problems to equipment malfunctions and weather conditions. However, the EPA's Roger O. Pfaff said Ashland had a raft of pollution problems including failure to obtain permits and meet emission limits.[6] Ashland's 1988 annual report stated plans to spend an additional $30 million in air and water quality controls in 1989. The company had spent $25 million during 1988 on air and water controls.

Safety incidents included an August 1984 explosion at a Freedom, Pennsylvania, facility, which killed three workers and resulted in citations for Occupational Safety and Health Administration (OSHA) violations. An August 1982 explosion at the Canton, Ohio, refinery caused that facility to close for 30 days.

Response to the Spill

Immediately after the collapse, the operator on duty radioed the barge to stop pumping and notified the terminal manager, the National Response Center, and the Coast Guard. An initial check revealed no oil in the nearby Monongahela River. The Coast Guard responded as the first federal agency on the scene and discovered oil in the river later that evening. After assessing the magnitude of the problem—approximately 750,000 gallons had escaped the containment dike and were flowing into the river through storm sewers—the Coast Guard Commander requested assistance from its National Strike Force, closed the Monongahela to river traffic, and directed boom placement in the river. An initial cleanup plan was formulated during a meeting of the Coast Guard and Ashland. Roger Shrum, Ashland's oil media relations manager, traveled to the scene within hours of the spill.

The firm hired by Ashland to clean up the oil spill arrived at 7 A.M. on Sunday, January 3, followed by the EPA and the Coast Guard Strike Force. However, cold temperatures (approximately 26°F), rapid currents, a system of locks and dams, and equipment designed for ocean spills (as opposed to river spills) hampered cleanup efforts. The oil slick flowed north with the Monongahela River into the Ohio River at Pittsburgh. Glen Cannon, Pittsburgh's public safety director, stated, "The problem is that this is so massive. It's bank to bank from here to Elizabeth [near Floreffe]."[7] Pennsylvania Governor Robert Casey declared a state of emergency on Monday, January 4, and mobilized the National Guard to help with water distribution.

[5] Don Hopey and Matthew Brelis, "Jefferson Spill 1st Major 'Black Mark' against Ashland Oil's Safety Record," *Pittsburgh Press*, Jan. 10, 1988.
[6] Schiller, op.cit., p. 124.
[7] "Collapse of Diesel Tank Pollutes Drinking Water Near Pittsburgh," *New York Times*, Jan. 4, 1988, p. A15.

Back at corporate headquarters, Ashland Chairman Hall and President Charles J. Luellen talked with staff both on and off site. They felt Ashland's emergency management team was handling the situation adequately. Lacy remarked, "He (Hall) didn't want to make an official appearance until he could provide some answers." Hall called Pennsylvania Governor Robert Casey late that evening; "I told him we intended to clear up the mess as fast as we could."[8]

On January 4, Ashland headquarters uncovered several disturbing details including the fact that the collapsed tank was reconstructed from 40-year-old steel, a proper permit had not been obtained for construction, and hydrostatic tests—complete filling of the tank with water—had not been performed. Also, the possibility of major water shortages for 750,000 people became apparent. Lacy noted, "That changed the situation completely. It was no longer a situation in which we could simply do everything to clean up the river. All of a sudden people were involved very directly and they needed answers." Ashland lawyers advised Hall to refrain from making a public statement because of liability considerations, but Hall decided, "Our company had inconvenienced the lives of a lot of people and I felt it was only right to apologize."[9] To reassure investors and the public, Ashland announced the company held $400 million in insurance with a $2.5 million deductible through OIL insurance, an oil industry mutual insurance company in Bermuda. The Bermudian company, with 49 members and $1 billion in assets, provided property, well control, and third-party pollution liability coverage.

On Tuesday, January 5, Hall flew to Pittsburgh, visited the spill site, and held a news conference. At the conference Hall stated:

> First, I want to thank everyone who participated in the cleanup activity. Many people have worked long hours—under difficult, cold, windy conditions—including voluntary organizations, government employees, and Ashland Oil employees. On behalf of Ashland Oil, its officers and directors, I want to apologize to the people of the Pittsburgh area for the inconvenience they have experienced as a result of this incident. The company is working with all appropriate government agencies in an effort to clean up the damage as rapidly as possible.

Hall acknowledged the tank was reconstructed from 40-year-old steel, admitted that no written permit was obtained, and said that hydrostatic testing had not been performed. He announced the hiring of Battelle Institute of Columbus, Ohio, to conduct an independent investigation into the collapse.

Meanwhile, at the scene, Ashland, EPA, the Coast Guard, and a number of state, local, and private agencies continued to work on two fronts: the cleanup of the river and the terminal, and the water-shortage problem. The Coast Guard Strike Force had been brought in at Ashland's expense, and approximately 130 contracted employees worked on the cleanup of 38 river miles on the Monongahela and the Ohio. They used 20,000 feet of boom and recovered about 204,000

[8] Clare Ansberry, "Oil Spill in the Midwest Provides Case Study in Crisis Management," *Wall Street Journal*, Jan. 8, 1988, p. 21.

[9] Ibid.

gallons of oil from the river and 2.95 million from the terminal. Despite these efforts, short-term environmental damage included the death of 10,000 fish and 2,000 birds. The cold weather minimized some effects because animals were hibernating or had migrated, but it hindered the cleanup. A Coast Guard spokesperson stated, "Cold is helping only in that it is congealing the oil. It makes it easier to contain. The basic problem is that it is miserable to work in this stuff."[10]

Ashland's efforts to minimize water shortages included providing boats for water testing and planes for flyovers of the spill. They also placed booms around water intake valves, bought carbon feeder for a number of water plants, and provided water barges and trucks. A total of 16 water facilities were affected but only the Robinson Township Authority could not maintain service. The Robinson Township Authority had 17,000 customers without water for up to five days and 200 customers waterless for a week. They were able to reopen intake valves eight days after the spill.

Ashland made advance payment against expenses to a number of local organizations that participated in the cleanup. These included checks of $210,000 to Allegheny County and $165,000 to Western Pennsylvania Water Company. Allegheny County Commission Chairman Thomas Foerster stated, "I can't recall, at any time in my government service, that I've found a company that was involved in something like this—that has been totally up front with us, cooperative. . ."[11] Ashland also gave a $250,000 grant to the University of Pittsburgh's Center for Hazardous Materials Research to assess the ecological and environmental impact of the spill. Ashland authorized long-range environmental-impact studies by Battelle Memorial Institute. On January 14, Ashland opened a Pittsburgh office under the direction of Corporate Vice President Phillip Block. This office coordinated with government agencies on the remaining cleanup and oversaw claims processing. By September 1988, Ashland had paid $15 million in cleanup costs and claims. Most of this amount was covered by insurance.

Regulations and Standards for Oil Storage and Spills

There were a number of federal, state, and local regulations applicable to oil storage and spills. The federal Clean Water Act of 1977 (CWA) specified strict and absolute liability for oil spills. The CWA authorized the federal government to remove a spill unless the owner or operator had properly undertaken its removal. Spills had to be reported to the National Response Center. Additionally, the CWA required a Spill Prevention Control and Countermeasures (SPCC) plan for any facility that stored more than 660 gallons of oil in an above-ground tank or had more than 1,320 gallons of combined storage. The site-specific SPCC plan had to identify potential equipment failures and contingency plans in case a spill reached water. Furthermore, the plan had to be certified by a registered professional

[10] Philip Shabecoff, "Tools' Mismatch to Task Hampering Oil Cleanup," *New York Times,* Jan. 6, 1988, p. A19.

[11] J. Dan Lacy, "How Ashland Oil Made the Best of an Unfortunate Situation," *AMC Journal,* August 1988, p. 8.

engineer and kept at the facility where the EPA could review it. Penalties for noncompliance could range up to $5,000 per day. After the collapse, the EPA found inconsistencies on tank volumes and containment areas in Ashland's plan as well as lack of a site-specific contingency plan for spills.

In practice there had been limited inspections of the estimated 650,000 facilities nationwide that were subject to SPCC regulations. The Floreffe terminal had not been inspected within the previous five years. EPA Region III had performed approximately 100 inspections per year. Nationally, inspections decreased from 3,412 in 1976 to 1,109 in 1987, while spills increased in the same period from 1,478 to 3,103. Of the inspections performed, about 60 percent of the plans were found to be deficient.

U.S. Representative from Pennsylvania Doug Walgren criticized these regulations at the hearing before the Committee on Merchant Marine and Fisheries on May 26, 1988:

> The greatest dismay was to find out that there really was so little federal regulation that we could have relied on to assume public safety in these circumstances. . . . The EPA spill containment regulations are broad and vague, and they essentially, at least until this point, have left the industry in the role of setting its own standards, and then policing its own response to those standards, and conducting whatever inspections are conducted.

A number of bills for new regulations were proposed in both the House of Representatives and the Senate, but none was passed.

OSHA also regulated oil storage, specifying that tanks should be no less than three feet apart, and foundations and supports had to be fire-resistant for two hours. The containment dikes were required to hold the contents of the largest tank and were restricted to an average height of six feet. Testing of tanks and compliance with American Petroleum Institute (API), Underwriters' Laboratory, or American Society of Mechanical Engineers standards also were required.

There were no federal construction standards for above-ground tanks in 1988. However, the Hazardous and Solid Waste Amendments of 1984 and the Superfund Amendments and Reauthorization Act of 1986 established a trust fund and regulations for underground storage tanks. The EPA had established an Office of Underground Storage Tanks and proposed design, installation, and release-detection requirements for underground tanks.

Another piece of federal legislation applying to oil spills was the Refuse Act of 1899. This act prohibited discharging refuse into navigable waters without permission of the Army Corps of Engineers. Additionally, the U.S. Coast Guard regulated transportation facilities that transfer oil in bulk.

At the state level, the Pennsylvania Clean Streams Law did not require a permit for oil tanks, but it did require a Preparedness, Prevention, and Contingency (PPC) plan for tanks over 50,000 gallons. The PPC plan included information about dikes, ability for cleanup, and a plan for notifying local emergency response officials. The Ashland PPC was prepared in 1970; the Department of Environmental Resources (DER) found it inadequate and out of date after the spill. The DER did not conduct routine reviews of tanks but estimated that out of the 6,500 tanks in this category in Pennsylvania, about 10 to 12 leaks were reported each year.

In Pennsylvania, the state fire marshal's office issued construction permits for oil tanks except in Allegheny County (where Floreffe was located) and Philadelphia county. The Allegheny County fire code based its construction standards on API standard 650. The code required notification of hydrostatic testing, so the fire marshall could choose to attend. Companies could be subject to fines of $200 for noncompliance. With a primary emphasis on fire prevention, the fire marshal's office did not employ engineers qualified to inspect tank construction.

The American Petroleum Institute, an industry association founded in 1919, issued a number of voluntary but generally recognized standards. These standards were frequently incorporated in fire code standards. The API-650 outlines standards for materials, design fabrication, erection, testing, and inspection of welded-steel oil storage tanks.

Reconstruction of Tank

The Pennsylvania Tank Collapse Task Force (TCTF), appointed by Governor Casey, investigated the reconstruction of the tank. They concluded, "Ashland, its employees, and some contractors displayed a pervasive pattern of negligence and ignorance in selecting, assigning, constructing, supervising, and inspecting the reconstruction project."[12]

The project originated in 1985 when personnel at the Floreffe terminal decided tank 1338 required repair or replacement. At the same time, Allied Oil, an Ashland subsidiary, sold their Whiskey Island, Ohio, terminal. The terms of the December 16, 1985, sale authorized Ashland to remove any of Allied Oil's tanks. The Floreffe staff evaluated the costs of repairing tank 1338, moving Allied Oil's tank WI-16 (48 feet in diameter and 120 feet high holding 96,000 barrels), or moving a smaller tank (55,000 barrels) from Birmingport, Alabama. Constructing a new tank was not considered. An inspector examined WI-16 and found it structurally sound except for the floor. He also recommended dismantling by cutting through the old welds. Floreffe staff decided to move WI-16 because this option was cheaper per barrel stored than the other two options.

After the Floreffe project engineer was assigned, he solicited verbal bids on the project from Ashland's qualified vendor list. The sole criterion for qualification was insurability. He accepted the lowest bid of $174,391, which was submitted by Skinner Tank Company. The contract with Skinner Tank stated that the tank would be constructed under the API-650 standard. However, starting with the dismantling, TCTF found many deviations from good construction practices: Skinner Tank cut down the tank to the right of the old welds instead of through the center, removed the insulation by driving over the steel plates with a small bulldozer, allowed a crane to fall on some of the plates, and may not have taken proper care with the transportation of the steel. TCTF also found Ashland did not take an active role in overseeing the project.

[12] Tank Collapse Task Force, *Report into the Collapse of Tank 1338,* June 22, 1988, p. iii.

Back at Floreffe, the project engineer talked with the Allegheny County Fire Marshal's office and sent them information on the project. Later, after checking on the permit application, he assumed verbal approval was given to begin construction without a written permit. After the collapse, Fire Marshal Martin Jacobs claimed his office had not approved construction. However, in October 1988, after the task force report was issued, a memo from Chief Inspector Charles Kelly was found stating he had inspected the Floreffe terminal and had given verbal approval.

During the reconstruction at Floreffe—which TCTF also found only loosely monitored by Ashland personnel—the Skinner Tank crew did not follow any written welding or construction procedures. After the tank was completed, Skinner Tank performed a diesel-penetration test; diesel oil was sprayed on the welds and the tank was checked for penetration. This test was not required by API-650 and it was unclear whether the whole tank or just sections were tested. Radiographs of the welds were required by API-650 and were performed. The project engineer calculated that 40 welds should be tested while the TCTF later calculated that the standard required 119 radiographs. Additionally, when the contractor who performed the radiographs reported that 22 of the 39 welds examined were substandard, no action was taken by the Ashland project engineer. Finally, a hydrostatic test—complete filling of the tank with water—was rejected by the Floreffe manager of facilities as taking too much time. The manager also incorrectly believed the oil-penetration test, not the hydrostatic test, was required by API-650. The tank was put into service in August 1987 with an initial load of 800,000 gallons of oil.

The TCTF concluded:

> At each step along the way, Ashland as an entity failed to take any active role in controlling its contractors or establish any procedures which might lead to a quality job. It was a passive consumer of the worst kind—apathetic as to potential problems, ignorant of actual events, unwilling to take any engaged role. Its employees were both institutionally and often personally unable to respond any other way. Both the details and big picture equally escaped Ashland's attention. Compared against the applicable standards, its industry peers, or even common sense, Ashland's conduct and procedures can only be considered grossly negligent. The structural collapse at Floreffe can be directly traced to the supervisory bankruptcy at Ashland.[13]

The task force's enforcement recommendations included pursuing civil action against Ashland, having the Attorney General consider criminal prosecution, and noting that Skinner Tank Company also was liable for civil prosecution.

Hall commented, "We clearly had a problem in the terminal department, which we've moved to correct. That doesn't say the rest of the company has a problem."[14] Ashland was disappointed with the tone of the report and felt that seeking maximum civil penalties was counterproductive since Ashland had made every effort possible to clean up the spill.

[13] Ibid., p. 79.

[14] Schiller, op. cit., p. 124.

Cause of the Tank Failure

There were a number of reasons why an oil storage tank could fail—tensile or strength failure, fatigue, or compression. In May 1988, Battelle determined that the tank collapsed because of brittle failure. This type of failure was related to the toughness rather than the strength of the material, and required three basic conditions—a notch or flaw, low toughness, and stress. The flaw was found to have been caused years before by a cutting torch. The tank's steel, which was over 40 years old, was found to have adequate strength for the application, but it lost its toughness at temperatures below 80 to 100°F as determined by a Charpy V-Notch test. The stress of filling the tank to capacity in cold weather brought all three requirements of brittle fracture together. At the Whiskey terminal, the tank had held a heavier type of oil, but it had been insulated and heated.

Senate Hearing

On February 4, 1988, the U.S. Senate Subcommittee on Environmental Protection held a hearing to examine federal, state, and company response to the spill. Current and proposed regulations as well as similar incidents were discussed. Hall, testifying on Ashland's role in the cleanup, summed up his remarks:

> In closing, let me say that Ashland Oil has operated in the Ohio River Valley for more than 60 years without an incident of this type, and we are proud of that record. We are embarrassed by this incident, but we are proud of the valiant efforts that our employees have made in containing the spill and in helping to keep the water supplies going.
>
> We hope you will agree that Ashland has handled this unfortunate incident in a responsible fashion. And let me assure you that we intend to continue to do so.

After Hall's statement, Senator Baucus commented:

> It's not often, in fact it's rare, that a major company like Ashland would come before this committee with such candor in such an apparent effort to try to find the causes of the problem and try to find the solution. I think all of us commend you very much.

Senator John Heinz of Pennsylvania spoke about a new bill that would regulate above-ground storage tanks more closely. Other senators felt that current regulations could be modified and pointed to the lack of resources available to the EPA and the Coast Guard for enforcement and cleanup.

In evaluating the response to the spill, the issue of whether the EPA should have declared the spill a "federal spill" was considered. In his written statement, Mark McClellan, deputy secretary of the Pennsylvania Department of Environmental Resources, stated:

> We found to our dismay that the procedures within which the federal officials operated hampered their ability to take action without extensive and delaying consultation with

> each other and with the responsible party. Specifically, because federal officials did not as we requested declare this a "federal spill" they had to receive authorization from Ashland Oil for every response action. Inability to reach the appropriate Ashland officials at the very early stages delayed response action that may have minimized the spill's impact.

James Seif, regional administrator of EPA Region III, gave a different perspective on this issue in his testimony:

> The fact is that it is not a federal spill except that they all are in terms of the regulatory jurisdiction: it's Ashland's spill. The spiller must clean it up. Appropriately enough, when the spiller doesn't, or can't, or won't, then a federal fund should be activated. In fact, I was confronted with a willing and apparently able responsible party who was working very hard, and I think in retrospect, effectively, to do the job.

Richard Golub, of the *Oil Spill Intelligence Report,* testified about other similar spills. The Floreffe spill was the largest since a well in Ranger, Texas, blew in November 1985, spilling 6.3 million gallons. He also cited nine major spills between 1978 and 1988 attributable to structural failures.

Legal Aftermath

In July 1988, Ashland entered into a consent decree with the EPA. The terms included Ashland paying $680,000 in costs, cleaning up the soil and groundwater, monitoring future discharges, creating a new SPCC plan, hydrostatically testing the remaining tanks, and undertaking an environmental compliance audit. Ashland was also fined $31,800 by OSHA: $30,000 for failing to repair the defective welds; $1,000 for an inadequate dike; and $800 for failing to establish a written safety plan. Additionally, Pennsylvania Governor Casey instructed state environmental officials to seek maximum civil penalties against Ashland.

In September, Ashland was indicted on two misdemeanor charges of violating the Refuse Act and the Clean Water Act. These were the most stringent charges possible. An Ashland press release stated, "The company is disappointed that criminal actions will be pursued in light of Ashland's efforts to mitigate the spill's impact and the fact that the company quickly accepted responsibility for the incident."[15] In Pittsburgh, U.S. Attorney J. Alan Johnson stated, "The criminal law is directed toward the conduct that brought it [the spill] about, not what happened afterward."[16] In February 1989, Ashland pleaded no contest to these charges and in March was fined $2.25 million. This was the largest fine for a fuel spill in the United States. Federal District Judge Gustave Diamond commented, ". . . it was something more than simple negligence that the company was guilty of." Ashland called the fine "excessive" and considered whether or not to appeal.[17] Ashland also faced 20 class action civil suits as a result of the spill.

[15] Ruth Marcus, "Ashland Oil Is Indicted in Pennsylvania Oil Spill," *Washington Post,* Sept. 16, 1988, p. A4.

[16] Ibid.

[17] "$2.25 Million Fine in '88 Spill," *New York Times,* Mar. 10, 1989, p. A16.

Changes at Ashland

At the May 26, 1988, hearing before the U.S. House of Representatives Committee on Merchant Marine and Fisheries, Phillip Block, vice president of Ashland Oil, testified about changes since the spill:

> Four employees from the engineering department and the trucks and terminals operating group subsequently were reassigned. Ashland has stated that all future tank construction will be in full compliance with the material, welding, and testing specifications of API-650.
>
> As a result of the collapse of the Floreffe tank, a review of Ashland's tank facilities was undertaken to determine their physical condition. While the review is not yet completed, 146 facilities with more than 1,000 tanks have been inspected to date. Where appropriate, remedial actions indicated by the review have been undertaken or scheduled for the near future. Organizational and procedural changes to strengthen environmental compliance efforts are under review, and several changes already have been made.

Ashland had closed the Floreffe terminal after the spill and reopened it in stages. Three additional tanks with storage capability of 272,000 barrels were built at the site with new steel in compliance with applicable industry standards.

J. Dan Lacy wrote about the less tangible effects on Ashland of the tank collapse:

> . . . The public's reaction to the decision to be open and to accept responsibility indicates that cooperating with officials and doing what it takes to make the situation right is a prudent course to follow in the management of a crisis. In fact, by quickly taking responsibility—by being a good corporate citizen—Ashland actually earned public trust rather than lost it.[18]

Discussion Questions

1. Assess Ashland Oil's activities as a socially responsible company. Did the company respond to the oil spill in a socially responsible manner? Was Ashland's record prior to the spill a socially responsible one? How do you account for differences before and after the spill?
2. Compare Ashland Oil's crisis management performance with the way Union Carbide handled the Bhopal industrial accident in India and Johnson & Johnson's crisis management in the Tylenol poisoning episodes. What differences do you see? How do you explain the differences?
3. How much responsibility for the Floreffe spill should be borne by state and federal regulators? Does their lax regulatory performance excuse deficiencies in Ashland's performance prior to the spill? Did public policy fail as a guideline for corporate conduct in this case?
4. Assume the role of the press, politicians, employees, members of local communities, and shareholders. Discuss John Hall's actions and statements from each point of view. How do you rate his leadership?

[18] Lacy, op. cit., p. 10.

CASE STUDY NESTLE: TWENTY YEARS OF INFANT FORMULA CONFLICT

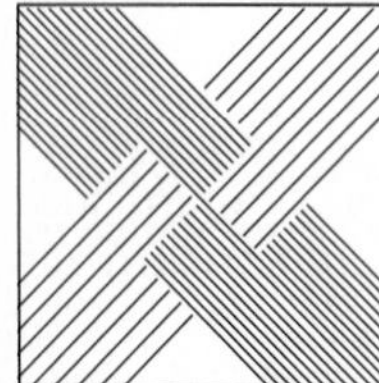

Few companies have found themselves embattled for so long over an issue that generated so much passion. Nestle, the world's largest manufacturer of infant formula, has been embroiled in controversy since the early 1970s, when its marketing practices in the developing nations were first criticized. For twenty years, Nestle managers have dealt with activists, government officials, and health experts who questioned the company's ethics and business judgment.

"I thought we would exist for two or three years, but instead, we have gone on for nine years. At some point—I don't know when—this Commission, and this issue, just has to end." According to former Secretary of State and U.S. Senator Edmund Muskie, chairman of the Nestle Infant Formula Audit Commission (NIFAC), the controversy surrounding Nestle and infant formula marketing has gone on well beyond most people's expectations. A Nestle manager who is 30 years of age in 1992 would have been only 20 years old when Senator Muskie's Audit Commission began, and only 10 years old when the infant formula marketing issue first arose in the early 1970s. Some Nestle employees have known this controversy throughout their entire careers with the company. Two different chief executive officers (called "managing directors" according to European tradition) have devoted thousands of hours to the controversy; Nestle also has spent millions of dollars over two decades. According to one close observer, "An entire generation of Nestle managers in more than 140 countries have been affected by this issue. Infant formula defines Nestle's history since the 1970s."

Key events in a company's history exert a powerful influence on the organization. They change how the company does business, how it relates to its internal and external stakeholders, and how it is seen by others, including its own employees. Key events can redefine corporate values and the common understanding of what is important and what is not. For Nestle, the infant formula controversy has been all of these things.

The Controversy

> Can a product which requires clean water, good sanitation, adequate family income and a literate parent to follow printed instructions be properly and safely used in areas where water is contaminated, sewage runs in the streets, poverty [is] severe and illiteracy is high?

With these words United States Senator Edward M. Kennedy, chairman of the Senate Health and Scientific Research Subcommittee, opened the 1978 Senate Hearings on Infant Formula. These hearings were organized in response to outcries from health professionals and consumer groups who claimed that the increased use of infant formula was detrimental to infant health in developing nations. The purpose of the hearing was to hear testimony from individuals involved in the controversy, including industry representatives and their critics, and to develop a plan of action to protect infant lives.

The first official action to halt the trend away from breastfeeding had come six years earlier. The Protein-Calorie Advisory Group, an organ of the United Nations that coordinated other nutrition-related agencies, issued a statement in June 1972 suggesting that governments monitor the use of formula. The statement also urged formula companies to avoid aggressive marketing and to instruct consumers in the safe use of the product.

Critics of formula use in developing countries usually cite three principal causes of product misuse which lead to infant morbidity (illness) and mortality (death). The first is low family income. The purchase of infant formula in adequate quantities to feed a growing baby often represents a large portion of the family's income: the incentive is to overdilute it. The real cost of the formula is masked when the mother receives her first few cans of formula at no cost while she is in the hospital. In 1980, a week's supply of formula equaled about half of a laborer's weekly wage in Nigeria and other African nations. A study in Barbados found that about three-quarters of low-income families who relied on bottlefeeding were making a four-day supply of formula last between five days and three weeks. The result of overdilution is slow starvation and/or inadequate physical and mental development.

Second, critics allege that the huge majority of third world residents do not have the sanitary systems necessary for safe formula use. Available water is often contaminated and homes lack facilities for sterilization and refrigeration. A sad reality of these poor hygienic conditions is that mothers, eager to protect their children from the "unsafe" environment, are more likely to be influenced by outside opinions on what is "best" for their babies. A marketer or health care worker can have tremendous influence on her. Infants fed formula under these poor hygienic conditions are more likely to contract debilitating bacterial diseases and diarrhea. As James P. Grant, executive director of UNICEF, said in a special report:

> (T)he low-income mother who is persuaded to abandon breastfeeding for bottlefeeding in the developing world is being persuaded to spend a significant proportion of her small income in order to expose her child to the risk of malnutrition, infection and an early grave.

The third major criticism of formula use in developing nations stems from the low literacy rate. Mothers who can barely read are at risk of not following the instructions correctly. These same women also are likely to be very vulnerable to pictorial representations of healthy, happy babies. The illiterate or semiliterate woman becomes an easy target for marketers.

A subtler aspect of the infant formula controversy was related to a common socioeconomic trend. In most developing countries, harsh economic conditions of the countryside were forcing many families to seek a better life in the city. There the low-income mother comes into more frequent contact with women from higher social classes. Many of these women have already abandoned breastfeeding in favor of the "more modern" methods of infant feeding. Bottlefeeding became identified with the "better life" they had come to the city to find. The text of a can of Enfalac, sold in Peru, illustrates the themes of modernization and quality:

> From Mead Johnson (owned by Bristol Myers) . . . the most modern infant formula . . . similar to mother's milk . . . the most modern and perfect maternalized infant formula, physiologically similar to mother's milk.

The label carried a picture of a white North American mother and baby.

Marketing in the Third World

As the birthrate in the industrialized nations leveled off or declined, formula companies began to look for new markets. They found them in developing nations where the birthrate was soaring and the media were reaching more and more people every day. The major formula companies (Nestle, Bristol-Myers, American Home Products, and Abbott Labs) focused their attention on the foreign market.

Formula promotion in developing nations became very intense by the early 1970s. Whereas in their home countries food companies tended to advertise directly to consumers while pharmaceutical companies promoted mostly to health professionals, formula companies marketed to both consumers and health workers abroad. An expert familiar with the industry spoke of this marketing strategy during the 1978 congressional hearings:

> This promotion to both consumers and medical personnel has positioned the industry to take advantage of other development-related trends. Concentration of population in urban areas pays dividends for a radio advertising program; growth in medical services, hospitals, and live births in health clinics coincides with medical promotion and endorsement policies; and market presence in developing nations where births are rising is opportune when birth rates in industrialized nations are stable or falling. It is true, as the manufacturers assert, that many trends contribute to increases in women bottlefeeding their babies, but it is naive to believe that these firms have not deliberately positioned themselves to take advantage of such social change.

Marketing to the consumer meant changing knowledge and beliefs about infant feeding. All the media were used extensively—radio, television, billboards, and magazines. Labels on formula cans carried the message that formula use was ideal "for those who can't" breastfeed and for "when breast-milk isn't enough." Critics alleged that mothers who accepted these messages would not be able successfully to breastfeed their children.

Formula cans also carried pictures of perfectly healthy babies, the race of the child usually dependent on where the product was to be sold. The implication clearly was that by drinking that formula, the newborn could be healthy and happy. Critics claimed that this message was not only misleading but also very dangerous. Formula use in economically depressed areas frequently took the child farther from good health rather than closer to it.

The formula industry also marketed through the health care system. Salespeople regularly visited physicians and hospital staffs, briefing them on new products and leaving generous amounts of samples. In many poverty-stricken areas, the formula companies donated supplies to the hospitals. Health care personnel would then, at their own discretion, pass the supplies to new mothers. During these crucial first few days while the mother was receiving free formula in the hospital, she would lose her ability to produce milk. The supply of free formula usually did not extend after the mother left the hospital, and the baby would then have to be fed on formula or some other breast milk substitute.

Many formula companies also employed "milk (or mothercraft) nurses," women who were trained in nursing but whose primary responsibility was to promote formula use, both to mothers and to the professional community. They ran workshops and distributed educational material to health care workers, and they visited new mothers at home and in the hospital. Although called "nurses," these women were actually the mainstay of the infant formula salesforce.

Formula companies also supported hospitals and individual physicians with grants. Many maternity departments depended on these grants as part of the compensation package for their personnel.

The Boycott

By 1977, there was sufficient outrage over infant formula marketing to form a large coalition of consumer groups and international health agencies. Much of the protest focused on Nestle, a company that controlled about half of the third world (developing nations) infant formula market. The next seven years were marked by court and media battles as Nestle, the unwilling representative of the entire formula industry, fought the boycott and tried to minimize the damage being done to sales and its corporate image.

Nestle's initial strategy to cope with the boycott was to try to discredit its leaders and to refute the allegations. At the Senate hearings, for example, Dr. Oswaldo Ballarin, president of Nestle/Brazil, testified that "a worldwide church organization, with the stated purpose of undermining the free enterprise system" was heading the boycott. Under the direction of the world's largest public relations firm, Hill and Knowlton, Nestle carried out a direct mail campaign where it mailed information packets to over 300,000 clergy and community leaders. Never recanting Ballarin's conspiracy allegations, Nestle continued to challenge the factual bases for attacks on its marketing in the developing nations.

In October 1979, the World Health Organization (WHO) and UNICEF jointly sponsored a conference on infant feeding practices. Representatives from the formula industry, including Nestle, and from different activist groups participated. Two major outcomes resulted from these meetings: the first was a preliminary set of guidelines for the marketing of breast milk substitutes; the second was the recommendation that the director general of WHO should attempt to develop an international code of marketing behavior.

After the WHO/UNICEF meeting, Nestle entered into its second phase of resistance. It contracted a different public relations firm, the Daniel Edelman Company, and adopted a new "low profile" strategy. Now the company steadfastly refused to acknowledge any wrongdoing in its marketing practices or to talk to boycott organizers. Instead of confronting its critics directly, Nestle sent out hundreds of thousands of new press releases stating that its marketing practices were in accordance with recommended standards. It hoped to convey the message that the boycott was no longer necessary.

Leah Margulies from the Interfaith Center on Corporate Responsibility, a leading activist group in the campaign to change industry practices, objected to Nestle's claim that it was abiding by the new recommendations:

> The pattern that emerges is that even after ten years of debate, the infant formula industry continued aggressive promotion of infant formula that competes with breast-milk. While some of the most flagrant forms of promotion have been suspended (e.g., mass media advertising), overall promotional effort has, if anything, intensified. The health institution and health care provider are now the central focus of an increasingly sophisticated campaign to promote artificial feeding in general and loyalty to a company's brand names in particular.

The third and final phase of Nestle's resistance was characterized by its efforts to strengthen "the new right," a political coalition that strongly believes public welfare is advanced through private sector freedom. Nestle supported organizations such as the Ethics and Public Policy Center (EPPC), headed by "the new right" philosopher Ernest Lefever. For its part, Lefever's organization publicized Nestle's cause. In a mass mailing to potential donors, the EPPC included a reprint of an article entitled "Crusade against the Corporations" by Herman Nikel. In this article, the author called the churches' support for the boycott "Marxists marching under the banner of Christ." Four months later the *Washington Post* revealed that Nestle had given $25,000 to the EPPC in 1980.

During this phase the company also funded "independent" research with the hope of improving its image and credibility. It formed a research foundation in Washington called the Nestle Coordination Center for Nutrition, Inc. (NCCN). Raphael Pagan, Jr., formerly vice president of public affairs at Castle & Cooke, Inc., was chosen to be its president. Favorable results from NCCN-sponsored studies were sent to the media, health professionals, and government agencies.

While the WHO Code was being drafted, Nestle worked separately with an industry council to develop plans for self-regulation. To assist in this effort, they hired Dr. Stanislaus Flache to be the Secretary General of the International Council of Infant Food Industries (ICIFI). Dr. Flache had previously been assistant director general for WHO.

Ratifying the Code

The WHO Code underwent several drafts and numerous revisions between 1979 and 1981. During that time all parties worked hard to advance their own positions.

Activists recruited more churches, labor unions, and other organizations to publicly join the boycott. They stepped up their information dissemination and advertising in order to persuade more individual consumers to boycott Nestle. They attended all WHO meetings where the new code was being discussed and achieved official nongovernmental organization (NGO) status, a very important recognition in international affairs.

Nestle, for its part, was also busy. It recognized that regardless of how strict the final WHO Code was, the company would actually have to abide by national laws, not international recommendations. It was therefore in the company's best interest to support national adoption of less stringent marketing codes. The International Baby Food Action Network (IBFAN)—the international activist organization—accused Nestle of pressuring local governments to adopt the ICIFI codes rather than the emerging WHO Code. In Zimbabwe, Nestle attorneys were able to cause a six-month delay in that country's Ministry of Health report on the dangers of bottlefeeding. When the report was finally published, Nestle attacked it for being "erroneous" and "tendentious."

WHO is the staff organization for the World Health Assembly, which is composed of more than 100 member nations. It is the assembly that actually adopts actions such as the marketing code. The days immediately before the actual vote in the assembly were marked with partisan efforts. Industry lobbyists and activists lobbied specific members to sway their opinions. The companies also were accused of playing "dirty tricks." For example, industry representatives circulated a letter among members of the Indian delegation that was supposedly from the "All India Medical Students Associations." The letter suggested that Prime Minister Indira Gandhi did not completely support the code. The head of the Indian delegation countered with a communique suggesting that the first letter was not authentic. A similar example was a letter allegedly from the International Pediatrics Association withdrawing its support from the code. The president of IPA publicly repudiated that claim.

Besides lobbying at the WHO Assembly, industry members voiced their opinions in the media. Among many statements released to the press, the following were representative:

> We oppose the universal code and some believe it is a sign that the UN system is moving to control multinationals.[1]
>
> The medical premise underlying the code is fundamentally faulty. . . . The WHO's proposed Code contains many unwarranted restrictions and prohibitions that are unconstitutional and represent a dangerous precedent. . . . We believe that the United States should vote "no" on the proposed code.[2]

The three United States infant formula manufacturers suggested that even if the WHO Code were passed in the World Health Assembly, they would not consider themselves bound by it. They argued that the decline in breastfeeding

[1] ICIFI Secretary General Stanislaus Flache, *International Herald Tribune*, May 4, 1981.

[2] Bristol-Myers (Mead Johnson) Co., *Washington Post*, May 7, 1981.

was due to changing life-styles, not to any sales efforts on the part of formula manufacturers.

Other food companies and organizations joined the formula companies in resisting the WHO Code, most notable among them Heinz, Kraft, Gerber, and the Grocery Manufacturers of America. Jointly, these companies lobbied officials in Washington to convince them that passage of the WHO Code would imply new laws, and these laws would violate both the First Amendment and U.S. antitrust laws.

Amid all this battling, the WHO Code came up for vote in May 1981. Of the 118 member nations voting, 114 voted in favor of it, 3 abstained, and only 1 voted against it: the United States. Representatives from the Reagan administration said the code violated the right of free speech and showed strains of being "totalitarian." The Secretary of Health and Human Services, Richard Schweiker, explained the U.S. position: "The administration honestly does not believe the WHO should be an international Federal Trade Commission. . . . The Code runs contrary to our Constitution."

Reactions to the Vote in the WHO Assembly

Two pointed resignations quickly followed the United States' lone negative vote in the WHO. Dr. Stephen Joseph, a leading pediatrician, and Eugene Babb, a nutritionist, both resigned in protest from their posts at the U.S. Agency for International Development. Babb commented: "What we're saying to the world (with this vote) is that narrow commercial interests are more important to us than the health of infants in developing countries." Protests from the public were immediately seen in the media. *Newsweek* called the WHO Code vote the Reagan administration's first foreign policy disaster.

The WHO Code

The final version of the International Code of Marketing of Breastmilk Substitutes underlined the joint responsibility of all international, national, and private sector parties in the fight to promote infant health. The responsibility was shared, but actual implementation of the code had to be done on a local level; WHO had no jurisdiction within national boundaries.

The code applied only to marketing of breastmilk substitutes. It put no restrictions on sales or distribution except where those tactics were used for promotional purposes.

Two major themes were bedrock for the rest of the code. The first was that all direct advertising and sampling to consumers be stopped. Billboards, point-of-sale advertising, and all manner of outreach to new mothers was proscribed. Consistent with this idea was a set of guidelines for product labeling. Article 9 of the code specified that all packaging carry the message that "breastfeeding is best" for the baby and that formula should be used only on the advice of a health care worker. The label was not to carry any pictures or text that idealized formula, including pictures of infants.

The second central theme of the WHO Code dealt with the manner through which the formula companies could promote and distribute their products. Marketing could continue but only if it in no way undermined breastfeeding and if all efforts were filtered through health care personnel. Health authorities in member states were called upon to educate health workers on the benefits of breastfeeding.

The marketing practices that were allowed to continue were carefully spelled out in the code. Educational materials now had to include information on the benefits of breastfeeding and the potential dangers of bottlefeeding. Donations of informational and educational materials could be made only with written permission of the appropriate governmental agency. Donations or low-priced sales of supplies could be made to health care professionals but not as sales inducements. If the health care worker thought it was appropriate to pass the free product on to the mother, both the institution and the formula company had the responsibility to ensure a continued supply of that product as long as the baby needed it. All manner of support to individual professionals (fellowships, research grants, attendance at conferences) had to be disclosed to the institution with which that person was affiliated.

Other marketing practices were strictly prohibited. The health care facility could not be used for any sort of advertising or promotion, including displays, posters, or demonstrations by industry personnel. "Milk nurses" were no longer permitted. Industry personnel could not be compensated on the basis of sales volume of formula. Sampling and gift giving to health care workers were curtailed.

The responsibility for monitoring compliance with the WHO Code and whatever local legislation resulted from it was left to the individual governments. Nongovernmental groups were encouraged to call attention to the infractions they saw. The industry itself was called upon to "apprise each member of their marketing personnel of the Code and of their responsibilities under it."

Nestle Agrees to Comply with the Code

The bitterness of the fight to pass the WHO Code in the World Health Assembly left industry executives, critics, and WHO officials disappointed and exhausted. There was no quick action to transform the code into national laws by the governments that had voted for it. It seemed that the fight to pass the WHO Code had simply created a massive stalemate.

On March 16, 1982, ten months after the WHO Code was passed, Nestle publicly announced that it would abide by the code. Telegrams poured into Nestle's headquarters in Vevey, Switzerland, congratulating the company on its new direction. Raphael Pagan, head of the Nestle Coordination Center for Nutrition, was quoted in *The Baltimore Sun* as saying:

> It's a quantum jump on the whole issue, the whole infant formula controversy. . . . I can assure you Nestle is implementing a very stringent code of checks and balances to make sure it works.

Nestle's critics were much less impressed with the "quantum jump." They wanted proof that the announcement would lead to real compliance in specific markets. The leaders of the Nestle boycott vowed to continue action against the company until there was clear evidence of implementation of the code throughout the developing world. Douglas Johnson, an Infant Formula Action Coalition (INFACT) leader, said:

> Nestle has now made a promise to all of us. We intend to see that they keep it. We will continue to monitor Nestle's activity in the field, through our network of nearly 100 allied organizations in 65 countries. We will continue to report industry violations of the Code every month to the World Health Organization, UNICEF, national health ministries, our allied groups, and industry.

New Directives and INFACT'S Response

Nestle issued a set of instructions to all its field personnel regarding the sale of infant formula one month before the company announced its intention to bring its marketing practices into line with the WHO Code. Although the new directives used the WHO Code as a starting point, they contained several major modifications. The result was a vague, and at times contradictory, set of instructions. To those eager to see operational compliance from the big formula company, it seemed that Nestle's new strategy was to confuse the issue of infant formula marketing while creating an appearance of compliance.

INFACT renewed its efforts to influence Nestle's marketing practices. It took exception to what it saw as the company's loose interpretation of the code. The critics did not trust Nestle and were wary of any ambiguous language ("loopholes") in the company's instructions.

Nestle's desire to end the boycott and INFACT's desire to see a major commitment to the WHO Code implemented by the infant formula manufacturers did help move the parties toward renewed negotiation. Although INFACT had a long list of criticisms of Nestle marketing instructions, four areas were singled out as pivotal for bringing the boycott to an end: the use of educational materials, the distribution of samples, the provision of formula supplies, and the giving of gifts to health workers. Each presented a difficult dilemma for the negotiators.

Educational materials

The WHO Code specified that informational and educational materials of any type should provide positive information on the value of breastfeeding and information about the health hazards associated with bottlefeeding. Article 4.2 of the code is quite detailed about the content of these messages. Nestle proposed a set of statements that it claimed struck a balance between factual information on formula feeding and appropriate warnings about the risks of bottlefeeding. INFACT argued for much stronger language to warn mothers about the risks of bottlefeeding. Whereas Nestle sought to communicate the message that infant formula was a nutritionally satisfactory alternative to human milk, when used properly, INFACT sought a stronger message that effectively urged mothers to breastfeed because of the significant risks associated with bottlefeeding. Interpretation and implementation of this article of the WHO Code was the most difficult point in the Nestle boycott negotiations.

Samples

Article 5.2 of the WHO Code said:

> Manufacturers and distributors should not provide, directly or indirectly, to pregnant women, mothers or members of their families, samples of products within the scope of this Code.

Nestle's directive stated:

> In accordance with existing instructions, samples (or free samples) may only be given to health workers . . . and not to mothers.

INFACT claimed that the company's instructions violated the code, because the giving of samples to health workers is simply an indirect way of ensuring that these product samples would be passed on to mothers. Thus the end effect would be product promotion that the code sought to ban.

Supplies

The WHO Code defines supplies as "quantities of a product provided for use over an extended period, free or at a low price, for social purposes, including those provided to families in need." It was intended to allow supplies only for the purpose of social relief.

The use of supplies was among the most difficult facets of the code to implement. Many hospitals depended on donations of infant formula—both to help in their fight against malnutrition and to simplify the job of maternity ward nurses. The code implied that the formula companies themselves were to initiate changes in their lucrative relationships with hospital personnel by changing the nature and purpose of formula donations. If one supplier acted and others did not, however, a competitive disadvantage could result.

Nestle's method to implement this new policy was to change the distribution process of its supplies. No longer would the company decide on the amount of formula to distribute. Henceforth doctors would have to request supplies. Nestle provided special request forms, hoping this new method would put the responsibility of formula use in the hospital upon medically trained personnel.

INFACT was critical of Nestle's directives. It claimed that they did not explicitly make the distinction between supplies (given for the purpose of social relief) and samples (given as sales inducements). The recipient of the product was not likely to perceive the difference. Thus a tighter control system was necessary.

Gifts

Gift giving to professionals took two forms prior to the WHO Code: giving "business" gifts to ensure a close working relationship, and giving supplies that doctors could use at home with their own babies. Both were discouraged by the code. The Nestle directive stated that the former was allowed on special occasions, but they "must not be given or accepted as a condition or inducement for recommending the use of any Nestle product."

Nestle put the latter form of gift giving under the conceptual umbrella of sampling for the purpose of professional evaluation. "Recognizing that there is a legitimate interest on the part of doctors to familiarize themselves with the characteristics of a specific formula, samples of infant formula to be used for feeding doctor's own baby may be given." INFACT rebutted by saying that any gift, by its very nature, is an inducement for the use of a product. Thus all personal gifts should be disallowed.

Nestle Infant Formula Audit Commission (NIFAC)

Nestle recognized the need to have a credible third party assess its efforts to implement the WHO Code. The company's senior management agreed to a bold idea: an independent commission that would review marketing policies to ensure they complied with its public commitments and review complaints from the public about breaches of conduct. Former Senator Edmund Muskie agreed to chair the commission, and a group of ten church leaders and public health experts was assembled. Their work began in 1982, with the expectation that it would take 18 months to two years to accomplish the objectives. But the long, frustrating controversy kept the commission in existence into the 1990s.

The Boycott Ends . . . And Resumes

In 1984, the Nestle boycott ended. Despite lingering distrust of multinational companies, the boycott sponsors concluded that adequate mechanisms assured Nestle's compliance with the code. Aggressive international monitoring of marketing activity would occur through a network of affiliates (this became IBFAN, the International Baby Food Action Network) and complaints would be forwarded to the Nestle Audit Commission.

Of the four central issues in the 1984 negotiations, free supplies proved the most difficult to resolve. Because hospitals needed and used free supplies of formula, companies felt obliged to supply them. Hospitals would not stop the practice without additional money to buy the formula through normal procurement channels. Governments were unwilling or unable to provide more funds to the hospital or to ban free supplies. In 1987, the remnants of the old boycott organization created a new group, Action for Corporate Accountability (ACA) to press the companies to stop the flow of free supplies. A new boycott was announced: Nestle and American Home Products were targeted.

The new boycott had very limited support. The issue, constituencies, and companies' behavior were different. Although ACA pressed the effort into 1990, momentum was difficult to build and sustain.

Industry Responses

By 1989, the infant formula industry was searching for an industrywide mechanism to shape its standards. The International Association of Infant Food Manufacturers was created. The group was designed to deal with issues affecting the entire infant formula industry. A process to respond to complaints was created, with an "ombudsman" to be named as an arbiter in cases not otherwise settled. The members also agreed to focus on developing a free supplies policy that would meet critics' concerns.

Numerous negotiations occurred in Europe and the United States. Nestle actively sought an industrywide agreement. In December 1990, the company announced it would phase out free supplies; American Home Products made a similar announcement. At last, it seemed that some solution to the international controversy might be at hand.

Nestle in the United States

Nestle is a major seller of food products in the United States. In 1984, after the boycott was settled, Nestle made one of its most important U.S. acquisitions when it purchased Carnation for $4 billion. Carnation enhanced Nestle's sales in many areas and its milk business gave Nestle a platform from which to enter the U.S. infant formula market.

In 1991, retail sales of infant formula in the United States were estimated to be about $1.6 billion. Abbott Laboratories, through its Ross Laboratories subsidiary, and Bristol Myers Squibb, through its Mead Johnson subsidiary, dominated the U.S. market with shares of approximately 53 and 33 percent, respectively. Wyeth Laboratories, a subsidiary of American Home Products, held approximately 8 percent of the market. The shares of these companies had remained stable for more than a decade, with Ross and Mead Johnson having dominated the market since the early 1970s. Nestle's acquisition of Carnation was believed to be a potential threat to Ross and Mead Johnson's control of the market.

In 1989, Carnation announced that it was introducing two formula products into the United States market: Good Start, a "hypoallergenic" formula for infants (under six months) and Good Nature, a "follow-up" formula for babies over six months. The company claimed that Good Start would be especially helpful to babies who showed signs of colic, upset, or discomfort with usual formulas. Good Start was manufactured through a special process that eliminated the chemical bases for most infant allergic reactions. Ross and Mead Johnson responded immediately, arguing that Carnation's claim was unsupported by scientific evidence and that the claim "hypoallergenic" had to be approved by the Food and Drug Administration. FDA was drawn into the fight and halted Carnation's claim until scientific proof could be reviewed. Newspapers carried extensive coverage of the dispute, and Good Start's sales suffered.

Carnation also had intended to advertise Good Nature on television, using mass media in a market that had been dominated by promotion to health care professionals, not to mothers directly. The American Academy of Pediatrics (AAP) issued a letter sharply critical of Carnation, claiming that mass media promotion would distort consumer understanding of the advantages of breastfeeding and thereby ultimately harm babies.

Carnation fought back, claiming that the academy was acting as an agent of Ross Laboratories and Mead Johnson, both of whom contributed large sums of money to the academy and its members. In fact, the three largest infant formula companies each made multi-million-dollar contributions to the building of a new headquarters for the academy. One angry pediatrician called the building "the house that infant formula built." Carnation's effort to market through the health care system by using medical representatives who call upon doctors and health administrators ran into difficulty at the same time its mass marketing efforts were being thwarted. After months of spending, it was barely able to show a 1 to 2 percent share of formula sales.

By 1990, Carnation was reassessing its position. Amid the furor about mass marketing and media promotion, Mead Johnson entered into a joint venture with Gerber, the nation's leading seller of prepared baby food. Gerber did not sell infant formula, although it had once tried to enter the market and was driven out by Ross and Mead Johnson. The joint venture with Mead Johnson used a 1983 M-J product formulation and packaged it under the name Gerber Infant Formula. The product was advertised on national television and print media with price coupons and other inducements. Mead Johnson continued to emphasize medical promotion for its formula, Enfamil. Mass marketing of the Gerber formula proved effective as the brand built a 6 percent share of the market by early 1991. Carnation's management was incensed. The American Academy of Pediatrics, which had been highly critical of Carnation, said virtually nothing about the Gerber–Mead Johnson promotion. The implication of AAP coziness with Mead Johnson was supported by decisions to exclude Carnation's officials from academy committees on which the industry was otherwise represented.

Antitrust investigation began at the federal and state levels. A Senate Antitrust Committee hearing, chaired by Senator Metzenbaum, was held to review the situation. Shortly thereafter, in later 1990, the state of Florida filed an antitrust lawsuit against the three largest infant formula companies. California, Texas, Pennsylvania, Oregon, and Wisconsin also launched investigations.

The antitrust inquiries focused on both promotional behavior and the companies' bidding on federal contracts to supply to the WIC—Women, Infants, and Children—nutrition program. Administered through the states, WIC was estimated to have spent more than $400 million to purchase infant formula for eligible babies in 1989. That made the U.S. government the single largest purchaser of infant formula in the world! Curiously, however, until the late 1980s, the companies gave no price discounts for quantity to WIC. In fact, analyses of pricing patterns through the 1980s showed that formula companies raised prices in ways that suggested "consciously parallel" behavior. Antitrust investigators stated that there was a basis for assuming price conspiracy. The lawsuits threw a new element of chaos into the business. Advocates of social welfare programs accused the industry of price gouging and exploitation of the poor to get an inflated subsidy for their products. Several states had used competitive bidding procedures to force the manufacturers to provide rebates on WIC sales. This approach helped control expenses, but the pattern was uneven across the United States. The largest states—California, Texas, and Florida—received favorable rebate terms while smaller states received less favorable bids or none at all. At one point, a Mead Johnson official wrote to a Montana health department officer that the company would not give more than 75 cents rebate per can. The letter signaled M-J's intentions, and other companies began to bid 75 cents as well. This also suggested conspiracy to some antitrust officials.

The 1990s: Will This Ever End?

As the early 1990s unfolded, it appeared that infant formula battles would continue in both the United States and the developing nations. Competitors from Japan and Europe threatened to undermine implementation of the WHO Code's provisions on sampling and free supplies. Health officials also worried that if the mass marketing strategies emerging in the United States proved successful, they would spread to other nations including the developing world. That would undermine the efforts of government and industry leaders to make the WHO Code effective as a standard of ethical marketing practice.

Discussion Questions

1. Evaluate the underlying problems of infant formula use in a risky environment. Then discuss and evaluate the basic strategies applied by Nestle to deal with these problems. Is it a company's responsibility to aggressively discourage its customers from misusing its product?
2. What should Nestle do regarding national governments? Should it abide by their individual codes, the WHO Code, or its own policies? Is consistency necessary? What can Nestle do if national governments will not act to control the worst practices of its competitors?
3. How should the WHO Code be monitored and enforced? How can Nestle headquarters guarantee compliance by its field staff? How can it demonstrate its compliance to external critics and governments? What will happen if NIFAC ends?
4. How should NIFAC evaluate Carnation's infant formula marketing in the United States? Does Carnation's marketing violate the WHO Code? If so, what does this imply about Nestle's future marketing in developing nations?
5. Do the antitrust concerns in the United States undermine the industrywide collaborations that seem necessary to deal with international issues? Can Nestle cooperate with the same companies that are opposing them in the United States?

CASE STUDY BHOPAL[1]

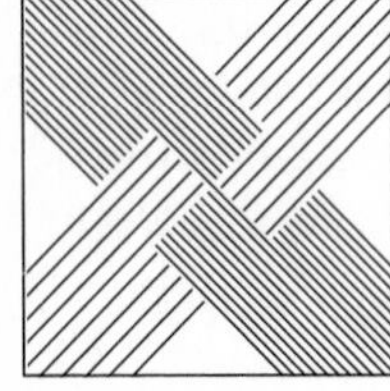

by **James Weber** *Marquette University*

It began without public warning at 12:56 A.M., December 3, 1984. As 900,000 people slept in and around the city and slums of Bhopal, India, a cloud of toxic gas consisting of methyl isocyanate (MIC) leaked from a storage tank at a Union Carbide pesticide plant. The evening's brisk winds pushed the cloud, within minutes, through the nearby dwellings, and within an hour agony had engulfed the lives of tens of thousands of Indians. Hundreds died in their beds, most of them children and the elderly weakened by hunger and frailty. Thousands more awoke to a nightmare of near suffocation, blindness, and chaos. They stumbled into the streets, choking, vomiting, sobbing, their eyes burning. Dogs, cows, and buffalos were stricken. Chaos filled the city, as death and panic spread.

By week's end more than 2,500 people were dead. Over 150,000 received medical care in the first week, and twice that many were treated by year's end. It was the world's worst industrial disaster. Lingering effects of the poisonous gas were felt for months after the leak. Many residents suffered shortness of breath, eye irritation, and depression, and continued to flock to hospitals, clinics, and rehabilitation centers. As many as 40,000 were estimated to be permanently injured from inhaling the poisonous fumes; many of these were so weakened as to be incapable of working or earning their livelihood.

Union Carbide Corporation

At the time of the accident, Union Carbide was the nation's third largest chemical producer, after Du Pont and Dow Chemical. The firm earned revenues of over $9 billion in 1982 and in 1983, though its net income fell from $310 million in 1982 to $79 million in 1983, which was its poorest performance in over a decade. One year before the disaster, Union Carbide had assets exceeding $10 billion, 99,506 employees worldwide, and a book value per share of $69.95.

In 1984, its strategic focus shifted away from the big cash generators of basic petrochemicals, which were swamped by global overcapacity, and metals and carbons products, which were hurt by poor conditions in the beleaguered steel industry. The firm announced in October 1984 an increased concentration of investment in three other lines of business—consumer products, industrial gases, and technology services and specialty products—all earmarked as growth areas. Just as this new corporate strategy was unfolding, the Bhopal disaster struck.

Union Carbide's operations in India go back to the beginning of this century,

[1] Information for this case was drawn from the following sources: the *Wall Street Journal; Business Week; Time; Newsweek;* the *New York Times;* Union Carbide Corporation news releases and annual reports; Paul Shrivastava, *Bhopal: Anatomy of a Crisis*, Cambridge, MA: Ballinger, 1987; and R. Clayton Trotter, Susan G. Day, and Amy E. Love, "Bhopal, India and Union Carbide: The Second Tragedy," *Journal of Business Ethics*, 1989, vol. 8, pp. 439–454.

when it began marketing its products there. In 1934, an assembly plant for batteries was opened in Calcutta. By 1983, Union Carbide had fourteen plants in India that manufactured chemicals, pesticides, batteries, and other products. The plant in Bhopal was built in 1969 to formulate a range of pesticides and herbicides derived from a carbaryl base. In 1979, the company commissioned the Bhopal plant to manufacture MIC. At the time of its construction, the plant stood well away from most of Bhopal's population, but in intervening years many poor people had settled near the plant.

Union Carbide was one of a few foreign firms in India in which the parent company was permitted to hold a majority interest. Normally foreign investors are limited to minority ownership of equity in Indian companies, but the Indian government waived this requirement in the case of Union Carbide because of the sophistication of its technology and the company's potential for export. Union Carbide Corporation owned 50.9 percent of the Indian subsidiary (known as Union Carbide India), with the remaining 49.1 percent distributed among Indian shareholders. However, the direct involvement of the parent company in the Bhopal plant was limited, and the operations were supervised and staffed by Indian workers.

The Chemical Industry and Public Safety

Every day in the United States the chemical and petroleum industries produce about 275 million gallons of gasoline, 2.5 million pounds of pesticides and herbicides, and nearly 723,000 tons of dangerous wastes. Many of these hazardous materials, chiefly petrochemicals, are shipped across the country. Yet, in spite of the high potential for disastrous consequences, the safety record of these industries in the United States is exceptionally good. The chemical industry's safety record in the year prior to the Bhopal disaster showed 5.2 reported occupational injuries per 100 workers versus a 7.5 average for all manufacturing.

Although chemical companies insisted that they applied the same standard of safety and environmental protection in foreign facilities as at home, leading chemical industry executives were aware that, when operating in a third world country, they faced many problems in attempting to reach the same standard of safety achieved in the United States. Most experts agreed that chemical companies building plants in the third world rarely were seeking to dodge environmental rules at home. Nevertheless, weaker regulations and enforcement abroad when combined with difficulties in maintaining quality control posed worrisome possibilities for disaster.

Host governments' efforts to respond to the growing need for safety and environmental safeguards had been minimal. The number of environmental control agencies in developing countries had soared from 11 in 1972 to 110 in 1984. However, many of these were small, underfinanced, and only meagerly supported by their governments. In India, for example, the federal environmental department had a staff of about 150 persons, compared with the U.S. Environmental Protection Agency's headquarters staff of 4,400. A study by the International Labor Organization found that labor inspectors in developing countries had little status, poor pay, and huge territories to cover.

These conditions had contributed to disasters prior to the Bhopal tragedy. In Mexico City in November 1984, liquefied-gas tanks exploded in a storage facility. The resulting fire took 452 lives and injured 4,248, and 1,000 people were reported missing. In Cubatao, Brazil, in February 1984, gasoline from a leaky pipeline exploded into a giant fireball that killed at least 500 people. Near San Carlos de la Rapita, Spain, in July 1978, an overloaded 38-ton tank truck carrying combustible propylene gas skidded around a bend in the road and slammed into a wall. Flames shot 100 feet into the air, engulfed a tourists' campsite, and killed 215 people.

These and other incidents demonstrated the broad potential for danger since few of the developing nations had the elaborate system of safety regulations and inspections found in the United States. Yet workplaces in the third world were fast acquiring many of the same kinds of complex industrial processes present in the United States. An environmentalist commented, "We're thrusting 20th-century technology into countries which aren't yet ready to deal with it. We've gotten away with it so far because there have been only minor tragedies. But the Union Carbide accident has really torn apart the whole cover on this, and things will never be the same again."[2]

Union Carbide's Response

As soon as the wire services carried news of the spreading tragedy in Bhopal, Union Carbide called an immediate halt to worldwide production and shipment of MIC. A company official explained that the firm took this precautionary step to determine if safety processes and devices were fully operational at their plants worldwide. To offset community fears near one of its MIC-producing plants in West Virginia, the company launched a public relations campaign that stressed the plant's excellent safety record and efficient safety equipment and procedures. On the day following the tragedy, Warren M. Anderson, Union Carbide's chairman, flew to India to provide relief and compensation to the victims. On December 6, Union Carbide employees around the world stopped work at noon to join in a moment of silence to show their grief and sorrow for those afflicted in the Bhopal disaster.

According to a Union Carbide fact sheet, the company responded to the Bhopal accident in three phases: immediate responses, intermediate responses, and long-term relief efforts.

Immediate relief efforts included Warren Anderson's trip to Bhopal on December 4; sending internationally recognized pulmonary and eye experts to treat survivors; dispatching a five-person medical relief and technical investigation team to Bhopal; offering a $1 million contribution to the Bhopal Relief Fund; contributing (through Union Carbide India) medicine, medical equipment, blankets, and

[2] *Wall Street Journal,* Dec. 13, 1984, p. 1.

clothing; and treating 6,000 persons at the plant's dispensary immediately after the incident.

Following these initial steps, the corporation focused on "intermediate" needs. These included collecting $120,000 through the firm's Employee Relief Fund; donating $5,000 toward a Bhopal eye center; sending additional donations of food, medicine, and clothing; and offering financial support for community rebuilding projects. However, the Indian subsidiary found its offers—of fully equipped medical care and research centers; facilities for rehabilitation, vocational education, and job training; a mobile medical van; and educational scholarships—rejected or ignored by the state government of Madhya Pradesh where Bhopal was located. It was at this time that Union Carbide Chairman Anderson commented that the company was in a "negotiation mode."

According to Union Carbide the company's long-term relief efforts were aimed at meeting health and welfare needs. U.S. Federal District Court Judge John Keenan, who held temporary legal authority over Bhopal matters, ordered the firm to disburse $5 million of Union Carbide's funds to assist survivors. Union Carbide began working with American investors to establish a prototype factory in Bhopal to manufacture low-cost prefabricated housing, but this project was later abandoned. Union Carbide India proposed to build dwellings for 500 residents, plus a job training center, a school, and a community center. In conjunction with Arizona State University, the U.S. firm developed a project to establish a Bhopal Technical and Vocational Training Center; this effort was not welcomed by the Madhya Pradesh state authorities, who subsequently accused the project's management of fraudulent use of Union Carbide funds.

In addition, a pledge of $10 million was made by Union Carbide to establish a hospital in Bhopal, modeled on U.S. Veterans Administration hospitals that had been initially created to care for war-injured personnel. Some observers believed that this gesture was part of Union Carbide's efforts to establish a stronger negotiation position regarding legal settlements.

Explanations and Causes of the Gas Leak

The safety of the plant's design and operations was the subject of an internal report by Union Carbide (U.S.A.) in May 1982, two and a half years before the accident. Ten major deficiencies were reported. They included a potential for materials to leak from storage tanks, the possibility of dust explosions, problems with safety valves and instruments, and a high rate of personnel turnover at the Bhopal plant.

Union Carbide India responded to this report with an "action plan" to correct the deficiencies. Progress in upgrading the plant was described in three separate reports. The final report, dated June 1984, six months prior to the disastrous leak, said that virtually all the problems at the plant had been corrected. The two remaining deficiencies, however, involved the operation of a safety valve used in the methyl isocyanate manufacturing process and the possibility that the tank storing MIC could be mistakenly overfilled. The report concluded that work on these two deficiencies was almost complete and depended on delivery of a control valve which was expected in July.

Human factors may have played a role. Employee morale was said to be low; some believed there were not enough staff, that training was inadequate, and that managerial experience was insufficient.

Various strategic factors and operating policies and procedures may have contributed to the accident and its aftermath. The Bhopal plant represented less than 3 percent of the parent firm's worldwide profits and thus was not critically important. Union Carbide's top management endorsed a plan in July 1984 to sell the plant because of the declining and increasingly competitive pesticides market. The facility had had eight plant managers in fifteen years, and it lacked contingency plans for dealing with major accidents. Indian insistence, like that in other developing nations, on placing operational control in the hands of host-country nationals may have worked perversely to reduce home-country headquarters control of the plant.

Finally, technological factors may have been involved. Various experts pointed to flaws in plant or equipment design, defective or malfunctioning equipment, the use of contaminated or substandard supplies and raw materials, and reliance on incorrect operating procedures. These failures might have been inadvertent, deliberate, or caused by negligence.[3]

Several investigations were conducted, and accusations surfaced regarding the cause of the accident.

On December 20, 1984, Union Carbide researchers arrived in Bhopal and conducted a three-month-long effort to reconstruct the sequence of events leading to the accident. They began by drilling into the remains of the MIC storage tank. Samples were sealed in 20 small glass vials and carried by courier to a West Virginia Union Carbide laboratory. The team's report was released in March 1985. It concluded that multiple systems failure and lapses, themselves linked to neglect of safety, maintenance, and operating procedures, appeared to have combined to cause the accident. The report stated that a safety valve opened as a result of a chemical reaction in the storage tank that contained 90,000 pounds of MIC. The valve remained open for nearly two hours before it resealed. During that period over 50,000 pounds of MIC in vapor and liquid form were discharged through the safety valve.

Other experts thought that the plant's scrubber system was not functioning or that the MIC gas leaked into the air through a loosened valve or ruptured tank without ever reaching the scrubber. The scrubber, a cylinder which washed the MIC with a caustic soda solution and converted it into safer substances, was the main safety device for preventing MIC gas from getting into the atmosphere.

In August 1985, Union Carbide suggested yet another possible cause of the disaster: sabotage. The company called attention to a wire service report that a group of Sikh extremists had claimed credit for the disaster. Sikh factions were pitted against the Gandhi government in a bitter political struggle that earlier

[3] For a discussion of these human, organizational, and technological possibilities, see Paul Shrivastava, *Bhopal: Anatomy of a Crisis*, Cambridge, MA: Ballinger, 1987, pp. 48–57.

had included armed repression of the Sikhs and the assassination by Sikhs of Prime Minister Indira Gandhi, whose son, Rajiv Gandhi, succeeded her as prime minister. The company said that it did not necessarily endorse the report, and a Union Carbide representative later said that the company now believed that a large volume of water had been deliberately introduced into the storage tank, perhaps by a disgruntled employee. Previously the company had said the water could have been inadvertently allowed into the tank. But a three-year investigation by Arthur D. Little, Inc., a U.S.-based engineering consulting firm hired by Union Carbide, confirmed Carbide's claim that a disgruntled employee may have tampered with the storage tank, causing a chemical reaction which led to the gas leak.

The Role of the Indian Government

The Indian government, like Union Carbide, was active in responding to the anguish and devastation following the tragedy. In his first official pronouncement regarding the disaster Prime Minister Rajiv Gandhi called the incident "horrifying" and established a $400,000 government emergency relief fund. A year later the Indian government had spent nearly $40 million on food and medical care for the 300,000 victims.[4]

Besides this direct assistance the Indian government took an active legal role. Responding to the earliest reports of the tragedy, police arrested five plant officials on negligence charges and sealed off the factory. More arrests followed. On December 7, 1984, as Chairman Warren Anderson stepped out of the plane at the Bhopal airport, police arrested him on charges of death by negligence, criminal conspiracy, causing air pollution, and killing livestock. Two of the firm's top Indian executives were seized when they arrived at the airport intending to investigate the disaster. After Anderson posted $2,500 bail, he was ordered to leave the country.

On December 6, the Indian government, on behalf of the Indian people stricken by the tragedy, filed a criminal complaint against Union Carbide's Indian unit over the poisonous gas leak. Pursuant to the complaint, Indian police conducted an investigation to determine whether to prosecute. State authorities closed the plant in December 1984, declaring that it would never be allowed to reopen.

In March 1985, Union Carbide began talks with the Indian government in an attempt to resolve the growing number of liability claims against the firm which totaled over $15 billion in compensation and punitive damages. In an interview published in the *Financial Times of London,* Rajiv Gandhi said his government had rejected as inadequate a settlement offer by Union Carbide. The offer included an immediate payment of $60 million and an additional $180 million over the next 30 years. Three days later the Indian government filed suit against Union Carbide (U.S.A.).

Other negotiations also were under way between Union Carbide and lawyers for the Bhopal victims. On March 23, 1986, they agreed to settle the litigation

[4] *Business Week,* Nov. 25, 1985, p. 96.

claims, with Union Carbide paying $350 million. When the Indian government heard of this agreement they proclaimed, "It has to be pointed out that there cannot be any settlement without agreement by India."[5] The Indian response further clarified that Union Carbide's proposed settlement was simply inadequate. There was pressure upon the government to push hard with its demands. A group of activists, the Poison Gas Episode Struggle Front, was calling for the nationalization of Union Carbide's Indian factories and for punitive damages equal to the total assets of the parent Union Carbide Corporation.

A critical legal question emerged shortly after the Bhopal tragedy. Should the claims be heard in United States courts, since Union Carbide was a U.S.-based corporation and the majority owner of the plant where the disaster occurred? Or should the claims be settled in Indian courts, since the disaster occurred on India's territory?

The lawyers for the victims and the Indian government favored a trial in U.S. courts, presumably because these courts traditionally delivered larger awards to accident victims and delivered them faster than their Indian counterparts. The landmark decision handed down in May 1986 by U.S. Federal District Judge John F. Keenan, which had significant implications for all U.S.-based multinational corporations, ruled that the claims were to be decided in India, not in the United States.

Judge Keenan stated that to retain the litigation in the United States would be an example of imperialism, where an established sovereign inflicts its rules, its standards, and its values on a developing nation. The Indian courts, according to Keenan, have the proven capacity to mete out fair and equal justice.

After this court decision was handed down, the Indian government found itself in a weakened negotiating position. As settlement talks dragged on, the government took another bold step. On September 8, 1986, it sued Union Carbide in a Bhopal district court for an unspecified amount of damages arising from the poison gas leak. The suit said the firm failed to provide the required standard of safety at its Bhopal plant. It also blamed the company for highly dangerous and defective plant conditions. Two months later the Indian government disclosed that it would seek at least $3 billion from Union Carbide. Criminal charges of homicide were later filed against former Union Carbide chairman Warren Anderson and eight other Carbide officials.

In 1987, Judge Deo, in an Indian court, ordered Union Carbide to pay $270 million in damages. This decree surprised the business community since, without a trial and presentation of evidence, responsibility for the deaths and injuries attributed to the gas leak had not been established. Carbide won their appeal of this decision and Judge Deo was later dismissed from the case because of bias.

Over four years after the accident, in February 1989, a settlement between Carbide and the Indian government was reached and approved by India's Supreme Court. Carbide agreed to pay $470 million in compensation to the Bhopal victims, with $5 million already having been distributed at the time of the accident.

[5] *Business Week*, Apr. 7, 1986, p. 39.

Since the settlement was reached before a trial was held, no blame for the Bhopal gas leak was legally assigned.

Worldwide Ramifications

Following the tragedy in Bhopal, fears spread through the community near Union Carbide's West Virginia plant, producer of MIC and other potentially hazardous chemicals. Three days after the Bhopal tragedy a gas bomb explosion rocked a Union Carbide plant in West Germany. The words "Poison Killer" and "Swine" were spray-painted on the plant's walls. A shipment of MIC, bound for France, was barred by the French Environment Ministry. Several European government agencies balked at continuing negotiations with Union Carbide over proposed plant construction plans.

Initially, the Union Carbide employees showed their sympathy and support for the tragedy's victims by contributing $150,000. Two years after the tragedy, a survey of Union Carbide employees in the United States discovered that many did not know how much was collected or what was done with the funds. Few knew, or seemed to care, about the progress of lawsuits or negotiations with the Indian government. They seemed to feel no personal responsibility for the tragedy and believed that the company was a victim of circumstances. "India forced the company not only to build a plant there but also to give control to its local subsidiary. We're bitter. A few incompetent, casual Indians put a black mark on my name," claimed one U.S. Union Carbide employee.[6]

The "black mark" also extended to the chemical industry and to U.S.-based multinationals operating in developing countries. "If I were a corporate manager, I would reexamine my profile of global activities, and in some cases I might pull out some products or processes where the risk is great and the profit marginal," said Ingo Walter, a professor at New York University's Graduate School of Business.[7]

These thoughts were echoed throughout the chemical industry. Ray R. Irani, president of Occidental Petroleum, said that the Bhopal incident meant that corporations must evaluate the reasons for establishing such operations in underdeveloped nations and search their souls as to the benefits to the corporation and to the country. Both Du Pont and Dow Chemical noted difficulties in conducting hazardous operations abroad, and many chemical companies reviewed their safety operations and emergency response procedures, reduced the storage of some toxic chemicals, reevaluated the risks of operating in developing countries, and initiated programs for informing area residents about hazards. Union Carbide announced in March 1985 that it was tripling the number of safety inspections of all its plants.

These changes in corporate operations were a result of various external pressures. The insurance industry sharply reduced coverage for toxic waste sites, while increasing premiums. This placed the chemical industry in a bind since

[6] *Business Week,* Nov. 25, 1985, p. 45.

[7] *Business Week,* Dec. 24, 1984, p. 27.

the law required them to buy insurance, but the insurance companies either would not sell it or its cost was prohibitive.

Governments of several third world countries imposed new curbs on chemical firms. For example, in Brazil, the world's fourth-largest user of agricultural chemicals, state authorities immediately restricted use of the deadly methyl isocyanate. The European Economic Community's regulation, developed as a response to a 1976 dioxin accident in Italy, required chemical plant operators to demonstrate that they had adequate safety measures and emergency plans and to inform residents in danger zones of the potential perils of accidents. In Germany new demands were made for stricter controls or even for plant closures.

Thousands of Americans living near chemical plants worried about their safety. The push for chemical right-to-know laws increased. These laws require companies to list and label all toxic or potentially hazardous workplace chemicals, so that employees, transport companies, and public safety officials are informed about actual and potential risks. The city of Akron, Ohio, passed such a law just one week after the Bhopal disaster, and similar measures were considered in hundreds of other communities and in nineteen state legislatures. Studies to develop federal legislation were begun shortly after the tragedy. "There's definitely heightened awareness," said Sandy Buchanan, director of the Toxic Action Project in Ohio. "Bhopal made it difficult for anyone to argue against people needing to know."[8]

Long-Term Impact On Union Carbide

Bhopal weakened Union Carbide in a number of ways. In the week following the accident, the company's stock dropped to $35 per share from $49, wiping out 27 percent, or almost $1 billion, of its market value. Eighteen months later, Union Carbide announced a massive restructuring plan. The plan involved a wave of plant closings and the dismissal of 4,000 employees, about 15 percent of the company's white-collar workforce.

Analysts were divided on whether the restructuring was primarily due to the massive Bhopal lawsuit claims filed against the company or to an attempted takeover by GAF Corporation. Some observers thought Union Carbide's lowered stock value had increased its attractiveness as a takeover target. In August 1985, GAF increased its stake in Union Carbide to 7.1 percent and rumors of a takeover circulated on Wall Street. In January 1986, GAF formally offered $5 billion for Union Carbide.

Union Carbide suppressed the hostile takeover with a defense that was upheld in the courts. The company's defense included putting on the selling block one of the firm's prime assets, the $2 billion Consumer Products Division, doubling Union Carbide's debt to $4.5 billion, and cutting the company's equity value to one-fourth of what it had been. Though Union Carbide claimed victory in this fight, the company emerged as a shadow of its former self.

[8] *Business Week,* Feb. 18, 1985, p. 36.

Continued Rumblings

The settlement for $470 million was appealed by the new Indian government of Prime Minister V.P. Singh, which was still seeking $3 billion in civil damages and criminal charges against Carbide officials. Some Bhopal victims, wanting additional compensation, continued to target Union Carbide. Protesters at Carbide's annual stockholders meeting in 1989 were arrested for unlawfully distributing a report critical of Union Carbide's performance in Bhopal since the accident. At a protest commemorating the fifth anniversary of the gas leak in Bhopal, 800 people were arrested when they tried to hold a meeting inside the vacant pesticide plant. Carbide spent over $24 million in legal fees, substantially changed its safety precautions at its plants worldwide, and has restructured its worldwide holdings as a result of the accident in Bhopal.

Discussion Questions

1. Assess the corporate social strategy of Union Carbide both before and after the Bhopal accident. Identify the company's strategic goals prior to the accident, and tell how they were changed after the accident. Were these goals appropriate for the company and for its stakeholders?
2. Develop a stakeholder map for Union Carbide, based on the Bhopal incident. Include each stakeholder's major interest, and rank the stakeholders in terms of their relative power. How would such information help Union carbide management in dealing with this crisis?
3. Of the various possible causes of the accident, which one do you believe to have been the most important? What could Union Carbide management have done to reduce or eliminate this causal factor? In your opinion, why did the company not take such action before the accident?
4. Over 2,500 deaths and 300,000 injuries are attributed to the effects of the gas leak. Is the $470 million settlement paid by Union Carbide "fair compensation" to the survivors of the Bhopal accident? If not, what would be a "fair settlement?"
5. What are the main ethical issues of this case? Show how you would use utilitarian reasoning, rights reasoning, and justice reasoning to analyze these ethical issues.

CASE STUDY DU PONT FREON® PRODUCTS DIVISION: CFCs AND OZONE DEPLETION[1]

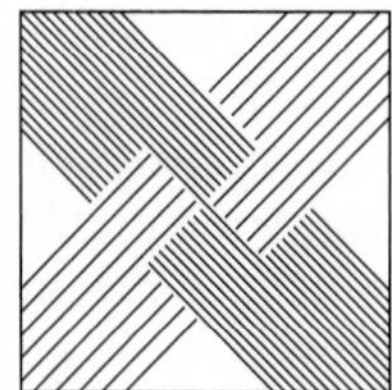

by **Forest Reinhardt** *Harvard Business School*

"Evidence of Ozone Depletion Found Over Big Urban Areas; Pattern Widens; Severity Surprises Experts," ran a front-page headline in *The Washington Post* on March 16, 1988. The day before, atmospheric scientists from an interagency governmental research team, headed by the National Aeronautics and Space Administration (NASA), released new information linking chlorofluorocarbons (CFCs) to the destruction of stratospheric ozone. The scientists reported that ozone depletion was more severe and widespread than had been previously anticipated. Furthermore, there was now hard evidence that CFCs contributed to ozone depletion over Antarctica. Since stratospheric ozone shielded the earth from ultraviolet radiation, the depletion of the ozone layer allowed increased levels of radiation to reach the earth's surface. This was likely to cause increases in skin cancer rates and damage crops and fisheries.

Invented in the 1930s, CFCs were widely used in a variety of industries because they were chemically stable, low in toxicity, and nonflammable. CFCs were the leading heat-transfer agent in refrigeration equipment and air-conditioning systems for buildings and vehicles. They were used in the manufacture of various kinds of foam, including building insulation. And they were used as solvents and cleaning agents in semiconductor manufacturing and other businesses. In Europe and Japan, CFCs were widely used as propellants in aerosol containers, although this practice was banned in the United States.

While no substitute existed for many of these commercial uses, concern for stratospheric ozone led, in September 1987, to an international accord under which CFC production is held at its 1986 level, and production is cut half by 1990. But the newest scientific evidence cast doubt on whether even these reductions would protect the ozone layer.

For Joe Glas, who ran the Freon® Products Division of E. I. du Pont de Nemours and Company, these new findings posed an extraordinary challenge. As the world's largest manufacturer of CFCs, Du Pont earned $600 million in revenues from this business in 1987. In the early 1980s, Du Pont led CFC producers and users in opposing CFC regulation, citing the uncertainty of the science. Recently, though, Du Pont took the opposite tack and pushed industry to support the international regulatory accord.

Despite its reversal in position, Du Pont was severely criticized in the press and in Congress for not doing more. A New York University physician, testifying

[1] By Forest Reinhardt. © 1989 National Wildlife Federation. Used with permission. This case is adapted from DuPont Freon® Products Division (A) prepared by Forest Reinhardt under the direction of Professor Richard H. K. Vietor, Harvard Business School, for the National Wildlife Federation.

at a House of Representatives hearing on ozone depletion, described a "near epidemic" increase in skin cancer rates. Senate hearings on the issue were scheduled for March 30, and Du Pont officials would have to testify. Glas needed to decide whether the Freon® Products Division should do nothing and let the regulatory process runs its course, take an active role in support of or in opposition to further controls, or take some unilateral action such as cutting back its own CFC production.

The CFC Business

CFCs were a class of chemical compounds containing carbon, fluorine, and chlorine. There were two main classes of CFCs: chlorofluoromethanes and chlorofluoroethanes. The Du Pont Company, which had invented most CFCs, marketed them under the trademark "Freon."

Chlorofluoromethanes consisted of two commercially important variations, CFC-11 and -12. In the United States, CFC-11 was used primarily as a blowing agent for foams. The end product ranges from the soft foams used in mattresses, furniture, and car seats (about 20 percent of blown foam applications) to foams used in food packaging and as the insulation in refrigerators (about 20 percent) to the rigid foams used as insulation in the construction of new buildings (60 percent). CFC-11 was also used in the United States in special, unregulated aerosols.

CFC-12 was used primarily as the coolant in refrigeration systems, including home refrigerators and air conditioners for buildings, cars, and trucks. Its secondary uses included foam blowing. In Europe and Japan, CFC-11 and -12 were widely used as aerosol propellants.

The chlorofluoroethanes consisted of CFC-113, -114, and -115. CFC-113 accounted for more than 95 percent of the total use of chlorofluoroethanes. They were used primarily as solvents in the electronics and defense industries to clean high-value electronic components such as printed circuit boards. In the United States, this use accounted for about half of CFC-113 demand; other applications included metal degreasing, dry cleaning, and cleaning medical implants and guidance systems.

A similar class of compounds, HCFCs, was composed of carbon, chlorine, fluorine, and hydrogen. Although not strictly CFCs, HCFCs were sometimes lumped into the same category. The most important HCFC was HCFC-22. About a third of HCFC-22 production was used as raw material in the manufacture of Teflon and other polymers. Significant end uses of HCFC-22 included air conditioning for buildings (but not for vehicles) and commercial refrigeration equipment.

A third class of compounds, called Halons, shared many of the same properties of CFCs and HCFCs, including the propensity to deplete stratospheric ozone. However, production of Halons was small relative to that of CFCs. They were mainly used in commercial and military fire protection systems.

CFCs and Ozone Depletion

CFCs were widely used because of their distinctive properties. CFCs did not react readily with other materials during manufacture of final products or while those products (such as refrigerators) were being used. Their stability also meant that, once released to the atmosphere, CFCs would not react with other effluent to form smog. Further, CFCs were nontoxic to humans.

CFCs could immediately be released to the atmosphere upon use (if, for example, they were used as solvents and then allowed to evaporate), or they might remain locked into a final product (a rigid foam, for example, or a refrigerator) for several years after manufacture. But sooner or later, all CFCs created were released into the environment.

Because of their stability, what happened to CFCs after their release was a matter of little concern. In 1972, an industry consortium was formed to study the environmental fate of CFCs. Then, in 1974, Mario Molina and Sherry Rowland, two chemists at the University of California at Irvine, postulated that CFCs could be responsible for widespread destruction of stratospheric ozone. According to their theory, CFCs tended to migrate slowly to the stratosphere, the upper level of the atmosphere between 15 and 30 miles above the earth's surface. There, they were broken into their constituent elements by ultraviolet radiation from the sun. The released chlorine atoms of CFCs then acted as a catalyst in a series of reactions that convert ozone (O_3) into oxygen (O_2). Because the chlorine acted as a catalyst rather than a reagent, a single chlorine atom could destroy large numbers of ozone molecules. And because CFCs persisted for long periods before breaking down to form free chlorine, the effects of today's use of CFCs would not be felt for decades or even centuries.

As an artificial pollutant in the lower atmosphere, ozone was one of the most unhealthy constituents of smog. Societies spent billions of dollars trying to control its levels. However, in the upper atmosphere, ozone blocked out some of the sun's ultraviolet radiation and prevented it from reaching the earth's surface. Therefore, stratospheric ozone depletion allowed *higher* levels of ultraviolet radiation to reach the earth. Higher rates of skin cancer in humans, as well as damage to crops and fisheries, were likely to result. A 1 percent decrease in stratospheric ozone concentrations could result in a 2 percent increase in the amount of ultraviolet radiation reaching the earth's surface. In turn, a 1 percent increase in cumulative exposure to ultraviolet radiation was expected to result in a 2 percent increase in the incidence of skin cancer.

The ozone depletion mechanism postulated by Rowland and Molina was only a theory. Empirical verification was unavailable in 1974 and could not be expected for years because of the difficulties in measuring actual levels of stratospheric ozone. Some 300 million tons of ozone were created and destroyed each day in a dynamic stratospheric equilibrium. For natural reasons, ozone levels in the stratosphere vary widely over the course of each day, each year, and each multiyear sunspot cycle. Further, even if a trend toward lower ozone concentrations could be detected, it would be difficult to be sure that CFCs were responsible.

To simulate the chemical and physical processes that determined ozone levels in the stratosphere, computer models were built by government agencies, academic institutions, and industry groups. These models used data on estimated chlorine-ozone reaction rates, the persistence of chlorine in the stratosphere, the effects of other stratospheric contaminants, and global meteorological patterns as inputs, and used the data to assess the effects of various levels of CFC loadings. The goal was to confirm modeling results by the empirical data.

The problem of matching observations to models was significant. Ozone concentrations were affected by a host of other natural and manufactured gases, including carbon dioxide, oxides of nitrogen, and methane. This difficulty was compounded by the "one-dimensional" nature of the models. Actual ozone concentrations over time were different not only at different altitudes but at different latitudes; since the models predicted only averages across all latitudes, they were difficult to verify by using empirical data. In response, scientists tried to develop models that predicted ozone concentrations at different latitudes and altitudes over time. These models were more difficult to create, more expensive to run, and even more sensitive to scientific uncertainty.

Almost as soon as the news of Rowland and Molina's work reached the press, U.S. consumers began switching to nonaerosol packing for common household products such as deodorant. The U.S. Environmental Protection Agency (EPA) considered it prudent to ban certain "nonessential" uses of CFCs. The ban took effect in 1978; its main impact was to stop the use of CFCs as an aerosol propellant, except for essential medical and military uses. In 1973, the United States consumed about half of all CFCs manufactured worldwide, and aerosol uses accounted for about half of this consumption. Manufacturers of products that used aerosol containers switched to other propellants, including carbon dioxide, propane, and butane. U.S. sales of CFCs peaked in 1973. With the exception of Canada, Norway, and Sweden, other governments did not impose bans on aerosol uses of CFCs. The European Economic Community promulgated voluntary, nonbinding guidelines for CFC aerosol uses in 1980, and this led to gradual reductions in these uses over time. However, these reductions were not enough to offset western European and Japanese trends toward increasing CFC use. CFC use grew apace in the developing world. In the United States, consumption of CFCs fell by 50 percent when aerosols were banned but climbed slowly back toward its mid-1970s level as demand in the nonaerosol sectors grew.

Shortly before the 1980 presidential election, the EPA announced it was investigating the need for further restrictions of CFCs. Following the Reagan victory, with "regulatory relief" an important item on the new administration's domestic agenda, EPA's investigation was curtailed, although not formally terminated.

During the early 1980s, refinements of the computer models led many scientists to believe that Rowland and Molina had overstated the ozone depletion problem. These scientists claimed that depletion from CFCs was likely to be less than the 1974 predictions. In 1979, the National Academy of Sciences (NAS) predicted that continued growth in CFC use would lead to a loss of 16.5 percent of the stratospheric ozone by the time a new equilibrium was reached (perhaps 100 years later). In 1982, NAS reduced its estimate to a depletion level of 5 to 9 percent. Two years later, the estimate fell again to between 2 and 4 percent. At the same time, actual monitoring of stratospheric ozone levels produced no hard evidence that any depletion was occurring. Finally, CFC production during this period was flat because of restrictions on aerosols and the worldwide recession in the early 1980s.

The Montreal Protocol

Then, in 1985, with CFC production again on the rise as the world economy recovered, British scientists working in Antarctica reported a dramatic decrease in springtime stratospheric ozone concentrations above that continent. The presence of this "hole" in the ozone layer called into question a whole generation of scientific models. The new findings hinted that model results had been too optimistic and raised the possibility that ozone depletion might be occurring more rapidly than even Molina and Rowland predicted.

Reactions to this new information varied widely. The Natural Resources Defense Council and other environmental groups called for a worldwide production ban. Congress held hearings, and *The New Yorker* published an article that was highly critical of the CFC industry and especially of Du Pont. Interior Secretary Donald Hodel drew some ridicule for suggesting that ozone depletion problems could be mitigated through the use of suntan lotion and sunglasses.

Government and industry scientists hurried to update their models, while diplomats held a series of meetings to bring about an international consensus on the ozone problem. A report by NASA and the United Nations World Meteorological Organization said that, based on new model calculations, it might be possible to allow CFC production to increase by 1.5 percent per year without any deleterious effects on the ozone. However, in the prevailing political climate, controls tighter than a cap on the growth rate were inevitable. In Montreal in September 1987, virtually all of the world's industrial nations pledged to cap production of CFC-11, -12, -113, -114, and -115 in their respective countries at its 1986 levels by 1989. Total production levels were to be cut back to 80 percent of 1986 levels by 1994 and to 50 percent of 1986 levels by 1999. Halon production was to be capped in 1993. The Montreal Protocol allowed certain exemptions for developing countries. It also provided for amendment should the scientific conclusions about the effects of CFCs change.

The protocol was to take effect when countries responsible for two-thirds of global CFC production had ratified it. Individual countries could decide how to allocate CFC production among producers, subject to an overall ceiling for each country that was expressed in terms of ozone depletion potential.

Even before the treaty was negotiated, a suit by the Natural Resources Defense Council forced the EPA to resume its investigation into further CFC regulatory controls. After the protocol, the EPA proposed mandatory cutbacks of production on the same schedules as the international protocol.

According to the EPA, failure to make such cutbacks could lead to an increase of about 150 million cases of nonmelanoma skin cancer among current and future U.S. populations born before 2075 and an increase of about three million cases of premature deaths from skin cancer among these populations. EPA also predicted large increases in cases of cataracts (a debilitating eye condition) as a result of increased exposure to ultraviolet radiation. Damages to crops and aquatic organisms, including several commercially important fish species, was also predicted. According to the EPA, CFCs also played a small role in the trend toward global warming. Finally, the EPA concluded that while the costs of mandatory substitution would be significant, the costs of doing nothing were substantially greater.

In December 1987, EPA proposed its regulations for implementing the protocol, which set limits on the amount of CFCs each firm could sell in the U.S. market. The limit for each firm was based on the firm's 1986 production, weighted according to the ozone depletion potential of each compound. Under that limit, firms could choose how much of each CFC to produce; a firm with permits to make 1,000 tons of CFC-11 could instead produce 1,250 tons of CFC-113 (or 250 tons of CFC-11, 250 tons of CFC-12, and 625 tons of CFC-113). Firms also could transfer production and sales rights among themselves to take advantage of scale economies in production.

In the absence of regulation, CFC use was expected to grow at about the level of GNP in the industralized world and somewhat faster in developing countries. Capping production, much less cutting production, could lead to substantial price increases, particularly in the short run when users had not yet switched to other substances or otherwise curtailed their consumption of CFCs.

EPA expressed concern about the large "windfall profit" that could accrue to CFC producers as regulatory shortages drove prices upward. These profits might be as high as $600 million per year for the first few years after the protocol took effect, with a discounted value of $9 billion over the period 1990–2010. EPA considered a fee or tax to capture these profits for the U.S. Treasury instead of allowing them to fall to CFC producers; however, EPA's statutory authority to do so was unclear.

Du Pont's Business Strategy

E. I. Du Pont de Nemours and Company was founded in the early 1800s as an explosives manufacturer. One hundred years later, Du Pont was the world's first firm to adopt the divisional structure which became standard for large corporations; it also developed modern management techniques for analyzing and controlling decision making in a large, decentralized operation. By 1987, Du Pont ranked ninth in the Fortune 500, with over $30 billion in revenues. Its products ranged from gasoline, plastics, and pesticides to sophisticated biomedical equipment.

In addition to modern management, Du Pont's name was synonymous with the harnessing of science for commercial ends. Nylon and Teflon were invented in the firm's laboratories in 1938. Later, Orlon and Dacron fabrics, Lycra Spandex fiber, Tyvek packaging materials, and Kevlar for bulletproof vests were developed by Du Pont chemists. The influence of science on the company extended beyond the product line, pervading the corporate culture. Du Pont managers routinely spoke of the company as being "science-driven" and were unimpressed with companies that could not be described this way. Du Pont did not ignore the marketplace, as its $30 billion in sales attested. But its middle managers saw themselves fundamentally as scientific problem solvers with the tools to serve an increasingly technological society.

Joe Glas embodied this scientific culture. An Iowa native, Glas earned a Ph.D. in chemical engineering from the University of Illinois and joined Du Pont in 1964 as a research engineer. After holding nine positions in five states, Glas became the director of the Freon® Products Division in 1985. At important meetings, Glas listened not only to his business managers, but to Ph.D. chemists Mark McFarland, who was hired to appraise and develop ozone science, and Joe Steed, who headed the team responsible for the division's scientific, governmental relations, and public affairs policies.

The Freon® Products Division, with 1,200 employees involved in the production and sales of CFCs, was a microcosm of the Du Pont scientific and managerial culture. It was a self-contained profit center with its own production, marketing, and R&D staffs. Virtually all of its revenue came from the sales of CFC-11, -12, -113, -114, and -115, and HCFC-22.

Du Pont enjoyed international patent protection of CFCs through the late 1940s. Just as the patents expired, demand for CFCs skyrocketed as building and vehicular air conditioning and household aerosols became common. Du Pont did not begin manufacturing CFCs in Europe and Japan until after indigenous firms had become entrenched. Still, by virtue of its early scientific leadership in CFCs, it was by far the world's largest producer and the only firm with a significant worldwide presence.

Manufacturing and Marketing

Du Pont maintained the largest CFC manufacturing facilities in the world. In 1987, it operated eleven plants, including six in Europe, Japan, and Latin America, and five in the United States. The company made CFC-11 and -12 in New Jersey and California, HCFC-22 in Kentucky and Michigan, and CFC-113 in Texas. The Freon® Products Division accounted for 2 percent of Du Pont revenues in 1987 (the figures for the preceding years were 2.2 percent, 1.7 percent, and 1.8 percent), about 2 percent of corporate assets, and about 0.9 percent of Du Pont's employees.

Profitability in the CFC business resembled that of other oligopolistic organic chemicals businesses, at least until Rowland and Molina ignited concern about effects on the ozone. The drastic decline in aerosol demand left all U.S. producers with substantial overcapacity in CFC-11 and -12. Du Pont lost a third of its CFC business. The losses were even heavier for the smaller U.S. producers that did not make HCFC-22 or CFC-113 or have significant international operations.

Du Pont, Allied, and Pennwalt each closed a CFC-11/12 plant after the aerosol ban; only one of six producers left the market. Real list prices fell by about 20 percent during the late 1970s; actual prices, which reflected discounts given by manufacturers, fell even further. After-tax operating income for the Freon® Division was only 1.6 percent of sales during 1974–1979, and by 1984 recovered only slightly to about 3 percent. Efforts by Du Pont to lead CFC-11 and -12 prices upward met with failure. Small producers cut prices to achieve higher-capacity utilization and thereby offset Du Pont's scale economies. As a result, Du Pont's capacity utilization was the most cyclical in the industry.

In the early 1980s, when Du Pont management concluded that costs were too high and that the CFC business was "not earning its keep," it slashed costs. At an expense of some $75 million, Du Pont extended the scope of its backward integration into chlorocarbon production. Total annual capital expenditures peaked in 1984 at $68 million. Ironically, the new capacity was never used as Du Pont's suppliers scrambled to accommodate the company, offering to sell it chlorocarbons at a lower price than Du Pont could offer itself. Although the $75 million investment was written off, Du Pont's operating profits improved somewhat as a result of its improved raw materials cost position, averaging 4 percent in 1984–1987 even after accounting for the write-off. Since 1984, the Freon® Division's annual capital expenditures declined at a rate of about 30 percent a year through 1987. Du Pont continued the efforts to cut costs after the mixed success of the backward integration effort. Most of the cost-cutting efforts centered on incremental improvement of yields and on continuing reductions in operating and maintenance costs. By 1987, Du Pont managers felt their efforts enabled them to become the United States's lowest-cost CFC producer.

The picture was brighter for CFC-113. Du Pont and Allied were the only U.S. producers. Many CFC-113 users were quite price-insensitive; the cost of CFC-113 to clean a printed circuit board was trivial compared with the price of the board itself. CFC-113 buyers were more willing than CFC-11 and -12 consumers to regard the chemical as part of a broadly defined service that included troubleshooting and training. With weak currencies in the early 1980s, some Japanese and European firms tried to invade the U.S. CFC-113 market, but, since Japanese manufacturers had limited capacity, only British and French imports were significant. Pretax operating profits for Du Pont and Allied in CFC-113 were thought to exceed 20 percent of sales.

During the Montreal Protocol negotiations and after the protocol was passed, Du Pont shunned a short-term profit-maximization strategy. Rather, Du Pont's strategy tempered the protocol's regulatory effects so as not to drive price-sensitive customers out of the market. "If we raise price to the market-clearing price, we may drive some of the low-value consumers out of business," said one Du Pont official; "then they won't be around when we introduce the substitutes. We might instead want to maximize the number of current customers so we can switch them to other products later."

"We now see the ozone and regulatory situation as a marketing opportunity for substitutes," another manager said. "If we can show them [customers] we have a leadership position in alternatives, then they see that as a contribution to their current business." Some other CFC makers, however, managed their businesses for maximum short-run cash flow, knowing that the usefulness of their plants was limited.

Substitute Development

As of late 1987, the status of substitute development in each of the major CFC applications was as follows: for foam blowing, HCFC-22 could be substituted for CFC-11 and -12 in some applications. Some chlorocarbons could also be used for foam blowing and were widely available, but many were thought to be carcinogenic, and some were ozone precursors (i.e., they led to higher ozone levels in the lower atmosphere and contributed to the health problems caused by smog).

Du Pont was ahead of its competitors in developing other chemicals that could be used in foam blowing. Attempts focused on two substances, HCFC-14b and HCFC-123. These were chemically similar to CFCs but reacted faster upon release to the environment and did not reach the stratosphere. No viable large-scale manufacturing process had been devised, however. In the case of HCFC-123, the Freon® Divison was still searching for an effective catalyst for production. These substances were estimated to cost from 1.5 to 4 times as much to produce as CFC-11.

In some solvent markets served by CFCs, chlorocarbons could be substituted. Furthermore, chlorocarbons did not meet the technical specifications of the electronics manufacturers, and no substitutes for this use had yet been identified.

Chlorocarbons could not be used in air-conditioning systems. HCFC-22 was a possible substitute, but its application to automobile air conditioning was problematic. The automobile industry estimated it would take a billion dollars in research and from five to seven years to redesign mobile (vehicular) air-conditioning systems to use HCFC-22 rather than CFC-12. Du Pont was testing a possible substitute, HFC-134a, which was likely to cost three to five times as much as CFC-12. It contained no chlorine and hence would not affect stratospheric ozone. In the refrigeration market, no substitutes for CFCs were commercially available in 1988, although Du Pont was optimistic that HFC-123a could serve this market as well.

Finally, numerous substitutes existed for the remaining aerosol applications of CFCs. In 1978, most American makers of aerosol packaging switched to simple compounds like propane and butane rather than more expensive propellants made by Du Pont. Because of the short time between the aerosol ban's promulgation and its effective date, aerosol producers had little time to test other products (propane and butane were flammable, an undesirable characteristic for a propellant). Du Pont hoped the longer lead times of the Montreal Protocol would allow European and Japanese aerosol producers to try Du Pont's more sophisticated, less flammable, but more expensive substitutes.

Du Pont's Political Strategy

Du Pont subscribed to a companywide "Safety, Health and Environmental Quality Policy," which read, in part, the company "will comply with all applicable laws and regulations" and "will determine that each product can be made, used, handled, and disposed of safely and consistent with appropriate safety, health, and environmental quality criteria." Adopted in 1971 at a time when Earth Day and new pollution control legislation focused public attention on industrial pollution, the environmental parts of the policy formalized what Du Pont managers saw as an ethos of corporate responsibility. In the Freon® Products Division, this policy was paraphrased, "If we can't make it safely, we won't make it at all." In practice, the policy meant that Du Pont would comply with governmental regulations or with its own standards, whichever were more strict.

In 1974, when ozone depletion first came to light, Du Pont felt the science was too weak to justify the widespread regulation of demonstrably useful chemicals. At the same time, Du Pont publicly promised to change its position if the scientific case against CFCs solidified. In advertisements in newspapers and magazines, Du Pont's chairman, Irving Shapiro, said that "should reputable evidence show that some fluorocarbons cause a health hazard through depletion of the ozone layer, we are prepared to stop production of these compounds." Dr. Raymond McCarthy, a Du Pont scientist, testified in Congress to the same effect: "If credible scientific data . . . show that any chlorofluorocarbons cannot be used without a threat to health, Du Pont will stop production of these compounds."

Beginning in 1972, Du Pont invested in basic ozone science. Under the auspices of the Chemical Manufacturers Association, Du Pont and other CFC makers formed the Fluorocarbon Program Panel to pool funds for science and oversee industry research on ozone depletion. Total Du Pont expenditures on atmospheric science, aimed at a better understanding of the ozone depletion problem rather than at any immediate commercial advantage, averaged $1 million per year through the ensuing decade.

After aerosols were banned in the United States, Du Pont and other U.S. CFC manufacturers continued to sell CFCs for use as aerosols in non-American markets. These sales were not precluded by U.S. or foreign regulation, and the company felt that science did not warrant the elimination of aerosol uses. Thus continued sales were seen as consistent with Du Pont's environmental policy. But as one manager put it, "We don't actually chase that kind of business very hard."

In 1980, when EPA threatened further restrictions, Du Pont was instrumental in forming the Alliance for Responsible CFC Policy. This trade association, which was unusual in that it included both CFC producers and consumers, lobbied Congress and EPA for what it deemed a measured response to the ozone issue. In 1980, the Alliance orchestrated a flood of 2,000 letters to EPA opposing further regulation. Alliance literature placed great emphasis on the essential nature of CFC uses—electronics manufacture, energy conservation, and air conditioning—and on the high cost and relative unattractiveness of substitutes. One Du Pont executive estimated that Du Pont spent several million dollars per year on research for alternatives, responses to EPA proposals, contributions to the Alliance, and other expenditures related to CFC policy. From 1980 to 1986, Du Pont led industry opposition against further CFC controls. Du Pont felt that if more regulatory action were taken it should be international; U.S. industry had suffered from its government's unilateral restrictions on aerosols.

By mid-1986, models of ozone depletion showed that significant sustained increases in CFC emissions were likely to decrease ozone. These new model results, combined with the disturbing new evidence of the Antarctic "hole," were sufficiently worrisome that Du Pont changed its position. According to a press release written by Steed's ozone policy team, "It would be prudent to limit worldwide emissions of CFCs while science continues to work to provide better guidance to policy makers." Because Du Pont felt that only international action would be effective, the company supported "the development and adoption of a protocol under the United Nations Vienna Convention for the Protection of the Ozone Layer to limit worldwide CFC emissions." Du Pont worried that further unilateral action by the United States would provide an excuse for other nations to delay regulating their producers, as had occurred with the aerosol ban.

Other Alliance members at first resisted this change in policy. Most thought that restrictions on the rate of growth of CFC production, not on the actual levels of production, would be sufficient. However, as scientific and public concern over ozone depletion continued to mount, the Alliance acknowledged the need for production caps. The Alliance, like Du Pont, was emphatic in its support for international action. It supported an international accord partly out of fear of the competitive advantages that could arise if the United States acted alone, and partly because some members felt that once the issue reached the international negotiating table, the Europeans and Japanese would reject any measures stronger than a production cap. By the time the Montreal Protocol was enacted, however, it went far beyond the cap that most observers anticipated, with reductions in total output scheduled for the 1990s. Nonetheless, Du Pont and the Alliance supported its ratification. Du Pont's reading of the available science at the time was that the protocol's measures would protect the ozone layer, with a significant safety factor.

The Ides of March

In late February 1988, three senators from the Environment and Public Works Committee wrote to Du Pont CEO Richard Heckert, reminding him of Du Pont's promise to stop production should reputable evidence show that fluorocarbons cause a health hazard. The senators suggested the time had come. "We request and urge," they wrote, "that within the next twelve months, the Du Pont Corporation cease all further production and sale of chlorofluorocarbons 11, 12, 113, 114, and 115," unilaterally if necessary.

Heckert restated Du Pont's position on the ozone issue. "Du Pont stands by its commitment," he wrote in a letter drafted by the Freon Division staff, but "at the moment, scientific evidence does not point to the need for dramatic CFC emission reductions." The Freon Division did not want to buckle under pressure if that pressure had no scientific basis, so the letter they wrote for Heckert emphasized the continuing uncertainty of the science. The letter pointed out that there was no certain linkage between CFCs and ozone depletion, that recent empirical studies had shown decreases in ultraviolet radiation at the earth's surface, and that the health effects of ozone depletion also were uncertain. Because of the importance of many CFC uses, the senators' proposal for a unilateral Du Pont cutback was "both unwarranted and counterproductive." CFC markets needed time to develop and adapt to improved substitutes. To interfere with a smooth transition through drastic production cutbacks would be "irresponsible," Heckert wrote.

Ten days after Heckert sent his letter, the United States became the first major nation to ratify the Montreal Protocol. The Senate voted 83–0 in favor of ratification. The next day, March 15, scientists on the interagency Ozone Trends Panel issued the executive summary of their report. The report described a fundamental change in the scientific understanding of the CFC-ozone connection. First, there was hard empirical evidence of reductions in stratospheric ozone concentrations, not just over Antarctica but over temperate, populated regions as well. Second, the causal link between CFCs and ozone depletion over Antarctica was finally established: the patterns of ozone depletion strongly indicated that CFCs were responsible for the ozone "hole." Third, ozone levels over Antarctica were lower not just during the Antarctic spring, but year-round. Fourth, improved models forecast continuing ozone decreases even if the Montreal Protocol were implemented.

Steed and McFarland attended the Ozone Trends Panel press conference on March 15 and conferred with other team members. McFarland, a member of the Ozone Trends Panel, had been prohibited from revealing data from the panel's investigation prior to the public release. As the only industry representative on the panel, however, he read the entire draft report, not only the executive summary. The two men phoned Glas and other Du Pont executives in Wilmington with an assessment that the findings were accurate. This appeared to mean that several of the statements Heckert had made to the Senate about ozone science had been overtaken by events.

Glas heard national coverage of the report on the evening of March 15. He summoned Steed and McFarland to his office early next morning. Glas needed to decide whether Du Pont should now change its strategy—and he needed to decide quickly. Heckert had called and wanted to know *that day* what the Freon Products Division intended to do.

Discussion Questions

1. What choices does Joe Glas have at the end of the case? Which option would you choose? Why?
2. What are the likely effects of the Montreal Protocol on the market for chlorofluorocarbons? What are the likely effects on the political environment? Distinguish between the domestic and international settings.
3. What will happen if some nations do not adopt the Montreal Protocol? Will Du Pont's business strategy be jeopardized? What can companies such as Du Pont do under those circumstances?
4. What ethical considerations should Du Pont's management weigh in deciding how to respond? What justice and rights arguments can be applied to this situation? Would a cost-benefit analysis provide sufficient answers?

Glossary

This glossary defines technical or special terms used in this book. It may be used by students as a quick and handy reference for terms that may be unfamiliar without having to refer to the specific chapter(s) where they are used. It also can be a very helpful aid in studying for examinations and for writing term papers where precise meanings are needed.

Acid rain. Naturally occurring rain containing dilute solutions of nitric acid and sulfuric acid that are formed when nitrogen oxides and sulfur oxides combine with atmospheric water vapor.

Acquisition. (See **Merger.**)

Administrative costs. The direct costs incurred in running government regulatory agencies, including salaries of employees, equipment, supplies, and other such items. (Compare with **Compliance costs.**)

Administrative learning. A stage in the development of social responsiveness within a company during which managers and supervisors learn the new practices necessary for coping with social problems and pressures.

Advocacy advertising. (See **Public issue advertising.**)

Affirmative action. A positive and sustained effort by an organization to identify, hire, train if necessary, and promote minorities, women, and members of other groups who are underrepresented in the organization's work force.

Agrarian society. A society in which agricultural activities dominate work and employ the largest proportion of the labor force.

Ambient air quality standard. (See **Environmental-quality standard.**)

American dream. An ideal goal or vision of life in the United States, usually including material abundance and maximum freedom.

Annual meeting. A yearly meeting called by a corporation's board of directors for purposes of reporting to the company's stockholders on the current status and future prospects of the firm.

Best available technology. A regulatory concept that describes the type of technology that business is sometimes expected to use in cleaning up or preventing pollution.

Biodiversity. The multitude of genetic variations of plants, animals, and other living organisms in an ecosystem.

Biotechnology. The use and combination of various sciences, including biochemistry, genetics, microbiology, ecology, recombinant DNA, and others, to invent and develop new and modified life forms for applications in medicine, industry, farming, and other areas of human life.

Blowing the whistle. (See **Whistle-blowing.**)

Board of directors. A group of persons elected by shareholder votes to be responsible for directing the affairs of a corporation, establishing company objectives and policies, selecting top-level managers, and reviewing company performance.

Bottom line. Business profits or losses, usually reported in figures on the last or bottom line of a company's income statement.

Bubble concept. A pollution control plan that determines compliance by measuring combined total emissions from an industrial installation, rather than from each of the plant's individual pollution sources.

Business. The activity of organizing resources in order to produce and distribute goods and services for society.

Business and society. The study of the relationship of business with its entire social environment.

Business ethics. The application of general ethical ideas to business behavior.

Central state control. A socioeconomic system in which political, social, and economic power is concentrated in a central government that makes all fundamental policy decisions for the society.

Certificate of incorporation. A certificate, usually issued by a state government, authorizing a group of individuals to establish a business in the legal form of a corporation. (See **Federal chartering.**)

Charity principle. The idea that individuals and business firms should give voluntary aid and support to society's unfortunate or needy persons, as well as to other (nonprofit) organizations that provide community services.

Coalitions. Groups of organizations or corporate stakeholders who work together to achieve a common goal.

Codetermination. A system of corporate governance providing for labor representation on a company's board of directors.

Commercial speech (in media presentations). The messages contained in paid commercial advertisements. Courts have ruled that commercial speech, unlike free speech generally, is only partially protected by the United States Constitution.

Commons. Traditionally an area of land on which all citizens could graze their animals without limitation. The term now refers to natural resources that are held for the benefit of all members of a society. (Compare with **Global commons.**)

Community relations. The involvement of business with the communities in which it conducts operations.

Comparable worth. The idea that different kinds of jobs can be equated with each other in terms of difficulty, training required, skills involved, effort made, responsibility involved, and working conditions, for the purpose of equalizing the wages paid to people holding jobs that are approximately equal in these ways.

Competition. A struggle to survive and excel. In business, different firms compete with one another for the customer's dollars.

Compliance costs. The costs incurred by business and other organizations in complying with government regulations, such as the cost of pollution control machinery or disposing of toxic chemical wastes. (Compare with **Administrative costs.**)

Concentration (corporate, economic, industrial, market). When relatively few companies are responsible for a large proportion of economic activity, production, or sales.

Consumer movement. (See **Consumerism.**)

Consumer rights. The legitimate claims of consumers to safe products and services, adequate information, free choice, a fair hearing, and competitive prices.

Consumer sovereignty. The idea that consumers, through their purchases, decide what will be produced by business firms.

Consumerism. A social movement that seeks to augment the rights and powers of consumers.

Corporate crime. Illegal behavior by company employees that benefits a corporation. (Compare with **Occupational crime.**)

Corporate culture. The traditions, customs, values, and approved ways of behaving that prevail in a corporation.

Corporate governance. Any structured system of allocating power in a corporation that determines how and by whom the company is to be governed.

Corporate legitimacy. Public acceptance of the corporation as an institution that contributes to society's well-being.

Corporate policy ethics. Companywide ethics problems and situations that require top-management policy decisions.

Corporate restructuring. The reorganization of a corporation's business units and activities which often involves the closing of current facilities and reduction of workforce.

Corporate social involvement. The interaction of business corporations with society.

Corporate social policy. A policy or a group of policies in a corporation that define the company's purposes, goals, and programs regarding one or more social issues or problems.

Corporate social responsibility. A business obligation to seek socially beneficial results along with economically beneficial results in its actions.

Corporate social responsiveness. The ability of a corporation to relate its operations and policies to the social environment in ways that are mutually beneficial to the company and to society.

Corporate social strategy. The social, political, and ethical parts of a company's plans and activities for achieving its goals and purposes.

Corporate stakeholder. A person or group affected by a corporation's policies and actions.

Corporate strategic management. Planning, directing, and managing a corporation for the purpose of helping it achieve its basic purposes and long-run goals.

Corporate strategic planning. A process of formulating a corporation's basic purpose, long-run goals, and programs intended to achieve the company's purposes and goals.

Corporate takeover. The acquisition, usually by merger, of one corporation by another.

Corporation. Legally, an artificial legal "person," created under the laws of a particular state or nation. Socially and organizationally, a complex system of people, technology, and resources generally devoted to carrying out a central economic mission as it interacts with a surrounding social and political environment.

Cost-benefit analysis. A systematic method of calculating the costs and benefits of a project or activity that is intended to produce benefits.

Crisis management. The use of a special team to help a company cope with an unusual emergency situation that may threaten the company in serious ways.

Crossownership (of media). The simultaneous ownership by one company of several different types of media, such as television stations, radio stations, newspapers, magazines, book publishing companies, and motion picture studios.

Cultural distance. The amount of difference in customs, attitudes, and values between two social systems.

Cultural shock. A person's disorientation and insecurity caused by the strangeness of a different culture. (Also known as *culture shock.*)

Debt rescheduling. Rearranging the dates and periodic payments to be made on a debt owed to a creditor (which usually is a bank).

Deregulation. The removal or scaling down of regulatory authority and regulatory activities of government.

Discrimination (in jobs or employment). Unequal treatment of employees based on *non-job-related* factors such as race, sex, age, national origin, religion, color, and physical or mental handicap.

Disinvestment. Withdrawing a direct investment of funds and other resources that are used to operate a business or a portion of a business. A company that withdraws its operations from South Africa normally disinvests in this manner.

Divestment. Withdrawing and shifting to other uses the funds that a person or group has invested in the securities (stocks, bonds, notes, etc.) of a company. Institutional investors sometimes have divested the securities of companies doing business in South Africa.

Dividend. A return-on-investment payment made to the owners of shares of corporate stock at the discretion of the company's board of directors.

Ecological balance. A natural equilibrium maintained among any group of living things and the environment they occupy.

Ecology. The study, and the process, of how living things—plants and animals—interact with one another and with their environment.

Ecosystem. Plants and animals in their natural environment, living together as an interdependent system.

Electoral politics. Political activities undertaken by business and other interest groups to influence the outcome of elections to public office.

Emission standard. A legally defined, specific amount of a pollutant permitted to be *discharged* from a polluting source in a given period of time. (Compare with **Environmental-quality standard.**)

Employee stock ownership plan (ESOP). A company plan that encourages employees to invest money in that company's stock.

Enlightened self-interest. The view that social responsiveness and long-run economic return are compatible and are in the interest of business.

Environmental impact statement. A report on the expected environmental effects of a planned development; such reports are required when federal funding or federal jurisdiction is involved.

Environmental-quality standard. A legally defined, specific amount of a pollutant permitted to be *present* in an area, such as a plant where toxic substances are used or a region where auto traffic is heavy. (Compare with **Emission standard.**)

Environmental scanning. Examining an organization's environment to discover trends and forces that could have an impact on the organization.

Equal-access rule. A legal provision that requires television stations to allow all competing candidates for political office to broadcast their political messages if one of the candidates' views are broadcast.

Equal employment opportunity. The principle that all persons otherwise qualified should be treated equally with respect to job opportunities, workplace conditions, pay, fringe benefits, and retirement provisions.

Ethical climate. The prevailing, often unspoken ethical attitudes and beliefs of an organization that tend to guide the behavior of organization members when confronted with an ethical dilemma.

Ethical egoist. A person who puts his or her own selfish interests above all other considerations, while ignoring or denying the ethical needs and beliefs of others.

Ethical relativism. A belief that ethical right and wrong are defined by personal opinion, a society's traditions, various periods of time in history, or the special circumstances of the moment.

Ethics. A conception of right and wrong conduct, serving as a guide to moral behavior.

Ethics audit. A systematic effort to discover actual or potential unethical behavior in an organization.

Ethics code. A written statement that describes the general value system and ethical rules of an organization.

Ethnocentric business. A company whose business standards are based on its home nation's customs, markets, and laws.

Export of jobs. A loss of jobs in a business firm's home nation, and a creation of new jobs in a foreign nation, caused by relocating part or all of the business firm's operations (and jobs) to the foreign nation.

Expropriation. (See **Nationalization.**)

Face-to-face ethics. The personal interactions people have with each other at work that involve ethical issues; the human, individual dimension of ethics that is part of most working relationships.

Federal chartering. A proposed plan for giving the federal government power to issue certificates of incorporation for private business corporations.

Fiduciary responsibility or duty. A legal obligation to carry out a duty to some other person or group in order to protect their interest.

Flextime. A plan that allows employees limited control over scheduling their own hours of work, usually at the beginning and end of the work day.

Foreign direct investment (FDI). The investment and transfer of funds by investors in one nation into business activities or organizations located in another nation.

Free enterprise ideology. A set of beliefs about one way to organize economic life that includes individualism, freedom, private property, profit, equality of opportunity, competition, the work ethic, and a limited government.

Free enterprise system. A socioeconomic system based on private ownership, profit-seeking business firms, and the principle of free markets.

Free market. A model of an economic system based on voluntary and free exchange among buyers and sellers. Competition regulates prices in all free market exchanges.

Functional-area ethics. The ethical problems that typically occur in the various specialized operational areas of business, such as accounting, marketing, finance, etc.

Functional regulation. Regulations aimed at a particular function or operation of business, such as competition or labor relations.

Future shock. A human reaction to rapid technological change whereby individuals experience difficulty in coping with the new conditions of life brought on by new technology.

Gender pay gap. The difference in the average level of wages, salaries, and income received by men and women.

Genetic engineering. (See **Biotechnology.**)

Geocentric business. A company whose business standards and policies are worldwide in outlook including multinational ownership, management, markets, and operations.

Glass ceiling. A barrier to the advancement of women, minorities, and other groups in the workplace.

Global commons. The idea that certain types of natural resources, such as the earth's atmosphere, tropical rainforests, and oceans, are vital for all living organisms.

Government and business partnership. A subtype of socioeconomic system in which government and business work cooperatively to solve social problems. (See also **Public-private partnership.**)

Grassroots politics. Political activity directed at involving and influencing individual citizens or constituents to directly contact government officials on a public policy issue.

Green consumerism. An attitude of consumers that considers the ecological effects of their purchase, use, and disposal of consumer goods and services.

Green management. An outlook by managers that emphasizes the importance of considering ecological factors as management decisions are made.

Green marketing. A concept that describes the creation, promotion, and sale of environmentally safe products and services by business.

Greenmail. The practice of paying a premium over the market price of a company's stock as part of a settlement with investors who wish to take over a company.

Hazardous waste. Waste materials from industrial, agricultural, and other activities capable of causing death or serious health problems for those persons exposed for prolonged periods. (Compare with **Toxic substance.**)

Home country. The country in which a multinational corporation has its headquarters.

Host country. A foreign country in which a multinational corporation conducts business.

Ideology. A set of basic beliefs that define an ideal way of living for an individual, an organization, or a society.

Individualism. A belief that each individual person has an inherent worth and dignity and possesses basic human rights that should be protected by society. Each person is presumed to be a free agent capable of knowing and promoting his or her own self-interest.

Industrial resource base. The minerals, energy sources, water supplies, skilled labor force, and human knowledge necessary for industrial production.

Industrial society. A society in which the building and mechanical processing of material goods dominates work and employs the largest proportion of the labor force.

Industry-specific regulation. Regulations aimed at specific industries, such as telephone service or railroad transportation, involving control of rates charged, customers served, and entry into the industry.

Inflation. Decline in the purchasing power of money.

Insider trading. The illegal practice of buying or selling shares of corporate securities based on fiduciary information which is known only to a small group of persons, e.g., executives and their friends ("insiders"), and which enables them to make profits at the expense of other investors who do not have access to the inside information.

Institutional investor. A financial institution, insurance company, pension fund, endowment fund, or similar organization that invests its accumulated funds in the securities offered for sale on stock exchanges.

Institutionalized activity (ethics, social responsiveness, public affairs, etc. An activity, operation, or procedure that is such an integral part of an organization that it is performed routinely by managers and employees.

Intellectual property. Ideas, concepts, and other symbolic creations of human intelligence that are recognized and protected under a nation's copyright, patent, and trademark laws.

Interactive model of business and society. The combined primary and secondary interactions that business has with society.

Interactive system. The closely intertwined relationships between business and society.

Interlocking directorate. A relationship between two corporations that is established when one person serves as a member of the board of directors of both corporations simultaneously.

International regulation. A form of regulation in which more than one nation agrees to establish and enforce the same rules of conduct for international business activities.

Issues management. Identifying, analyzing, and developing recommendations and implementing policies concerning issues that have special meaning and importance for a company.

Justice. A concept used in ethical reasoning that refers to the fair distribution of benefits and burdens among the people in a society, according to some agreed-upon rule.

Knowledge society. A society in which the use and electronic manipulation of knowledge and information dominate work and employ the largest proportion of the labor force. (See **Postindustrial society.**)

Laissez faire. A French phrase meaning "to let alone," used to describe an economic system where government intervention is minimal.

Laws. A society's formally codified principles that help define right and wrong behavior.

Leveraged buyouts (LBOs). The acquisition of a corporation by a group of investors, often including top executives, that relies on debt financing to pay the purchase price. The value of the company's assets is used as a "lever" to borrow the necessary amount for the purchase.

Lie detector. (See **Polygraph.**)

Lobbying. The act of trying to directly shape or influence a government official's understanding and position on a public policy issue.

Luddites. Groups of early-nineteenth-century English workers who, believing that machines took away jobs from workers, destroyed factory machinery.

Megacorporation. One of the very largest business corporations.

Merger. The joining together of two separate companies into a single company.

Mixed state-and-private enterprise. A socioeconomic system in which government owns some key industrial and financial enterprises but most businesses are owned and operated by private individuals and corporations.

Moral development stages. A series of progressive steps by which a person learns new ways of reasoning about ethical and moral issues.

A condition in which the most fundamental human values are preserved and allowed to shape human thought and action.

Multinational corporation. A company that conducts business in two or more nations, usually employing citizens of various nationalities.

National competitiveness. The ability of a nation to engage in business in international markets through its publicly owned and privately owned enterprises.

Nationalization. Government taking ownership and control of private property with or without compensation. (Also known as *expropriation.*)

Network television (or radio). A group of affiliated television or radio broadcasting stations that reach a certain percentage of the viewing or listening public. The affiliated stations agree to broadcast programs arranged by network officials.

Nomadic society. A society in which food gathering, hunting, and fishing dominate work and where human groups move as necessary to find such food.

Occupational crime. Illegal activity by a business employee intended to enrich the employee at the expense of the company.

Occupational segregation. The practice or custom of employing only men or only women in a particular job category.

Offset policy. A pollution control plan that permits excess pollution from one source if another polluting source reduces its emissions by an equal or greater amount.

Opportunity costs. The various opportunities that cannot be realized because money is spent for one purpose rather than for others.

Organizational commitment. A stage in the development of social responsiveness within a company when social responses have become a normal part of doing business. Therefore, the entire organization is committed to socially responsible actions and policies. (Compare with **Institutionalized activity.**)

Patriarchal society. A society in which men hold the dominant positions in organizations, the society's values reflect and reinforce male-oriented privileges, and women tend to hold subordinate positions.

Performance-expectations gap. The perceived distance between a corporation's actual performance and the performance that is expected by the corporation's stakeholders.

Philanthropy (corporate). Gifts and contributions made by corporations, usually from pretax profits, to benefit various types of nonprofit community organizations.

Plant closing laws. Legislation that requires employers to notify employees in advance of the closing of a facility in order to allow time for adjustment, including negotiations to keep the plant open, to arrange an employee buyout, to find new jobs, etc.

Pluralism. A society in which numerous economic, political, educational, social, cultural, religious and other groups are organized by people to promote their own interests.

Policy decision. A stage in the public policy process when government authorizes (or fails to authorize) a course of action, for example, by passing (or failing to pass) a law, issuing a court opinion, or adopting a new regulation.

Policy evaluation. The final stage in the public policy process when the results of a public policy are judged by those who have an interest in the outcome.

Policy formulation. A stage in the public policy process when interested groups take a position and try to persuade others to adopt that position.

Policy implementation. A stage in the public policy process when action is taken to enforce a public policy decision.

Political action committee. A committee organized according to election law by any group for the purpose of accepting voluntary contributions from individual donors and then making contributions in behalf of candidates for election to public office.

Pollution charge. A fee levied on a polluting source based on the amount of pollution released into the environment.

Pollution rights. A legal right to exceed established pollution limits; such rights may be bought, sold, or held for future use with approval of government regulators.

Pollution trade-offs. Accepting one form of pollution rather than another when it is not possible to eliminate both.

Polygraph. An operator-administered instrument used to judge the truth or falsity of a person's statements by measuring physiological changes that tend to be activated by a person's conscience when lying.

Populism. The preference for a democratic political system, family-operated farms, small-size business firms, and small-town life.

Postindustrial society. A society combining the features of a service society and a knowledge society. (See **Service society** and **Knowledge society.**)

Preferential hiring. An employment plan that gives preference to minorities, women, and other groups that may be underrepresented in an organization's workforce.

Pressure-response model of social responsiveness. A model of corporate behavior that emphasizes the need for stakeholder pressure to stimulate corporate activity.

Primary interactions or involvement. The direct relationships a company has with those groups that enable it to produce goods and services.

Primary stakeholders. The people and groups who are directly affected by a corporation's economic activities and decisions.

Principle of national sovereignty. The idea that the government of each nation is legally entitled to make laws regarding the behavior of its citizens and citizens of other nations who are acting within the nation.

Priority Rule. In ethical analysis, a procedure for ranking in terms of their importance the three ethical modes of reasoning—utilitarian, rights, and justice—before making a decision or taking action.

Privacy. (See **Right of privacy.**)

Private property. A group of rights giving control over physical and intangible assets to private owners. Private ownership is the basic institution of capitalism.

Privatization. The process of converting various economic functions, organizations, and programs from government ownership or government sponsorship to private operation.

Product liability. A legal responsibility of a person or firm for the harmful consequences to others stemming from use of a product manufactured, sold, managed, or employed by the person or firm.

Product recall. An effort by a business firm to remove a defective or sometimes dangerous product from consumer use and from all distribution channels.

Productivity. The relationship between total inputs and total outputs. Productivity increases when the outputs of an organization increase faster than the inputs necessary for production.

Profit maximization. An attempt by a business firm to achieve the highest possible rate of return from its operations.

Profit optimization. An attempt by a business firm to achieve an acceptable (rather than a maximum) rate of return from its operations.

Profits. The revenues of a person or company minus the costs incurred in producing the revenue.

Proxy. A legal instrument giving another person the right to vote the shares of stock of an absentee stockholder.

Proxy statement. A statement sent by a board of directors to a corporation's stockholders announcing the company's annual meeting, containing information about the business to be considered at the meeting, and enclosing a proxy form for stockholders not attending the meeting.

Public affairs function. An organization's activities intended to perceive, monitor, understand, communicate with, and influence the external environment, including local and national communities, government relations, and public opinion.

Public issue. A problem or concern of corporate stakeholders that has the potential to become a politicized matter, leading to legislation, regulation, or other formal governmental action.

Public issue advertising. An advertisement appearing in the media that expresses the sponsor's viewpoint about a public issue. (Also known as *public policy advertising* or *advocacy advertising.*)

Public issue life cycle. The sequence of phases through which a public issue may pass.

Public policy. A plan of action by government to achieve some broad purpose affecting a large segment of the public.

Public policy agenda. All public policy problems or issues that receive the active and serious attention of government officials.

Public policy process. All of the activities and stages involved in developing, carrying out, and evaluating public policies.

Public trustee. A concept that a business owner or manager should base company decisions on the interests of a wide range of corporate stakeholders or members of the general public. In doing so, the business executive acts as a trustee of the public interest.

Public-private partnerships. Community-based organizations that have a combination of businesses and government agencies collaborating to address important social problems such as crime, homelessness, drugs, economic development, and other community issues. (See also **Government and business partnership.**)

Publicly held corporation. A corporation whose stock is available for purchase by the general investing public.

Questionable payments. Something of value given to a person or firm, which raises significant ethical questions of right or wrong in the host nation or other nations.

Quotas (job, hiring, employment). An employment plan based on hiring a specific number or proportion of minorities, women, or other groups who may be underrepresented in an organization's workforce.

Regulation. The action of government to establish rules by which industry or other groups must behave in conducting their normal activities.

Re-regulation. The imposition of regulation on activities that were deregulated earlier.

Reverse discrimination. The unintended negative impact experienced by an individual or group as a result of legal efforts to overcome discrimination against another individual or group.

Right (human). A concept used in ethical reasoning that means that a person or group is entitled to something or is entitled to be treated in a certain way.

Right of privacy. A person's entitlement to protection from invasion of one's private life by government, business, or other persons.

Rule of Cost. The idea that all human actions generate costs.

Secondary interactions or involvement. The relationship a company has with those social and political groups that feel the impact of the company's main activities and take steps to do something about it. These relationships are derived from the firm's primary interactions.

Secondary stakeholders. The people and groups in society who are indirectly affected by a corporation's economic activities and decisions.

Service society. A society in which the provision of services, rather than the production of material goods, dominates work and employs the largest proportion of the labor force. (See **Postindustrial society.**)

Sexual harassment. Unwanted and uninvited sexual attention experienced by a person, and/or a workplace that is hostile or threatening in a sexual way.

Shareholder. (See **Stockholder.**)

Shareholder resolution. A proposal made by a stockholder and included in a corporation's notice of its annual meeting that advocates some course of action to be taken by the company.

Shareholder suit (individual). A lawsuit initiated by one or more stockholders that attempts to recover damages *they* (as stockholders) *personally* suffered due to alleged actions of the company's management.

Shareholder's derivative suit. A lawsuit initiated by one or more stockholders that attempts to recover damages suffered *by the company* due to alleged actions of the company's management.

Social accountability. The condition of being held responsible to society or to some public or governmental group for one's actions, often requiring a specific accounting or reporting on these activities.

Social audit. A systematic study and evaluation of an organization's social performance. (Compare with **Social performance evaluation.**)

Social forecasting. An attempt to estimate major social and political trends that may affect a company's operations and environment in the future.

Social involvement. (See **Corporate social involvement.**)

Social overhead costs. Public and private investments that are necessary to prepare the environment for effective operation of a new business or other major institutions.

Social performance evaluation. Information about an organization's social performance, often contained in a company's annual report to stockholders and sometimes prepared as a special report to management or the general public. (Compare with **Social audit.**)

Social regulation. Regulations intended to accomplish certain social improvements such as equal employment opportunity or on-the-job safety and health.

Social responsibility. (See **Corporate social responsibility.**)

Social responsiveness. (See **Corporate social responsiveness.**)

Society. The people, institutions, and technology that make up a recognizable human community.

Socioeconomic system. The combined and interrelated social, economic, and political institutions characteristic of a society.

Solid waste. Any solid waste materials resulting from

human activities, such as municipal refuse and sewage, industrial wastes, and agricultural wastes.

Specialized learning. A stage in the development of social responsiveness within a company during which managers and supervisors, usually with the help of a specialist, learn the new practices necessary for coping with social problems and pressures.

Stakeholder. (See **Corporate stakeholder.**)

State-owned enterprise (SOE). A business organization whose ownership is largely or entirely held by a national government.

Stateless corporation. A multinational corporation whose activities are conducted in so many nations as to minimize its dependence on any single nation and enable it to establish its headquarters' activities virtually anywhere in the world.

Stewardship principle. The idea that business managers should act in the interest of all members of society who are affected by their business decisions, thus behaving as stewards or trustees of the public welfare. (Compare with **Public trustee.**)

Stockholder. A person, group, or organization owning one or more shares of stock in a corporation. (Also called *shareholder.*)

Strategies of response. (See **Corporate social strategy.**)

Sustainable development. A concept that describes current economic development that does not damage the ability of future generations to meet their own needs.

Technology. The tools, machines, skills, technical operations, and abstract symbols involved in human endeavor.

Technology assessment. An analytic attempt to understand, beforehand if possible, the economic and social effects of new technology, particularly the unintended, indirect, and possibly harmful impacts that may occur.

Telecommuting. Performing knowledge work and transmitting the results of that work by means of computer terminal to an organization's central data bank and management center, while the employee works at home or at some other remote location.

Tender offer. An offer by an individual, group, or organization to buy outstanding shares of stock in a corporation, frequently in an effort to gain control or otherwise benefit themselves.

Third Wave. A period of widespread social change characteristic of high-technology, service-oriented, knowledge-based societies.

Third world nations. Developing nations relatively poorer than advanced industrial nations.

Toxic substance. Any substance used in production or in consumer products that is poisonous or capable of causing serious health problems for those persons exposed. (Compare with **Hazardous waste.**)

Trade association. An organization that represents the business and professional interests of the firms or persons in a trade, industry, or profession; for example, medical doctors, chemical manufacturers, or used car dealers.

Trade-offs, economic and social. An attempt to balance and compare economic and social gains against economic and social costs when it is impossible to achieve all that is desired in both economic and social terms.

Unanimity Rule. In ethical analysis, a procedure for determining that all three modes of ethical reasoning—utilitarian, rights, and justice—provide consistent and uniform answers to an ethical problem or issue.

Utility (social). A concept used in ethical reasoning that refers to the net positive gain or benefit to society of some action or decision.

Values. Fundamental and enduring beliefs about the most desirable conditions and purposes of human life.

Wall Street. A customary way of referring to the financial community of banks, investment institutions, and stock exchanges centered in the Wall Street area of New York City.

Whistle-blowing. An employee's disclosure to the public of alleged organizational misconduct.

Work ethic. The belief that human labor and work are inherently worthwhile, admirable, and both personally and socially valuable. The work ethic is sometimes called "the Protestant ethic" or "the Protestant work ethic" because of its origin among early Protestant theologians.

Bibliography

PART ONE (Chapters 1–5)

Ackerman, Robert, *The Social Challenge to Business,* Cambridge, MA: Harvard University Press, 1975.

Bowen, Howard R., *Social Responsibilities of the Businessman,* New York: Harper, 1953.

Bradshaw, Thornton, and Vogel David, (eds.), *Corporations and Their Critics: Issues and Answers to the Problems of Corporate Social Responsibility,* New York: McGraw-Hill, 1981.

Cavanagh, Gerald F., *American Business Values,* 2d ed., Englewood Cliffs, NJ: Prentice-Hall, 1984.

Chamberlain, Neil W., *The Limits of Corporate Social Responsibility,* New York: Basic Books, 1973.

Chamberlain, Neil W., *Social Strategy and Corporate Structure,* New York: MacMillan, 1982.

DeGeorge, Richard T., *Business Ethics,* 3d ed., New York: MacMillan, 1990.

Dickie, Robert S., and Rouner, Leroy S. (eds.), *Corporations and the Common Good,* Notre Dame, IN: Notre Dame University Press and School of Management Boston University, 1986.

Donaldson, Thomas, *Corporations and Morality,* Englewood Cliffs, NJ: Prentice-Hall, 1982.

Donaldson, Thomas, *The Ethics of International Business,* New York: Oxford University Press, 1989.

Drucker, Peter, *The New Realities,* New York: Harper & Row, 1989.

Etzioni, Amitai, *The Moral Dimension: Toward a New Economics,* New York: Free Press, 1988.

Freeman, R. Edward, and Gilbert, Daniel R. Jr., *Corporate Strategy and the Search for Ethics,* Englewood Cliffs, NJ: Prentice-Hall, 1988.

Freeman, R. Edward (ed.), *Business Ethics: The State of the Art,* New York: Oxford University Press, 1991.

Freeman, R. Edward, *Strategic Management: A Stakeholder Approach,* Marshfield, MA: Pitman, 1984.

Guy, Mary E., *Ethical Decision Making in Everyday Work Situations,* New York: Quorum Books, 1990.

Heath, Robert L. et al., *Strategic Issues Management: How Organizations Influence and Respond to Public Interests and Policies,* San Francisco: Jossey-Bass, 1988.

Jackall, Robert, *Moral Mazes: The World of Corporate Managers,* New York: Oxford University Press, 1988.

Kuhn, James W., and Shriver, Donald W. Jr., *Beyond Success: Corporations and Their Critics in the 1990's,* New York: Oxford University Press, 1991.

Miles, Robert, *Managing the Corporate Social Environment: A Grounded Theory,* Englewood Cliffs, NJ: Prentice-Hall, 1987.

Mitchell, Neil J., *The Generous Corporation: A Political Analysis of Economic Power,* New Haven, CT: Yale University Press, 1989.

Mitroff, Ian, and Pauchant, Thierry, *We're So Big and Powerful, Nothing Bad Can Happen to Us,* New York: Carroll Publishing Group, 1990.

Nader, Ralph, and Taylor, William, *The Big Boys: Power and Position in American Business,* New York: Pantheon, 1986.

Naisbitt, John, and Aburdene, Patricia, *Megatrends 2000: Ten New Directions for the 1990's,* New York: William Morrow, 1990.

Nash, Laura L., *Good Intentions Aside: A Manager's Guide to Resolving Ethical Problems,* Boston: Harvard Business School Press, 1990.

Post, James E., *Corporate Behavior and Social Change,* Reston, VA: Reston, 1978.

Preston, Lee E., and Post, James E., *Private Management and Public Policy,* Englewood Cliffs, NJ: Prentice-Hall, 1975.

Rion, Michael, *The Responsible Manager: Practical Strategies for Ethical Decision Making,* San Francisco: Harper & Row, 1990.

Sethi, S. Prakash, and Falbe, Cecelia M., *Business and*

Society: Dimensions of Conflict and Cooperation, Lexington, MA: Lexington Books, 1987.

Toffler, Barbara Ley, *Tough Choices: Managers Talk Ethics,* New York: Wiley, 1986.

Vogel, David, *Lobbying the Corporation: Citizen Challenges to Business Authority,* New York: Basic Books, 1978.

Werhane, Patricia H., *Persons, Rights, and Corporations,* Englewood Cliffs, NJ: Prentice-Hall, 1985.

PART TWO (Chapters 6–8)

Brown, Lester R., *State of the World, 1990,* New York: Norton, 1990.

Ehrlich, Paul R., and Ehrlich, Anne H., *The Population Explosion,* New York: Simon & Schuster, 1990.

Harding, Harry, *China's Second Revolution: Reform After Mao,* Washington: Brookings, 1987.

Kennedy, Paul, *The Rise and Fall of The Great Powers,* New York: Random House, 1987.

Laaksonen, Oiva, *Management in China During and After Mao in Enterprises, Government, and Party,* Berlin: Walter de Gruyter, 1988.

Lenway, Stefanie Ann, *The Politics of U.S. International Trade: Protection, Expansion and Escape,* Marshfield, MA: Pitman, 1985.

Reich, Robert B., *The Next American Frontier,* New York: Penguin Books, 1983.

Savas, E. S., *Privatization,* Chatham, NJ: Chatham House, 1987.

Vachani, Sushil, *Multinationals in India,* New Delhi: Oxford & IBH Publishing Co. Pvt. Ltd, 1991.

Veljanovski, Cento, *Selling the State: Privatisation in Britain,* London: Weidenfeld & Nicholson, 1987.

PART THREE (Chapters 9–11)

Ford Foundation Project on Social Welfare and The American Future, Executive Panel, "The Common Good: Social Welfare and the American Future." Policy Records of the Executive Panel, Ford Foundation Project on Social Welfare and the American Future. New York, NY: The Ford Foundation, 1989.

Berry, Jeffrey M., *The Interest Group Society,* Boston: Little, Brown, 1985.

Cranston, Ross, *Law, Government and Public Policy,* New York: Oxford University Press, 1987.

Dewey, Donald, *The Anti-Trust Experiment in America,* New York: Columbia University Press, 1990.

Eagleton, Thomas F., *Issues in Business and Government,* Englewood Cliffs, NJ: Prentice-Hall, 1991.

Epstein, Edwin M., *The Corporation in American Politics,* Englewood Cliffs, NJ: Prentice-Hall, 1969.

Fugate, Wilbur L. (Assisted by Lee Simowitz), *Foreign Commerce and The Anti-Trust Laws,* 4th ed., Boston: Little, Brown, 1991.

Galambos, Louis, and Pratt, Joseph, *The Rise of Corporate Commonwealth: United States Business and Public Policy in the 20th Century,* New York: Basic Books, 1988.

Garvey, George E., and Garvey, Gerald J., *Economic Law and Economic Growth: Anti-Trust, Regulation, and the American Growth System,* New York: Greenwood Press, 1990.

Lipset, Seymour Martin, and Schneider, William, *The Confidence Gap: Business, Labor, and Government in the Public Mind,* Baltimore: Johns Hopkins University Press, 1987.

Lodge, George C., *Perestroika for America: Restructuring Business-Government Relations for World Competitiveness,* Boston: Harvard Business School Press, 1990.

Lodge, George C., *Comparative Business-Government Relations, Englewood Cliffs, NJ: Prentice-Hall, 1990.*

Maitland-Walker, Julian, (ed.), *Toward 1992: The Development of International Anti-Trust,* Oxford, England: ESC Publishing, 1989.

Marcus, Alfred A., Kaufman, Allen M., and Beam, David R., *Business Strategy and Public Policy: Perspectives from Industry and Academia,* Westport, CT: Quorum Books, 1987.

Oxford Analytica, *America in Perspective: Major Trends in the United States Through the 1990's,* Boston: Houghton Mifflin, 1986.

Peters, B. Guy, *American Public Policy: Promise and*

Performance, 2d ed., Chatham, NJ: Chatham House, 1986.

Porter, Michael, *The Competitive Advantage of Nations*, New York: Basic Books, 1991.

Reich, Robert B. (ed.), *The Power of Public Ideas*, Cambridge, MA: Ballinger, 1988.

Reich, Robert B., *The Work of Nations*, New York: Free Press, 1991.

Vietor, Richard H. K., *Strategic Management in the Regulatory Environment*, Englewood Cliffs, NJ: Prentice-Hall, 1989.

PART FOUR (Chapters 12–15)

Bloom, Paul, and Smith, Ruth Belk (eds.), *The Future of Consumerism*, Lexington, MA: Lexington Books, 1986.

Gale, Anthony (ed.), *The Polygraph Test: Lies, Truth, and Science*, London, England: Sage, 1988.

Gunderson, Martin, Mayo, David J., and Rhame, Frank S., *AIDS: Testing and Privacy*, Salt Lake City, UT: University of Utah Press, 1989.

Herman, Edward S., *Corporate Control, Corporate Power*, Cambridge, England: Cambridge University Press, 1981.

Kester, Carl W., *Japanese Takeovers: The Gobal Contest for Corporate Control*, Boston: Harvard Business School Press, 1991.

Linowes, David F., *Privacy in America: Is Your Private Life in the Public Eye?* Urbana, IL: University of Illinois Press, 1989.

Lorsch, Jay William, *Pawns or Potentates: The Reality of America's Corporate Boards*, Boston: Harvard Business School Press, 1989.

Puckett, Same B., and Emery, Alan R., *Managing AIDS in the Workplace*, Reading, MA: Addison-Wesley, 1988.

PART FIVE (Chapters 16–19)

Adler, Nancy, and Israeli, Dafna N., (eds.), *Women in Management Worldwide*, Armonk, NY: Sharpe, 1988.

Barcus, F. Earl, *Images of Life on Children's Television: Sex Roles, Minorities, and Families*, New York: Praeger, 1983.

Brown, Lester R. et al., *State of the World, 1991*, New York: Norton, 1990.

Buchholz, Rogene, Marcus, Alfred, and Post, James E., *Managing Environmental Issues: A Casebook*, Englewood Cliffs, NJ: Prentice-Hall, 1992.

Corrado, Frank M., *Media for Managers: Communications Strategies for the Eighties*, Englewood Cliffs, NJ: Prentice-Hall, 1984.

Dates, Jannette L., and Barlow, William (eds.), *Split Image: African-Americans in the Mass Media*, Washington, D.C.: Howard University Press, 1990.

Dertouzas, Michael L., Lester, Richard K., and Solow, Robert M., *Made in America: Regaining the Productivity Edge*, Cambridge, MA: MIT Press, 1989.

Goldin, Claudia, *Understanding the Gender Gap: An Economic History of American Women*, New York: Oxford University Press, 1990.

Gray, Barbara, *Collaborating: Finding Common Ground for Multiparty Problems*, San Francisco: Jossey-Bass, 1989.

Gutek, Barbara A., *Sex and the Workplace: The Impact of Sexual Behavior and Harassment on Women, Men, and Organizations*, San Francisco: Jossey-Bass, 1985.

Hochschild, Arlie, *The Second Shift: Working Parents and the Revolution at Home*, New York: Viking, 1989.

Hoffman, W. Michael, Frederick, Robert, and Petry, Edward S. (eds.), *The Corporation, Ethics and the Environment*, Westport, CT: Quorum Books, 1990.

Morrison, Ann M., White, Randall P., and Velsor, Ellen Van, *Breaking the Glass Ceiling: Can Women Reach the Top of America's Largest Corporations?* Reading, MA: Addison-Wesley, 1987.

Oskamp, Stuart (ed.), *Television as a Social Issue,* Newbury Park, CA: Sage Publications, 1988.

Powell, Gary N., *Women and Men in Management,* Newbury Park, CA: Sage Publications, 1988.

Rix, Sara E., *The American Woman 1990–91: A Status Report,* New York: Norton, 1990.

Ten Berge, Dieudonne, *The First 24 Hours: A Comprehensive Guide to Successful Crisis Communications,* Cambridge, MA: Basil Blackwell, 1990.

United Nations, *The World's Women, 1970–1990: Trends and Statistics,* New York: United Nations Publications, June 1991.

Indexes

Name Index

Subject Index